Hostile Acts

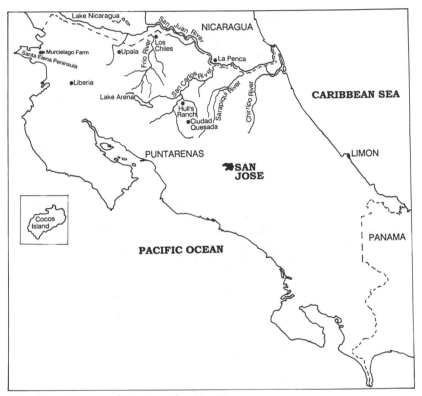

Costa Rica. Courtesy of Roy Arguedas, *Tico Times.*

Hostile Acts

U.S. Policy in Costa Rica in the 1980s

Martha Honey

University Press of Florida
Gainesville/Tallahassee/Tampa/Boca Raton
Pensacola/Orlando/Miami/Jacksonville

Copyright acknowledgments appear on the last printed page of this book.

Library of Congress Cataloging-in-Publication Data

Honey, Martha.
    Hostile acts: U.S. policy in Costa Rica in the 1980s / Martha Honey
       p.   cm.
    Includes bibliographical references and index.
    ISBN 0-8130-1249-X (cloth : alk. paper).—ISBN 0-8130-1250-3 (pbk. : alk. paper)
    1. United States—Foreign relations—Costa Rica. 2. Costa Rica—Foreign relations—United States. I. Title.
E183.8.C8H66   1994
327.7307286—dc20   93-31188

The University Press of Florida is the scholarly publishing agency for the State University System of Florida, comprised of Florida A & M University, Florida Atlantic University, Florida International University, Florida State University, University of Central Florida, University of Florida, University of North Florida, University of South Florida, and University of West Florida.

University Press of Florida
15 Northwest 15th Street
Gainesville, FL 32611

To Tony, Shanti, Jody, and Fran
For your unending support, patience, and love

Un gran abrazo
Martha/Mama

Contents

Tables

Preface

In January 1989, Costa Rica charged CIA operative John Hull with the crime of "hostile acts." Hull was accused of contravening the country's policy of unarmed neutrality by using Costa Rican territory to run the contra war against neighboring Nicaragua. Sadly, the term "hostile acts" seems appropriate to describe the overall impact of U.S. policies on Costa Rica during the 1980s. Cosa Rica, Latin America's oldest and most stable democracy, is arguably the best example of the kind of country the United States says its foreign aid and foreign policy are intended to promote. But during the 1980s, as the Reagan and Bush administrations set their sites on wiping out communism in Central America, Washington used its economic, political, and military might to undermine, not strengthen, Costa Rica. Although a sideshow to the overt U.S. interventions in Nicaragua, El Salvador, and Panama, Costa Rica, too, became a victim of Washington's misguided strategy.

This book is based on three different types of information: that which I learned firsthand as my husband and I got drawn personally into the web of the Iran-contra scandal; that which I investigated and reported on as a journalist; and that which I studied in a more detached, scholarly manner. These are different methods of acquiring knowledge. I had hoped, in this book, to weave these different voices—the personal, the popular, and the academic—into a unified resonance. The result, I feel, is less than satisfactory, but it is perhaps an accurate reflection of how I have not always so easily balanced these different roles. The "journalistic" style is dominant throughout the opening and closing sections, while the first-person account is largely confined to chapter 1 and the economic chapters reflect more academic researches.

I also hoped, through this book, to give voice to people in one Third World country, Costa Rica, and to describe how they have experienced the impact of U.S. foreign policy. For this reason, the text is sprinkled with quotes, and the content is heavily based on interviews collected during my eight years as a journalist in Costa

Rica and scores more that were done specifically for this book. (Quotations and facts not footnoted come from these interviews.) Some individuals agreed to talk only off the record, so I am obliged to guard their identities for the sake of candor. A number of people, including Oscar Arias, John Biehl, Guido Fernández, Ottón Solís, Edén Pastora, Carol Prado, and Modesto Watson generously gave me many hours of their time, and the text has been enriched with their information and insights. The book has also been completed despite the unwillingness of several key players—most important, Luis Alberto Monge and Daniel Chaij—to be interviewed.

Obviously, Costa Ricans do not speak with one voice, and my analysis is heavily dependent upon and indebted to those whom I think of as "the good Costa Ricans." For me, these are Costa Ricans who value and want to protect the finest of their country's traditions: its nonmilitarism, respect for human rights, democratic political system, and commitment to social justice and equality through strong public institutions. Among these many friends and colleagues, I am especially grateful to Mitzi Spesny and Pedro León, Oto Castro, Carmen Araya, Roberto Cruz, Miguel Martí, Sheila Ugalde, Carlos Rojas, Edgar Ulate, Manuel Monestel, and Rubén Pagura.

This book was only possible through the efforts of several fortuitous "walk-ins." Ken Ward stopped by to volunteer for a few weeks while he was in Costa Rica recovering from hepatitis. He ended up staying for more than two years, working on many aspects of the research and writing the substance of the agriculture chapter. He not only made the day-to-day work less lonely, but together we shared an enthusiasm and commitment for what we came to call "the Damn Book." Ken came to me via another walk-in, Paul Sonn, a bright, gentle, and inquisitive Dartmouth graduate who came to work for a year just as I was beginning the research. Soon after he was joined by Cyrus Reed, a recent Princeton grad with excellent Spanish and a great sense of humor. Together they worked long hours for no pay, other than my husband Tony's excellent lunches, to transcribe interviews, translate and summarize documents and books, organize newspaper files, and compile chronologies of drug-trafficking cases, Southern Front military activities, and right-wing organizations.

Over the years, a number of other people contributed by helping to research or review various sections. These included, in alphabetical order, Carmen Araya, Fran Avirgan, Tony Avirgan, Jake Bernstein, Karen Brown, Mario Carazo, Bob Carty, Alvaro Chávez, Mary Clark, Michael Conroy, Colin Danby, Cam Duncan, Gordon Durnin, Mario Fernández, Roanna Foreman, Jack Harris, Linda Holland, Alicia Korten, Miriam Lefkowitz, Felipe Montoya, Lynn Morgan, Sandy Munro, David Myers, Chris Rosene, Peter Rosset, Ann Marie Saidy, Lezak Shallat, Carlos Sojo, Tom Thacher, Alex Todorvic, Carol Weir, Walter Willett, Bruce Wilson, and Rosalind Wiseman.

I am also greatly indebted to a number of people at the Christic Institute who generously helped me get documents and articles and shared their knowledge, particularly of the Southern Front. My thanks go to Irene Abrago, Carl Deal, Rick Emrick, Richard McGough, Joanne Royce, Susan Steinberg, and Doug Vaughan. Carl Deal, in particular, was invaluable during the final editing process. Peter Kornbluh of the National Security Archive generously devoted many days and his good judgment to correcting and critiquing the manuscript. I am grateful to Dery and Dick Dyer of the *Tico Times* for kindly providing most of the photos used in this book and for the map, as well as for setting high professional standards in responsible reporting and for their friendship over the years.

I was able to undertake this project only because the University of California at Northridge generously invited me to be a visiting professor, with no teaching responsibilities, so that I could begin my writing. This wonderful opportunity was worked out through the efforts of the chair of the Journalism Department, Michael Emery. While there I was greatly assisted and encouraged by a number of faculty members, most importantly Susan Henry.

I am eternally grateful to both my agent, Gloria Loomis, and to Walda Metcalf, editor and chief at the University Press of Florida, who showed an early interest in the project and for nudging me through all the stages, even as I missed one deadline after another. Michael Senecal calmly and competently shepherded the manuscript through production. I appreciate the time and thought the publisher's two readers, Marc Edelman and Andrew Reding, gave the manuscript. Their excellent comments and critique have, I am sure, made the final product more worthwhile. I am indebted as well to Elizabeth Johns, who undertook the enormous task of editing down my original manuscript. Her professionalism and personal knowledge and interest in Central America helped immeasurably to whittle down my unwieldy draft into a more refined and readable manuscript.

Finally, my family—Tony, Shanti, Jody, and Fran—has been far too tolerant and kind through these last few years. It has taken a toll on all of us, which I regret. We all celebrate the end of this project in the hope that it will make some small contribution to a better future for Costa Rica, a country we all love.

ONE

Coming to Costa Rica

What U.S. policy makers call their backyard, I call my living room.
—Rodrigo Carazo, president of Costa Rica, 1978–82

"Costa Rica, here we come!" Jody shouted as he pressed his nose and mop of blond hair against the airplane window to catch his first glimpse of the brilliant green mountains surrounding San José. Nearby passengers laughed at the enthusiasm and joy of our two-year-old son. It was January 1983. We had decided to relocate halfway around the world—from Tanzania in East Africa to Central America.

We had spent a decade in Tanzania, where I had completed a Ph.D. and my husband, Tony Avirgan, and I had begun our careers as free-lance journalists, covering the anticolonial struggles in Southern Africa, Tanzania's nonaligned socialist development strategy known as *ujamaa* ("familyhood"), and the overthrow of Idi Amin in Uganda. Now "the story" had moved beyond Tanzania, and we decided to move on as well.

By the early 1980s, Central America—a string of tiny countries connecting Mexico to South America—was aglow with conflicts, and that, from the perverse perspective of the press, was good news. Scores of journalists were converging on the region, which had rapidly moved onto the Reagan administration's political front burner. Fixated by Cuban and Soviet "subversion" in the isthmus, Washington right-wingers failed to comprehend the roots of the region's rebellions: poverty, hunger, landlessness, militarism, and human rights abuses.

From the outset, a major obsession of the Reagan administration was to overthrow the Sandinistas, a broad-based military and

1

civilian front which in July 1979 had succeeded in ousting the U.S.-backed Somoza dictatorship in Nicaragua. Like many other Americans who lived in Central America, I was personally sympathetic to the goals of the Sandinista revolution. Certain of their policies troubled me, including their suppression of press freedom, compulsory military service, and heavyhanded efforts to integrate the Atlantic Coast peoples into the rest of Nicaragua. But the Sandinistas' commitment to helping the poorest of the poor contrasted sharply with the Reagan administration's cynical championing of the richest of the rich. And I was convinced that without the CIA-run war, Nicaragua would be a more economically thriving and politically open country. While the Sandinistas struggled to implement desperately needed social reforms—land redistribution, literacy programs, health care, job training, and cooperative farms—Washington's covert operatives quickly regrouped remnants from Anastasio Somoza's notoriously repressive national guard. The principal counterrevolutionary or "contra" force was the Honduran-based FDN (Nicaraguan Democratic Force), which at its peak was said to number around 20,000. Despite its size and U.S. backing, the FDN had little military capability or popular support. It never succeeded in establishing a "liberated zone" or rebel "capital" inside Nicaragua. As one contra leader lamented toward the end of the decade, "We never managed to hold even one telephone booth inside the country."

In contrast, 6,000 to 8,000 leftist guerrillas in El Salvador were waging an impressive civil war against that country's oligarchy ("the Fourteen Families") and its 10,000-man, U.S.-trained and -equipped army. During the early 1980s, the FMLN (Farabundo Martí National Liberation Front) succeeded in winning widespread popular support and gaining control of 20 percent or more of the countryside. Washington charged that the Salvadoran guerrillas were being armed by the Sandinistas, Cuba, and the Soviet Union. But while some arms did come from the outside, the FMLN was a home-grown guerrilla force, equipped as well with U.S. weapons captured from the Salvadoran army. Together with the FDR (Democratic Revolutionary Front), its civilian wing, the FMLN challenged a series of military-backed and U.S.-supported Salvadoran governments, including that of José Napoleón Duarte, a right-of-center businessman elected in 1984. Right-wing death squads tied to the military and oligarchy responded by murdering thousands of suspected guerrilla supporters, including Archbishop Oscar Romero, four U.S. churchwomen, and, in November 1989, six prominent Jesuit theologians.

In Guatemala, as well, the region's oldest and most brutal guerrilla war—which dated from a 1954 CIA-engineered coup—continued to simmer in the early 1980s. In 1981, the army launched a counterinsurgency campaign, destroying an estimated 440 highland towns, killing or "disappearing" between 50,000 and 75,000, and forcing guerrilla sympathizers into military-controlled "model villages." Unable to put down the armed guerrillas, death squads targeted trade unionists, peasant organizers, students, liberal clerics, and left-of-center politicians. Despite Guatemala's horrific human rights record, Reagan lifted the U.S. arms sale embargo in 1983 and, in 1985, resumed military aid and increased economic assistance fivefold.

Honduras, the region's poorest and least industrialized country, became the main staging area for Washington's war against Nicaragua. Beginning in 1981, the Reagan administration carried out almost continuous air, naval, and ground military maneuvers in Honduras and off its coast. The United States constructed several large military bases for U.S., Honduran, and contra forces and stationed about one thousand U.S. military personnel permanently in the country and thousands more in ships off the coast. Honduras's military-controlled government exchanged use of its national territory for hundreds of millions of dollars—what Hondurans called "a rain of dollars" (*una lluvia de dólares*)—in the form of U.S. economic and military assistance.

Panama, at the tip of the Central American isthmus, housed the Southern Command (SouthCom), the largest U.S. military complex in Latin America. It included eleven army, navy, and air force bases, about thirteen thousand U.S. military personnel, and the 'School of the Americas, which had trained most of Latin America's military elite. (In 1984 the School moved to Fort Benning, in Georgia.) A major mission of the U.S. forces was to protect the Panama Canal and the Canal Zone, which constituted a virtual U.S. colony inside Panamanian territory. Reagan hardliners opposed a treaty signed by President Jimmy Carter to turn the canal over to Panama by the year 2000 and greatly diminish the U.S. presence in Panama. In the late 1980s, tensions mounted between Washington and Panama's military chief, General Manuel Noriega, who had been the CIA's most important and longest serving intelligence "asset" in the region. In December 1989, the Bush administration, suspecting Noriega of disloyalty and charging him with drug trafficking, launched a massive military invasion into Panama City. After the United States bombed and leveled large sections of the capital, killing hundreds—perhaps thousands—of civilians, Noriega finally surrendered. He was flown to Miami, where he was tried and convicted on charges of drug trafficking and money laundering. Throughout Central America, the Reagan and Bush administrations responded to popular unrest with an array of low-intensity and high-tech warfare, which many Latin Americans viewed as simply modern-day variants on "gun-boat" and "big stick" diplomacy.

Within this context, Costa Rica appeared to be an oasis of tranquility. We chose Costa Rica believing it would be a safe haven for our two children, Jody and seven-year-old Shanti, and a centrally located base from which to cover the region's wars. Unknown to us, Washington also set its sights on Costa Rica about this same time. Prior to the 1980s, the United States had generally viewed Costa Rica as a benign backwater, of little strategic or economic importance.

But two events—the Sandinista victory and Costa Rica's internal economic crisis—caused the newly elected Reagan administration to reevaluate Costa Rica and to decide that, for geopolitical reasons, Costa Rica *was* important. While U.S. officials stressed the supposed threat posed by Nicaragua, Costa Ricans were far more worried by the collapse of their economy. In the late 1970s, a steep rise in the cost of gasoline and oil imports and plummeting agricultural export prices plunged Costa Rica into unprecedented economic chaos, with 100 percent inflation, massive currency devaluations, a sharp rise in unemployment, the highest per capita debt in Latin America, and the beginnings of social unrest.

The Reagan administration quickly struck a deal with the Costa Rican government: to bail out Costa Rica economically in return for support in Washington's war against the Sandinistas. U.S. dollars started to flow, and within a few years Costa Rica became the second highest per capita recipient of U.S. economic assistance, surpassed only by Israel. Along the remote northern border with Nicaragua and on isolated farms in the western province of Guanacaste, U.S. military and intelligence operatives built up the "Southern Front"—clandestine operations to challenge the new leftist government in Managua. From the heavily guarded embassy complex in downtown San José, U.S. technocrats and State Department bureaucrats quietly doled out millions of dollars to create new private institutions which were later collectively dubbed the "Parallel State." These initiatives became central, interconnected pieces of the ideological framework of the New Right in power in Washington, which set out to combat communism and spread U.S.-style capitalism around the globe. Their eyes focused on distant goals, the ideologues and implementors of these policies acted with a proselytizing zeal and arrogance. They had little understanding, concern, or respect for the national character, history, and traditions of Third World countries such as Costa Rica.

While most Costa Ricans hold a deep love and admiration for the United States, during the 1980s officials of the Reagan and Bush administrations (when not confusing Costa Rica with Puerto Rico or San José with San Juan) tended to view this tiny country simply as a pawn in its chess game against international communism. These functionaries showed scant regard for Costa Rica's admirable history as Central America's only stable, peaceful, truly democratic, and relatively prosperous country. For a century, with two brief lapses, Costa Rica has been a well-functioning, multiparty, Western-style democracy. In 1948, it took the highly unusual and eminently sensible step of abolishing its army and has since been protected by a small, lightly armed police and border patrol known as the Civil and Rural Guard. Under the constitution, it is illegal to re-create a military cadre, and guard members must all resign at the end of each administration. Costa Rica justifiably fears a standing army.

While its neighbors poured much of their scant resources into military training and hardware and suffered a succession of coups, Costa Rica was able to pump a large portion of state funds into expanding its middle class and assisting and protecting the country's urban and rural poor through progressive legislation and a welfare state. Social reforms begun before World War II included a labor code and eight-hour workday, a social security system, and social assistance programs.

After World War II and accelerating in the 1960s, Costa Rica followed an economic development strategy common in much of Latin America: it used foreign investment and loans to expand its manufacturing sector and to develop new agricultural exports, particularly beef. But the expanding role of the state in democratic reform—including the nationalization of the banking system, and growth of government-owned services—set Costa Rica apart from its neighbors. The country's public services are the best in Latin America; they include excellent government-run health and insurance systems, public education through the university level, efficient and inexpensive mass transportation, and well-run public utilities throughout most of the country. It has a literacy rate of 93 percent, among the highest in the world, and a life expectancy of seventy-six years for females and seventy-one for males. Over 80 percent of households have electricity and televisions, and 95 percent have running water.

Costa Rica has been an anomaly for other reasons as well. In contrast with other Central American countries, at the beginning of the 1980s Costa Rica had no death squads, no "disappearances," no political prisoners, only occasional human rights abuses, and no significant left- or right-wing guerrilla movements. A century ago it abolished capital punishment, and as a tribute to these traditions the Organization of American States' Human Rights Court has been based in San José since 1979. In 1980 the United Nations founded its World Peace University here.

Costa Rica's welfare state, economic stability, and political democracy are rooted in the country's comparatively egalitarian colonial origins. Costa Rica, meaning "rich coast," is really a misnomer; unlike other parts of the region, it had no inherent wealth. When Christopher Columbus first landed in 1502, he found little gold, silver, or other great mineral deposits and no large native population to exploit. For the next several centuries, while the *conquistadores, latifundistas,* and Catholic clerics carved up the more lucrative parts of the continent, it remained a backwater. Eventually it was settled by poor farmers, mainly from Spain, who staked out small homesteads in the fertile highland areas of the Central Valley.

Costa Rica's self-image is that of a nation built by fiercely independent but essentially egalitarian yeoman farmers. But during this century, the place of the small, independent farmer who produces for the family and the local market has gradually eroded. There has been extensive consolidation of land, especially around coffee, bananas, and (since World War II) cattle. By 1980, two-thirds to three-quarters of the economically active rural population was landless,[1] and Costa Rica's land distribution had become as skewed as it was in El Salvador, Guatemala, or Honduras. According to a U.S. government report, "The number of landless poor represents a higher proportion of the rural population in Costa Rica than in any country in Central America."[2] For this reason, one of the strongest and best organized—though largely nonviolent—social movements in Costa Rica has become that of the squatters who "invade" under- or unutilized land. The government has generally treated squatters—who are known as *precaristas* because of their precarious legal status—benignly, often giving them title to land and providing social services. And, unlike elsewhere in the region, Costa Rica's welfare system and relatively high wages for laborers have provided the lower and middle classes with a social "safety net," thus defusing violent political and economic unrest.

Costa Rica's population of 2.9 million is largely homogeneous, with only about 30,000 indigenous people and a nearly equal number of blacks (most of whose ancestors came from Jamaica). Costa Rica's blacks and Indians have historically been treated as second-class citizens, and Costa Ricans generally view themselves as racially, culturally, and politically superior to their neighbors, particularly Nicaraguans.

The country's well-established political democracy, respect for human rights, antimilitarism, and economic stability meant that, prior to 1980, Costa Rica had become a haven for political exiles and economic refugees fleeing dictatorships in Nicaragua,

El Salvador, Guatemala, Cuba, Chile, Uruguay, Argentina, and elsewhere. Prior to World War II, Jews, mainly from Poland, fled to Costa Rica, which became the first country after the Pearl Harbor attack to declare war on Japan. In the early 1950s during the Korean War, a group of American Quakers migrated to Costa Rica to avoid paying U.S. war taxes. They settled in a mountaintop community known as Monteverde, where they raise cows, make cheese, and help protect a world-famous rain forest reserve. This influx of immigrants enriched the country culturally, artistically, and politically and gave it a more international and broad-minded character. During the 1980s, tens of thousands of Nicaraguan political and economic refugees came to Costa Rica. They formed the backbone of the contra operations and helped shift the political climate to the right.

Costa Rica's democratic reformism and respect for human rights have been tempered by other crosscurrents—traditional religious values, anticommunism, and racism—which have worked to create a largely conservative society. Despite the country's long democratic tradition, blacks and women did not gain full voting rights until after World War II, and indigenous people were not granted Costa Rican citizenship until 1991. The Catholic church, which represents the state religion, has helped to legitimize the reformist role of the state while at the same time keeping a lid on popular movements that challenge the authority of either the church hierarchy or the government. Although Costa Rica's Popular Vanguard Party (PVP) is one of the oldest Communist organizations in Latin America (it was founded in 1931), it was banned in 1950 and remained illegal until 1975. In the years following the 1959 Cuban Revolution, several thousand Cubans fled to Costa Rica, many hoping to emigrate to the United States. Costa Rica became one of the bases for anti-Castro activities, with some Cuban emigrés working for the CIA while others trafficked in arms, drugs, and false passports. Costa Rica supported the CIA's 1961 Bay of Pigs invasion and, after the fact, helped legitimize the 1965 U.S. invasion of the Dominican Republic, which crushed a popular uprising and fortified the right-wing military dictatorship that had ousted the progressive president, Juan Bosch.[3] In 1961, an anticommunist paramilitary organization, the Free Costa Rica

Movement (MCRL), was formed, and for the next twenty years it raged against Castro's Cuba and the internal "communist threat." But, until the 1980s, its membership was small and without significant political influence.

Costa Rica and Nicaragua have a long history of territorial and political hostilities, stemming from 1824 when Costa Rica annexed the Nicaraguan province of Nicoya. This touched off a series of border disputes and squabbles. In the 1850s, North American adventurer William Walker invaded Costa Rica from Nicaragua in an unsuccessful bid to set up a slave state. Following Costa Rica's 1948 civil war, the losing side twice—in 1948 and 1954—launched attacks on the central government with the help of the Somoza dictatorship. Likewise, anti-Somoza forces staged several abortive invasions from Costa Rica, and in the late 1970s, Costa Rica gave arms, political support, and military bases to the Sandinista rebels fighting against Somoza. All these events gave rise to the popular saying that "in Costa Rica there are three seasons—the dry season, the rainy season, and the season for conflict with Nicaragua" and helped pave the way for the creation of the contras' Southern Front during the 1980s.

Many Costa Ricans proudly call theirs the "most pro-Yankee country" in Latin America. One reason, undoubtedly, is that Costa Rica is one of the few countries in the hemisphere never to experience a sizable U.S. military presence (it successfully repelled William Walker's invasion). Costa Ricans prefer to view themselves more as an appendage of the United States—mainly Miami—than as part of the Third World.

As a result, Costa Rica has developed a national character which is a curious blend of smug self-contentment, social enlightenment, humanistic values, anticommunism, and pro-Americanism. It has had a rather charmed, if somewhat uneventful, history in a region where revolutions, civil wars, grave injustices, and massive economic disparities have forced people into drastic actions. While years of struggle have fortified the backbones, fired the spirits, and created strong passions in Nicaraguans, Salvadorans, and Guatemalans, Costa Rica's "good life" has, in comparison, created a somewhat dull, parochial people.

In both their personal and political behavior, Costa Ricans are nonconfrontational. They prefer accommodation to conflict. They often appear to be diplomatic fencesitters, unwilling to struggle to defend their political values. With the exception of the 1948 revolution and some infrequent strikes and land takeovers, social conflict has been rare. Costa Ricans have tended to rely on the pervasive, paternalistic welfare state, rather than grass-roots organizing, to solve their social problems.

While we gradually came to recognize these sometimes conflicting values, Tony and I continued to feel a spiritual and political affinity to Costa Rica's traditions of nonmilitarism, political democracy, social justice, and economic equality. When we first arrived, we had no idea how rapidly the U.S.-backed war against Nicaragua would engulf Costa Rica and alter the course not only of its history but also of our own lives. This book is largely about the impact of U.S. policies on Costa Rica, but it is heavily influenced by our personal experiences, which taught us a great deal about the underbelly of U.S. foreign policy.

A central argument underlying my analysis is that Costa Rica probably represents the world's best example of the type of country our government says it's trying, through political and economic policies, to foster around the world. As Costa Rica's former Planning Minister, Ottón Solís, put it, "Costa Rica is an important model for the U.S. We are the only Third World country to prove that the combination of a capitalist economy and a democratic political system can be successful." But, sadly, like the rest of Central America, Costa Rica suffered at the hands of Washington. During the decade of the eighties, U.S. foreign policies weakened and undermined, rather than strengthened and nurtured, this country's admirable political and social traditions.

Although from the outset we reported from other Central American countries, we quickly found that our biggest running story was at home—the creation of the contras' Southern Front. The Southern Front consisted of a number of small anti-Sandinista armies assembled along the border with Nicaragua and an elaborate support and resupply network run through Costa Rica. It paralleled the Northern Front, built up in Honduras from the remnants of Somoza's defeated National Guard and assembled into the FDN, the largest contra army. The game plan was for the Northern and Southern Fronts to push their way gradually across Nicaragua and eventually topple the leftist Sandinistas in power in Managua.

While the Northern Front operated fairly openly, those involved with the Southern Front denied it existed. In part this had to do with U.S. congressional funding regulations. The Reagan administration was barred by Congress from taking military actions aimed at toppling the Sandinista government and was permitted to use the contras only to interdict the supposed flow of arms north, from Nicaragua to the FMLN guerrillas in El Salvador. The military front out of Costa Rica, to the *south* of Nicaragua, violated this congressional mandate. Furthermore, Costa Rica's constitution prohibited the presence of any foreign military group—contra or U.S.—without the legislature's prior approval. Costa Rica's President Luis Alberto Monge had adopted an official policy of "unarmed neutrality," under which the thousands of Nicaraguan exiles in the country could engage in peaceful political activity but not in armed resistance. The Southern Front's main contra commander, Edén Pastora, and other militants within his coalition movement called ARDE (Revolutionary Democratic Alliance) were officially barred from entering Costa Rica. They therefore played hide-and-seek with authorities. Protected by a network of CIA operatives and collaborators within the Monge government, they were periodically "discovered" and expelled for the sake of appearances.

By 1984 we had developed a number of excellent sources within ARDE, the Costa Rican government and legislature, and among European diplomats and refugee workers. From them we began to learn the extent of U.S. and contra penetration of Costa Rica. We heard, for instance, that a network of government collaborators and local journalists was being built up and put on the CIA payroll to facilitate the contra war machine; that poor families in northern Costa Rica were being paid 2,000 colones a month (some $45 at that time) to send their sons to fight with the contras; that contra planes were fueled, repaired, and stored at Pavas, an airport for light aircraft near our house; that a rabidly anticommunist *gringo* farmer named John Hull was running contra operations from his ranch near the Nicaraguan border; and that other landowners—Americans, Cuban Americans, and right-wing Costa Ricans tied to the paramilitary Free Costa Rica Movement—were permitting contra planes to use their landing strips.

Several times we and other journalists were taken by ARDE to interview commander Edén Pastora at contra camps just inside Nicaraguan territory. On route to the camps we got a glimpse of the extensive contra support network in Costa Rica's northern zone: police and rural guardsmen warmly greeted the rebels; small workshops repaired and fueled ARDE boats and vehicles; shop owners regularly sold food, clothing, hammocks, batteries, beer, soda, and staple foods to the combatants; and dirt-poor rural homesteaders lent their front porches, fields, and sometimes their women to the contras.

In early 1984, Tony and I decided to try to go along on a military operation with another Southern Front group, UDN-FARN (Nicaraguan Democratic Union-Nicaraguan Revolutionary Armed Forces), led by Fernando "El Negro" Chamorro. Although officially part of Pastora's coalition, El Negro was actually working closely with the FDN (Nicaraguan Democratic Force), the CIA-created contra army based in Honduras. To our delight, we were told our request had been accepted and we could go in a few days. Just by chance, I mentioned the invitation to an experienced local television journalist whose judgment I trusted. He was shocked and warned us that he had learned UDN-FARN planned to take some journalists to the border area, have them killed, and then capture headlines by announcing that they had been murdered by the Sandinistas. We then told our UDN-FARN contacts that we could not go. Shortly afterward reporter Dial Torgerson and photographer Richard Cross were killed by a land mine along the Nicaraguan-Honduran border, and U.S., Honduran, and contra officials immediately blamed the Nicaraguan government. We became convinced that the certain elements of the CIA and contra leadership were intentionally plotting to kill journalists, blame Managua, and label the Sandinistas as "terrorists."[4]

Gradually Tony and I were getting a clear picture of how the CIA was organizing the Southern Front. It seemed to us that the contra story was there, just below the surface, waiting to be fully uncovered. But neither the Costa Rican nor the foreign press seemed to be vigorously pursuing it. The local press was, by and large, very conservative, and it was being aggressively courted by U.S. Embassy information officers to take a strongly anti-Sandinista line and not to disclose contra operations inside Costa Rica. With some notable exceptions, the U.S. media were still unwilling to believe that the Reagan administration was running a massive covert war against Nicaragua. At this point, I was working as a stringer for the *New York Times,* the London *Times* and *Sunday Times, Time* magazine, BBC and CBC (Canadian) radio, and ABC television and was doing occasional pieces for the *Philadelphia Inquirer* and the *Miami Herald.* Tony also reported for BBC as well as National Public Radio, and he worked as a cameraman for ABC, CBS, and WTN. Often we were challenged by editors or senior reporters who said our information didn't jibe with what they were being told in Washington. Gradually, I found myself becoming cautious, doubting sources who had been reliable and questioning the scope of the U.S. covert operations we were finding.

I was told by high-ranking contras, for instance, that the mining of Nicaragua's ports in early 1984 was purely a CIA operation and that ARDE and the Honduran-based FDN had been ordered to take the credit. Based on detailed information from two excellent sources within ARDE and bits and pieces from several others, I wrote what was scheduled to be a front-page story for London's *Sunday Times.* But when I talked again with ARDE's political spokesman, Alfonso Robelo, he denied the story with such conviction that, at the last minute, I got cold feet and asked the *Times* to withdraw it until the following week so I could do further checking. A few days later the *Wall Street Journal* broke the story, out of Washington, that the mining had been done by the CIA.

In March and April 1984, we worked on a series of exposés for the *New York Times* and ABC's "World News Tonight," including shooting video for the first time of Edén Pastora's clandestine command post in a large house nestled in the hills of the upper-class San José suburb of Escazú. We climbed to the field above the ARDE compound and took pictures of dozens of men (some in partial military fatigues), mud-covered jeeps, and a large tower for ARDE's clandestine radio station, "Voice of Sandino," which was officially located, its broadcasts said, "in the mountains of Nicaragua." ABC ran the piece, and the embarrassed Costa Rican government immediately raided and dismantled Pastora's Escazú headquarters.

For us and other American journalists in Costa Rica, such covert and illegal U.S.-sponsored activities were the most important story. Less apparent from our Costa Rican vantage point were the secret Sandinista operations to track and target contra leaders and CIA agents in various Latin American countries. These included assassinating deposed dictator Anastasio Somoza in Paraguay and a former National Guard major in Honduras, and plotting against Edén Pastora and other contra leaders in Costa Rica. While I harbored no illusions that the Sandinista security and intelligence apparatus was benign, I believed that it was not politically suicidal and therefore would not want to attack civilians and provoke confrontations with Costa Rica. The evidence of Sandinista atrocities was also wantonly thin. Again and again, shrill accusations by U.S. diplomats, the Reagan White House, and Costa Rican officials of mass murders of Miskito Indians, Sandinista army cross-border aggression, and guerrilla training camps in Costa Rica proved false. Costa Rica's left was tiny and factionally divided. It was incapable of threatening either the Costa Rican government or U.S. interests. Only much later, after the Sandinistas were out of power, did a fuller picture begin to emerge of the Sandinista counterintelligence operations inside Costa Rica, operations which seemed in part corrupted by isolation and secrecy, an addiction to violence, personal vendettas, and probably infiltration (see chapters 2 and 11)

By early May 1984, Pastora's troubles were coming not only from the Sandinista's, the Costa Rican government, and the press, but also from his main patron, the CIA. We and other journalists following the contra beat were well aware that Pastora's umbrella movement ARDE was deeply divided over a CIA ultimatum that it unite with the Honduran-based FDN. On May 1, the Agency sent word that Pastora had thirty days to make up his mind whether to subordinate his guerrilla forces to the command of the FDN and CIA. If he refused, the CIA would cut its support. Throughout the month there were heated clandestine meetings in San José between the anti-unity Pastora faction and the pro-unity Alfonso

Robelo faction. And toward the end of the month the ARDE commander and his supporters took out a paid advertisement to warn that "dark forces" were trying to force an alliance "by means of pressure, manipulation and false expectation."

May 30, 1984, promised to be newsworthy, but we had no premonition of danger. We woke that morning to find that Edén Pastora had summoned the press to his riverside contra camp, La Penca, to reveal publicly the CIA's ultimatum that he join forces with the FDN and to announce his intention to carry on a guerrilla war independent of U.S. support. ARDE had not asked us to the press conference; we heard it announced on the radio. We were annoyed at not being invited but not surprised, since we knew Pastora's people were angered by our recent participation in the ABC and *New York Times* series. Tony was confident he could talk his way in, and ABC news wanted him and his soundman, Edgar Ulate, to cover the event. Orión Pastora, ARDE's press officer, tried to stop Tony from going, but backed down when other journalists intervened, accusing ARDE of press censorship. Tony offered to take our jeep, since ARDE had not arranged enough transportation. There was no security check of the journalists' gear—an oversight we later came to suspect was intentional.

Over breakfast at the Hotel Irazú, Tony chatted briefly with one of the few journalists he did not know, a bearded man toting a large silver camera case who introduced himself as Per Anker Hansen, a Danish photographer. When Tony threw out the names of a couple of prominent Danish journalists he had met in Africa, he was somewhat surprised that the photographer hadn't heard of them.

Finally, close to noon, the press caravan pulled out of town, heading for the Costa Rican border hamlet of Boca Tapada about four hours away. From there they would board motor-powered canoes for the two-hour ride up the coffee-colored San Juan River to the La Penca, a one-hut encampment on the Nicaraguan bank. It was a sunny day, and most of the press corps was in a good mood. Associated Press reporter Reid Miller later said the trip began "like a Sunday picnic."

At the last minute I had decided to stay home because I

already had an assignment to do a piece for the *New York Times* on the CIA's thirty-day ultimatum against Pastora. I knew from interviews over the previous days that Pastora was going to use the press conference to denounce CIA pressure for ARDE to unite with the FDN and to declare that he would continue to fight the Sandinistas on his own. I worked all day on the piece, and about 7 P.M., the *Times* foreign desk told me it was running on the front page of the next day's paper.

Jody was asleep, and I was sitting in the living room with Shanti, our eight-year-old daughter. I was beginning to relax and calculate whether Tony and the others might get back into town that night. Just then the phone rang, and a journalist for Reuters asked if I had the radio on. I said no, and, after a pause, he said, "I'm sorry to tell you this, but there's been an explosion at the press conference. Many journalists have been injured and some killed. But they are not saying who."

I recall thanking him, putting down the phone, and turning to find Shanti standing close by, looking at me silently. Deep inside my brain a voice was saying, in a slow cadence, "Okay. This is it. The end of an era. Tony is dead. You have to carry on alone." I felt my heart contract, and an uncontrollable trembling began. I put my arm around Shanti, told her there had been an explosion, and said we needed to go downstairs to the office and try to find out what had happened. Over the next hours, Shanti stayed at my side, hardly saying anything, until she finally curled up and fell asleep on the office floor.

I put on the radio and heard anguished live reports from Edgar Fonseca, a reporter for the leading daily *La Nación,* who by chance had taken a two-way radio with him. As he described the destruction, confusion, and injuries of many of his colleagues, I could hear moans in the background. He urged Costa Rican or U.S. authorities to send helicopters and fast boats to La Penca to evacuate the wounded. He mentioned the names of many of the injured but not Tony's; the radio kept saying they were withholding the names of the dead. I called everyone I could think of— Pastora's aides, the U.S. Embassy, other journalists, Costa Rican officials, diplomats—but I couldn't get any news about Tony. Dery

Dyer, editor of Costa Rica's English-language weekly newspaper, the *Tico Times,* was assured by an embassy consular officer, Lynn Curtain, that he had "checked through channels," and "you can breathe a sigh of relief because there are no Americans dead. That we know." Dery conveyed this conversation to me, but somehow neither of us felt relieved. We learned later that at that very moment, *Tico Times* reporter and U.S. citizen Linda Frazier, whose legs had been blown off, was slipping toward death.

Then the phone started ringing, with calls coming from various news media around the world, wanting details, wanting me to get and send footage, wanting radio reports and newspaper copy. At first I tried to handle it all professionally, telling what I knew. Be detached, objective, cool, I kept telling myself. Then I could hear myself beginning to lose control, my voice rising and breaking, saying this was not a good time. I was sorry, but I couldn't file a piece just then; I didn't know if my husband were dead or alive. Some distant voices were, of course, sympathetic and apologetic, others pushed for my cooperation. I recall hanging up as someone started to discuss a financial bonus if I could get exclusive footage.

At some point during the evening I also went next door to talk with our neighbor Jack, who said he was a communications operator at the embassy but who we knew worked for the CIA. We, of course, had never discussed his real work with him, but as I explained the situation and pleaded for his help, our eyes met and it seemed clear he realized that I knew who he was. He said he would try his best, and after a while he called to say he was sorry but he had been unable to get the names of the dead. He offered to come and stay with me, a gesture that seemed to come from genuine concern, but I declined.

Finally I called our good friends Chris Rosene and Sheila Katz, who immediately offered to bundle up their two sleeping children and come over. Shortly after 10 P.M., Chris and I decided to drive to the hospital in the town of Ciudad Quesada, where the wounded were arriving. I hastily packed a change of clothes for Tony, wondering if I would bring them back unused. Sheila stayed behind with Jody and Shanti and their two children and took over the thankless job of monitoring the incoming calls and trying to contact contras, government officials, and diplomats for more information.

It was a two-hour drive through light rain, thick fog, and total blackness on twisting mountain roads. Guided only by the yellow flash markers down the center strip, Chris drove and I kept the radio tuned to an all-news station which had live reports from La Penca. The Red Cross was sending ambulances to Boca Tapada, the nearest point in Costa Rica which could be reached by road, but there were no helicopters or fast boats. The announcer described the condition of many of the journalists and said one foreign woman had died.

We arrived at the hospital just after the first ambulance, carrying *Newsweek*'s Susie Morgan, had pulled into the emergency entrance. There were already dozens of family members and friends of other journalists standing silently outside the hospital. Chris and I managed to persuade a nurse to let us see Susie, who was lying on a stretcher, for the moment unattended, outside an operating room. She was my friend, but I couldn't recognize her. Her whole, thin body was burned and covered with deep cuts, mud, and soot; her eyes were bandaged with surgical gauze, and her blond hair was singed away. I said her name softly. "Oh, Martha, am I going to live?" she asked in her high, precise British accent. Relieved by her voice, I said, "Of course you are," without having anything but my own determination to back it up. When I asked if she knew about Tony, she said vaguely that she thought she had seen him after the explosion. Then a nurse came to take her into the operating room. Later that night Susie was evacuated on a medical plane to Florida, and over the next several years she underwent a series of operations. She recovered, although she remained badly scarred and slightly crippled.

Outside the hospital, Chris and I joined the quiet vigil of family and friends of other journalists. At intervals, Red Cross workers with walkie-talkies would receive word that another ambulance bringing in the wounded was about to arrive. A white-uniformed nurse with a clipboard was keeping track of those who had arrived. At one point she pointed to a bearded man, dressed in hospital garb, sitting in a wheelchair just outside the swinging doors leading into the emergency entrance. "Do you know him?"

she asked me. "No," I said, "Who is he?" She checked her list. "He's Per Anker Hansen, a Dane," she said. "He wasn't injured, and he says he's waiting for a woman to come and collect him. Are you the woman?" "No," I answered. "I don't know him. I'm just waiting for news of my husband." She checked her list for Tony's name, but it wasn't there.

Throughout the night, I would occasionally glance at the uninjured journalist, Hansen, as he sat calmly in his wheelchair, chain-smoked cigarettes, and watched the scene in front of him. At one point, someone came and whispered to me that Linda Frazier was dead. I was already so emotionally numbed that I felt this news was being passed to another person and that my real self was viewing the scene from the sidelines—somewhat like the detached Danish journalist in the wheelchair.

Then, just at dawn, I heard Tony's name spoken over a crackly Red Cross walkie-talkie; he was arriving in the last ambulance. As they lifted him out on a stretcher, I could see wounds and cuts all over his body. He had a hole the size of a tennis ball in his side and the skin had been stripped away from several fingers on his right hand. But as he smiled faintly at me, the curtain of numbness lifted, and I felt confident he would survive. As I followed his stretcher through the swinging doors, into the emergency room, I glanced to my side and noticed that the wheelchair was empty. Hansen was gone.

TWO

The Road from La Penca

Some five days later, Costa Rican authorities announced that "the Danish journalist Per Anker Hansen" had become the bombing's prime suspect and issued an international arrest warrant for him. By piecing together the remnants of the bomb, video footage that miraculously survived the explosion, and information from the victims, investigators learned that the terrorist was traveling on a stolen Danish passport, with credentials from a nonexistent Paris photo agency, "Europe 7." The phony journalist had carried the bomb to La Penca concealed in his large metal camera case. There, as the press conference began, he set the case down in the midst of the journalists and left the room. Chillingly incriminating video footage taken by Jorge Quirós, a young Costa Rican cameraman who died in the explosion, shows the bomber easing his way through the crowd of journalists and out of the wooden shack where the press conference was being held. It shows an animated, angry Pastora denouncing CIA pressure and vowing never to align with the FDN. Then the picture disappears, but the sound continues for a few seconds: moans and cries over a blank screen.

Costa Rican investigators interviewed an ARDE sentry who said "Hansen" told him he'd come outside to "take a leak." In reality, he had gone to nearby bushes and detonated the bomb with a remote-control device later found by investigators. The bomb, made of C-4 plastic explosive and concealed below a false bottom in the camera case, was powerful enough to kill everyone in the wooden building. However, just before it went off, a contra radio operator, "Rosita," accidently kicked over the metal case as she was handing Pastora a cup of coffee. The force of the explosion went up and down instead of sideways, thus saving the lives of most of the journalists. Three died, along with Rosita. Seventeen other journalists were injured, many very seriously.

Pastora, whose legs were badly cut by shrapnel, and two of his wounded lieutenants were quickly carried to ARDE's one speed-boat and evacuated, along with the only doctor at the scene. The contras ignored the journalists' pleas to take the most seriously wounded—Linda Frazier and Jorge Quiros—in the same boat. Both died shortly afterward, and another Costa Rican journalist, Evelio Sequeira, died a few days later.

In the chaos after the explosion, the bomber propped himself against some gasoline barrels outside the building, smeared dirt on his face and arms, and feigned injuries. (Ironically, a photo of "Hansen" with a pained, stunned expression on his face subsequently ran in newspapers around the world to portray the horror of the event.) When the first canoe was being loaded with injured, he got aboard, leaving behind the most seriously wounded journalists. Doctors at the hospital said his only wounds were two small cuts on one arm, apparently self-inflicted. They put him in a wheelchair.

At the hospital, he asked again and again if a woman had come for him, and twice during the night nurses found him down a darkened hospital corridor, making a call from a pay phone. Investigators later determined that for several years Hansen had traveled with a woman who used a stolen French passport in the name of Patricia Anne Boone Mariscot. They had been in Panama during part of 1982 and had visited Mexico, Ecuador, Peru, and Honduras in the months before the bombing. They spoke French with each other. Hansen spoke accented but almost flawless English to those he met. Although he usually spoke Spanish like a South American, he could change his accent and imitate Mexican or European Spanish. Curiously, he knew almost no Danish. He said it was because he had grown up in Venezuela, where his father was a medical doctor. He was tall, well built, with a receding chin, high forehead, sagging eyes, and a sharp, slightly curved, distinctive nose. At times he had a full beard; other times he was clean shaven, and his hair color varied from brown to an odd almost-reddish shade.

In early May, Boone dropped from sight and Hansen teamed up with Swedish journalist Peter Torbiornsson and his young Bolivian cameraman, Luis Fernando Prado. They were seeking an interview with Pastora, and Hansen said he also needed photos of the contra leader for his Paris photo agency. Through this ploy Torbiornsson said later, the Swedish crew unwittingly provided cover for the terrorist.

Hansen also used Torbiornsson to assist his escape from the country after the bombing. At dawn Hansen finally persuaded the Swede, who was not seriously injured, to leave the hospital. Dr. Max Pacheco, a contra and CIA collaborator who was conveniently in charge of the hospital's emergency operations, arranged for Hansen and Torbiornsson to leave and take a taxi back to the Gran Vía Hotel in San José, where they had been staying. Once there, the bomber quickly paid his bill and checked out, telling Torbiornsson he had a plane to catch to Miami. He walked out to the street and disappeared.

Costa Rican investigators with the Organization of Judicial Investigation (OIJ) determined little else in their original investigation into the bombing. Right after this, any serious local investigation was virtually closed down (it was only reopened four years later, under the Arias government), and a series of false stories and dead-end leads, put out by Costa Rican and U.S. government officials, were planted in the press. The first came out within hours of the bombing: journalists in Washington began receiving calls from their contacts in the Pentagon, CIA, and State Department's Office of Public Diplomacy, "tipping" them that the bomber was Spanish, a Basque from the separatist organization ETA (Euzkadi Ta Askatasuna) who had received military training in Nicaragua and had been hired by the Sandinistas. Major U.S. news media, including ABC "World News Tonight," ran this story, and for most of the U.S. press this became the "answer" to the crime.

But within a few days, those of us seriously investigating were able to determine that the ETA man named by Washington, José Miguel Lujúa Gorostiola, had been under house arrest in southern France since January. There was no way he could have been in Central America. Yet none of the major U.S. media ran retractions of the ETA story or tried to discover why the U.S. government was issuing false information.

For other reasons as well, we sensed almost immediately that the investigation was somehow being manipulated. Over the first few days, press reports mentioned Tony and other so-called leftist

foreign journalists as suspected accomplices. Quoting unnamed
Costa Rican officials, the local press said the bomb was believed to
have been planted in Tony's metal camera box and that Linda
Frazier had close ties to ETA.

My brother Tim had heard a report of the bombing on the radio
in Portland, Maine, and had literally bounded out of bed and caught
the next plane down to Costa Rica. The morning after he arrived, I
read the local headlines and said I feared the ground was being
prepared to blame Tony for the bombing. Tim said I was paranoid.
But, the next day, as we were loading Tony from an ambulance onto
a medical jet, Costa Rican security officials intervened. They said
Tony was a prime suspect and couldn't leave the country.

It took two full days, while the Lear jet and medical crew sat
on the runway of the international airport, to clear Tony's departure. From his hospital bed, he gave hours of testimony to the
Costa Rican investigators. We had to get documents showing we
owned property in Costa Rica. We had to convince them that the
children and I were staying in the country, and that, after he
recuperated, Tony planned to return. And we had to get the U.S.
Embassy doctor to verify that Tony needed to leave. Finally he was
permitted to depart for the Philadelphia hospital where he underwent further medical treatment.

Shortly after the bombing I was contacted by the Committee to
Protect Journalists, a New York–based human rights group which
lobbies for press rights and safety worldwide. They asked if I would
be interested in undertaking an investigation into the bombing, on
their behalf and that of two other U.S.-based press organizations, the
Newspaper Guild and the World Press Freedom Committee. I
readily accepted, and they put up a small sum of money. The object
was to find out the true identity of the bomber, who hired him, and
why. We estimated the investigation would take no more than a few
months to complete. At the time we had no idea that we were
entering another sort of nightmare, one that would go on for years,
consume most of our time and financial resources, further disrupt
our family and professional lives, endanger those around us, lead to
the murder of our most important informant, and involve the
mysterious death of another key witness.

It never occurred to us that by pursuing a journalistic investigation we would end up being accused of drug trafficking, of murder, of bribing witnesses, of espionage; that we would be twice sued for libel; that our media clients would be pressured to stop hiring us and our colleagues would be told we were communist agents; that our names would be sprinkled through the diaries of a then-unknown lieutenant colonel Oliver North at the National Security Council; or that a CIA operative would be sent to Costa Rica with orders to "dig up dirt" on our personal lives. We viewed solving the La Penca crime as an important journalistic endeavor, but we had no indication at the time of how many unexpected turns the investigation would take. We did not foresee that in the progress of investigating this terrorist bombing we would stumble upon a much larger criminal enterprise, one that eventually became known as the Iran-contra scandal. Nor did we realize that when we ultimately found the identity of the bomber this would reveal another dirty operation, this one run out of Managua by Cuban intelligence and the Sandinista's Interior Ministry.

We began with the assumption that the bombing could have been the work of either the left or the right: the Sandinistas, Pastora's opponents within the contra movement, or the CIA. A day or two after the bombing, my brother, journalist Lyle Prescott, and I had a clandestine meeting in a deserted restaurant with "Andrés," the ARDE intelligence officer who was one of our best sources. He said that it was as yet unclear who was behind the bombing, that "Pastora has many enemies." However, he suggested some lines for further investigation. He said that while in 1983 the Sandinistas had indeed plotted to kill Pastora, it appeared that they had recently concluded the ARDE commander was more useful alive, because he was causing deep divisions within the contra ranks. Andrés recommended that we try to learn more about both John Hull, who had cut his ties with Pastora in the weeks prior to the bombing, and the Cuban American Felipe Vidal. This was the first time I had heard Vidal's name. Andrés explained, "We suspect he works for the CIA. In the days before La Penca, he talked about eliminating Pastora with a bomb."

These leads proved propitious. Within a short time, we managed, with the help of a Canadian writer, Hugh Graham, to locate

Felipe Vidal. For a period of about eight months we had a great deal of contact with him, with Hull, and with their contra network. Why Vidal met with us is something of a mystery: either he assumed we could be used to write sympathetic articles about the contras and his so-called International Brigade or he was keeping an eye on us, trying to determine just how much we knew. From him and others we learned many details of how this Hull-Vidal operation was linked to the CIA, Oliver North, the FDN, and Colombian drug lords. And we gradually gathered pieces of evidence indicating that this network was plotting to get rid of Pastora.

Through interviews in Costa Rica and Miami we collected other evidence. For instance, a Costa Rican businessman with good connections in Miami told us that Cuban extremists, including some persons connected to the 1976 car-bomb murder in Washington of Chilean diplomat Orlando Letelier, were claiming credit for the La Penca bombing. An American businessman told us that he had met a Cuban American who ran a Miami-based seafood import business which was a cover for "mercenary" activities and CIA operations. The American said this man, who used the name Ricardo Martinez, was ultra-right wing, hated Pastora, and boasted that "his group did La Penca and he seemed to know a great deal about it."

We gathered information that a group within the Costa Rican government, including Alan Solano, Albert Llorente, Minor Calvo, Colonel Rodrigo Paniagua, Colonel Francisco Tacsan, and a CIA dirty tricks unit called The Babies had put out false leads and concealed evidence after the bombing. We learned that just days before Oliver North had made a covert stop at Costa Rica's international airport to meet with an Embassy official and contra leader, and that North's "trusted courier," Robert Owen, was in Costa Rica at the time of La Penca. The night of the bombing, Owen was huddled in a CIA safe house in San José with John Hull and the CIA station chief. Persons linked to four different intelligence services—Venezuelan, Uruguayan, Israeli, and Vatican—all said it was a CIA operation. "The boys with the blue eyes were responsible" was the cryptic message from an official at DISIP, the Venezuelan intelligence service. Gradually the evidence began to indicate that the intellectual authors of La Penca included self-proclaimed American patriots, anti-Castro Cubans, right-wing and corrupt Costa Rican officials, and Nicaraguan contras from the FDN, all of whom worked under the direction of officials from the U.S. Embassy, CIA, and National Security Council.

Nearly a year after the bombing, we had what seemed to be a major breakthrough. We made contact with a young Nicaraguan named David, who, through a Costa Rican intermediary, Carlos Rojas, passed us a great deal of information. Carlos, a carpenter and small restaurant owner, was a neighbor of our office-mate, Julia Meeks, whom he contacted in late April 1985 with a most unusual story. He said that one Friday evening at the end of March he had stopped by the Rendezvous Bar near the U.S. Embassy to have a beer before heading home. The bar was empty, and as he sat there three men entered. He could hear by their accents they were Nicaraguans. Two of them ordered the third to wait, saying they would return in a few minutes. As soon as they left, the young, dark-skinned Nicaraguan turned to Carlos. "You must help me," he whispered. "Hide me. I want to get away. I don't want to be involved anymore in their things. They are going to dynamite the U.S. Embassy and assassinate high functionaries. Many innocent people will die. I want to get out."

For the next ten minutes the young man, who said his name was David, poured out his story, all the time watching the doorway for the return of his companions. He trembled as he spoke. "I'm an anti-Sandinista," he said, "but these people are much more evil than the Sandinistas." He said he had been a Sandinista soldier and had received military training in a "socialist country." He had defected and become part of an ultra-right-wing terrorist group, a dirty tricks unit within the FDN which took orders from the CIA and included John Hull and other North Americans, Cuban-Americans, foreign mercenaries, Costa Ricans, and contras. They operated from one of Hull's farms near the Nicaragua–Costa Rica border and also had safe houses and camps in Honduras, Panama, Miami, and Nicaragua, including in Managua. They had connections in high places and moved "in and out of Costa Rica like a dog from its own house," David told Carlos.

They trafficked in cocaine, marijuana, and arms, as well as specializing in terrorism: "They are using our cause [the contra war] to get rich," he said bitterly. David described himself as "a traitor to a dirty cause" and said he wanted to arrange for himself and his brother—who belonged to the group's cell in Honduras—to escape.

He explained that this group had carried out the La Penca bombing, and even though the assassination attempt against Pastora failed, the group was still intact and planning a new series of attacks, both in Costa Rica and Honduras, which would also be blamed on the Sandinistas. "The same people who committed the bombing against Pastora are the ones in charge," he told Carlos. Their next targets included the U.S. embassies in Costa Rica and Honduras, the presidential offices in San José, U.S. personnel, and several prominent contra leaders aligned with Pastora. He said he and his two companions were part of a reconnaissance team casing the U.S. Embassy. The plan was to put explosives in the electrical box outside the building. Many passersby would be hurt or killed in the explosion, and the U.S. would retaliate against Nicaragua.

Carlos, unfamiliar with the details of contra politics, listened intently and tried to remember as much as possible of David's rapid-fire monologue. He studied David's round, smooth face, his straight, black hair, and his concise descriptions punctuated with pauses as he tried to hold back his emotions. The young Nicaraguan seemed intelligent and sincere, and he was clearly very frightened. He said he knew it was risky to ask Carlos, a total stranger, for help, but he had not alternative. He was being closely guarded by his cellmates, who suspected he was losing his commitment to their terrorist mission. He said he was almost never left on his own. He had no independent contacts in Costa Rica. He needed Carlos's help to work out an escape plan for himself and his brother. Carlos said he was sorry but he could not hide him, that he lived in a row house with three small children. His wife ran a beauty parlor in the front room. The neighbors and clients would quickly detect a stranger in hiding.

The other two Nicaraguans reappeared in the doorway. David and Carlos quickly agreed to try to meet again. The trio left. Carlos followed them out and watched as they walked around the corner in front of the U.S. Embassy. A large gray American car without license plates stopped, and the three got in. Carlos could see another man and a woman inside the car.

Carlos took the bus home and told his wife, Mari, of this strange encounter. He was worried about David, about the innocent people who could be hurt in an embassy bombing, about what this meant for his country. What should he do? Mari's advice: "You heard nothing, you saw nothing, you do nothing."

A month after this meeting, on April 25, 1985, Costa Rican Rural Guardsmen raided a contra camp on one of Hull's properties and arrested nine Nicaraguans and five foreign mercenaries—two Americans, two Englishmen, and a Frenchman. Something clicked in Carlos's mind: David had mentioned this camp. Maybe his story was true. He contacted his neighbor, Julia, the only North American he knew, believing that she could warn the U.S. Embassy. At the time, he did not know that she was working with journalists. She recognized the potential importance of his information and asked Carlos if he would be willing to talk with us. He agreed, never dreaming that this act of responsible citizenship would alter the entire course of his life. Years later, as he and his family sat in their small apartment in exile in Canada, he looked at me and shook his head. "All I wanted was one beer before heading home. And look where it led."

The day the five mercenaries were arrested, Felipe Vidal happened to be in our office. "Oh, shit," he said as we heard the news on the radio. "Do you know them?" we asked, trying not to reveal what an important story we sensed this was. "Yeah," he said. "They're part of our group." He made some calls, including one to Hull, who told him the gringos had left most of their clothing at his ranch. We quickly got news assignments to cover the story. Vidal said he couldn't show up at the prison and asked if we'd mind taking their clothing and a note from him to the gringos. We readily agreed, thinking this might serve as a useful entry for interviews. Vidal's note, written in stilted and ungrammatical English, read in part, "One word of caution, though. Be careful of what comes out of your mouth. Too many words errantly spoken to the wrong ears is creating a stumbling block for your release. Either you people watch what you speak or you will continue in that limbo like state."

Fortunately, two of the mercenaries—Peter Glibbery, a studious-looking Brit, and Steven Carr, a wayward middle-class kid from Florida—didn't follow this advice. Within a few weeks, when no legal or financial help had come, this pair began to spill the secrets of their operation to a steady stream of journalists calling on them at La Reforma Prison. They told of military and paramilitary training in the United States, Britain, and South Africa; of their recruitment as military trainers for the contras; of their dealings with Hull, Tom Posey of Civilian Military Assistance, Cuban American organizations in Miami, and others in the so-called private aid network; of Hull's links to the CIA; of contacts with Oliver North's courier Robert Owen; of arms shipments to Ilopango Air Force Base in El Salvador and Hull's farms in northern Costa Rica; and of collaboration with U.S. Embassy and Costa Rican officials. There were also hints of involvement in drug trafficking and the plot to bomb the Embassy. The information helped fill in the picture of Hull's operation and its ties to high officials in the U.S. and Costa Rican governments.

In mid-May 1985, shortly after Carlos first talked with us, he again made contact with David, and over the following weeks a pattern was set: the two met at prearranged spots—a park near the university, a plaza or street corner in the city, a hotel, or on a bus—and Carlos tape-recorded when possible, took notes, or simply tried to remember the details he heard. Before each meeting, we prepared a list of questions for Carlos to ask David. Immediately after, Carlos came to us to be debriefed. David maintained that it was too risky for him to meet directly with the gringo journalists; he was being closely watched and we were too well known.

Through this method David passed much information. He said the La Penca bomber was supposedly a right-wing Libyan hit-man known as "Amac Galil,"[1] who had been trained by DINA, Chile's secret police, and hired for $50,000, which he received in cash from FDN political chief Adolfo Calero. David told us that the bomber had been flown out of the country to Panama and had since been living with a woman in the Cuban community in Miami and traveling to both Honduras and Nicaragua.

David said that there was an anti-Sandinista group in Managua, including some former Somocistas and a relative of President Daniel Ortega who "gave money to erase Pastora. They are the ones that from the beginning planned the attempt at La Penca and the intention was to plant differences between Nicaragua and Costa Rica." He said there were also some anti-Sandinista agents inside the Nicaraguan embassy in San José who "pass money for these terrorists to commit actions" and that some people in the U.S. Embassy were also involved. He stressed, however, that his group was more interested in profits than politics. "The main objective of this group in Managua is arms and cocaine trafficking. The war benefits the group's profits."

David confirmed our suspicion that the ETA lead and other false stories had been planted in the press to mislead investigators He said that one of Felipe Vidal's tasks had been to work with Costa Rican journalists on the CIA payroll to orchestrate the media cover-up. He also identified a number of Costa Rican officials who he said were part of a CIA-paid ring of collaborators assisting in the La Penca attack.

David's most startling information was that the La Penca network was still intact and was actively planning new terrorist attacks. In mid-July David passed word that the Embassy bombing and other actions in Costa Rica and Honduras would occur the last week of the month. He said that his group was waiting for the new U.S. ambassador, Lewis Tambs, to arrive in Costa Rica before beginning operations. Tambs was one of those targeted for assassination. He had just been transferred from Colombia, where drug traffickers had put a $1 million bounty on his head. David said his group, which had links to the Colombian cartel, planned to murder the ambassador, quietly collect the $1 million reward, and publicly blame the Sandinistas.

Our fears increased as we sensed a cover-story was being planned. For several months, certain Costa Rican security officials and the ultra-rightist paramilitary group, the Free Costa Rica Movement, had claimed to possess evidence that Costa Rican leftists and Sandinista agents were planning to bomb the U.S. and other embassies in San José. A left-wing member of the Legislative Assembly, Sergio Erick Ardón, said that security officials raided his home and seized his files. When they later showed him what they had taken, he says he was surprised to find a drawing of the U.S. Embassy among the papers. He concluded that his political party was to be framed for some terrorist act.

Then, on July 19, the day after we received word from David that the bombings were about to occur, the Reagan administration sent a warning to Nicaragua that it had "intelligence reports" indicating that the Sandinistas were planning terrorist attacks against U.S. personnel in Honduras and possibly elsewhere in Central America. In a diplomatic note delivered to Managua, the U.S. government warned that Nicaragua would be held responsible and there would be "serious consequences for the perpetrators and for those who assist them."[2]

Stunned by David's tale and these official statements, which appeared to lay the groundwork to blame the Sandinistas and escalate the war, we decided we must inform some Costa Rican authority, even though we knew government functionaries were involved. We met with Vice Minister of the Presidency Manuel Carballo, a strong supporter of neutrality and an opponent of contra activities within Costa Rica. He said our information fit what he had learned from his own investigation into John Hull's contra- and drug-trafficking activities. He proposed assigning a Rural Guard intelligence officer, Major (later Colonel) Harry Barrantes, to work with us. We also prepared several news reports linking this latest terrorist scheme to the La Penca bombing and the CIA. These reports appeared over the weekend, just before (according to David) the terrorist attacks were set to begin.[3]

Before we met with the Vice Minister, Carlos told us that David had proposed they spend several days together, making a tape recording of all the remaining details, photographing various safe houses and arms caches around San José and in northern Costa Rica, and preparing a map, including locations of camps and airstrips where weapons and drugs were moved through Costa Rica. David said that his brother was due to arrive the following week, at which point they both planned to escape from the group and leave the country. This seemed much riskier than their earlier rendevous, and we urged Carlos not to meet with David this time, but he insisted; David had assured him it was safe, because the rest of his group had gone to Honduras to make final preparations. Finally we agreed and gave Carlos a camera, map, tape recorder, and funds for the proposed trip.

Several days passed. Then, late one night, Tony received an hysterical call from Carlos, who said he was at a pay phone in La Sabana, the large park on the edge of San José and we must come for him at once. Carlos, usually an impeccable dresser, was filthy, covered with dirt and brush, and he was shaking so badly he could hardly talk. He finally managed to tell us that late one evening when he and David were in La Merced Park, they were suddenly jumped by three men, all Costa Ricans, who stuck guns at their throats. The attackers pushed them into a green jeep, saying, "We caught you, we've caught the informers." Carlos and David were held to the floor of the jeep, forced to pull their shirts over their heads, and driven for several hours to what David recognized as a contra camp located near John Hull's ranch house at the northern town of Muelle.

At the camp they saw other Costa Ricans wearing green Rural Guard uniforms with the national flag on the armband. They also saw a large number of partially opened crates labeled "medicines" that actually contained bullets and weapons. The guardsmen immediately confiscated Carlos's wallet and identification card. They huddled around a two-way radio to contact Hull and Colonel Rodrigo Paniagua, a retired Guard official who we knew worked with Vidal and the CIA. David whispered to Carlos that they would surely be killed and must try to escape. When the guard watching them was not looking, David kicked him hard in the groin, and they both jumped out through an open window.

As they ran for cover into the trees, shots rang out. All that night, and all the following day and night, they ran and walked over rough, isolated terrain. Wanting to get rid of any evidence in case they were recaptured, they threw their cloth bag containing four tapes, tape recorder, camera, and maps into a stream. Finally they got a lift into San José on a banana truck. They were dropped off late at night at La Sabana Park, and Carlos urged David to come with him to our house. But David said he needed to organize his escape and reach his brother. He promised to telephone the next day.

Early the next morning, we notified Major Barrantes about what had happened. At his request, Carlos made a long tape-recorded interview in which he detailed all he had learned from David and described the kidnapping. Barrantes took the tape to study it, first agreeing that its contents and Carlos's identity would remain confidential. Carlos, Barrantes, and Tony then went to Muelle, where Carlos managed to identify the location on Hull's main farm where his kidnappers had taken David and him.

No terrorist attacks occurred the following week, and we later learned from sources in Costa Rica and Miami that the hit team called the operation off once they realized that the press knew about it. They began to look for other possible leaks in their network. In Miami, Jesús García, a portly, loose-tongued Cuban American who months earlier had been invited to take part in the Embassy bombing, was set up and arrested on an illegal weapons charge. He told his lawyer, public defender John Mattes, that he had refused to participate in the plot to bomb the U.S. Embassy because he did not want to be involved in killing fellow Americans. "I told them I'd picked up too many bodies of Americans while serving in Vietnam." But he knew too much and was something of a wild card, so a scheme was hatched to put him in jail. Fortunately we heard of the case, contacted Mattes, and, by comparing notes, concluded that García and David were part of the same group. I went to Miami to talk with García and see what he knew about La Penca. He claimed to know quite a bit: "It's common knowledge in the Cuban community that we did it. Pastora is a communist." He said he understood that the man responsible was "Amac Galil" or "the Arab," that he was "from the Middle East," and that he was "hanging around Miami with René Corvo." He added, "There are probably one hundred people who know a lot about the Pastora bombing, and there are probably forty who know Amac."

In early August 1985, our first real indication that something was horribly amiss came when David failed to call as scheduled;

instead we started receiving telephoned death threats in our office. They said: "Carlos Rojas, Tony, Martha, Julia, and the others, stop your investigation or you all could die." Then cars without license plates and with two-way radio antennas started passing slowly by our house and Carlos's, sometimes parking for hours just down the street, taking photos, or following us when we left the office. We managed to identify several of the cars as belonging to Costa Rica's Ministry of Security and to the U.S. Embassy. Strangers—a Nicaraguan with a gold tooth, a tall man with a South American accent, and others—stopped Carlos and warned him to "stay away from his communist journalist friends." They threatened to kill him and his family.

Every day we waited for David to call. Carlos was becoming increasingly apprehensive. Then one day Major Barrantes arrived to tell us he had learned from an informant that David had been recaptured, taken to Hull's ranch, tortured for information, and murdered. Carlos, who had developed a close friendship with the young Nicaraguan, wept uncontrollably, saying over and over that David's death was his fault.[4]

Vice Minister Carballo suggested that Major Barrantes place armed guards in our houses. It was an arrangement we all quickly found intolerable: the guards lounged around our homes and disrupted our family life, lived in the office where we had all our files, made free use of our phone, had to be fed meals, and failed to show up when they did not have transportation. Finally we all agreed that we needed another form of security.

But before we could find one, Major Barrantes, Costa Rica's clean cop, disappeared. One day in early August 1985, he failed to appear for a prearranged meeting. We made some phone calls and learned that the day before, Barrantes had been summoned to the U.S. Embassy to meet with the military attaché. There he was offered a scholarship for a three-month course in counter-terrorism at Fort Benning, Georgia, and a plane ticket, on the condition that he leave the following day. It was an offer Barrantes later said he could not refuse.

Just after Barrantes left, an article appeared in the local press saying that the Costa Rican authorities had "new leads" about La Penca, based on a taped interview with a Costa Rican named

Carlos Rojas. The article said authorities had learned that the bomber was a Libyan, that he had collaborated with certain unnamed Costa Ricans, and that, after the bombing, he had been flown out of the country—to Managua![5] Barrantes had broken his pledge, had made Carlos's identity public and had, with the clever change of one word—Managua for Panama—totally changed what David said was political nature of the La Penca bombing. He made the Sandinistas, not the CIA, responsible. From a local journalist, we also learned that Hull had a copy of the tape, as well as a photo of Carlos sitting in our house. We guessed that one of Barrantes's "guards" had secretly taken the photo. Not surprisingly, at this point both Vidal and Hull completely cut any contact with us (for more details, see chapter 11).

In the wake of Barrantes's departure, the Costa Rican investigation into John Hull, La Penca, the plot to bomb the Embassy, and David's death closed down. When Tony went to meet with Manuel Carballo at the Presidential House, he was told by the Vice Minister that it would be better to speak outside. Once in the garden, Carballo explained that he suspected that his office was bugged by the CIA's The Babies. He said that he had met with several other top Costa Rican officials, all part of the proneutrality faction in the Monge government. Carballo said they had analyzed the situation carefully and concluded that they were locked into a confrontation with the CIA, and that they could not win. He said it was too dangerous to investigate these matters further, that he and the others feared their families, careers, and their political party (the National Liberation Party) would be hurt. He was sorry, he said, but they could offer us no further help or protection.

We were disappointed by this response, but we understood that it was also classically Costa Rican. Living as they do in a tiny country deeply dependent on the colossus to the north, Costa Ricans are survivors, not fighters. For Carballo's small, proneutrality faction, La Penca was but one piece in an increasingly complex and dangerous puzzle. Perhaps they viewed our investigation and its fallout as a fight between the gringos—John Hull and the CIA, versus Tony and me. There is a saying in East Africa, "When the elephants fight, the grass gets trampled." Carballo and the others feared that they could be personally and politically trampled by aligning with us. So they got off the field; they cut their ties with us.

Suddenly the price tag on our investigation had become extremely high. David had been killed, we feared Carlos and others might be in danger, and we had lost our support within the Costa Rican government. Even though we felt we knew much about La Penca and other covert operations, there was no end in sight. We had been living on the fringes of normality ever since the bombing, but it seemed that the more we learned, the more dangerous our situation became. We heard colleagues saying to us, either explicitly or implicitly, "You've gotten too involved, too obsessed; you're becoming part of the story." They suggested we move on to another story, maybe another part of the world.

While part of me longed to do so, it wasn't that easy. Other peoples' lives were in even more danger than ours. We calculated that our adversaries knew that, because we were Americans and journalists, killing Tony or me would precipitate a public outcry and an investigation. So instead of making major changes in our lives, we took a number of personal precautions and continued our investigation. We sent our children to stay with my parents in the States; put a burglar-alarm system in our house, office, and cars; tried to vary our driving routes; and began looking under the hood and body of our cars before starting them. But our most immediate concerns were two-fold: to get Carlos and his family out of the country, and to publish the findings of our investigation. With the help of friends and Amnesty International, we resettled the Rojas family first in Norway and then in Canada.

Simultaneously, we faced the task of compiling and publishing the results of our La Penca investigation as quickly as possible. We believed, on a personal level, that publicity would give us a form of protection. We worked day and night for several weeks to prepare the report in English and Spanish. In late September we sent it to the U.S. press organizations that had asked us to investigate La Penca.

We also presented the report at a press conference in the office of Dr. Fernando Cruz, Costa Rica's chief prosecutor (the equivalent of the attorney general in the United States), whose office was in charge of directing the government's La Penca investigation. Cruz, a soft-spoken, scholarly, and incorruptible judicial official had told us that he feared the government's investigation was being tampered with and intentionally closed down by powerful forces he did not fully understand. He courageously opened the press conference by saying that ours had been the only serious investigation of the bombing, and he urged the press and government to consider our findings carefully. His support meant a great deal to us—and it infuriated the U.S. Embassy, which retaliated by canceling several scholarships due to be awarded to people in his office. In a Costa Rican television interview just after our press conference, Ambassador Tambs called Tony and me "traitors" to our country.[6]

Those we named moved to counterattack as well. Right after the press conference, both Colonel Rodrigo Paniagua and John Hull sued us for libel and defamation of character, serious charges that carry both stiff financial penalties and jail sentences. We hired one of Costa Rica's most prestigious and high-priced attorneys, who managed to get the Paniagua case dismissed on a technicality. While we were glad to have avoided going to court, we did not merely want to evade the charges. We felt our reputations as journalists were at stake; we wanted the court to rule that the findings in our La Penca report were legally sound.

After a series of strategy sessions on how to handle the Hull lawsuit, we replaced this attorney with Oto Castro, one of a handful of Costa Rican lawyers committed to public-interest cases. He told us he would willingly handle ours and would not accept a fee, because he supported what we were trying to do. Oto, an unpretentious, open-hearted man who is driven by a love of life and sense of outrage at power misused, quickly became both our trusted legal counsel and dear friend. We all agreed that we should turn the tables and put Hull and the CIA on trial by calling witnesses who would substantiate and expand upon the evidence we had presented in our La Penca report.

We assumed that Hull had sued us with the conviction that we could never get witnesses to testify in open court, and at first we feared he was right. After all, David had been killed, and other key witnesses were being threatened. Much of our original report had been based on sources who requested anonymity. But between the time Hull sued us in October 1985 and the trial in late May 1986, the political climate had begun to shift, and gradually a number of sources expressed a willingness to go on the record. Those who finally testified on our behalf included Edén Pastora, Peter Glibbery, Carlos Rojas (who courageously returned from Canada), Jesús García's Miami public defender John Mattes, and a number of journalists. Our surprise witness was soldier of fortune Jack Terrell, who agreed at the last moment to testify. Terrell had worked with the mercenary recruiting outfit, the Civilian Military Assistance (CMA), and he says that after the La Penca bombing he had attended meetings to lay plans for a second assassination attempt on Pastora. He knew Hull, Bruce Jones, Felipe Vidal, Rob Owen, and other key members of Oliver North's network, and he claimed to have seen the La Penca bomber at one Miami meeting. Hull appeared visibly shaken when Terrell entered the courtroom as our witness.

We convinced the judge to accept Terrell as a substitute for another of our witnesses, mercenary Steven Carr, who did not show up. Carr and Glibbery had both agreed to testify for us and had received court orders to do so. Then, about a week before the trial, the Costa Rican courts suddenly granted bail to Carr, Glibbery, and the other three mercenaries. Hull had received the bail money from James Keyes, a Boston businessman who worked with North and the CIA, and had posted it with the expectation that the mercenaries would come to stay with him, so he could prevent them from testifying on our behalf.

Both Carr and Glibbery, however, told us they felt threatened by Hull and Vidal. They chose instead to stay at our house in the days before the trial. Carr, who got out of jail a few days before Glibbery, called an uncle in the United States who he told us worked for the CIA. Carr said the uncle arranged for him to see a top CIA official in the Embassy. For several days Carr had meetings at the Embassy, where they insisted that he speak with Hull as well. All urged him not to testify at our trial. He said they told him, "There's a 90 percent chance that Avirgan and Honey will lose the court case and that, whether they win or lose, you'll go back to jail if you testify."

This was a lie—under a court order to appear, Carr risked legal penalties for failing to appear—but his Embassy contacts succeeded in terrifying him. Two nights before the trial I was alone in our house, and Carr returned, saying he'd come from a bar where he was talking with Embassy people. Perceiving that he was drunk and feeling pressured, I asked if he intended to testify. He said he wanted to, that he wanted to tell the truth, to do the right thing, and try to put his life back together. After a brief conversation, he left the house, saying he was going to visit a friend.

That was the last we saw of him. He did not return to our house, and the next day we learned he had not reached the friend's house. On the day of the trial, when Carr's name was read out, he was not in the courtroom. Concerned for his safety, we asked the court to order Hull and the U.S. Embassy to clarify his whereabouts and to assure us he was all right.

We heard nothing from Carr until two weeks after the trial, when he called from jail in Naples, Florida. Apologizing for having caused us worry, he explained his disappearance from Costa Rica. He said Embassy officials and Hull had pressured him to jump bail and leave the country. He said the Embassy provided him with a bus ticket to Panama and arranged for a border guard to help him across, since he had no passport and was under court order not to leave the country. In Panama he was assisted by U.S. and Panamanian officials and put on a plane to Miami. The Embassy in San José had promised he would not go to jail in the United States, but as soon as he landed he was arrested and thrown in jail in Naples for a previous parole violation.

Carr was released in November 1986. But during his six-month term in prison, he continued to cooperate with journalists and congressional investigators. He did not change his story of illegal contra and CIA activities. Two weeks after his release he was found dead in a suburban Los Angeles driveway, victim of an apparent cocaine overdose. While in jail he had told us and other journalists that he was giving up his drug habit and also that he feared for his life. A number of mysterious circumstances surround his death and, shortly afterward, Peter Glibbery said that Hull had threatened that "the CIA will kill you like they killed Carr," if he didn't recant his story. When questioned about this,

Hull said Glibbery had misunderstood, and he had actually said that "the communists," not the CIA, had killed Carr, and would kill Glibbery as well.[7]

Despite the disappearance of Carr, the trial in late May 1986 was, in retrospect, an historic event. For two days, our witnesses testified about covert CIA and contra activities, drug trafficking, La Penca, and other terrorist plots. These were largely unknown, almost-taboo subjects about which the Costa Rican public had been told little. Security was very tight: court officials told us there had been telephone threats to bomb or otherwise disrupt the proceedings, and several of our witnesses were threatened as well. Pastora testified in a basement cell, under heavy guard, because it was deemed too risky for him to appear in public. Spectators were thoroughly searched three times, and the entire courthouse took on the appearance of a building under siege.

The courtroom was packed with our friends and supporters and local journalists. When the youthful, studious judge, Jorge Chacón, read his lengthy ruling, concluding that "this Tribunal absolves Anthony Avirgan and Martha Honey of all penalty and responsibility for the crimes of injuries, falsehoods, and defamation for damaging John Hull," the audience erupted with wild cheering. A grim-faced Hull quickly packed up his papers, gathered his small coterie of supporters, and left the courtroom, vowing, "This isn't over yet."[8]

Indeed it wasn't. For years we continued to do battle journalistically and legally with Hull's network. A week after the libel trial, we initiated a civil suit in U.S. Federal Court in Miami through the Christic Institute, a Washington-based public interest law firm. We sued for financial compensation for Tony's injuries, the loss of his camera equipment, and the harassment we both suffered during our investigation of the bombing. The suit charged Hull and twenty-seven other defendants with criminal conspiracy and other illegal acts for their involvement in the La Penca bombing and drug and arms trafficking.[9] On the advice of our lawyers we did not name any persons officially working for the U.S. government, since the courts could then dismiss the case on grounds of national security. Instead, we named people who were part of Oliver North's so-called "private aid network" to the contras, even though we knew that many of them worked clandestinely for the CIA or National Security Council. Many of those named in the suit subsequently emerged as key players in the Iran-contra scandal.

This case was filed six months before the Iran-contra scandal finally broke wide open in Washington. The defendants publicly called it "a fairy tale," but they were clearly worried. We learned, for instance, that in March 1986, almost two months before we had filed the case in Miami, Richard Secord and others knew of our plans and hired a retired CIA operative, Glenn Robinette, to come to Costa Rica and "dig up dirt" on us. He spent a great deal of money, hired some taxi drivers to spy on our office, and found nothing. We did, however, have several mysterious break-ins; files were rifled while valuables were left untouched. Just about this time, our names, that of our lawyer, Dan Sheehan, and key witnesses such as Jack Terrell began to crop up in Oliver North's diary entries. North ordered increased surveillance of all of us and set out to neutralize Terrell as a witness by falsely accusing him of plotting to assassinate President Reagan.[10]

The more we investigated, the more aggressively Hull and his associates tried to silence us and our sources. Some forms of harassment were remarkably crude. At one point, for instance, we were mailed a packet of cocaine concealed in books supposedly sent to us from Nicaragua by Sandinista Interior Minister Tomás Borge. Inside the package was an absurd letter in which "Tomás" talked about a cocaine-smuggling ring involving us, the Christic Institute, Nicaraguan President Daniel Ortega and his brother, Defense Minister Humberto Ortega, and Massachusetts Senator John Kerry. When our secretary, Carmen Araya, collected the package from the post office, she was immediately arrested by Costa Rican narcotics police, who raided our house later that day, detained one of our lawyers, and began legal action against us. It took a year and a half to get that case dismissed. In the meantime, we learned that the cocaine package had not been mailed from Managua, but rather had been inserted into the postal system in San José by members of the Costa Rican narcotics police, and that the scheme was hatched at a dinner meeting between

Vidal and another Cuban-American drug trafficker, Dagoberto Núñez.

At the same time in mid-1987, an ultra-right-wing, CIA-financed organization, misnamed the Costa Rican Democratic Association, brought a suit demanding that we be charged with espionage and expelled from Costa Rica. The Democratic Association held press conferences and took out paid ads denouncing us. Their accusation was lengthy—about six hundred pages of mostly irrelevant material—and legally ridiculous. It proved embarrassing nevertheless and took time for our lawyer, Oto Castro, and us to fight. In December 1988 this case, like the cocaine case, was dismissed for lack of evidence.

The U.S. Embassy also helped orchestrate a smear campaign intended to ruin us professionally and break us financially. U.S. diplomats "warned" journalists who did not know us (as well as Costa Rican officials and a number of our sources) not to talk with us because we were "communists" or worked for some unnamed "non-Western intelligence agency." Once, at a breakfast press conference, contra official Alfonso Robelo publicly identified me as "a known Sandinista agent." Privately he admitted U.S. officials had told him to say this.

There was a smear campaign against us and the Christic Institute in the United States as well. The right-wing press had a field day, spurred on by the flamboyant style and cockiness of our lawyer, Dan Sheehan, as well as by our antiwar activism during the 1960s and early 1970s, which "proved" we were anti-American. There was besides a sustained campaign to get our news clients to stop using us. The day after the bombing, when the New York Times ran my piece about the CIA's ultimatum against Pastora, I was abruptly informed that I was, in essence, fired. I subsequently learned that an enraged senior executive had berated the Times foreign editor, demanding to know why the paper had published a politically sensitive front-page story written by a mere stringer in Costa Rica. The standing policy, I was later told, was that any CIA stories, especially ones implicating the Agency in illegal activities, had to be written by staffers. I was also told that the powers-that-be had concluded I was a "leftist" and should be let go.

While I do not know whether the New York Times executive

was propelled into action by a phone call from Washington, we do know that, over the next few years, other editors were. National Public Radio (NPR) in Washington, for instance, received complaints from the State Department and its propaganda arm, the Office of Public Diplomacy, that its Central American coverage was too left wing. NPR executives made a decision not to use us to cover the contras, saying that they believed our lawsuit made us players in the story, and in part, we suspected, because some Reagan administration officials pressured top executives at both ABC and CBS television to stop using us, which, fortunately, they did not.

Despite such attacks, from the time of our victory in the Hull libel case, we could feel the balance beginning to shift. Within the United States there were growing numbers of journalists probing the illegalities of Washington's war against Nicaragua, including the role of Oliver North and other officials, the use of so-called private companies and individuals, the diversion of Iranian arms sales profits and other funds to the contras, and the connection with drug trafficking. Six months after we won our trial with Hull in Costa Rica and filed our La Penca case in the United States, the Sandinistas shot down Eugene Hasenfus's arms-laden plane over Nicaragua, and Attorney General Edwin Meese admitted to the illegal Iranian arms sales and the diversion of covert funds to the contras. The Washington press corps and Congress finally sat up and took notice. The Iran-contra scandal was front-page news.

The fallout—the Tower Commission report, the Iran-contra hearings, Senate Foreign Relations Committee reports and other congressional inquiries, Special Prosecutor Lawrence Walsh's trials and other court proceedings, and, for a time, a flood of investigative press reports—allowed the American public a glimpse into the world of covert operations and CIA dirty tricks. But the official inquiries largely turned out to be attempts at damage control and cover-up. They did not investigate what we believe were the worst of the illegal deeds: the La Penca bombing and other terrorist plots, and the CIA- and contra-related drug trafficking.

We hoped our lawsuit would help expose these issues. As originally crafted by Christic Institute attorney Rob Hager, it was a brilliant, pioneering, and courageous case that held great legal and political promise. From the outset, however, we had severe conflicts with the Institute's chief lawyer, Daniel Sheehan, who early on muscled aside Hager and a number of other competent lawyers, insisting upon pursuing a broad-based conspiracy theory involving the so-called "Secret Team" and stretching back to the Bay of Pigs. Tony and I wanted a much more narrowly focused and tightly argued case, centered on the illegal U.S. war against Nicaragua. We became increasingly disturbed by Sheehan's sloppy attention to the investigative and legal aspects of the case, his cavalier and often rude behavior before the court, and his conspiratorial and cultist mind-bent, which eventually degenerated into viewing anyone critical of his approach—including Tony and me—as being part of the enemy camp. Over the years we struggled, together with a group of extremely dedicated and competent Christic Institute employees, to try to concentrate on building a solid investigation and to keep the case focused upon the facts surrounding the La Penca bombing.

In the end, we lost—both to Sheehan and, ultimately, in court. In June 1988, just three days before the trial was scheduled to begin, the Miami judge rejected our case, saying we did not have sufficient evidence. Declaring that the case was "frivolous," the judge subsequently ruled that we had to pay court costs for all the defense lawyers—a total of about $1.2 million, most of which had been donated by a very generous couple in Los Angeles. We lost, repeatedly, various appeals, and the Christic Institute ultimately ended up paying close to $2 million in court costs and legal fees to the Hull-North network. This was a devastating personal and political defeat from which Tony and I are only slowly beginning to recover.

In contrast, the political climate in Costa Rica improved in the late 1980s. President Oscar Arias took office in May 1986, just two weeks before our libel trial with Hull. Arias had been elected on a "peace" platform, and he immediately set about trying to end the Nicaraguan conflict. Through the Central American Peace Plan, a regional diplomatic initiative for which he won the 1987 Nobel Peace Prize, and through his government's crackdown on contra operations inside Costa Rica, he worked toward a negotiated cease-fire, demobilization of the rebel forces, and new presidential elections in Nicaragua. During his tenure, Costa Rica's Legislative Assembly sponsored investigations that finally implicated Hull, Panama's General Manuel Noriega, Robert Owen, Ambassador Lewis Tambs, CIA station chief Joe Fernández, and National Security Council adviser Admiral John Poindexter and his deputy Oliver North in contra-related drug trafficking and other illegal acts. The Legislative Assembly commission report ordered that all these individuals be declared *persona non grata* and never again be permitted to enter Costa Rica.[11] And, with Arias's blessing, Costa Rica's judicial authorities reopened investigations of Hull and La Penca and ultimately brought murder charges against both Hull and Felipe Vidal.[12] Both fled the country, thus preventing a trial, while the whereabouts and true identity of the bomber "Per Anker Hansen" remained a central mystery of the La Penca case.

This mystery was not finally solved until mid-1993. But the findings brought a new twist which, in turn, raised more questions. By the early 1990s, all serious investigations into the La Penca bombing pointed toward the CIA. These included, in addition to our original investigation and successful defense in the Hull libel trial, two documentary films, scores of articles, several books, and the Costa Rican judicial investigation. While evidence and testimony pointing toward the CIA filled many file drawers, all tips and theories implicating Managua had led, one after another, to dead ends.

Then, just about the time we were getting ready to move from Costa Rica and I was completing a draft of this book, we decided to check, once again, the story of one of our original sources, Peter Torbiornsson, the Swedish television journalist with whom "Hansen" traveled in the weeks leading up to the bombing. Over the years, Torbiornsson had consistently maintained that he had first met the bomber by chance in early May 1984, at a San José hotel, and that he had naively accepted him as a Danish free-lance photographer on assignment to cover Pastora. Torbiornsson repeatedly argued that he had unwittingly facilitated "Hansen" attending the La Penca press conference and aided his escape from Costa Rica afterward.

Somehow this story failed to hang together. We were troubled, for instance, by the failure of a Swede to detect a phony Dane, by Torbiornsson's apparent lack of concern for his young, badly wounded Bolivian soundman, whom he abandoned when he himself hastily left Costa Rica, and his failure to join aggressively with those of us who were determined to get to the bottom of this terrorist act. So we decided to reinterview Torbiornsson and see if we could pick up anything that might help to determine the bomber's identity.

I tracked Torbiornsson down in southern France and asked if he had anything new to add to his previous declarations. "I'm now certain he was working for the Sandinistas," Torbiornsson responded in a slow monotone. Stunned by this about-face, I asked for an explanation. For the first time Torbiornsson admitted that he had been introduced to the bomber beforehand in Managua, that he was now convinced he was working for Nicaraguan and possibly Cuban intelligence, and that he assumed from the outset that "Hansen" had been sent to spy on Pastora's operations.

I worked hard to control my frequently hot temper as I asked Torbiornsson why he had not revealed this information years ago, right after La Penca. "I really didn't think at first that 'Hansen' was the one who did it," he replied.

My colleagues and I realized we needed to get the full story face to face and so persuaded Torbiornsson to fly to Miami. For two days, journalist Doug Vaughan and private investigator Richard McGough and I talked with Torbiornsson. He was remorseful—"I have a strong sense of guilt at some level"—but argued he had tried to handle this situation in his own way because, he said, he had not wanted to mix publicly "the Sandinistas with this bombing." Torbiornsson said he therefore had set off on his own solo journey to try and find out the truth. Over the course of several years he told us, he had met with top Sandinista officials and demanded answers. He said he received vague admissions that Sandinista intelligence had a hand in La Penca. But the officials he spoke with had not given the bomber's real identity or any other details.

Torbiornsson seemed unaware of the full gravity of his declarations and of his behavior. He had concealed evidence, lied under oath and on camera to Costa Rican authorities and his colleagues, and set back the investigations for years. In Miami, he did agree to go again to Managua with Tony, to knock on doors, and try to get answers. Several months later, Doug Vaughan and another colleague Carl Deal also went to Managua and made the same rounds. These two trips produced some tidbits of information, some promises of help, but no hard evidence and certainly no admissions that the Sandinistas had a roll in La Penca. Frustrated, short of funds, and uncertain Torbiornsson was telling the truth, we filed away our notes.

Soon after this a new source appeared. In Paris, Jorge Masetti, a former Argentine leftist who had begun denouncing Castro, told *Miami Herald* foreign editor Juan Tamayo and several other journalists that he recognized photos of the La Penca bomber as someone who had been part of his cell and had worked for Sandinista counterintelligence. Eventually seven other Argentine former leftists who were located by journalists in Buenos Aires also identified the bomber as someone they had kown as "Martin." Through a process of elimination they concluded that his real name was Vital Roberto Gaguine. Gaguine had reportedly been among twenty-eight leftist guerrillas killed in a 1989 attack on La Tablada, Argentina's largest military barracks outside the capital.

In late July 1993, Vaughan succeeded in locating Gaguine's father and brother who live in Miami Beach. For days they refused to talk with him by telephone or in their homes. So early one morning Vaughan walked unannounced into the Gaguine's upscale men's clothing store and showed the two men a half dozen photos. "Yes, that's my brother," said Eduardo Gaguine, viewing the famous photo of the bearded "Per Anker Hansen," clad in hospital garb, sitting in a wheelchair at the San Carlos hospital.

Vaughan then showed Samir ("Sami") Gaguine, a frail man in his seventies, two other photos—one of "Hansen" beardless and wearing a floppy hat, and the other a mug shot from Panama immigration records of a curly headed, mustached youth starring straight at the camera. "My son," acknowledged the older man. "He's dead. What worse news can you tell me?"

Plenty. As Vaughan explained La Penca, the father and son broke down sobbing. They had never heard, they said, of La Penca.

They did not know that Vital Roberto had been involved in Nicaragua. They had seen him, they admitted, in Miami in the mid-1980s, but they claimed to know little of his political activities. Vital Roberto had told them only a sad personal story: that his wife, America García Robles, had committed suicide and killed his only child. She had jumped out of a ninth-story window in Buenos Aires holding their young daughter in her arms.

Two days after this encounter, Vaughan and Juan Tamayo obtained further confirmation through fingerprint identification that the La Penca bomber was Vital Roberto Gaguine. Costa Rica's badly bungled original investigation into the bombing had failed to recover any fingerprints of "Hansen" from his hotel room or from searches of immigration records in several countries. For years we and other colleagues tried, without success, to turn up a paper trial for Hansen in Panama where he had lived for much of 1982 and had been involved in a minor traffic accident. Panamanian officials insisted documents must have been prepared, but someone, it seemed, had made them disappear.

Then in the rubble of the 1989 U.S. invasion, Vaughan, a bulldog of an investigator, spent a week turning Panama's remaining immigration files upside down and came up with two sheets of paper, misfiled under "Anker." They contained a photo of the bomber taken in 1982 and the only known fingerprint of "Per Anker Hansen." In mid-1993, journalists in Argentina managed to retrieve fingerprints of Vital Gaguine from Argentine police files. The two sets were brought to Miami and shown to a police expert. "Absolutely, to a certainty, the same person," was his conclusion.

At last we had, we believed, the true name of the illusive La Penca bomber, whom we and a handful of others had doggedly tracked for nearly a decade. He had become a phantom with more sightings than Elvis and a man of many names and pseudonyms— "Per Anker Hansen," "Amac Galil," "The Arab," "El Turco," "Martin El Inglés," and, finally, Vital Roberto Gaguine. Over the years the CIA and others had identified him as being a long list of real people—José Miguel Lujua Gorastiola, Arturo Nestor Figari, Hector Amodio Perez, Per Arvid Hansen, and Vigelio Paz, among others. His nationality had been variously said to be Danish, Basque, Libyan, Venezuelan, Uruguayan, Israeli, Palestinian, Cuban, and, finally, Argentine. His affiliation had molted from that of a free-lance photographer to a mercenary hired by the CIA and cocaine cartel to an Argentine guerrilla working for Cuban and Sandinista intelligence.

But the identification of the bomber did not add up to a resolution of the La Penca case. He was, conveniently, said to be dead. So we were instead left with a set of matching fingerprints, a dozen photos, a voice recording, some video footage, several distraught family members, scores of witnesses and informants of varying credibility, and two trails of leads that went, geographically and politically, in opposite directions. We now knew "who" had planted the bomb, but we still do not have clarity about "how" or "why" (see chapter 11).

In the process of this long search for the La Penca bomber we and others stumbled upon a viper's nest of other illicit goings-on inside Costa Rica. Many of these activities were linked to Washington's covert war against Nicaragua. But the more we dug, the more we uncovered evidence that U.S. economic and political policies were also eroding Costa Rica's democratic institutions and social fabric. The following chapters are an attempt to look systematically at what happened in Costa Rica during the 1980s and to examine how policies of the Reagan and Bush administrations undermined the stability of this tiny, democratic, pro-American ally.

THREE

AID's Privatization Solution

We are not Santa Claus. It's obvious with resources come responsibilities.
—AID official in Costa Rica, 1984

In San José's most fashionable nouveau-riche suburb, the U.S. Agency for International Development (AID) compound stands as an oversized monument to one of the Reagan administration's most generous and controversial foreign assistance programs. AID, which is part of the State Department, disburses most of the United States' economic assistance around the world. AID assistance to Costa Rica began in 1946, but it wasn't until the 1980s that Costa Rica became a major recipient of U.S. funds.

The AID complex in Costa Rica, which opened in 1988, was constructed to conform to Washington's worldwide security standards. Its twin buildings, set one hundred feet back from the road and without windows on the lower floors, are surrounded by a fifteen-foot steel-reinforced concrete fence said to be tank-proof and impossible to scale. "A grenade or mortar would barely scratch the paint," said one of the site engineers.

The compound includes a warehouse, maintenance shops, motor pool, and commissary. It contains office space for 300 to 500 workers, although AID employed only 129 people in Costa Rica in 1992 and announced plans to close the program entirely by late 1996. On the top floor of the office building is a vault-like emergency room intended to hold about a dozen diplomats. Guarded by a special combination lock, it has its own communications system, air conditioning, electrical generator, and fully stocked refrigerators. There are no windows. The ceiling contains an escape hatch to the roof, which, dotted with red landing lights, can serve as a heliport.

Contractors for the AID compound and the enormous American Embassy building located a few blocks away say that U.S. officials minutely monitored the construction of both buildings and, in following Washington's prescribed specifications, insisted that the cement be mixed to meet mid-winter Michigan building standards, not those of tropical Costa Rica.[1] This is ghetto or Beirut-style architecture in a tranquil upper-class San José suburb. It is a concrete fortress laced with sophisticated security equipment in a peaceful country that has no tanks, army, guerrillas, death squads, or significant civil strife.

AID is meant to put the U.S. government's best foot forward overseas. Its logo during the 1980s was a friendly handshake, portraying the institution as serving the needs of the Third World. But in Costa Rica, it was difficult to get in AID's front gate. Appointments must be arranged in advance. Cameras and tape recorders are not permitted inside without advance arrangements. Visitors must pass through four security doors and a metal detector before entering the building, and, once inside, they are escorted everywhere and watched by video cameras. A number of areas are off-limits, including to staff without special clearance.

Officially, AID says the compound cost $9.2 million;[2] Costa Ricans involved in the construction estimate the real cost must have been several times higher. The Agency says that, under a joint AID–Costa Rican government agreement signed in 1984, local currency—*colones*, not dollars—from an AID "trust fund" account in Costa Rica's Central Bank were used to cover nearly all the costs of the building. Not so, say Costa Rican government officials and contractors involved in the project. They say *everything* was imported to construct both the AID complex and Embassy building except the cement and the wooden doors. The dollars used to purchase these imports were obtained by asking Costa Rica's Central Bank to convert colones in this AID account into dollars, a practice which violated AID's own policy. As discussed below, the main rationale for AID's Costa Rica program in the 1980s was balance-of-payment support—that is, giving Costa Rica hard currency to meet its import needs. Reconverting colones into dollars to pay for construction of U.S. government facilities actually drained off Costa Rica's foreign exchange.

Just as AID's architecture conforms to worldwide security regulations having little bearing on local reality, so its gargantuan program during the 1980s fit a Reaganomics mold that paid little attention to Costa Rica's specific economic problems and needs. AID's program in Costa Rica was a virtual carbon copy of the free-market prescriptions pushed throughout the world by the Reagan and Bush administrations. During the 1980s AID shifted emphasis away from projects designed to lessen Third World poverty and toward funding for the private sector. President Reagan signaled this shift in 1981 when he urged a joint meeting of the International Monetary Fund (IMF) and World Bank "to believe in the magic of the market place."[3] The standard package of policy changes—dubbed "structural adjustments" and advocated by AID, the IMF, and World Bank—included promotion of private enterprise, new exports, foreign investment, currency devaluation, and food imports, coupled with cutbacks in government employment, welfare programs, state-owned institutions, trade barriers, and subsidies protecting the internal market. As Colin Danby writes in his study of AID's Central American programs, "[N]ever before has so much pressure been exerted on Third World countries to follow a relatively uniform set of structural adjustment measures dictated by the United States, IMF, and World Bank. U.S. policy has *always* emphasized private sector development and openness to trade and investment, but never before has it been maintained that development is the same as, and limited to, these policies."[4] In 1984, as President Reagan told AID officials, "The success of our overall policy [in Central America] is directly linked to what the private sector can accomplish."[5]

In the post–World War II period, Washington has used economic aid and military might to try to ward off Soviet and Cuban influence in the region. In the 1960s, the Cuban revolution helped spawn two distinct responses toward Latin America from the Kennedy and subsequent administrations. One was the ambitious promotion of economic "modernization" through the Alliance for Progress, Peace Corps, and AID projects and then, in the

1970s, a shift in aid both toward "the poorest of the poor" and toward countries which complied with certain human rights criteria. The other was counter-insurgency and covert military operations such as the Bay of Pigs, the coup against the Rafael Trujillo government in the Dominican Republic, and the overthrow of democratically elected President Salvador Allende in Chile.

In the 1980s, the Sandinista revolution also provoked a dual response from Washington. The military response included the contra war against Nicaragua, counter-insurgency operations in El Salvador and Guatemala, U.S. military build-ups (particularly in Honduras), low-intensity warfare strategies throughout the region, and the invasion of Panama. The Reagan administration's economic response, as outlined in 1983 in AID's "Four Pillars" program, called for "greater use of the private sector in solving development problems."[6] It postulated that the private sector is, ipso facto, efficient, competitive and democratic, while the public sector is corrupt, sluggish, and antidemocratic. At a 1986 AID conference on privatization, Agency Administrator Peter MacPherson bluntly proclaimed, "Statism has failed."[7]

Behind the rhetoric of private enterprise and free trade, the poor were not targeted for help; they were to benefit from the supposed trickle-down of loose change from the bankrolls of big manufacturers, growers, and exporters. It was a raw, survival-of-the-fittest policy, shorn of the humanistic trappings of the 1960s and 1970s. This change was reflected, for instance, in a sharp decline in U.S. Development Assistance (DA), the traditional channel for project funds targeting the poor. In 1980, 97 percent of the AID budget for Costa Rica went for Development Assistance, while after 1985 it was only about 12 percent and in 1990 just 13.5 percent.

AID was able to push its private sector policies and structural-adjustment programs most aggressively and to claim the greatest success in implementation in Costa Rica, which Washington viewed as politically more stable and militarily less important than the rest of Central America. The Reagan administration wished to support the "fragile democracies" in El Salvador, Honduras, and Guatemala and did not dare tinker drastically with existing structures for fear of provoking a right-wing military coup or, worse, left-wing guerrilla victory. In these countries, an overriding goal was stabilization, not transformation of the economy. U.S. funds were used in part to reinforce rather than dismantle the state, as well as the military sectors.

In contrast, Costa Rica's well-established democracy, economic and political stability, and nonmilitarism enabled it to undergo substantial changes without risk of political or economic collapse. Costa Rica therefore became the showcase for pushing economic innovations that were adopted more gradually and more cautiously in the other Central American countries. In Costa Rica, AID's gigantic structural adjustment package emphasized recovery and growth through sell-offs of government enterprises, creation of new private institutions, cuts in government spending and social services, expansion and strengthening of private banks, nontraditional exports, foreign investment, currency devaluations, importation of basic grains, tightening of credit and subsidies to small farmers, and tax and tariff incentives to agricultural and industrial exporters. These policies were implemented through AID's creation of what has been called the "Parallel State": a set of private institutions and enterprises which duplicate and weaken the state sector.

Just as the AID compound in Costa Rica was apparently financed in an unorthodox manner, so AID's entire Costa Rican program was carried out with unique and highly irregular twists. The AID account in Costa Rica's Central Bank, for example, was kept in the name of AID, while normal procedure would have been to turn the account over to the host country. Also unusual was AID's requirement that the Costa Rican government pay interest, averaging 21 percent annually, on the undisbursed portions of this account. These unconventional and costly practices gave enormous discretionary power to then-AID director Daniel Chaij, whom several prominent Costa Ricans referred to sardonically as "the proconsul." In addition, irregularities in the allotment of AID funds in Costa Rica became the subject of a devastatingly critical State Department memo which concluded that Chaij and other AID officials had mismanaged and misappropriated millions of dollars in foreign aid to Costa Rica.

AID's Economic Quid Pro Quo

As the Reagan administration took office in January 1981, it viewed with dismay what one diplomat called "the mounting storm clouds" over Central America. In El Salvador and Guatemala, leftist guerrillas appeared on the verge of toppling pro-U.S., right-wing military regimes. But it was the Sandinistas' 1979 triumph over the Somoza dictatorship in Nicaragua that most worried the new Reagan administration that a "communist beachhead" had been established in Central America. The 1980 Santa Fe report, which formed the ideological framework for Reagan's Latin American policy, warned, "The Americas are under attack. Latin America [and] the Caribbean rim and basin are spotted with Soviet surrogates and ringed with socialist states. . . . The United States must remedy the situation."[8] The 1980 Republican National Convention called for a cutoff of U.S. aid to the "Marxist government" in Nicaragua and pledged to "support the efforts of the Nicaraguan people to establish a free and independent government."[9]

Parallel with Central America's political turmoil, the region entered a severe economic crisis, with declining terms of trade and living conditions and a virtual collapse of the Central American Common Market (CACM). This economic collapse was precipitated by the so-called second OPEC (Organization of Petroleum Exporting Countries) crisis of the late 1970s, during which prices of gasoline and petroleum products rose steeply, hitting hardest Costa Rica and other non-oil-producing Third World nations. Like the rest of the region, Costa Rica's economy had been built on a few traditional agricultural exports—coffee, bananas, beef, and sugar—and on highly protected local industries producing for internal and Central American markets. At the end of the decade, the country plunged into its most serious economic slump in this century, with coffee prices plummeting, oil import prices doubling, and inflation skyrocketing 100 percent. As the terms of trade shifted, Costa Rica was forced to borrow heavily from foreign banks and lending institutions. International interest rates shot up, increasing Costa Rica's foreign debt to more than $3 billion by 1980, the highest per capita in Latin America. The situation was particularly acute because almost half of Costa Rica's debt was in high-interest, short-term loans from commercial banks.

Meanwhile, the Reagan administration had moved swiftly to implement its anti-Sandinista policy. Within weeks of taking office, Washington suspended more than $60 million in aid to the Nicaraguan government, and the CIA began covertly funding and training anti-Sandinistas rebels—the contras—in Honduras. In late 1981, Assistant Secretary of State Thomas Enders proposed that the United States step up economic aid to its Central American allies: Costa Rica, Honduras, El Salvador, and Guatemala.[10] According to a Senate Democratic Policy Committee report, "The Reagan Administration . . . placed high priority on greatly increased aid to Central America as a means of countering the threat posed to other Central American countries by the Sandinista government of Nicaragua."[11] In 1979, Central America had received less than 1 percent of total U.S. foreign aid. In 1986, 8.7 percent of AID's worldwide allotment went to the four U.S. allies in Central America and to the contras. The dollar amount grew almost ten-fold, from $103.9 million in 1979 to $995.5 million in 1986. The percentage of military aid also rose sharply. Between 1946 and 1980, U.S. military assistance to Central America averaged only 7.7 percent of the total, while between 1981 and 1987, military aid ranged from 18 percent to 36 percent of the total aid package to these countries.[12]

The Reagan administration also set out to prevent close congressional and host-country oversight of its massive Central American aid programs. By their nature, foreign-aid procedures give an administration a relatively free hand in how the funds are spent. Each year Congress votes overall levels for U.S. economic and military assistance programs, but in most cases it is left to the administration to determine allotments for each country. Particularly after congressional debate over the U.S. war against Nicaragua heated up, administration critics threw their energies into blocking contra aid rather than scrutinizing the assistance programs to Costa Rica and other allies in the region.

In addition, congressional oversight was made more difficult because under the Reagan administration the type of foreign aid shifted away from Development Assistance allotted for specific programs to a heavy reliance on Economic Support Funds (ESF) or cash transfers of dollars. During the 1980s, ESF funds to

Central America were used almost exclusively for balance-of-payment support—that is, financing imports from the United States, general budget support, and foreign-debt servicing, rather than for projects.[13] In Costa Rica, ESF cash transfers represented a new form of assistance. Between 1975 and 1981, Costa Rica received no ESF funds, the bulk of the money being Development Assistance project loans. Of the more than $1 billion in aid given between 1982 and 1988, $830 million were in the form of ESF cash transfers. Just over $30 million were used for ESF project aid, while the rest—nearly $800 million—were cash transfers, mostly in the form of grants rather than loans.[14] According to an AID evaluation, cash transfers to Costa Rica "have been large in relation to population ($55 per capita), large in relation to GNP (peaked at 5 percent), and large in relation to imports (an average of 13 percent)."[15]

The Senate Democratic Policy Committee found that, by their nature, these cash transfers could easily be used for "inappropriate" purposes. Its report says, "Some argue that the [ESF] program has grown so rapidly primarily because the executive branch is trying to avoid congressionally-imposed restrictions and guidelines that govern other assistance programs. . . . Considerable concern has been raised about the increase in ESF assistance, largely because of cash transfers, for which there is the least amount of accountability as to how the countries spend the money."[16] As detailed below, in Costa Rica disbursement was overseen by the AID mission and a handful of Costa Rican technocrats; the Legislative Assembly, public, and government as a whole had very little say over how AID funds were spent.

The Reagan administration also bypassed Congress and regularly increased AID appropriations to Central America by utilizing the system of "reprogramming"—changing appropriated funding levels, supposedly to meet emergency needs. In 1981, for instance, the administration used reprogramming to "drastically increase" the aid flow to Central America, including a 43 percent increase to Costa Rica.[17]

The administration also turned off the AID pipeline when Costa Rica balked at accepting Washington's economic and political preconditions. In November 1983, for example, both AID and the IMF suspended disbursement just after Costa Rica declared its neutrality policy and voted in the United Nations against the U.S. invasion of Grenada. In mid-1984, AID withheld funds in order to pressure Costa Rica into passing a bank-reform bill. Then, in both 1986 and 1987, AID withheld funds after President Oscar Arias spoke out against U.S. aid to the contras and launched his Central American Peace Plan.

Congress, for its part, could increase annual aid allotments through supplemental authorizations and appropriations. Later in the decade, the Democratic majority in Congress used this power several times to increase funds to Costa Rica, after the administration had slashed the aid package in order to show its displeasure with the Arias peace plan.

Ironically, when the Reagan administration took office, the AID mission in Costa Rica was preparing to pack up and go home. In the 1970s, U.S. assistance to Costa Rica was comparatively modest, fluctuating between $.7 million and $20.7 million per year,[18] and the Carter administration had concluded that Costa Rica was largely middle class and therefore undeserving of further assistance. But when Liberation Party candidate Luis Alberto Monge won the presidency in February 1982, the Reagan administration took a fresh look at tiny Costa Rica. "The U.S. saw Costa Rica as an ally, a model of democracy. There were tensions in the region. So we said, 'We're going to support Costa Rica in a big way,'" explained Carl Leonard, who was AID director in Costa Rica from January 1988 to mid-1990. Quietly, behind closed doors, the Reagan and Monge governments struck a deal.

Just a month after his inauguration, Monge went to Washington. Although the pink-cheeked, rotund Monge had had ties in the past to CIA-financed labor and political-front organizations,[19] some doctrinaire Reaganites were concerned that, as a long-time trade unionist and as one of the architects of Costa Rica's social-welfare state, Monge would prove too left-leaning. They quickly found there was no need to worry: the Costa Rican President understood how to strike a political bargain. A strong social democrat, he is also staunchly anticommunist, and he quickly showed that he was willing to use democratic Costa Rica as a regional rubber stamp for Reagan's anti-Sandinista policies. In return, Monge wanted Washington to pour in aid and bail Costa Rica out of its economic crisis.[20]

Monge was an old-style, Tammany Hall–type politician, a coarse, heavy-drinking, womanizing, back-room deal maker who had spent the previous fifteen years embroiled in party politics, playing off and balancing the different factions in Liberation's broad-based political spectrum. He came to office when Costa Rica was in its worst economic crisis and when the country was rapidly moving from the sleepy shadows to center stage in Washington's political arena. While Monge understood his party and his country to their core and had years of experience in international trade-union activities, he did not fully grasp the complexities of big-power politics or the full implications of the Reagan agenda for Costa Rica. A pragmatist and realist, he was short on idealism or political vision. His cabinet was a balance between the right and left wings of his party, between those who supported Washington's war against Nicaragua and those who supported Costa Rican neutrality. In earlier, calmer times, these opposing factions could have functioned with minimal friction, but in the mid-1980s, the Nicaraguan war reverberated in Costa Rica, causing deep, irreconcilable divisions in the government, a near coup d'etat, and finally the marginalization of the pro-peace group.

Monge intended for Washington to play a balancing act as well, using Costa Rica to take verbal swipes at Nicaragua and to help isolate the Sandinistas internationally, while in return respecting Costa Rica's traditions of nonmilitarism, strong public-welfare institutions, and the government role in the economy. But he found again and again the right-wing ideologues in Washington had virtually no understanding or appreciation of Costa Rica's unique political traditions. They pushed Costa Rica relentlessly to adhere to their political and economic policies; every concession Monge made only brought new demands from Washington. Costa Rica had been accustomed to doing a slow minuet with Washington, in which Washington led, but usually benignly and subtly. Suddenly Costa Rica was forced to follow a new, faster-paced number in which there were no breaks. By the time Monge furtively tried to establish a bit of political space—in September 1983, declaring his lofty principle of "perpetual unarmed neutrality" and, in May and June 1984, making a twelve-nation "Operation Truth" tour in Europe—it was too late. Costa Rica was already doing Washington's bidding.

This new dance between Washington and Costa Rica began with Monge personally assuring President Reagan and other top officials that he was a man whom Washington could work with—for a price. Monge came to office at a time when the Reagan administration was isolated from Latin America because it had supported Britain in the Malvinas/Falkland Islands war with Argentina. Monge was the first Latin leader to call on Reagan since Washington had sided with London. Monge also used the state visit to voice harsh attacks upon Cuba and the leftist Salvadoran guerrillas, but Washington most appreciated his remarks concerning Nicaragua. Standing on the steps of the White House, the short, portly Monge, dressed in a somber three-piece suit and reaching only to Reagan's armpits, warned that the Sandinistas represented "a massive offensive by Marxist-Leninist totalitarianism."[21]

Over the next four years, the Reagan administration repeatedly summoned Monge to Washington to help push various contra aid proposals through the reluctant Congress. According to Fernando Zumbado, who served as Monge's ambassador to Washington and then to the United Nations, on one occasion "Monge was in Miami, in some sort of medical facility, resting and having a check-up, and there was a vote that was coming up on contra aid. They sent an airplane to take Monge to Washington to talk to President Reagan and he was then sent over to Congress. He found he was in the middle of a propaganda effort by the White House. He tried to be as complex and ambiguous as possible in his explanations, taking ten minutes or so to answer each question, but they always got something they wanted to get from him."

Monge did manage to use these trips to Washington to solicit economic support for his country. During his first visit he called on the IMF, inviting them back to Costa Rica. By the end of 1982, a new $100 million IMF standby agreement had been approved. Over the next few years, Costa Rica received increased assistance as well from the World Bank, the Inter-American Development Bank (IDB), Canada, and several western European countries. But

Table 1. Costa Rican Foreign Aid, 1980–90[22]
($US millions)

	1980	1981	1982	1983	1984	1985	1986	1987	1988	1989	1990
AID[a]	14	13	50	212	168	207	157	181	102	115	75[c]
World Bank	30	29	0	25	0	84	0	26	100	95	4
IDB	133	29	61	36	87	0	174	120	61	189	63
IMF	60[b]	330[b]	100	0	0	52	0	66	0	53	0

Source: Statistics provided to author by AID Mission/Costa Rica and Costa Rican Central Bank.

a. AID funds consist of Economic Support Funds (ESF), Development Assistance (DA), and PL-480 food aid, but not military assistance.

b. The IMF suspended disbursements in both 1980 and 1981, after the Carazo government failed to meet IMF requirements.

c. No agreement was reached during 1990 on an additional $15 million in PL-480 food aid. Instead this was rolled over and sent in 1991.

the Reagan administration and AID rapidly stepped forward to become Costa Rica's major donor. By 1983, AID assistance had soared to $212 million, a 27-fold increase over 1978. U.S. funding for the three-year period 1983 though 1985 equaled 35.7 percent of the Costa Rican government's operating expenses and averaged about 25 percent of export earnings.[23] Between 1982 and 1989 Costa Rica received over $1.2 billion in economic, military, and food aid, six times more AID support than in the previous three decades combined.[24] During the 1980s, Costa Rica became the world's second-largest per capita recipient of U.S. economic aid, surpassed only by Israel.

The massive influx of aid to Costa Rica was a short-term salve: it stabilized the economy, lowered inflation, and reduced unemployment. Monge became immensely popular within the country, hailed for having rescued Costa Ricans from further economic hardship. Largely hidden from public view, however, were more fundamental economic problems that seemed to grow worse. One of the main rationales for AID's balance-of-payments support and emphasis on increased exports was so that Costa Rica could pay off its foreign debt. Yet Costa Rica's foreign debt rose from $1.1 billion in 1978 to $3.8 billion in 1984 to $4.5 billion in 1989, surpassing the gross domestic product (GDP), which hovered around $3.1 billion. As Monge left office, interest payments on the foreign debt were suspended and the country went into technical default.[25]

Also largely hidden from public view were the political and

economic conditions tied to U.S. economic assistance. U.S. diplomats repeatedly denied any political strings, but the "quid pro quo" document introduced in Oliver North's trial in the spring of 1989 provides irrefutable evidence that the Reagan administration repeatedly used AID funds as a carrot to win Central American support for the contra war.[26] The forty-two-page document details how the White House doled out funds to a number of countries, including Costa Rica, in return for their support for "the Nicaraguan Resistance." The document cites, for instance, a meeting on June 25, 1984, at which CIA Director William Casey proposed to Ronald Reagan, George Bush, and other top administration officials that the United States "provide Honduras and Costa Rica with increased economic assistance as an incentive for them to assist the Resistance."[27] Perhaps as a direct result of this meeting, Costa Rica was allotted an additional $73.2 million in 1984, $60 million of which were for balance-of-payment support and $7 million—three and a half times the original $2 million earmarked—were for military assistance.[28]

While denying there were any political preconditions, U.S. officials were frank about the economic quid pro quo for these dollars. AID used a variety of methods to compel the Monge and Arias governments to accept its package of economic "reforms." A leading Costa Rican economist recalls, "Through AID we were presented a possible way out of the crisis. They said, 'Don't worry. We will finance everything.' But under very special and very specific circumstances and conditions."

In carrying out its economic policies, AID and its powerful director, Daniel Chaij, worked closely with influential local businessmen, leaders of the various chambers of industry, commerce, and export, and prominent editorial writers and columnists who were ideologically committed to and personally benefited by the Agency's private-sector programs. What one businessman dubbed "Chaij's inner circle" included Ernesto Rohrmoser, Luis Liberman, Samuel Yankelewitz, Alberto Dent, Jr., Mario Rojas, Carlos Araya, Rodolfo Cortes, Guillermo von Breyman, and Richard Beck. AID also helped the government put together a relatively small and stable "team" of Costa Rican ministers and economic technocrats—Eduardo Lizano, Carlos Manuel Castillo, Fernando Naranjo, Federico

Vargas, Jorge Manuel Dengo, and Armando Aráuz, among others—
who oversaw implementation of AID's policies. These AID collaborators in the government were neo-liberals who viewed Costa
Rica's existing economic model—based on consumer goods industries, production for the local and regional market, a large state
sector, and a few traditional agricultural exports—as incapable of
pulling the country out of its economic crisis. The AID network
paralleled and in some cases overlapped with the CIA-run network
of Costa Rican collaborators assembled to support U.S. political and
military objectives during the 1980s.

U.S. officials and AID maintained a sort of veto power over
certain appointments. This system of control was informal, with
the Costa Rican president recognizing that certain top officials
must get along well with Washington, and U.S. officials expressing
displeasure if someone they considered hostile was named. U.S.
influence began during the election campaigns with, it is widely
said, the selection of the two vice-presidential candidates for each
major party. "In this country we must have two vice presidents,"
quipped one top politician, "because one is for Costa Rica and the
other is for the U.S." During the 1980s, Vice President Armando
Arauz in the Monge administration and Vice President Jorge
Manuel Dengo under Arias were close confidants of the U.S.
Embassy and AID. The Costa Rican cabinet, as well, was said to be
divided into two camps. As one Monge government minister
recounted in an interview, "Once jokingly in a cabinet session
someone said, 'Well, as you know we have two kinds of ministers
here: ministers of the state and ministers of the AID mission.' And
really that's what we had."

AID viewed the presidency of the Central Bank as another
essential post. During the 1980s, bank presidents Carlos Manuel
Castillo and Eduardo Lizano had extremely close relations with
the U.S. government, and Lizano became the most important
official assuring implementation of AID's policies. When Lizano
briefly resigned in 1987, the U.S. Embassy and AID voiced their
disapproval. After President Arias announced that Lizano was
being reinstated, the AID administrator in Washington, Peter
MacPherson, made a point of telling a visiting Costa Rican government delegation that this was "very useful news."

AID helped finance the salaries of Costa Rican officials, including, during the Monge administration, some Ministry of External Trade (MINEX) functionaries[29] and, under Arias, the head of the government's export-promotion institution, CENPRO. These payments were funneled through the AID-financed institution CINDE (Coalition for Development Initiatives) or through the United Nations Development Program (UNDP), thereby circumventing an AID prohibition on paying salaries of employees of foreign governments. One minister, who says he was offered but declined such a salary, claimed this indirect arrangement also provided cover for Costa Ricans who "did not want it known they were paid by AID."

AID worked not only with its local network of collaborators, but also with the IMF, Inter-American Development Bank, and World Bank to impose "structural adjustments" and economic "reforms" in Costa Rica. AID agreements, as well as those of the IMF and World Bank, laid down "mutually supportive" conditions which the Costa Rican government had to meet.[30] As U.S. ambassador Curtin Winsor explained, "[W]hat we created was a cascading conditionality where we got the Costa Ricans to agree to do what the World Bank wanted, with what the IMF wanted, and with what the commercial banks wanted, and with what we wanted. And we coordinated the whole thing so that they got a loan package . . . and they in turn did what was necessary to make what all of us wanted to see done, work."[30] As noted earlier, AID, although not required by law to do so, several times cut off funding when Costa Rica failed to meet IMF or World Bank conditions. Despite the 1984 Kemp-Kasten Act, which prohibited cross conditionality—that is, tying U.S. assistance to compliance with IMF, World Bank, or other multilateral donor agreements—a close relationship continued.[31]

AID documents refer benignly to the "extensive dialogue" between the mission and the Costa Rican government, but AID often had to play hardball, including cutting off funds and exerting heavy pressure on Costa Rican legislators and government officials, to win approval for its reforms and projects. According to a minister in the Monge administration, "Because of our enormous debt and economic crisis, we were pushed as a country to a very critical situation in which our independence was really lost. And from that moment on we were more in the hands of the IMF or the AID mission and less on our own feet, with our own possibilities to make decisions."

AID's assistance agreements clearly show the multiple layers of preconditions for such aid. The second Economic Stabilization and Recovery Agreement, dated December 13, 1982, was for $64.5 million ($56.5 million in loans and $8 million in grants), and it laid the foundation for AID's privatization and export-oriented policies implemented over the next eight years.[32] Despite the economic crisis, the thirteen-page agreement, signed by AID director Daniel Chaij and Central Bank president Carlos Manuel Castillo, provided no support for government social programs such as health or education and only $5 million for mortgage financing to families below the poverty line. This latter was added at the Monge government's insistence. The rest of the agreement concentrated on bolstering the private sector. It required, for instance, that by February 1983 the government present to the legislature a bank-reform law allowing private banks access, for the first time, to funds previously funneled solely to state financial institutions. The agreement also stated that the entire $64.5 million AID package be loaned, interest free, to private entrepreneurs to import goods from the United States. These businessmen, in turn, were to repay an equivalent amount in colones which, as explained below, was then deposited into a special AID account.

The agreement goes on to detail how these colones must be spent: $8 million were earmarked to create the private-sector export-promotion agency CINDE; $10 million were for "a special credit line" to private banks to be loaned to private producers and manufacturers; and the remaining $41.5 million in colones were to be lent in "unsubsidized" loans to small and medium-size private businesses and (at Costa Rica's insistence) to cooperatives. Thus while subsidized or low interest rates were eliminated for small and medium producers and cooperatives, under AID's terms, importers/exporters, large manufacturers, and private bankers were guaranteed access to U.S. funds at concessional rates. Finally, the AID agreement required that the Monge government negotiate and comply with an

IMF accord and that, within a year, it devalue the colón so that the official rate was on par with the black-market rate.

This agreement and those that succeeded it were almost never submitted to the Legislative Assembly for approval. Under Costa Rican law, the legislature must approve only loans (such as from the World Bank, IMF, and IDB, and from AID's special PL-480 food assistance program) and not grants, which accounted for the bulk of AID funds. The rationale is that because loans must be repaid, the legislature should approve them. The Central Bank president also has the right to contract for loans on his own, without Legislative Assembly approval, so that even some AID loans were not put up for debate and approval. As one AID economist told the U.S. General Accounting Office (GAO), "[Grants] avoided a Costa Rican Assembly debate over US conditions, while a loan would require approval and debate, and could have resulted in unwanted anti-American rhetoric."[33]

Over the years, however, a handful of legislators looked closely at AID's conditions and raised a cry of alarm. One of the most persistent critics was the independent-minded Liberation Party congressman José Miguel Corrales. In June 1987, he sent letters to both President Reagan and President Arias denouncing the "illegalities" and "inconsistencies" in the six agreements signed between 1982 and 1986. Although Corrales found little official support for his views, his candor won considerable popular support. In both 1988 and 1989 he was voted in public opinion polls as the "best legislator."

Daniel Chaij's Extraordinary Powers

As AID director from February 1982 to June 1987, an unusually long term, Dan Chaij carried out Washington's privatization policies with a missionary zeal. In fact, he was the son of Seventh Day Adventist missionaries who had served in Uruguay and Costa Rica while he was growing up. Chaij had been an AID functionary in a number of Latin American countries, spoke excellent Spanish, and knew how to get along with the country's economic and political elite. A vice-minister recalled that "in dealing person-to-person

Chaij was very approachable. He wasn't arrogant, although he was also very insistent."

Others, such as Fernando Zumbado, who held top posts in both the Monge and Arias governments, were less flattering: "Dan Chaij was a guy that accomplished things on his own. Many times he didn't respect the rules. He had a lot of power in Costa Rica and he got used to that type of power. He was like the finance minister." Even Central Bank president Lizano, who supported the AID-imposed privatization and austerity measures, was lukewarm in assessing Chaij: "He was very much interested in getting things done and he was quite impatient with the bureaucracy all over the place for postponing or putting obstacles, stones in the road."

An Arias minister went even further in his criticism: "Chaij and the American Embassy threw money around. They had so much money that people—politicians, reporters—were afraid to talk. Many people live from these funds so they behaved themselves." He added, "If they [the Embassy or AID] viewed someone as a good minister they might say, 'You need a car? OK.' He gets a car. 'You need computers?' You get computers. 'You need a scholarship for your son?' Your son gets a scholarship." A 1987 AID audit and State Department memo documented such illegal practices.

In addition to a loose and partisan management style, the AID mission also adopted several highly irregular administrative procedures which greatly enhanced Washington's hand in reshaping the Costa Rican economy. One was the creation of a local currency equivalency account, known as the "Special Account." Dollars given via AID's ESF cash transfers were deposited in installments to the government's account in the Central Bank, so long as Costa Rica satisfactorily implemented the AID-prescribed reforms. These dollars were lent to private importers, again following AID guidelines, and importers then repaid these loans with colones deposited into AID's Special Account in the Central Bank. These funds were used for AID-specified projects and programs. In effect, this allowed AID to disburse its funds twice—once in dollars and a second time in colones.

Such local currency equivalency accounts, while required by AID missions in other countries, are not used by the World Bank, IMF, or most other international agencies.[34] Much of Costa Rica's other foreign assistance has been in the form of loans earmarked for specific projects; those grants were simply deposited in the Central Bank without requiring an equivalent local currency account. In the late 1980s, however, both Canada and Spain gave some modest balance-of-payment grants for which local equivalency accounts were set up.

The AID Special Account had, until the Arias administration demanded a halt, two other unique and possibly illegal features. One was that the local currency account in the Central Bank was kept in the name of AID, while normal Agency procedure would have been to turn it over to the host country. Costa Rican officials and U.S. investigators say that, under this extraordinary procedure, the AID mission was able to select the projects and private enterprises to be funded with little Costa Rican government oversight. AID officials feared, as one told Colin Danby, that if the Costa Rican government controlled the account, AID funds would be "sopped up in social programs"[35] such as public health care and education. AID wanted to funnel the money mainly to the private sector. According to a 1988 evaluation of AID's Costa Rican program, "Most local currency projects were private sector–oriented (42 percent of expenditures), and many of them supported export-oriented production."[36]

In addition, because these funds were held by AID and therefore not included in the Costa Rican government's annual budget, the Legislative Assembly was not able to review most AID projects. AID documents clearly reveal that this unusual policy was intended to bypass the legislature, because this body was certain to raise questions about AID's programs. A 1988 AID study noted, "In practice, AID had almost complete control of local currency funds. This procedure is in sharp contrast to the normal Costa Rican practice of heavy legislative involvement and close ministerial control of all expenditures."[37]

While both U.S. and Costa Rican government officials complain that submitting projects for Legislative Assembly approval can be a slow and cumbersome process, it has also historically been an important feature of Costa Rica's democratic system. The system of checks and balances, so highly praised as a cornerstone of U.S. democracy, was bypassed by AID and Costa Rican technocrats who rightfully believed that the Legislative Assembly was likely to balk at AID's privatization program. Those few AID projects that went to the Legislative Assembly for approval—the EARTH university and the two bank "modernization" laws—were heatedly debated, and AID had to exert vigorous behind-the-scenes arm-twisting to secure their passage.

This system gave enormous discretionary power to a handful of people, most importantly to AID director Chaij. As one of his strongest critics, Arias adviser John Biehl, charged, "Nobody here ever managed the amount of money he has managed. He was not accountable to the U.S. because under American law, the money was Costa Rican. But AID, along with certain Costa Ricans said no, it belongs to the U.S. so it didn't have to go through the Legislative Assembly. Together they managed to work about a billion dollars for just exactly what they wanted."

A final reason for keeping the Special Account in AID's rather than the Costa Rican government's name was so that the AID mission could impose another extremely unusual, very costly, and apparently unique requirement. Beginning in 1982, AID administrators required the Costa Rican government to pay the going interest rate, averaging 21 percent annually, on the undisbursed colones in the AID Special Account. (In contrast, AID frequently lent money to private Costa Rican banks at subsidized interest rates, sometimes as low as 2 to 3 percent.) According to Lizano, "The Central Bank never pays interest on the government accounts," so only by keeping the account in AID's name could interest be collected.

These interest payments were deposited into the AID colones account and became part of the enormous pool controlled and dispensed by the mission. According to U.S. Embassy statistics, between 1984 and 1988, the government paid the AID account over 8.5 billion colones in interest or more than $169 million at the exchange rate for those years. Of this, AID "programmed" (spent) 4 billion colones during this period, while the rest remained undisbursed. This meant that AID had even more funds to work with in its drive to restructure Costa Rica's economic policies.

U.S. officials in Costa Rica attempted to portray these interest payments as routine. They produced a copy of an AID cable, sent to all AID missions, saying that, "AID policy favors that local currency be placed into an interest bearing account." In fact, Costa Rica was the only country in the world making interest payments prior to 1988. In addition, these interest payments were suspended for several brief periods in order to reduce Central Bank losses, an indication, Costa Rican officials say, that the policy was "flexible" and locally imposed.

The AID cable cited by Embassy officials to justify the interest payments is dated October 1987, five years *after* the Costa Rican mission began this procedure.[38] The date of this cable also coincides with the period when Arias government officials, congressional Democrats, and AID auditors were beginning to take a critical look at AID's activities in Costa Rica. It is impossible to avoid the conclusion that AID sent out this cable retroactively to cover up its questionable policy in Costa Rica. AID officials in Washington indicate that only after this point did AID begin to charge interest in selected other countries.

Even after this scheme had been exposed as far from routine, U.S. officials in Costa Rica contended that it was of no import, implying that the Arias government was making much to do about nothing. One Embassy official, who asked not to be named, arrogantly argued, "The interest issue was a phony issue in my view. You can debate it either way and it doesn't make much difference. It's Costa Rican money whether they pay themselves interest into a bank account or not. What difference does it make? It has accounting implications and nothing else." However, Arias government officials argued that the paying of interest certainly did have grave implications, since AID controlled the Special Account and this account was enormous, totaling 25 percent of the Costa Rican national budget. "It was a trade-off. If AID used the account a lot it meant the Central Bank could not use its other funds for items like credit for production, subsidizing agriculture, or building a hospital. As long as we paid interest on the AID account, the government had to spend less on its own social programs," explained former Planning Minister Ottón Solís.

Not only was the charging of interest neither routine nor insignificant, the reasons the AID mission cited for this practice—to offset devaluation of AID funds due to inflation and to encourage Costa Rica to use the money in the Special Account quickly—

did not make economic sense. In reality the impact of the interest payments was just the opposite. The interest payments were so enormous that the Central Bank met them, in part, simply by printing more colones, an inflationary practice that worked against the AID mission's stated rationale. An AID-commissioned study admitted that if all the Special Account money had been disbursed at once, it would have had "devastating consequences" on inflation, import demand, and the government's "general economic stabilization objectives." The IMF, therefore, imposed limits on the amount—between $60 and $80 million of local-currency funds that could be disbursed each year—of local-currency funds that could be disbursed each year from the AID Special Account. The remainder stayed in the Special Account, and the government was compelled to pay over 20 percent interest on it.

In the end, according to AID statistics, only about half of the interest payments paid into the Special Account were ever disbursed.[39] The balance was eventually returned to the Arias government. According to an AID official in Washington who asked to remain anonymous, charging interest was counterproductive: "The problem in Costa Rica was that there was too much local currency floating around, and there wasn't any point in creating more by charging interest."

These interest payments also added to the Central Bank's deficit, which both AID and the IMF were demanding that the government reduce. When the Arias administration took office in May 1986, it found to its horror that interest payments to the AID account equaled one-third of the Central Bank deficit, a figure so high that it was causing stumbling blocks in negotiations with the IMF. As a result, the Arias administration moved to stop the interest payments and get rid of Chaij. In May 1987, Arias bluntly told Reagan's special envoy Philip Habib that the interest payments were "a thorn in the side of Costa Ricans" and urged that Dan Chaij be removed from Costa Rica.

The next month, Chaij was hurriedly recalled to Washington and no replacement was sent until early 1988. Contrasted to his high-profile tenure in Costa Rica, his departure was low-key; there were no farewell parties, no testimonial dinners by the business chambers, and no official send-off from the airport. Chaij did, however, give each of his closest friends and collaborators a parting gift—a brightly colored tin plate, with a picture of himself in the center, his years of service in Costa Rica, and words to the effect of "thanks and good luck" imprinted on it—a sort of crass replica, several officials noted, of the Roman proconsul coins. For several years after his return to Washington, Chaij's status with the State Department was described as "under administrative review," although no disciplinary action was ever taken against him.

Also in June 1987, Finance Minister Naranjo told the press that Costa Rica planned to propose to AID that the interest payments be stopped during 1987 and 1988. Bank president Lizano later said in an interview that no interest had been paid in either of these years. But, according to AID statistics, over 1.5 billion colones in interest payments were put into the Special Account from 1987 to mid 1988. Then, in 1988, Arias adviser John Biehl and a handful of other government advisers and officials began lobbying to halt the interest payments permanently and to put the Special Account in the name of the Costa Rican government. Even those officials who had for years acquiesced to the interest payments now came out in opposition.

Costa Rican officials raised this issue in mid-1988 during AID agreement negotiations. AID and Costa Rica reached an Agreement that the Special Account would be overseen by a commission composed of key Costa Rican economic officials. This victory on paper for the Costa Rican government was undercut by the fact that the commission was composed of AID's closest economic collaborators.[40] While many people believed that, once the account was in the government's name, disbursement of funds would have to meet approval by the Legislative Assembly, this did not happen. A Central Bank official handling the disbursement said that, in practice, there was no real change in procedures. The Arias administration did, however, win victories in getting the account put in the government's name, in canceling the interest payments, and in securing the removal of Director Chaij.

About this same time AID received another publicly embarrassing black eye. In January 1988, a manager-to-manager memo from the State Department's Inspector General Herbert Beckington to AID Administrator Peter MacPherson was leaked to the press.[41] Such memos are intended as red flags to alert top management to problems that auditors have found in particular AID programs. The twenty-five-page memo, based on a 1987 audit of the Costa Rican program, documents cronyism, favoritism, and mismanagement. It found that the actions of those running the Costa Rican AID program "closely approach criminal conduct," that "all systems of checks and balances seem to have failed," and that supervision from Washington "was non-existent."[42] Asked about it, one AID project officer—who asked to remain anonymous—said, "I've been with AID for eighteen years and I've never seen such a strong letter."[43]

The Parallel State

On the heels of the Inspector General's memo came more embarrassing disclosures about the AID program. In the spring of 1988, John Biehl, President Oscar Arias's closest and most outspoken adviser, gave an interview to Lezak Shallat, a reporter for the small Chilean magazine *APSI* in which he said that Washington wanted to use "Costa Rica as a military base and transform the economy so that it is in total agreement with Reagan's economic policies, with 'Reaganomics.' " Biehl, a Chilean who had known Arias since their days at the University of Sussex and who worked in Costa Rica as a United Nations Development Program (UNDP) technical adviser assisting the Arias government with economic planning and analysis, had been a forthright critic of Reagan's contra policy.

In the *APSI* interview, however, Biehl went a step further, publicly denouncing the impact of AID's policy and claiming that U.S. aid has been used in Costa Rica to build what he called "a Parallel State."[44] Biehl described the Parallel State as a set of AID-created and -financed private institutions—banks, a foreign investment agency, a university, a road construction company, and so forth—which duplicated and weakened existing government institutions. According to Biehl, Washington was trying to dismantle Costa Rica's quiet socialism not by attacking it head-on, but by undermining it through a set of well-financed, competing private-sector institutions loyal to the United States. This was a powerful charge, especially in Costa Rica, where liberal politicians publicly deny and privately grumble about U.S. interference. But until Biehl spoke out, no one as close to the seat of power had given such a detailed and graphic critique of the AID program.

At the time the *APSI* article appeared, the Reagan administration and Costa Rica's right wing were already gunning for Biehl, whom they perceived as the brains behind Arias's Central American Peace Plan and the main stumbling block to their successful pursuit of a military "solution" in Nicaragua. In mid-1987, at the apparent instigation of Vice President Bush, UNDP head William Draper requested Biehl's resignation because, Draper said, the Chilean "got involved in political activities and that's a violation of UN rules." Afterward, Biehl continued to serve as an unofficial adviser to Arias, and his opponents continued to watch for another opportunity to renew the attack. When Biehl exposed the Parallel State, the right wing denounced him as a foreigner who had no right to meddle in Costa Rica's internal affairs. In a well-orchestrated press campaign, the right demanded Biehl be expelled from the country.

Arias refused to expel his friend, and Biehl refused to retract his statements. In an opinion column in *La Nación* Biehl expanded on his theory of the Parallel State: "The US economic aid is conditioned on the creation of certain institutions and on modifying Costa Rican legislation to facilitate a predetermined economic model. . . . [T]he millions of dollars which finance this new bureaucratic structure are in fact public resources which belong to the Costa Rican people."[45] But by July 1988, Biehl, worn down by the vicious personal attacks, announced that he was returning to his native Chile.

Curiously, while most U.S. Embassy officials had no kind words to say about John Biehl, Richard Rosenberg, head of AID's private-sector programs in Costa Rica, frankly admitted in an interview with researcher Ken Ward, "Biehl was dead right." He said creating a Parallel State "was the intention of the AID mission [and] of the Costa Rican government participants. They reached the conclusion that it was impossible to do this kind of work within the structure of the Costa Rican government. That conclusion is still sound. . . . [I]t is a Parallel State; that criticism is perfectly valid."

Richard McCall, who during the late 1980s was chief aide to Senator John Kerry, argued that U.S. officials built the Parallel State without understanding the economic foundations of Costa Rica's democracy. He stressed that Costa Rica has been able to maintain democracy because its public institutions have created economic and social stability. McCall argued that Reagan and Bush administration officials seemed to regard democracy "as just holding elections" and gave "no thought to the long term implications of what they were advocating down there."

Gradually, through the 1980s, AID's privatization strategy succeeded in permanently altering the economic structures on which Costa Rica's democratic institutions rest. According to the Centro de Estudios para la Acción Social (CEPAS), a Costa Rican social and economic research center, privatization has meant "not simply the dismantling of the state, but the redefinition of its functions."[46] The result has been, as one Costa Rican politician put it, "the Central Americanization of Costa Rica." Washington has managed, he said, to set this historically unique country on a path toward becoming "just another right-wing, politically pliant, economically dependent banana republic." AID began this process first by denationalizing parts of the banking sector, and this, once accomplished, paved the way for building a pantheon of other private, parallel institutions.

FOUR

Privatization of the Banks

Costa Rica nationalized its banking system in 1948, after the end of its civil war. In announcing the decision, its principal architect, José (Don Pepe) Figueres, who was leader of the postwar junta and founder of the National Liberation Party (PLN), told the nation, "The administration of money and credit ought not to be in private hands, any more than the distribution of water and the mail."[1] While a few private banks continued to carry on restricted functions, only the four state banks[2] could handle government funds, receive foreign currency from overseas, and offer checking and savings accounts. The state banks also provided almost all loans to both the government and the private sector. Costa Rica thereby developed the most extensive nationalized banking system outside the Soviet bloc, and it served as a model for subsequent bank nationalizations in El Salvador, Peru, Mexico, and to some extent Venezuela.

The state-run banking system, along with the abolition of the army and building of the social-welfare system, became the cornerstone of Costa Rica's unique social-democratic form of government and of the National Liberation Party, a broad-based, multiclass party which dominated politics in the postwar era. Indeed, the three were very much interrelated: the Costa Rican government was able to channel through its Central Bank the funds it saved by not financing an army and use the money to build an impressive welfare system which provided the best social services in Latin America and served as a buffer against impoverishment and political unrest. These elements, coupled with postwar Costa Rica's relatively high wages, high percentage of wage earners, and high per-capita gross domestic product (GDP) gave the government a greater capacity to undertake social programs.

Table 2. GNP per Capita, 1949–82 (in 1950 U.S. dollars)

	Costa Rica	El Salvador	Guatemala	Honduras	Nicaragua
1949	286	185	220	152	182
1959	309	192	243	158	262
1969	390	256	300	175	363
1979	558	289	377	193	251
1982	493	196	353	177	263

Source: James Dunkerley, *Power in the Isthmus: A Political History of Modern Central America* (London: Verso, 1988), p. 174.

The state banking system also enabled the government to set up or purchase scores of enterprises, including the electricity and telephone company (ICE), the housing authority (INVU), and the National Production Council (CNP), which has assured farmers and consumers stable, subsidized prices for basic foods and established agricultural infrastructures such as powdered-milk factories and grain elevators. In the 1970s, the state-owned Costa Rican Development Corporation (CODESA) was created through government and foreign financing, and it made major investments in cement, sugar, cotton, aluminum, oil refining, fertilizer, and transportation. By 1978, there were 182 autonomous state-owned institutions receiving almost 50 percent of the government's budget.[3]

Hailed as providing for the "democratization of credit," the nationalized banking system also helped the country diversify from its two traditional exports, coffee and bananas. Beginning in the 1950s, bank credit went into cattle production and the export of beef. After Costa Rica joined the Central American Common Market (CACM) in 1963, bank credit flowed into a number of new consumer industries aimed at the domestic and regional market. The banks also made low-interest loans available to small and medium-size farmers; funneled government resources into education, health care, social security, transportation, and other public services; and directed development funds to the poorer regions of the country.

With the economic crisis of the early 1980s, many Costa Ricans came to believe that the state banks had become overly bureaucratic and needed to be streamlined and modernized. Some argued that the system should be reformed "to strengthen, not destroy it."[4] Other businessmen and bureaucrats began to urge an expanded role for private banks. Contended Eduardo Lizano, who throughout most of the 1980s was Central Bank president, "You cannot expect to have a vigorous business sector if you don't have a vigorous banking system, and you cannot build a modern industrial sector based on the four state banks."[5] He was among a group of prominent members from both major political parties who approached U.S. ambassador Curtin Winsor to propose that AID tie its contributions to a "liberalization" (partial privatization) of the banking system and the sell-off of the state-run industrial conglomerate, CODESA.[6]

The ambassador and AID officials, who themselves had nary a kind word to say about the national banking system, readily obliged. Ambassador Winsor publicly denounced the state banking system as "scandalous," charging that it had "become so politically involved and so inefficient that it's calcified and frozen."[7] AID documents described the state banks as "plagued by political interference and inefficiency,"[8] "burdened with excessive regulations," suffering from "processing delays" and "poor discipline,"[9] "noncompetitive," and forced to "comply with development guidelines rather than commercial considerations."[10] The state banks had become overly bureaucratic, but they needed streamlining and modernization, not privatization. U.S. officials paid lip service to "reforming" the nationalized banks, but as AID reports reveal, the Agency set "promotion of private sector banking" as one of its "highest priority conditions,"[11] and a strong symbiotic alliance quickly developed between U.S. officials and powerful local businessmen and politicians.

During the 1980s, AID stipulated that large portions of its funds go to private banks and other private-sector enterprises, particularly nontraditional exports. A 1986 AID agreement, for instance, required that the Central Bank open a $120 million low-interest credit line to private banks to be used for "private business capital, with preference to exporters."[12] AID also used its financial might to fund and on occasion create new private banks, which grew in number from five to more than twenty during the 1980s. In 1981, AID lent $10 million at bargain-basement interest rates of 2–3 percent to BANEX, a newly established agro-industrial and export bank. In 1982 and 1983, the Agency lent a total of $10 million in dollars at 2–3 percent, plus $5 million in colones at 5 percent interest to COFISA, a new private bank set up to receive AID funds. Then in 1984 AID created a new private merchant and investment finance company, the Private Investment Corporation (PIC), with a $1 million grant and a $20 million long-term, low-interest loan. AID claimed that PIC was "the first of its type to be established in Latin America."[13] In fact, PIC's functions were already being carried out by the holding company of the state-owned conglomerate CODESA, which AID was simultaneously forcing the government to dismantle.

According to a banker involved in these deals, PIC, COFISA, and BANEX all received the AID loans in dollars through "paper companies" set up in Panama. The banker described these Panamanian transactions as "a trick" to get around regulations then in effect that prohibited private banks from directly receiving foreign funds. After the 1984 bank reforms were passed, private banks could receive dollars directly from overseas, so it was no longer necessary to funnel AID loans through Panama.

AID worked with local interests to set up the legal framework for denationalization through two pieces of legislation: one, passed in 1984, midway through the Monge administration, reformed the existing bank law; the other was a new law passed in 1988, halfway through Arias's term. The campaigns mounted to secure passage of these two bills were backed by powerful coalitions that cut across party lines, including conservative government technocrats, the major media, and large private finance and business associations. They both became intertwined with parallel U.S. political pressures aimed at involving Costa Rica more deeply in Reagan's war against Nicaragua. The controversy surrounding both bills helped precipitate cabinet reshuffles that resulted in more conservative governments and caused grave splits within the Liberation party, which by the end of the decade was suffering from deep ideological ruptures.

1984: A Technical Coup d'Etat

This bank privatization drive began in July 1982 with an AID agreement requiring that the Monge government "take measures and seek legislative changes" to allow private banks "to participate in any local currency credit program."[14] The next AID agreement, signed in December 1982, gave the government until February to submit to the legislature an amendment allowing private banks to participate on an equal basis with public banks in "the Central Bank's rediscount and other lending programs."[15]

In May 1983, President Monge, backed by private bankers, presented the legislature with a proposal to reform subsection 5 of Article 62 of the existing Central Bank law, the *Ley Orgánica del Banco Central*. Under the reform, private banks were to be given access to funds that the Central Bank received from international lending agencies. In August 1983 Monge presented a second proposal to the Legislative Assembly calling for a reform of Articles 6 and 7 of the country's currency law, *Ley de la Moneda*, and Article 100 of the Ley Orgánica. These changes would permit private banks to receive, for the first time, term deposits of 180 days or more and would allow certain commercial transactions in dollars.

For sixteen months, from May 1983 to August 1984, the government and the American Embassy engaged in what one U.S. report euphemistically called "extensive policy dialogue"[16] to secure passage of the complete Ley de la Moneda and Ley Orgánica reforms. This banking debate took place during Costa Rica's most tumultuous political period of the decade.[17] The United States was not only demanding economic reforms, but also political and military support for its war against Nicaragua. The Monge government, the ruling Liberation party, and public opinion were all deeply divided over the war. Contra operations out of northern Costa Rica had peaked, and several border incidents nearly precipitated the intervention of U.S. troops. The American Embassy was pressing the government to accept military aid, training, and engineers.

During this period, United States–Costa Rican relations were further strained by the crude declarations and heavy-handed interferences of the new U.S. ambassador, Curtin Winsor, an arch-conservative lacking in political finesse or previous diplomatic experience. In July 1983, Winsor replaced career diplomat Frank McNeil, who understood the country well and who, with the help of his Costa Rican wife, had ingratiated himself with the Liberation party leadership and Costa Rican elite. Winsor, on the other hand, was the overweight son of a banking and coal-mining magnate who had made large contributions to Republican party campaign coffers. As Winsor himself explained "As a Reagan appointee, as a conservative who believes that political democracy requires free economics as a topsoil in which to grow, I was horrified by what I saw in Costa Rica." In abysmal Spanish, cold-warrior Winsor repeatedly warned of the dangers of Sandinista aggression and the "cancer of communism," causing irritated Costa Ricans to label him "a cancer specialist."

In May 1984, while the Ley de la Moneda was being vigorously debated, the ambassador paid what he termed a "courtesy call" to the Legislative Assembly to discuss "aspects of the international monetary system."[18] When questions arose publicly about the appropriateness of the ambassador's interventions, Winsor declared, "We're asking that Costa Rica come up with its own development program. But due to their democratic, and therefore inefficient, government, they have been unable to put together that program."[19]

AID Director Dan Chaij, for his part, used somewhat less public tactics. Rather than appear in person at the Legislative Assembly, he worked through friendly government officials and legislators, several of whom he would meet Friday afternoons at a Turkish bath.[20] Winsor and Chaij also received support from an increasingly powerful coalition that included private business associations, government economists and technical advisers, the right wings of both major political parties, the major media, and the Free Costa Rica Movement (*Movimiento Costa Rica Libre*). The country's leading daily, *La Nación,* ran editorials denouncing the "dogma of the nationalized banking system" and the Legislative Assembly's delays in approving the reform measures. The major media and business chambers warned that unless the bill was passed, $300 million in funds from AID and the IMF would be suspended.[21]

That is just what happened. The IMF conditioned renewal of its expired $100 million standby credit agreement on passage of the Ley de la Moneda, layoffs of 3,300 government employees, and cuts in the higher-education budget and government deficit.[22]

From late 1983 into 1984, AID halted disbursement of funds over a technical infraction,[23] and in June 1984 AID delayed delivery of $58 million, and Winsor announced that another $200 million already in Costa Rica would not be disbursed from AID's Special Account because the full bill had not passed.[24] AID Director Chaij informed Central Bank president Marcos López that Costa Rica "could forget U.S. economic aid if the bill was not approved."[25]

In late May, in the midst of this economic and political turmoil, Monge and a large entourage left on a month-long, twelve-nation European tour, the longest official trip ever taken by a Costa Rican head of state. Dubbed "Operation Truth," it was aimed at soliciting aid and polishing the tarnished image of Monge's Neutrality Proclamation. Just prior to this trip, there were widespread rumors that the United States was preparing to invade Nicaragua, using both Honduras and Costa Rica as bases. At the insistence of a group of Liberation party legislators and moderates in his cabinet, Monge convinced First Vice President Alberto Fait to assume the presidency, thus bypassing right-wing Second Vice President Armando Aráuz, who many suspected would support a U.S. invasion. Three days after Monge's departure, the invasion rumors gained credence with the La Penca press conference bombing, which Washington quickly blamed on the Sandinistas. But because the May 30, 1984, bombing was bungled and its main target, contra leader Edén Pastora, survived, it did not provide sufficient provocation for a direct U.S. invasion.

Unsuccessful in his attempts to raise sufficient support in Europe and facing a worsening economic crisis at home, Monge telephoned Reagan from Brussels asking him to release the AID funds. As Monge recounted, "I assured him that the requested [bank] modifications would be approved eventually."[26] Reagan did intervene and, in early June, AID agreed to release $23 million on the condition that Monge not announce it publicly. Winsor said the United States wanted to give Monge "the leverage to do what he knew had to be done" to get the law passed.[27] Both Winsor and Monge feared that if the legislature knew that some AID funds had already been released, it would vote down the bill.

Monge's return from his tour in early July did not quell the internal unrest, particularly from the right. Almost daily, full-page paid ads predicted economic disaster if the bank reform package was not ratified. The Union of Private Business Chambers and Associations accused the legislators of "destabilizing" the country and acting like "communists,"[28] and the Chamber of Exporters said its members would stop paying taxes unless the reforms were passed.[29]

Government and party officials interviewed say that U.S. arm-twisting behind the scenes intensified on the political and military front as well. The United States began pressuring Monge to accept what one official described as "a broad program to convert Costa Rica" into a war front against Nicaragua, including permitting construction of "more than one" secret contra airstrip, allowing the anti-Sandinista rebels to operate "freely" in the border zone, and "creating trouble at the border so there would be Sandinista attacks" and Costa Rica would call for U.S. military protection.

Then, on August 8, the pro-neutrality Security Minister Angel Edmundo Solano told reporters as he left a stormy Council of Government meeting that he had ordered the metropolitan police and OPEN—Costa Rica's equivalent to a national guard—on "maximum alert" following "rumors of a coup" by "groups on the far right as well as on the far left who want to destabilize the country." Reports circulated that Civil Guard units were massing to oust the heavy-drinking Monge "for health reasons" and install the U.S. Embassy's favorite, Armando Aráuz.

Although Monge publicly retorted that Solano was "the only one who believes [the coup rumors]," something was clearly afoot. A Legislative Assembly member explained in an interview at the time that "the government did have information that made them fear an intervention from the right." A high government function-ary says he had learned that Aráuz was in close touch with U.S. Embassy officials and had met at the house of a former Supreme Court president, together with Interior Minister Alfonso Carro and leaders of the opposition Unity party to discuss ousting Monge. It was ex-President "Pepe" Figueres who stepped in and took decisive action. A close Figueres associate recalls receiving a call from "a large group of colonels and majors who said that something was cooking, that they felt there was a possibility of a coup and a delivering of power to Aráuz." He relayed the message to Figueres, who quickly moved to "cool everybody off." The diminutive elder statesman called together several politicians, influential business people, and about a dozen Civil Guard commanders, mostly colonels, who were said to be involved in the plot. He told them they were "under oath to defend the constitution and he didn't see any real necessity . . . for a coup." Thus challenged, the plotters pleaded innocence. Figueres informed Monge that the crisis was over.[30]

Then, Information Minister Armando Vargas proposed to Monge a strategy aimed at overcoming the political divisions within his Cabinet without appearing to knuckle under to external or internal pressures. On August 10, Monge asked that his entire government step down. He dispatched his driver to collect letters of resignation from all the ministers, legislators, and heads of government-run institutions. On August 16, after a week of suspense, Monge announced the changes on national television and radio. The Costa Rican president appeased the right by replacing two neutrality advocates: Security Minister Solano with arch-conservative Benjamín Piza, and Fernando Berrocal (who was accused of corruption) with centrist Danilo Jiménez. He balanced this by removing two of the government's strongest contra supporters, the Minister and Vice Minister of Interior, Alfonso Carro and Enrique Chacón, and replacing them with two moderates, Enrique Obregón and René Castro. Monge also named Eduardo Lizano to head the Central Bank in place of Marcos López.[31]

At the time, it was said that Monge had astutely regained political equilibrium within his administration. The press praised the selection of Lizano, former head of the University of Costa Rica economics department, and of Benjamín Piza, former Seagrams liquor company executive, terming both men well-respected and competent administrators. Only later did it become clear how important these two appointments were to Reagan administration efforts to reshape Costa Rica. Lizano (who was named a governor of the IMF, World Bank, and IDB) played a central role in denationalizing the banks and building the Parallel State, while Piza (who had been a founding member of the Free Costa Rica Movement) became an important collaborator in the construction of the secret airstrip and the Southern Front. Monge's reshuffle amounted to a "technical coup d'etat" which moved the political spectrum to the right and in which Washington emerged as the real winner.

Monge next stepped up pressure on the Legislative Assembly to pass the full bank-reform package. Within days of the government reshuffle, Monge ordered the legislature cloistered in a special emergency session to debate the law. On Sunday, August 19, after twenty-three straight hours of debate, the bill passed, 30 to 10. Liberation party legislator Rodolfo Navas told the press, "We considered it the lesser of two evils." He noted that the changes would undoubtedly lead to abuses and a concentration of wealth, but he said he felt compelled to vote for the bill in order "to avoid hunger, impoverishment and unemployment," which would result if IMF and AID funds were cut off.[32]

1988: AID Stays on the Sidelines

Following the 1984 reforms, the Arias administration came under extreme pressure to pass another bank denationalization law, the *Ley de Modernización del Sistema Finánciero.* The impetus for this new denationalization was the 1987 economic failure of numerous finance companies—the Costa Rican equivalent of the American S&L scandal. Like private banks, the number of finance companies mushroomed during the 1980s, growing from none in 1969 to thirteen in 1979 to sixty-eight by 1987. Under existing laws, these companies could function with little capital or control, and many were plagued with poor accounting and bad management. Thousands of unsuspecting Costa Ricans, mainly lower- and middle-class retirees, housewives, and professionals, were lured into investing their small life savings by promised returns as high as 42 percent.

Suddenly, however, a number of these finance companies or *financieras* began to fold. Between September 1987 and March 1988, at least fifteen declared bankruptcy and, according to the failed companies themselves, nearly sixteen thousand investors lost 5.7 billion colones. Other estimates range from 8 billion to as high as 11 billion colones in losses. A number of companies had been open for less than two years.

AID blamed the failures on the Central Bank's sudden decision to "throttle back on the money supply" (restrict credit), which squeezed the financial institutions.[33] Others said the collapse was linked to "Black Monday," the Wall Street crash of September 1987. There were also reports that some of the finance companies were tied to drug-trafficking and money-laundering operations. The failures coincided, for example, with the seizure in Miami of three tons of cocaine concealed in a shipment of wood. This was the largest cocaine shipment seized to date in the United States, with an estimated street value of $120 to $340 million. The ship's last port of call had been Costa Rica, and it was rumored that the capture of the cocaine shipment helped precipitate the bankruptcies of Costa Rican finance companies.[34]

Lack of official controls and regulations was certainly a primary cause of the failures. Many of the finance companies were involved in questionable financial activities. Costa Ricans referred to them as *garroteras,* slang for "loan sharking." The finance companies' capital was frequently used by directors and shareholders for their personal business interests or for conspicuous consumption, such as expensive new cars and homes. Owners of several companies loaded millions of colones of investors' money into suitcases and skipped the country after their companies collapsed. Two representatives of one failed company had previously been caught in Belize trying to pass off half a million dollars in false bills.[35] The largest of the bankrupt finance companies, IBESA, was owned by an Iranian, Hojabar Yazdani, a former associate of the deposed Shah who had fled to Costa Rica with his wealth and his family. IBESA's 7,080 investors lost 2.27 billion colones, an average of about $5,000 per account (calculated at 60 colones per dollar).[36] Yet, because of weak legislation and controls and despite protests by irate depositors, neither Yazdani nor any other owner had, by the end of the decade, been prosecuted or forced to repay their investors.

The Ley de Modernización represented the government's answer to the *financiera* crisis. Its main purpose was to shore up public confidence in the private financial institutions and to prevent future bankruptcies. But while everyone accepted the need to protect investors, critics argued that this was accomplished at the public's expense. In addition, under the rubric of "professionalizing" and streamlining the banking system, the new law further strengthened and consolidated private banking. It also changed the make-up of the Central Bank's board of directors, removing the Ministers of Planning and the Economy and, for the first time, giving the majority of seats to the private sector, a move that eliminated voices that favored social development over purely fiscal and monetary considerations. In addition the law guaranteed that deposits in private banks and finance companies would be insured by the state-run National Insurance Institute (*Instituto Nacional de Seguros* or INS). This meant, as Ottón Solís put it, that "profits are privatized while losses are the responsibility of the state." Yet another section of the law penalized directors and managers if state banks did not function properly, while not making officials of private banks similarly responsible. Critics argued that state banking officials would become even less aggressive and innovative, while private bankers could act with impunity, knowing their mistakes would be covered either by the state insurance company or the Central Bank. Finally, the law also called for the total elimination of subsidized funding for the National Production Council, an important state institution which provides guaranteed prices and other forms of assistance to farmers.

In essence, with these "modernizations," state institutions were to be used to protect private financial institutions while not making these institutions or their directors legally responsible for malpractice or failures. An article in the progressive Catholic magazine *Aportes* charged that the new banking system changes amounted to "nothing more than another example of how 'market forces,' of which so many legislators have become ardent admirers, demand the help of the state."[37]

In contrast to 1984, AID played a much more oblique role in the bill's passage. A December 1987 AID report noted that, given "the intense political sensitivity of AID's role in the public/private bank issue, . . . the prevailing sentiment among private bankers is that it would be better right now to allow the political waters to settle, rather than stir them up with provocative arm-twisting on the state-vs-private-bank issue."[38] Instead, the local interests that had benefited from the AID- and IMF-orchestrated structural changes to the economy were, by 1988, powerful enough to fight successfully on their own for the new law. They had support from most of Arias's key economic advisers, including Central Bank President Lizano, Finance Minister Naranjo, Minister of the Presidency Rodrigo Arias, and First Vice President Jorge Manuel Dengo.

Of Arias's economic team, only Planning Minister Ottón Solís vigorously and publicly objected to the law. However, he had become isolated, and when it became clear that Arias supported the bill, Solís tendered his resignation. Others within the Cabinet who had objected to Arias's acquiescence to AID-prescribed economic reforms—Vice Minister of Exports Eduardo Alonso and Agricultural Minister Alberto Esquivel—were also eased out. By mid-term, the composition of Arias's administration, like his predecessor Monge's, had shifted sharply to the right.

People close to Arias say that he decided to support the law, and other economic policy changes, for both personal and political reasons. Unlike Monge, who had been a long-time trade unionist and party functionary, Arias hailed from Costa Rica's coffee and business oligarchy, which favored the law. Ideologically, Arias and, even more so, his brother Rodrigo, the Minister of the Presidency, agreed with many of AID's economic prescriptions for Costa Rica. Further, those close to Arias say that he could not simultaneously oppose Washington's economic and political strategies. The Reagan administration and local right-wing were in 1988, as they had in 1984, exerting strong pressure on Costa Rica to support the war against Nicaragua. A peasant-union leader said that Arias told him in 1987 that AID had, in essence, presented an ultimatum: accept either "liquidation" of the state banking system or "eighteen thousand contras in the country." Arias, he said, chose the former. Overall AID funding levels were down by almost half, and AID disbursement had been suspended during much of 1987 to show White House displeasure with Arias's Central American Peace Plan and with the crackdown on contra activities inside Costa Rica. The major media, particularly *La Nación*, were attacking Arias relentlessly both for his peace plan and for the country's economic woes. According to a well-placed observer, Arias backed the new banking law "to win internal support and breathing space from the editorial writers" in the local press. When Arias made his support for the law known several months before the final vote, the negative editorials abruptly stopped. After weeks of debate, the legislature passed the bill on October 24, 1988, by a vote of 34 to 10.

Impact of Bank Privatization: *"Un Golpe de Estado"*

By the end of the decade, private banks and financial institutions were greatly strengthened, and AID boasted enormous success in implementing its bank privatization policy. Costa Rica's four long-time state banks remained. But the number of private banks grew rapidly—from two in 1969 to five in 1979 to twenty-one in 1990. During the same period the number of private finance companies grew from zero to thirteen to fifty-eight.[39] All these private banks and at least two finance companies, COFISA and the Private Investment Corporation (PIC), received AID funds.[40] Over a three-year period in the mid-1980s, private bank capital increased 5.5 times.[41]

It is difficult to get a breakdown of how much AID money was channeled to private banks or what percentage of private bank funds have come from AID. The Central Bank claimed not to have these statistics since the Special Account was in AID's name, and AID would not provide a detailed breakdown. According to one Agency study, "nearly half" of AID's balance-of-payments (ESF) transfers have gone to Costa Rica's financial sector, and of this amount "most" has been channeled to the private banks.[42] Another report states that between 1982 and late 1988, "AID programs pumped some $200 million worth of credit into the local [private] banks," of which two-thirds were in local currency.[43] Yet another AID study states that "roughly 40%" of the private banks' total assets came from AID.[44]

While these official figures are impressive, Costa Rican and U.S. officials say that the amount of AID funds channeled to the private banks is, in reality, considerably higher—in the range of 80 percent of total U.S. appropriations. A Liberation party official says Central Bank officials told him that "80% of the resources given to Costa Rica by AID passed directly to the private banks." A well-placed Costa Rican official says he was told informally by one of Chaij's associates that "more than 75% of the private bank funds came from AID's Special Account in the Central Bank." If correct, this figure would amount to some $590 million between January 1985 and September 1988. "This was much more extensive than we had been led to believe," commented one Costa Rican ex-minister.

Former president José Figueres, the man who nationalized Costa Rica's banks back in 1948, proclaimed on various occasions, "I shall consider [even] one step backward in the bank nationalization as *un golpe de estado* [coup d'etat], with all its consequences."[45] While Figueres's concern was perhaps overstated, AID's bank privatization drive during the 1980s did pave the way for a gradual transfer of power, which worked in various ways to undermine the role of the state and with it the country's social and economic stability:

1. It has facilitated a concentration of wealth and the rise of an oligarchy of private bankers, large agricultural exporters, and industrialists who have been spoon-fed with AID funds. During the 1980s, the rich got richer while the poor got poorer. In 1973 the richest 10 percent of the country earned an average income sixteen times greater than the poorest 10 percent. By 1990, the gap had become thirty-one times greater.

   Among the elite were the old oligarchy of *cafetaleros* (coffee growers), who began moving into private banking. Coffee exporters owned a number of finance companies and were on the boards of directors and partners in two of AID's most pampered banks, BANEX and COFISA, as well as private banks such as the *Banco de Fomento Agrícola* (Bank of Agricultural Development) and Bank of America.[46] Large, politically connected industrialists also used AID funds to expand into private banking. Several Chambers of Industry presidents during the 1980s were owners of private banks.

   AID played an important role in the creation of this new class of private bankers by hand-picking who would receive AID funds. According to one knowledgeable Costa Rican, "AID has been a major factor in explaining the growth of private banks. AID has given subsidies to the private banks, and it has created a handful of big shots who control this private banking system. Competition is not there," he stated.

2. While competition between the public and private sectors is not intrinsically bad, the growth of private banks has limited the government's capacity to undertake socially important projects and has shaped the government's decisions about how the nation's funds are used. Historically, the goal of the state banks was to use their resources for the egalitarian development of the entire country. However, state banks are now forced to compete with the private banks, which are much less willing to finance projects that, despite their social benefit, may involve high risks or low profitability. Therefore, state banks have also become reluctant to make small, risky, or potentially difficult-to-collect loans, particularly to small farmers and entrepreneurs. Instead, both government and private banks now exhibit a bias toward bigness even though, economists say, Costa Rican farmers have a relatively good repayment record compared with large growers or cattlemen.

AID has supported this shift in emphasis, demanding that government banks alter their lending policies to conform to "market forces" and not to "political" considerations. In a March 1988 report on Costa Rica, AID was highly critical of the "historical use of the state banks as government development tools instead of [as] conventional financial institutions. . . ."[47] But many Costa Ricans argue vigorously that it was precisely this factor—the government's ability to make financial decisions based on policy objectives and social concerns rather than simply on profitability—that greatly accelerated the country's development as a stable, largely egalitarian democracy.

One critic of denationalization told his colleagues in the Legislative Assembly, "When I see an official of a private bank in [a remote village such as] Brus Malis de Limoncito de Coto Brus . . . searching for a peasant to lend money to, to buy a cow or plant a hectare of corn, then I will come here to advocate that the private banks be allowed to handle public savings. But no, what interests them is commercial activity, lucrative activity, which gives them profits but which produces nothing to develop the country."[48]

The private banks' preoccupation with profits has affected, in turn, the operations of state banks. Costa Rican journalist Lidiette Brenes writes that, "It is noticeable the little interest private banks have in expanding their operations to the interior of the country because the core of their clients are the big and well established." In contrast, the national bank system, which has maintained services throughout the country, has now begun closing some of these branches. In 1986, state banks had 248 rural offices, or one for every ten thousand individuals.[49] Between 1988 and March 1990, branches in seven remote communities closed.[50] and in October 1990 the National Bank of Costa Rica closed seven more rural offices "because they were not producing profits for the home office."[51] By the end of 1990, the poorest sections of the country, as well as the poorest parts of the population, had less access to banking facilities.

Through its promotion of exports, AID has required a cutback in traditional subsidies (low-interest loans to small farmers, manufacturers, and businessmen) and the imposition of a broad package of so-called "incentives" (in reality also subsidies) to industrialists and producers of nontraditional agricultural crops for export. In 1981–82, the government was giving low-interest loans to fifty-four predetermined categories of borrowers, including those who otherwise would have no access to loans and credit. While many agreed that the system had serious weaknesses, including excessive rigidity, redundancy, and high administrative costs, it had been an important tool for assuring a broad distribution of credit, local food production, and assistance to the poorer sectors of society.

AID, however, set out to eliminate much of this in order to facilitate the shift toward production for export. A 1988 AID report explains, "As a result of ESF conditionality . . . subsidized credit has been reduced to less than 16 percent of available credit. In addition, the Central Bank has phased out its special credit allocation categories for specific activities, thus allowing credit to flow more efficiently to the most productive sectors of the economy." The result, according to the AID study, has been: (1) a decrease in credit available for production for the local market and traditional exports; (2) an increase in credit available to private sector producers of nontraditional exports; (3) an increase in credit available to export industries in general; and (4) expansion of private banks, which while still providing a minority of total credit, now do the majority of export-related banking.[52] Parallel with this, bank lending to the public sector dropped from 43.3 percent of all money lent in 1982 to just 23.3 percent in 1987.[53] "The banks have moved," as one Unity party economist noted, "from subsidizing the poor to subsidizing the rich." Brenes states that this "liberalization" process has "totally removed the campesino from the credit system" and left "the market wide open for the survival of the fittest."[54]

3. Having been wholly created or greatly propped up with multimillion dollar loans from AID, private financial institutions now give the appearance of functioning better than state banks. By 1987, for instance, AID was proudly reporting that the "return on investment in private banks is about 11%, compared to 6% for the nationalized banks." But this same study notes that AID "has pumped" millions of dollars exclusively to private banks and, it concludes, "These credit lines have been a major contributor to the strong recent growth of private banking in Costa Rica."

AID argues that by building up the private sector it has helped force the state banks to respond by becoming more efficient and competitive. According to one AID analysis, the Agency's strategy of encouraging the development of private-sector banking "creates an incentive for improvements in the nationalized banks by providing a competitive alternative."[55] In reality, however, the overall effect of AID's privatization drive has been to weaken, not strengthen, the state banks through a distorted form of competition. While the flowering of private banks forced the state system to adopt some efficiency methods in accounting and customer service,

AID also imposed "efficiency" by forcing the national banks to cut services to the country's poor and rural populations.

The private banks also appear more successful because they concentrate on servicing the least risky and most lucrative financial sectors—large commercial, industrial, and nontraditional export enterprises—while the state banks are left carrying out the high risk but often socially important functions. Also, the majority of private bank credit is lent for corporate operational costs, which are generally short-term, quick-turn-over loans with higher profitability. In contrast, state banks must handle most of the long-term credit for investment.[56]

Because the private banks have been spoon-fed by AID, there is no way to judge if private is more efficient than public. According to Ottón Solís, "Even the Chicago boys [conservative free-market economists from the University of Chicago] would be upset because AID does not respect market forces. They give funds to the banking system at subsidized interest rates and the private banks are not induced to go to the market to compete for funds because they have guaranteed funds from the Central Bank."

When, however, toward the end of the decade AID began cutting back on assistance to Costa Rica and with it credit to private financial institutions, the effects were quickly felt. In 1989, the private Weeden International Bank went bankrupt and closed. By 1990 another bank, International Bank of Exportation, was in the process of liquidation and a third, the Bank of Construction, had been taken over by the Auditor General of banks. By 1992, five private banks had closed, and the total number had dropped to nineteen. No new banks were opening, and economists predicted that over the next few years there would be more bankruptcies as AID phased out its program.[57]

4. In pushing through the bank privatization measures, AID and its local collaborators tried to undermine and short-circuit public and legislative debate. The question of Costa Rica's state banking structure is a major issue which should have been

decided through an open political process. Instead, AID and
U.S. Embassy officials viewed Costa Rica's democratic form of
government not as an institution to be protected and fostered,
but rather as an obstacle blocking implementation of the
Reagan administration's economic and political agenda. They
sought to minimize public discussion; cut deals with
government technocrats; pressure the Legislative Assembly
behind the scenes; whip up popular support through the press,
the commercial and industrial chambers, and other
conservative organizations; prop up powerful local
businessmen who personally benefited from these changes;
condition AID funds on approval of the banking bill and other
major economic reforms; and instill public fear about the
economic consequences of not passing the banking laws or
implementing structural changes.

5. As detailed in the following chapter, bank privatization
   facilitated privatization in other areas. AID saw it as the
   necessary first step in the building of the Parallel State. Walter
   Coto, a former Central Bank president and secretary general of
   the Liberation party, argued that AID and its local collaborators
   saw bank privatization as "a strategic element in the slow
   imposition of a new economic and financial model . . . designed
   for Costa Rica from the outside."[58] In an interview, former
   legislator Julio Jurado added, "The road toward privatization
   begins first with the privatization of the banks because from
   there come the resources to privatize other sectors and to create
   what they've now called the Parallel State."

FIVE

The Parallel State

In building the Parallel State, AID and other U.S. government funds were used to dismantle existing public institutions, to construct a pantheon of new, private organizations, and to bypass authorization and oversight by the Costa Rican government and legislature (see table 3). The AID-created private institutions do not simply operate independently from the state sector; they also serve to drain much-needed financial and human resources away from already existing public institutions. "The phrase 'parallel' is an unfortunate misnomer," one government official told the *Tico Times*. "Parallel assumes equal growth in equal conditions. The more exact term is 'parasitical,' because duplicated efforts detract from the public sector by redirecting potential resources to the private sector."[1]

The parallel institutions set up or strengthened by AID include: the Private Council on Agriculture and Agro-Industry (CAAP), which duplicates the Ministry of Agriculture; the Private Finance System (SFP) built, together with AID-financed private banks, to compete with the government's national banking system; the Private Investment Corporation (PIC), which was set up to replace the banking functions of the Costa Rican Development Corporation (CODESA); and the private Association of Highways and Roads in Costa Rica (ACCCR), which parallels the government's Ministry of Public Works and Transportation (MOPT). Other AID-created institutions include the private agricultural school EARTH, which duplicates other educational institutions in Costa Rica and the region; FINTRA, the AID trust fund used to sell off the government industries controlled by CODESA; and the private export-promotion institute CINDE, which overshadowed the state-run Center for the Promotion of Investment and Exports

Table 3. Costa Rica's Parallel State: Government and AID Developmental Organizations in Costa Rica, 1980s.

Costa Rican Organizations	USAID Organizations
CODESA: Costa Rican Development Corporation	PIC: Corporation of Private Investments
CENPRO: Center for the Promotion of Investments and Exports	CINDE: Costa Rican Coalition for Development Initatives
MOPT: Ministry of Public Works and Transport	ACCR: Association of Highways and Roads of Costa Rica
MAG: Ministry of Agriculture	CAAP: Private Council on Agriculture and Agroindustry
UCR: University of Costa Rica UNA: National University CATIE: Center for Tropical Agronomy Research and Training EGA: School of Livestock ITCR: Technological Institute of Costa Rica	EARTH: School of Agriculture for the Humid Tropics
SBN: National Banking System	SFP: Private Finance System

(CENPRO). CINDE also doubled as a conduit for funneling AID resources to private-sector projects and parallel-state institutions.

The Association of Highways and Roads in Costa Rica, which is made up of private contractors, received AID contracts for building and improving roads and bridges, despite the fact that it replicated the government's Ministry of Public Works and Transportation (MOPT). ACCCR was used in part because the Monge government balked at repeated Embassy demands that U.S. military engineers be permitted to construct roads and bridges in northern Costa Rica. These Green Beret- and ACCCR-constructed roads and bridges, while useful to residents of the area, were also part of U.S. strategic planning for the build-up of contra forces in the border zone and a possible ground invasion of Nicaragua. They are capable of accommodating military vehicles, tanks, and cargo planes. According to a *campesino* (peasant) organizer in northern Costa Rica, ACCCR builders of the Upala and other roads boasted, "These are super roads. They have a base that can handle vehicles of any weight. And the bridges have removable sides to let wide, unstable vehicles pass."

These roads and bridges in northern Costa Rica not only facilitated contra and U.S. military operations; they also benefited ranchers and farmers in the region, including, in particular, the businesses of CIA operative John Hull. Hull lobbied both ambassadors Frank McNeil and Curtin Winsor for new roads and bridges and flew each of them around the area in his light plane. Subsequently, AID and Inter-American Development Bank funds built roads and bridges which doubled the value of Hull's 1,750-acre cattle ranch and made timber on other previously inaccessible property marketable. The roads also enabled Hull to start a new citrus business.[2]

Another AID-created organization, the Association of Costa Rican Development Organizations (ACORDE) was created as an umbrella foundation for financing nongovernmental organizations (NGOs). Set up in 1986 with a $4.9 million AID grant, ACORDE sought to exert influence over the growing number of Costa Rican NGOs, particularly those involved in private enterprise and profitable, productive projects. ACORDE quickly overshadowed the private but more liberal coalition, the Federation of Voluntary Organizations (FOV), which funded mainly women's organizations, as well as the government's own National Directorate of Community Development (DINADECO), an umbrella organization that channels resources to local groups. DINADECO had received AID funding until the early 1980s. According to an official with an AID-funded NGO, by the end of the 1980s ACORDE had become "the only show in town when it comes to getting big bucks for NGO work." CINDE served as a conduit for AID funds to a number of export-oriented NGO projects involving cooperatives, small business, peasants, artisans, labor, and women.

While recognizing the public relations value of these programs, some AID and CINDE officials also viewed ACORDE as a sort of antidote to the economic and social impact the private-sector, export-oriented strategy. According to a Costa Rican representative of PACT (Private Agencies Collaborating Together), a

U.S.-based NGO funded by AID, ACORDE was created as "a shock absorber." He explained, "AID director Dan Chaij strongly supported ACORDE because he thought that the AID economic program for Costa Rica was certain to impoverish some people and that ACORDE could help reduce the social impact of AID policies." In interviews, CINDE officials said that AID, including director Chaij, were in reality indifferent to ACORDE, but that some prominent Costa Ricans recognized its value.[3]

Reagan administration officials tried to impose their conservative, private-sector orientation on other U.S. organizations, such as the Inter-American Foundation, which provides grants to grassroots development projects in Latin America and the Caribbean. Several knowledgeable persons at the foundation said that it became "much more ideological" and "hard-line" during the 1980s, with the Reagan appointees on its board of directors "trying to reorient [the foundation] towards business and a private-sector approach." The foundation, which claims to be "apolitical and non-partisan," receives funding from Congress, and its nine-member board of directors—six members from the private sector and three from government—is appointed by the President and confirmed by the Senate. President Reagan named Victor Blanco, a conservative Cuban-American described as "a hardball player in Washington politics," as chairman and Harold Phillips, a wealthy California Republican seafood exporter and business professor who resides in Costa Rica, as vice chairman. Officials interviewed say Blanco and Phillips "were put into the foundation to give it a strong private enterprise thrust" and to weed out "the anthropologists and sociologists and other liberals" on the staff. Several associates described Phillips as "a very outspoken contra supporter" and a close friend of former ambassadors Winsor and Tambs. Winsor was one of several ultraconservatives appointed by Reagan to the foundation's advisory board. According to a former foundation employee, "The organization did shift during the 1980s. There was a battle between the old liberals and new management. It was messy, protracted, and one-sided because the new management had all the power. A lot of people gracefully abandoned ship and the foundation did change its course."

Table 4. Uses of AID Funds in Local Currency Account, 1982–87 (in millions of colones)

	1982	1983	1984	1985	1986	1987	Total	%
Agricult./Nat. resources	278	1,000	349	858	1,670	0	4,155	9.74
Housing	36	224	325	626	994	741	2,946	6.90
Education	132	369	433	0	246	0	1,180	2.76
Health	19	0	305	0	0	0	324	0.76
Sanitation	0	356	0	850	0	0	1,206	2.83
Trans./Roads	0	386	0	794	0	0	1,180	2.76
Comm. dev.	0	148	24	59	0	0	231	0.54
Bus./Industry	342	484	150	1,328	2,260	1,989	6,553	15.35
Democracy	4	94	5	12	172	0	287	0.67
Central Bank losses	0	10	0	326	2,288	3,785	6,409	15.02
Disaster relief	0	7	0	12	10	0	29	0.07
EARTH	0	3,651	0	2,473	0	0	6,124	14.35
CODESA divestment	0	11	7,022	2,032	0	0	9,065	21.24
Program support	273	214	766	316	1,421	0	2,990	7.01

Source: U.S. Embassy, Costa Rica. See chapter 3 for an explanation of local currency account. This table does not represent the total AID budget per year. It lists only the funding appropriated in colones, from AID's Special Account. Other programs, such as CINDE, were financed in dollars. Many programs were financed partly in dollars and partly in colones. Figures for "program support" refer to AID's local currency administrative costs for Costa Rica.

While AID imposed its private-sector bias on nongovernment organizations, it largely ignored Costa Rica's historically strong social services in the areas of health, education, and low-cost housing. When AID funds did go to these sectors, they were often channeled to private rather than to public-sector projects. For instance, in housing, AID provided a $20 million loan and a $300,000 grant to the savings-and-loan system for private low- and middle-income housing; it hired private contractors for public works and housing construction; and it gave another $5 million grant for housing projects through the private bank COFISA. In the field of education, AID put up $118 million for the private university EARTH, funded a private religious school cofounded by Daniel Chaij's father, supported library improvements in other private institutions, and financed the printing of textbooks and "democracy" books by private firms. In health, AID provided an $8.5 million grant for family planning, part of which went to the private Costa Rican Demographic Association for marketing subsidized contraceptives through private pharmacies and clinics.

The massive AID and United States Information Service (USIS) scholarship program for study in the States also "emphasizes the private sector."[3] In 1987, AID auditors and the State Department Inspector General's Manager-to-Manager memo severely criticized the USIS scholarship program for selecting relatives of a number of wealthy businessmen and politicians with close ties to the Embassy or AID projects. Auditors pinpointed seventeen questionably awarded scholarships totaling $558,415. Among those receiving scholarships were the sons and daughters of President Monge, Monge's brother-in-law and wealthy businessman Samuel Yankelewitz, and Monge's Vice President Armando Arauz. The Manager-to-Manager memo says that a number of the scholarship recipients did not go through proper applications procedures and were not academically qualified. In an interview, former ambassador to the United States and director of CINDE Federico Vargas candidly confirmed these irregularities in explaining how Chaij arranged a $51,081 scholarship for his own son based solely on his telephoned request for help.

Chaij acknowledged to the magazine *Aportes* that the granting of scholarships was "politically motivated."[4] He and other officials argued that it was proper to choose candidates deemed to be pro-American, since the program was aimed at countering a modest Soviet scholarship program being given to Costa Ricans. Embassy officials threatened, for example, to revoke an AID scholarship from a young Costa Rican pianist if he performed at a cultural event protesting the Pinochet dictatorship in Chile. The pianist withdrew from the performance. The Inspector General's memo concluded that the U.S. Embassy and AID had a bias toward "the socially advantaged who already had pro-U.S. inclinations."[6]

There are numerous cases of Costa Ricans from poor or even middle-class families who managed, on their own, to obtain scholarships or private American sponsorship for study in the States, but were denied visas because consular officials suspected they would stay there permanently. José Hernández, for instance, came from a poor family of twelve children, but he managed to get sponsorship for study in the United States from a University of Delaware chaplain. But when he returned home to visit his ailing mother, the U.S. Embassy refused to reissue his visa, despite assurances from Delaware religious leaders, educators, politicians, and businessmen that Hernández's studies and living expenses in the United States were fully covered. With only a partial education, Hernández ended up working odd jobs in San José. One angry U.S. citizen who had arranged a six-month scholarship and financing for another Costa Rican, only to have the visa denied, charged sarcastically that "these highly-paid" Embassy officials were "America's first line of defense in the war against poverty." In a letter to the *Tico Times,* he wrote, "This is a tale of . . . civil servants who aren't civil, of public servants who don't serve the public, and of diplomats who aren't diplomatic."[7] In the wake of the AID audit scandal and after Chaij's departure, the AID mission did agree to bar relatives of prominent Costa Ricans from receiving scholarships, but its preference for selecting economically advantaged Costa Ricans continued.

United States Information Service (USIS) funds were used as well to finance construction of a large radio transmitter in northern Costa Rica which beamed Voice of America broadcasts into Nicaragua. Since foreigners cannot own media in Costa Rica, USIS created a private corporation, the Costa Rican Association for Information and Culture (ACIC), composed of influential, conservative businessmen and politicians.

AID funds went not only to undermine Costa Rican government institutions but also to strengthen the conservative Unity party, the main opposition to the ruling National Liberation party, which the Reagan and Bush administrations viewed as responsible for both Costa Rica's "socialist" welfare system and the Central American Peace Plan. For instance, AID funded the Center for Political Investigation and Training (CIAPA), a private think-tank employing critics of Arias's peace plan. AID also partially financed new headquarters for the National Association for Economic

Development (ANFE), an ultraconservative research institute "devoted to the defense of private enterprise." In addition, AID funds supported COUNSEL, a group of legal and economic consultants closely associated with the Unity party. Several COUNSEL members were named to prominent positions in the Calderón government which took office in May 1990. These included Central Bank president Jorge Guardia, Finance Minister Thelmo Vargas, and Miguel Angel Rodríguez, leader of the Unity faction in the Legislative Assembly.[8] When Senator John Kerry raised objections about these partisan AID appropriations, AID stopped this funding.[9]

During Costa Rica's 1990 election campaign it was revealed that a Unity party political think tank, the Association for the Defense of Liberty and Democracy in Costa Rica, had received, between 1986 and 1989, $434,000 from another U.S. government institution, the National Endowment for Democracy (NED). The funds, which were channeled via the Republican party's National Republican Institute for International Affairs, included at least $50,000 in salary payments to presidential candidate Rafael Angel Calderón, who had been the Association's executive director for two years. NED, a nonpartisan organization, receives congressional appropriations to strengthen democratic institutions overseas but is specifically barred from involvement in partisan politics. U.S. Congressman Jim Leach (R-Iowa) called it "mind-boggling" that taxpayer money would fund "the opposition of the strongest democracy in Central America."[10]

By channeling resources to private institutions, forcing the dismantling of state enterprises, and withholding funds from important public projects, AID and other U.S. government programs helped to build up a privileged, powerful, and politically conservative elite while simultaneously weakening the economic underpinnings of Costa Rica's social-welfare system and democratic institutions. At the same time, the AID-created and -supported private institutions gave virtually no public accounting of how their funds were spent. Viewing the results of AID's massive program during the 1980s, one prominent Unity party economist asked, "Where is the balance sheet for the Parallel State? Where have all the millions gone?" Three projects which took a sizable chunk of these millions were CODESA, EARTH, and CINDE.

CODESA: Sell-off or Sell-out?

The dismantling of CODESA, the state-run Costa Rican Development-ment Corporation, was one of AID's earliest, costliest, and most ambitious projects. In targeting CODESA, AID picked a vulnerable spot in the Costa Rican public sector. Most Costa Ricans had come to agree that the financially troubled conglomerate was in need of an overhaul. Under the banner of "economic democratization,"[11] AID has overseen the liquidation, transfer, or sell-off of several dozen government industries and businesses once part of CODESA.

This was AID's first such divestiture operation, and propo-nents praised it as an "impressive success" that served as a model for other countries.[12] But critics say the divestment process was riddled with ideological zealousness, indiscriminate sell-outs, fi-nancial waste, and administrative sloppiness. AID's own audit report concluded that the CODESA divestment was "far from successful," and, in mid-1989, a *Tico Times* editorial noted that "a full accounting is long overdue" of where AID's tens of millions of dollars actually went.[13]

In demanding that the Costa Rican government denationalize CODESA, AID struck at the heart of the state's direct involvement in economic activities. CODESA, similar to a number of govern-ment holding companies (parastatals) set up by other Latin Ameri-can governments, represented the entry of the Costa Rican govern-ment as a participant in economic activities, and not just a promoter. The government, and in particular the Liberation party, argued that state ownership of certain areas of production was desirable in order to impede concentration of economic power, diversify the economy, provide basic goods and services, and avoid excessive influence of foreign capital.

CODESA was created in 1972 as a government holding company and development bank. It was to be financed through handling, at a commission, foreign funds channeled through its development bank. However, this never proved profitable, and by the 1980s CODESA was operating at a huge deficit.[14] CODESA's function was both to assist private enterprises and to provide complete or partial government financing for socially important industries that were either financially risky or so costly that the private sector was reluctant to undertake them. It was expected to sell its ownership in these companies once they were on sound financial footing. By the early 1980s, CODESA owned thirty companies outright and had partial interest in twelve others. Over 90 percent of its assets were invested in seven enterprises: aluminum, sugar, railroad, bus, and fertilizer firms and two cement companies.[15] In CODESA's first ten years, it had not transferred any enterprises to the private sector.

CODESA's mandate was also to help, through a wide variety of other economic services and activities, to strengthen private enterprise within the framework of a mixed economy. It provided administrative and technical assistance to old and new firms, assisted import-substitution and export-diversification projects, extended loans and capital, guaranteed businesses against bankruptcy, and took over several failing private enterprises.

CODESA was initially favored by industrialists and businessmen, but by the early 1980s they began to perceive some of its operations as competing with and not complementing private capital. Politicians doled out CODESA posts as political patronage, and nearly all its operations were running in the red. Yet it enjoyed virtually unlimited access to government credit. Private entrepreneurs and bankers were also annoyed that all foreign funds had to be channeled, at a commission, through CODESA's bank. Therefore, the demands of AID privatization planners that CODESA be swiftly and completely sold off found support among big business, the opposition Unity party, the right wing of the Liberation party, the conservative mainstream press, and certain technocrats.

But while AID and its local supporters decried CODESA as an uneconomical, politically motivated white elephant incapable of reform, Costa Rican supporters of a mixed economy contended that CODESA's troubles were due in part to the country's severe economic crisis in the early 1980s and that, while CODESA needed to be overhauled and pruned, it should not be totally dismantled. They argued that, like the nationalized banks, it was an important tool for social and economic development that should not be judged solely in terms of profits and efficiency. An AID-commissioned report conceded, "Despite all the negative signals produced by CODESA, an important number of legislators and politicians actively defended the institution."[16]

The CODESA divestiture followed the pattern of other AID-orchestrated privatization projects undertaken during the 1980s. First, an AID-commissioned report by the Arthur D. Little consulting firm found that CODESA had accumulated a debt of over $180 million and was consuming a lion's share—one-third—of government credit. The IMF and World Bank conditioned their loans on a CODESA sell-off,[17] and beginning in 1984 AID agreements barred any further government loans to CODESA. However, to begin the sell-off, AID had to engineer passage of the wide-ranging "Law of Financial Equilibrium of the Public Sector," popularly known as the Emergency Law. A CODESA divestiture study admits that approval of this law, passed by the Legislative Assembly in February 1984, "required a great deal of political maneuvering as [it] generated great resistance and a prolonged debate among supporters of CODESA." In the end, the legislature passed the bill, but, as AID evaluators concluded, the legislature's approval was "less the result of political agreement than an acceptance of the clout AID's grants enjoyed."[18]

AID next set out to minimize further the public and legislative debate over CODESA and to work behind the scenes with both presidents Monge and Arias and AID-created private-sector organizations to implement the divestiture. AID's most imaginative move was to set up FINTRA (Fiduciaria de Inversiones Transitorias, S.A.), a private-sector "trust fund" financed with some $175 million from AID's special local-currency account in the Central Bank. By 1987, this amounted to over 20 percent of AID's local-currency funds, making the CODESA divestiture AID's largest program (see table 4). FINTRA's five-member board of directors was "selected with significant input by Mr. Chaij and the President of the Republic" (Monge).[19] The board had complete authority to handle the divestiture and select new buyers.

FINTRA's function was to purchase, one after another, CODESA's enterprises and to run them until buyers could be found. FINTRA would function until all of CODESA's business had been sold off. Under the law, the "legal price" of CODESA holdings was fixed by the Comptroller General's office and government tax assessors. FINTRA would pay this official price and then look for buyers who would pay the considerably lower market value, minus depreciation. The proceeds from the final sale were to go into the FINTRA trust account.[20] FINTRA's first purchase was the aluminum-fabricating company, ALUNASA, for $52 million—almost one-third of its total budget. Eighteen months later FINTRA sold it for a mere $7 million to businessman Rodolfo Guardián. Although eyebrows were raised in Washington about this scheme, because it underwrote a private purchaser, AID justified it as a way of warding off political criticism in Costa Rica, since the government was paid ALUNASA's full assessed value. According to the Center for Privatization study, "FINTRA and USAID served to diffuse some of the . . . accusations of selling the 'national patrimony' at apparent distress prices."[21]

While CODESA companies were originally scheduled to be sold off rapidly, over a thirty-two-week period ending September 1985, this timetable proved unrealistic. By May 1987, only four of CODESA's forty-two companies and subsidiaries had been sold to the private sector, and ownership of another six had been turned over to other government agencies. The Manager-to-Manager memo concludes, "The causes for this lack of progress are many, but totally unrealistic planning by supposedly experienced AID personnel would have to be high on the list."[22] As a result, FINTRA funds sat idle in its Central Bank account, and despite complaints by some Central Bank officials, AID compelled the government to pay interest on the undisbursed balance. According to the AID audit, this amounted to a massive $61.6 million in interest payments over a two-year period and it enabled FINTRA to carry out its limited activities using only the interest and not the principal in the account.

According to the AID Inspector General's memo, a large chunk of FINTRA's funds was soaked up in high administrative costs. Like other AID-sponsored private-sector operations, FIN-TRA was no financial bargain: salaries for board members ranged from $2,000 to $3,600 per month, and four of the five board members devoted just five to eight hours per week to FINTRA. In addition, they received $250 per-diem travel expenses and were not required to file vouchers. The FINTRA board members made enough trips to contact 140 potential overseas buyers, yet no purchases resulted from these junkets. The Inspector General's memo concluded, "The FINTRA Trust is an expensive, ineffective mechanism which has not noticeably contributed to the divestiture process."[23]

By the end of 1992, still only ALUNASA of CODESA's seven largest companies had been sold to a private buyer. The sugar mill, CATSA, had been sold to cooperatives, two other companies were transferred to different government agencies, one was liquidated, and no buyers had been found for the remaining two, FERTICA and CEMPASA (of which only 40 percent was to be legally sold off). After Rafael Angel Calderón assumed the presidency in May 1990, AID agreements repeatedly demanded that all CODESA assets be promptly sold off. This did not happen, and so CODESA continued to run them and FINTRA continued to look for buyers. AID officials admitted they were completely disillusioned because the process had become "completely stagnated."[24]

A separate question to be sorted out was the fate of CODESA's merchant and investment bank. The bank had gradually been deprived of access to Central Bank credit, eliminated by law from receiving and lending foreign funds to the private sector, and barred by a Cabinet resolution from making new investments or forming new companies, but it was not slated to be sold off.[25] It was, instead, being slowly starved as CODESA's assets were dismantled. CODESA President Alfonso Campos admitted that, with the full sell-off of CODESA's holdings, the investment bank would be left without any specific functions and the institution would disappear.[26]

However, AID officials quietly worried that if the shell corporation remained, the government might in the future try to "fill up the CODESA stable with new parastatal companies."[27] To prevent this possibility, they moved instead to create a parallel, private institution to perform just the sort of merchant banking activities CODESA had done. With a $1 million grant and $20 million loan in dollars (payable over twenty years at 2–3 percent interest), plus $5 million in local currency, AID created the Private Investment Corporation (PIC), which was "intended to fill an institutional gap by providing a blend of traditional merchant banking and investment banking services."[28] In fact, there was no institutional gap. As with the other AID-created parallel institutions, PIC's aim was to duplicate and eventually replace a government institution. Like other parallel-state institutions, PIC was designed to conform to AID's private sector, export-oriented strategy. According to a PIC annual report, this AID-financed merchant bank could only loan to private (not state) enterprises producing for the export (not internal) market.

The Center for Privatization, a coordinating office for consulting firms selected by AID to provide technical services to AID divestment and privatization programs worldwide, concluded that the CODESA divestiture, although extremely costly and lengthy, was successful on an ideological plane. A Center report states that the cost of FINTRA was offset "attitudinally in the increasingly favorable view toward privatization in general that has developed, reflected not only in the Government but in the press and the views of the general public. As an important element of a private sector program it must be regarded as having justified the cost and effort invested in it."[29] This process is, however, more accurately described as a denationalization, since, by 1992, less than one-quarter of CODESA had ended up in private hands.[30] The Center for Privatization report makes clear that, in fact, AID's real intent was to remove the government from ownership of industries. It states that the CODESA sell-off and use of the FINTRA trust "serves to assure that, whether or not investments are ultimately sold into private hands, they do not remain under government control."[31] The $175 million price tag for scoring this ideological blow was inordinately high: the CODESA divestiture was AID's most costly program, consuming over 20 percent of AID's budget. In the end, questions remained about what really happened to all these millions, and, more fundamentally, about whether the Costa Rican government couldn't have used these funds for more socially beneficial projects.

EARTH: Dan Chaij's Retirement Scheme

While the CODESA denationalization was AID's most costly and ambitious project, the so-called EARTH school (Escuela de Agricultura de la Región Tropical Húmeda or School of Agriculture for the Humid Tropical Region) became its most controversial institutional creation. This private U.S.-style, four-year undergraduate university specializes in the humid tropics and trains managers for private-sector jobs such as farm managers through a "learn by doing program."[32] Located at Guácimo on Costa Rica's lowland Caribbean coastal plain, EARTH cost $118.4 million to build and staff, but it provides only the most marginal benefit to Costa Rica. Although the school is international and no more than twenty Costa Rican students are admitted each year, 78 percent or $92 million of the cost was financed through AID's Costa Rica program. The rest—$26.4 million—came from AID's Regional Office for Central America and Panama (ROCAP) program, based in Guatemala. EARTH consumed nearly 15 percent of all AID grants to Costa Rica during the period 1983–87. Yet clearly the benefits to Costa Rica were extremely limited.

During this same period, AID used less than 3 percent of its local currency funds for other education programs, most of which also helped private institutions (see table 4). One of the most questionable was the Adventist Center of Higher Education (CADES), an unaccredited religious school in Alajuela cofounded and run by Dan Chaij's father, which received a $300,000 AID grant and six scholarships for study in the United States. According to the State Department Inspector General's memo, at the time of the loan CADES "lacked legal status under Costa Rican commercial laws. . . . Moreover, no evidence was shown that CADES had proper accounting systems and controls to effectively administer grant funds." Chaij, who had grown up partly in Costa Rica, was himself a graduate of the school and a prominent member of the Seventh Day Adventist Church, which has jurisdiction over the school.[33]

The creation of EARTH was a pet project of the AID Director. Costa Rican insiders referred cynically to the EARTH school as Chaij's "retirement scheme," since it was widely believed that he hoped to leave AID and to be appointed as its first director. Costa Rican officials recall that Chaij's lobbying for the project was extremely persistent. At one point he called one of Arias's ministers to say that U.S. approval of a new PL-480 food-aid package "would be smoothed out" as soon as the government sent the EARTH project to the Legislative Assembly.

Officially, the EARTH project began with an October 1984 letter from President Monge to U.S. Ambassador Curtin Winsor. But knowledgeable government officials, academics, and legislators say that Chaij convinced Monge (who was subsequently named to EARTH's board of directors) to write the letter formally requesting that AID finance the project. Such a school had never before been a priority of top educators. The Embassy's law firm, Vargas, Jiménez and Peralta, actually drafted the bill that was presented to the Legislative Assembly in September 1985, and Chaij personally orchestrated the campaign over the next year to secure its passage.

Chaij assembled the predictable panorama of local promoters to take out paid newspaper ads, lobby the Legislative Assembly, and give public speeches supporting the project. They contended that EARTH was unique because of its "hands-on" approach to education—it was to feature learning through manual labor on the school's 3,200-hectare farm—and because of its specialization in the humid, as opposed to dry, tropics.

EARTH opponents included a handful of outspoken legislators, Rector of the University of Costa Rica Fernando Durán and other leading academics, the University Employees Union (SINDEU), and the Federation of Students of the University of Costa Rica (FEUCR). They contended that if AID was really concerned with Costa Rica's higher education, it should support the existing and well-respected agricultural school at the University of Costa Rica (UCR), which already had three experimental research stations, including one emphasizing humid tropic studies. In addition, these opponents argued that EARTH's curriculum could be handled by other institutions in the region, including the United Fruit Company's long-established Pan-American agricultural school, El Zamorano, in Honduras and the Organization of American States' internationally recognized Centro Agronómico Tropical de Investigación y Enseñanza (CATIE) in Turrialba, Costa Rica. A University of North Carolina study reportedly concluded that existing Central American institutions like the University of Costa Rica could be strengthened to serve an international student body for less than half EARTH's projected cost per student.[34]

Coincidentally, the Legislative Assembly debated EARTH just as the 30,000-student University of Costa Rica was facing a severe economic crisis resulting from AID/IMF/World Bank prescribed cuts in public-sector spending. These cuts forced a sharp rise in tuition and layoffs of about five hundred faculty members. But AID, with its obsession for the private sector, gave less than $700,000 to the University of Costa Rica between 1983 and 1987, most of which went to purchase electronic equipment.[35]

Others questioned why the school and its farm, which was intended to be run as a commercial venture, should be awarded the same status as a foreign embassy, including diplomatic immunity for its non-Costa Rican staff, duty-free import privileges, and exemption from local taxes. Critics also objected to AID's selection of California Polytechnical University at San Luis Obispo (Cal Poly), an institution with no expertise in the humid tropics, to oversee the design and construction of EARTH's campus, write the curriculum, and handle other aspects involved in launching the new school. Nineteen U.S. universities submitted proposals, including a number that had long academic relationships with Costa Rica and expertise in the humid tropics.

Despite these objections, Chaij, Monge, and other proponents set about to railroad the project through the Legislative Assembly in hopes that it would be approved before Monge left office. Opponents managed to block its passage during Monge's administration, but in August 1986, after the Arias government came into office, the new Legislative Assembly passed the EARTH bill. Many in the new government, unacquainted with the project, supported it out of a general commitment to higher education.

Although approved, the project remained controversial. The Inspector General's memo found that in buying land for the school and its farm, AID paid over $9 million and "engaged in activities that are in violation of both AID's regulations and sound management practices." The property belonged to the politically influential Rojas family, which includes Rodolfo Cortes Rojas, an ex-member of CINDE's board of directors who became president of EARTH's board of directors and a member of its board of trustees.

Despite AID Director Chaij's fast-paced drive to get the project underway, once officially approved, EARTH moved forward at a snail's pace. By late 1989, it had hired only two faculty—a general director (not Chaij, who had fallen from grace) and an academic coordinator—and it had received applications from only sixty-three students. It finally opened in March 1990 with just sixty students (about half its intended class size), nineteen of whom were Costa Ricans.

EARTH's campus and farm cost a total of $37.7 million, and the complex stands out conspicuously in the poor Caribbean coastal farming region of Guácimo. According to the *Tico Times,* "The brilliant white and red buildings of EARTH rise from Costa Rica's northern plains like a freshly-minted California suburb, complete with a paved four-lane divided access road."[36] Each building sports the AID shield. Its annual operating cost was expected to be seven times more per student than the University of Costa Rica.[37]

EARTH's cost led to another scandal: the tuition. The annual tuition per student was initially set at $15,200 per year, making EARTH the most costly school in the region. Students at the University of Costa Rica, for instance, paid only $275 per year, a figure frequently reduced by full or partial scholarships. For unexplained reasons, AID initially stated that "no scholarships are proposed for the students" at EARTH—this despite its stated intention to attract students from rural areas.[38] But when general director Dr. José Zaglul took a look at the meager stack of applicants, he ordered that tuition be cut and scholarships be given for at least the first few years. EARTH therefore lowered its tuition to $9,600, with AID subsidizing the difference. Even so, by 1991, 90 to 95 percent of the students were receiving scholarships, 80 percent of these full scholarships. So long as EARTH offers so many scholarships, officials said, it can never become self-sustaining.

CINDE: The Flagship of AID's Parallel Institutions

Created in 1983 by AID officials and a small group of prominent businessmen, CINDE (Coalition for Development Initiatives) became the centerpiece of the Parallel State and the flagship institution for AID's strategy of private-sector-led growth through new industrial and agricultural exports outside the Central American market. Wholly financed by AID with a total of some $40 million by the end of the decade, CINDE overshadowed CENPRO (Center for the Promotion of Investment and Exports), an existing government institution with virtually the same mandate. CINDE operated seven offices overseas and spawned three AID-funded divisions in Costa Rica: PIE (Investment and Export Promotion Program), intended to attract foreign investors into Costa Rica's new nontraditional export businesses; CAAP (Private Council on Agriculture and Agro-Industry), to promote and provide technical assistance to nontraditional agricultural exporters; and PROCAP (Private Sector Training Program), to run courses and seminars designed to improve the productivity of the private sector. In 1989 CINDE set up a new Industrial Development Program to "assist local industries in making the conversion from import-substitution to exporting."[39] AID has channeled millions of dollars through CINDE for other projects, including the EARTH university.

AID officials boast that CINDE is a shining example of how Third World nations can use foreign investors to diversify and expand their moribund economies and lessen their dependence on AID handouts.[40] In a 1988 interview, U.S. ambassador to Costa Rica Deane Hinton termed CINDE "a great success. The expansion of investment in this country dates from the CINDE operation. The data shows a tremendous growth of jobs, growth of exports, at a rather astonishing rate." In the latter half of the 1980s, AID financed CINDE-like institutions in six other countries, including El Salvador,[41] Honduras, and Guatemala.

CINDE itself boasts of spectacular achievements. In April 1990, CINDE claimed that over the previous five years, it had attracted 120 foreign companies to invest $353 million in Costa Rica and export $305 million in nontraditional products. By late 1989, CINDE claimed to have created thirty thousand new jobs.[42] A letter written to the international press at the time of the Hemispheric Summit on Democracy in October 1989 proclaimed, "Thanks to efforts of CINDE and governmental specialized institutions, Costa Rica has achieved the lowest rate of inflation and unemployment and has better indexes on health and literacy rates than the rest of Latin America."[43]

The reality is less rosy. For one thing, CINDE-created jobs in Costa Rica are often jobs that are lost to American workers when U.S. companies move south looking for cheap, unorganized labor and tax and import concessions. While this constitutes a clear loss to U.S. workers, the supposed benefits to Costa Rica are also dubious. Foreign companies in Costa Rica receive enormous tax breaks, their products are exported, and they import almost all their materials. The only real financial gain for Costa Rica is from wages. From its inception, CINDE has been highly controversial. CINDE was never voted upon by the Legislative Assembly, has had no oversight by any branch of the Costa Rican government, and (at least initially) spent millions of dollars with little effective supervision from the AID mission or Washington. Despite its public-relations claims, CINDE played no role in bolstering Costa Rica's public health and education systems and, by the early 1990s, annual inflation had climbed steeply, to over 20 percent.

From the start CINDE has promoted a costly development strategy that is not generating long-term, sustainable economic growth or a more egalitarian distribution of wealth. As one top government economist observed in 1989, "The Reagan and Bush administrations, through CINDE, have had a lot of leverage to subsidize the private sector in Costa Rica. But their methods have violated even their own ideology of free trade, market forces, and democratic participation. We are induced to sacrifice money donated by the U.S. to Costa Rica to promote exports instead of channeling these resources to internal social development. This has not been done through competition because the private sector is subsidized heavily, the market forces are violated completely. It's not democratic because no one discusses it openly. CINDE officials are not elected and are not accountable. Free trade, competition, and democracy are all violated."

Just as AID funds fortified the private banks, they also created and fed CINDE as a private institution in order to sidestep, rather than reform, Costa Rica's existing export promotion agency, CENPRO. CENPRO was founded by the government in 1968 to promote nontraditional exports to countries outside Central America. During the 1970s, when the Central American Common Market (CACM) was functioning well, there was little incentive for exporters to seek new nonregional markets, and CENPRO's success rate was modest. The economic crisis of the late 1970s brought it near bankruptcy, and it lacked funds for investment promotion. One private banker voiced the popular view that, over the years, CENPRO had grown "bumbling and bureaucratic." Yet a number of Costa Rican analysts argued that AID should have used its resources to streamline, modernize, and professionalize CENPRO, which had fifteen years of experience in export promotion, rather than build a new, parallel institutional giant.

While former ambassador Hinton argued that "CENPRO was not on any hit list," a 1988 CINDE evaluation reiterated AID's underlying "belief that the private sector is more efficient in the promotion of national development goals."[44] AID therefore chose to by-pass and weaken rather than reform and promote CENPRO. Despite hair-splitting attempts by U.S. and CINDE officials to delineate their differences, the purpose of both institutions was essentially the same.

AID contends that private institutions are more efficient than state ones, but CINDE itself turned out to be expensive, wasteful, and fraught with illegal administrative procedures. This was the conclusion of the Manager-to-Manager memo sent by the State Department Inspector General to the AID Administrator in Washington following a 1987 audit of AID's program in Costa Rica.[45] While the lengthy memo detailed a host of irregularities in the AID program, its harshest critique was of CINDE. In 1983, CINDE was established with $11.25 million in colones from AID's Special Account. This money was illegally transferred before AID submitted a project plan or approved budget. The memo stated that AID files contain "little explanation" as to "why the mission Director [Chaij] authorized a grant of $11.25 million to an institution that could not ensure that the funds would be managed properly." It continued, "CINDE not only lacked the capacity to effectively administer AID funds at the time it was created, it did not acquire an acceptable managerial ability for a number of years after it came into existence."[46] Both the memo and a 1988 AID evaluation[47] concluded that CINDE never really got off the ground in terms of promoting foreign investment and nontraditional exports until 1986.

At the time the audit was done in 1987, CINDE still lacked proper accounting and control procedures to manage its growing portfolio and activities. The memo stated that even though AID "was aware of this situation," the mission continued to fund CINDE to the tune of $33.8 million by December 1986. It concluded that during its first five years, CINDE's "operations and activities were poorly monitored, if monitored at all, and no measures were taken to prevent waste and abuse of AID-granted funds. . . . It appears that CINDE has produced few tangible developmental results and that long-term goals as outlined in its Charter is [sic] illusory."

The lengthy memo listed a number of CINDE's "serious operational deficiencies," including the organization's inability to balance its books in 1985, its failure to prepare interim financial statements to assess its accomplishments, and its lack of accounting for travel expenditures. The memo claimed that "AID-granted funds were used for questionable purposes"; that CINDE's travel allowances, per-diem rates, public relations, and entertainment expenses were "excessive"; and that the organization could show "little tangible results" from these investments. It stated that, contrary to AID regulations, CINDE paid for personal gifts and parties for Ambassador Winsor, Director Chaij, and other U.S. officials, and that CINDE officials were not required to file travel reports. In 1986 alone, CINDE spent some $200,000 on travel. Then-CINDE director Federico Vargas told the auditors that CINDE board members, all Costa Rican VIPs, "would feel offended" if required to submit expense accounts.[48]

The Inspector General's letter stated further that twenty-three top CINDE officials were involved in a tax-evasion scheme designed by Chaij, Fernando Naranjo, and Guido Fernández, and that "virtually all of [CINDE's] top officials" illegally avoided paying Costa Rican taxes by diverting part of their salaries to companies they owned. "CINDE created contracts with these companies for consulting services which were not actually provided," the memo states.[49]

The Inspector General's letter added that "AID handpicked the Board of Directors so that CINDE would act according to AID's goals and not take on its own character." It concluded that many

Costa Ricans view CINDE as "too inbred" and as "a closed institution," aimed at benefiting a few "wealthy and influential" Costa
Ricans "to advance their own personal and political interests . . . at
the expense of the United States government and Costa Rica." In
an interview former ambassador Frank McNeil defended AID's
selection process for CINDE. McNeil said that he and Chaij
personally "went through the names of the movers and shakers,
particularly in business," because they agreed that "if CINDE were
to succeed, it was absolutely essential to get first-class people for
the board and to run the program." He added that "it is false to
intimate that Mr. Chaij sort of set up CINDE in the dead of night."

Other Embassy, AID, and CINDE officials charged that the
Inspector General's memo was inaccurate and amounted to a
vendetta against Chaij. In private, though, a number of well-
placed Costa Rican and U.S. officials conceded that the audit
report and memo was largely accurate.

What seems equally clear is that the memo was intentionally
leaked to the press by Reagan administration officials in an effort
to undercut President Arias's peace initiatives. The original story
syndicated by Scripps Howard on January 21, 1988, presented the
AID scandal as a tale of high-level corruption within the Arias
administration, rather than one of gross mismanagement and
favoritism in a major U.S. overseas program.[50] The story sparked
an uproar in both Washington and San José.

Responding to the AID scandal, Costa Rica opened two
official investigations into possible illegal activities by CINDE and
misuse of AID funds. One inquiry, by the public prosecutor's
criminal investigations branch, the OIJ, was short lived and incon-
clusive, grinding to a halt after CINDE officials flatly refused to
open the organization's books to judicial investigators. The other,
by the Legislative Assembly, was more substantive and public. The
Assembly voted unanimously to form a five-member bipartisan
special commission on CINDE and AID, and during the spring of
1988, this body took testimony from several dozen persons.
Initially CINDE stonewalled again, refusing to turn over documents and accounts, on the grounds that as a private company it
was not accountable. The commission countered that the funds
CINDE received from AID were donations to the Costa Rican

government and that CINDE, as a recipient, qualified as a public institution. In May, CINDE relented and presented several volumes of documents to the commission.

The legislative commission collected a thick dossier of testimony basically substantiating the Inspector General's memo, but it produced no concrete changes and the controversy gradually died down. In January 1989, United Press International quoted AID Inspector General Beckington as saying that "the Costa Rican government made no attempt to discipline its officials or recover the funds."[51] Neither, for that matter, had AID.

The findings in the audit report and State Department memo are particularly shocking, since AID officials in Costa Rica argued that one of the rationales for setting up CINDE as a parallel private institution was that, given Costa Rica's economic crisis, there was no time to reform CENPRO, an institution they characterized as riddled with corruption, cronyism, and inefficiency. Instead, CINDE and CENPRO existed uncomfortably side by side, with CENPRO increasingly marginalized by CINDE's aggressive, well-financed operations. CENPRO's annual budget of 45–55 million colones (or less than $1 million) between 1984 and 1989 was on average seven times smaller than CINDE's. Because of financial constraints, CENPRO was forced to close its only overseas offices in the United States, while CINDE opened new offices in the United States, Europe, and Asia and in 1990 moved into a luxurious new office complex in San José.

As it did with the banking sector, AID set out to remold Costa Rica's laws and government structure to facilitate CINDE's objectives. CINDE faced an immediate problem: it was an independent and wholly private institution, but it needed government cooperation to implement its investment and export schemes. In 1983, therefore, AID played a key role in creating a new government body, the Ministry of External Trade (MINEX), which was designed to be, as one former AID official put it, a sort of "czar of exports." To carry out its new export strategy, AID, along with the first MINEX minister, Mario Carvajal, helped orchestrate passage in 1984 and 1985 of three major export-incentive laws—on free-trade zones, *maquila* industries, and export contracts—designed to attract foreign investors and promote new industrial and nontraditional agricultural exports. The rationale behind this strategy, which was pushed as well by the World Bank and the IMF, was that economic recovery and growth depended on expanded exports and foreign exchange earnings. Beginning with the Monge administration, Costa Rica's longstanding bias toward production for the domestic and regional markets was systematically shifted and its laws and government institutions restructured to promote private sector exports, primarily to the United States. These policies went beyond simply creating an equal playing field between producers for the domestic and the export markets. They promoted export-oriented growth rather than simply free-market development. They reorganized the economy to favor production for foreign markets, imports of previously produced goods including of basic foods, and foreign investment. As such these export-oriented policies were tailor made to benefit U.S. and other foreign companies. They turned out to provide very little to Costa Rica, other than income from wages. These economic reforms represent an early version of free-trade policies advocated throughout the Americas by the Bush administration in the early 1990s.[52]

The first bill, the Free Trade Zone Law, modified existing legislation to allow private developers to own and run export-processing industrial parks or free-trade zones and to permit these parks to be built in the economically well developed Central Valley. Under this revised law, industries in the free trade zones must export at least 51 percent of their product and in return they are given a ten-year renewable contract guaranteeing duty-free import of raw materials and capital goods, no local taxes for the first six years, and relative freedom in taking profits out of the country. They are not even required to maintain a local bank account.

The original legislation, passed in 1979, only permitted the government to administer industrial parks that were designed for foreign manufacturing companies. It also specified that the parks be located in the poorer regions of the country. In 1981, the government's Free Zone Corporation, a subsidiary of the state holding company CODESA, established two manufacturing zones in the economically depressed port cities of Limón and Puntarenas. But these industrial parks, located away from the large labor force, the international airport, good roads, schools, comfortable climate, and other conveniences, attracted few foreign investors.

In the mid-1980s, MINEX, CINDE, and a private firm, *Grupo Zeta,* teamed up and successfully pressured the government to modify the legislation. In 1985, the Free Zone Corporation declared *Grupo Zeta*'s industrial park in the Central Valley town of Cartago as a privately administered free zone, and over the next few years, a number of other privately owned industrial parks were built. By the end of the decade the government was selling off its two parks, making all the free-trade zones totally private enterprises located in the Central Valley.

A second, far more sweeping piece of AID-backed legislation was Law #6955 or the *Ley para el Equilibrio Financiero del Sector Público* (Law for Financial Equilibrium in the Public Sector), popularly known as the Emergency Law. A portion of this law modified the existing *maquila* (or assembly-plant) regulations to allow foreign-owned companies outside the free trade zones to import raw materials and manufacturing equipment, purchase local inputs, and export their products without paying any taxes. Grouped into something known as the Temporary Admission Regime, the *maquila* industries cannot sell their products locally.

The Emergency Law also created the Export Contract and the National Investment Council (CNI), an interagency body that awards the contracts. CINDE-hired consultants drew up the Export Contract which gives an extraordinary package of benefits intended to attract foreign investors and promote new, so-called nontraditional exports. The incentives, which are subject to renewal in 1996, are based on the percentage of production exported. They include:

1. Income-tax exemption for profits earned on nontraditional exports sold outside Central America.
2. Import-duty exemption for machinery, raw materials, and other inputs invested in the exporting process.
3. Exemption from local taxes for nationally purchased production inputs.
4. Abolition of export duties on nontraditional products. (Exporters of traditional products such as bananas and coffee continued to pay a government tax.)

5. The CAT (Tax Credit Certificate) bonus from the government worth 15 percent of the total value of exports to the United States and up to 20 percent of the value of exports to Europe and Asia.

This costly and controversial export-incentive package has provided massive government subsidies to exporters. In 1988, for instance, the government awarded export companies 5,395 billion colones (or about 8 percent of its budget) on CATs, and these exporters also paid no import, export, or income taxes. In addition, they can take out of Costa Rica all profits and capital investments at the current exchange rate. Wealthy local business-men were given breaks as well, including a law passed during President Arias's term which reduced the highest tax rate from 50 percent to 30 percent of gross profits for the corporate sector. In addition, the World Bank, Inter-American Development Bank, and Latin American Export Bank set up the Export Financing Fund (FOPEX), a $140 million line of credit in the Central Bank to help exporters expand their production.[53]

OPIC: Another Support for U.S. Investors

With the creation of MINEX and the passage of the three export-incentive bills, CINDE had, as one former vice-minister put it, "everything it needed to promote exports and attract foreign investors." The influx of new U.S. investors into Costa Rica was also facilitated by the Overseas Private Investment Corporation (OPIC), which provides both insurance and loans to American business ventures in "politically risky" parts of the world. A U.S. government agency, OPIC is run like a business: it is self-sustaining and designed to make a profit. During the 1980s, OPIC's Costa Rican program grew to become the largest in Latin America, and OPIC developed a close working relationship with both the U.S. Embassy and CINDE.[54]

In 1989, OPIC had nine loans and between twenty-six and thirty insurance contracts in Costa Rica, about half in nontraditional exports. OPIC-supported companies in Costa Rica include a number of multinationals—Holiday Inn, Firestone Tire, Borden—

as well as a number of smaller investors, many of whom were from
Florida. These included five fern-exporting companies that were
part of a single U.S. consortium of thirteen companies owned
by John Marsell, Joseph Master, and Kenneth Lanier, all of De-
land, Florida. They use separate names to evade taxes but often
share offices, secretaries, and phone lines. OPIC statements
make no mention of these linkages, and OPIC officials denied
knowing about the multiple ties of the Marsell, Master, and Lanier
trio.

OPIC's most controversial project in Costa Rica was a
$375,000 loan in March 1984 to CIA operative John Hull, a central
figure in the Iran-contra scandal. The loan, whose irregularities
were investigated in U.S. Senate hearings, was given to Hull and
two partners, William Crone and a Costa Rican named Alvaro
Arroyo, to set up a factory, Maderas Tropicales (Tropical Woods),
making axe and wheelbarrow handles for sale in the United States.
By the end of 1985, Hull had made only one interest payment, and
the loan lapsed into default.

The report of a U.S. Senate investigation into the matter concluded, "What appears to have happened is that Hull simply took
most of the money, inasmuch as no equipment was purchased for
the factory, no products were shipped from it, and Hull's partner,
Crone, testified that he never saw the money."[55]

OPIC Vice President Eric Garfinkel said the agency made the
loan on the strong recommendation of Embassy officials who
argued it would "strengthen American relations with Costa
Rica."[56] Robert Owen, Oliver North's liaison to the illegal contra
operation out of Costa Rica, also met with OPIC officials several
times on Hull's behalf. Bill Crone complained that "John even
bragged to the OPIC lady who came to Costa Rica about what he
was doing. He would show military supplies that he had there on
his farms—boots and things like that. And he would tell about the
contras coming in to get people there and flying out."[57]

There were numerous other irregularities in OPIC's handling
of the Hull loan. Although OPIC requires investors to match loans
with at least half the cost of implementing the project, Hull put
almost nothing into the venture. The land Hull offered as collateral did not actually belong to him, but OPIC never conducted an

audit of the loan, on which accounting records were found to be "seriously amiss."[58]

In April 1987, after Hull's involvement in the contra war against Nicaragua was made public in the Tower Commission report, OPIC referred the case to the Justice Department for collection and possible civil and criminal-fraud charges. However, despite the fact that U.S. judicial authorities say it is still open and there is a subpoena out for Hull, the case has remained dormant. In July 1989, Hull jumped bail to avoid prosecution in Costa Rica and returned to the United States, but the Justice Department made no effort either to prosecute him for the OPIC loan or to extradite him back to Costa Rica.

Caribbean Basin Initiative: Creating the Right Climate for U.S. Investment

CINDE pursued its strategy of attracting foreign investment and promoting nontraditional exports under the umbrella of the Caribbean Basin Initiative (CBI), the Reagan administration's much-heralded trade act giving certain commodities from specific countries duty-free access to the U.S. market. Covering Costa Rica and twenty-seven other Central American and Caribbean countries, CBI was announced in June 1982 and extended and broadened in 1990 to expand export incentives and cover more products.

While CINDE claims that the CBI promotes "economic revitalization and expanded private sector opportunities,"[59] its principal benefits go to the U.S. market and American investors in the region. "With all the CBI propaganda, everyone said, 'Now the U.S. is really helping the region,' " recalled one Costa Rican economist. In reality, however, Costa Rica and other developing countries already enjoyed virtually the same market access to all the industrialized nations—Japan, European Economic Community countries, Canada, and the United States—through the little-publicized Generalized System of Preferences (GSP). Under the GSP, the United States and other developed nations negotiate, on a country-by-country basis, tariff relief and reduction packages with the Third World.

On the other hand, CBI protects U.S. business, for instance, by excluding certain key products also produced in the United States—textiles, leather goods, petroleum derivatives, refined sugar, and canned tuna—from duty-free access to the U.S. market. Ironically, these are exports that Costa Rica and other CBI countries could most easily have expanded. Products which *are* allowed duty-free access to the U.S. market under CBI must include at least 35 percent value added, that is, they must contain local materials (including wages) totaling 35 percent of the export price. The stated intent of this provision is to stimulate use of local raw materials in producing export products. However, under CBI, 15 percent of these local compenents can be of U.S. origin—a provision that helps the United States and reduces benefits to the local economy. CBI has also helped make Latin America more attractive than Asia for U.S. as well as Asian investors wanting cheap labor, geographic proximity, and guaranteed access to the U.S. market.

U.S. investors have indeed flocked to Costa Rica (the country CINDE boasts has "the Right Business Climate for your Caribbean Basin Investment")[60] to set up assembly plants or grow nontraditional agricultural projects. More than any other CBI country, CINDE propagandists were able to sell Costa Rica's political stability, economic reorientation toward the private sector and exports, good infrastructure, educated and nonunionized labor force, proximity to the United States, and massive AID program to lure U.S. investors. Foreign investors made high profits, but Costa Rica received minimal benefit. Costa Ricans could not buy most of the new manufactured goods and nontraditional crops, the government could not tax the foreign exporters, few of the new firms used local raw materials, and most took their profits out of the country. The principal residue of these operations was jobs, and even these were not usually skilled enough to make good use of Costa Rica's well-educated work force. As one Costa Rican economist put it, this was not a real development program, it was "a pacification program to keep people quiet."

CINDE's "Development" Strategy

The AID/CINDE "pacification" program has concentrated on attracting U.S. assembly-line industries, particularly clothing manufacturers, to Costa Rica. CINDE's initial goal was quick success through the apparel industries,[61] which were viewed as the fastest way for the new institution to win approval and replace CENPRO. Textiles have historically been the easiest and cheapest industry to set up in the Third World, as well as the most easily moved when economic conditions change. As a 1988 AID evaluation critically noted, CINDE's "strong emphasis on creating jobs—any jobs—has resulted in the program attracting mostly low technology, low capital intensive, relatively temporary apparel/textile companies that can move their investment around on short notice."[62]

While CINDE hailed its textile strategy as new, it was, in a sense, a step backward, since Costa Rica already had a substantial industrial base—36 percent of total production in 1980—and a highly literate, healthy work force. Costa Rica's textile-manufacturing sector was already well developed, with most of its firms nationally owned and producing for the local and Central American markets.

CINDE's textile strategy represented a short-term, quick fix designed to create jobs and increase exports. Almost immediately, textiles became the country's fastest-growing industrial sector. CINDE officials say that, in 1986, 87 percent (or 4,667) of the jobs created by new foreign investment were in textile factories. From 1986 through the first quarter of 1990, new textile jobs totaled 19,250 or almost one-third of the industry's total 60,000 jobs. By the end of the decade, Costa Rica had about seventy large clothing manufacturers, each employing one hundred or more workers. Eighty-five percent of these companies were foreign, mainly U.S., owned; the rest were owned by Asian investors. Ninety to 95 percent of textile exports were going to the United States. Textile exports proved so profitable that even some long-established companies manufacturing for the domestic market began producing for export, a transition assisted by CINDE's Industrial Development Program.[63]

Most of the new U.S. manufacturers were runaway shops, seeking in Costa Rica nonunionized, cheap labor with, a CINDE brochure boasts, "the longest regular work week—48 hours—in the area."[64] According to Costa Rican law, salaries for garment workers averaged $.60–$1.00 per hour for a forty-eight-hour week. But industry officials say that with fringe benefits and Social Security, they actually pay about $1.50 per hour. Either figure constitutes poverty wages for workers and a real attraction for manufacturers in the United States who, by 1991, were paying a minimum wage of $4.15 per hour.[65] According to a former CINDE official, "CINDE's investment officers look through the Dun and Bradstreet listings of American corporations, pinpointing labor-intensive manufacturers in the U.S. Once they've targeted a manufacturer, a CINDE rep calls the firm and sends them a packet of promotional literature." The ex-official termed CINDE "just a well-oiled job-stealing machine—maintained and financed by U.S. taxpayer dollars." Not only is this detrimental to U.S. workers, but it is also, as the former official put it, encouraging a "new form of dependence" in which Costa Rica's export market is increasingly controlled by U.S. capital.[66]

Almost as soon as it began, the bonanza for textile exporters began to evaporate. In 1988, Costa Rica signed the Multi-Fiber Agreement (MFA), an accord among garment and textile producing countries to allow certain levels of imports or quotas for foreign goods. The MFA is designed to protect domestic manufacturers, and once Costa Rica joined, the U.S. textile industry immediately began lobbying to impose quotas on Costa Rican imports. U.S. manufacturers claimed that Costa Rican skirt exports to the United States—which grew from just .33 percent of the total in 1986 to a still minute .44 percent in 1988—constituted a "market disruption" and therefore violated MFA. While the textile manufacturers' claim of excessive competition from Costa Rica was absurd, this U.S. lobby is extremely powerful, and Costa Rican officials were forced to spend months trying to defend their exports. In the wake of this dispute, CINDE executive Federico Vargas said the organization had stopped promoting certain textile sectors because "if we brought in more (to the American market) we would probably invite the establishment of more quotas on the part of the U.S. So we are definitely lessening our emphasis on textiles." By the end of the decade, Costa Rican Chamber of Industry official Maurillo Aguilar said in an interview that growth of textiles and apparel had "come to a standstill."

There have been other instances (cement in 1984 and cut flowers in 1986) where Costa Rican exports have raised the ire of U.S. producers, sending chills of fear through Costa Rican–based exporters, many of whom wonder when and how often such disruptions will happen in the future. According to a Costa Rican official involved in the textile negotiations, "U.S. policy has a big contradiction in it. AID, CINDE, and CBI have told us to develop our exports to the U.S. We've done that. Now pressure from American industries and the Department of Commerce is blocking our exports. It's a Catch-22." In an effort to minimize such problems, in 1991 Costa Rica joined GATT (General Agreement on Tariffs and Trade), an international accord which seeks to liberalize world trade and to assure non-discrimination of member countries.

Costa Rica's textile industry faced a second serious problem. By the end of the decade, textile production in Costa Rica had become expensive relative to other CBI countries. When CINDE began its textile-promotion strategy, unemployment stood between 10 percent and 18 percent, but by the end of the decade it had fallen below the 5 percent mark. While CINDE hailed low unemployment as a victory, it is a two-edged sword. With nearly full employment, wages continued to nudge upward. "The moment that real wages start increasing, your textile 'máquila' companies become nonprofitable," explained Ennio Rodríguez, an economic consultant and former Minister of External Debt in the Monge government. Chamber of Industry officials say that as a result, small and medium-size textile manufacturers are beginning to shut down, and larger ones are considering relocating in Mexico, El Salvador, the Dominican Republic, and other countries with even lower wages. In the early 1990s, the North American Free Trade Agreement (NAFTA) between the United States, Canada, and Mexico threatened further to cripple Costa Rica's chances of attracting and keeping American investors, who were expected to opt for Mexico's even lower wages, duty-free status, and closer proximity to the United States.

Thus CINDE's first development project, which had scored so quickly, appeared to be stalled. But CINDE's cheerleaders remained ever upbeat, arguing that textiles should be viewed simply as a transitional industry paving the way for more sophisticated apparel manufacturing and nontraditional agricultural exports. Chamber of Exporters President Sylvia Fletcher, for instance, credits CINDE's textile strategy with creating "a spirit of expansion and a spirit of success in exports" which is "contagious" and will spread to new commercial activities. But these CINDE apologists generally fail to note that such conversions take capital, and that small and medium-size enterprises, mostly Costa Rican-owned, cannot afford the shift. An industrial sewing machine, for example, costs only $1,000, while the knitting machine required for finer garments costs $125,000. Pursuing this strategy means going after new foreign investors, and indeed some from Korea and Japan did move in, attracted by Costa Rica's political stability and high-quality work force.[67] "We want Costa Rica to be the Rolls-Royce of textiles," said Christián Villegas, an official in CINDE's Textile Section. But, she conceded, "It's a completely different ball game."[68]

While a long-term, well-planned modernization strategy for Costa Rica's industrial sector remained at decade's end largely on the CINDE drawing board, AID and CINDE had begun a big drive to increase nontraditional agricultural exports (NTAEs), including luxury fruits, vegetables, ornamental plants, and flowers. The initial expansion was rapid, but a number of economists and producers cautioned that this growth could also prove temporary.

CINDE/CENPRO Merger

As the decade closed, CINDE faced an apparently insurmountable problem: the AID financial pipeline was being turned off, and AID began to lay plans to divest itself of CINDE. The export-promotion agency had been wholly created and funded by AID and, as one AID official put it, "The privatization zealots didn't carefully consider how CINDE could become self-sufficient." Instead, AID's game plan was to attempt to orchestrate an institutional merger with CENPRO, the government agency it had initially muscled aside.

One sign of AID's merger scheme was the naming in 1988 of Carlos Torres as CENPRO's director. A Puerto Rican American who had worked for AID and directed CINDE's investment-promotion program, PIE, Torres was described by one top CINDE official as "the real father of the [CINDE] program." Earlier, Torres had also worked for Arthur D. Little, the international consulting firm commissioned by AID in 1982 to perform an evaluation of CENPRO. According to an AID report, Torres's principal task at CENPRO was "preparing the way for the reorganization," and "his presence at CENPRO has effected a truce in the turf wars that prevailed in earlier years between CENPRO and CINDE."[69] Torres became the first non-Costa Rican—and a U.S. citizen at that—to hold this government post, a fitting symbol of growing U.S. domination in Costa Rica's export sector.

In the wake of the AID audit report criticizing cronyism in AID programs, U.S. officials were understandably nervous that Torres's appointment could become yet another embarrassing faux pas. Off the record, an AID official expressed concern over the "political implications" of naming Torres, because his salary with CENPRO was paid by AID. The rest of the CENPRO staff was on much more modest government salaries. An AID study notes that Trade Minister Luis Diego Escalante "braved considerable opposition" in naming Torres.[70]

In negotiations with Arias government officials, AID outlined several proposals for a CINDE/CENPRO merger. Under the scheme AID hoped to create a "multi-lateral endowment" of about $120 million, whereby a consortium of AID and other foreign donors would initially put up funds and the new CENPRO/CINDE would operate from the interest. The new trust fund, called FUNDEX, was to be run by Costa Ricans. But the scheme never got off the drawing board; Japan and several European countries were not interested in contributing.[71]

Between 1986 and 1990, AID had given $7 million to CINDE's training program and an additional $3.5 million plus 500 million colones for promotion of nontraditional exports. After 1990 there were no more new AID funds, and CINDE was forced to exist on unspent funds from early grants. The fiesta was ending, staff was being laid off, and its budget was slashed, but none of this was apparent from the outside; early in 1990, CINDE moved into a multimillion-dollar, new glass-and-chrome office complex on the edge of San José. And, a year later, AID tapped one of its oldest and closest Costa Rican collaborators, businessman Ernesto Rohrmoser, to become general manager and try to keep the flagship of AID's Parallel State from sinking.

Through it all, CENPRO, like the little engine that could, was still plugging along and picking up programs that CINDE could no longer handle. All of this indicates that there is no evidence to support the Reagan and Bush administrations' presumption that private institutions are, by their nature, better than state ones. Given sufficient resources and good management, CENPRO has always been capable of modernization and streamlining. AID argued that CENPRO was moribund based largely on its inability during the 1970s to promote large-scale Costa Rican exports to Europe and the United States. But in those years the domestic market was healthy and the Central American Common Market flourishing, so manufacturers and growers did not need new markets. CINDE came into being as the tide was turning, and exporters were being forced, because of the economic and political turmoil in Central America, to seek new markets. It is therefore unfair to pronounce CENPRO a failure given the economic context of the 1970s, or to claim CINDE's success based on that of the 1980s. What is clear is that AID would have better served Costa Rica if it had put resources into the government institution CENPRO rather than create, at great expense and with tremendous waste, the enormous, private, parallel white elephant, CINDE.

SIX

Health Care in the 1980s: Making Chocolate with Only a Little Cocoa

Costa Rica rightfully boasts of the best health care system in Latin America and the Caribbean, one that is rivaled only by Cuba and Jamaica. As in Cuba, Costa Rica's health infrastructure is almost totally state run: 90 percent of the country's doctors and most hospitals are state controlled, and the social security system covers 89 percent of the population. By 1990, life expectancy in Costa Rica was seventy-five years and infant mortality was 15.3 per thousand, less than among the nonwhite population in the United States. Ninety percent of children were fully immunized, 90 percent of pregnant women received prenatal care, and there were virtually no cases of severe malnutrition. According to the World Bank, Costa Rica's health status is "comparable to [that] of the developed nations and better than [that] of 80 percent of the countries of the world."[1]

But the economic crisis at the beginning of the 1980s had made the high standards of Costa Rica's remarkable health system difficult to maintain. AID, in alliance with the International Monetary Fund (IMF), World Bank, and Inter-American Development Bank (IDB), required Costa Rica to cut back on spending for health and other social programs.[2] As a result, Costa Rica's medical personnel were forced into, as President Arias put it, "making chocolate with only a little cocoa." By the end of the decade the gap between services to the rich and the poor had widened.

Costa Rica's system of health and other basic social programs dates from the early 1940s. Swimming against the tide of anti-reformist dictatorships elsewhere in Central America, the populist, reformist President Rafael Angel Calderón, Sr. (1940–44), aligned himself both with Costa Rica's progressive Archbishop Víctor Sanabría and the Communist party (Partido Vanguardia Popular or PVP), pledging to use public resources for social welfare programs to help the poor. Calderón, a medical doctor, founded new hospitals and clinics as well as the country's social security system, the *Caja Costarricense de Seguro Social* (CCSS). Popularly known as the *Caja,* the CCSS provides accident, sickness, dental, disability, maternity, old age, and unemployment coverage to workers and their families. In 1943, Calderón amended the constitution with a set of social guarantees—a sort of Bill of Rights—including a pledge that "the State will work for the greatest well-being of Costa Ricans, affording social protection to the family, the foundation of the nation, assuring aid to mothers, and to children."[3]

Costa Rica's national budget reflected the government's growing commitment to health and other social programs. In 1938, 20 percent of the budget went to health and social welfare programs, while in 1958 they received 45 percent. By the 1960s, Costa Rica was spending twice as much per capita on health and social security as any other Central American country. At the same time appropriations for defense went from a modest 7 percent in 1938, to a peak of 25 percent in 1948, and then down to a mere 2 percent in 1958 and 2.2 percent in 1966.[4]

Between 1940 and 1970, the main health care emphasis was on eliminating both malnutrition and infectious and parasitic diseases and on reducing morbidity and mortality rates.[5] During this period, the government created a large nutrition department within the Ministry of Health to carry out food-distribution programs, and the number of hospital beds steadily increased. By 1965, Costa Rica had approximately 420 hospital beds per 100,000 people, more than double the average elsewhere in Central America. Over these three decades, adult death rates fell from 18.8 to 6.6 per thousand, while infant mortality declined less dramatically.[6] These nutrition and hospital-expansion programs, while impressive, were also costly, consuming 90 percent of Costa Rica's health budget.

Early in the 1970s, the Costa Rican government embarked on an ambitious new modernization strategy designed to extend low-cost health care to the entire population through the Caja, to eradicate infectious diseases, and to reduce infant mortality— all within the decade.[7] To help implement this program of preventative and primary health care, the government passed a series of new measures: the first national health plan (1971), the law of universal social security (1971), the law transferring all public hospitals to the Caja (1973), the general health law (1973), and new rural and community health programs (1973 and 1976).[8] The University of Costa Rica doubled its admissions to both the medical and nursing schools. The government nationalized all but two hospitals,[9] transferred administration of these public hospitals to the Caja, and extended social-security coverage to a majority of the population. Most doctors were contracted to work for the state system, although they are also permitted to maintain private practices not covered by the Caja. Comprehensive new health programs included hot-meal programs in schools, centers for mothers and preschool children, improvement of housing and drinking water, latrine and sewer construction, and an expansion of medical services and vaccination programs.

The results demonstrated that proper state planning can produce dramatic results. Between 1970 and 1980, infant mortality fell 69 percent (from 61.5 to 18.6 deaths per 1,000 live births),[10] deaths from infectious and parasitic diseases declined by 98 percent, and communicable diseases such as polio and diphtheria were totally eradicated. But, as in previous decades, these successes were costly. Between 1974 and 1979, the percentage of the national budget spent on health rose from 7.1 percent to 13.6 percent. During the 1970s, the Caja's budget increased by 689 percent, and health expenditures became a major reason for the government's chronic budget deficits.

Until 1977 the Ministry of Health was heavily dependent on AID and other forms of foreign assistance.[11] In the first half of the 1970s, the annual budgets for AID's modest program in Costa Rica included a significant percentage for the categories of health, population control, and nutrition: 18.8 percent in 1972 (or $313,000 out of a total AID package of $1.66 million); 29.3

percent in 1973 ($379,000 out of $1.29 million); and 5 percent in 1974 (or $411,000 out of $8.9 million).[12] In 1977, however, AID, which had been the most consistent source of foreign assistance, pronounced Costa Rica "too healthy" to qualify for further health-care programs.[13]

From Costa Rica's perspective, this was a time to reshape its health-care strategy rather than to be satisfied with its past success. By the end of the 1970s, Costa Rica stood, according to Dr. Edgar Mohs, director of the prestigious children's hospital in San José and later Minister of Health during the Arias administration, "at a crossroads": it was a small, relatively poor country which needed to focus on health problems typical of more developed societies, including heart disease, cancer, alcoholism, and obesity. While Costa Ricans boast of having "more teachers than soldiers," they also have far more *cantinas* and *tabernas* (bars) than schools. Costa Rica has the world's fourth-highest level of alcohol consumption per capita, surpassed only by Russia, Chile, and France. Costa Rica also has the world's highest per-capita rate of stomach cancer, and heart attacks have become the leading cause of death. Costa Rica's medical establishment proposed that, during the 1980s, the emphasis needed to be on improvements in the quality of life and preventative medicine.[14]

But as the health sector was gearing up for this new strategy, Costa Rica was hit broadside by its worst economic crisis, forcing the government to cut back on state medical programs. "As a result," writes medical anthropologist Lynn Morgan, "health services were reduced and the health model called into question, just after an expensive health infrastructure was erected and when people most needed health services."[15] The impact reverberated through the health sector, particularly affecting programs for poor and rural Costa Ricans. Whereas the great advances in the 1970s were due in large part to primary-care programs targeted toward the poor, in the 1980s underprivileged parts of the country and population experienced the severest curtailment in services and programs. A number of health clinics closed or went understaffed; childcare and food-distribution centers and community health programs were cut; and installation of sanitation, sewage treatment, and potable-water systems was curtailed.

The effects of such cuts were quickly apparent. Between 1981 and 1982, the number of children treated for malnutrition doubled, and between 1980 and 1983 the number of abandoned children tripled.[16] Infectious diseases such as malaria, measles, whooping cough, and hepatitis, which had been controlled or eradicated in the previous decade, reappeared. By 1990, 89 percent of Costa Ricans were covered by the social-security system, a figure which, while impressive, fell short of the target of 94 percent set a decade earlier.[17]

Massive monetary devaluations caused the salaries of social security doctors to plummet from an average of $1,744 per month before 1980 to just $278 in 1982. That year doctors paralyzed the public-health system with a forty-two-day strike in which they won salary increases of $40 per month and subsequent adjustments for inflation.[18] The devaluations also led to a 400 percent rise in the cost of importing medical supplies and equipment, forcing the Caja to leave $6.5 million worth of imported supplies unclaimed in customs and greatly cut back its subsequent orders.[19] Costa Rica's health-care system was also taxed by an influx of refugees, particularly from Nicaragua.

The Costa Rican government, constrained by the economic crisis and compelled by new AID and IMF agreements, reduced overall spending on health, nutrition, and sanitation. The national health budget, excluding social security, declined from a high of 11.4 percent of the total GNP in 1979 to 5.7 percent in 1989. More startling was the 56 percent decline of real per-capita health expenditures from 1979 to 1989. Per-capita spending (in 1966 constant colones) dropped from 361.3 in 1979 to 160.5 in 1989. Between 1980 and 1985 the budget of the Family Allowance Agency was reduced by more than 30 percent.[20] The Caja was forced to trim benefits to its employees, encourage voluntary resignations, impose a freeze on hiring, increase payroll taxes for employees from 6.75 percent to 9.25 percent, and require, for the first time, that its 22,000 employees contribute 4 percent of their salaries to obtain coverage. A law granting full severance and retirement benefits to those who voluntarily resigned from government service led three thousand health workers, mainly nurses and technicians, to quit. Due to a hiring freeze, they could not be replaced.

Budget cuts for health care continued, even after the worst of the economic crisis of the early 1980s was over. The *Caja's* income from sales taxes was eliminated and, beginning in 1986, the government's contribution was reduced from 1.25 percent of the total budget to only .75 percent in an effort to reduce the state's deficit. But even this minimal amount was not fully paid each year.[21]

In the late 1970s, the government had announced its intention to wean itself fully from foreign aid and become self-sufficient in health care. But by 1982 the Caja's deficit totaled more than 30 percent of its operating budget, and medical officials reluctantly called for foreign assistance.[22] Two years later the Ministry of Health proposed a $207 million health budget, $148 million (71 percent) of which was to come from overseas. By 1985, Costa Rica's health system was receiving aid from UNICEF, the IDB, the Kellogg Foundation, and AID.[23]

AID: Health Care through Privatization and Trickle-Down

Health programs everywhere were a low priority for the Reagan administration. The 1985 foreign-assistance budget for Central America included only 3 percent for health[24] and AID showed a clear bias in favor of private medicine. When the AID spigot was turned on full force in the early 1980s, Costa Rica's health care system received barely a sprinkle. According to an October 1988 breakdown of its then-current Costa Rican portfolio, AID was spending a mere 2.3 percent of its funds on health and 1.6 percent on family planning. Most of these funds were loans: between 1983 and 1987 an infinitesimal .38 percent of AID's total grants went for health projects.[25]

During the decade AID financed just three health programs in Costa Rica, all of which had private-sector components. One was a $10 million loan and $300,000 grant to revamp the Caja's administrative procedures and to import and distribute drugs through both private and state-run pharmacies. A second was an $8.5 million grant to state and private family-planning programs. The third was a $600,000 grant to the conservative U.S. medical organization Project Hope to upgrade emergency medical services and occupational therapy with Costa Rica's Red Cross, another private-sector organization. No AID funds were appropriated for health projects in 1989, 1990, or 1991, and the Agency announced it was phasing out its health programs in Costa Rica.[26]

U.S. officials in Costa Rica appear to have maintained a sort of love/hate relationship with the state-run health-care system. On the one hand they conceded, as one AID officer put it, that Costa Rica's health achievements were "mind boggling" and provided an important social and economic cushion for the country's poor. On the other hand, this same official said in an interview that "social programs in any country are wretchedly inefficient. And basically the situation Costa Rica got into in the eighties was that it couldn't begin to pay for them."

U.S. officials argued that the AID-orchestrated privatization and export-expansion measures would put Costa Rica on the path to economic recovery, thereby generating enough funds to pay for health and other social services. One high-level U.S. diplomat asserted, "The actual effect of our assistance through the years has been to make it possible for these people to run their public sector programs. Privatization bailed them out. It kept the welfare state going." In an interview, AID official Richard Rosenberg concurred, arguing that in most cases, "You can demonstrate pretty clearly that if you can get the economy here to go, the poor people will share [the benefits]. Trickle-down works in this country."

By 1990, the cuts in public spending, coupled with AID's broad-based privatization drive, were bringing into question the efficiency, cost and quality of the state health system and positing privatization and a variant, decentralization,[27] as the answer. Such views found support among Costa Rica's conservative press and business and medical elites. As the decade of the 1980s closed, a series of newspaper articles and radio commentaries discussed the growing problems of the country's public health care system. A piece in La Nación headlined "Grave Situation of Hospitals in the Country" portrayed long lines in government hospitals, shortages of personnel, faulty diagnostic and treatment equipment, and suspension of elective surgery operations.[28] According to medical anthropologist Morgan, "Underlying their argument was a plea for class-based medical care, with access to services contingent on ability to pay."[29]

While Costa Rica's neediest were most hurt by the cutbacks, influential groups were proposing private-sector "solutions" destined to widen rather than reduce the health-care gap between the rich and poor. From the beginning of the decade the chambers of commerce and industry and some people within the medical establishment had argued that the state-run health-care system had become too costly, cumbersome, and bureaucratic. They lobbied for a "reprivatization" of health care through elimination of the compulsory social-security system (the Caja) and promotion of free-market competition.

Under the banner of decentralization, some doctors began a drive to regain their elite status and lucrative incomes, which had continued to fall during the decade.[30] Medical specialists, spearheaded by doctors at San José's large Calderón Guardia Hospital, succeeded in gaining financial and administrative autonomy for the major urban government hospitals which they built into ultramodern, state-of-the-art, and inevitably very costly institutions. "The risk," noted former Caja Board Vice President Alvaro Chávez, "is that the big-city hospitals will become sort of islands unto themselves, and rural hospitals will be almost abandoned." Other privatization plans nibbled away at the perimeters of the national health system. AID gave financial support and technical advice to proposals to privatize auxiliary services such as hospital laundries, food services, and pharmacies.[31]

Another variant was a plan to privatize Caja clinics by turning ownership over to the doctors and nurses working in them. Patients were still to receive free treatment, but the medical staff would contract with the Caja to form a cooperative and would receive set government payments for each patient treated. By 1990, there were three such Caja-financed, staff-owned clinics operating in working-class areas near San José, and plans were being laid for further expansions. Supporters argued these clinics would be more efficient because staff with a personal stake in the profits would work harder to put the money to efficient use. Critics warned that the quality of health care in these clinics would decline as the medical staff, in order to make profits, cut back on medicines and visitation lengths and perhaps even began to demand that some patients pay for some types of services.

While those supporting privatization argue that Costa Rica cannot afford to continue financing its public-health system, statistics show that the nationalized system has provided high-quality health care that is, in fact, less expensive than medicine in other countries in the hemisphere. Comparing World Bank health indicators for infant mortality and life expectancy Dr. Walter Willitt of the Harvard School of Public Health found that Costa Rica's system (along with Jamaica's) is both the best and the most economical in the Western hemisphere. Willett concludes that "privatization will almost surely cause more inefficiency because it will concentrate resources in expensive high-tech facilities that provide very low health benefits at great expense."

Other findings support the contention that moving toward privatization and advanced care at the expense of the public system will adversely affect Costa Rica's health sector. As early as 1981, UNICEF and the World Health Organization (WHO) warned, "Private medicine is maldistributive of a country's limited health care resources." The UNICEF/WHO study states that private medicine cannot be seen as separate from the national health service, because its costs go toward making "the total health care 'cake.' " This report concluded that in a variety of ways private medicine has an adverse impact on the public sector: "[T]he private medical sector absorbs scarce health personnel trained mainly at the state's expense. It is predominantly curative in character, and its expensive practices lead . . . to inflated medical expenditure [and] . . . excessive foreign exchange cost for pharmaceuticals. . . . It has negative influence on medical education. . . . Private medicine undermines . . . attempts to rationalize . . . procedures on a cost-effective basis. . . . For these reasons the private medical sector now has negative effects on primary health care implementation."[32]

A decade later, while privatization was being aggressively pushed worldwide as the cure for all economic, social, and political ills, another health study reached similar conclusions. A 1990 paper by Milton Roemer and Ruth Roemer published in the *American Journal of Public Health* presented evidence that "the

Table 5. Health Statistics Adjusted for GNP, 1986

Country	Infant Mortality (per 1,000 births)	Life Expectancy Female	Life Expectancy Male	GNP ($ per capita)
Argentina	32.11	74.22	67.17	2,920
Bolivia	105.71	56.82	53.41	600
Brazil	62.14	68.71	62.55	1,810
Canada	46.71	70.35	65.54	13,160
Chile	15.34	76.16	68.90	1,320
Colombia	42.02	69.24	63.96	1,230
Costa Rica	13.93	77.01	71.78	1,480
Dominican Republic	60.11	69.72	65.33	710
Ecuador	58.76	69.31	65.01	1,160
El Salvador	54.51	67.62	58.25	820
Guatemala	54.92	64.52	59.17	930
Honduras	65.22	67.69	63.31	740
Jamaica	12.51	77.62	72.25	820
Mexico	45.32	72.67	65.52	1,860
Nicaragua	58.40	64.64	61.27	790
Panama	23.04	74.24	70.18	2,330
Paraguay	37.17	70.45	66.12	1,000
Peru	84.50	63.37	60.06	1,090
USA	56.90	67.31	61.96	15,400
Uruguay	25.47	74.63	68.49	1,900
Venezuela	38.20	72.70	65.77	2,920

Source: Compiled by Dr. Walter Willitt, Harvard School of Public Health. Based on statistics in World Bank, *World Development Report,* 1988. Rate adjusted for GNP by regression analysis, a statistical method of determining the relationship between variables. Statistics are not available for Cuba.

private sector in national health systems has had largely anti-egalitarian effects. The contention that private spending releases government health funds for the poor simply ignores the inequities of private claims on scarce social resources." The study contends that major health gains in developing countries have invariably been made by the state, not the private sector. It concludes, "Further improvements will depend on greater strength in public sector health services rather than private sector services which aggravate inequities."[33]

Other studies done in Costa Rica and elsewhere dispute the

contentions of U.S. officials that "trickle down" works. These studies conclude that private sector growth and stimulation of the economy are not enough to insure improvements in health areas. In his study of infant mortality, Luis Rosero-Bixby states that "the decrease in mortality in Costa Rica during the first half of this century cannot be explained by economic factors alone. . . . Despite economic stagnation from 1910–1949, mortality rates decreased substantially during this period. Improvements in social services, such as education and public health, and imports in technology apparently influenced mortality independently of economic conditions." Rosero-Bixby estimates that during the 1970s, Costa Rica's dramatic reduction in infant mortality was mainly due to "health interventions, especially primary care programmes. Up to three quarters of the decline was evidently attributable to contemporary improvements in public health services" which included targeting the country's poorest regions and most underprivileged sectors of the population.[34]

Likewise, the United Nations Development Program (UNDP) found that, in 1991, although Costa Rica and Oman had similar-size populations, and Oman's income was four times higher, Oman's life expectancy was only fifty-eight years compared with seventy-five (other studies calculate seventy-six) years in Costa Rica. The UNDP credited Costa Rica's success to its relatively "high public expenditure" for a social security system, primary health care, and compulsory education.[35]

These studies demonstrate that advances are readily made when a country develops a multifaceted public-health-care strategy, with sufficient resources and proper planning, and these improvements can be made even though the economy as a whole is not healthy. In other words, trickle-down does not work, and a policy of benign neglect toward health and other social services is not enough; state planning and public resources directed into the health sector are imperative.

Thanks to the solid foundation built by the health system over the previous decades, by 1990 Costa Rica's traditional health indicators—including infant mortality and life expectancy—were at the same level as in the 1970s. However, these aggregate figures did not adequately reflect the impact of the health budget cuts upon the urban and rural poor. The 1988 World Bank report found that "there are still areas which are extremely under-served and where health and nutrition status is still similar to that of most low-income countries." An AID Action Plan for 1990–91 acknowledged that "population and cost increases have strained the GOCR [Government of Costa Rica's] ability to deliver the same level of services as has been the case in the past, a problem exacerbated by the simultaneous need to cut public sector expenditures."[36] (Not surprisingly, this AID report ignored the role of the United States in compelling Costa Rica to cut health and other social service spending.) In addition, new health problems emerged: by 1990, suicide rates had quadrupled, the divorce rate had risen six times, and child abuse had increased tenfold over 1970; mental illness and prostitution (along with sexually transmitted diseases) had increased; 10 percent of the population was alcoholic, and heart disease and cancer had become the leading causes of death. Most importantly, the final tally was not yet in. The more profound, long-term impact of the economic crisis and belt tightening during the 1980s had not yet been seen or measured.[37]

As the 1990s began, Costa Rica appeared headed in the direction of further privatization. In June 1990, just after the conservative Calderón government took office, the Association of Doctors and Surgeons, the professional medical organization, endorsed the concept of eliminating the Caja's monopoly on medical treatment and establishing specialized private institutes and clinics whose services would be financed by the Caja.[38] The Calderón government set up a large commission of hospital administrators and experts from Costa Rica and the World Bank to examine the whole issue of privatization of health care services. At the same time the government announced a 25 percent cut in the government health budget,[39] a move that will certainly worsen state medical services and bolster the demand for more privatization. This trend ignores the historical and medical evidence that Costa Ricans are best served by strengthening their state health system.

Poverty is up, real wages have fallen, and the health budget is down: between 1984 and 1989, health spending dropped 12 percent in real terms and 27 percent in per-capita terms. While by

1990 the effects of "making chocolate with only a little cocoa" were already evident, the worst was yet to come. "The more enduring effects," Morgan forecasts, "will result from long-term structural readjustment policies which will inevitably change the character of the country's extensive, nationalized health system. Many such changes are now in initial planning stages but, if implemented on a national scale, they will profoundly affect the country's health service structure. The trend, in short, is toward privatization of health services and reducing the state's role as health provider."[40] This, inevitably, will seriously undermine Costa Rica's high-quality, egalitarian, and cost-efficient public health system and will widen the gap between the haves and the have-nots.

Health Care for the Contras

The Reagan and Bush administrations' love/hate relationship with Costa Rica's public health system was also evident in Washington's persistent attempts to use Costa Rica as a rear base for treating wounded and sick contras and caring for Nicaraguan refugees. Costa Rica was the country in Central America most capable of handling an influx of refugees and war wounded. Washington recognized that it was more economical and politically palatable to treat the combatants in Costa Rica than to send them to the United States. In addition, the administration viewed Costa Rica's health care system as a tool for shoring up the country's commitment to the war against Nicaragua. There was a realization, particularly by the Pentagon, that medicine could be, as Maj. Gen. William Winkler, commander of the Academy of Health Sciences, put it, the "least controversial, most cost-effective means" of pursuing U.S. military objectives, including the contra war in Nicaragua. According to another expert, Lt. Col. James Taylor, who was chief of the U.S. Army's Southern Command Humanitarian Services Division, military medicine has "a new exciting role [to play] in supporting US national interest."[41]

Costa Rican officials from the Monge and Arias governments say that U.S. envoys and diplomats—including William Casey, Alan Fiers, and Joe Fernández from the CIA, Elliott Abrams and

Morris Busby from the State Department, and ambassadors Winsor, Tambs, and Hinton—repeatedly demanded that Costa Rica provide elaborate facilities for Nicaraguan refugees, permit wounded contras to be treated in government and private hospitals and clinics, train doctors to treat the war injured, and upgrade medical centers in the northern zone to support the war effort. In doing so, Washington exploited both Costa Rica's outstanding health infrastructure and its humanitarian traditions of opening its borders and providing a safe haven to political dissidents, exiles, and refugees from other Latin American countries.

However, like most U.S. policies in Costa Rica, caring for Nicaragua's war victims was never openly debated, either before the Legislative Assembly or within the press. Interviews revealed that government officials were divided: a majority supported treating war injured on humanitarian grounds, and some (such as Dr. Max Pacheco in Ciudad Quesada, Dr. Luis Federico Lamicq in San José, and security ministers Benjamín Piza and Hernán Garrón) actively worked with the CIA-contra network to do so. A minority within the government and legislature argued that treating military combatants violated the country's neutrality policy and, later, jeopardized the Arias peace plan. Initially, virtually everyone in Costa Rica supported admitting Nicaraguan refugees, although as the numbers grew, so, too, did public resentment.

While U.S. officials pressured for Costa Rican cooperation in certain medical-related contra projects, many were carried out clandestinely and without permission by the North network, CIA, AID, or private right-wing organizations. Some of these activities were eventually uncovered by the press or the police, but many undoubtedly remained hidden. The best known of the U.S. Congress's "humanitarian" aid packages, a $27 million appropriation passed in June 1985 and distributed by the State Department's Nicaraguan Humanitarian Assistance Office, did not utilize the Caja or Costa Rican hospitals or clinics. This scandalously corrupt program was liberally used by the North network and contras in the field as a cover for arms shipments and personal embezzlement. Part of a $47.9 million nonlethal aid package approved in March 1988 was, however, used by a special AID Task Force on Humanitarian Assistance for a variety of medical and other contra-support projects in Costa Rica. In carrying out most of these operations, the United States often bypassed or manipulated not only Costa Rica's public health and refugee systems, but also a number of the international relief and humanitarian aid agencies, including the United Nations High Commission for Refugees (UNHCR).

Attempts to bring war wounded and sick into Costa Rica began virtually with the opening shots of the war. Within a month of the Sandinistas' July 1979 victory, John Hull claims he led a team of medical doctors into Nicaragua to assess health needs. Once the contra war started, Hull and his partner Bruce Jones say that they regularly flew light planes into Nicaragua to evacuate injured and ailing fighters. In 1984 and 1985, contra collaborator Dr. Max Pacheco helped arrange for personnel at the San Carlos government hospital outside Ciudad Quesada to receive training in treating war wounds. Costa Rica's Red Cross also trained a dozen or so Nicaraguan contra paramedics.[42] In addition, Hull worked with the CIA and contras to convert rented houses into clandestine contra clinics. Among this network was a large, two-story house outside Ciudad Quesada which Hull rented in 1983 from a Costa Rican schoolteacher, Javier Ugalde, who was working in the United States. Hull told Ugalde that the tenants would be an elderly American couple, but when the teacher returned unannounced over Christmas, he found his house wrecked and full of wounded and sick contras.

Hull vigorously protested that he broke no laws by ferrying wounded combatants to Costa Rica, but this is not so. Neither the combatants nor Hull went through immigration procedures. The secret contra clinics were unlicensed and unregulated by Costa Rica's health ministry. And these operations were geared toward sending combatants back to the war as quickly as possible, in violation of Costa Rica's neutrality policy. In fact, the CIA and contras set up their private clinics to by-pass government red tape and restrictions.

By July 1988, AID's special Task Force on Humanitarian Assistance was operating eleven "recuperation houses" as part of an extensive "combatant medical assistance" program inside Costa Rica." On a number of occasions, Costa Rican guardsmen and reporters discovered these clandestine hospitals and forced them to close or relocate. A U.S. Embassy cable complained of "raids by local authorities and evictions by irate landlords which have plagued the program since its inception."[43]

The largest of these secret hospitals was discovered in September 1988 by a group of foreign journalists. Hidden behind an eight-foot-high, padlocked metal gate, several hundred wounded combatants and their families were being cared for on the grounds of an abandoned lead foundry in Curridabat, a one-time industrial suburb to the east of San José. "Vicente," a young Nicaraguan contra, told reporters that this was an AID-financed medical clinic under the control of "the high command of the Nicaraguan Resistance." He said wounded contras were being brought in from camps in Nicaragua, Honduras, and El Salvador, and that, once recovered, the contras frequently returned to camps in Nicaragua to resume fighting.

Although located just a mile from the Presidential House, Information Minister Guido Fernández said neither he nor President Arias had any knowledge of the clinic. Fernández added that Costa Rica "would not grant permission for any foreign government to establish such a facility." Surprisingly, the usually tight-lipped U.S. Embassy readily supplied details of the clinic, which a spokeswoman said had been approved by Security Minister Hernán Garrón. The Embassy released a written statement saying that this "centralized Recuperation Center" was part of the $47.9 million "Humanitarian Assistance Medical Supply and Service Program in Costa Rica to finance medical services, outpatient consultations, medical supplies and pharmaceuticals for sick and wounded individuals of the Nicaraguan Resistance and family members."[44]

As soon as its existence became known, Nicaraguan Vice Foreign Minister Víctor Hugo Tinoco denounced the hospital as a "violation" of the recently signed Sapoa ceasefire agreement between the contras and the Nicaraguan government.[45] It seemed probable that the U.S. Embassy had released details with the intention of exposing divisions within the Arias government and scuttling the peace proposals. As a *Tico Times* editorial lamented, "By raising doubts about Costa Rica's sincerity and re-opening questions about its commitment to neutrality, the clinic affair has imperiled the peace process for which Arias has struggled so long and hard."[46]

A Security Ministry press release said that Minister Garrón had approved plans for the contra clinic after meetings with U.S. Ambassador Deane Hinton, AID officials, a bipartisan U.S. congressional delegation, and Special U.S. Envoy to Central America Morris Busby. The statement added lamely that "the Minister of Public Security didn't consider it necessary to consult with the President of the Republic . . . considering it a logical consequence of the permission to treat the sick and wounded [and] at no time was this an arbitrary or clandestine decision."[47]

Off the record, Costa Rican officials revealed that for many months, U.S. officials had been pressuring the Arias government to permit treatment of wounded contras. Arias finally agreed that wounded children and contras could be treated free in any of the twenty-nine Caja facilities, and AID would have to cover the cost for treatment at the Catholic Clinic in San José and other government-approved private hospitals.[48] Arias's concession did not include medical facilities not approved by the Health Ministry, such as the Curridabat center. Both Garrón and Ambassador Deane Hinton assured Arias that this and all other private contra clinics would be closed, but again Arias's orders were ignored. The Curridabat clinic did not finally close until July 1990. By then, this and other contra hospitals in Costa Rica had spent approximately $2.4 million treating sixteen hundred persons.[49]

In a similar vein, contra supporters attempted to use the Caja to smuggle into Costa Rica medical and, the evidence indicates, military supplies for the contras. In August 1987, socialist legislator Javier Solís revealed that in 1985, Hull and Max Pacheco, through a hitherto-unknown organization, the Association for the Development of the Northern Zone, were involved in soliciting thirty tons of hospital supplies and equipment, plus 45,000 bags of rice, from private U.S. donors. The shipment, destined for state-run hospitals and clinics in the north, arrived at Costa Rica's Pacific Coast port of Caldera in August 1985. Addressed to the Office of Medical Services for the Northern Zone in Ciudad Quesada, the shipment valued at

$1.187 million came with instructions to notify John Hull of its arrival. Hull's name set off alarms, and Costa Rican security officials impounded the sealed containers.

If Hull's name was not enough to raise suspicions, that of the donor organization, the National Defense Council (NDC), certainly was. Headquartered in Alexandria, Virginia, with a chapter in Miami, the NDC was set up in 1978 as a nonprofit think tank and lobbying group aimed at drumming up support for and funneling supplies to the contras and other right-wing military operations in Central America. The NDC's leadership included Maj. Gen. John Singlaub of the World Anti-Communist League and the vice president's son Jeb Bush, who was a key link in Miami between covert contra operations and the White House.[50] In February 1985, Jeb Bush presided over the NDC's first shipment of "humanitarian" aid—47,000 pounds of medicines destined for distribution by Guatemala's military—and the organization announced plans to send aid to the contras.[51]

In an interview in late 1985, Jorge González, a Cuban American NDC official in Miami, said that the organization coordinated its Central American medical "relief efforts" with two evangelical, contra-connected organizations, the Christian Broadcasting Network and World Medical Relief.[52] He said the NDC would not work with either the United Nations High Commission for Refugees or the U.S. Red Cross because they were too liberal.

Why the NDC, whose slogan is "In Defense of Free Enterprise, Country and Constitution" would want to give over a million dollars in supplies to Costa Rica's state-run hospital system was never explained. When Costa Rican officials finally inspected and released the shipment, they announced that it contained no weapons. However, they estimated the contents were worth only $254,000—more than $900,000 short of its declared value. This discrepancy was also never explained, leading to lingering suspicions that some supplies were covertly siphoned off for the contras. The released goods were turned over to Dr. Pacheco's organization for distribution to northern-zone hospitals, charities, and refugee camps. Antibiotics, syringes, wheelchairs, surgical instruments, and cots were given to a new Caja clinic in Boca Tapada, a Costa Rican hamlet and contra staging post just minutes from the Nicaraguan border. Indirectly, at least, the NDC shipment aided the war effort, since the contras used the northern hospitals and clinics, as well as the refugee camps.[53]

There is evidence of other U.S.-based attempts to get contra supplies into Costa Rica disguised as medicines for Costa Ricans or for Nicaraguan refugees. Carlos Rojas, our Costa Rican informant who was kidnapped and taken to a contra camp on Hull's farm in July 1985, reported seeing there partially opened wooden crates of rifles and ammunition stamped "medicine." Earlier, in mid-1983, a group of Miami-based Cuban Americans, hired by the CIA to work with Hull, accompanied a shipment labeled as medical supplies into the Atlantic port of Limón. According to one of the Cubans, Felipe Vidal, the group managed to get into Costa Rica disguised as "Puerto Rican nurses," but the crates with military hardware hidden under clothing and medicines were opened and confiscated. In one of his memos to Oliver North, Robert Owen reported on an October 1984 meeting at the U.S. Embassy with Ambassador Curtin Winsor and two unnamed, retired lieutenant generals. He wrote, "One of the Generals wants to start a distribution program of medicines to Nicaraguan refugees and less fortunate Costa Ricans. As some of the supplies might find their way to the freedom fighters, the meeting [with Pastora] was suggested [by Winsor]." The generals and Owen did visit Pastora's camp and meet with Hull.[54] It is possible that this trip led to the million-dollar-plus NDC shipment to Hull and the Caja.

The Reagan and Bush administrations also tried to manipulate refugee policies in Costa Rica to serve its war effort. In addition to its medical clinics, the 1988 AID Task Force on Humanitarian Assistance also gave stipends, medical care, clothing, housing, and vocational training to several hundred contras and their families living in Costa Rica. This was a clandestine operation, constituting "a parallel AID program to circumvent the UNHCR's refugee program," according to one foreign refugee-agency official who asked to remain anonymous. Under Costa Rican law, all refugee programs were supposed to be administered by the UNHCR, the Costa Rican government's refugee organizations, and designated foreign humanitarian agencies such as Catholic Relief Services. In an interview, AID Task Force official

Pat Irish justified not working with UNHCR since "the target group" (the contras) did not fall within the UN's definition of refugees—that is, civilians who are fleeing for their lives. Irish admitted, however, that AID was also "totally out of our element. This is just not AID's field."[55]

For years before mid-1988, when Congress authorized the special AID Task Force to handle medical and other assistance to the contras, the CIA and Oliver North's operation had been secretly supporting rebel leaders and their families operating out of Costa Rica, as well as others in Honduras and the United States. The help ranged from monthly allowances of thousands of dollars for top political leaders like Alfonso Robelo ($10,000) and Arturo Cruz, Sr. ($7,000), to several thousand colones ($20 to $50) for minor players in Costa Rica. After the AID Task Force's program expired in July 1990, Nicaragua agreed to give amnesty to former combatants, and the United States agreed to help finance their repatriation through a new institution known as the International Commission on Verification and Support (CIAV). According to international relief workers, the UNHCR in effect took over AID's "caseload" of several hundred contra families in Costa Rica (and far greater numbers in Honduras) and administered their documentation and repatriation.[56]

Over the years the Reagan administration undercut UNHCR efforts by working closely with several ultraconservative refugee groups closely linked to the contras. These included the Friends of the Americas in Honduras[57] and Jim Woodall's Trans World Mission and Concerned Women of America[58] projects in Costa Rica. These groups, which were part of the contra private-aid network overseen by Oliver North, distributed medicines, food, clothing, seeds, and other relief aid to Nicaraguans living in the border areas. This violated UNHCR policy of protecting refugees by moving them away (preferably at least 50 kilometers) from troubled international boundaries.

Jim Woodall, a former Cadillac salesman turned right-wing missionary, solicited clothing and funds in the United States based on highly exaggerated claims of twenty thousand or more "naked starving Nicaraguan refugees" along the Costa Rican border.[59] A Woodall associate said that the Embassy illegally used its diplomatic privileges to bring in from the U.S. several shipments of this clothing duty free. In addition, an AID Task Force memo revealed that some of this "donated clothing" was then distributed to wounded and sick contras entering candestinely from Nicaragua so that they could "avoid attracting unfavorable attention" and "present a clean, neat appearance when traveling" from the border to the clandestine clinics inside Costa Rica.[60]

While the CIA and AID maintained their own contra-relief operation paralleling the UNHCR's refugee program, Washington also sought to manipulate the UN's refugee work in Costa Rica.[61] Indirectly, Washington's refugee strategy put additional strains on Costa Rica's health and other social services, as well as on the UNHCR and other international relief organizations. The United States gave no direct funding to Costa Rica's official refugee programs, but it did exert pressure on the Costa Rican government and the UNHCR (23 percent of whose budget was contributed by the United States) to reshape refugee policies to serve its war against Nicaragua.

This process began shortly after the Monge government took office with an aggressive, covert campaign by U.S. officials to encourage Costa Rica to open the door wide to would-be Nicaraguan refugees, while closing down access to other nationalities except Cubans. As one government official explained, "Costa Rica has prided itself on unbiased and humane treatment of refugees. In the past it has given support to Argentineans, Uruguayans, Chileans and others fleeing right-wing military dictatorships. Now only refugees supposed to be fleeing communist countries—Nicaragua and Cuba—are being admitted."

Hardest hit were Salvadoran refugees, an estimated sixteen to twenty thousand of whom had fled their homeland's vicious civil war to Costa Rica by the early 1980s. Beginning in 1983, the Costa Rican government required any Salvadoran to enter as a tourist, with a passport, visa, round-trip air ticket, and two hundred dollars in cash. The numbers of Salvadoran refugees permitted into Costa Rica dropped dramatically—from over two thousand per year in 1980 and 1981 to under fifty between 1985 and 1988.[62]

Simultaneously, the Reagan administration was orchestrating

a campaign to "increase and exaggerate the number of Nicaraguan refugees," according to an European aid worker interviewed in 1983. U.S. Embassy and Costa Rican refugee officials predicted that by mid-1983, between fifty and one hundred thousand Nicaraguan refugees would have entered Costa Rica. In January 1983, two months before the first Nicaraguan refugees crossed into northern Costa Rica, the government established a network of receiving stations along the border, providing food and medicines to those crossing from Nicaragua and chartering planes to fly them to inland reception centers. There was considerable suspicion at the time that this "red carpet treatment" (as one disgruntled aid worker termed it) was also being used to aid the contras.[63]

U.S. and Costa Rican officials had, it soon became apparent, drastically miscalculated. By September 1983, only 440 Nicaraguan refugees had entered the UNHCR camps, and some of these turned out to be bogus cases.[64] The camps, which had unusually high numbers of young men, quickly became recruiting grounds and "R&R" stations for the contras. In 1985, the Dutch government withdrew a donation of some $1 million (25 million colones) for Nicaraguan refugee projects in Costa Rica after a Dutch journalist visiting the Tilarán refugee camp in Guanacaste filmed an interview with an armed Nicaraguan who vowed he would soon return to fight.[65]

Propelled by the expanding war, compulsory draft, and economic deterioration, the numbers of Nicaraguan refugees did grow tremendously. By the end of the 1980s, just over thirty-five thousand Nicaraguan refugees had officially registered with the United Nations, and the numbers of undocumented refugees were estimated to be several times higher. About a third of those registered—10,581—went into six UNHCR camps, which were gradually closed after December 1989.[66] As the numbers grew, Costa Rican public opinion changed from initial support to caution to near hysteria, with the press fanning the anti-Nicaraguan prejudices that had historically existed in the country. Increasingly the Nicaraguan refugees, rather than the country's economic woes or the U.S. war against Nicaragua, were blamed for the country's ills: the rising crime rate, black marketeering, unemployment, and a reemergence of various diseases such as malaria, typhoid, and measles that had been virtually eradicated in Costa Rica. Government doctors were deployed to treat the refugees and, between 1985 and 1988, infant mortality in the refugee camps fell from seventy to fifteen per thousand and malnutrition dropped from five cases per thousand to practically zero.[67] Even though the cost of supporting these refugees was largely paid by foreign donors, Costa Ricans came to view themselves as overburdened by the Nicaraguan refugees.

U.S. attempts to use Costa Rica's refugee facilities and state-run medical services to support the war effort and to set up clandestine contra clinics reflected Washington's cynical lack of respect for the country's impressive health-care system and humanitarian traditions. Precisely because Costa Rica's medical infrastructure was the best in the region, the United States argued publicly it did not need AID assistance. Yet behind the scenes Washington attempted to place this system, together with Costa Rica's open-door refugee policy, at the service of the contra war.

SEVEN

Nontraditional Agricultural Exports: An Agriculture of Desserts

By the early 1980s, consensus was growing among international financial institutions, as well as sectors within Costa Rica, that the country had to diversify its traditional agricultural exports and food-crop production. This convergence of opinion was precipitated by a number of factors, including the virtual collapse of the Central American Common Market (CACM), plummeting world prices for Costa Rica's main export crops, skyrocketing costs of oil imports, the country's heavy borrowing from international banks, and its soaring foreign debt. While in the past AID programs in Latin America and the Caribbean concentrated on expanding production of staples—coffee, sugar, cotton, bananas, and beef—in the 1980s it began to promote the expansion of what it termed "nontraditional agricultural exports" or NTAEs, to "third markets"—that is, markets outside Central America.[1] These luxury crops included melons, strawberries, macadamia nuts, pineapples, flowers, and ferns destined principally for the U.S. market and secondarily for Europe. Together with textile exports, they were perceived as having the potential to become the Costa Rican economy's main engine for new growth.

The new strategy was embodied in various AID agreements containing specific requirements designed to expand export incentives, including a unified exchange rate, market-based interest rates, cuts in subsidies to growers of food crops for the domestic market, and removal of many price controls.[2] AID also required cuts in government support for the National Production Council (CNP), which subsidized the production and sale of "*granos básicos*" (basic grains), the staple food crops, including rice, corn, sorghum, and beans. Along with the IMF and World Bank, the Agency argued that the CNP was too costly and that it would be cheaper for Costa Rica to import basic grains rather than subsidize local producers.

This dovetailed with AID's Public Law 480 or PL-480 program, which provided food imports from the United States. U.S. food aid, together with cutbacks in the CNP and bank loans to food producers, worked to undermine Costa Rica's basic grain farmers and weaken the country's commitment to a policy of self-sufficiency in food production.

Increased quantities of AID funds flowed to support the new exports; between 1982 and March 1988, over $110 million were earmarked specifically for NTAEs and related projects.[3] AID funneled tens of millions of dollars into private banks and finance companies such as COFISA, PIC, and BANEX for nontraditional export projects. The lion's share of funds appropriated for AID's $30 million Northern Zone Development and Northern Zone Consolidation projects went to support the promotion of nontraditional export crops and construction of infrastructure to ease access to outside markets. In addition, AID pumped an estimated $40 million into CINDE through its entirely AID-funded Private Council on Agriculture and Agro-Industry (CAAP) subdivision, set up in 1985 to promote nontraditional agricultural exports as a complement to CINDE's textile promotion.

This package of policy changes, new programs, and multi-million-dollar funding amounted to giving a multitude of benefits to private exporters for new products, while drastically curbing support to small and medium-size food producers and growers of some traditional exports. While NTAE backers contended that the new program was designed to help Costa Rica's "inefficient" food producers make the transition to new export crops, by the end of the decade it was evident that the NTAEs were dominated by big capital (often foreign) and that small growers[4] were being squeezed out. Costa Rican proponents of the new strategy argued further that new investors would only be lured into producing nontraditional exports if the government provided wide-ranging subsidies. Said Central Bank President Eduardo Lizano, "If one desires a great increase in exports, it is an indispensable requirement that such activities earn satisfactory profits, even more, that export activities become like golden eggs."[5]

But rather than admit it was giving "golden eggs" to the new exporters, the Monge and Arias administrations maintained the rhetoric of supporting Costa Rica's traditional small farmer.[6] Political support for the small independent farmer runs deep in Costa Rica, where it is popularly accepted that the foundation of the country's democracy and social tranquility has been a rural egalitarianism based on family-run homesteads. Yet the self-supporting yeoman farmer has increasingly become a rarity. By 1980, between two-thirds and three-fourths of the economically active rural population was landless, and the campesinos and poor bore the brunt of the economic crisis of the early 1980s.

During the Arias administration, the value of nontraditional agricultural and agro-industrial exports rose from $90.9 million in 1986 to $188.3 million in 1989, an increase of over 100 percent, while traditional agricultural exports declined slightly for those years, although they rose modestly over the entire decade.[7] By the late 1980s, advocates of the so-called "agriculture of change" were trumpeting its enormous success. Costa Rica, along with the Dominican Republic, was touted as having the region's most successful agricultural diversification and growth rates for nontraditional exports.[8]

But there is a flip side to this glowing picture of success. Costa Rica's foreign debt, which the new exports were supposed to help pay off, soared from $2.7 billion in 1980 to $4.7 billion in 1987, in part because of the host of duty and tax breaks given to NTAE producers. By 1987, interest payments alone on this staggering debt were eating up 35 percent of all export earnings. (If Costa Rica had not received an IMF loan, debt payments would have consumed 80 percent.)[9] In the 1980s, as well, big capital—both foreign and national—began consolidating its hold over the export sector, widening the gap between the rich and poor. The country has had to import food staples; and small and medium-size farmers have lost their financial security, economic independence, and, in a growing number of cases, their land.

During the Arias administration, campesino organizations protested this AID-prescribed medicine. On various occasions, corn and rice farmers blocked roads, built barricades, and halted traffic for days along major highways. Peasants and small farmers camped out for two weeks in San José's central park and threw rotting nontraditional products—melons, flowers, and strawberries—at the doors of the Central Bank. They carried signs saying, "Peace with Hunger is Not Peace" and chanted, "We don't eat flowers, we eat beans." Squatter organizations, which had initially declared a moratorium on protest because of the Arias government's pledge to construct eighty thousand houses, broke their silence and occupied a plaza in front of the Ministry of Housing, took over unused or underutilized lands, and clashed with Rural Guardsmen sent to evict them. "Small farmers are being squeezed out for bigger producers, who convert farms into huge industries. The agriculturalist, except in the Central Valley, is handing over all his land," says Carlos Campos, leader of the campesino organization UPAGRA.[10]

In the 1990 election, campesinos abandoned the Liberation party of Oscar Arias and threw their votes behind the populist platform of Unity party candidate Rafael Angel Calderón, who promised economic and social justice to the country's rural farmers and poor. Calderón won overwhelmingly in the rural areas of Puntarenas, Guanacaste, and Limón provinces. Although Arias left office as the most popular president in the country's history, primarily because of the success of his peace plan,[11] his Liberation party lost in large measure because small and medium-scale farmers decisively rejected its agricultural policies.

Despite the Unity party's populist campaign platform, once in office Calderón's extremely conservative economic team continued the same strategy: cutbacks in government spending, more privatization, expansion of nontraditional exports, increased foreign investment, and closer integration into the U.S. market. Implementation of these policies accelerated after June 1990, when the Bush administration unveiled its "Enterprise for the Americas" program, which proposed establishing a free market throughout the hemisphere.

NTAEs: Old Wine in New Bottles

AID's agricultural strategy for the 1980s—crop diversification and production for export—is simply the latest twist in the Agency's traditional agenda. While in the past AID in Latin America and the Caribbean concentrated on expanding production of staples demanded by the average North American consumer, its NTAE strategy for the 1980s was a sort of yuppie variant, intended to supply an all-season potpourri of luxury agricultural products to the upscale American market.

In some cases, what AID hailed in the past as "new" agricultural exports are today labeled "traditional." In Costa Rica and elsewhere in Central America, the most striking example is beef. In the early 1960s, as a result of the booming fast-food hamburger market in the United States and the Kennedy administration's Alliance for Progress, which called for Central America to diversify its exports, the U.S. government began heavy promotion of beef production for export. Expansion of cattle raising and beef exports were facilitated through a variety of mechanisms: AID and other international assistance; state bank credit and subsidized loans; tax and modernization incentives; and new roads, refrigeration facilities, packing plants, and other infrastructure projects.[12] Costa Rican beef exports increased dramatically, rising from $4.3 million in 1960 to $81.7 million in 1979. After a steep decline in beef export earnings due to Costa Rica's currency devaluations in the early 1980s, beef exports rose to average $56.3 million in the latter half of the decade.[13]

Costa Rica's rapid expansion of cattle production caused severe social, economic, and ecological consequences, many of which are now being repeated with the new NTAEs. Land converted to cattle farms increased an average of 60,000 hectares per year between 1963 and 1973. By the end of the 1980s, 54 percent of all farmland was in cattle production, and in large part because of this, Costa Rica had the highest deforestation rate in the world.[14] A concentration of farmland and capital in the hands of large cattle farmers led to the creation of a "cattle elite," with foreign, mainly North American, capital controlling a sizable number of the largest ranches and the packing plants, the industry's most profitable sector.[15]

Similarly, AID's ostensibly "new" emphasis on growth through the private sector and foreign investment is also an old and well-worn policy. A 1983 AID strategy paper for Latin America and the Caribbean stated, "In the 1950s, we regarded the private sector as the major engine of development, and thus saw a greater role for US private investment." But in the early 1970s this development strategy was rejected because of "widespread disappointment with the growth performance of the 1960s and [because of] our concern about the social and political consequences of not fulfilling the growing aspirations of middle and lower income groups."[16]

Recognizing the failure of this private-sector strategy, the U.S. Congress in 1973 amended ended the foreign aid legislation to target funds directly to the poorer classes.[17] However, with the advent of the Reagan administration, the AID pendulum again swung strongly toward the private sector, free-market capitalism, and export promotion as the prescriptions to spur economic growth, with the poorer sectors required to settle for "trickle-down" from the top rather than direct assistance.

By the end of the 1980s, economists were once again cautioning Latin America about the rush to privatize. Meeting in Caracas in May 1990, the United Nations Economic Commission for Latin America and the Caribbean released studies questioning heavy reliance on the private sector and its ability to distribute wealth fairly. Gert Rosenthal, head of the UN Commission, warned against indiscriminately reducing the state role in development: "Making the state smaller," he said, "does not resolve certain basic issues like equity. Who is going to take care of the people who are left out? Privatization is fine in certain instances, but it is not something to put on a pedestal and venerate."[18]

NTAEs: "Window of Opportunity" into the United States?

Not only is AID's nontraditional export-promotion program in Costa Rica simply a variant of earlier policies, but it is also a carbon copy of the Agency's export package being pushed throughout Latin America and the Caribbean. Proponents contend that nontraditional crops are going after "new market niches" and therefore have a "window of opportunity" into the United States and Europe, one that traditional exports no longer have because their markets have been exhausted. An AID strategy paper argued, "The traditional exports represent 'mature' markets, where all the production possibilities have been explored, and where the resulting intense competition keeps profit levels relatively low."[19]

A number of experts, however, dispute whether the markets for Costa Rica's traditional export crops have, in fact, "matured." While falling export prices did contribute to Costa Rica's economic crisis in the late 1970s, throughout much of the 1980s the market price for the country's traditional exports—coffee, bananas, beef, and sugar—remained fairly constant, while total earnings increased from about $560 million to $660 million per year. The multinationals' aggressive expansion of banana cultivation in Costa Rica in the late 1980s also belies AID's claim that markets for all traditional exports were permanently exhausted.

A regional study on agricultural diversification comparing four nontraditional crops—melons, pineapples, cucumbers, and cashews—with Central America's five traditional products—coffee, bananas, beef, sugar, and cotton—found that two of the nontraditional crops, melons and cucumbers, had "considerably greater" price fluctuation than any of the traditional products except sugar. Only one nontraditional export, pineapples, showed an upward trend in trade prices.[20] Such fluctuations can be disastrous for small farmers who have no financial cushion and have been led to believe that NTAEs will bring higher, more stable prices. As Peter Rosset, an agronomist who worked for the Costa Rica–based Center for Tropical Agronomic Research and Education (CATIE), put it in an interview, "We gringos will always eat rice, sugar, and beef, drink coffee and wear cotton shirts, but we won't always pay twenty-five bucks a pound for macadamia nuts." President Arias, an advocate of increasing Costa Rica's exports, caustically referred to the new crops as an *agricultura de postres* ("agriculture of desserts"), meaning that they are luxuries the developed world can and will do without in times of recession.

If AID's NTAE drive is successful, Costa Rica will also face intense competition, because virtually the same list of new crops is being advocated in all twenty-eight countries covered by the Caribbean Basin Initiative (CBI), as well as in many other tropical and temperate-climate countries around the world. All these products must try to fit through the same "window of opportunity" into the U.S. and European markets. A 1986 U.S. General Accounting Office (GAO) report on the CBI acknowledges this predicament, stating, "These countries are following similar export strategies predicated upon non-traditional exports. The countries export similar products which could lead to increased competition and thus potentially reduced prices and foreign exchange earnings."[21]

This has already begun to happen for certain crops. In 1988, hundreds of Costa Rican farmers who had planted cardamom on the advice of the Ministry of Agriculture, found themselves in financial ruin as the world price plummeted. A generally positive 1989 evaluation of AID's NTAE strategy in Costa Rica predicted an overproduction of macadamia nuts during the next decade. The report stated that "there are a number of countries coming into production in 1990," and this was likely to cause "a world surplus of macadamia nuts for marketing at that time." In addition, with Hawaii as the world's largest macadamia producer and its production increasing, it appeared likely that these U.S. growers would lobby to bar imports from Costa Rica and other foreign countries.[22] This problem is compounded by the fact that macadamia trees take nine years to reach full maturity and cost an estimated $1 million per hectare to plant.[23] The future therefore does not look bright for Costa Rican macadamia producers and their multi-million-dollar investments.

This same AID report says there is likely to be an overproduction of mangoes as well, since "half the developing countries are going to take a shot at exporting mangoes." It goes on to state that "Costa Rica's growing season now corresponds to the growing season in Mexico and throughout the rest of Central America and the Caribbean."[24] This, of course, presents a problem not just for mangoes, but for all of Costa Rica's agricultural exports. Viria Araya, a Ministry of Agriculture extension officer in the Atlantic coast canton of Pococí, contends that AID and the other promoters of NTAEs are not addressing the problem of overproduction. "No one knows how many hectares are cultivated, how many the market can support, nor is there any attempt to restrict production to avoid over-production."[25]

As export levels of certain of these new crops rise, they also threaten established producers in the United States, who are likely to respond by throwing up trade barriers. AID predicts this could happen with macadamia; it has already happened to cut flowers, with drastic results. In 1986, the Association of North American Flower Growers, claiming unfair trade practices, brought suit against Costa Rican flower growers. The suit charged that the export bonuses known as CATs and other benefits received under their export contract represented a subsidy from the Costa Rican government, and that the Costa Rican growers were therefore selling or "dumping" their flowers at artificially low prices. During the nine months it took to resolve the conflict, the Costa Rican exporters had to pay both import and countervailing duties into the United States, as well as give up the CATs bonuses and other Costa Rican government tax breaks guaranteed under the Export contract. The U.S. courts finally ruled to drop the tariffs but, in return, Costa Rican exporters of three specific categories of flowers—roses, carnations, and chrysanthemums—had to give up CATs and their other benefits.

At the time this suit was filed, Costa Rican flower growers included a mixture of large producer-exporters and medium and small growers, including two export cooperatives, COOPEFLOR and COEXFLOR, comprising over fifty small producers. Then-CENPRO Director Carlos Torres, himself a flower grower, said in an interview, "Flowers are one of the few industries where you had that many small people. It was actually touted as something that the small producer could get into." But that changed when CATs and other export incentives were removed. By May 1988, twenty-four medium and large growers were at the point of bankruptcy, fifteen small producers had abandoned production, and both cooperatives failed, along with all their members.[26] Most large exporters and about half the medium-size growers survived by switching to different species or new export crops, but about 90 percent of the small growers went under. According to an AID study, production became concentrated in the hands of fifteen large companies which control 75 percent of the market, with one producer controlling 50 percent.[27] The market is unlikely to reopen to small and medium growers, because both producers and bankers now consider flower exports to be a risky business. Financial credit and loans have become scarce and, as an official at the private Banco de Comercio told researcher Tom Thacher, "*Flowers* is now a dirty word in the banking sector."

During the 1980s, Costa Rica not only shifted emphasis from traditional to nontraditional exports, but also shifted away from Central America and toward new or "third" markets, most importantly the United States. For several decades prior to 1980, Central America, as organized under the Central American Common Market (CACM), had been Costa Rica's main market for its nontraditional exports. (In contrast, Costa Rica's traditional exports have always been sold mainly outside the region.) By 1980, the worldwide economic crisis and the region's political instability caused the CACM serious problems. In addition, the Reagan administration, which was building up its war against the Sandinistas, had no political interest in strengthening Costa Rica's participation in the Common Market, because this would indirectly help Nicaragua, Costa Rica's largest trading partner.[28] These reasons, coupled with requirements under AID, CBI, and IMF agreements and the government's export-subsidy package, forced a dramatic reorientation toward the United States. In 1980, 63 percent of Costa Rica's nontraditional exports went to other Central American countries (excluding Panama), while by 1989, that figure had dropped to less than 20 percent. At the same time, Costa Rica's nontraditional exports to the United States nearly tripled, from 15 percent of total nontraditional exports in 1980 to 42 percent in 1989. By the early 1990s, the United States had become by far the largest market for Costa Rica's new exports—over twice the size of the next biggest market.[29] Thus, while Costa Rica diversified its export crops, it did not expand its markets; it has simply shifted nontraditional exports away from the CACM to the United States.

Table 6. Costa Rican Exports by Markets, 1984–89 (in thousands of U.S. $)

Year	CACM	% of total	United States	% of total	ECC	% of total	All others	% of total	Total
1984: Traditional	19	2	262,815	40	233,029	36	153,610	24	649,473
Nontraditional	185,311	55	81,219	24	12,398	4	57,493	17	336,421
1985: Traditional	0	0	252,014	42	148,398	25	193,713	33	594,125
Nontraditional	134,351	40	109,852	33	13,881	4	75,306	22	333,390
1986: Traditional	11	1	304,224	42	294,051	41	123,425	17	721,711
Nontraditional	91,948	25	160,336	43	20,717	6	95,079	25	368,080
1987: Traditional	7	1	294,985	43	279,165	41	104,279	15	678,436
Nontraditional	98,012	22	214,222	48	31,931	7	98,877	22	443,042
1988: Traditional	9	1	250,963	37	266,237	40	154,283	23	671,492
Nontraditional	114,893	22	233,206	45	55,087	11	109,417	21	512,603
1989: Traditional	1,200	1	274,248	39	300,642	42	131,229	18	707,319
Nontraditional	128,381	20	304,190	46	66,889	10	155,004	24	654,464

Source: CENPRO computer database, "Costa Rica: Principales Productos de Exportación No Tradicionales en Miles de US $. Período 1984–1989."

Table 7. Costa Rica's Major NTAEs:
Relationship with U.S. Market, 1987

Crop	Costa Rica exports to U.S. by crop (% of total exports)	U.S. imports from Costa Rica by crop (% of total imports)
Vegetables	88	2.00
Macadamia nuts	70	1.17
Cocoa powder	92	0.92
Cocoa butter	100	1.34
Pineapples	89	25.44
Strawberries	58	insignificant
Flowers	91	1.73
Ornamental plants	40	insignificant

Source: U.S. Dept. of Commerce, Bureau of Census, "US General Imports & Imports for Consumption," Washington, D.C., 1987.

Not only do AID's agro-export policies tie Costa Rica to the U.S. market, they also compel growers to purchase inputs mainly from the United States. Many of the new export crops are not native to the region and therefore require hybrid seeds, pesticides, and fertilizers. This has meant a growth of raw-material inputs for NTAE production, all of which enter duty free under the terms of the Export contract. Under CBI, 15 percent of the required "local" 35 percent value added may be made up of inputs from the United States, a clause that helps U.S. producers while it substantially reduces benefits to Costa Rica. AID agreements stipulate that Economic Support Funds (ESF) be used to buy imports from the United States, and many AID projects require that *all* imports be bought from the United States. A GAO report on the impact of U.S. assistance to the region notes the complaints of even some AID officials that " 'buy American' provisions often prohibit beneficiaries from purchasing less expensive foreign-made goods that meet their needs."[30]

But while Costa Rica has become increasingly dependent on U.S. buyers, Costa Rican exports into the United States constitute a miniscule fraction of the U.S. import market. As table 7 shows, of its major nontraditional exports to the United States, only Costa Rica's pineapples constitute a large share—25 percent—of the U.S.

import market. However, not even this is significant, since most—90 percent of U.S. consumption—is of domestically grown pineapples, mainly from Hawaii.

Such an imbalance gives Costa Rica little or no clout in influencing U.S. import prices and policies and makes producers and exporters vulnerable to North American quotas, import duties, quality standards, and other trade barriers. Since Costa Rica's NTAEs are luxury products which are facing increased competition from other countries in the region, their prices will drop or the U.S. market will become problematical when there is overproduction or economic recession. All of this indicates that Costa Rica's NTAEs are likely to find increasing difficulty squeezing through the "window of opportunity" into the U.S. market.

NTAE: AID's "Quick Fix" Approach

A 1988 AID-contracted evaluation of the nontraditional export strategy in Costa Rica and fourteen other Central American and Caribbean countries concluded that the Agency's NTAE strategy constituted "a short-term, 'quick fix'" approach with the aim of getting fast results. Just as the Inspector General's audit report and memo was devastatingly critical of AID-created parallel institutions and financial management in the Costa Rican program, so this study found that AID's NTAE program was hastily implemented without careful research, planning, technology, training, extension services, environmental and marketing studies, infrastructure, or host-country input. The study states, "In most of the countries surveyed . . . production-related issues . . . [including crop monoculturing, soil and water conservation, and use of chemicals] were treated only as secondary considerations in the rush to produce and profit" from the new exports. It says, "Most local agronomists in the countries surveyed do not have training or experience" in the new crops, and AID funds for training "seem low and do not include significant amounts for the long-term training of horticulturalists—something which is basic to the development of CD/NTAE (Crop Diversification/Non-Traditional Agricultural Exports)."

The study also states that, in its obsession with the private sector, AID "has ignored or put little attention to host country public entities—especially Ministries of Agriculture—in the design and implementation of [nontraditional export] projects."[31] Agronomist Peter Rosset concurs, arguing that historically Costa Rica's Ministry of Agriculture has provided important extension services which, along with subsidized bank loans and guaranteed crop prices, "have kept small farmers in Costa Rica from being as poor as in El Salvador or Guatemala. Today, [these services] have been gutted."[32] The AID study concludes that "it is too early to determine unequivocally that one or another of AID's projects or approaches to CD/NTAE development can ensure sustainable success over time."

Another problem, which clearly has long-term implications, is that many of the new crops prescribed by AID are not native to Costa Rica and so require heavy use of fertilizers and pesticides to meet the high quality standards of the U.S. market. An AID evaluation report on NTAEs found that "increased production of nontraditional crops has already led to increased incidence of crop pests and disease. In the absence of proper preventive and corrective action, pest and disease incidence will grow at a rapid pace." Campesino organizer Wilson Campos explained that small farmers in his northern region have long had problems with a particular type of insect. "We have lived with this bug all our lives," he said. "It eats certain plants but not our corn, beans, and rice. Then we plant cardamom and the bug decides that it tastes good. The next thing we know, we have a plague."

While pesticides, along with fertilizers and hybrid seeds, are often necessary to make these new crops grow in Costa Rica, they can present health and marketing problems. According to two 1990 General Accounting Office reports on pesticides, Latin America, which supplies nearly 80 percent of U.S. fruit and vegetable imports, rates fourth in the world (behind Japan, the United States, and Europe) in pesticide use per hectare. The study found that while multinational corporations have ready access to information and employ full-time agronomists to monitor pesticide levels, independent growers in Costa Rica, Guatemala, and the Dominican Republic, who are relatively new to the nontraditional export business, "tend not to have management practices in

place that specifically consider U.S. safety and quality requirements for their export crops. They have fewer resources, including
less access to information on US pesticide requirements, and the
information they obtain may be inconsistent or inaccurate."

The study further found that for crops not produced commer-
cially in the United States, such as Costa Rican–grown yucca and
chayote (a type of squash), the U.S. Environmental Protection
Agency has not set residue tolerance levels for pesticides used on
these crops. This means that determining acceptability for the U.S.
market is left to the discretion of individual customs inspectors,
who can reject the crops for even slight amounts of pesticide
residue. In addition, Costa Rican growers currently use over forty
pesticides, including eight of the world's most dangerous pesticides whose use is either totally banned or strictly regulated in
industrial countries.[33] Crops using these pesticides can be rejected
by the importing countries, and some already have been. In the
latter half of 1988, for instance, five thousand tons of Costa Rican
agricultural products, worth $4.5 million, were refused entry into
the U.S. and European markets because of "contamination" by
pesticides or insects. Most were nontraditional crops.[34] A 1989
AID evaluation of Costa Rica's NTAE program found that "chemical residues have become a serious issue for food products," and it
predicted that "a problem with residues on Costa Rican mangoes
could be disastrous."[35]

Of course, pesticide use presents hazards to Costa Ricans as
well. Since the 1950s, Costa Rica's traditional exports, particularly
bananas, cotton, and coffee, have been heavily dependent on
pesticides (some of which are banned in the United States), and
this has caused serious health problems. Costa Rica suffers the
world's highest rate of stomach cancer, and many scientists and
environmentalists suspect this is caused by high toxic residues on
locally grown fruits and vegetables. The dangers have accelerated
in recent years with the expansion of the new export crops.
Between 1985 and 1987, Costa Rica spent an estimated $40
million per year on pesticides. According to María Aguilar of the
Pesticide Program at Costa Rica's National University, pesticides
have become "like gods for farmers," and government regulation
of their use is limited and easily circumvented. For instance, the

pesticide Lindane, which is widely used on Costa Rican pineapples, causes miscarriages, nervous-system damage, and possibly
leukemia.[36] In the late 1980s, AID conducted a study on pesticide
levels in strawberries; when asked for a copy of the study, an AID
official said it was not public. But, he added, "I can tell you one
thing. I won't eat the strawberries."

Ross Wherry, an AID rural-development officer in Costa Rica,
admitted that at least three deaths per year can be attributed
directly to improper use of pesticides. Several peasant organizations say the problem is much more serious, and that pesticides
are causing not only deaths, but also sickness, sterilization, nervous-system damage in humans and animals, and contamination
of groundwater, rivers, ocean shorelines, and soils. They argue
that AID's nontraditional export strategy is only worsening the
country's already serious pesticide problem.

NTAEs: Real Earnings

When AID and local proponents of the NTAE strategy boast of its
"spectacular growth," they invariably fail to count the cost to the
government of producing the new exports. These costs are hidden
behind the bevy of new programs, infrastructures, and "incentives" (in reality, subsidies) given to exporters. These include
low-interest AID and government loans, storage and transportation facilities, new roads and airports, as well as exemptions
guaranteed by the contracts between exporters and CENPRO.
These export contracts, which give nontraditional exporters exemptions on income taxes, import duties, and local taxes, as well
as export bonuses, have greatly reduced state revenues. Over 90
percent of exporters hold export contracts.[37] This meant that for
1988 alone, the Costa Rican government lost almost 1.7 billion
colones (about $21 million, or 2.7 percent of government spend-
ing) in revenues solely in exporters' exemptions from import
taxes.[38]

The most controversial incentive program for nontraditional
exports has been CAT (*Certificados de Abono Tributario* or Tax
Credit Certificate). Under this program exporters of nontraditional products (agricultural and manufactured) who sell all or

part of what they produce outside Central America receive a government bonus equal to 15 percent to 20 percent of the value of those exports. The government issues exporters certificates in colones that are negotiable on the local stock exchange. To qualify for CATs, exporters must have 35 percent value added (that is, in the value of labor and local components) in those products sold in the United States and 20 percent in their exports to Europe. The stated aim of this program is to reward companies that benefit the economy through job creation and use of local raw material.

Costa Rica first set up the CATs program in 1972 to stimulate exports outside the Central American Common Market, but with the nontraditional export drive in the 1980s it grew dramatically: from $240,000 in government payments to exporters in 1973, to $8.3 million in 1983, to $65 million in 1989.[39] By the end of the 1980s, CATs had become, to use Eduardo Lizano's term, a "golden egg" for exporters and a substantial financial burden for the government. The cost of CATs since its inception was staggering—equivalent to nearly $40,000 million. In 1989, for instance, CATs payments equaled 8 percent of all government expenditures and 22 percent of the budget deficit,[40] figures that raised the ire of both the World Bank and the IMF. In 1990, the World Bank conditioned a $120 million loan partly upon Costa Rica's devising an alternative incentive scheme to CATs.[41]

Some local economists, politicians, and businessmen also raised strong objections to the CATs program and called for its modification or limitation. For example, a special Legislative Assembly commission studying CATs found in 1990 that 70 percent of exporters, including those producing traditional exports and companies based in the free zones, did not receive CATs,[42] and yet they still found it profitable to sell their products abroad.

In fact, the bulk of the CATs bonuses have gone to a small portion of those involved in the export sector. As designed, they are paid solely to an exporting company, thereby excluding growers who work on consignment or intermediaries who sell to exporters. A number of nontraditional agricultural companies contract production in order to shift risks and costs to the producer (often smaller farmers), while maintaining control of the most lucrative processing and export functions. For instance, over half (3,500 hectares in 1988) of PINDECO's pineapples are grown on contract by small farmers, yet the whole CATs bonus goes to the multinational exporter. In the San Carlos area, increasing amounts of citrus fruits are grown by individual farmers who then sell to Ticofrut, a processing plant jointly owned by U.S. and Costa Rican investors. Ticofrut handles exports and thus receives all the CATs.[43] In contrast, for some of Costa Rica's traditional agricultural products, including coffee, meat, and milk, the government has established regulations to distribute profits more equitably among exporters, processors, cooperatives, and individual producers. According to former Agriculture Minister Rodolfo Navas, "There are sectors where we have established a whole infrastructure of protection and fairer distribution of benefits. But this is not taking place with CATs. It is being concentrated in a few hands, and if we don't control that, there won't be any benefit for Costa Rican society as a whole."

Even among those companies getting CATs, a few have collected the lion's share of the benefits. A confidential report done for the Ministry of External Commerce and leaked to the press found that, in 1989, 26 companies—less than 5 percent of the 526 companies earning CATs that year—received over 50 percent of the value of CATs. The largest beneficiary, PINDECO, received $6.25 million (paid in colones), equal to nearly 10 percent of all CATs and more than three times the amount awarded the next largest recipient. Government statistics showed a similar imbalance in 1991.[44]

Corporate cheating on CATs became commonplace. When the Calderón government took office in May 1990, it found that 40 percent or more than 500 of the 1,200 companies applying for CATs and other incentives under export contracts were doing so improperly. They had either failed to file proper papers with the government or to meet the value-added requirement.[45] Some of the largest recipients of CATs benefits have been implicated in fraudulent behavior, including drug trafficking, money laundering, and fraud.[46] Under pressure from the World Bank and IMF, as well as exporters of traditional crops, the Calderón government

Table 8. Costa Rican Imports, Exports, and Trade Deficit, 1983–90 (in millions of U.S. $)

Year	1983	1984	1985	1986	1987	1988	1989	1990
Exports	862	998	939	1,086	1,114	1,245	1,437	1,670
Imports	993	1,102	1,111	1,163	1,385	1,409	1,743	2,181
Deficit	−131	−104	−172	−77	−271	−164	−306	−511

Note: In 1986, the deficit fell more than 50 percent, but this was mostly the result of an increase in the value of a traditional export, coffee, which jumped almost 25 percent. ,

Source: AID, "Strategy Update," Costa Rica, March 1988, p. 11; CENPRO, "Costa Rica: Balanza Comercial. Período 1984–1989"; Ronald Bailey, "Exports Rise, but Trade Deficit Worsens," Tico Times, March 8, 1991.

lowered the rebates to a range from 8 to 12 percent of the export value. In November 1992, the National Investment Council eliminated payment of CATs to new exporters and announced that the entire CATs program would be terminated by 1996.[47]

While many Costa Ricans had also come to view CATs as a financial windfall for unscrupulous entrepreneurs, it is probably the small and medium exporters who will be most hurt by these reductions. According to both an AID study and former CENPRO Director Carlos Torres, it was the loss of CATs bonuses that forced many small and medium flower grower-exporters out of business. As the AID report states, "These CATs represented the entire margin of profit for many of the inefficient [read small] farmers." Torres predicted that cuts in CATs could precipitate similar crises in other agricultural sectors.[48]

Even without CATs, nontraditional exports have been a drain on the national coffers. A main pillar in AID's argument for increased nontraditional exports has been that export growth will help reduce Costa Rica's trade deficit, that is, the discrepancy between imports and exports. In a March 1988 report, for instance, AID projected that Costa Rica's trade deficit would fall to $105.6 million in 1989 and a mere $84.4 million in 1990.[49] AID was wrong: the deficit grew nearly twofold between 1988 and 1989 and more than threefold by 1990.

Exporters point to 1986 as the year nontraditionals "took off" in a spurt of "spectacular growth." Overall, however, exports grew an average of only 9.9 percent annually between 1986 and

1989, while imports increased by an annual average of 14.8 percent over the same period. Mario Mora, director of the Economic Analysis Department in the Ministry of Planning (MIDEPLAN), said that three principal factors have led to this sharp increase in imports: (1) AID/IMF/World Bank tariff reduction requirements that make all imports cheaper; (2) structural adjustment policies that make no effort to use locally made materials or to vertically integrate agricultural and industrial production; and (3) the nontraditional export drive, which requires large amounts of imported raw materials.[50] A 1990 report by the Planning Ministry conceded, "Even though the promotion of [nontraditional] exports has diversified production, the growth of exports, although satisfactory, is not sufficient to finance the level of imports that the current development model requires."[51] By the early 1990s, the overall impact of nontraditional agricultural exports was far from "spectacular"; at best it represented a modest financial gain and possibly even a net loss to the Costa Rican economy.

NTAEs: Foreign Domination and the "New Oligarchy"

The AID-promoted new agro-exports, like the textile stitching and other export assembly plants, are dominated by large, often foreign, investors. A precise breakdown of foreign ownership is not publicly available. However, according to Central Bank and other officials interviewed by the *Tico Times,* more than 50 percent of Costa Rica's agribusinesses are foreign owned or controlled.[52] A confidential National Bank report leaked to the local press in 1988 disclosed that 40 percent of the hectares planted in macadamia and 80 percent of those in citrus are owned by foreigners.[53] In the flower industry, the largest grower, American Flowers, is U.S.owned and accounts for 50 percent of all exports. Of the fourteen "second tier" flower companies representing 25 percent of the market, only two are completely national.[54] Likewise, over 90 percent of fern exports are foreign- (mainly U.S.-) owned or controlled, and only three companies, producing in 1989 about 9 percent of the exports, are totally Costa Rican.[55] By 1988, over 95 percent of pineapple exports were being handled by the Del Monte subsidiary PINDECO.[56] Other nontraditional crops heavily dominated by foreigners include ornamental plants,[57] papaya, mangoes, and melons. Costa Rican growers, including small farmers, are found in several sectors: chayotes, plantain, tubers, and yucca—all traditional crops that are now being promoted as nontraditional exports. There is also some Costa Rican capital in strawberries and melons as well as in fishing. Statistics compiled by AID reflect the imbalance between foreign and national investments in nontraditional export crops. In 1988, foreign investment in NTAEs hit AID's projected annual goal of $2 million, but NTAE investment by Costa Ricans was only $850,000, a mere 11 percent of AID's $7.6 million target.[58]

One reason foreign capital is dominating the nontraditional export sector is that initial investments are often very costly. They can range from almost $2,000 per hectare for cardamom, over $3,500 for melons, more than $5,400 for pineapples, and nearly $12,000 for strawberries, to over $1 million per hectare for macadamia.[59] This is well beyond the means of Costa Rica's independent farmers, who in 1989 earned on average less than $2,000 (about 170,000 colones) per year, while salaried farm workers made less than $1,400 (about 119,000 colones).[60]

In contrast, foreign investors in agriculture have a myriad of advantages: they have direct access to foreign currency, loans, technology, and destination markets, plus the economic means to establish new types of crops, produce the quantity and quality demanded for export, purchase necessary imports, hire technicians and marketing experts, get bank credit, CATs, duty-free imports, and other incentives, safely and swiftly export their crop, and shift production to keep up with changes in the international market. José María Figueres, Oscar Arias's last agricultural minister and a close collaborator with AID strategists, conceded in an interview that "our shift toward nontraditional export items has helped the larger companies, both foreign and national, much more than the small producer."

A detailed study of ornamental plants, flowers, and foliage which, in 1988, accounted for 42 percent of nontraditional exports found that foreign investors have had advantages in all key areas—marketing, technology, and financing—and that, increasingly, they are consolidating their hold and frustrating efforts by national companies to enter their fields. In addition, the study found that the government's "institutional policies," most importantly the export contract, "indirectly discourage the growth of the unsubsidized small national producer, placing them in competition with subsidized large established export companies, the majority of which are foreign controlled." Those Costa Ricans who are involved either on their own or as partners with foreign companies are usually wealthy industrialists, experienced international businessmen, or persons with previous dealings with foreigners. In joint ventures, a CINDE official explained, the Costa Rican component "is only land, labor and infrastructure. The technology, working capital, marketing and overall control of the operation is held by the foreign partners."[61]

This preference for foreign over national firms is evident, for instance, in the allocation of bank loans. Costa Rica's private banks, particularly those that have received special AID credit lines, have been a main source of financing for nontraditional exports. These banks require strict conditions for loans that invariably exclude small and medium growers of the new exports.[62] Borrowers must usually put up collateral (other property, companies, or bank accounts), provide a feasibility study, hire a technical assistant, possess a marketing contract, and demonstrate the ability to self-finance between 40 and 65 percent of the cost of the project. An official with the private Banco Interfín bluntly declared, "I would not loan to a national alone because I have serious doubts about his ability to sell his product."[63]

As researcher Thomas Thacher documents, U.S. businessman John Marsell's fern consortium, Helechos Internacionales, illustrates how a foreign firm has aggressively and astutely established dominance in Costa Rica's nontraditional export sector. Marsell, whose father was a fern pioneer in Florida, began growing ferns in Costa Rica in the 1970s, eventually building up a consortium of thirteen companies. The consortium exports to a central processing plant in Florida, also controlled by Marsell, which handles all marketing and purchasing. Marsell's operations have been financed by U.S. investors, three OPIC loans, and AID funds funneled through private banks, including about $2 million in credit from BANEX and $1 million from PIC. By maintaining the separate companies, Marsell is able to manipulate his export contracts and other incentives, shelter income from taxes, and purchase inputs for unsubsidized production. As Thacher concludes, Marsell's "expansion is easily financed and his company holdings grow while others are not able to initiate for lack of technical experience, marketing and credit. By the time a national producer acquires the[se] three basic ingredients, he must compete against a concentrated fully developed foreign investor such as Marsell."[64]

By the end of the 1980s, it became clear that Costa Ricans were losing control of another sector of their economy: tourism. During the Arias administration, tourism grew to become the country's third-largest foreign-exchange earner, behind coffee and bananas, and by 1992 it was the country's most rapidly expanding sector. This was mainly because of accelerated foreign investment in hotels, tour companies, travel agencies, condominiums, car rentals, light aircraft and boating companies, beach-front resorts, and vacation homes. In the late 1980s, tourism was classified as a nontraditional export because, CENPRO director Torres argued, tourism brings in dollars which "most of the time" are changed legally in banks and hotels. Businesses involved in tourism were given incentives and tax breaks administered by the Costa Rican Institute of Tourism (ICT). These included exemptions from property taxes, as well as from import taxes for construction and remodeling and duty-free import of vehicles such as vans and cars, fishing and pleasure boats, jet skis, dune buggies, and golf carts.[65]

In 1990 an ICT document warned that "the majority of Costa Rican beaches are private property." It said that in recent months foreigners, including Japanese, Taiwanese, and North Americans, had bought hotels and beach-front property at a feverous pitch equal to all foreign property investments over the previous twenty to thirty years. By the early 1990s, foreigners owned much of the property along the country's prime beaches, including Bahía Culebra and Flamingo, Hermosa, Portero, Grande, Junquillal, and Samara beaches. Alarmed by this trend, legislator Gerardo Rudín asked the Ministry of Tourism to investigate this "privatization of the coasts," which, he said, included illegal sales within the "sea-land zone" intended to protect public access to all beaches.[66]

The growth of nontraditional exports has coincided with illegal activity as well: the increased use of Costa Rica as a bridge for moving cocaine from Latin America to the United States. In 1990, the U.S. Drug Enforcement Agency (DEA) estimated that two tons of cocaine were being shipped through Costa Rica each month. Increasingly, these drugs are being concealed among perishable nontraditional agricultural exports, an ideal front because U.S. customs officials are under pressure to inspect them quickly to avoid spoilage. Drugs have been found hidden in a variety of new exports, including plantains, squash, and fresh pineapples, as well as handicrafts and wood. One of the largest busts occurred in April 1989, when U.S. customs agents in Miami found 1,346 kilos of cocaine in a shipment of Costa Rican frozen yucca. One of the most notorious companies involved was Frigoríficos de Puntarenas, a once-legitimate Costa Rican seafood company that was taken over by a group of Miami Cuban drug traffickers and CIA operatives in 1982 and used for running contra-related covert operations.[67] Alarmed by the drug traffickers' penetration of Costa Rica's export trade, CINDE and the Chamber of Exporters convened a conference in early 1990 titled, "How to Prevent our Exports from Being Used as a Trojan Horse." Experts warned that unless the drug-smuggling problem was checked, the United States would classify Costa Rica as a "top-risk" country (as had been done with Colombia and Jamaica), thereby subjecting Costa Rican products to minute, time-consuming, and costly customs inspection.[68]

At the same time, one of Costa Rica's traditional exports, bananas, were making a big comeback. Spurred by the package of export incentives and an expanding international market, particularly in Eastern Europe, well-established multinationals such as Del Monte and United Fruit and new venture capital from Colombia and elsewhere began investing in bananas. In 1986, the banana industry started buying up land at a rate of two thousand hectares annually, particularly on the Atlantic coast. By the early 1990s, the Calderón government had set a target of ninety million boxes for export annually, bananas had become the number one export earner, and Costa Rica was on the verge of becoming the world's leading banana producer.

This is, however, a dubious distinction, as researcher Alicia Korten points out. Intercropping and seed variety have given way to monocropping that is heavily dependent on imported seeds and pesticides. In fact, pesticides account for 50 to 55 percent of the cost of the banana industry's material inputs. Tropical forests and farmlands are being plowed under for banana plantations. Prior to 1980, the Atlantic coast produced 70 percent of Costa Rica's corn; by 1990, it produced only 5 percent, largely cause of banana expansion. And in the process, landowners are being turned into laborers, a transition which means "the breakdown of a whole social structure," writes Korten.[69] Like the drive to expand nontraditional exports, the banana expansion moved into high gear without proper planning for its long-range effect on the environment and the people of the region.

NTAEs: Impact on Small Farmers

In 1987, Agricultural Minister Antonio Alvarez Desanti glibly asserted that "the government desires to better the standard of living of the small producers through the establishment of 'agriculture of change' crops with higher profitability."[70] But the reality has been altogether different. Small and medium-sized farmers trying to break into the new exports face a myriad of obstacles, particularly a lack of capital and credit to purchase costly inputs (seeds, fertilizers, and pesticides), as well as inadequate technical skills, overseas contacts, and marketing know-how.

In Costa Rica, there are numerous examples of how small farmers have been enticed into switching to new crops without adequate feasibility studies, financing, or technical assistance. Wilson Campos, head of a farmers' organization in northern Costa Rica, says, "The problem with the 'agriculture of change' is that the country was not ready to jump into it. AID and the government didn't do any planning." Campos says that farmers in northern Costa Rica were being forced through propaganda, contraction of credit for food crops, and government pressure to switch to nontraditional crops. While AID did not heavily target the small farmer for assistance in growing NTAEs, in 1989 the Agency provided $10 million to the National Bank for subsidized loans to campesinos who planted new export crops such as cardamom, passion fruit, and black pepper. No AID credit was given for traditional food crops. Loans were restricted to farmers with three hectares or less, but many of the new crops require more sizable operations to be financially viable. Organizer Campos says there is a shortage of people who know how to grow the new products, and farming has become "a game of trial and error," with the producer taking all the risk. "Corn, rice, beans are all known crops. We've grown them for many years. The new crops, nobody knows how. The technicians are learning right beside the farmers," Campos explained. "The difference is that we depend on the crops to survive; the technicians are on salary."[71]

There are other examples. In 1983, for instance, the demand for *tiquisque,* a tuber or root vegetable, was high. That year the few farmers at an AID-funded farming project in El Indio, in the northern Atlantic region, switched to *tiquisque* and made a good profit. Other farmers hurriedly switched to the new crop, and within two years the market was saturated. As one farmer lamented, "My neighbor made 80,000 colones per hectare, so I planted. The next year the price went down, but I got by. Then the third year, no one would buy it."[72]

Even when AID did provide financial and technical assistance, it was often insufficient or sporadic. For instance, through Costa Rica's agrarian reform institute, IDA (Instituto de Desarrollo Agrario or Agrarian Development Institute), AID provided funds to a group of twenty small farmers in Guácimo on the Atlantic plains to grow squash (*ayote*) for export. The first year IDA provided these farmers, who had a reputation for hard work, with healthy seeds imported from the United States, a guaranteed export contract with a U.S. company, and two advisers. That year they had a very successful crop. The second year there was no contract, the advisers were not rehired, and the farmers growing ayote, who now numbered one hundred, could not obtain the same disease-free seeds. Sixty percent of the farmers failed, and by the following year the rest had gone under.[73]

Whether cases such as these represent simply short-term

glitches in implementation of the NTAE program or more long-term structural and competency problems remains to be seen. While failures with new crops are common, the problem is that poor people cannot afford such risks and the government, AID, and other institutions have not extended crop insurance or taken other measures to reduce the risks.

Not only were many small farmers finding it tough to make the transition to the AID-promoted NTAE program, but their efforts to continue as producers of food crops or traditional exports were also being crippled by three other policies promoted by AID during the 1980s: (1) a restriction of bank credit for small and medium growers of traditional crops, (2) cutbacks in government support for the National Production Council (CNP), and (3) an influx of PL-480 food imports from the United States.

Restriction of Credit to Small Farmers

While the Monge and the Arias administrations called on small and medium-scale farmers to increase their technical efficiency and levels of production, both governments, in league with AID, IMF, and the World Bank, moved to drastically curtail low-interest bank credit. Traditionally, Costa Rica's national banks were the main source of credit to farmers, but between 1983 and 1987, credit for the agricultural sector plummeted from 80 percent to 20 percent of total credit.[74]

In an Orwellian manner, AID played with language and definitions to argue that the benefits historically given to small growers of traditional crops were negative "subsidies," while the new benefits it demanded for nontraditional exporters were positive "incentives." AID contended that government price controls and low-interest credit to traditional agriculture "distort the market," contribute to the government deficit, act as "disincentives to production," and prop up "uneconomic" farmers.[75] It argued that by restricting such "easy money," small farmers could be forced to adopt new production techniques and become "efficient."[76]

But the results have often been opposite from what AID projected: credit cuts have proved to be a "disincentive," not a stimulus, to production. Since such cutbacks have frequently not been coupled with training programs to teach farmers how to adopt new technologies, the result has sometimes been lower productivity. The U.S. Embassy report admitted that "the difficulty small [corn] farmers have had in obtaining credit for the 1986/1987 crop year" caused a "decline in input use [which] is reflected in the drop in yields."[77] A 1988 U.S. Embassy report confirms the negative impact of the new bank policies on the agricultural sector, while conspicuously omitting AID's role. The report states, "In making interest rates more responsive to market conditions, the Central Bank hoped to introduce greater rationality and competition into a highly distorted credit environment; in practice, this led to a reduction in credit available to the agricultural sector, and some traditional crops were either not planted or planted in insufficient quantities. Between 1982 and 1987, bank credit available for small producers of corn, beans, and other crops dropped more than three fold, from 515 million to 148 million colones. By mid-1988, traditional exports of rice and meat were being imported."[78]

The expansion of the private banking system and cutbacks in traditional credit categories have created a threefold problem for small and medium farmers. These farmers do not meet the criteria for private bank loans, less AID and other funds are being channeled through the state banks, and the conditions for borrowing these funds have been greatly tightened. As Rolando Rivera, sociologist with the research organization CEPAS (Centro de Estudios para la Acción Social) said in an interview, "Not only are farmers getting a smaller slice of the pie, but now there is less pie." Soon after taking office, Calderón's Agricultural Minister Juan Rafael Lizano conceded that "the biggest problem" facing small and medium farmers "is that they have no credit."[79]

Chopping the National Production Council

Small farmers and food producers have also faced hardships as their traditional supports with the National Production Council (CNP) have been cut back. The CNP was created in 1949 to promote self-sufficiency in basic grains (corn, beans, rice, and sorghum) and insure that Costa Rican growers would not be undercut by lower international prices for food crops produced by heavily subsidized U.S. and European farmers. By purchasing grains at guaranteed prices and subsidizing their sale on the local market, the CNP maintained a class of small farmers in these traditional food crops, stabilized prices, and generally kept the country self-sufficient in basic grains. Over the years the CNP became an important part of Costa Rica's social welfare system.

Critics complain that, like the subsidized bank loans, the CNP is expensive and wastes scarce public resources by underwriting "inefficient" small farmers. They argue that if these crops can be bought more cheaply on the international market, then Costa Rica should import them, and traditional food growers should look for new, more profitable crops. "There is no reason for the country to produce that which is cheaper to import. It should produce only that which creates the most profits," Central Bank president Eduardo Lizano, the country's most powerful proponent of this argument, said in 1989.[80]

One obvious problem with such facile axioms is that prices on the world market fluctuate. While in the late 1980s, U.S. basic grain prices were below production costs in Costa Rica, in 1990, droughts raised U.S. prices, making it more economical for Costa Rica to grow its own grains. However, with small and medium food farmers in Costa Rica lacking credit and squeezed off the land, the country cannot increase grain production quickly when world prices go up. Many Costa Ricans argue that, given the uncertainties of the international market and the political implications of being dependent on basic food imports, the country must maintain self-sufficiency in grain production, even if during certain years it is uneconomical to do so. The government maintains the rhetoric of food self-sufficiency, but the reality is different: in the 1987–89 growing seasons, Costa Rica imported over 57,000 tons of rice, 267,000 tons of yellow and white corn, and 8,000 tons of beans, the latter from both the United States and Nicaragua.[81]

Food dependency has been one of the consequences of the policies pushed by AID and the other international lending agencies. In negotiations with the IMF, World Bank, and AID, the Costa Rican government was compelled to cut funds to the CNP, the most important vehicle guaranteeing food self-sufficiency. The May 1984 AID agreement specifies that "the National Banking System will not provide credit to the CNP if such credit is to be used to cover losses incurred by CNP subsidies."[82] As part of the 1985 World Bank structural adjustment agreement, Costa Rica agreed to reduce the CNP deficit by (among other measures) no longer allowing it to purchase yellow corn and reducing the price paid for white corn and beans.[83] Also the 1986 PL-480 food-aid agreement with the Costa Rican government called for an end to subsidized consumer prices.[84] Between 1984 and 1987, retail prices increased 130 percent for white cornmeal, 100 percent for rice, and 164 percent for beans.[85] In 1988, under the World Bank's second structural adjustment package, the government agreed to eliminate all consumer price subsidies for beans, rice, and corn, leading to new price hikes of 40 percent. In addition, the government promised to take "all the necessary steps to permit private businesses to import beans, corn and rice in case of insufficient internal supply."[86] Between 1985 and 1988, the CNP's budget was slashed by a third. All these moves created difficulties for both consumers and local producers of basic grains and other food crops.

The number of basic grains covered by the CNP has also been cut back. In 1984 and 1986, faced with a surplus rice harvest, the CNP sold the excess on the international market at a price below what had been paid to Costa Rican growers. As a result, the CNP's losses soared, causing raised eyebrows in AID and the other international lending institutions. Pressure mounted for the Costa Rican government to remove rice from CNP protection and force producers to fend for themselves on the free market. In 1986, a Rice Office, representing producers and millers, was set up to replace some of the functions previously handled by the CNP, including importing and distributing unprocessed rice and determining the amount of acreage to be planted to meet national needs. By 1991, private entrepreneurs, not the CNP, were purchasing all rice from local producers.[87]

The impact of this privatization was swift and dramatic. In 1987 and 1988, Costa Rica had to import rice to meet internal demand,[88] as local production was concentrated in the hands of a few large mills. With the CNP cutbacks and restriction of credit to small growers, the rice mills have taken over buying and banking functions. According to Antonio Capella, president of the Chamber of Basic Grain Producers, "The most corrupt thing is that the big mills are well capitalized, so they get bank credit at 21 percent and turn around and distribute the money to small growers for about 40 percent."[89] The mills, not the CNP, also set the price and sell seeds, chemicals, and other supplies to the farmers. In just three years, the number of rice growers fell from about 2,400 to 350, dominated by two dozen big growers. A number of the small growers were forced off their land and into San José, "looking for some place to throw up a shack," says Capella. Other small growers were absorbed by five big mills, only two of which are wholly Costa Rican owned.[90]

By the early 1990s, the CNP's function had been radically reduced from a broad program to promote basic grain self-sufficiency, stability, and fair farmer and consumer prices to that of a "basic grains policeman," which warehoused basic foods, purchased unprofitable crops, and handled grain imports. As with rice, the CNP was no longer buying most corn or selling it to the public at subsidized prices. Rather, private buyers were purchasing the corn from farmers and selling it to speculators, causing consumer prices to rise steeply. The CNP's role had been reduced to purchasing unprofitable crops such as beans and mounting a publicity campaign trying to get people to eat more beans (as if that were possible). The CNP's most important function had become managing wheat imports which, as explained below, had skyrocketed, thanks to AID's "Food for Peace" program.[91]

The CNP *has* cost the government a lot financially, but the blame can hardly be placed completely on the shoulders of the small basic grain producers. In 1988 almost half the CNP deficit was attributable to wheat imports. As is argued in the following section, AID, through its PL-480 food program, has helped Costa Ricans develop a dependence on wheat, a grain it does not grow.[92] Despite its losses, the CNP should not be judged in pure economic terms. The idea behind the CNP was not to make money but to guarantee the price of staple foods and assure social stability. As one CNP official put it, "The CNP has lost a lot economically. The country has gained a lot politically. It has been one way in which a climate of tranquility and well-being has been maintained here."[93]

It became evident that the cutbacks in CNP have threatened

Costa Rica's social tranquility and economic stability when, in September 1986, over a thousand small farmers blocked Central Avenue in San José. They were protesting the government's decision to remove CNP subsidies, cut back on production of white corn and beans, and totally eliminate the production of yellow corn. Costa Rica's elite new, U.S.-trained antiriot squad attacked the demonstrators with clubs and teargas, and, predictably, the conservative local press denounced the farmers as "provoked by extremists in coordination with the Sandinistas."[94]

Flooding the Market with "Food for Peace"

Accompanying the cuts in the CNP and in credit to small farmers has been the complementary policy of increasing U.S. imports, mostly wheat, under AID's "Food for Peace" or PL-480 program. PL-480 has been the carrot, while credit and the CNP reductions have been the stick; together they have worked to undermine local food production. The PL-480 program, which supplies U.S. agricultural products to the Third World, comes in two forms: Title I, under which the United States sells surplus food overseas through long-term, low-interest loans, while the recipient government, in turn, sells the food on the local market and uses the funds for AID-approved projects; and Title II, under which U.S. agricultural surplus is donated to countries to be distributed to the needy, usually through development or charitable organizations.

Like U.S. economic and military assistance, PL-480 shipments to Central America skyrocketed in the 1980s. From 1956, when the program started, until 1979, Central American countries received a total of only $10 million worth of U.S. food assistance, but during the next decade, that figure leapt to more then $600 million.[95] PL-480 assistance to Costa Rica—wheat, yellow corn, husked rice, beans, and oil—grew from a modest $400,000 in 1980 to a peak of $28.2 million in 1983. For 1990 the amount was $15 million, but because of Costa Rican objections to the terms of the agreement it did not arrive until 1991. During the 1980s the vast majority of food assistance—over 98 percent—has come under Title I, with the dollar value of Title II reaching only $300,000 in 1986.[96]

Under PL-480 Title I, the United States provides fixed

amounts of dollar credit so that Costa Rican importers can cheaply buy U.S. agricultural surplus for resale within Costa Rica. AID pays the U.S. growers in dollars, while the local importer repays the Costa Rican government an equivalent amount in colones, which go into a PL-480 account in the Central Bank. The Costa Rican government eventually repays these loans in dollars under easy credit terms: low interest, a six-month grace period, and up to forty years repayment time. Like AID's local-currency Special Account, which is generated by the ESF funds, the PL-480 account is used for AID-approved projects, but there are several significant differences between the two accounts. While the Special Account was, for years, kept in the name of AID, the PL-480 account has always been in the name of the Minister of Planning, and, unlike the AID Special Account, no interest has ever been charged. PL-480 loan agreements are also supposed to be submitted to the Legislative Assembly for approval (while AID grants are not), although this has not been done.

AID officials contend that PL-480 has multiple benefits: it pays U.S. farmers for their agricultural surpluses, saves Costa Rica and other recipient governments foreign exchange, and generates local-currency funds for projects. However, a number of studies caution that both the intent and impact of PL-480 must be more carefully scrutinized. Viewed globally, political considerations, rather than purely humanitarian ones, are the driving force behind the selection of countries to receive PL-480 aid. During the 1980s, the five countries with the lowest average per-person caloric intake in the world—Chad, Ghana, Mozambique, Mali, and Ethiopia—were among those receiving the least amount of U.S. food aid per capita, because the Reagan and Bush administrations viewed these African countries as communist and/or of little strategic import. At the same time, Central America's strategically important "democracies"—Guatemala, El Salvador, Honduras, and Costa Rica—received massive amounts of PL-480 food aid, even though they were not among the world's most needy countries. In 1985, El Salvador received more PL-480 dry milk than the country's annual consumption capacity.

Although former Planning Minister Ottón Solís maintains that the Costa Rican government (through his ministry) had substantial control over the PL-480 local-currency account and appropriated the funds for a number of useful programs, including rural roads, land titling, and small producer projects, U.S. officials clearly saw the program as a means of influencing policy. According to a 1983 AID regional paper, PL-480 "increases, sometimes substantially, the magnitude of the total assistance package we are able to offer governments, and thus increases our ability to influence their decisions."[97] Several of Costa Rica's PL-480 projects were double-edged: they provided infrastructure in poor parts of the country but also facilitated contra activities in the border region. Some $7 million in PL-480 funds went toward the $30 million Northern Zone Development Project, a long-term, multi-dimensional program that built roads, airstrips, bridges, schools, and irrigation ditches and promoted nontraditional exports in the region closest to Nicaragua.[98] Another $3 million in colones from the PL-480 account was allotted for bridges constructed by U.S. military engineers in both the northern and southern zones. According to Planning Minister Solís, not only was subsidizing the U.S. army "reprehensible," but the bridges themselves could have been constructed by Costa Rican engineers and the materials supplied by local companies, thus giving the PL-480 funds to nationals.

The most profound and adverse effects of the PL-480 food imports have been on the small farmers and on the country's ability to be self-sufficient in food production. By U.S. law, PL-480 food aid is prohibited from harming local producers. But, in practice, PL-480 food aid has undermined basic grain farmers by injecting millions of dollars' worth of wheat and other grains into the market, directly and indirectly competing with local production. Wheat cannot be grown in Costa Rica's tropical climate, but cheap wheat imports from the United States are changing Costa Rican diets away from corn and rice and toward wheat bread, pastries, cakes, and pastas. In recent decades commercial wheat imports to Costa Rica have increased over twentyfold.[99] A 1987 U.S. Embassy report states that "Costa Ricans are now consuming more pasta than ever before." It continues, "Low income people living in rural areas have begun to substitute pasta for rice for about two meals a week," and wheat now directly competes with corn as a flour base.[100] While Costa Rica's wheat consumption predates the large PL-480 imports of the 1980s, this U.S. food aid has accelerated the trend toward the country's permanent dependency on wheat imports. In 1988, because of delays in ratifying that year's PL-480 agreement and a substantial decline in PL-480 wheat in 1987, the CNP was forced to buy wheat on the international market; these wheat imports amounted to almost half the CNP's deficit for that year.[101] This problem will become increasingly serious, because AID is cutting back on its assistance to Costa Rica during the 1990s.

The flood of PL-480 food aid during the 1980s, coupled with cutbacks in credit to small farmers and the CNP, precipitated an ongoing political debate over Costa Rica's food policy and the role of the small farmer. The so-called "comparative advantage" group argued that because Costa Rica's small grain growers are "inefficient," it is frequently more economical to receive food subsidies from PL-480 or buy food on the international market. This faction included the conservative wing of the Liberation party, much of the Unity party, neoliberal economists, big businessmen, importer-exporters, and industrialists and was backed by AID and the other international lending agencies.

   Another faction, including farmer and worker organizations, the liberal wing of the Liberation Party, and left-leaning politicians, academics, and economists, argued that the country should be self-sufficient in basic foods, even if producing locally is, at times, more expensive. They point out that international grain prices are artificially low because the United States and other developed countries give subsidies to their own farmers.[102] And they contend that it is better to keep small farmers on their own homesteads and to assist them in improving their efficiency in food crops than to force them to become squatters, peons, or assembly-line factory workers.

   This food aid versus food self-sufficiency debate came to the fore in 1987, when Agriculture Minister Alberto Esquivel clashed with Central Bank president Lizano and AID director Chaij over a proposed donation of 1,400 tons of U.S.-surplus powdered milk. Esquivel argued that such a large PL-480 food shipment "would

Table 9. Yellow Corn Imports, 1983–90
(all markets, metric tons)

Year	Commercial Imports	PL-480/other donations
1983–84	—	26,222
1984–85	—	43,348
1985–86	—	—
1986–87	11,500	10,955
1987–88	74,439	47,440
1988–89	145,247	—
1989–90	177,147	—

Source: National Production Council computer data supplied at author's request.

have broken all Costa Rica's dairies." Comparative-advantage advocate Lizano countered by criticizing Esquivel as someone who "thinks we should raise all our own food and has other such fancy ideas." Although a drought in the U.S. dairy lands forced Chaij to withdraw his offer, the controversy degenerated into personal attacks, and in April Lizano quit. AID officials, fearing their whole Costa Rican program was in jeopardy, quickly lobbied for his reinstatement. Under pressure, President Arias asked Esquivel to resign, and Lizano agreed to return to his post at the Central Bank.[103] Since then Costa Rica has, in practice, opted to become a food importer. That year the Arias administration announced plans to halt production of yellow corn, saying PL-480 and private importers, not the CNP, would handle imports to cover all consumption needs. Immediately imports of yellow corn, which is used for animal feed, skyrocketed, but most has been bought on the open market by private importers rather than supplied via PL-480.

This short-sighted decision was one of the reasons for peasant protests in September 1987. In a letter to then-President Oscar Arias, a union of campesino organizations accurately charged, "The PL-480 program is designed to subject us to food dependency and to implement what are clearly political/economic objectives. Yet it has been presented in our country as an 'assistance program.' "[104]

As the decade ended, the debate continued. Just before leaving office in May 1990, the Arias government quietly agreed to a

$15 million PL-480 loan agreement, including $9 million worth of wheat imports. In return, Costa Rica was compelled to eliminate import taxes on rice, beans, and yellow corn, thereby cutting back on both government income and protection for local food producers. However, the newly installed Legislative Assembly balked at ratifying this accord. Liberation party legislator Israel Avila charged that AID was trying to "co-govern" the country by asking that the Costa Rican government consult with AID every third month. The new Calderón government urged ratification, arguing that vital road, bridge, and water projects in the northern zone would have to be scrapped if the agreement was not approved. Then, in late August 1990, the PL-480 package was suddenly declared unconstitutional by Costa Rica's new and aggressively independent Constitutional Court, known as the *Sala Cuarta*.[105] After further negotiations between the government and the AID mission, the accord was modified by the Sala Cuarta to conform with Costa Rica's constitution, and it was approved by the Legislative Assembly. The PL-480 package finally came in 1991. In 1992, a similar situation occurred: AID approved $15 million under PL-480, but Costa Rica's legislature did not approve the terms and it was never delivered.[106]

AID's Nontraditional Exports: A House of Cards

Although AID and its local collaborators claim that the NTAE strategy has been an enormous success, both Costa Rica's small farmers and the available data suggest a much more cautious assessment. In February 1990, Costa Rica's rural population used their ballots to declare a resounding "No" to the nontraditional export strategy, and since then a new coalition of peasant organizations has vowed to step up militant demonstrations unless these policies are changed. The Calderón government, while publicly acknowledging the need for increased credit, better technical assistance, processing of agricultural exports, and more cooperatives to help the campesinos, rapidly signed new AID, PL-480, World Bank, and IMF agreements which continue the same neoliberal strategies, including expansion of free trade, NTAE promotion, and reduction of traditional supports and subsidies to small farmers.

Available data do not indicate that nontraditional exports will lead to greater stability and expanding profits for the government. In 1990, NTAEs grew by only 3 percent, after increasing between 15 percent and 30 percent during the several preceding years. In comparing the growth rates of nontraditional and traditional exports, the indications are that because nontraditionals are largely perishable luxuries whose selling prices fluctuate widely in U.S. markets, they will prove less stable than Costa Rica's traditional exports, with the possible exception of sugar.[107] In addition, although it is diversifying its products, Costa Rica is becoming more, not less, dependent on a single market—the United States—whose "window of opportunity" could be shut for a variety of reasons, including high levels of pesticides, insect damage, poor quality, overproduction, or competition with U.S. growers and manufacturers. Since Costa Rica is becoming less important strategically to the United States in the 1990s, it will have neither the economic clout or political bargaining power to push for space in the U.S. market.

While proper statistics on real earnings of the NTAEs have proved difficult to get, they are certainly well below what is claimed by AID, the Chamber of Exporters, or CINDE and CENPRO. The cost of duty-free imports and of CATs has proved a tremendous drain on the Costa Rican government and has contributed substantially to the government and trade deficits. The neoliberal theory of trickle-down is not working. Rather, profits from the new exports are being accumulated by a new class of largely foreign exporters, agro-industrialists, and manufacturers and are not being redistributed in any significant measure to either the government or the small farmer.

While privatization and free-market policies dominated in the 1980s, in previous economic crises the Costa Rican government played an active and positive role in protecting the country's middle and lower classes. For example, during the first so-called OPEC crisis of the early 1970s, the Costa Rican government, over the objections of the country's large landowners, exporters, and foreign investors, took a number of steps to cushion the impact on small farmers and the country's poor. These measures included increased land reform, minimum-wage adjustments targeted at the lowest income groups, price ceilings on basic foodstuffs, subsidies on utilities and public transportation, increased spending on health, education, and other social services aimed at the poor and middle-income groups, and export taxes to increase government revenues.[108]

During the 1980s, the Monge and Arias administrations paid lip service to small producers, but their policies clearly supported the emerging new oligarchy of investors, exporters, producers, manufacturers, and private bankers and financiers and the requirements of international lending agencies. Rather than weeding out "inefficient" farmers, the "agriculture of change" is rapidly wiping out small producers in general. A 1988 World Bank study warned that "smallholders unable to move into the new [nontraditional crop] activities might have to sell their land and become landless workers."[109] This, indeed, is what was happening. In 1984 there were 70,000 basic grain farmers. Just four years later, in 1988, only 27,000 remained.[110] And the trend continues, as small farmers sell their land to large NTAE growers, banana companies, or tourist developers. They and their families are becoming integrated into AID's new export strategy, not as independent producers but as agricultural laborers or factory workers.

The nontraditional export policy was most aggressively pushed during the Arias administration, despite the president's commitment to peace and social justice. "There was a lot of double-talk. Arias said he wanted self-sufficiency, but some of the policies, like eliminating subsidized interest rates, go against this," says Ottón Solís. Some critics, such as peasant leader Carlos Campos, believe that Arias fully endorsed this strategy, including its logical outcome of turning campesinos into factory or agro-industrial laborers. "Small farmers are being squeezed out for bigger producers, who convert farms into huge industries," Campos says. He contends that the aim of the AID/Arias agricultural policy is to change peasants into "cheap labor for industry, like in Brazil, El Salvador, or the Dominican Republic."[111] Others, including several officials who served in the Arias government but are critical of his economic strategy, argue that the Costa Rican president was forced to choose where to fight the United States—on economic or political and military policies. "Deep in my heart," former Agriculture Minister Esquivel said in an interview, "I believe that Oscar [Arias] knew the problem of agriculture much better than he seemed to. And that he just had to choose." Arias chose to oppose instead Washington's other broad policy: the war against Nicaragua and, within Costa Rica, the building of the Southern Front.

EIGHT

The Southern Front: "Honduras South"

While AID technocrats in Washington and Costa Rica were build-ing the private Parallel State, the "boys across the river" at Langley and in the Old Executive Office Building next to the White House were laying plans for "privatizing" the contra war. Privatization became the buzzword for the New Right's political, military, and economic strategists for Central America. Just as AID funds were funneled to strengthen Costa Rica's private sector, so U.S. funds were covertly channeled through private individuals and organiza-tions, as well as other countries, to bankroll the contra war against Nicaragua.

The Southern Front, like AID's Parallel State, was created largely without public debate in either Costa Rica or the United States; was implemented in a manner which circumvented public and congressional scrutiny; was dependent upon a network of collaborators, a steady flow of U.S. dollars, and an elaborate infrastructure; and served to undermine, rather than strengthen, Costa Rica's democratic traditions and political stability. But the motivation for these two privatization strategies—the Parallel State and the Southern Front—differed. Washington's economic strategy was part of a broader resurgence of neoliberalism, which openly promoted development through private enterprise; in con-trast, Washington's political and military strategy against Nicara-gua was highly unpopular, and privatization became the cover for waging the war while evading congressional scrutiny and circum-venting public opposition.

Early on, the planners of the Nicaraguan war foresaw that they would have to find a way to hide the government's hand in the unpopular war. At first, the CIA had hoped it could run the war by convincing Congress that it was carrying out only a limited operation against Nicaragua. In March 1981, just six weeks after taking office, Reagan signed a "Presidential Finding," authorizing a $19.5 million CIA operation to support Sandinista opponents inside Nicaragua and interdict arms supposedly flowing from the Sandinistas to leftist guerrillas in El Salvador.[1] The creation of the contra armies quickly got underway, with training carried out in Argentina, Honduras, and the United States. In December 1981, Reagan signed a new finding officially authorizing the CIA to organize, fund, and train this rebel force. At the same time, CIA Director William Casey assured the House and Senate Intelligence committees that the CIA was merely engaged in a small paramilitary operation in the Nicaraguan-Honduran border region. He falsely testified that no Americans were involved and that the aim was merely to hit Cuban targets inside Nicaragua and to capture arms flowing from Nicaragua to the Salvadoran guerrillas.[2] It eventually became evident, however, that this official story was a lie. In May 1983, the House Intelligence Committee issued a report asserting that the contra build-up was really aimed at overthrowing the Nicaraguan government.[3]

Overseeing the contra war was a small interagency committee known as the Core Group, made up of CIA Latin American chief Duane (Dewey) Clarridge, Assistant Secretary of State for Inter-American Thomas Enders, Nestor Sanchez from the Defense Department, General Paul Gorman of the Joint Chiefs of Staff, and, beginning in early 1983, Oliver North, who replaced Roger Fontaine, from the National Security Council (NSC). The Core Group or RIG (Restricted Interagency Group), as it was later called, reported to the National Security Planning Group, an elite committee composed of President Reagan, Vice President Bush, CIA Director Casey, Secretary of State Alexander Haig, Secretary of Defense Caspar Weinberger, NSC adviser Richard Allen, and top White House aides.[4]

With the December 1982 passage of the first Boland amendment (named after its sponsor, House Intelligence Committee chairman Edward Boland), Congress prohibited CIA or Defense Department funds from being used to topple the Nicaraguan government. A year later, Congress passed a $24 million cap on the contra operation and stipulated that when this money ran out, the CIA would have to close down its paramilitary program in Central America.

The Administration countered congressional moves to restrict contra aid by taking three actions:[5] First, it set up an Office of Public Diplomacy (OPD) for Latin America and the Caribbean, an interagency operation whose mission was to "sell" the contras and other Administration projects to the American public. The OPD was based in the State Department but overseen by the NSC and (illegally) by the CIA.[6] Second, the CIA sought to stockpile supplies for the contras. And third, the Agency arranged for President Reagan to sign a new Finding on September 19, 1983, which stated that contra aid could be used not just to interdict arms to El Salvador or to curb Cuban support for the Sandinistas, but also to pressure the Nicaraguan government to hold free elections. Administration operatives used the Finding's "essential ambiguity" to authorize paramilitary actions aimed, they argued, at forcing Managua to "democratize"—an administrative metaphor for overthrowing the Sandinistas.[7]

Within the Reagan administration, operational command of the Nicaraguan war as well as the diversion of funds to the contras shifted from the CIA to a "shadow CIA" within the National Security Council (NSC). Day-to-day operations were handled by a three-person RIG (Restricted Interagency Group, sometimes referred to as the Riglet or mini-RIG) made up of Oliver North, CIA Central American Task Force director Alan Fiers ("Cliff Grubbs" or "Albert Fenton"), and Assistant Secretary of State for Interamerican Affairs Thomas Enders and then after mid-1985 Elliott Abrams. According to his boss Admiral Poindexter, North became the "switching point that made the whole system work" and "the kingpin to the Central American opposition,"[8] thereby allowing other officials to argue they were "out of the loop." But in practice, as journalistic and governmental investigations later revealed, a broad, interagency network of high- and middle-level administration officials continued to be consulted and to play a role in the surrogate supply network that North dubbed "Project Democracy."

By December 1984, when Congress passed the second Boland amendment, banning "direct and indirect" support for the contras

from any U.S. "intelligence agency,"[9] the Reagan administration's
plan to "privatize" the war was already in place, and the war
continued without missing a beat. This privatization cover went one
step beyond the concept of "Vietnamization," the strategy adopted
late in the Vietnam war of sending mainly pro-U.S. Southeast Asian
troops rather than American GIs into combat. In Nicaragua, not only
were no North American boys supposed to die on the battlefield, but
no American taxpayers' dollars were supposed to finance the battle.

Beginning in late 1983, administration officials set up a financial pipeline with friendly foreign countries and American right-
wing "humanitarian" and paramilitary groups to assure that, as
Oliver North testified, the contras were kept together "body and
soul." Over a three-year period from 1983 to 1986 CIA director
William Casey organized what later became known as a "vest
pocket" operation outside normal channels to funnel millions of
dollars and thousands of tons of war materiel to the contras.
Administration officials tapped a number of allies, including Israel,
South Africa, Brunei, Taiwan, Chile, Guatemala, Panama, and El
Salvador to provide funds, weapons, advisers, and logistical support
for the contras. In financial terms none was more important than the
oil-rich kingdom of Saudi Arabia, which helped to underwrite
Washington's covert foreign adventures in Afghanistan, Angola, and
Nicaragua. By mid-1984, Saudi Arabia was depositing a million
dollars a month for the contras into secret bank accounts in Switzerland and the Cayman Islands. After a meeting with President Reagan
in early 1985, Saudi Arabia's King Fahd agreed to double the
amount. By 1986, the Saudis had contributed more than $30 million
to the contra cause. In return the Reagan administration sold the
Arab state $8.5 million worth of AWAC radar reconnaissance
planes—a controversial transaction brokered by Air Force Major
General Richard Secord, a covert operations specialist who was
deputy assistant secretary of defense for the Near East, Africa, and
South Asia.

Secord, who left the military in 1983 under a cloud of
financial scandal, quickly resurfaced as one of several key "retired"
intelligence officials and military officers providing "private aid"
cover for the contra operation. Other retirees included Lieut. Col.
Richard Gadd, Col. Robert Dutton, Gen. John Singlaub, and

ex-CIA officer Thomas Clines. These men, along with Iranian-born arms dealer Albert Hakim, became the principals behind a maze of international front companies and secret bank accounts used to channel money and arms, illegally and secretly, to the contras, contra-related projects, and a variety of other covert schemes. These offshore bank accounts and shell companies constituted what Secord termed "the Enterprise," "an off-the-shelf, stand-alone, self-sustaining entity" that operated without congressional appropriations or authorization. The Enterprise was the covert business structure for North's Project Democracy.[10]

While CIA operations were ostensibly subject to congressional oversight, the Enterprise was not. But, as the Iran-contra congressional panel concluded, "Its income-generating capacity came almost entirely from its access to U.S. government resources and connections." Just as Costa Rica's Parallel State institutions were financed and assisted by AID, so too did the North/Secord Enterprise—while hidden from Congress and the American public—have indispensable support from the White House, NSC, CIA, and other government agencies, and its operatives understood that their actions were sanctioned by the president. The Enterprise's profits—what Secord and North euphemistically called its "residuals"—were, its directors contended, strictly private. The U.S. congressional report concluded that, without risking any of their own money, the Enterprise's directors made "extraordinary profits," and its revenues exceeded expenses by $12.2 million.

As Albert Hakim testified during the 1987 congressional Iran-contra hearings, "whoever designed this structure, had a situation that they could have their cake and eat it too. Whichever [sic] they wanted to have: a private organization, it was private; when they didn't want it to be a private organization, it wasn't."[11] Again and again, those involved tried to have it both ways. When caught, the "private" persons invariably protested that they had been led to believe the operation was "sanctioned by the White House," while government officials claimed they were simply assisting private citizens.

The Iran-contra testimony of Lewis Tambs, U.S. ambassador to Costa Rica from mid-1985 to early 1987, is a classic illustration of this sort of official doublespeak. He told the congressional panel that the 1984 Boland amendment (which he admitted he had never read) "forbade use of appropriated US Government funds to aid the freedom fighters, and any aid in opening a Southern Front would come from what we casually called 'private, patriotic Americans.' And obviously, neither I nor anyone in that mission, as far as I was concerned, was going to violate the law. But if private individuals were going to aid the freedom fighters, that certainly was their business." Asked if he was instructed by North to "open a southern military front along the Costa Rican/Nicaraguan border, Tambs replied, "It is correct in the sense that I aided the private, patriotic Americans."[12]

The history of the Southern Front and the privatization of the contra war out of Costa Rica went through several stages and faced particular circumstances that ultimately gave it a different trajectory from the Northern Front in Honduras. At first Reagan ideologues and war strategists had hoped to turn Costa Rica into "Honduras South." The game plan was to mold Costa Rica's Civil and Rural guards into a standing army, to station U.S. military forces in the country, and to create in Costa Rica one large conventional contra army aligned with the Nicaraguan Democratic Force (FDN), the main contra force operating out of Honduras. But U.S. cajoling and arm-twisting was never wholly successful in Costa Rica. War strategists in Washington were constrained by their own cover story: Southern Front contras could not be said to be involved in arms interdiction between Nicaragua and El Salvador, since both were *north* of Costa Rica. They were also constrained by Costa Rica's policy of neutrality, its constitutional ban on recreating an army, and its prohibition against hosting foreign troops, all of which made militarization more difficult than in Honduras.

Further, Washington faced problems with the contra leadership in Costa Rica, which was less willing to subject itself to CIA control than were the remnants of former Nicaraguan dictator Anastasio Somoza's repressive National Guard, which made up the FDN leadership in Honduras. The Southern Front contra leaders were mainly former Sandinistas who, while anticommunist, were also anti-Somoza, nationalistic, and, at least rhetorically, anti-imperialist. They believed, wrongly, that they could take CIA funds but run their own war.

On top of this, Washington had to be even more secretive in building the Southern Front than it did in building the Parallel State. While Costa Rican officials and businessmen could publicly endorse AID's free-market economic prescriptions, none dared argue openly in favor of creating the contras' Southern Front or its adjuncts, a Costa Rican army and U.S. military bases. The right wing, including even the extremist Free Costa Rica Movement (MCRL), which was aligned internationally to the World Anti-Communist League or WACL,[13] was therefore confined to publicly railing against "communist oppression" in Nicaragua and "infiltration" into Costa Rica, and to demanding political tolerance for anti-Sandinista exiles and organizations while covertly assisting contra military operations.

For a combination of reasons, therefore, the Southern Front never became the mirror image of the Northern Front. By the second half of Monge's administration, U.S. strategists had dropped the idea of building "Honduras South," complete with a large conventional contra army and a U.S. military presence in Costa Rica. Instead, they decided to capitalize on Costa Rica's nonmilitarism by hyping each Sandinista attack against rebel forces in the border region or against contra leaders in San José into a fevered pitch and by building an image of unarmed, democratic Costa Rica about to fall to Sandinista-style communism. But U.S. operatives running the contra war went a step further: they decided to carry out their own terrorist attacks, border clashes, and internal sabotage and blame these incidents on the Sandinistas. They adopted a strategy of what can be termed "unconventional warfare," which was intended to turn U.S. public and congressional opinion against Managua and provide the rationale for escalating the war. In pursuing this strategy, the CIA and "private aid" operatives set out to dismantle the existing contra armies in Costa Rica headed by Edén Pastora and Brooklyn Rivera and create instead a small clandestine network working under the direction of John Hull, Cuban American Felipe Vidal, and other CIA operatives. They partially financed their activities through drug trafficking (see chapter 11). The two fronts—Honduras with the large, conventional contra army and sizable U.S. military presence, and Costa Rica with a clandestine "dirty tricks" network—became like opposite sides of the same coin, rather than mirror images of one another.

The Southern Front's contra activities were built upon a multifaceted infrastructure, and the net effect was to move Costa Rica politically to the right. Through military aid and training, gifts, covert payments, and propaganda, the United States helped to remold Costa Rica from a country that had actively supported the Sandinistas' protracted war against Somoza and enthusiastically celebrated the fall of the dictatorship, into one that was strongly anti-Sandinista. A particular target was Costa Rica's traditionally conservative mass media, which became a strident proponent of the U.S. war against Nicaragua. Journalists were enticed with trips and scholarships to the United States and, in the case of a dozen or more, with monthly CIA stipends to supplement their meager Costa Rican salaries. By 1983 former Security Minister Juan José Echevarría was warning, "There is an anti-communist hysteria in this country, which has been developed, maintained and stimulated by the press and also by the conservative wings of both traditional parties."[14] In addition, Costa Rica became a regional center for anti-Sandinista propaganda, home of a powerful Voice of America (VOA) transmitter, several clandestine CIA and contra radio stations, and *Nicaragua Hoy,* the contras' weekly newspaper supplement syndicated throughout Latin America.

U.S. funds and personnel were used as well to set up an array of right-wing Costa Rican civic, political, and paramilitary organizations. Some of the most active included the Costa Rican Democratic Association (ADC), which ran a popular, pro-contra music station, Radio Impacto; the North Huétar Democratic Association, a paramilitary group made up mainly of northern zone ranchers and linked to the Free Costa Rica Movement and the contras; *Libro Libre* (Free Book), an anticommunist publishing house; Pro-Democracy Association (APRODEM), a civic group that held round tables and placed newspaper ads opposing the Arias peace plan and denouncing the Sandinistas; and the Organization for National Emergencies (OPEN), later known as the National Reserve, a large, anticommunist paramilitary organization trained and armed by the Civil Guard to defend Costa Rica against terrorism, subversion, and outside attack. Costa Rica also became headquarters for dozens of Nicaraguan exile groups—human rights, labor, women, business, students, journalists—many of which received covert American financing. Middle- and upper-class Nicaraguan exiles found that San José, with its pleasant climate, relatively high standard of living, social-welfare benefits, and human-rights tradition, offered both political space and economic possibilities. They set up political offices in rented houses scattered throughout San José's suburbs and clandestinely housed their light aircraft "air force" at the Tomás Bolaños international airport on the west edge of the city.

During the 1980s, Costa Rica began to receive U.S. military aid, using it to "professionalize" and "modernize" (and greatly expand) its Civil and Rural guards, police, security forces, intelligence services, narcotics squads, and volunteer reserve force, all under the guise of protecting the country from Nicaraguan aggression and internal leftist destabilization. Behind the pretext of preparing for a Sandinista invasion, large landowners organized and trained armed vigilante squads which battled land squatters and hunted for leftists. The United States also greatly expanded its CIA operations in Costa Rica and sent Green Berets to train Civil Guardsmen at the Murciélago camp just a few kilometers from the Nicaraguan border. In the dry, flat cattle country of Guanacaste province, the scores of private landing strips and large fenced-off farms were ideal for covert operations. Beginning in 1982, the CIA clandestinely built or improved several dozen contra landing strips, including the two-kilometer-long Santa Elena runway which received arms and, on occasion, shipped out cocaine.

On the other side of the country, the steamy Caribbean port town of Limón became the unofficial capital for black and Miskito Indian contras and refugees. About a thousand Nicaraguans were housed in the refugee camp on the edge of town, and at least that number had settled in the area, making a living from the contra war or petty businesses. Through Limón harbor moved crates of arms and supplies for the contras, much of it concealed as agricultural equipment consigned to a contra front company, Ladivia, S.A. A network of contras, mainly Miskito Indians, and CIA operatives like boat pilot Eugene Strickland, moved these war supplies by helicopter, road, and sea up to the contra camps. Using CIA-supplied fiberglass boats with powerful outboard engines, contra captains traversed the tranquil canals running up the coast from Limón to Tortugüero and Barra del Colorado. Once they reached the Nicaraguan border, they were forced to go far out into the often-rough Caribbean ocean to avoid Sandinista patrol boats.

These fiberglass boats, CIA-supplied Zodiacs, and local fishing craft were also used to unload military supplies from large CIA "mother ships" which would anchor about ten miles out at sea. In an interview at the time, one contra official described how, on March 2, 1984, an unidentified ship anchored near the mouth of the rebel-controlled San Juan River and unloaded sixty thousand pounds of arms, including 1,200 M-14 rifles, into small fishing boats. "It was a very professional operation," the contra explained. "No one even spoke so we did not know if there were North Americans aboard the supply vessel."

Ciudad Quesada, a sun-baked farm town of fifty thousand in northern Costa Rica, was the home of John Hull and the main staging area for the war as well. In the 1970s, the town experienced an economic boom from the growing cattle business; in the 1980s, it seemed nearly everyone carved out a niche in the contra supply chain. There was a wild-west atmosphere, as merchants and farmers hustled to sell food and supplies to the contras; truckers hauled sacks of rice and beans, woven baskets filled with fruits and vegetables, and crates of soda and beer to the border; wounded contras arrived at the government hospital and clandestine contra clinics; and the contra leadership gathered in local restaurants and hotels. In the shady town square, with its adobe gazebo, young Nicaraguans wearing combat boots hung out, flirting with the local girls and making calls from the pay phone.

Costa Rica as a whole, but most intensely its northern region, was affected by the war effort, which brought in its wake an influx of thirty-five thousand refugees, arms and drug trafficking, black marketeering, war profiteering, political killings, and increasing crime and hooliganism. Historically poor, the northern zone is inhabited mostly by Nicaraguans who over the decades fled the oppression and turmoil in their homeland. Young men from dirt-poor farming families in Costa Rica were recruited to fight with the contras; their parents were promised two thousand colones a month. The war spilled over into the border outposts of Upala and Los Chiles, where anti-Sandinista fighters, frequently drunk and brandishing weapons, occasionally robbed local stores, raped women, and shot farmers. Schools shut down, frontier dwellers abandoned their farms, and several mysterious assassinations and fire bombings along the border were blamed on rival pro- and anti-contra factions.

Arias government officials say that when they took office in May 1986, they were horrified to discover how far covert U.S. and contra activities had penetrated Costa Rica. Arias confidant John Biehl bluntly accused U.S. officials of using what he labeled the "tip of the penis" argument to get further and further into Costa Rica. "They had told Monge just a little more an airstrip, a few military trainers, some contra medical facilities, an intelligence center, etc., etc. By the time Oscar [Arias] took over, Reagan's war against Nicaragua was operating deep inside Costa Rica."

The day Arias took office, he called Ambassador Tambs and ordered that the largest of the contra runways, Santa Elena airstrip, be closed. Over the next four years the Arias government worked to end the Nicaraguan war through his Central American Peace Plan, a crackdown on contra operations at home, and Costa Rican judicial and legislative investigations of drug trafficking, the La Penca bombing, and CIA operative John Hull. A staunch anticommunist and anti-Sandinista, Arias was motivated not by a desire to salvage the Sandinista government, but by a determination to save what he considered Costa Rica's unique way of life—its traditions of unarmed neutrality and political stability, its relatively high standard of living, and its concern for social justice. In an interview at the time of his inauguration, Arias declared, "If the war continues I fear we in Costa Rica will be forced to build an army, not to fight the Sandinistas, but to defend ourselves against the foreign standing army—the contras—based in our territory."

Four years later, when Arias left office, the contra war was essentially over, the Sandinistas had been voted out, and the Southern Front had been largely disassembled. Arias accomplished his main objective, ending the U.S.-contra war, and for this he has gone down as the most popular president in recent Costa

Rican history. But the Southern Front, although dismantled as a military force, has left a profound mark on Costa Rican society.

Edén Pastora, ARDE, and the CIA

Edén Pastora was the man originally chosen by the CIA to be the military commander of the Southern Front. Almost from the outset, it was a rocky marriage of convenience, in which both sides needed but did not respect one another. Born in Nicaragua in 1937 into a poor Matagalpa province farming family, Pastora was the youngest of five children. When he was seven his father was murdered on orders of a general in Somoza's National Guard who wanted their family farm. This left Pastora with a lifelong hatred of Somocistas and with a stubborn refusal, later on, to align himself with the CIA's reincarnation of the National Guard, the FDN.

Pastora's upbringing was conservative, Catholic, and pro-American. He says it was not until he went to study in a prestigious Jesuit boarding school in Grenada that he "discovered the true history" of General Augusto Sandino, who waged a guerrilla war against the U.S. military occupation of Nicaragua in the 1920s and 1930s. In the future, Pastora would consider himself, not the Sandinistas, to be the true ideological descendant of Sandino.[15]

After completing three years of medical school in Guadalajara, Mexico, Pastora returned home to join the growing armed struggle against the Somoza dictatorship. In 1959, he helped organize the Sandino Revolutionary Front (FRS), a precursor of the Sandinista National Liberation Front (FSLN), which was founded in 1961. (In the 1980s, he also named his anti-Sandinista movement out of Costa Rica the FRS.) He quit the struggle in 1973 because, he says, of opposing ideological interpretations between his nationalist *sandinismo* and the international Marxist-Leninist line taken by other Nicaraguan revolutionaries who were part of the FSLN.

Pastora took up what became his fallback profession whenever he dropped out of the political struggle: fishing. For the next few years he managed a modest commercial fishing operation at Barra del Colorado, a run-down, rain-soaked northern Costa Rican coastal hamlet near where the San Juan River empties into the Caribbean. In 1976, Sergio Ramírez and Carlos Coronel, two representatives of the FSLN's directorate, trekked to Pastora's riverside encampment to propose that he rejoin the Sandinista Front as part of the *tercerista* or "third way" faction, which was considered the most moderate of the political tendencies within the Front. They explained that *terceristas* advocated overthrowing Somoza through a general insurrection of many sectors and all classes of the population. Its leaders included Daniel and Humberto Ortega, who were in exile in Costa Rica.[16]

Pastora liked the *tercerista* line and was persuaded to return home. He again became a guerrilla leader, fighting throughout much of Nicaragua and eventually taking command of the Sandinista's southern flank, based in Costa Rica. The high point of Pastora's military career and a turning point in the war against Somoza came in August 1978, when Pastora captured world headlines and the hearts of Nicaraguans with his takeover of Somoza's National Palace in downtown Managua. This was the war's boldest and most dramatic episode. Pastora, known as *Comandante Cero* (Commander Zero), and two others led twenty-five guerrillas dressed in National Guard uniforms into the palace in broad daylight. Moving from room to room, they quickly rounded up an estimated one thousand five hundred government officials, including the entire Congress.

Over a tense two days, Nicaragua's Archbishop Miguel Obando y Bravo worked to strike a deal. In the end, the guerrillas' demands were largely met: Somoza's newspaper published a lengthy Sandinista communiqué and a half million dollars in cash were handed over (Pastora had demanded $10 million), together with about fifty political prisoners, including FSLN co-founder Tomás Borge. In return for release of the palace hostages, Somoza guaranteed safe passage out of Nicaragua for Pastora, his comrades, the cash, and the most important of the freed prisoners. Thousands of Managua residents, chanting "Viva el Comandante Cero," lined the boulevard to the airport. The revolutionary entourage boarded the planes and flew to Panama City. The image of Pastora brandishing his rifle became etched into Nicaragua's revolutionary folklore. Pastora's charisma, dramatic gestures, colorful language, loud voice, and hearty laugh commanded center stage and won him popular appeal. As author Christopher Dickey puts it, Pastora's bravado in capturing the National Palace made him the star of the Sandinista revolution. He never, however, succeeded in becoming its leader.[17]

In Panama, Pastora was welcomed by the country's populist leader, General Omar Torrijos. Himself a moderate nationalist, Torrijos took an instant liking to Pastora and offered him the services of two of his best aides: Colonel Manuel Noriega, a short, ugly man with a badly pock-marked face who was head of the G-2 intelligence branch, and Deputy Health Minister Hugo Spadafora, a handsome, green-eyed medical doctor and political adventurer. Noriega supplied Pastora with arms and ammunition for five hundred men, which he siphoned off from Panama's military arsenal. Spadafora, who had participated with Amilcar Cabral in Guinea Bissau's anticolonial struggle in West Africa, had raised an international brigade of three hundred volunteers to fight with Pastora on the Southern Front against Somoza.[18]

Less than a year later, in July 1979, the Sandinistas' third attempt at a national uprising succeeded in bringing down General Somoza and the National Guard. For months beforehand, Pastora and his troops had been bogged down in heavy fighting, taking the war's highest casualties on the Southern Front. Fearing that the more radical Sandinista factions would seize power and exclude him, Pastora appealed to Costa Rica's Vice Minister of Security, Enrique Montealegre, and CIA agent Max Singer to force Somoza to withdraw his troops from the south, so that Pastora could reach Managua. Singer promised an answer, but Pastora heard nothing. On July 19, 1979, when the Sandinistas marched triumphantly into Managua, Pastora and his troops were still trapped in southern Nicaragua.[19]

When Pastora finally arrived, it was clear that the other Sandinista leaders didn't quite know what to do with him. He was named Vice Minister of Security under Tomás Borge and then Vice Minister of Defense under Humberto Ortega. And, in early 1981, he was dispatched to command troops fighting against the newly formed contra army, which was making raids in northern Nicaragua from base camps in Honduras. He was not made part of the inner circle of power, the nine-member National Directorate, although his right-wing enemies would later accuse him of being "the tenth comandante."

Despite his mass popularity, Pastora began to feel personally short-changed and marginalized by the other revolutionary leaders. And life in Managua presented Comandante Cero with other problems: bureaucratic structures and office buildings made him feel confined and claustrophobic. By nature impulsive and undisciplined, he was never comfortable pushing papers, and he has an almost infantile inability to manage finances or deal with day-to-day problems. He is at heart an anarchist, more at home in the mountains, on the river, or in exile, fighting with weapons and diatribes against whatever government happens to be in Managua. Pastora also became troubled by the Sandinistas' increasingly close ties to the Soviet bloc and Cuba and by what he called the development in Managua of a "new, high-living class of Marxist bureaucrats." Years later, he recounted, "When I was in the government I knew the sweet honey of power. I lived in a mansion which I got from a general of Somoza. My freezers were full of food. I had three new Mercedes Benzes. There were gardeners taking care of my mansion. The whole world smiled at me. But we were not carrying out the promises that we had made to the people."[20]

For these reasons, Pastora says, in mid-1981, just two years after the Sandinistas' triumph, he broke with his former comrades, drove into self-imposed exile, and again became a guerrilla leader. Pastora left Managua in secret late one afternoon in July 1981, heading a small caravan of the three Mercedes Benzes and one Fiat out of Managua, through Costa Rica, and down the Pan American highway into Panama, there to seek help from his old friends General Omar Torrijos and Hugo Spadafora. Pastora says that Torrijos, along with another moderate nationalist leader, Venezuelan President Carlos Andrés Pérez, had urged him to break with Managua. Although Pastora is reticent to admit it, the CIA may have played a role in his decision as well. In early 1981, while still a government official, Pastora had received a message from the CIA, sent via an old contact, Enrique Montealegre, who was by then Costa Rica's ambassador to Nicaragua.[21]

At first Pastora did not split completely with the Sandinista directorate. Instead, he said he left, in the style of guerrilla leader Che Guevara, to work for revolution elsewhere, specifically to aid the Guatemalan guerrilla movement ORPA (Revolutionary Organization of the People in Arms), a largely Indian guerrilla group with a similar nonaligned political philosophy. However, in a private letter to his old boss, Defense Minister Humberto Ortega, Pastora spelled out his real intention: to force the Sandinistas to appoint more moderates to the directorate and give his former Southern Front fighters more prominent positions in the FSLN. Later Pastora grimaced when called a contra, arguing instead he was a "true Sandinista" who stood for democratic, nonaligned socialism and respect for human rights.[22]

On arriving in Panama, he held secret talks with two long-time friends and former Southern Front fighters, Leonel "Comanche" Póveda and Carlos Coronel. Both still held positions in the Nicaraguan government, Póveda as Vice Minister of Internal Commerce and Coronel as Minister of Fisheries, and according to associates, both had connections with the CIA. Coronel stayed in exile with Pastora, while Póveda, a U.S.-army-trained artillery specialist, went back to Managua and organized a spray-painting campaign proclaiming Comandante Cero would return.[23]

Many view Coronel as the brains behind Pastora and the main architect of the tercerista line. From a respected Nicaraguan family, he is the son of a celebrated poet. His mother and brothers continued as Sandinista officials even after Carlos joined the contras. A lover of political strategy and intrigue, Coronel acted as Pastora's main go-between to Cuba and was widely said to be dealing simultaneously with the KGB, CIA, the Sandinistas, and Castro. He was brilliant, secretive, and highly complex, where Pastora was blunt, aggressive, and direct. As one colleague put it, "Carlos was playing chess. Pastora played only checkers."

A few weeks after Pastora arrived in Panama, he found himself not only broke but also without his main mentor. On July 30, 1981, Torrijos was killed when his private plane crashed in northern Panama. Pastora was supposed to have gone on the flight, but missed it because he had spent the night with a mistress. His first reaction was that a bomb must have been planted by the Sandinistas—and intended for him.[24] While the cause of the crash remains a mystery, no one but Pastora ever blamed Managua.

Shortly after Torrijos's death, Pastora flew to Libya, via Cuba, seeking a new source of financial support. In Tripoli, Pastora met with Colonel Muammar Qadhafi and convinced him to contribute $3 million (some say $5 million) to ORPA. The money was transferred directly to the Libyan embassy in Managua, and from there to a Nicaraguan government bank account. Pastora returned to Havana, where, to his surprise, he was held under virtual house arrest while Fidel Castro attempted to convince him to reconcile his differences with the Sandinistas and return to Nicaragua. Pastora refused. Finally, in late August 1981, Martín Torrijos, the dead General's son, who had fought with Pastora in the war against Somoza, came to his rescue. The Cubans agreed to release Pastora.[25]

Working again out of Panama as well as Costa Rica, Pastora tried to collect Qadhafi's millions for his ORPA campaign, without success[26] So, once again, he went to see his old go-between, Enrique Montealegre, who facilitated new contacts with the CIA. Pastora says he authorized two of his top aides, Carlos Coronel and Sebastián González ("Wachán"), a veterinarian and business-man who was briefly the Sandinistas' Vice Minister of Agriculture, to develop "contacts with members of the CIA." Like Coronel, Wachán maintained complex and shifting alliances—with the CIA, the Israelis, Panama's General Manuel Noriega, and later Noriega's opponents.

The Agency arranged for Pastora to go to California to buy arms for ORPA. On September 10, 1981, Pastora, along with Jorge Molina and Raúl Arana, two Nicaraguans who worked for the CIA and the FDN, arrived at a Lake Cahuilla police firing range near the Cabazon Indian reservation outside San Diego. There the trio found a group of Saudi Arabian government officials and an odd assortment of local politicians and policemen, Christian mission-aries, real estate developers, Indian "consultants," arms manufac-turers, gun-runners, and dope dealers—many with organized crime and CIA connections. They were shown a demonstration of military hardware, including night-vision equipment. The display was part of a joint scheme by Wackenhut International, a Florida-based security firm headed by former CIA, NSC, Defense Depart-ment, and FBI officials, and Cabazón reservation entrepreneurs to manufacture and sell weapons on the Indian lands.[27] Using CIA funds, Pastora purchased some one hundred rifles, which he sent via truck to ORPA in Guatemala.[28]

In February 1982, Pastora met face-to-face for the first time with the chief of the CIA's Latin American division, Duane "Dewey" Clarridge. Code-named "Moroni," Clarridge was a large, rough-edged, heavy-drinking, cigar-smoking CIA veteran who had only rudimentary knowledge of both Spanish and military tactics and no previous experience in Central America. Clarridge set out to impress Pastora and his aides, Coronel and Wachán, inviting them to meet at a luxury resort hotel in Acapulco, Mexico. The CIA executive brought along two other agents, one of them the CIA station chief in Costa Rica, who went by the name "John Hull." Soon after, Pastora met the other John Hull, the elderly Indiana farmer who was running contra operations off his farms in northern Costa Rica. To his astonishment, Pastora learned that "the CIA was working with two John Hulls"[29] (see chapter 9).

Pastora tried to sell Clarridge on his "revolutionary concern"—backing the non-Communist ORPA guerrillas in Guatemala—but Clarridge wanted to open the contras' Southern Front, using the old network developed in the war against Somoza. Pastora agreed, contingent, he says, on the CIA's accepting his ground rules: that Pastora's organization, the Sandino Revolutionary Front (FRS), would adhere to the tercerista political line; that there would be no alliance with the FDN; that Pastora, not the CIA, would run the operation; and that, initially, Pastora would carry out only political protests while clandestinely training his military front in Costa Rica. Clarridge accepted these conditions, and promised adequate military and financial support. A deal was struck.

Pastora and Clarridge also agreed on another point: that the CIA's role in Southern Front military operations had to be kept secret. The Agency was treading on thin ice, because the White House had not officially authorized a Southern Front. Costa Rica was geographically not on the supposed arms route from the Sandinistas to the Salvadoran rebels. The CIA-contra operation was also illegal under Costa Rican law, which prohibited any foreign army, either regular or guerrilla, from being based within the country. There was further the issue of maintaining Pastora's credibility, which rested on his image as a nationalistic, non-aligned leader. Therefore, all parties involved—Pastora and his aides, the Reagan administration, and the Costa Rican officials—worked to maintain several fictions: that Pastora's operations in Costa Rica were purely political, that all Southern Front military operations were within Nicaragua, and that Pastora's movement was financed by sympathetic, moderate governments and organizations, not by the CIA.

At the beginning, Clarridge sought to ingratiate himself with Pastora. He gave him a phony Brazilian passport in the name of Wanderley P. Dos Santos. In the passport photo, Pastora is wearing CIA-supplied false teeth to broaden his jaw. Pastora used the document to travel to Europe and twice to Washington, where Clarridge arranged two "photo opportunities" with CIA director William Casey. (Pastora says Casey fell asleep at both meetings.) But Clarridge's enthusiastic support for Pastora soon began to sour, and his strategy changed. Pastora recalls that "the pressure from the CIA started for us to go into armed combat" and quickly open a military front out of Costa Rica.

By early 1984, when the armed conflict was at its peak, Pastora found he was still under intense pressure from Clarridge and others in the CIA. They wanted him to develop a conventional military chain of command and align the Southern Front under the control of the Honduran-based FDN. In fact, the CIA wanted it both ways: they wanted the contras to be a guerrilla force capable of penetrating deep into Nicaragua, living off the land, winning hearts and minds, and so on; but they never trusted the military capabilities or politics of the Southern Front contras, and so they wanted Agency operatives to maintain tight control over all aspects of the operations. In the end, concerns over control became paramount to the CIA, and Pastora came to view Clarridge as one of the key architects of the campaign to destroy him.[30]

At the same time Clarridge was cutting his deal with Pastora, the CIA hedged its bets by creating a small, parallel FDN army in Costa Rica. Even earlier, in December 1980, the FDN's predecessor, known as the "15th of September Legion," carried out the first contra attack of the war by hitting a leftist Argentine-run radio station in Costa Rica. The FDN was officially founded in Guatemala in August 1981, and the bulk of its troops and Argentine military trainers moved to Honduras. Small groups of those trained in Argentina, the United States, and Guatemala were sent into Costa Rica, as well as to Panama and El Salvador. By early 1982, FDN-aligned groups were establishing political offices in San José and clandestine training camps and supply bases on farms in the Guanacaste area, while FDN teams were launching cross-border attacks from Costa Rica. Between February and April 1982, months of transition from the Carazo to the Monge administrations when the central government was barely functioning, the FDN consolidated its logistical network, strengthening ties with Costa Rican security and right-wing groups such as the Free Costa Rica Movement. By June 1982, Costa Rican security estimated there were three hundred FDN contras training on eight farms in the northern zone.

From the outset, this FDN force was involved in sabotage and bombings, with targets that included Managua-bound airliners, Nicaraguan trucks passing through Costa Rica, and a Costa Rican–based leftist radio station. By mid-1983, the FDN on the Southern Front was brought under the control of CIA agents John Hull, Felipe Vidal, and other Cuban-American operatives, and Oliver North's network. It became the centerpiece of the "dirty tricks" unit and was also involved in drug trafficking. Ultimately, this FDN operation replaced Pastora's "conventional" army as the main force on the Southern Front.

On April 15, 1982, Pastora ended his public silence at a press conference outside San José. Standing in front of an FRS banner, he was flanked by his closest aides: Hugo Spadafora, Leonel Póveda, Carlos Coronel together with his brother-in-law Ian Kinnock, Sebastián González ("Wachán"), Harold Martínez (Comandante Ramón), and Carol Prado, an engineer who quickly became Pastora's closest aide.[31] Pastora declared he was giving the Sandinistas one year to return to what he called their original ideals of democracy, nonalignment, economic pluralism, and respect for civil liberties. He did not call for armed struggle against the Sandinistas, in part because to do so in neutral Costa Rica would have prompted his expulsion. He hoped, however, to provoke an uprising among middle and upper levels of the Sandinista army, many of whom had earlier fought with Pastora on the anti-Somoza Southern Front.

Instead, only seventeen Sandinista border guards crossed into Costa Rica to seek political asylum. Pastora went to Barra del Colorado to meet them and made the mistake of giving the deserters a smart military salute. The little ceremony was recorded by Costa Rican television and embarrassed the Monge government, which had taken office just two weeks earlier. It immediately announced Pastora was expelled from Costa Rica, because the salute indicated he must be involved in military as well as political activities.

After his expulsion, the CIA sent Pastora first to Europe, where he solicited political and financial support from Social Democrats and the Socialist International, and then to Tegucigalpa to discuss uniting the disparate anti-Sandinista movements in Honduras and Costa Rica. Pastora laid out his position to Honduras's military strongman, General Gustavo Alvarez Martínez and to Donald Winters, the tall, blond CIA station chief. Pastora said he wanted all the former Somocista guards out of the FDN army before he would sign a unity agreement. Alvarez and Winters demanded unity, with no changes in the FDN's make-up. The meeting quickly turned raucous, with Alvarez shouting that Pastora was a "communist son of a bitch" and Pastora retorting that the Honduran military chief was a "fascist son of a bitch." Winters intervened, and hastily arranged for a private plane to fly Pastora secretly back into Costa Rica. But the conflict was not resolved. The Somocistas in the FDN, the CIA, and General Alvarez became increasingly convinced that Pastora had to be replaced.

Up in Washington, some of those in the know were becoming uneasy about the CIA's unauthorized funding of the Southern Front. Donald Gregg, the man in charge of covert action projects for the National Security Council, drafted a new Finding that dropped the phony cover story of arms interdiction and authorized the training, arming, and financing of Pastora's forces with several "rationales": launching attacks against Cuban advisers working in Nicaragua, provoking an uprising within the Sandinista military, and rallying anti-Sandinista support among key European and Latin American governments. A memo from Gregg to National Security Adviser William Clark stated that "the urgency in dealing with the Finding derives from the fact that the opposition group under Edén Pastora has been developing quickly." This Finding was never signed by President Reagan, a ploy that meant that Congress continued to be deceived about the contra war. But the finding's "rationales" became the publicly articulated intentions of the Southern Front.[32] Still left unstated was the contras' real objective: overthrowing the Sandinistas.

Just as the Southern Front appeared to be taking off, Pastora announced that he was quitting, the first of several times he did so. Pastora had become incensed when a group of former National Guardsmen with the FDN attacked San Francisco del Norte (a small village in northern Nicaragua), executed a group of captured prisoners, and wrote "Viva Cero" on the walls, implying they were with his FRS. To disassociate himself from these atrocities, Pastora took out paid ads in the Costa Rica press, announcing he was dissolving the FRS and blaming ex-Somocista Guardsmen for the murders. Once again Pastora had tipped his hand publicly that he was in Costa Rica, and several weeks later President Monge again demanded that he leave.

In late August 1982, Pastora, having had second thoughts about his resignation, traveled to the Dominican Republic, where he met with Monge (who was on an official visit) and asked permission to return to Costa Rica for "humanitarian reasons": to see his family and take part in anti-Sandinista "civic" activities. Monge agreed.[33] This sort of shadow-boxing between Pastora, the CIA, and the Costa Rican authorities continued: Pastora would quit, then return; the Monge government would expel Pastora and other contra military leaders or raid a camp or office, and then turn a blind eye to subsequent activities; and the CIA increasingly twisted the screws, trying a wide variety of tactics to force Pastora and the Southern Front into an alliance with the FDN. Pastora was unpredictable and childish, the CIA charged. The CIA was domineering and ruthless, Pastora retorted.

Back in San José in September 1982, Pastora called a press conference with the leaders of three other anti-Sandinista groups: Alfonso Robelo, head of the businessmen's MDN (Nicaraguan Democratic Movement); Fernando "El Negro" Chamorro, commander of the UDN-FARN (Nicaraguan Democratic Union–Nicaraguan Revolutionary Armed Forces), a tiny group closely aligned with the FDN; and Brooklyn Rivera, leader of the Atlantic coast–based Misurasata (Unity of Miskito, Sumu, Rama, and Sandinistas), which comprised the three coastal Indian tribes and, like Pastora's FRS, claimed to be adhering to the original ideals of the Sandinista revolution. These leaders announced the formation of their new contra movement, the Revolutionary Democratic Alliance (ARDE), which became the main contra force on the Southern Front. Arturo Cruz[34], the silver-haired, urbane former Sandinista ambassador to Washington, also signed the accord as the "moderator," without any institutional affiliation. Publicly, things were still at the political stage. But behind this façade of civic responsibility, the CIA was stepping up both preparations for war and pressure for unity with the FDN.

Beginning in late 1982, several contra officials as well as John Hull and Bill Crone, North Americans who owned farms in northern Costa Rica, were asked by the CIA to indicate which airstrips and farms were most suitable for contra training and supply drops. Shortly afterward, even though Pastora had not officially declared war on Managua, some of his lieutenants, including Wachán, José Robelo ("Chepón"), Luis Rivas Leal ("Wichard"), and Harold Martínez, began training combatants. According to one contra leader, during late 1982 the CIA made two airdrops of guns, sights, and ammunition. The flights were coordinated by CIA personnel in the U.S. Embassy. The supplies were dropped onto several Guanacaste farms, some used by Pastora's FRS, others by the FDN, and still others by El Negro Chamorro's UDN-FARN. These included *Las Ciruelas* ("Plums"), owned by a North American; *El Alamo*, a farm owned by a Costa Rican doctor where ARDE also set up clandestine transmitters for Radio Sandino Libre; and *El Pelón*, another Costa Rican–owned farm.

By early 1983, the contras were using several other Guanacaste farms for both training and supply drops. These included

Horizonte, owned by a wealthy American, Cecil Hylton; the farms of Adolfo Jiménez, a Cuban American and long-time CIA agent; and, near the town of Cañas, *Las Loras* ("Parrots"), the farm of Victor Wolf, a Costa Rican of German parentage. The CIA installed communications equipment between Las Loras and the CIA-contra supply depot at Ilopango Air Base in El Salvador. Wolf, an ideological right-winger and long-time CIA and DEA (Drug Enforcement Agency) collaborator,[35] also permitted the paramilitary group *Patria y Verdad* ("Fatherland and Truth") to train on his farm. This group, headed by Juan José Saborio, had ties to death squads such as *Mano Blanca* ("White Hand") in Guatemala and constituted a nascent death squad in Costa Rica.

On April 15, 1983, a year after Pastora had announced the start of his political struggle against the Sandinistas, ARDE issued its first "call to arms." A statement from Pastora put out, it was said, "from the mountains of southern Nicaragua" denounced the Nicaraguan government for failing to moderate its policies. In press interviews, Alfonso Robelo spelled out the new cover story: ARDE was respecting Costa Rica's neutrality by fighting entirely inside Nicaragua[36] and was adhering to Pastora's "third way" by not receiving any CIA or other U.S. assistance.

On May 1, 1983, ARDE forces launched their first military action, hitting the San Juan River town of El Castillo Viejo. Pastora's men held a Sandinista military post for two hours before, fearing a counterattack, they retreated. The Southern Front war had officially begun. Over the next three years, between May 1, 1983, and May 16, 1986, when Pastora officially stopped fighting, Southern Front contras carried out 163 recorded attacks against Nicaragua.

The ARDE Alliance
Alfonso Robelo: The Money Man

Within the ARDE alliance Pastora was the public personality, but Alfonso Robelo, a millionaire agro-industrialist and industrial engineer with a neatly trimmed beard, was Washington's man of confidence. Articulate, sophisticated, and U.S.-educated, he moved more comfortably in elite political and business circles in Washington, Miami, and San José than he did among the contra fighters. In March 1978, soon after Somoza agents murdered of one of the dictatorship's most articulate opponents, newspaper editor Pedro Joaquín Chamorro, Robelo formed the Nicaraguan Democratic Movement (MDN) to spearhead private-sector opposition to the dictator. After the Sandinista triumph, Robelo became a member of the ruling junta. He resigned in April 1980 (just three days after the newspaper editor's widow, Violeta Chamorro, resigned), becoming an opposition leader inside Nicaragua before moving to Costa Rica in April 1982.

In San José, Robelo immediately re-created the MDN as an organization of Nicaraguan businessmen and professionals in exile. From this platform he assumed a leadership role in organizing the Southern Front, acting as the key link to the U.S. Embassy, where he met frequently with the ambassador, political and military officers, and the various CIA station chiefs. He became one of the Southern Front's most important liaisons with Washington and part of what was jokingly called the "Contras' Frequent Flyers Club." Robelo says that, according to his agenda, he met with Oliver North thirty-six times.[37] Even after the Iran-contra scandal had broken wide open, Robelo would proudly show visitors a sort of rogues' gallery on the wall of his home study: a collection of photos of himself with Reagan, Bush, Casey, Poindexter, North, Robert Owen, and others.

Robelo served as ARDE's chief accountant, personally collecting each month packets of neatly tied $100 bills from the CIA station chief and doling funds out to the military and political forces. He set up several San José bank accounts and front companies for ARDE and the MDN that were used for renting houses and offices and buying planes and vehicles. He also acted as ARDE's chief press spokesman, giving the organization's (and the CIA's) official line on various events, which sometimes meant giving out the official lie. In September 1983, for instance, he told the press that the ARDE planes that had bombed Managua "took off from airfields inside Nicaragua"; they had actually left from Ilopango Air Force Base in El Salvador. In early 1984, he told the press that ARDE had mined two of Nicaragua's ports; CIA operatives had mined the ports and told ARDE and the FDN to claim responsibility. In May 1984, he declared, "we receive no money from the

Reagan administration"; at that point, ARDE was wholly financed by the CIA. And several weeks after the La Penca bombing, he told AP correspondent Joe Frazier, whose wife Linda was one of those killed, that the bomb had been planted by a Libyan agent working for Colonel Qadhafi and Tomás Borge (one of the phony cover stories circulated by the CIA). Although capable of lying calmly and convincingly, in private Robelo could candidly distinguish between his public role and his personal views. In one such conversation, he admitted that he was ordered to give out these stories by either CIA operatives or other contra leaders.

In carrying out his multiple duties within ARDE, Robelo walked a tightrope along the Costa Rican government's somewhat unclear line between admissible political and inadmissible military activities. Although deeply involved in all aspects of ARDE's affairs, he cultivated the public perception that he was active solely in ARDE political matters. Robelo managed to maintain a fairly secure and prominent place in Costa Rican high society, including with the Arias family.[38] He dined in San José's best restaurants, socialized and conducted business with the country's elite, and lived in a Spanish-style villa tastefully decorated with Latin American art. Only its sliding solid metal gate and the presence of armed guards denoted that his line of work might be dangerous. In fact, at least twice during the contra war, assailants tried to kill Robelo in San José. In June 1983, a bomb carried by two Sandinista Interior Ministry agents exploded prematurely as they were en route to an ARDE office to meet Robelo. In November 1984, Robelo and his girlfriend were injured when a young contra who may have been working for the Sandinistas threw a hand grenade into their parked car.[39] Within ARDE Robelo rapidly emerged as the focal point for those support-ing an alliance with the FDN. His cousin Alfonso Callejas was a top FDN political leader, and, according to another contra official, "the two wanted to control the political side of a unification" between ARDE and the FDN. By early 1983, Robelo had emerged as the counterpoint to Pastora, publicly arguing that "the FDN is not our enemy."[40] In the fall of 1983, Robelo sent some of his loyalists to Honduras for military training under CIA/FDN auspices, a move which greatly angered Pastora. As the CIA tightened the screws on Pastora in the months proceeding the La Penca bombing, Robelo withheld money from Pastora's faction. He officially broke with Pastora a few days before the bombing and afterward announced that his faction of ARDE was joining the FDN and backing the military forces led by "El Negro" Chamorro.

In September and October 1984, Robelo and Adolfo Calero, political leader of the FDN, met in Panama and announced the formation of UNIR (Nicaraguans United for Reconciliation), a short-lived political organization intended to isolate Pastora and Brooklyn Rivera and unite the Northern and Southern fronts. UNIR was supported by Oliver North, Robert Owen, and John Hull, all of whom saw contra unity as necessary to obtaining more congressional aid for the contras.

By March 1985, UNIR had disappeared, and in June, Robelo, Calero, and Arturo Cruz announced they would lead the United Nicaraguan Opposition or UNO, another U.S.-created alliance. It soon turned out to be as rocky as ARDE, with Robelo and Cruz complaining they had no authority or funds. In March 1987, Cruz quit contra politics for good. Robelo threatened to do so, too, but in the end he remained loyal to Washington and became a leader of a new, expanded umbrella organization, the Nicaraguan Resistance (RN), created in April 1986.

It was finally an ultimatum from President Arias, rather than the CIA manipulations or Sandinista attacks, that forced Robelo into official retirement. In January 1988, Arias suddenly issued an order expelling from Costa Rica Robelo and two other UNO leaders, Alfredo César and Pedro Joaquín Chamorro, Jr., unless they publicly opposed further military actions and supported the Central American Peace Plan. Robelo, citing personal reasons (business interests and a pregnant wife), renounced the armed struggle and several months later officially resigned from the Nicaraguan Resistance. He remained in San José, playing a behind-the-scenes role in contra politics and later campaigning for his old friend Violeta Chamorro in Nicaragua's February 1990 national elections.

In the mid-1980s, when Robelo's political influence in Washington was at its peak, he dreamed of returning as Nicaragua's next president or foreign minister. But his political hopes were circumscribed by personal factors, a degree of political disillusionment, and the more calculated maneuvers of Alfredo César, an articulate, U.S.-educated former banker. César, who moved to Miami and stuck with the Resistance, increasingly took over Robelo's role on the Southern Front and in Washington. After the Sandinistas' 1990 election defeat, Robelo hoped to be named Nicaragua's ambassador to Washington. Instead he was given the more modest post of Managua's envoy to Costa Rica.

Fernando "El Negro" Chamorro

In contrast with Pastora and Robelo, the tall, balding, mustached Fernando "El Negro" Chamorro, a former Managua Chevrolet salesman, was the weak link in the alliance, a man with little political clout, military success, or personal charisma. "The American press was never turned on by him," lamented Arturo Cruz, who described El Negro as "a genuine Nicaraguan hero" for his twenty-year (1959–79) struggle against Somoza. Journalist Christopher Dickey gives a more modest assessment, describing Chamorro as "a bourgeois revolutionary whose greatest claim to fame" was a July 1978 attack "where he rigged up a mosquito coil to a rocket launcher and lobbed a shell from a [seventh-floor] balcony of the Intercontinental [Hotel] into Somoza's conference room at the EEBI" (the basic-training military academy in Managua). The artillery killed no one, but Somoza's National Guard fatally shot two bystanders in a counterattack against the hotel. Back in November 1962, Chamorro had, in fact, commanded a much more significant military operation, leading rebel attacks against the towns of Jinotepe and Diriamba and holding Somoza's garrisons there for about three days. This event, forgotten by most involved in the contra war, may well have marked the high point in El Negro's military career.

In 1980, El Negro and his cousin José Francisco ("El Chicano") Cardenal, whom Dickey describes as "conspirators and talkers who never seemed, quite, to go to war,"[41] formed the Nicaraguan Democratic Union–Nicaraguan Revolutionary Armed Forces (UDN-FARN), a small, Honduras-based, political/military organization which received CIA funds and Argentine military training. Cardenal went on, in 1981, to form the FDN, while El Negro, buffeted by his disputes with the CIA, Pastora, and the

Honduran and Costa Rican authorities, shuttled UDN-FARN between the Honduran and Costa Rican war front.

In late 1981 and early 1982, Chamorro's forces in Costa Rica were aligned with the FDN. In February, El Negro narrowly escaped an assassination attempt at his home in San José. A masked assailant threw a fragmentation bomb into his apartment, injuring his son and a Canadian woman. The lone attacker was never captured, but Pastora says he later learned the man was sent by a special "dirty tricks" unit working for Nicaragua's Interior Ministry.[42] From Costa Rica, UDN-FARN took part in several small border raids, including an April 1982 attack on Peñas Blancas. In November 1982, just after the ARDE political alliance had been publicly announced, Costa Rican security forces captured weapons belonging to UDN-FARN, and Chamorro was expelled from the country. El Negro and his small band of fighters went to Honduras to fight with the FDN.

In early 1983, El Negro began pushing the CIA for permission to launch an attack along the Honduran-Nicaraguan border. The CIA ordered UDN-FARN to keep away from border posts to avoid embarrassing Honduras and jeopardizing the FDN's operations there. El Negro went ahead anyway, attacking the El Espino border crossing along the Inter-American highway. When his small, poorly equipped force rapidly became trapped in a fierce fight with the Sandinistas, El Negro went to the nearest telephone booth and called (collect) CIA official Dewey Clarridge to ask for reinforcements and mortars. Outraged, Clarridge refused to send more supplies and ordered the Honduran authorities to disarm UDN-FARN, arrest El Negro, and hold him at a safe house in Tegucigalpa. Word quickly leaked to Pastora, who frantically tried to arrange for a plane to fly from Costa Rica to Honduras to liberate El Negro from the CIA. Before this could happen, El Negro obtained his own release by agreeing to leave the country. He went, once again, to Costa Rica to work with ARDE.

In Costa Rica, El Negro continued to specialize in border attacks. UDN-FARN's small army—several dozen young Nicaraguans and Costa Ricans—repeatedly attacked the tiny, twelve-house hamlet of Fátima located on the banks of the San Juan River. El Negro contended that it was a strategic target, because it contained a garrison of one hundred-odd Sandinista soldiers and a warehouse full of food and ammunition for the Sandinista forces stationed up and down the river. While the American press never found El Negro much to write home about, several Costa Rican journalists took up his struggle like ardent groupies, giving UDN-FARN feature play each time it attacked the beleaguered Fátima outpost.[43] Over the years El Negro's forces never totaled more than several hundred men.

In June 1983, soon after ARDE officially announced the opening of its military operations, El Negro broke publicly with Pastora and announced an alliance with the FDN. He rejoined the ARDE alliance in January 1984, siding with Robelo's pro-FDN faction. After the May 1984 La Penca bombing, the CIA picked Chamorro to head the new ARDE alliance, with Robelo as political leader. This became known as the "rich ARDE"—the one with continued U.S. financing—as opposed to Pastora's "poor ARDE," the one that had been cut off. In October, El Negro became one of the military commanders of Robelo and Calero's UNIR. Throughout all these twists and turns of alliances, UDN-FARN combatants continued to hug the Costa Rican–Nicaraguan border, presenting a constant headache for Pastora, Robelo, their CIA handlers, and (later) North, Robert Owen, and Joe Fernández. As Owen wrote in a memo to North, "Negro believes in a border war. He is not schooled in tactics nor does he see the importance of taking the war deeper into Nicaragua. He wants to be able to use Costa Rica as a sanctuary."[44]

Somewhere along the road from his battles against Somoza to his battles against the Sandinistas, El Negro took up the bottle. By the time the Southern Front opened, Chamorro had acquired a love of whiskey and another nickname, "Johnny Walker." He went less and less often to the war front and became lazy and irresponsible, spending most of his time in San José, in an upper-middle-class house with a statue of a large nude woman in the front yard. (As a military commander, he was not supposed to enter Costa Rica, and Security Minister Solano expelled him three times.) His dwindling band of contras worked closely with the FDN and CIA-run operations of John Hull, and fought separately from the remnants of Pastora's forces.

El Negro appeared to be personally honest but was clearly a

poor judge of character; his closest aides were unsavory types who had their hands in the till and were involved in drug trafficking. As Owen wrote North, "The concern about Chamorro is that he drinks a fair amount and may surround himself with people who are in the war not only to fight, but to make money." Owen listed nine of Chamorro's associates who were suspected of drug running and rip-offs of funds and supplies.[45] Among them was René Corvo, a Cuban American CIA operative based at El Negro's main camp near the border town of Upala. Another, Felipe Vidal, was involved in embezzling the "humanitarian aid" money appropriated by Congress. Vidal and Corvo were part of a contingent of Miami Cubans whom El Negro had invited to come to Costa Rica as contra military trainers. These Cubans, who arrived in 1983 and were linked to the CIA, became involved in drug and arms trafficking and other illegal activities. The first public linkage of the CIA and contras to drug trafficking, the February 1983 "Frogman case" in San Francisco, involved UDN-FARN officials accused of moving cocaine from Colombia through Costa Rica to California. Subsequent drug cases implicated El Negro's brother Edmundo Chamorro, who was also a leader of UDN-FARN. Edmundo Chamorro had had, since his days in Nicaragua, a reputation for gambling, drug use, and immoral behavior, and in San José he got involved in trafficking as well.

In March 1986, El Negro announced he was quitting the war. But, typically, he equivocated. In May, when the CIA finally succeeded in forcing Pastora to abandon the battlefield permanently, El Negro agreed to return. Once again, he became Washington's hand-picked Southern Front commander, but by then the CIA and North's network were in the process of dismantling all remnants of the Southern Front's conventional armies. In 1987, El Negro resigned for good. His health, after years of neglect and self-abuse, began to decline. He accepted the Sandinista's amnesty offer and went to Managua to work, for a time, with the Conservative Party.

Brooklyn Rivera and the Miskito Coast
ARDE's fourth leader was Brooklyn Rivera, head of the Atlantic coast contra movement, Misurasata. Brooklyn, as everyone called

him, was the junior partner in the ARDE alliance. A curly-haired, racially-mixed student leader from Puerto Cabezas, he never lost his youthful appearance and shy manner. Soft-spoken and timid, he always seemed out of his depth in the midst of the intense infighting within ARDE, the maneuvers by the CIA, dealings with international Indian rights activists, and many rounds of negotiations with the Sandinistas. Even more than Pastora and El Negro, Brooklyn fell prey to this complex web of pressures and manipulations, which probably helped give him his perpetually worried countenance. His relations with the CIA in many ways mirrored Pastora's: the Agency viewed his independence and nationalism as a sign that he, too, was a Sandinista agent—"a closet leftist," as one U.S. official put it—and retaliated by buying off his commanders, forming rival movements, cutting off his finances and military supplies, attempting to kill him, and sabotaging his peace talks with the Sandinistas.

Misurasata fought on Nicaragua's Atlantic coast, a region that was colonized by the British in the 1600s, only unified with the rest of Nicaragua in the 1800s, and still remains distinct from the country's Pacific coast. Ethnically, it is similar to Honduras's Miskito coast; historically, it is closely linked to Britain and the United States, whose companies exploited the region's timber, minerals, and fish; and religiously, it is predominantly Protestant (the Moravian church dominates) rather than Catholic. Thinly inhabited—it has only about 10 percent of Nicaragua's population—its people are a mix of Miskito Indians and two much smaller tribes (the Rama and Sumu), as well as Creoles, blacks, and descendants of the Spanish (ladinos).

The Sandinista revolution against the Somoza dictatorship left the Atlantic coast largely unaffected. Somoza collected taxes from the multinational timber, fishing, and mining companies, but kept a low political and military profile in the region, and many Atlantic coast people viewed the fight against the dictator as a battle among "the Spaniards" on the Pacific coast. After coming to power, the Sandinistas set out to try to incorporate the coast into the new revolutionary society, sending in thousands of youthful volunteers, Managua functionaries, and foreigners (including Cubans sent in solidarity by Castro) to undertake an extensive literacy campaign, open health clinics, create new security forces and militia, and set up local governments. These efforts were often hastily executed, heavy-handed, culturally insensitive, and at times violent. The Atlantic coast quickly became the Sandinistas' Achilles' heel—an area with long-standing but complex grievances that was aggressively targeted by the CIA and closely watched by the international community.

In November 1979, Brooklyn Rivera, another young Atlantic coast activist Steadman Fagoth, and other activists founded Misurasata as a mass organization to press for autonomy with the Managua government. In December 1980, Misurasata drafted its "Plan of Action 1981," which included proposals for communal land rights, mineral and timber rights, and the use of indigenous languages and English, as well as Spanish, in the literacy campaign. Initially, the Sandinistas indicated a willingness to negotiate on many of these points, but talks broke down in February 1981, when Misurasata laid claim to more than a third of the country's territory, based on their survey of native land titles. The government denounced "Plan 1981" as a CIA program intended to provoke a separatist insurrection, outlawed Misurasata, and arrested thirty-three of its leaders, including Brooklyn and Fagoth. In one scuffle, said to mark the start of the anti-Sandinista war on the Atlantic Coast, four FSLN soldiers (including, Misurasata officials said afterward, two Cubans) and four unarmed Miskitos were killed at the Moravian church in Prinzapolka.[46]

Within two weeks, the Sandinistas released all those arrested except Steadman Fagoth; security archives documents revealed he had worked as an informant for Somoza. Fagoth was finally freed in May on the proviso that he accept a scholarship to study overseas. Followed by about a thousand other Miskitos, Fagoth went instead to Honduras, where he formed another contra organization, Misura (by dropping the Sandinista affiliation of Misurasata), which became aligned with the FDN. In November 1981, Misura cadres, trained by Argentine military instructors and equipped by the CIA, launched the "Red Christmas" offensive, a series of attacks across the Coco River. Their intention was to seize control of some piece of territory and declare a provisional government, which would receive U.S. military support. (Permanently capturing a piece of Nicaraguan territory continued to be an unrealized goal of Washington's war strategists and the various contra leaders.) The Sandinistas responded to this attack by launching a massive counter-offensive. Beginning in January 1982, FSLN soldiers burned crops, destroyed homes, and forcibly moved 8,500 Indians from their riverbank communities to a resettlement camp with the unfortunate name of *Tasba Pri* ("Free Land"), located fifty miles from the border. As a result ten thousand Miskitos fled to Honduras.

For five months after Fagoth's departure for Honduras and before the Red Christmas offensive, Brooklyn, who was the area's most popular leader, had stayed in Nicaragua trying, he says, "to save the situation, not let the conflict increase, and promote a peaceful solution." In August 1981, however, he threw in the towel, concluding that he could not reach detente with the Sandinistas. He left for Honduras with the intention of organizing an anti-Sandinista guerrilla force. As he crossed the border, he was arrested by the Honduran military acting on orders of Fagoth[47] and the CIA, who correctly feared he might set up a rival movement to Misura. Brooklyn was held in Puerto Lempira for nine days, then transferred to Tegucigalpa, where he was kept in isolation for seven months, through the Red Christmas upheavals. After his release he stayed in Honduras, was arrested again, and on one occasion was, he says, nearly killed by former Nicaraguan National Guard officer Colonel Enrique Bermúdez, commander of the newly formed FDN. In June 1982, Rivera was finally expelled and went to Costa Rica.[48] Other Indian exiles in Honduras, as well as dissidents from the Atlantic coast, began arriving in Costa Rica to join up with Brooklyn.

In Costa Rica, Brooklyn quickly reconstituted Misurasata as a rival to Fagoth's Misura and as a part of the ARDE alliance. Like Pastora and his FRS, Rivera chose to keep his organization's original name as a sign that he adhered to what he said were the true goals of the Sandinista revolution. By early 1983, Misurasata had established its military base at the junction of the Sarapiquí and San Juan rivers, where ARDE had a military training camp, and just a few hundred yards from a Costa Rican guard post. Brooklyn and others in Misurasata claimed they had upwards of three thousand armed combatants on the Atlantic coast, but around one thousand appears more accurate. It is undoubtedly true that, if weapons had been plentiful, Misurasata could have armed several times this number, at least during its first few years. But within the ARDE alliance, Misurasata was always the stepchild, receiving the most meager and poorest quality of supplies. As one Misurasata leader complained soon after the alliance was announced, "Pastora controls the arms and Robelo the finances. We—Misurasata—have to beg for everything we get."[49]

Judging by appearances, Misurasata and its leaders in San José were hardly living an easy life on Washington's war chest. Misurasata had use of a few battered jeeps and, over the years, occupied a series of barren offices scattered around the working-class suburb of Pavas. Often the telephone would be disconnected for nonpayment, and at times there were no unbroken chairs in the place. Brooklyn would sit behind a completely empty desk and, for a while, the only wall decoration was a large military-type topographical map of Nicaragua. After Brooklyn had a falling-out with the CIA, the map also disappeared. Perhaps the only advantage of these spartan furnishings was that it was easy to move offices quickly, which Misurasata had to do, not for security reasons, but because the organization was often evicted by landlords unable to collect the rent.

While Misurasata received the least resources within the ARDE alliance, it got the most international sympathy. Groups in Europe, Canada, South America, and the United States showed interest in working out an autonomy plan acceptable to the Nicaraguan government, the Atlantic coast people, and the guerrillas of Misurasata and Misura. International pressure and widespread discontent on the Atlantic coast did gradually compel the Sandinistas to admit they had made grave errors and to undertake political talks aimed at reaching an autonomy agreement. By 1985, the Sandinistas had rebuilt many of the destroyed villages and moved about 150,000 Indians back to their homelands. Thousands of Indians began returning from Honduras under the amnesty plan, and by 1987 fighting had virtually ceased.

Within this atmosphere, and with international backing, Brooklyn became the first contra leader to begin political talks with the Sandinistas. In August 1984, the Sandinistas offered amnesty to Brooklyn, and in October Senator Edward Kennedy facilitated a secret meeting at a New York City hotel between Brooklyn and Nicaraguan president Daniel Ortega. In November, Brooklyn returned to Nicaragua, and in December the two sides held talks in Bogotá, Colombia. Over the next four years, Kennedy's staff, as well as the Moravian church, Indian-rights groups such as the Washington-based Indian Legal Resource Center, and several foreign governments including Sweden, Colombia, France, Canada, and Holland, continued to play an active role as intermediaries in these on-again, off-again negotiations between Misurasata (and, as it was later called, Yatama, a Miskito acronym standing for "children of the motherland") and the Nicaraguan government.

Also involved as a key adviser to Brooklyn was Bernard Nietschmann, a goateed Berkeley geography professor who had worked for more than twenty years on the Atlantic coast. Nietschmann's prolific writings were widely circulated on Capitol Hill and contained some highly exaggerated claims accusing the Sandinistas of a Nazi-style "occupation" and of setting up "concentration camps" on the Atlantic coast.[50] Although he contended he was merely an academic, a memo from Oliver North reveals that Nietschmann worked with the National Security Council and its disinformation department, the Office of Public Diplomacy.[51] In mid-1988, Nietschmann, who was part of Brooklyn's delegation, provoked a confrontation on the Atlantic coast which undermined the delicate peace negotiations with the Sandinistas, according to Moravian church officials who were mediating the talks.

The CIA, as well as the FDN, was clearly hostile toward Brooklyn's peace talks with the Sandinistas, and the Agency tried from the start to sabotage them and undermine Brooklyn's authority. The CIA channeled the bulk of its funding to Fagoth's Misura, and in 1985, Oliver North and Robert Owen oversaw the creation of a group to rival Misurasata, KISAN (Coast Indians All Unite in Nicaragua), to which they illegally funneled monies that Congress had earmarked for Misurasata. In addition, several CIA operatives, led by Cuban American Felipe Vidal (using the nom de guerre Max Vargas), bribed Brooklyn's commanders to desert and plotted to assassinate him (see chapter 11). These maneuvers parallel the CIA and FDN campaign against Pastora.

Although Rivera clashed with Pastora over the equitable distribution of resources, he supported Pastora's refusal, prior to the La Penca bombing, to accept a CIA ultimatum to align with the FDN. After the bombing, Pastora and Brooklyn joined together, along with representatives of the workers' movement and Christian Democrat José Dávila, in "the poor ARDE." Rivera himself resisted CIA pressure to align Misurasata with Misura and submit to Agency control over his military operations. "The CIA cowboys want us to be their little Indians," Brooklyn told the *Wall Street Journal* in 1987.[52]

Ironically, despite the multifaceted pressures to break Misurasata and destroy him personally, Brooklyn emerged from the war as the ARDE leader who most closely achieved his goals. In September 1989, he returned to the Atlantic coast to campaign politically for Yatama, which was aligned with the anti-Sandinista political coalition, UNO, headed by Violeta Chamorro.[53] After the election, Brooklyn began working closely with the Chamorro government on reconstruction plans for the Atlantic coast.

NINE

The Southern Front: Its CIA Network, Surrogates, and Collaborators

We were told funds and supplies were coming from "friendly" countries and organizations in Latin America and Europe. But we eventually realized there are really only two possible sources for these quantities of money: the KGB and the CIA. And we certainly weren't getting anything from the KGB. —ARDE official

For years, Edén Pastora and the other ARDE leaders denied receiving money and supplies directly from the CIA. They claimed—and a number genuinely believed—that the support came from certain Latin American and Western European countries, as well as from organizations such as the Socialist International. ARDE did get some limited non-CIA funding. Its earliest and biggest windfall of apparently "independent" funding came, ironically, from the Nicaraguan government. In December 1982, Nicaragua's ambassador to Washington, Dr. Francisco Fiallos Navarro, announced his resignation, took $630,000 from the Embassy kitty, and personally gave it to Pastora, who used it to buy four airplanes, munitions, and other military supplies.

However, from the outset—from February 1982 to the La Penca bombing in May of 1984—the bulk of the Southern Front's funds came directly from the CIA. The funds were passed by the station chief in monthly allotments ranging from a low of $90,000 to a peak of $625,000 in the final few months. (In addition, the CIA supplied the Southern Front with a dozen or more light aircraft and sent airdrops and shipments of munitions, weapons, food, and uniforms.) These funds were used to run ARDE's expanding bureaucracy and military force. ARDE's go-between with the U.S. Embassy, Alfonso Robelo, says that he gave "about 85 percent" of the funds to Pastora to be distributed to the various Southern Front military factions—FRS, Misurasata, and UDN-FARN—and used the rest for the San José–based operations. Pastora the military commander and Robelo the political leader were each required to provide the CIA chief with a cost breakdown and vouchers for food, rent, salaries, office supplies, vehicles, planes, military equipment, and so on. Contra officials used to joke that this was "the only guerrilla organization in the world with a corporate accounting system."

After the La Penca bombing, ARDE began to fall apart. Almost none of the congressionally approved "humanitarian aid" or Oliver North's so-called "private aid" was distributed to Pastora's and Brooklyn's remaining forces. The numbers of contra foot soldiers dwindled and those who remained became increasingly impoverished, living in isolated, riverside encampments, perpetually short of uniforms, boots, rifles, ammunition, and food. Some tried to fight a guerrilla-type war by moving farther inside Nicaragua; El Negro's forces hugged the border near Los Chiles; and, overall, Southern Front military actions became smaller and more sporadic. Meanwhile, some of the CIA handlers and contra leaders aligned with the FDN put their energies into "unconventional warfare," which combined terrorist plots and border incidents with drug trafficking, while other contra politicians concentrated on forming a string of "umbrella" organizations designed to win congressional funding, despite having little connection to the guerrillas in the field.

In addition to the monthly CIA stipends handled by Robelo, the Southern Front also received money passed through several conduits, that is, other countries and organizations that appeared to be financing the contras but who were usually acting simply as conduits for CIA funds.

Venezuelan Conduits

According to an ARDE intelligence officer who knew details of the covert supply operation, "In 1983, the principal funds arrived from Venezuela and the Germans. It was CIA money, sent through covert channels." As Robelo admitted in early 1984, "We get money from Venezuelans on a regular basis. We have a man there, a Nicaraguan, who collects the money." In a September 1983 interview, Pastora indicated that military hardware was also being funneled via Venezuelans: "A man came to me, a Venezuelan, and put me in touch with [another man who] said to me, 'Comandante, I come to offer you one thousand rifles with one condition, that you don't ask me where they come from.' And I asked him, 'Is that the only condition?' And he said, 'Yes.' So I accepted."

Despite the fact that Venezuela was one of the "impartial" countries making up the Contadora Group[1] of the eight Latin American nations seeking a negotiated end to the war, there are indications that the government, under President Jaime Lusinchi, supplied funds and perhaps military trainers to the contras.[2] Pastora's old backer, former Venezuelan president Carlos Andrés Pérez (a vice president of Socialist International), frequently acted as mediator between the contras and the Nicaraguan government and may also have channeled money to the contras. One of Pérez's relatives, a man known as Iván Gómez, was a CIA operative working inside Pastora's organization and, after the La Penca bombing, Pérez sent a private plane to evacuate Pastora and a wounded comrade to a Caracas hospital.

One of the early go-betweens for CIA funds to the contras was Tor Halvorsen, a heavy-drinking, free-spending Venezuelan of Norwegian origin who had headed the Venezuelan Tourist Corporation and was a close friend of Pérez.[3] In the early 1980s, Halvorsen became president of the Committee in Defense of Democracy in Nicaragua (CDDN), a CIA-financed organization used to rally regional public opinion against the Sandinistas and support, in particular, the FDN. The CDDN in Caracas held lavish gatherings for contra leaders and through its press office, run by Venezuelan businessman/playboy Fernando Campbell, worked to undermine Sandinista support in the region and in the Socialist International.

In 1982, the CDDN also opened an office in downtown San José. Run by Nicaraguan lawyer Francisco Aviles (who was later implicated in a ring trafficking cocaine to California) and by Costa Rican accountant Orlando Castro Murillo (who was subsequently arrested for illegally operating a strip-tease parlor with a counterfeit liquor license), the office established contacts with influential Costa Ricans, including ex-presidents Daniel Odúber, Luis Alberto Monge, and Oscar Arias.[4] The CDDN went on to use CIA funds to set up in San José the pro-FDN radio station Radio Impacto and the ultrarightist Costa Rican Democratic Association (ADC), which rallied Costa Rican support for the contras and carried out witch-hunts against supposed leftist subversives in Costa Rica.[5]

West Germany: The Konrad Adenauer Foundation

Another early channel for CIA funds was the Konrad Adenauer Foundation, a political education organization affiliated with West Germany's Christian Democratic party. Laurence Birns, Director of the Council on Hemispheric Affairs (COHA), a liberal Washington-based research group, says that in 1984 his CIA contacts told him that the Agency was financing Pastora through the Adenauer Foundation. Birns was told that "the guiding light" in disbursing these funds was Aristides Calvani, a former Venezuelan foreign minister and an extreme right-winger.[6]

In an interview at the time, Alfonso Robelo admitted, "We have received money from members of the [German] Christian Democratic Party and the Foundation may be helping [José] Dávila," head of ARDE's Christian Democratic Solidarity Front (FSDC). While Dávila denied receiving Adenauer funds, he did not deny receiving a foundation scholarship to study in Germany and "having a very tight relationship" with its leaders. According to a journalist close to the foundation, Adenauer funds in Costa Rica were passed to the Nicaraguan Assembly of Democratic Unity (ANUDE), a contra political organization founded in 1982 to work for unity between the FDN and ARDE. This journalist said Dávila was the Adenauer Foundation's "main contact man" in ANUDE. ANUDE worked out of the office of Agro Invest, which Dávila admitted in an interview was a "cover name [that] doesn't mean anything."

Israel's Covert Aid

Of all the U.S. surrogates in the contra war, none was more important than Israel. Both the Israeli government and Mossad, its intelligence agency, provided various types of support to the Southern Front contras.[7] The full extent of Israeli involvement in the Iran-contra scandal has remained a closely guarded secret. The 690-page report of the Iran-contra congressional hearings, for instance, included only a few brief references to Israel's covert support for the contras.[8] More enlightening was the forty-two-page "memorandum of facts," or so-called "quid pro quo" document introduced in Oliver North's 1989 trial, which provided new details on the triangular relationship between the United States, Israel, and the contras.[9] Nevertheless, much information remains hidden.

Israel had a history of assisting Central America's military dictatorships, especially when the United States withdrew. In the late 1970s, mass killings and other human-rights violations drove the Carter administration to cut off aid to the military dictatorships of El Salvador, Guatemala, and Nicaragua. Israel, seeking both Central American support within the United Nations and markets for its military and security hardware, stepped in to fill the void. Until the Reagan administration resumed funding, Israel supplied El Salvador with over 80 percent of its weapons (including napalm), installed a computerized intelligence system, and supplied counterinsurgency advisers. In Guatemala, Israel provided crucial assistance to every phase of the military's war against leftist guerrillas, which resulted in at least ten thousand deaths and tens of thousands of "disappearances." Israeli support included small arms such as Galil rifles, artillery, antiterrorism equipment, transport planes, and counterinsurgency aircraft. Israeli experts installed two computer centers for monitoring dissidents and compiling death lists and provided advice and training for Guatemala's increasingly sophisticated intelligence operations. In both Guatemala and El Salvador, Israel assisted in the forced relocation of peasants into military-controlled "model villages," where inhabitants were coerced into growing nontraditional luxury exports instead of corn and other food crops. Perversely compared to Israeli *kibbutzim*, these villages received support from South Africa and U.S. evangelical and right-wing organizations, including the National Defense Council.

Between September 1978 and July 1979, when the Somoza dictatorship fell, Israel was supplying 98 percent of the National Guard's weapons. These included Uzi submachine guns, Galil assault rifles, ammunition, surface-to-air missiles, nine combat-equipped aircraft, and two machine-gun-equipped helicopters.[10]

Israel's role in Costa Rica is not that of a U.S. proxy. Its ties are deep and long standing, explained in part by Costa Rica's early declaration of war against Hitler and by the country's small but influential Jewish community. One Israeli diplomat described it as "a true, stable friendship." The administration of President Rodrigo Carazo (1978–82) sought security assistance from Israel, West Germany, and Panama. According to Carazo's Security Minister, Juan José Echevarría (who had been Costa Rica's ambassador to Israel), "The Security Ministry here was created by the CIA. But I felt it was better to have advisers from Israel than the U.S. It was smaller, farther away, and less interested in our internal problems."

Publicly, Israel denied providing military training or weapons to Costa Rica during the Monge and Arias administrations. Costa Rican officials say, however, Israel supplied Galil and Uzi rifles, communications equipment, and tear gas, as well as advisers to train Costa Rican forces in security, intelligence, and anti-terrorism. Israel helped establish (along with the CIA) a new Special Intervention Unit (UEI) or SWAT team.

Israeli government categorically, and falsely, denied supporting the contras. Yet by late 1981, Mossad was providing training and support to the first contra units, and after the Falklands/Malvinas war when Argentine military advisers began withdrawing from Central America, Israel sent its first major arms shipment to the contras. In February 1982, U.S. National Security Adviser Robert McFarlane and senior Israeli Foreign Ministry official David Kimche (a thirty-year Mossad veteran) worked out a deal for Israel to provide military advisers and to sell millions of dollars of Israeli-made military equipment to Guatemala, Honduras, and Costa Rica, some of which was to be funneled to the contras. In return, the White House agreed to increase its aid to Israel by an equal amount (without telling Congress).[11]

In December 1982, Defense Minister Ariel Sharon, another defense ministry official, and Mexican-based Israeli arms dealer David Marcus Katz turned up unannounced in Honduras, where they met with Honduran and FDN officials. Arriving in Tegucigalpa shortly after a visit by President Reagan to both Honduras and Costa Rica, they arranged to provide military advisers and sell military equipment (some Israeli-made and some captured PLO weapons) to Honduras. Some of these arms and trainers were to go to the contras. Contra leaders estimate that during 1983 alone, Israel supplied their Southern and Northern Fronts with six thousand weapons. In late 1983, after Congress passed a spending cap on CIA contra operations, journalists saw captured PLO weapons—including artillery, antitank weapons, and heavy machine guns, all painted with light tan desert colors and marked with Russian lettering—in Pastora's contra camps along the San Juan River.

The secret deal, code-named Tipped Kettle, was endorsed by CIA Director William Casey, who asked the Defense Department to help make the arrangements. General Richard Secord, then Deputy Assistant Secretary of Defense, was chosen by the Pentagon to handle the transfer of an estimated $10 million in PLO hardware. The CIA then arranged a second Israeli shipment to the contras (dubbed Operation Tipped Kettle II) in the summer of 1984, as U.S. congressional funding was being cut off.[12]

Besides these Israeli "donations," ARDE also used CIA funds to purchase weapons from Israel. These deals were brokered by international arms sellers, and most of the weapons passed through Panama. ARDE's arms purchaser in Panama was Sebastián González ("Wachán"), who made one trip to Tel Aviv, where Israeli officials showed him warehouses full of captured PLO weapons. In interviews, Wachán and Rodrigo García, a Costa Rican involved in the deals, gave first-hand details of the Israeli supply operation out of Panama, which, they said, was organized by the CIA and run by Mossad agent Michael Harari and Panamanian National Guard officials. In early 1983 the CIA asked Wachán to be the chief supplier through Panama for the five Northern and Southern Front contra organizations: ARDE, the FDN, the Atlantic coast groups Misurasata and Misura, and El Negro Chamorro's UDN-FARN. Wachán explained, "Panama was the CIA's first choice because they wanted to involve as many countries in Central America as possible in the U.S. operations against Nicaragua."[13]

Wachán was first approached about the Israeli deal by an American agent known as "Frank," who, he recalls, "tried to give the impression of a university professor: intellectual, athletic, bearded, with glasses." Also involved in the operation were Dewey Clarridge and, Wachán believes, Oliver North, whom he once saw with Frank at the Marriott Hotel in Panama City. As "a sign of good will," the CIA gave Wachán a Cessna 404 airplane. Wachán then used his contacts in Noriega's defense forces to obtain a Panamanian registration number, which was given on condition that the plane not be used inside Nicaragua. Wachán says he then turned the plane over to ARDE; to his dismay it was used in the September 1983 attack on Managua's international airport. His Panamanian contacts were furious: "After this I was led to believe the Panama military people did not want to go along with this deal" of funneling Israeli hardware through Panama to the contras.

There was also the problem of the nosy U.S. senator. Neither Panama, because of its diplomatic role within the Contadora Group, nor General Noriega, because of his ties to the Sandinista military, wanted public exposure of the contra supply operation. But Panama's duplicity was nearly exposed in early 1983, when a U.S. congressional delegation headed by Senator Patrick Leahy discovered and detailed to the Senate Intelligence Committee the CIA's massive, covert contra operation out of Panama and other countries in the region. During a stormy confrontation at Panama City's Marriott Hotel, Leahy told Dewey Clarridge what he had found out. Not only was Panama being used as a transshipment point, but the CIA was also pressuring Noriega to allow construction of a large facility on Coiba Island for training the Southern Front contras. It was clear, the Senator told Clarridge, that the CIA had gone far beyond the congressional authorization permitting interdiction of arms from Nicaragua to the Salvadoran guerrillas. The real intent, the Senator said, was to topple the Nicaraguan government.[14]

For this combination of reasons, Wachán said that, "After this point, in Panama we saw only uniforms, boots, and raincoats, not weapons for the contras." In mid-1983, the military resupply operation was moved to Ilopango Air Force Base in El Salvador, where it was facilitated by colonels Lobo and Bustillo and other Salvadoran officers. Preference was given to the FDN and, Wachán says, "Pastora was hung out to dry."

As the CIA began to cool on Pastora, Israeli supplies for ARDE were cut back. The tap was turned off for the first time in about October 1983 when, in an attempt to force Pastora to unify with the FDN, contra officials say the CIA halted shipments of money and captured PLO military supplies. In an interview in one of his river-front base camps, Pastora complained at this time that his several thousand troops were short of arms, ammunition, food, and clothing. After the La Penca bombing and the virtual collapse of military operations along the Southern Front, Israeli supplies went mainly to the FDN in Honduras and to the non-ARDE forces based in Costa Rica.

The Argentines: The First Cut-Outs in Washington's Dirty War

Just as the CIA used a variety of conduits—Venezuelans, West Germany's Adenauer Foundation, and Israel—to funnel money and arms to the Southern Front contras, so it built a complex network of collaborators and "cut-outs"(Agency lingo for surrogates) inside Costa Rica. The earliest of these were the Argentines, who first trained and organized the remnants of Somoza's National Guard into an anti-Sandinista fighting force.

The Argentine military was a logical ally in Washington's war against Nicaragua. Since 1976, Argentina's military dictatorship had waged what was known as "the Dirty War" against its own population. Between 9,000 and 30,000 "subversives," including *Montonero* and ERP (*Ejército Revolucionario Pueblo* or People's Revolutionary Army) guerrillas, political opponents, clergy, human rights activists, trade unionists, peasants, students, artists, and journalists had been killed or "disappeared" by the military and security forces. Having brutally mastered the techniques of social control at home, the Argentine armed forces were ready by 1980 to export these skills to help roll back the communist insurgencies in El Salvador and Guatemala and topple the Sandinistas in Nicaragua. As Argentine trainers boasted to contra leader Edgar Chamorro (who later quit in disgust over contra brutalities), "We're the only people in Latin America who've beaten the communists in a war. The way to win is to fight a 'dirty war' like we did in the 1970s."[15]

Even before Ronald Reagan's electoral victory, high-level U.S. intelligence agents, powerful right-wingers in Washington, and former Nicaraguan National Guard officers began negotiations with the Argentine military to organize the contras.[16] Argentine officers had worked as advisers, instructors, and agents in Somoza's secret police, and a number of Nicaragua's top National Guardsmen had received training in Argentina. Thanks to Washington's official and unofficial contacts in Buenos Aires, by late 1980 some fifty former Somoza Guardsmen were undergoing military and intelligence training in Argentina. This nucleus, along with Argentine military officers and trainers, went to Central America to help pull together the FDN in Honduras and to begin organizing the FDN's Southern Front in Costa Rica.[17]

While Argentine military killers were assembling a contra army, in Managua, Argentine militant leftists were offering their services to the Sandinista's newly formed state security apparatus. Several dozen Argentines, along with scores of other foreign revolutionaries, had fought against Somoza on Pastora's Southern Front and then settled in Managua when the Sandinistas won power. A handful of Argentine ERP guerrillas (including the La Penca bomber, Vital Roberto Gaguine) became part of an ultra-secret section of the Sandinista's Interior Ministry which handled special missions, including sabotage and assassinations (see chapters 2 and 11).

This cell's first mission was a spectacular success. On September 17, 1980, in broad daylight along one of Asunción, Paraguay's largest boulevards, an ERP hit team fired machine guns and a rocket-propelled grenade into a Mercedes-Benz limousine. Killed instantly were deposed Nicaraguan dictator Anastasio Somoza, his financial adviser, and chauffeur. The hit team had been sent by Nicaragua's Interior Ministry, and the killing of Somoza marked the close of the Sandinistas' war against the dictatorship.[18]

Three months later—and just a few weeks after Reagan's election—Nicaragua's new war opened, and once again, Argentines were involved. The Argentine military officers in Guatemala outlined the first mission for their contra trainees, the "15th of September Legion" (the FDN's precursor). Curiously, the first target was not some Sandinista military installation inside Nicaragua; instead it was a powerful privately-owned, shortwave radio station deep inside Costa Rica. Located in the picturesque mountain town of Grecia, *Radio Noticias del Continente* was run by Argentine leftists and it broadcast programs sympathetic to Latin America's revolutionary movements and critical of the continent's dictatorships. To the annoyance of the Argentine military, four attacks over the previous year had failed to knock out the station. "If you do this job for us, we will help you," 15th of September Legion Captain Hugo Villagra ("Visage") recalls being promised by the Argentine intelligence officers.

In Costa Rica, the Free Costa Rica Movement (MCRL) and the fledgling contra infrastructure worked with the CIA to plan the radio station attack. In the early morning hours, before the heavy mountain mist began to rise, Villagra and his commando team crept up to the fence of the well-fortified radio compound and hurled homemade Molotov cocktails towards the transmitter. Costa Rican guards inside opened fire. When the battle was over, two contras were wounded, one was captured and the rest managed to flee. The radio transmitter was not damaged. Several days later, Costa Rican guardsmen captured Villagra and six other contras. The contras' first military operation—like many that followed it—ended in disaster.

Shortly after the attack, Costa Rican security moved in and permanently close *Radio Noticias*. A year later, FDN commandos hijacked a Costa Rican airliner on a domestic flight and exchanged the passengers for Villagra and the other imprisoned contras.

Arrangements were made for safe passage to Guatemala, but the plane mistakenly landed in El Salvador and Villagra was again arrested. He spent another year in jail, and then in October 1982, his friend, Salvador's ultra-rightist politician Roberto d'Aubuisson, secured his release. On orders from the CIA, Villagra was taken to Honduras and made the FDN's "theater commander" in charge of combat operations.[19]

Although the Argentine military trained the 15th of September commandos who attacked *Radio Noticias,* no Argentine operatives appear to have been based permanently in Costa Rica until December 1981, when immigration records show that Estánislao Valdez, the head of the Costa Rican–based Argentine team, first arrived. Valdez, who operated under the name "Héctor Francés,"[20] was a wiry, mustached young Argentine army lieutenant and intelligence officer. Francés (whom one contra official recalls as having "a completely criminal gorilla mentality"[21]) worked under the control of Argentine officers in Honduras[22] and traveled frequently to Honduras, Guatemala, El Salvador, and Panama. But his primary task was to set up an FDN front based in Costa Rica.

Francés's persona in Costa Rica was that of a journalist and architect. He entered the country as a tourist, lived quietly with his wife and infant child in the posh San José suburb of Los Yoses, and "socialized with conservatives."[23] On October 7, 1982, the Costa Rican press reported that Francés was seized at gunpoint by a Sandinista commando team—four men and a woman—as he walked in his neighborhood. He was forcefully thrown into a stolen beige-colored microbus that later turned up abandoned on the other side of town. In late November, the journalists' association in Mexico City, FELAP, showed an hour-long videotaped interview with Francés, and in the following days copies were distributed in Bogotá, Caracas, Havana, and Lima. Francés said he had arranged his own "kidnapping," had defected to the Sandinistas, and had revealed CIA and contra activities because he was disillusioned by U.S. support for Britain in the Falklands/Malvinas war. But journalists familiar with the story believe that Francés was forcibly abducted and compelled to give the taped interview. Francés was never heard from again.[24]

In his recorded confession, Francés described his covert mission in Costa Rica,[25] naming scores of Costa Ricans and Nicaraguans said to be involved. Francés said he and fellow Argentine military officers[26] were working for the FDN "under the permanent oversight and direction of the CIA." He argued that during these early years, "Costa Rica perhaps [had] an even more important role in the counterrevolution than Honduras."[27] In Costa Rica, he said, the CIA was "playing two cards," creating two military structures, one under Pastora and the other under the FDN. Francés concentrated on setting up FDN cells; Pastora says he knew Francés but had little contact with him. While Washington and the contra leadership, as well as many journalists, dismissed Francés's declarations as Sandinista propaganda, over time many of the allegations he made—concerning individuals, organizations, structures, and modes of operation—proved accurate.

His statement reveals that, from the start of the contra operations, the CIA was running its own dirty war out of Costa Rica, plotting terrorist acts to cast blame on the Sandinistas and escalate the war against Nicaragua. He described, for instance, how he and two Costa Rican Ministry of Foreign Affairs officials, Juan Antonio Simón and Rogelio Castro, "studied the possibility, based on [the Agency's] proposal, for carrying out an operation in the area of Limón . . . to prove the presence there of Nicaraguan patrols." He said that in Washington right-wing businessman and political lobbyist Nat Hamrick and Costa Rica's conservative Foreign Minister Fernando Volio were preparing to protest this "Sandinista aggression" and request U.S. troops to "defend its [Costa Rica's] sovereignty."

Francés also described plans (beginning as early as 1982) to kill Edén Pastora because, he said, certain officials in Washington and in the contra ranks already felt the rebel commander would be more useful as a martyr than as a living and divisive leader. Francés stated that "the possibility of his [Pastora's] physical elimination has been suggested in various meetings," and contact had been made "with Toruno and Pineda [ex-National Guardsmen involved in setting up the Southern Front] to see what people we had in Costa Rica capable of carrying this out."[28]

Two John Hulls, Two Joe Fernándezes, Two Felipes, Two Papis, and Many Tomases

Even before Héctor Francés disappeared from Costa Rica, CIA *gringos* were already on the scene organizing the Southern Front. In 1982, Pastora, Robelo, and the other leaders of the new ARDE say the CIA station chief whom they dealt with was "John Hull," who worked under cover as a political officer in the U.S. Embassy. They describe this "John Hull" as about forty-five years old, rather tall and slim, and with blue eyes, straight brown hair, and a scarred complexion. He was considered a good family man, with a *gringa* wife and three children, and "a gentleman" who had previously been posted in Europe, always wore a sports jacket, was polite, and never raised his voice. In late 1983 or early 1984, he was transferred to Bolivia.

"He was delicate and intellectual," Pastora recalls. "He was the only educated person of the CIA I ever met. Maybe that's why I noticed. The only one who blushed when someone said a bad word." A Costa Rican CIA confidant described this station chief as "the last political man they sent. We could discuss strategy and ideas. All the [rest were] gorillas, only wanting a military solution." Clearly, "John Hull" in the Embassy bore no resemblance to the rough, crude, elderly farmer John Hull who was soon running contra operations out of the border region. "They didn't even seem to be from the same litter," was how Pastora put it. He and others gradually learned that the CIA liked to "play the trick" of giving several agents the same name.[29]

"John Hull" the station chief had an assistant named Phil Holts (known to many simply as "Felipe"), whose cover was second secretary in the Embassy's economic section. Holts became station chief when "John Hull" left Costa Rica. According to a Costa Rican intelligence official who knew him, "Felipe" Holts was a gringo, about thirty-eight years old, short, with clear skin. This official described him as "a polite, decent man, an Evangelical. He was patient, calm, never in a rush." Holts established a close relationship with farmer John Hull's network and was in a CIA safe house with Hull and Oliver North's envoy Robert Owen on the night of La Penca. Part of this network was another Felipe, Cuban American Felipe Vidal. Shortly after the bombing "Felipe" Holts was transferred to Brazil, to the disappointment of John Hull.[30]

A CIA agent who spanned both the pre– and post–La Penca periods was Dimitrius Papas ("Papi"), an older Greek American who trained the CIA-controlled group of intelligence agents known as "The Babies" (see chapters 10 and 11). ("Papi" was also a nickname for John Hull, the farmer.) Papas worked closely with Costa Rican intelligence officials in both the DIS and the OIJ and was involved in the cover-up of the La Penca bombing. One of his agents said of Papas that he was "about fifty-five, white-haired with a big mustache, short, fat, loved women, drinking, night clubs, and high living. He did not try to hide himself."[31]

When "John Hull" the CIA chief left Costa Rica, he was temporarily replaced, according to some accounts, by "Tomás," who had served under him as the CIA's chief of security. Information about this "Tomás" (almost certainly not his real name) is sketchy. He was described as a "very military-like" North American in his late forties, about six feet tall, somewhat heavy, athletic, with short, curly, dark blond hair and glasses and who spoke Spanish poorly. At the time of La Penca, it appears that Phil Holts had become station chief and both "John Hull" and "Tomás" had left.

"Tomás" was also the code name for every CIA agent working out of the Embassy. According to contra collaborator Bill Crone, all the CIA officials were contacted by calling a special U.S. Embassy number and simply asking for "Tomás." The most famous "Tomás" was Joe Fernández or "Tom Castillo," who became CIA station chief in Costa Rica in July 1984. A big, burly, silver-haired, olive-skinned Latin[32] with a large family, he arrived (as he would leave two and a half years later) under a cloud. The Agency had put him on probation for his role in preparing both the CIA comic book, "Freedom Fighters Manual," which described scores of ways to sabotage the Nicaraguan economy, and the so-called CIA manual, *Psychological Operations in Guerrilla Warfare*, which advocated a mix of political propaganda and terrorism.[33] Fernández was already known to many of the contras. He had been based at CIA headquarters in Langley, Virginia, where he had served as the CIA's main liaison to the anti-Sandinistas. Fernández convincingly pulled off his alias. Until the Iran-contra scandal broke, most contra leaders believed that there were two different CIA people: Tom Castillo, whom they frequently dealt with and who appeared to work out of a San José high-rise office building, and Joe Fernández, who they heard was the CIA station chief within the Embassy.

To add to the confusion, there was another CIA agent in Costa Rica named Joe Fernández. This was José Luis Fernández, a Puerto Rican who had been a consular officer in the U.S. Embassy in San José in the 1970s and returned periodically afterward. In 1985, he worked as a CIA operative inside the political campaign of Rafael Angel Calderón.

After the Iran-contra scandal broke in late 1986 and station chief Joe Fernández was removed, contra leaders say they dealt mainly with Charles Harrington, a youthful, sandy-haired operative who was listed as an Embassy political officer. Unlike his predecessors, the lanky, awkward Harrington was widely known to be a CIA agent, and television crews made a game of trying to capture him on camera. In late 1989, Harrington was transferred to Bolivia.

Contra officials and some of their American supporters say they had contact with an assortment of lesser CIA agents at the Embassy. One was named "Levine"; another, "Buck," was involved in helping to locate landing strips;[34] a third was Nelson Nugent, a political officer who left Costa Rica in September 1984. As in Washington, the contra war as run by the San José Embassy was an interagency operation, involving the ambassador, several DEA agents, the military attaché, and officers in the consular and press sections. Over the years these diplomats included ambassadors Curtin Winsor, Lewis Tambs, and Deane Hinton; "Bill," a tall Marine who was head of operations under "John Hull"; a large, brash, crewcut consular officer named Kirkpatrick Kotula; a short, hard-driving Latin DEA agent named Robert Nieves; and heavy-drinking military attaché Colonel John Lent, who had served in the same post in Managua and was married to the sister of Miskito contra leader Steadman Fagoth. Lent's predecessor, Colonel John Taylor, was one of the Embassy's most important covert operatives in the country throughout the 1980s. Described as crass, difficult, and temperamental, Taylor oversaw training at the controversial Green Beret base at Murciélago, Costa Rica, and met with North during his secret trip to Costa Rica just three days before the La

Penca bombing. After Lent's arrival, Taylor was moved to head of security for AID in Costa Rica.

As the contra war expanded, so did the number of agents based in Costa Rica and elsewhere in Central America. By 1987, U.S. officials said there were more than two hundred CIA agents and contract employees involved in the war against Nicaragua. Most of them had military experience in Vietnam, but many lacked political savvy.[35] In the spring of 1984, according to an ARDE intelligence officer, the CIA decided "to triple" the number of agents in Costa Rica within the course of just a few months.[36] Ten of the new agents (eight Americans, a Spaniard, and a Puerto Rican) were comfortably housed in the country club–style Golf Residence apartments outside San José. This CIA team had as its principal mission the training of a new antiterrorist brigade within Costa Rica's Civil Guard.

A youthful, bespeckled ARDE officer who called himself "Andrés" explained that the Agency was also moving a number of these new agents into my own neighborhood, Rohrmoser. (Rohrmoser is an upper-middle-class suburb preferred by Nicaraguan political exiles and Costa Rica's nouveau riche where, several years later, the new U.S. AID and Embassy buildings were built.) During a clandestine meeting on a picnic bench in the extensive La Sabana park, Andrés explained that the CIA was facing a problem, however, because most of its new agents were single males. "They will stand out like sore thumbs in your family-oriented neighborhood," Andrés explained. But in its wisdom, Andrés went on, the CIA had arrived at a solution: it worked a deal with its Costa Rican counterpart, the Ministry of Security, which agreed to supply these single male agents with "rent-a-families": Costa Rican women "of confidence" and their children to give "an appearance of family life. They will live with the men and receive a salary for their services." Most of these women and children, Andrés said, were the extramarital families of Costa Rican agents, so the arrangement benefited members of both security forces. Until this moment, I had considered Andrés an impeccable source. But as I related this story to Tony, we both agreed that it sounded incredible.

At the time this conversation took place, the house next door to ours was empty. Soon afterward, a Chevy sedan with Virginia license plates pulled up in front, followed by a moving van. When Tony and I went to meet our new neighbor, a black-haired, slightly overweight, middle-aged man emerged from the car. Speaking with a tinge of a southern accent, he said his name was Jack and that he worked in "communications" in the Embassy. He said he was in Costa Rica alone, that he and "the wife" were separated, and that his kids were grown.

About a week later, we were startled to see another moving van arrive next door, followed by the Chevy bearing Jack, a Costa Rican woman, and two young children. We went out to greet them, and, without missing a beat, Jack introduced us to his "wife," Carmen, and their two young "sons." The "family" lived next door to us for nearly two years, until Jack was transferred to Colombia. At that point, he bought Carmen and her sons a small house in the area and promised to return for her some day. We never saw him again.

Contrary to the CIA's game plan, Jack's presence caused considerable stir on the block. The neighbors buzzed about the gringo and his Costa Rican *compañera,* and the day-and-night passing of Embassy security cars and vans helped blow his cover. Security vehicles came by every fifteen minutes, and the uniformed, armed guards inside frequently stopped in front of Jack's or—after we came under surveillance—at our house to hold loud, coded conversations over two-way radios.

The Costa Rican Network

"Sadly, there are Costa Rican officials who take their orders from the U.S. Embassy and not from their President."

—Arias government official, 1987

One of the tasks of these CIA agents was to expand the network of Costa Rican collaborators and informants to facilitate the war effort and other U.S. political objectives in Central America. When the Reagan administration took office in 1980, it found that U.S. covert intelligence capabilities in Central America were very limited.[37] The Republican administration set out to correct this. As was the case in building the Parallel State, dollars and gifts were used to help bind the loyalty of those needed to assist the Southern Front's covert war. By the end of the decade, Washington had built an infrastructure of corrupt Costa Rican collaborators that ran from the border posts and ports of entry to the uppermost inner circle of the government. It included customs and immigration officials, regional Civil and Rural Guard commanders, Foreign Ministry officials, diplomats, ministers and vice ministers, journalists, and members of the President's staff.

Often the price for cooperation was pathetically modest—a trip to Washington, a scholarship for study at a military base, some new office equipment, a loosely monitored expense account, or a "topping up" of one's meager official salary. Robert Owen wrote Oliver North that President Monge's personal secretary requested "a small word processor or personal computer," in return for which she "would make duplicate disks of all information and correspondence and give them to our friends [the CIA]."[38] Other officials were apparently more handsomely rewarded. U.S. officials said they believe that Monge personally took a CIA "bribe" in return for his cooperation with Washington's covert schemes, including the Santa Elena airstrip. Monge repeatedly denied he accepted any payments.[39] José Ramón Montero, Monge's Civil Guard chief in Guanacaste, was also on the take. Bank records uncovered by U.S. congressional investigators found that during just the first half of 1986, Colonel Montero, who was overseeing the Santa Elena landing strip construction and other local contra activities, received nearly $200,000 from the secret Iran-contra bank account for his services.

One of the most important CIA collaborators was Colonel Rodrigo Paniagua, a tall, balding, elderly, alcoholic Security Ministry official who served as the first director of OPEN, Costa Rica's military reserve force. Paniagua used his position to become a sort of jack-of-all-trades in handling the complex relations between the Costa Rican government, ARDE, the FDN, other contra groups, the Cuban Americans from Miami, and assorted mercenaries. He worked with Colonel Antonio Pereira and several others at San José's international airport to help arriving mercenaries, CIA operatives, and drug traffickers avoid immigration and customs checks. Several mercenaries told how Paniagua cleared without inspection handguns, ammunition, dynamite, and other military gear, some of which was packed in seventy-pound boxes and sent as unaccompanied baggage on commercial flights from Miami on TACA (El Salvador's national airline) and LACSA (Costa Rica's national airline).[40] Security Minister Angel Edmundo Solano fired Paniagua in April 1984, because he had warned Pastora's lieutenant Popo Chamorro that Costa Rican authorities were about to raid ARDE's command post outside San José. Even after he was officially out of the government, Paniagua continued to act as a go-between for the CIA.

Benjamín Piza, Costa Rica's Security Minister from 1984 to 1986, was one of the most trusted confidants of the CIA, especially station chief Joe Fernández, whom he counted among his best friends. A white-haired, soft-spoken business executive, Piza had no previous government experience and limited military or police knowledge. His greatest qualification for the job was that he was unswervingly pro-American and staunchly anticommunist. His appointment represented a coup not only for the U.S. Embassy but also for the local right wing. Piza's grandfatherly mannerisms gave the impression that he was only casually aware of what was going on, but the records reveal that he was intimately involved in Southern Front operations. His most famous collaborative effort with the CIA and the Oliver North network was in building a two-kilometer runway, barracks, and fuel depot for the contras on the Santa Elena peninsula. In an interview, Piza admitted working with the CIA, but denied he received money for his services.

During Piza's tenure, the CIA rapidly expanded its influence and control over the Security Ministry. The main liaison to the Embassy was the Ministry's number three official, Francisco Tacsan, a slight, wizened-faced man of Taiwanese descent. One of Tacsan's functions was to help oversee the special dirty-tricks unit, "The Babies," run by CIA agent Dimitrius Papas. The Babies handled a variety of unsavory tasks including running smear campaigns against pro-neutrality Costa Rican government officials and manufacturing false documents blaming the La Penca bombing on Salvador guerrillas, "Communists" in the Costa Rican government, and the Sandinistas.

"The Army of the Media"[41]

"The upper classes of Latin American countries normally control by means of the army," observes Chilean theologian Pablo Richard, who lives in Costa Rica. "Since there is no army here, they do so through the media of communications." Washington, likewise, has historically imposed its will in Latin America from the top down, through the military hierarchies. Faced in Costa Rica with a nation lacking an army, the United States turned instead to the mass media as its main vehicle for social control. During the 1980s, the U.S. Embassy and Costa Rica's conservative business elite collaborated to fine-tune the press into a shrill propaganda tool supporting the war effort. The target was three-fold: (1) to convert Costa Ricans, who had enthusiastically welcomed the Sandinista victory, into militant anti-Sandinistas, particularly by playing on their conservative Catholic, anticommunist, and anti-Nicaraguan sentiments; (2) to penetrate and propagandize inside Nicaragua through private Costa Rican radio and television stations, the U.S. government's Voice of America (VOA), and CIA-created radio stations;[42] and (3) to carry the anti-Sandinista message throughout the hemisphere through the syndication of *Nicaragua Hoy* and by planting stories in the Costa Rican press that were picked up by other Latin American media.

While Costa Rica guarantees freedom of the press, the press has been the one major institution left untouched by the country's post–World War II social democratic reforms. The major newspapers, television stations, and radio networks remained in the hands of ultraconservative landowners and wealthy businessmen who tried to use the media to slow the pace of social transformation.[43] After 1979, the Costa Rican press perceived an urgent new mission: to stop the spread of revolution by targeting labor unions, the landless, and other real or imagined leftists at home, vilifying guerrilla movements in El Salvador and Guatemala, and supporting the U.S. war against Nicaragua. The press glorified the contras, depicting their fight as a holy war, while unrelentingly attacking peace efforts, including Monge's Neutrality Proclamation, the Contadora Group, and its successor, the Central American Peace Plan. The result was that despite Costa Rica's apparent diversity— three major daily and a half dozen other newspapers, five private and one state television station, and one hundred radio stations (medium wave and FM)—the political line of all the major media was remarkably uniform.

The headlines, photo captions, and editorials in Costa Rica's leading newspapers clearly reflected this right-wing bias. Following the September 1983 ARDE attack from Costa Rica against Nicaragua's border post at Peñas Blancas, the headlines read "Nicaragua Bombed CR" (*La República*) and "Civil Guard Attacked by Nicaraguan Army" (*La Nación*). A columnist in *La Nación* decried Monge's subsequent talks with Ortega aimed at reducing hostilities as "dialogue without reason" and called Ortega "a wolf in sheep's clothing." Other editorials denounced Monge's Neutrality Proclamation as "cowardly" and "dangerous." In a May 21, 1983, front-page story, *La República*, without citing any sources, reported that the Sandinista army was engaged in "repeated violations of official territory with the object of capturing [Costa Rican] citizens or Nicaraguan residents." The contras, on the other hand, were portrayed as fighting a just, religious war. Just prior to this both *La República* and *La Nación* both ran several pages of colored photos and long interviews with Pastora, describing the struggle as "a *campesino* war" to "liberate all completely all of Nicaragua from the dictator." On another occasion, caption on a photo of an FDN soldier in *La República* read, "The guerrillas that fight the Sandinistas in northern Nicaragua always say a prayer before going into battle."[44]

Among the most blatant examples of press manipulation was a doctored photo appearing in *La Nación* in June 1985 of Free Costa Rica Movement (MCRL) militants hurling stones at the Nicaraguan embassy. In the *La Nación* photo, someone had airbrushed out the Nazi-style trident insignia worn by the MCRL demonstrators. This was apparently intended to portray the attack as a spontaneous popular protest rather than an organized assault by this far-right group. At this time, MCRL had a special relationship with *La Nación*. The newspaper's vice director, J. A. Sánchez Alonso, was MCRL's vice president and the paper ran weekly full-page announcements of the organization's activities. When questioned, Sánchez Alonso dismissed the doctored photo—which *El Seminario Universidad* ran in its original form—as simply the work of some unnamed individual and not a result of the paper's bias.[45]

In a wide variety of ways, the U.S. Embassy helped to build a network of journalists who worked to weld this common ideological front. Local journalists say that in the late 1970s, U.S. Embassy officials began holding regular "coffee klatches" with top journalists and media directors to lay out a uniform editorial line. Once the Sandinistas were in power, U.S. Embassy officials began playing a more active role in these gatherings, and AID sought to shore up support through its Central America Peace Scholarship Program (CAPS). The United States Information Service section within the Embassy put out an array of press releases, bulletins, magazines, and other publications and held frequent seminars, lectures, receptions, and press conferences for the local press.

Covertly, as well, the CIA and contras built the network of press collaborators by putting certain Costa Rican journalists on their payroll.[46] Carlos Morales, editor of the weekly university newspaper, *El Seminario Universidad,* and former president of the journalists' association, said he personally knew at least eight journalists, including three "top editors," receiving monthly CIA stipends of about $300 to $500. This amount, passed either directly from the CIA or indirectly through the contras, nearly doubled their meager Costa Rican salaries. "Their job has been to get into the press stories, commentaries, or editorials attacking Nicaragua and sympathetic to the contras," explained Morales, a journalism professor who has taught most of Costa Rica's press corps. Another prominent Costa Rican journalist, who requested anonymity, named eight journalists—three with *La Prensa Libre,* three with *La Nación,* one with *La República,* and one with Channel 7—who he said received between $50 and $200 per month from the CIA.

An ARDE official said that he saw on the desk of press secretary Orión Pastora a list of "about half a dozen names of local journalists" with amounts of money listed alongside. "I don't know how frequently these people were paid, but my understanding was that they received payments regularly," the official said. The FDN in Costa Rica, through its press spokesman Oscar Montalbán, also gave "stipends" (bribes) to local journalists.[47]

The same situation developed in Honduras, the contras' Northern Front. In a 1985 affidavit submitted to the World Court, ex-FDN press spokesman Edgar Chamorro said that he also "received money from the CIA to bribe [about fifteen] Honduran journalists and broadcasters to write and speak favorably about the FDN and to attack the government of Nicaragua and call for its overthrow."[48]

A number of local journalists who refused to toe the line were fired, forced to resign, or marginalized. A television reporter at Channel 7, who later quit in disgust, recalled that "various times I interviewed Pastora under a big tree [at his clandestine command center] in Escazú. I had to say it was in a contra camp." In 1985, a woman reporter for *La República* lost her job after refusing to say that a contra camp she had visited in northern Costa Rica was located inside Nicaragua. Later, when the United States turned against Panamanian General Noriega, several journalists at *La Nación* found they were moved to less important stories after they refused a directive to write anti-Noriega pieces. Of Costa Rica's newspapers, only the small-circulation weeklies *El Seminario Universidad, Tico Times,* and *Esta Semana* (begun in 1989) supported Costa Rican neutrality, the Contadora Group peace negotiations, and the Central American Peace Plan, and criticized, on occasion, U.S. foreign policy.

Costa Rica gradually became the contras' main propaganda center in Central America. Under Costa Rican law, all media must be owned by nationals (although financing can be external), so the CIA had to create various associations to front its media operations. In 1982, for instance, the CIA set up a popular music station, Radio Impacto, with clandestine U.S. money channeled from Tor Halvorsen's CDDN in Venezuela. Radio Impacto beamed pro-FDN and, after the La Penca bombing, anti-Pastora as well as anti-Sandinista propaganda into Nicaragua. The CIA kept a very tight reign on the station, even faxing from Washington scripts for editorials. By the late 1980s Impacto, which transmitted from a small converted house in the San Pedro suburb of San José, had built a repeater and three large towers outside Puerto Viejo near the border with Panama. It beamed anti-Noriega programming southward in the months prior to the December 1989 U.S. invasion.[49] In mid-1990, with both Panama and Nicaragua again safely within the U.S. camp, Radio Impacto closed down.[50]

In January 1985, the U.S. Information Agency's Voice of America (VOA) opened a powerful $3.5 million, medium-wave transmitter at Pital, twenty kilometers from the Nicaraguan border, intended to counter, according to Ambassador Winsor, "the vile propaganda and hate spewed forth by the regime in Managua."[51] President Monge argued that he had requested the VOA transmitter so that Costa Rica could regain "sovereignty of the airwaves" in northern Costa Rica, but from the outset the target was clearly Nicaragua. In a clever end-run around Costa Rica's law requiring local ownership of all mass media, the project was fronted by a group of conservative media executives, journalists, and politicians who formed a private, nonprofit organization, the Costa Rican Association for Information and Culture (ACIC).[52]

When Radio Costa Rica went on the air, journalists and local residents invited to tour the compound's four broadcasting towers in Pital were stunned by its elaborate million-dollar security system. The one-square-kilometer installation was protected by high-tension wire, double storm fencing, microwave sensors, television cameras, sandbags, dogs, and armed guards. "It resembles a military fortress more than a radio broadcasting station," noted one local newspaper after the VOA's inaugural open house.[53] A number of Costa Ricans and contras close to the VOA operation say the transmitter was also being used for intelligence gathering in the border region and inside Nicaragua. Like Radio Impacto, the VOA closed down and dismantled its facilities in mid-1990. The transmitters from both stations eventually showed up in Europe, beaming procapitalist, pro-Catholic messages into the former Soviet Union. The transmitters had been sold to the Catholic Radio and Television Network in Belgium by the San José–based company Elcor Electronics, which had originally built them in the 1980s. An Elcor official termed the transaction, which was partially financed by a $90,000 grant from the U.S. Catholic Bishops' Conference, "confidential."[54]

The CIA also set up and financed several contra-run media outlets, including a pro-Pastora radio station, La Voz de Sandino (Voice of Sandino). Claiming to broadcast "from the mountains of southern Nicaragua," it was, in reality, beamed from ARDE's hillside command post in Escazú, just outside San José. Beginning in 1985, *La Nación* began carrying a four-page weekly pro-FDN supplement, *Nicaragua Hoy* (Nicaragua Today),[55] edited by Pedro Joaquín Chamorro, Jr., whose family owned and ran Managua's opposition paper *La Prensa*. However, the publication was fronted by several Costa Ricans whose names appeared on the masthead. *Nicaragua Hoy*, which carried as its logo a drawing of Nicaragua surrounded by barbed wire, said its objective was to "publish information and articles of opinion about the Nicaraguan reality to try to compensate for the well-orchestrated disinformation campaign of the Sandinista government." It had no advertising and was widely said to be financed by the CIA and by Reverend Sun Myung Moon's Unification Church and its financial affiliate CAUSA (Confederation of Associations for the Unity of the Societies of America). It was syndicated to seven major newspapers in other Latin American countries, with a total readership of 624,000.[56]

Carlos Morales terms the 1980s, particularly during the Monge administration, "a very sad, disagreeable period" when "the Costa Rican press practically put itself at the service of Washington's dirty policies." Through its network of press collaborators and an infrastructure of contra media outlets, the CIA took cynical advantage of what has been called Costa Rica's greatest weakness: its mass media.[57]

But while Washington managed to exert tremendous influence over the media it did not fully win over public opinion. Despite years of press propaganda denouncing the Sandinistas, praising the contras, opposing all peace initiatives, and subtly advocating rebuilding an army, the majority of Costa Ricans continued to adhere to their basic principles. Public opinion polls consistently showed that a majority of Costa Ricans did not want an army, supported peaceful negotiations, did not feel militarily threatened by the Sandinistas, and did not want foreign troops—

contras, U.S., or others—stationed on their territory. If Washington won the battle for control of the media, it never fully won the hearts and minds of the Costa Rican public.

The CIA Assets within ARDE

Besides the CIA network within the Embassy, the Costa Rican government, and the press, the Agency also had a group of Costa Rican–based agents working directly inside Pastora's organization. Contra officials say that by early 1984, a team of agents, mostly "Latin American assets," was based at ARDE's suburban command post (code-named "San Pedro") in Escazú and in ARDE's San Juan River camps. The head agent was Iván Gómez, a Venezuelan and cousin of former president Carlos Andrés Pérez. Other members of the team included "Armando," a Colombian military officer and engineer who was chief of operations; a North American known as "Omar," who coordinated the supply flights; a supplies specialist, "Manuel"; a communications specialist called "Carlos"; and a North American, "Jorge," who was a combat specialist. Their operations were coordinated by ARDE's logistics chief, Adolfo "Popo" Chamorro, who was also the chief liaison with Costa Rican government officials.

According to ARDE officials who worked with this CIA team, these operatives oversaw the "more important plans and specialized operations," not the day-to-day details of the contras' operations. They also helped intercept Sandinista and Costa Rican government communications. They were careful not to appear in public and spoke rarely to conceal their American accents. But although these CIA operatives were all supposedly specialists, they proved to be incredibly incompetent. Pastora finally got fed up and expelled them from his command post just before Costa Rican authorities raided and completely dismantled it in April 1984. "I fired them because it became apparent that they were not trying to really work but were trying to get a general picture of our organization," Pastora said. "I told them, 'You have no reason to come here; you haven't contributed anything.' Three days later they sent the police." Pastora and others believe that the CIA may have permitted Costa Rican security forces to raid and dismantle the "San Pedro" command post both as a retaliation for these firings and as part of the general crackdown on Pastora in the weeks leading up to the La Penca bombing.

The CIA had another special team within ARDE: a group of Agency-trained and -financed Nicaraguan pilots who operated out of Miami, El Salvador, and Costa Rica. From the inception of the Southern Front, the CIA considered a contra air force to be essential to move personnel and supplies, evacuate battlefield casualties, and, for a short period, to launch air strikes against Nicaragua. Many of the original contra pilots—Renato Torrealba, Mariano Montealegre, Marcos Aguado, Gustavo Quesado, Octavio Barrera ("Condorito"), Agustín Román, Sebastián Muller, and Guillermo Bolt—had flown for the Sandinista air force or Aero-Nica, the national airline, where they had been trained by a shadowy Panamanian American pilot, John Daly. Daly had worked for years with the Panamanian military; after the Sandinista triumph, the new government hired him to train pilots for their air force and airline. In the early 1980s, most of Daly's trainees "defected" and publicly joined with Pastora. Those involved say they suspect that Daly was a CIA operative assigned to set up an Agency cell among Nicaragua's pilots.

After defecting, members of this team underwent training at Ilopango Air Base in El Salvador, where they gained combat experience by going on bombing raids with the Salvadoran Air Force.[58] From late 1982 on, ARDE had munitions warehouses and transport planes at Ilopango. According to an ARDE official based at Ilopango, all the logistics were handled on a rotation basis by six CIA agents from the U.S. Embassy. The team of contra pilots was headed by former AeroNica pilot Torrealba (who was killed in an April 1984 crash) and they flew supply runs for both the Southern and Northern Fronts. They were well paid—about $5,000 a month each.

The CIA supplied light airplanes and helicopters to both ARDE and the FDN. These planes were "laundered" through the Salvadoran military, quietly passed from the Pentagon to the CIA as "surplus,"[59] "given" as gifts by "friends" (drug traffickers) in Miami, or, most frequently, supplied through dummy aviation companies.[60] On the eve of the La Penca bombing, Robert Owen described in a memo to North his meeting with "the commander of Pastora's air force." Owen wrote, "He has 15 Nica pilots, 1 Costa Rican and a Salvo [Salvadoran]. There are another 5–10 who pack the chutes and act as kickers. For aircraft they have: 1 twin engine Islander, 1 twin engine Queen Air; 1 Barron [Baron]; 1 Cessna 206; and I believe 1 Cessna 180 and a Maul [Maule] which they were using for wounded. They also have 3 helicopters, only one of which was working."[61] Owen was describing the ARDE air force at its height. By the time Pastora finally threw in the towel in late May 1986, ARDE did not have a single plane left; all had either crashed or been seized by John Hull and the FDN.

In addition to the CIA's team of pilots and the "Latin American assets" put inside ARDE, there were various Southern Front contras who worked directly for the CIA. Most of the top political leaders—Robelo, Alfredo César, Arturo Cruz, Sr., Arturo Cruz, Jr.,—received payments from the CIA. But a host of lesser officials were also strategically placed within Pastora's organization to help execute CIA directives. All had a personal devotion to the United States, where they had lived for years. Others, like Pastora's cousin Orión Pastora, ARDE's information officer and liaison with the CIA-paid Costa Rican journalists, began cooperating in return for a U.S. visa and other rewards. One of the most important CIA operatives was Pastora's second-in-command, Harold Martínez ("Ramón"), who had been one of the co-founders of the FRS.

Later, two other Pastora commanders—Adolfo "Popo" Chamorro and Roberto "Tito" Chamorro—became CIA collaborators. Both these Chamorros were cousins of Octaviano César, an important contra-CIA operative with multiple functions, including overseeing a ring of informants. Octaviano, who looked like a seedier version of his brother Alfredo, the urbane banker and smooth contra politician, was also involved in drug trafficking. In the spring of 1984, Octaviano (along with Popo and ARDE pilot Marcos Aguado) helped arrange a deal with Colombian drug trafficker George Morales to supply planes, pilots, and cash to the Southern Front. In return, Octaviano promised to use his influence in Washington to get Morales's indictment delayed or dropped[62] (see chapter 11).

Another contra with influence in Washington was Arturo Cruz, Jr., who worked with Oliver North and the CIA, dated

North's secretary Fawn Hall, and played a sophisticated game intended to give Pastora and ARDE an independent image. While his father served as ARDE's respectable elder patrician, the younger Cruz acted as its leftist intellectual, pushing Pastora to take a publicly anti-CIA posture.[63] Educated in Britain and at Johns Hopkins University, he became, until shortly after La Penca, Pastora's main ideological "handler" in Washington, arranging meetings with administration officials, Congress, and influential private individuals.

The Ugly American and *La Zona Norteamericana*

> *Hail Mary, Queen of Grace*
> *The Southern Front is a Horrible disgrace.*
> *Help us Lord to change the pace,*
> *So all of us might save face.*
>   —John Hull to Oliver North, May 1985[64]

Of all the CIA operatives in Costa Rica, none was more important than the balding, ruddy-faced, solidly built farmer, the real John Hull. Hull's public persona was that of a big-hearted, good-humored, plain-talking American patriot. He portrayed himself as "a simple farm boy," transplanted in the late 1950s from Indiana to Costa Rica. He had brought with him, he said, the best of North American values: hard work, know-how, charity, Christianity, and anticommunism.

Hull claimed his pioneering spirit had tamed the wilderness and carved profitable homesteads out of jungle. He boasted that he had brought civilization in the form of U.S. technology, new agricultural exports, and other North American investors. After his arrival with his father in 1956, Hull's enterprises grew to include 2,500 acres in ranches stocked with several thousand head of pure Brahman cattle, timberland, citrus farms, an orange-tree nursery, and a company, Inversiones Floyd (or Floyd Investments), that managed about 25,000 acres throughout the northern zone for absentee American landowners. An experienced pilot, Hull used his light aircraft the way most farmers use pick-up trucks—to haul passengers and supplies and to inspect his vast holdings. He once boasted, with considerable justification, "Nothing moves along the Costa Rican–Nicaraguan border without my knowledge."

From the front porch of his airy farmhouse at the crossroads town of Muelle, Hull would gaze out at his 1,700-acre cattle ranch and see, he told visitors, communist threats in various disguises: Costa Rican squatters, "leftist" journalists, liberal U.S. congressmen, Castro Cuban agents, Russian spies, and, most importantly, the Sandinistas. He was driven, he claimed, by a mission to defend U.S. and Costa Rican democracy from the imminent threat of "international communism." As he put it in early 1984, "If the U.S. doesn't help, I think Costa Rica will fall, and El Salvador. And then Mexico could well go. Then you've got the domino theory, and a scenario where they [the communists] can throw twenty or thirty thousand refugees into the States. They can break the U.S. economy and not even fire a shot. I think that's their plans, and I think they're doing a splendid job."

Hull contended that his help for the contras was purely humanitarian. Ad nauseam, he repeated that he gave only food, shelter, clothing, and band-aids to the "resistance fighters." He acknowledged flying mercy missions into Nicaragua to bring out the wounded for treatment in Costa Rican hospitals and contra-run clinics, claiming to be the Florence Nightingale of the Southern Front. He insisted that he violated no laws.

In reality, Hull was a man of many faces and disguises, as amoral and multifaceted as the Southern Front which he ran. Underneath his good-old-boy, cowboy image, Hull was crass, vindictive, miserly, greedy, vain, and ruthless. He was eventually charged by Costa Rica's judicial authorities with murder, drug trafficking, and "hostile acts"—violating Costa Rica's official policy of neutrality by making war against Nicaragua. But the list of accusations against Hull also includes fraud, bigamy, theft, embezzlement of U.S. government funds, holding both U.S. and Costa Rican citizenship illegally, black marketeering, and money laundering. Hull was known by various names —"*Papi*" (Father), "*El Patrón*" (The Boss), and "Santa Claus"—all reflecting the tremendous power he wielded. But by the end of the decade, many Costa

Ricans, former contras, and other North American residents in Costa Rica thought the most fitting name for Hull was "the Ugly American."

John Hull's right-wing connections and convictions were a family tradition. He grew up in Patoka, a rural town in the southeast corner of Indiana, where the state meets Kentucky and Illinois. This is fertile country, not only for farming, but also for fundamentalist religious sects and Ku Klux Klan activities. One of Hull's close friends and business partners in Costa Rica, Richard Shoff, had been the Indiana Klan's state secretary and was a frequent speaker at Klan rallies in the 1970s.[65]

Hull's father was a farmer and a World War I captain in military intelligence. In Indiana, the senior Hull ran a network of informers who infiltrated labor-union meetings during the Depression to gather data on suspected leftists. "He had men that could go into meetings that the Reds had and come out remembering more than 200 names," Hull recounted with pride to journalist Jonathan Kwitny.[66]

Prior to the U.S. entry into World War II, Hull was a flight instructor in the U.S. Air Force. During the war, he joined the Canadian Air Force and flew planes from Canadian factories to Britain for use by the Royal Air Force (RAF). Hull also claims that he flew fighters and bombers in the Ferry Command of Britain's Royal Air Force.[67] He liked to take visitors to his ranch into his small study and show them photos and memorabilia of his war exploits.

Back in Indiana after the war, Hull started a small timber and grain farm, which he built into a lucrative 500-acre operation, Floyd Investments. By the mid-1980s, this company which was managed by his legal wife, was described as "one of the most mechanized and highly productive farms in northern Indiana."[68]

He and his father began spending winters in Costa Rica in 1956; by 1968 they had settled permanently into farming in the San Carlos area. By the mid-1970s, Hull had set up Inversiones Floyd to purchase and manage land for absentee buyers. By this point he had already come to the attention of the local authorities and the press. Along with other ranchers and land speculators,

Hull became involved in intense, and not infrequently violent, struggles with peasant squatters and with other foreign investors over land in the expanding cattle zone between Ciudad Quesada and the Nicaraguan border.[69] As a consequence of these disputes, several U.S. investors sued Hull for fraudulently handling the land sales. Over the years, Hull's high-handed, sloppy, and illegal business practices led to a series of squabbles and lawsuits with his investors and business associates.[70]

There are indications that it was opportunities offered by the CIA rather than cheap farm land which lured Hull and his father to Central America. When they first arrived, Hull's father had a job with the U.S. Department of Agriculture that required the pair to fly their private plane all over Latin America. "I've heard Hull's father was connected with the CIA and for me that [Department of Agriculture] job would have been a perfect cover," said Hull's ex-business partner, Bill Crone. Hull acknowledges that his father "stayed with military intelligence until old age."[71]

Another businessman has identified John Hull as a CIA agent he worked with in Brazil in the mid-1970s. Robert Hayes, president of a Lakeland, Florida, engineering firm who admits to working for the CIA and other U.S. intelligence agencies, says that in 1987 he picked up a copy of *Time* magazine[72] and saw the photo of a man he had been trying to avoid for more than a decade. Hayes subsequently told journalists and congressional and legal investigators that the *Time* photo of John Hull looked exactly like a man he had known first as "Joe Sibley" and later as "John Joseph Michaels." Hayes, who in the 1970s ran a construction and engineering firm in Brazil, says that Hull/Sibley/Michaels worked out of the U.S. Consulate in Sîo Paulo and, between 1974 and 1976, recruited him for a series of clandestine "projects" that included interrogations, kidnappings, and assassinations—all sanctioned, he was led to believe, by the U.S. government.

Hayes says the relationship soured after this man tried to recruit him for acts of "simulated terrorism" (including the bombing of a Catholic cathedral, a theater complex, and the U.S. Consulate in Sîo Paulo), with the intent of planting phony evidence implicating Cuba. Hayes refused because civilians would be killed, but he says that Hull/Sibley/Michaels and two other CIA agents kept pressuring

him to participate. Finally, Hayes says, he fled for his life after two
CIA agents and four of his own associates were murdered.[73]

It sounded bizarre, but the tale had a familiar ring. This Sîo
Paulo plot was nearly identical to the 1985 San José plot in which
Hull's right-wing operatives were to bomb the U.S. Embassy and
other targets and leave behind evidence incriminating the Sandinistas. Investigators from the House Subcommittee on Crime and
Criminal Justice and journalists found Hayes and his wife, who
corroborated the story, credible, and Hayes successfully picked
out Hull's voice from a series of recordings. Associates in Costa
Rica say that Hull did have business interests in Brazil and traveled
there frequently in the mid-1970s, although neither he nor "Sibley" or "Michaels" are listed in the U.S. State Department's direc-
tory of employees for Brazil.[74] Hull's denial had a familiar ring as
well: he called Hayes's story "a communist disinformation deal to
discredit the contras."[75]

Several sources claim that Hull worked as a CIA agent along
the Sandinistas' Southern Front in the late 1970s, once the Agency
realized Somoza's days were numbered. Hull's sidekick Bruce
Jones says that he and Hull were involved in providing "humanitarian" aid to the Sandinistas from 1978 until the overthrow of
Somoza in July 1979. According to Jones, "On numerous occasions he [Hull] flew wounded Sandinista soldiers out from the
bush . . . into the hospitals in Ciudad Quesada. And we supplied
blankets, medical supplies for them, clothes for them."[76] Hull
himself admits that, within a week of the Sandinista victory (in
July 1979), he led a team of doctors into southern Nicaragua to
report on conditions for the CIA. Congressional investigators
found evidence as well that Hull worked for the CIA at least since
the early 1970s. Hull acknowledges that he regularly passed on
information to the U.S. Embassy in San José, but confesses to
working as a CIA "liaison" only since 1982.[77] At this point Hull
was put in charge of contra operations out of the northern zone. In
this position, he oversaw supply drops into the zone, established
contra camps on farms in the north, rented houses for the CIA and
contras in both San José and Ciudad Quesada, set up clandestine
clinics for treating wounded contras, organized supply lines to the
camps, served as a paymaster, and—together with contra com-

manders and Costa Rican colonels—planned rebel offensives. Although until May 1984 he claimed to be supporting Pastora and ARDE, from the outset his goal, like the CIA's, was to unify the Southern Front with the Honduran-based FDN.

Hull's curriculum vitae also included overseeing the foreigners involved in the war: the Miami Cubans who came in 1983, a group of five gringo mercenaries who arrived in 1985, and "private patriotic Americans" (fellow farmers, pilots, and investors), many of whom also had properties in northern Costa Rica.[78] Among the most important of these were Bruce Jones, who was expelled from Costa Rica after *Life* magazine identified him as a CIA agent and photographed him in camouflage gear leading a contra band across a river[79]; William Crone, who, in testimony to congressional and judicial investigators, detailed Hull's business and contra activities and admitted to his own role as pilot for the CIA[80]; and James Denby, another farmer-pilot who, in December 1987, was arrested and jailed by the Sandinistas when his plane made an unauthorized landing in Nicaragua.[81]

Scattered throughout Costa Rica were what contra and Costa Rican sources described as "lesser John Hulls" who also worked to support the war against Nicaragua. In the early 1980s, Cecil Hylton, a Virginia millionaire who owned extensive cattle and rice farms in Guanacaste, allowed at least one of these, Hacienda El Hacha, to be used for contra training and supply drops. In 1984, Hylton donated seventeen properties near the Nicaraguan border, including El Hacha, to the Assemblies of God ministry of U.S. television evangelist and contra supporter Jimmy Swaggart. In the early 1990s, when the contra war was over, Swaggart's ministry sold much of this property to Costa Rica's National Parks Foundation for incorporation into the Guanacaste Park.[82] Another *gringo* collaborator was Colonel Joseph Yurko, a retired military officer with a farm on the Nicaraguan border and a house in Washington who assisted ARDE on behalf of the Pentagon, several sources said. Over on the Atlantic coast port of Limón was another American, Eugene Strickland, a tugboat captain who met frequently with Hull and worked closely with the Miskito Indian contras. Near the border with Panama was an erratic German named Manfred Hoffman, who had close ties to the U.S. Southern

Command and worked for the CIA. Hoffman's presence came to light after the September 1985 murder of Panamanian doctor and contra commander Hugo Spadafora. At the request of CIA station chief Joe Fernández, Hoffman spread a transparently false story blaming the murder on Salvadoran leftists.[83]

Together with some of these other foreigners, Hull became deeply involved in two of the most closely guarded "projects" of the contra war: terrorist actions designed to be blamed on the Sandinistas and drug trafficking. How much Hull received for his services is unknown. He admitted to getting $800 a month from the CIA for five personal bodyguards, and he told soldiers of fortune Peter Glibbery and Steven Carr that his "friend" on the National Security Council (North) deposited $10,000 a month into his Miami bank account.[84]

Hull intermingled his business and contra affairs and managed the covert contra operation with a casualness that reflected his confidence that he was untouchable. Guns were bought, sold, and occasionally stored in his office on the edge of Ciudad Quesada. Hull used a crackly, hand-held radio to communicate with his ranch house and properties about both business and contra affairs. Cuban Americans, CIA operatives, and mercenaries frequented and sometimes slept in the office. He routinely had calls or visits from absentee U.S. investors, other American farmers, Costa Rican government officials, contra commanders, the CIA station chief in San José, Robert Owen, and the press.

Neighbors said the comings and goings at Hull's main ranch, half an hour's drive north from Ciudad Quesada, were "like Grand Central Station." Vehicles known to belong to the contras, covered trucks said to carry weapons, and taxis filled with an assortment of gringos—muscular mercenaries, pot-bellied southerners, and straight-laced Washington bureaucrats—passed in and out of Hull's gates at all hours of the day and night. Hull usually introduced American visitors as would-be investors in his citrus project, but they often turned out to be part of the contras' "private aid" network.

The farm abutted the San Carlos River, a tributary of the San Juan River along which the contra camps were scattered. Gradually it took on the appearance of a military encampment. Large storage tanks for aviation fuel were crudely concealed within a wooden shed. The road and nearby bridge were improved by AID, and there was a landing strip—the largest in the region—next to the main house.[85] According to a November 1987 *Time* magazine article, "Barricades have been installed along the perimeter of his main estate. The ranch-house roof has been reinforced to resist mortar attack; large mesh screens cover the windows to repel grenades. Until recently as many as five bodyguards, paid a total of $800 a month, watched over Hull and his [common-law] wife," Margarita Acosta.[86] On Sundays, Hull and other local ranchers and roughnecks who belonged to the North Huétar Democratic Association staged military maneuvers in his pastures. These vigilantes first organized in the 1970s to defend against squatters; in the 1980s they concentrated on preparing for the phantom Sandinista invasion.

In all his activities, Hull was very well protected.[87] He worked closely not only with top Costa Rican political and security officials, but more importantly with U.S. Embassy officials, including the various CIA station chiefs. He traveled often to Washington, where he called on his Indiana congressional delegation, including then-Senator Dan Quayle, as well as other congressional right-wingers and officials of the NSC, the Pentagon, and the CIA. Hull's name is sprinkled throughout Oliver North's notebooks, and North's assistant, Robert Owen, became the main courier between the NSC and the Southern Front. Those close to Hull said his company administered ranches in Costa Rica for important people including Rob Owen and Oliver North. In 1987, CIA station chief Joe Fernández told the CIA Inspector General's Office, "I've heard that Hull manages properties for several senators . . . [David] Durenburger, [Dan] Quale [*sic*] . . . and others in Washington." None of these names are found in Costa Rica's land registry records, but this is not conclusive since owners' identities are easily concealed behind corporations.[88]

Hull's connections went even higher. Costa Rican security sources say that during the Reagan administration Hull talked frequently with the office of Vice President Bush and that on one occasion Bush himself called Costa Rican President Monge to explain that an investigation into Hull's activities should be stopped because "this man is very important to us." CIA Station Chief Joe Fernández related that when he first met North in mid-1984, North told him to "take good care of him [Hull] because he has a close friend in the White House." When Fernández asked who, he recalls North replied, "The President . . . and he also has lots of other friends in Washington." Fernández was impressed: "I just didn't believe him. The President knew personally one of my station's assets! That was a new experience." He says shortly after this he met with his boss, William Casey, who also asked about Hull. "I had the idea that Hull was a special person," stated Fernández.[89] Indeed he was: so special that he was never compelled to testify before any of the U.S. government's Iran-contra investigations.

Over time, however, Hull's CIA and contra activities became so blatant that Costa Rican authorities could not continue to turn a blind eye. By March 1984, a local resident had brought suit against Hull, Bill Crone, and Bruce Jones for supporting the contras and for arms trafficking. Once, Hull and his lawyer even spent the night in the town jail, but judicial police say an urgent call from Ambassador Tambs succeeded in getting them released.

Costa Rican guardsmen raided Hull's farm several times, but he was invariably tipped beforehand. One raid in August 1985 was particularly ambitious. The Rural Guard launched a two-pronged attack—by land, through the front gate of his property, and by water, coming up the river on the back of his property. The land patrol arrived first, only to find a cheerful Hull waiting with a spread of lemonade and *bocas* (snacks). The amphibious flank hadn't arrived, so after searching Hull's house and finding $100,000 in cash but no arms, the troops turned to lemonade and small talk. Presently, someone spotted armed men creeping across the pasture toward the house. The guardsmen quickly put down their juice glasses, picked up their rifles, and crouched in readiness. Just before the orders to shoot were given, someone recognized that the assault force was the missing Rural Guard "amphibious" unit.

Despite Washington's protection and Hull's repeated refusal to cooperate with local authorities, in 1988 and 1989 the Costa Rican legislature's special drug commission presented evidence of Hull's cocaine trafficking, and the judicial branch indicted him for "hostile acts" and murder in the La Penca bombing. After his arrest in Costa Rica on January 12, 1989, nineteen U.S. Representatives signed a letter warning President Arias that U.S.–Costa Rican relations could be jeopardized if Hull were not treated properly.[90] Then, in July 1989, Hull jumped bail and was secretly flown to the United States, ironically by Drug Enforcement Agency (DEA) official Juan Pérez and a known drug trafficker, Dagoberto Núñez. Over the next several years, Costa Rican judicial authorities tried in vain to have Hull extradited from the United States so that he could be tried for murder and "hostile acts." Costa Rica's chief prosecutor José María Tijerino said that "according to the norms of international cooperation [extradition] shouldn't be complicated." However, after years of bureaucratic red tape and foot dragging, Tijerino sadly concluded that there was "no political will" to bring Hull to justice.[91]

The Cuban Network
and the International Brigade

In early June 1983, just after ARDE officially declared the start of Southern Front military operations, a contingent of seventeen private "volunteers" arrived from Miami. They had come, so they said, as military trainers for the contras. In return, they hoped to gain practical military experience fighting alongside the contras, intercepting shipments of arms and other supplies from Cuba to the Sandinistas, and attacking Cuban-run institutions and Cuban personnel inside Nicaragua. They also had a long-term objective: top FDN leaders had promised them that once Nicaragua was "liberated," they could use the Atlantic coast as a base for military operations against Cuba, just as Somoza had permitted during the Bay of Pigs invasion. These Miami fighters said they were motivated by a desire to build a worldwide anticommunist movement linking the fight in Nicaragua to the guerrilla wars against the Marxist governments in Angola, Mozambique, and Afghanistan. They claimed to be unpaid volunteers, supported by private donations from businessmen in Miami, and they denied having ties to any branch of the U.S. government, including the CIA.

Some were anticommunist soldiers of fortune, but two leaders of this "International Brigade"—Felipe Vidal and René
Corvo—were CIA operatives and drug traffickers. Their mission
was not to help build the Southern Front contras into a formidable
fighting force, but rather to remove both Edén Pastora and
Brooklyn Rivera and replace them with a small, politically control-
lable UDN-FARN army aligned with the FDN and directed by the
CIA. In pursuing these goals, they had a hand in the most
clandestine Southern Front operations: the formation in 1983 of
M-3, the first anti-Pastora splinter group; several plots to eliminate
Pastora; a 1985 plot to bomb the U.S. Embassy; several assassination attempts against Brooklyn Rivera; payoffs to contra commanders who joined UDN-FARN and the FDN; and efforts in the
late 1980s to sabotage Rivera's negotiations with the Sandinistas.
They used the contra infrastructure on Hull's farms, private airstrips in Guanacaste, and front companies such as the Cuban-run
seafood exporting company Frigoríficos de Puntarenas, to move
Colombian cocaine via Costa Rica to the United States.

While closely aligned with Hugo Spadafora and his handful of
Panamanian fighters, Vidal and Corvo worked under the control
of John Hull, a series of CIA station chiefs, and Oliver North. The
pair was also connected to Félix Rodríguez, Luis Posada and
Gustavo Villoldo, three other Cuban American CIA operatives
working in contra operations in El Salvador and Honduras. And
Vidal and Corvo had ties to Rafael Quintero, another Cuban CIA
agent who came to Costa Rica in 1985 to oversee construction of
the secret Santa Elena airstrip. Beginning in late 1984, they became linked with the Alabama-based Civilian Military Assistance
(CMA) and a group of American mercenaries sent to the Southern
Front. These foreign foot soldiers formed part of the private façade
designed to conceal Washington's role in the illegal contra war.

This International Brigade worked in Costa Rica until the
Iran-contra scandal broke and the Arias government finally forced
the closing of the Southern Front. At any time, there were never
more than twenty foreign mercenaries in Costa Rica, most of
whom were Miami Cubans. According to Vidal, the International
Brigade was supported by "fifty to sixty collaborators" in both
Miami and Costa Rica. Vidal describes his supporters as "dedicated

patriots" with years of service to the anti-Castro cause. The "rank and file" of this International Brigade came from the Miami milieu, where anticommunism and the love of combat and terrorism are intertwined with organized crime and CIA operations.

One of the Brigade's most elusive backers was Watergate burglar and long-time CIA agent Eugenio "Rolando" Martínez. In 1981, President Reagan pardoned Martínez (he was the only Watergate burglar to be so pardoned), and he and Vidal developed a close personal and professional relationship. Many others with the Brigade had been arrested and convicted on arms and drug violations and most had been members of various Cuban extremist terrorist groups—Alpha 66, Omega 7, the Cuban National Movement, CORU (*Comando de Organizaciónes Revoluciónarias Unidas*), the 2506 Brigade of Bay of Pigs veterans, the Cuban Legion, and others. Two of the Cubans who came to Costa Rica, Pedro Gil and Rafael Pérez, were implicated (along with some International Brigade supporters in Miami) in the May 27, 1983, bombing of Miami's Continental Bank building. Most felt no moral quandary about terrorism if it furthered their anti-Castro political aims. As advertising executive and soldier-of-fortune Eduardo Paz put it in an interview, "I would blow up [the state of] Maine with everyone in it if it would provoke a war with Cuba. We came to Costa Rica because we wanted to instigate direct U.S. intervention against both Nicaragua and Cuba."[92]

Several of these "internationalists" said that, during a 1982 visit to Miami, El Negro Chamorro had invited them to come to Costa Rica to fight with UDN-FARN. When the group arrived in Costa Rica the following June, Felipe Vidal Santiago (alias Morgan or Max Vargas),[93] a political activist with a string of arms and drug arrests and convictions,[94] quickly took charge of operations. Vidal's associates described him as "instinctively a killer," "a psycho," and a bomb expert. Several of the Iran-contra whistle blowers—Steven Carr, Peter Glibbery, Jack Terrell, and Jesús García—claimed that Vidal had threatened to kill them if they continued talking to the press. Despite Costa Rica's tropical climate, Vidal always wore a leather jacket to conceal a holstered pistol. He also kept a crossbow in a closet at Hull's ranch; it was, Hull told others, "Felipe's weapon of choice."

But Vidal's personality could belie his reputation and police record. Smart, humorous, hardworking, with a husky voice, pleasant smile, and direct penetrating eyes, he had a way with women. At times he sported a thick black beard which gave him a decidedly more sinister appearance. In a series of interviews over eight months, Vidal revealed many details of his personal history and political views. Born into a middle-class family in Havana in 1951, Vidal and his parents fled to Miami in 1961. While his mother worked in a factory putting plastic grapes in ornamental bouquets, his father, an ex-naval officer, helped found the Cuban National Movement (CNM), which Vidal termed "an independent organization that didn't take money from the CIA." Authors Warren Hinckle and William Turner describe the CNM as "a crypto-fascist . . . action group which looked fondly upon the Italy of Mussolini and the Germany of Hitler."[95] The senior Vidal, also named Felipe, made two dozen clandestine sabotage missions against Cuba before being captured and publicly executed by firing squad in 1964.

Vidal, who was twelve at the time, blames the CIA and the Kennedy administration for his father's death, as well as for the failure of the Bay of Pigs invasion and for cutting support to anti-Castro militants following the Cuban missile crisis. "Suspicion of the CIA was something engraved on me by my father," Vidal recalled. Yet Vidal, like his father, has worked for the CIA much of his adult life.

In the late 1970s, Vidal became involved in a variety of anti-Cuban terrorist actions, working throughout Central America and parts of the Caribbean. He recounted, for instance, assisting in the attempted kidnapping of a Cuban consul in Mérida, Mexico. (A Cuban fisheries technician was mistakenly killed.) Sometimes his references to past activities were more oblique. Once, when a discussion turned to the arrest of some anti-Castro militants who had attempted to blow up a Cuban diplomat's car in New York, Vidal shook his head and said, "I had told those guys to wear gloves when they fastened hand grenades under a car."

Another of those put on the CIA payroll once the Reagan administration took office was René Corvo, the other principal in the Southern Front's Cuban contingent. Known as "The Dwarf," Corvo (sometimes spelled Corbo) is a thin, aging man with a graying Ho Chi Minh–style wispy beard and the appearance of ill health brought on by alcoholism. A trained nurse and former U.S. Army paratrooper, Corvo was captured during the Bay of Pigs invasion and spent twenty-two months in a Cuban jail. He is an active member of the 2506 Brigade and was designated in 1983 as the organization's official "representative" to the contras.[96] Between January and August 1983, he had been the military commander of the "Commandos 307" contra-Cuban training camp in Naples, Florida, and had ties to another training camp in the Everglades.

Corvo, together with Frank "Papito" Hernández, who crewed on contra supply flights, came to Costa Rica in December 1983, but he continued to handle outside logistics, returning to Miami to recruit Cuban fighters, raise funds, and arrange shipments of arms and supplies.[97] He also supplied financial assistance, including cash and airline tickets, to some of his recruits. While Vidal instilled fear and respect in those around him, Corvo was looked upon as a wild card—incompetent, volatile, and careless about his involvement in illegal activities. In a memo to Oliver North, Robert Owen wrote bluntly, "Corbo is trouble."[98]

One of the International Brigade's backers in Costa Rica was Cuban exile Adolfo Jiménez, a Bay of Pigs veteran and long-time CIA operative. When Vidal's people first arrived in June 1983, they stayed in the San José hotel El Presidente, of which Jiménez is part owner. Jiménez had lived in Costa Rica for many years and the contras used his Guanacaste farm for military training and arms and drug flights. According to a contra leader who visited Jiménez's farm in the early 1980s, it was a well-organized operation in which top regional Rural and Civil Guard officials were paid to cooperate.

An early contra military trainer on Jiménez's farm was Armando López-Estrada, another Bay of Pigs veteran, long involved with the CIA and drug trafficking. While Jiménez operated in the shadows and shied away from the press, López-Estrada, a silver-haired, rather elegant-looking terrorist, seemed to relish taking credit for an impressive list of exploits. He is described as the military chief of the 2506 Brigade and a founding member of CORU; he was investigated by the FBI for possible involvement in the 1976 Air Cubana bombing; in 1978 he was tried and acquitted in Miami for making unauthorized commando attacks against Cuba; and in 1980 he was involved, along with Vidal, in the assassination of a Cuban official in Mérida, Mexico.[99]

In August 1986, López-Estrada was arrested by Costa Rican authorities after mechanics at a muffler shop discovered three live hand grenades strapped to the bottom of his late model Toyota. The Cuban told startled shop employees that he worked for the military section of the U.S. Embassy. In a four-page statement to Costa Rican authorities, López-Estrada said that he had been hired by Reagan administration officials in 1981 to recruit agents in the Cuban exile communities in Costa Rica and Panama. He said that in 1983 and early 1984 he worked as a CIA operative, supervising a group of Cubans who were training contras on Jiménez's farm and helping to secure military supplies for the contras. In early 1984, Hull proposed that he and René Corvo supply ARDE, but, angered by Pastora's anti-U.S. declarations, López-Estrada and Corvo both entered Costa Rica on May 31, 1984, the day after the La Penca bombing.[100]

Immigration records show he traveled frequently between Miami, Colombia, and Costa Rica. A top Costa Rican security official said in an interview that the government was convinced López-Estrada was involved in trafficking cocaine. The U.S. Embassy quickly denied any ties to López-Estrada, describing him as a "private businessman." In a crude attempt at damage control, *La República* accused the Sandinistas of planting the grenades, and Channel 7 refused "for reasons of national security" to sell video footage of López-Estrada's arrest to U.S. television networks. Rather than investigate further and risk turning up a CIA connection, the government first held him incommunicado and then put López-Estrada on a plane to Miami and barred him from reentering the country for ten years.[101]

One of Vidal's most important Cuban supporters was Dagoberto Núñez (or Moisés Núñez Ruíz), another Bay of Pigs veteran who had extensive U.S. military training and had lived in Costa Rica since 1977. In 1982, he and a group of Miami Cubans took over Frigoríficos de Puntarenas, an existing company that exported seafood from Costa Rica to its sister company, Ocean Hunter, in Miami. In an interview Núñez said he was simply an anticommunist businessman who had provided "economic support"—bags of rice, beef, and, on occasion, shrimp—to the contras. Núñez described his support as minimal and humanitarian, but a document written by Vidal lists Núñez as handling the International Brigade's "logistics" in Costa Rica and Núñez's Miami business partner Francisco Chánes as being in charge of logistics in the States.[102] A 1988 U.S. Senate report makes it clear that "logistics" included moving drugs and money laundering. It states, "Frigoríficos de Punterennas [sic] is a Costa Rican seafood company which was created as a cover for the laundering of drug money." In 1986, as its drug ties were being investigated, Frigoríficos received $261,937 in U.S. State Department humanitarian aid funds for the contras. This transaction was overseen by Robert Owen.[103]

Another supporter of the Cuban contingent was Tony Santiago, a CIA operative and the uncle of Felipe Vidal, who lived in Miami but spent much of his time in Costa Rica. Santiago, a well-educated, distinguished-looking man in his mid-50s, claimed a long and close friendship with President Monge. The two had worked, along with CIA agent Sacha Volman, at the San José-based Inter-American Institute of Political Education, a Liberation party think tank covertly funded by the Agency. In 1983 and 1984 Santiago described himself as doing advisory work for President Monge.[104]

These were some of the men behind the façade of this private, voluntary International Brigade. While within Costa Rica the Brigade operated in the shadows, keeping a very low profile, in Miami's Cuban community these men appeared on radio talk shows, at public rallies, and in the Spanish-language press, playing the role of great patriots going off to fight Cuba's proxy in Central America (the Sandinistas) and to build new bases from which to liberate their home island. But this, of course, was only their cover story. They did not mention their CIA or drug-trafficking connections.

From the outset their mission appeared star-crossed. "We began [in early 1983] by making a front organization and running a marathon supposedly to raise money for Nicaraguan refugees. We got a lot of donations, especially from factories," Vidal recounted. They mixed these "humanitarian" donations with military supplies for themselves and ARDE and put together a shipment of hospital equipment, tents, blankets, clothing, enough canned food for 150 men for two months, $250,000 in medicines, 133 uniforms and pairs of boots, and an unspecified quantity of weapons and ammunition—leftovers from past anti-Castro Cuban operations in the United States. The goods were loaded into a container in Miami and in September 1983 arrived by ship at the Costa Rican Atlantic port of Limón. Vidal and several other "volunteers" accompanied the shipment, dressed in white uniforms and "disguised as Puerto Rican nurses" coming to help in the refugee camps. But their advance work somehow went awry. The usually cooperative Costa Rican customs officials inspected the container, found the mortars, machine guns, ammunition, and uniforms hidden under the clothing and medicines, and seized the shipment. Vidal and the other "nurses" managed to slip quietly into Costa Rica.

These Cubans had other shipments arrive without difficulty, thanks to a network of Costa Rican collaborators. Most important was Colonel Rodrigo Paniagua, who was the godfather of one of Vidal's daughters, an indication of the two men's close personal relationship. Vidal estimated that his group brought into Costa Rica over a million dollars of military supplies, enough to outfit and equip five hundred fighters. Sometimes supplies arrived on commercial flights, but most came via light aircraft directly into the clandestine military camps in Costa Rica.

Most members of the Cuban contingent came, they said, to join El Negro Chamorro's UDN-FARN, which had been carrying out tiny skirmishes across Costa Rica's border. But by the time they arrived, Chamorro had broken with Pastora and had moved his base of operations temporarily to Honduras, where he formed an alliance with the FDN. Finding Chamorro gone, Vidal and some of the others sought to make contact with Pastora. Over the objections of Pastora and with the help of Hull, Bruce Jones, Colonel Paniagua, and Adolfo "Popo" Chamorro, the Cubans managed to be accepted as military trainers in the San Juan River camp of one ARDE commander, Comandante Tono. From there they monitored Pastora's activities. After the La Penca bombing, some of the Cubans regrouped at an FDN camp called Monico, on one of Hull's farms, while others went to the UDN-FARN's camp near Los Chiles. From there they continued to ply their twin skills of terrorism and drug trafficking.

While Vidal was maneuvering his way into an ARDE camp, others of these Cubans were helping foment a split within the Alliance. In October 1983, a handful of contras and their supporters, including Miami Cubans Eduardo Paz and Rafael Pérez, announced they were forming an anti-Pastora splinter group known as the Movement for a Third Way or M-3. This was, a top ARDE official later said, "the first attempt by the Company to make a new Southern Front without Edén," and it coincided with the first split between Robelo and Pastora (and Brooklyn Rivera) over CIA pressure for unity with the Honduran-based FDN and Misura.

From the outset M-3 appeared to be a CIA creation. The breakfast press conference at a San José hotel announcing its formation, the carefully prepared press releases, and the fact that many U.S. journalists had received calls from Washington informing them of the event, gave credence to speculation that this was more than a dissident grassroots movement. Most of M-3's five directors had strong ties to the United States. Only two were present that day. Its military commander was Eduardo Sánchez Renazco, who had fought with Pastora against Somoza and had briefly headed the Sandinistas' Air Force Militia Reserve before defecting and becoming ARDE's first intelligence chief. He had acquired the nom-de-guerre of "Alejandro el Gringo" because he had lived in the United States for years and had been a Green Beret in Vietnam. M-3's political director, Alvaro Taboada, was also present. He had been the Sandinistas' ambassador to Ecuador until November 1982, when he resigned and joined Pastora.

Not present was Luis Rivas Leal ("Comandante Roger Alemán" or "Wicho"), an engineer and (like Taboada) a Tulane University graduate who had long lived in the United States. A favorite of the CIA, the FDN, and later, Oliver North's network, Rivas had played an early role in locating Southern Front airstrips and later in schemes to remove Pastora. Also absent were the two other directors: Dr. Sergio Prado, a physician who was said to be "the real brains" behind the organization, and Sebastián González ("Wachán"), Pastora's old commander, who had close ties to the CIA, the Israelis, and Noriega.

According to press reports and the accounts of others, M-3 guerrillas saw very little combat against the Sandinistas. Most of their time was spent feuding with Pastora's forces and dodging Costa Rican authorities, who accused them of an assassination and cattle smuggling from Nicaragua.[105] This dissident movement only existed for about a year. It set up a camp, with just thirty-two fighters, near the famed Santa Elena airstrip and the Murciélago base (where U.S. Green Berets trained Costa Rican Civil Guardsmen). After a blitz of publicity, a few minor hit-and-run actions inside Nicaragua, a spray-painting campaign around Costa Rica, and some limited funding from the FDN, the CIA withdrew its support, choosing instead to back the Hull-Vidal network and to try to work inside the main body of ARDE to force a merger with the FDN and the removal of Pastora. The shortage of funds finally forced M-3 to give up any pretext of being a guerrilla movement.

The CIA Calls the Shots

What the CIA wanted, Pastora and others on the Southern Front gradually realized, was total control. Pastora's original agreement with Dewey Clarridge—that he would accept CIA money, arms, and training but run his own war—proved delusory. The Agency resisted even semi-independence. If the CIA could not fully direct Southern Front military actions, they would prefer no action at all. If they could not mold Pastora into a passive puppet, they ultimately decided, they would get rid of him.

Pastora, in contrast, had grandiose dreams of becoming a great military commander. He sought to build not only a large contra army, but also his own navy and air force. The ARDE commander wanted to use CIA-supplied boats for military operations, and, for a time, the Agency agreed with this strategy. In late 1983, the CIA set out to organize an ARDE navy. According to one of those involved, the training was carried out in Miami in boats supplied by the CIA through an Agency front company, "Monza" or ABC Marine. The navy was intended both to help supply the contras by sea and to carry out attacks along Nicaragua's Atlantic coast.

Likewise, Pastora wanted ARDE's CIA-trained pilots and CIA-bought planes used for more than supply drops, transporting contra and CIA officials, and evacuating wounded: he wanted them used for military attacks. But ARDE's first air attack in September 1983, against Managua's international airport and other targets,[106] was a military fiasco. Rather than marking the opening of the Southern Front's air campaign, the incident caused the CIA to order a halt.

Bombing Managua had seemed an excellent idea beforehand; Casey, Clarridge, and Pastora all endorsed it. They wanted to show that the contras were capable of moving from the sparsely populated border regions and striking deep into the heart of Nicaragua. Casey wanted to make headlines; Pastora wanted to prove his military prowess. They dubbed the air strike "*Voltaje al Sol,*" ("Voltage to the Sun") which, ARDE officials say, was intended to signify a "Strike at the Center of Power."

At Ilopango Air Base in San Salvador, the CIA outfitted four planes to carry bombs and rockets. Three were small Beechcraft Barons from the Salvadoran Air Force, and the fourth was the Panamanian-registered Cessna 404 that had been based at Pavas. In San José, Venezuelan Iván Gómez, the CIA agent in charge of the operation, called together top ARDE officials—Carlos Coronel (representing Pastora), Alfonso Robelo, chief of ARDE's air force José Robelo, and Brooklyn Rivera—to select the targets. José Robelo recalled, "It was like a board of directors meeting, and it seemed a curious way to make decisions such as this." He says that originally they planned to bomb the Security Ministry headquarters (which had been Somoza's old military bunker) but decided against it because it was "too close to the Intercontinental Hotel where all the press and gringos stay." Two days beforehand, the pilots were assembled at Ilopango.

Before dawn on September 8, 1983, three ARDE planes flew out of Ilopango and headed toward Managua. One Beechcraft Baron had engine trouble and turned back. A second dropped bombs in a Managua residential area, injuring no one and doing little damage. The intended target was the Sandinistas' Santa María telecommunications center run by the Soviets. Early press reports said the bombs were aimed at the home of Foreign Minister Father

Miguel D'Escoto. Neither was hit. At the time, Father D'Escoto, along with eight other Latin foreign ministers, was attending a Contadora Group meeting in Panama City, where they were striving to reach a negotiated end to the Nicaraguan war. D'Escoto correctly charged that the air attack was intended to escalate the war and cause the Contadora peace process "to fail."

As the third plane, the Cessna 404, neared Managua, there was a last-minute change of plans. It had been scheduled to attack the Presidential House and Central Bank, but en route the two pilots radioed Iván that they intended to hit the Sandino International Airport instead. Agustín Román, a former AeroNica pilot, and Sebastián Muller, a helicopter pilot and Sandinista Air Force deserter, decided on the change "because they knew all the guys at the airport and they wanted to do something spectacular at that spot," a colleague explained later. Their plane swooped very low over the airport and dropped its two 500-pound bombs near the AeroNica hangar, damaging the hangar and destroying four military vehicles. But the force of the explosion threw the propeller-driven Cessna off course, sending it crashing into the control tower.[107] The impact ignited a fire in the terminal building and VIP lounge, where scores of waiting passengers and airport employees ran for cover, four persons were injured, and one was killed. Román and Muller also died in the crash.

Also flying toward the Managua airport at this same time were two U.S. Senators, Gary Hart of Colorado and William Cohen of Maine, who were on a Central American fact-finding mission. At the last minute, CIA officials ordered their U.S. Air Force C-140 transport plane into a holding pattern and then diverted it to Honduras. The Senators arrived in Managua that afternoon. They were shocked by the destruction, and even more upset when the Sandinistas produced irrefutable evidence that the bombing was a CIA operation.

In the wreckage the Sandinistas had discovered incriminating papers pointing toward the Agency. The Cessna's tail numbers and log book led from the CIA proprietor Investair to the ARDE front company Servicios de Mar, Aire y Tierra in Panama City. On the body of Román, Nicaraguan officials discovered a handwritten note outlining arrangements for a covert meeting with a "David

Anthony" at a Texas burger restaurant in the San José suburb of Moravia. The card said "Anthony" would be sitting near the front entrance with an "umbrella and news magazine on the table." The other side of the card contained a listing of U.S. Embassy officials, including Ambassador McNeil, and an extension for David Anthony. When called, the switchboard said that no David Anthony worked in the Embassy, and the extension was "out of service." When pressed, the operator transferred the call to Nelson Nugent, the deputy political officer whom an American mercenary later identified as his CIA contact at the Embassy. Nugent said he was "in no position to either deny or confirm anything."[108]

At a bilateral meeting in San José, Nicaraguan security officials presented their Costa Rican counterparts with a dossier on alleged Costa Rican complicity in the airport attack and other contra activities. All this proved embarrassing to the Monge government, which was deeply divided between those trying to enforce the official policy of neutrality and those collaborating with the CIA and the contras. The pro-neutrality faction, including Security Minister Angel Edmundo Solano, quickly announced a "clean-up operation" against ARDE. Within a ten-day period, the Costa Rican government declared it had foiled a planned guerrilla attack on the border post of Peñas Blancas, seized several boatloads of arms, arrested three ARDE guerrillas at the port of Moín outside Limón, and fired four top Civil Guard officials for arms trafficking and collaborating with the anti-Sandinistas. They also sent more guards to patrol the border zone and seal off the contras' "clandestine arteries," and they posted machine-gun-toting guards at the Pavas airport to prevent "any more flights for Pastora taking off from here." In addition, the government announced it had expelled over eighty "volunteers," mainly Vietnam veterans and Cuban Americans who had arrived in Costa Rica and brazenly announced their intention to fight with ARDE. But ARDE officials interviewed at the time said the Monge government crackdown was temporary. They said they were holding private talks with their Costa Rican government collaborators and expected that "in a few days we'll have this straightened out."

While the Monge government shadow-boxed with ARDE, the CIA had to face two badly shaken and very angry Senators. In

Managua, Hart and Cohen had chewed out the CIA station chief; back in Washington, they confronted Casey. They charged that the bombing raid was politically stupid and militarily inept. Hitting a civilian airport would only turn Nicaraguans against the contras; the CIA's fingerprints were all over the remains of the plane and the pilots; and the Sandinistas, whose agents had penetrated Pastora's inner circle, had known of the plans beforehand. In Managua, the CIA station chief was evasive; in Washington Casey was emphatic: the Agency had not authorized the bombing. The Agency line was that this was an initial effort by Edén Pastora's "new air force," that the contras were free agents, and they had to be allowed to do their own thing.[109]

But behind the scenes, the CIA was taking steps to assure that ARDE could never do its own thing. In early October the orders came down the line to stop all military attacks against Nicaragua from Ilopango. The air base was to be used only for contra resupply runs. The Nicaraguan pilots were moved out of Ilopango, and soon afterward they were replaced with American, South African, and other foreign pilots supplied by Richard Secord's network. In his testimony to the Iran-contra congressional hearings several years later, Joe Fernández said the CIA had been forced to cut its ties with Pastora in part because the ARDE pilots had changed targets at the last minute and bombed the Managua airport. What most irked him, Fernández said, was that "two members of the Senate . . . almost lost their lives because of [this] erratic action on the part of Edén Pastora."[110]

The next major action of the war, the mining of Nicaragua's ports, was carried out wholly by specially hired CIA assets. ARDE and the FDN played no role: they did not know about it beforehand, and they were simply ordered to claim responsibility afterward. It was a script written and executed by Washington. And, much more than the Managua airport bombing, it became an international scandal, leading to a cutoff of congressional funding for the contras and a major Reagan administration defeat in the World Court. The CIA, left to its own devices, turned out to be much more "erratic" than ARDE ever was.

Covering an Elephant

Gradually, concealing the CIA and contra networks and operations in Costa Rica became like trying to shroud an elephant with a blanket: some part kept coming uncovered. Of all the Southern Front infrastructure, it was the contra air force that most often threatened to blow wide open the whole clandestine arms and drug operation. After September 1983, ARDE's planes and pilots were restricted to supply runs, but even these flights continued to attract unwanted publicity. In early 1984, the contra resupply operation for the Southern Front once again greatly increased. Most planes were dropping supplies at night into the contra camps and bases along the San Juan River.

Then on the night of March 24, 1984, at the height of the supply operations to the Southern Front, one of the planes crashed near Hull's farm. Coming on the heels of revelations that the CIA had mined Nicaragua's harbors, this plane crash could have been the smoking gun revealing, for the first time, the CIA-run resupply network and American combat-related deaths. But instead, as happened repeatedly on the Southern Front, the CIA managed to orchestrate a cover-up and conceal important information until the press lost interest.

The DC-3 cargo plane was loaded with weapons, mortars, 500,000 bullets, 400 pairs of military boots, and uniforms to be dropped by parachute into a contra camp on the Nicaraguan side of the San Juan River. It was a rainy and foggy night, and the aluminum plane, which was painted gunboat gray, was flying low, without lights, guided by newly installed navigation equipment. As it made a turn over Chamorrito de Cutrís in northern Costa Rica, the navigation equipment apparently stopped functioning and the plane slammed into the side of Cerro Valerio, a remote, jungle-covered mountain. Weapons, ammunition, bodies, and wreckage were scattered over several hundred square meters. Peasants living in the area saw the fireball in the night and, a few hours later, made their way to the crash site.

All seven men on board were killed. Only two, both Nicaraguans, were ever publicly identified by Costa Rican and contra investigators. They were the pilot, Renato Torrealba (head of the

CIA team of contra pilots), and the co-pilot, Milton Gutiérrez Sacasa. Five other persons on the plane were variously reported to be Salvadorans, Nicaraguans, and Americans, but the exact composition differs according to the source.[111] The tilt of evidence indicates there were Americans, probably four, on board. William "Tom" Golden, who was assistant army attaché in Managua in the early 1980s, says, "There's no question in my mind. There would have been Americans on board because the supply flights always use contract pilots hired by CIA front companies."

As soon as CIA officials in San José, who were monitoring the flight, lost radio contact, they suspected a crash. The CIA head of security, "Tomás," frantically called Hull, ordering him to take his plane and find the wreckage. Hull did manage to locate and overfly the crash site. Contras on the ground awaiting the airdrop also sent an urgent message that they had suddenly lost communication with the plane.

Pastora says he, too, was called by "Tomás" and ordered to send men to the site to destroy all the evidence. The next day local residents led about a dozen uniformed men, a mixture of contras and Costa Rican Rural Guardsmen, to the site. They carried cans of gasoline. As the bodies were pulled from the wreckage, peasants later told reporters that they heard one ARDE guerrilla exclaim, "Oh no, Americans! This will really drop us in the shit." They said that the dead included four blond gringos wearing camouflage uniforms.

The ARDE guerrillas proceeded to cut the jawbone from each body, following instructions given by CIA agents "Tomás" and Iván Gómez, who was handling the supply flight from Pastora's "San Pedro" headquarters. The bodies were then partially burned, placed in plastic bags, and buried in shallow graves marked with small wooden crosses tied together with parachute rope. Then they collected five loads of salvageable weapons along with the jawbones (which were sent to the United States so the CIA could identify those killed), drenched the wreckage in gasoline, and set fire to the site.

For almost two weeks, nothing appeared in the local press, although rumors of the crash rapidly circulated around San Carlos. Then, on April 6, José Loria, a reporter for La Prensa Libre, finally reached the site and, over the next few days, published a series of long articles.[112] Loria said he found seven bodies, four North Americans and three he believed were Nicaraguans, partially burned and buried. Peasants in the area told Loria they had been ordered by Rural Guard officials not to disclose what they knew. Several said they interpreted these warnings as "death threats."

When CIA chief "Tomás" and other Embassy officials saw Loria's story, they realized that the cover-up was in trouble. So the next day, Saturday, April 7, "Tomás," two CIA contract agents,[113] John Hull, and Bruce Jones took a larger twin-engine plane to the nearest landing strip, several hours from the crash site. Under orders, a group of ARDE guerrillas again burned the site and then brought the bags of corpses and loaded them onto the plane. Accounts as to their ultimate destination vary. Most say they were taken to El Salvador, Bruce Jones says they were buried inside Nicaragua, and several sources say the bodies of the Americans were flown to Miami.

When the official Costa Rican inspection team finally arrived the following day, April 8, they found the ground still smoldering from the second fire. They gathered up and took to San José some bones from the two graves, pieces of the plane containing the registration and serial numbers, parts of weapons, and a few sheets of paper written in English, including a child's poem and drawing with the name "Herick" on it. The authorities subsequently announced they had the remains of only two persons. They promised a full investigation.

U.S. Embassy officials and ARDE stonewalled, flatly denying any knowledge of the plane. The OIJ report released several weeks later concluded there were no North Americans on board. OIJ official Minor Calvo told the press that there was no evidence Costa Rican officials had "acted irregularly" or been involved in a cover-up. Vice Minister of Security Johnny Campos declared definitively, "There has been no hiding of information, neither has there been negligence." Only Security Minister Angel Solano spoke frankly. He said that it was impossible to determine who was on board because all the evidence had been destroyed by fire. No one was ever prosecuted.[114] The OIJ investigation went nowhere, and the press soon dropped the story.

Two footnotes on this story appeared later in the press. One was a story in mid-May which provided interesting details about the plane's history. An investigation by David Todd of the Canadian news agency Southam News found that the aging DC-3 had been seized by U.S. authorities during a drug investigation and was subsequently altered and refitted, partly at a Delaware military base. It was painted with false Canadian markings, converted into a cargo plane, outfitted with long-range fuel tanks, and designated for U.S. military use.[115] This seemed to indicate the official U.S. hand—military or CIA—in the contra resupply operation.

The second tantalizing tidbit on the DC-3 crash appeared in *Newsday* in December 1987. In attempting to investigate the identity of the Americans supposedly killed, reporter Brian Donovan had put in a routine request under the Freedom of Information Act for documents with government agencies, including the Department of the Army. To his surprise, Army officials replied that they had files pertaining to the crash at the Pentagon, but they refused to turn them over. When asked if the Army played a role in the incident, an Army lawyer told Donovan, "You know I'm not going to answer that."[116]

Despite a continuous string of aviation mishaps, it wasn't until October 1986, when the Sandinistas shot down another arms-filled plane over southern Nicaragua, that the contra war and resupply network came under extended public and congressional scrutiny. This time, not only incriminating papers, but also a crew member, Eugene Hasenfus, survived—and Hasenfus began talking.

1. Contra leader Edén Pastora in guerrilla camp. Photo by Mark Baille.

2. Pastora denouncing CIA maneuvers against him to journalists seconds before the explosion of the bomb at La Penca. Photo by José Antonio Venegas.

3. After the bomb exploded, wounded journalists lay for hours on the bank of the San Juan River waiting for rescue boats to arrive. Some, including Tony Avirgan (in the checked shirt), did not reach the San Carlos Hospital in northern Costa Rica for nearly twelve hours. Photo by José Antonio Venegas.

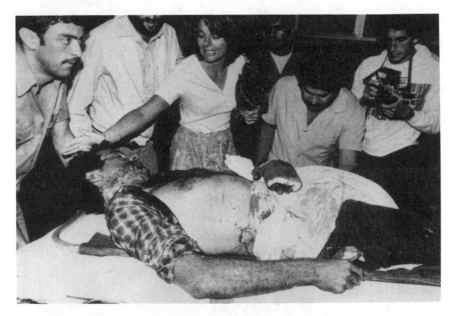

4. The author (center, carrying jacket) meeting Avirgan as he arrives at San Carlos Hospital at dawn on May 31. Photo by M. E. Esquivel.

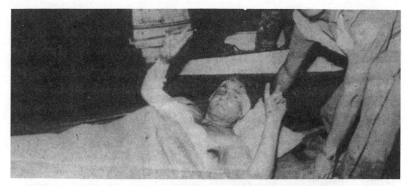

5. Edén Pastora giving the victory sign as he is evacuated to a San José hospital after the bombing. After the hospital received telephone threats, Pastora was taken to Venezuela. Photo by José Antonio Venegas.

6. The La Penca bomber, Vital Roberto Gagulne (alias Per Anker Hansen, alias Amac Galil, alias Martin El Inglés) feigning injury at La Penca minutes after the explosion. He had set a camera bomb in the midst of the gathered journalists and gone outside to detonate it using a remote-control device. Photo by José Antonio Venegas.

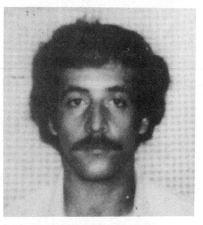

7. The bomber sitting in a wheelchair outside the emergency entrance at San Carlos Hospital. At dawn he checked out of the hospital, took a taxi to San José, and disappeared. Photo by Marvin Vega.

8. Photo of the bomber found in Panamanian immigration records. He had lived for several months in Panama City, posing as Per Anker Hansen and traveling with a female who used a stolen passport. Photo by Doug Vaughan.

9. Carlos Rojas, a Costa Rican who became a go-between passing information from an unidentified contra defector who called himself "David" to the author and Tony Avirgan. Rojas was later kidnapped and briefly held by the contras and their Costa Rican supporters and subsequently received death threats that forced him to leave Costa Rica. Photo by Julio Lainez.

10. Death threat that was slipped under a door at Carlos Rojas's home in January 1986. Translated it reads, "Carlos Rojas, if you, Tony Avirgan, Martha Honey and Edgar [Tony's camera assistant] continue with the investigation it is possible that someone will kill you." Author's files.

11. John Hull, the farmer, pilot, and CIA operative who helped run the contra war from his ranches in northern Costa Rica. Photo by S. G. Rubinow.

12. Scene from the May 1986 trial in which John Hull (far right, foreground) sued the author and Tony Avirgan (left, foreground) for criminal libel for publishing a report accusing him of being connected with the CIA, the La Penca bombing plot, and drug trafficking. The charges were dismissed. Photo by Julio Lainez.

13. The multimillion-dollar headquarters of the U.S. Agency for International Development (USAID) in Costa Rica, which opened in 1988 in an upper-class San José suburb. Popularly known as "the bunker," the heavily fortified complex contradicted the agency's self-perpetuated image as a friendly, helping hand from the United States. Photo by Julio Lainez.

14. Daniel Chaij, the controversial and powerful USAID director in Costa Rica from February 1982 to June 1987. During this period USAID's Costa Rica program became its second-largest per capita. U.S. Information Service.

15. Presidents Ronald Reagan and Luis Alberto Monge during Reagan's 1982 visit to Costa Rica. The Reagan administration leaned heavily on Monge to support the war against Nicaragua in return for military and economic aid. Photo by M. E. Esquivel.

16. Costa Rican campesinos protesting USAID and the Arias administration's non-traditional export program, known as Agriculture of Change. The program favored large, often foreign producers of luxury export crops over the small- and medium-sized farm operations that produced food for the local market.

17. ARDE commander Edén Pastora at one of his camps along the San Juan River in late 1983. At that time the Southern Front along the San Juan was the most militarily active area in the contra war. The approximately five thousand Southern Front guerrillas were united under the umbrella of ARDE (the Revolutionary Democratic Alliance).

18. Brooklyn Rivera, leader of the MISURASATA faction of ARDE, composed of Miskito and other groups from Nicaragua's Atlantic Coast. Like Pastora, Rivera was a strong nationalist who often clashed with his CIA advisers, trainers, and suppliers. Photo by M. E. Esquivel.

19. Fernando "El Negro" Chamorro, the heavy-drinking commander of the UDN-FARN, the smallest faction within ARDE. UDN-FARN was militarily ineffective, and some of El Negro's lieutenants were involved in drug trafficking.

20. Left to right: Alfonso Robelo, Arturo Cruz, and Adolfo Calero announcing the formation of UNO (the United Nicaraguan Opposition) at a June 1985 press conference in San José. UNO was a CIA-created umbrella contra organization uniting the Honduras-based Northern Front and the Costa Rica-based Southern Front guerrillas.

21. Left to right: Robelo, Cruz, and Calero meeting President Reagan in the White House, April 4, 1984, as Oliver North (far right) looks on. White House photo by Pete Souza.

HECTOR FRANCES
EX AGENTE DE LOS
SERVICIOS DE
INTELIGENCIA
ARGENTINA.

22. Photo of the videotaped confessional of kidnapped Argentine military intelligence officer and CIA collaborator "Héctor Francés" (Estánislao Valdez), who organized the early contra infrastructure in Costa Rica. Francés was kidnapped in San José in October 1982 by an Argentine leftist hit team that worked for Nicaragua's Interior Ministry.

23. Joe Fernández ("Tomas Castillo"), CIA station chief in Costa Rica from July 1984 to January 1987, when he was recalled in the wake of the Iran-contra scandal. Fernández oversaw the buying off of Pastora's field commanders and the construction of the Santa Elena airstrip used for contra resupply flights.

24. Robert Owen (right), with his lawyer, Leonard Greenebaum, testifying at the Iran-contra congressional hearings in May 1987. Owen was North's "trusted courier" to the contras and assisted in several Southern Front projects, including the construction of the Santa Elena airstrip. Author's files.

25. Southern Front contras at a camp on one of the farms controlled by John Hull. Journalists who were flown to the camp by Hull associate Jim Denby in mid-1984 were told that it was located inside Nicaragua, but later their hosts admitted that it was in northern Costa Rica. The crates contained rifles, bayonets, and other weapons. Photo by Chris Covatta.

26. Contras with North American and Cuban American supporters at a camp in northern Costa Rica in 1985. The Costa Rican government later charged Felipe Vidal (standing, second from left) with the crime of "hostile acts." Author's files.

27. Five foreign mercenaries—two American, two English, and one French—talk with the press at La Forma prison outside San José. The mercenaries had been arrested in late April 1985 at a contra camp on one of John Hull's properties. Peter Glibbery (center, with glasses) and American Steven Carr (in striped shirt) soon began talking openly about the activities of Owen, Hull, North, and the CIA concerning the contras.

28. Angel Edmundo Solano, President Monge's first security minister. Solano supported Costa Rican neutrality and was removed in August 1984 under pressure from the U.S. Embassy. Photo by M. E. Esquivel.

29. Benjamin Piza, President Monge's second security minister. Piza collaborated closely with the CIA and the contras, permitted the construction of the clandestine Santa Elena airstrip and the training of Costa Rican guardsmen by U.S. Green Berets. Photo by M. E. Esquivel.

30. Col. Harry Barrantes, the U.S.- and Israeli-trained Costa Rican intelligence officer who initially investigated and then collaborated with John Hull and the CIA. Photo by Julio Lainez.

31. Graduation ceremony for Costa Rican civil guardsmen trained by U.S. Green Berets at Murciélago near the Costa Rica-Nicaragua border. Photo by M. E. Esquivel.

32. Sandinista Interior Minister Tomás Borge with Fifth Directorate member Maria Lourdes Pallais, Cabazas, Nicaragua, May 1988, after Pallais was revealed as a Sandinista spy who had infiltrated the CIA and carried out several covert missions inside Costa Rica. Photo by Lou Demateus. Author's files.

33. The Santa Elena airstrip in northern Costa Rica, which was used not only for contra resupply operations but also for drug trafficking. Photo by Julio Lainez.

34. Presidents Ronald Reagan and Oscar Arias meeting at the White House, June 1987. During Arias's visit, Reagan and his advisers tried in vain to convince Arias to abandon negotiations for a Central American Peace Plan and to support the contras. Arias responded with a strong lecture about the realities of Central American politics.

35. Left to right: The five Central American presidents, José Azcona of Honduras, José Napoleon Duarte of El Salvador, Oscar Arias, Vinicio Cerezo of Guatemala, and Daniel Ortega of Nicaragua, at the August 1987 summit in Guatemala City where they signed the Central American Peace Plan, establishing a cease-fire between Nicaragua and the contras and marking the beginning of the end of the contra war.

36. President Oscar Arias in Oslo, Norway, December 1987, after he received the Nobel Peace Prize.

37. President George Bush greeting Oscar Arias after arriving in Costa Rica to attend the October 1989 Democracy Summit held in San José. At the summit Bush announced plans to restructure $1 billion of Costa Rica's $4.5 billion foreign debt.

38. The sixteen presidents of the Americas gathered at the October 1989 Democracy Summit. At the summit Daniel Ortega announced that due to increased contra activity Nicaragua would not renew the nineteen-month-old cease-fire with the contras. Bush commented, "We are not going to let this one little man, who is out of whack with the rest of the world, ruin a very good meeting."

TEN

Militarizing Costa Rica

We are a country of more teachers than soldiers, of more schools than cannons, of more books than rifles, and of more libraries than barracks. And these sentiments and this manner of being have formed a basic part of our national character for many generations.

—Oscar Arias, 1982

What Washington Wanted

Parallel to building up the contra forces, CIA networks, and political, press, and contra infrastructures inside Costa Rica, the Reagan administration also sought to use Costa Rica's police and security forces to support its war against Nicaragua. This was done through U.S. military aid and a stepped-up U.S. military presence in the country. Although Costa Rica had abolished its army in 1948, in 1981 the United States began providing, for the first time in thirteen years, "security" assistance to Costa Rica to upgrade and expand the existing forces and create a potpourri of new counter-terrorist, intelligence, and antidrug units. Quietly the United States also provided assistance to the quasi-governmental organization OPEN and to private right-wing groups such as the Free Costa Rica Movement. U.S. soldiers arrived to carry out a variety of "civic works" and security training, and Washington tried to involve Costa Rica in regional military maneuvers and alliances. The rapid increase in military aid, while moderate compared with U.S. military aid to Honduras and El Salvador, sparked a vigorous and divisive debate about whether Washington was trying to force Costa Rica into building an army. By the mid-1980s, many Costa Ricans were convinced that the Reagan administration was strong-arming their country into re-creating an army; but by the end of the decade, this had not fully happened. Washington was checked in part because the perceived threat from Nicaragua and internal leftists was too minimal to sway Costa Ricans from their deeply held antimilitaristic traditions.

In addition the Reagan and Bush administrations came to the conclusion that Costa Rica was more useful as a largely defense-less, democratic ally that could be perceived to need U.S. "protection" in the face of Sandinista aggression. While exhibiting no appreciation for the significance of the abolition of the army in Costa Rica's history, the Reagan administration came to find the country's nonmilitarism convenient in its war against Nicaragua.

Washington's hard-nosed view of Costa Rica was clearly articulated in a secret 1984 State Department memo regarding Costa Rican–Nicaraguan border incidents. The memo stated, "In public relations terms . . . Costa Rica . . . wears a white hat. Its commitments to democracy and regional peace are not challenged. Attacks against a small democracy with no standing army put Nicaragua in a bad light. . . . These incidents should be helpful in strengthening our case in Europe and Latin America where we are making a major diplomatic/psychological effort to win support for our policy [and should] give weight to our basic theme in the Congress on the need to stop the Sandinistas. They demonstrate why we must aid the Contras."[1]

The Reagan administration was, however, walking a precari-ous line. On the one hand, Washington was trying to exploit Costa Rica's nonmilitarism and neutrality to win international support in its war against the Sandinistas. On the other hand, it was trying to persuade Costa Rica to upgrade and expand its military capabil-ity, open its territory to both contra and U.S. forces, and line up militarily, as well as politically and ideologically, against the Sandinistas. Washington's intention was also to build up a stratum of Costa Rican government and security officials clearly aligned with—in essence loyal to and working for—the United States. These goals, while falling short of building an army, nevertheless brought considerable change to Costa Rica's social fabric. By the end of the 1980s Costa Rica's security forces had been substantially "modernized," "professionalized," and expanded, and appeared much more like a conventional army. The number of police and auxiliary forces had increased fourfold, there were at least nineteen different police bodies, and overall spending for police and security forces steadily expanded while budgets for government social programs were being cut. By the end of the decade, Costa Rica's security forces were armed and trained enough to suppress internal dissent, but the country was still dependent on the United States to defend it against any serious foreign aggression. Sadly, but predictably, judging from the experience of other Latin American countries, parallel to this U.S. "upgrading" of the security forces was a rise in human rights violations, including torture, illegal detentions, and repressive actions against protesters. All of this worked to undermine—not strengthen, as U.S. policy makers tried to argue—Costa Rica's unique postwar history as the hemisphere's only country without an armed force.

Costa Rica's pacific traditions began on December 1, 1948, when the diminutive José "Pepe" Figueres, commander of the victorious forces in the country's brief but bloody civil war, picked up a sledgehammer, smashed a stone turret on the main military fort, turned the keys to the fort over to the Ministry of Education, and sent the soldiers home. The following year, Figueres's ruling social democratic Junta adopted a new constitution that made it illegal to re-create a standing army. This historic decision,[2] taken in large part to prevent a military coup that would return to power the wealthy coffee oligarchy, became, together with the nearly simultaneous decree nationalizing the banking system, the foundation on which was built Costa Rica's postwar stability, relative prosperity, and well-functioning parliamentary democracy.

Externally, Costa Rica was protected by the 1947 Río Mutual Defense Treaty, which Costa Rica signed two days after abolishing the army. Under this treaty Costa Rica could seek multilateral military assistance through the Organization of American States (OAS), in case of external aggression. Costa Rica's new nonmilitary policy was tested just twelve days later, as forces loyal to ex-president Rafael Calderón Guardia invaded from Nicaragua, and the Figueres junta successfully appealed to the OAS to mediate an end to hostilities.

After December 1948, the army was reduced to a 1,200-man, lightly armed Public Security Force consisting of a Civil Guard police force and coast guard. The officers were drawn from the local elite and had little military background or training. Security force positions were doled out with each new administration as political patronage jobs, ranks were largely ceremonial, and there was no military rank higher than colonel. This effectively prevented the formation of a standing military, but also meant that each major party had a pool of loyal security forces.

Until 1974, Costa Rica received police assistance through AID's Public Safety Program. In that year Congress banned U.S. training of Latin American police forces because of massive human rights violations—torture, murder, and "disappearances"—in countries like Uruguay, Brazil, and Argentina.[3] Until 1974, the training of Costa Ricans emphasized combating communism and terrorism,[4] restructuring police units according to U.S. methods, officer training in U.S. schools like the International Police Academy (IPA) in Washington, and creating certain permanent units where, unlike the Civil Guard, positions were protected as part of the civil service. One of the new U.S.-created units was the 120-person Organization of Judicial Investigation (OIJ), organized in 1973. Roughly equivalent to the FBI, it was almost from the outset accused of human rights violations.[5]

In 1970, AID funds also helped set up another unit, the Office of Narcotics within the Security Ministry. Some of its agents quickly became embroiled in scandal, including charges of marijuana trafficking, torture, and murder. Two Cuban Americans worked as advisers to the unit: a CIA agent who worked for Interpol, Luis López Vega (or Luis Vega López), who later reportedly died in Angola; and a U.S. DEA agent, Carlos Hernández Rumbaut (known as "Papalucho"). Both were said to be members of the Miami-based, anti-Castro terrorist group Alpha 66.[6] In 1970, Hernández Rumbaut, a Bay of Pigs veteran, was appealing a fifteen-year conviction in Alabama for possession of 467 pounds of marijuana when the DEA took an interest in him. It arranged his bail and then recruited him for DEACON I, a new, top-secret, joint DEA-CIA intelligence unit composed mainly of South Florida Cuban CIA assets.[7] With the DEA's consent and a U.S. diplomatic passport, Hernández set himself up in Costa Rica, where, within a short time, he was made an honorary member of the Narcotics Office, then promoted to captain and second-in-command, and, soon after, became President José Figueres's bodyguard.

In 1973 he and the President's son, José María, and several others were implicated in the murder of a small-time marijuana dealer known as "Chemise." The case was covered up, but it resurfaced in 1991 after José María Figueres became a presidential aspirant. A 1976 *Washington Post Magazine* piece which cites Hernández's confidential DEA file identifies the U.S. agent and Figueres as "members of a death squad."[8] As discussed below, such activities again became visible in the 1980s with the exposure of the links between the contras, drug traffickers, and the CIA–Oliver North network.

While U.S. military assistance to Costa Rica was modest during the postwar decades, a relatively large number of Costa Ricans received training at the U.S. Army School of the Americas, located at Fort Gulick in the Panama Canal Zone's U.S. Southern Command. Between 1949 and 1967, over 1,900 Costa Ricans had to take courses, ironically giving it one of the highest (perhaps the highest) per-capita number of graduates in Central and South America. The school trained, according to one of its officers, "the leaders and managers of the armies of Latin America in the latest U.S. doctrine and use of U.S.-manufactured weapons." The official explained that students received "training in military, not police functions," including basic infantry, reconnaissance, commando operations, military intelligence, and a variety of technical courses.[9]

Between 1967 and 1981, the only U.S. military assistance to Costa Rica was a loan of five million colones to purchase patrol boats for the naval section of the Civil Guard. In 1978, the air and naval sectors between them had 109 men, six aircraft, and five coastal patrol boats. By 1980, Costa Rica had a combined Civil Guard and Rural Guard of seven to eight thousand men who had received riot control and counter-insurgency training. They were equipped with new radio transmitters, patrol cars, and computer facilities, salaries had been raised, and the forces had been professionalized. They lacked, however, the larger weapons found in conventional armies such as tanks, fighter airplanes, and heavy artillery. It was still a comparatively benign, low-key, lightly equipped force. City police officers often carried screwdrivers rather than pistols in their holsters, since one of their main duties was removing license plates from the vehicles of traffic offenders.[10] According to a 1981 Swedish study, this "Costa Rican version of the national guard model" adequately served the country's needs: "It responds primarily to problems of internal security; its military skills are police-like and managerial, and there are political restrictions on the scope of its actions." Training of the Civil Guard at the School of the Americas and within the country had made it, the study concluded, "one of the best trained forces in Latin America."[11]

Costa Rica's "Neutralist Tightrope Act" Unbalanced

That same year, 1981, Nicaragua became a target for U.S. subversion, and Washington had a decidedly different assessment of Costa Rica's security capabilities. According to a U.S. Embassy document, "By 1981 . . . faced with a heavily militarized and expansionist Nicaragua . . . the Public Security Forces were totally unprepared to react. Patrol boats, aircraft and vehicles were inoperative or too few in number. The border units were untrained, under-equipped and incapable of maintaining an effective presence on the northern frontier."[12]

U.S. officials hammered away at another theme as well: that Costa Rica faced a serious threat of internal leftist subversion, orchestrated by the Sandinistas. In the early 1980s, there was a spate of terrorist incidents, an occurrence almost unknown before then. The political violence began in December 1980 with the contra attack on *Radio Noticias del Continente,* and over the next twenty-three months there were fourteen incidents. Four involved primarily Costa Ricans from an ultraleftist group known as "La Familia." They were quickly arrested, tried, and given long prison sentences. The other attacks involved an assortment of foreigners, mainly Latin Americans. While more than half of the early actions were carried out by leftists, as the decade continued it was clear that the biggest internal threat came from the right—the contras and local paramilitary groups. But the U.S. Embassy continued to play up the threat from the left, including publishing a yearly list of terrorist attacks in Costa Rica.[13]

U.S. government documents implied that Costa Rica feared Sandinista aggression and internal leftists and was therefore all too eager for U.S. assistance. As the report cited above states, "In response, the Government of Costa Rica requested U.S. equipment and training necessary for Costa Rica to meet minimal security objectives." Indeed, documents outlining the history of U.S. "security assistance" to Costa Rica fail to mention that Costa Rica had abolished its army and is constitutionally proscribed from recreating an armed force. From 1981 on, Defense Department assistance and training to Costa Rica was resumed.

In doing so, the United States and Costa Rica had first to overcome a semantical problem. The Costa Rican government did not want to accept "military" aid; the Reagan administration was barred by Congress from giving "police" assistance in Latin America. Therefore, although the aid fell under the U.S. Military Assistance Program and was designated for the "non-police functions" of the Costa Rican forces, the funds were labeled "security assistance" when distributed in Costa Rica. In addition, the diplomatic post of U.S. military attaché at the Embassy was renamed the "political/military officer" and, later, the "defense representative," and military matters were handled by the Embassy's Office of Defense Cooperation. Costa Rica, in turn, called its defense department the Ministry of Public Security.

From the outset U.S. officials were said to have urged that Costa Rica's Civil and Rural Guards be put under the civil service system that would secure their jobs and permit the building of a permanent force. The Costa Rican government, however, resisted, in part out of fear of establishing a standing army and in part out of a desire to maintain its political patronage system.

During the 1980s, the United States gave four types of security assistance: (1) training of existing Costa Rican forces; (2)

military equipment; (3) training and equipment for new police and security units; and (4) U.S. military presence and projects in Costa Rica. The first three were financed through two U.S. programs—the International Military Education and Training Program (IMET) and the Military Assistance Program (MAP)—programs which spent $28 million between 1981 and 1990. The fourth, U.S. military projects in Costa Rica, were financed partly with U.S. funds and partly with covert moneys from the CIA or North operations. The total cost for U.S. military projects in Costa Rica is not known.

U.S. military aid began very modestly during the 1978–82 administration of President Rodrigo Carazo (whom Washington disliked), with only $80,000 in 1981 and 1982 for training fifty-two Civil Guard officers at the School of the Americas. The Monge administration took office in May 1982, and funds for training quickly grew. Police and security forces received training from U.S. instructors at the School of the Americas, the Regional Military Training Center (CREM) in Honduras, Fort Benning in Georgia, and other locations in the United States, and, locally, at the Costa Rican Academy of Public Forces located in Alajuela. Training was also provided at Murciélago, on the Santa Elena peninsula near the Nicaraguan border, and at separate schools for the OIJ, Rural Guard, and transit police. By 1988 mobile training teams composed of U.S. military, police, antinarcotics, and intelligence instructors had also given short courses in Costa Rica to about twelve hundred security-force members.

U.S.-supplied military equipment (which peaked at $9 million worth in both 1984 and 1985) included uniforms and field equipment, weapons, ammunition, mortars, vehicles, patrol boats, two Hughes 500-E unarmed transport helicopters, four Cessna unarmed observation planes, communications networks for the Civil and Rural Guards, and prefabricated barracks. Some of this equipment was conspicuously inappropriate: fifty "police" vehicles that turned out to be U.S. Army jeep-type troop carriers, and uniforms for the city police that were camouflage combat fatigues.[14]

While, during the 1980s, U.S. aid and training was the most sizable and most important in reshaping Costa Rica's police forces, the Monge and Arias governments received assistance from a number of other countries as well. These included Israel (1,500 Galil rifles and military instructors); Taiwan (M-16 rifles, gas masks, shields, helmets, radios, blankets, and camouflage cloth for uniforms, plus several hundred scholarships);[15] South Korea (riot-control gear and night sticks); Argentina (patrol cars); Venezuela (M-14 rifles); Chile; Panama; Japan; Spain; and West Germany. Only one socialist country—Rumania—was approached, and it gave some limited assistance to the Security Ministry when Angel Edmundo Solano was its head.

During the 1980s, foreign assistance from the United States and other countries was also used to create a variety of new security and police units. Pointing to a rash of terrorist attacks, Monge government officials created an elite new antiterrorist force called the Special Intervention Unit (UEI), which was financed and trained by the United States, West Germany, Israel, and Taiwan. Composed of about one hundred specially chosen men "with no family obligations," the group reportedly received a $2 million donation of antiriot gear and small arms from Taiwan. Israel supplied three antiterrorist trainers, and some members were trained by special SWAT police in Washington. Also formed in 1982 was the one-hundred-person Directorate of Intelligence and Security (DIS), roughly equivalent to a combined CIA and Secret Service, which was charged with intelligence gathering and protecting dignitaries. Beginning with a special decree in 1985, DIS investigations, documents, and reports are considered "state secrets" and therefore not public, a practice previously unknown in Costa Rica. DIS quickly became one of the most notorious of the police bodies. The Costa Rican human-rights organization CODEHU found evidence that DIS was frequently responsible for illegal detentions and other violations of human rights.[16]

The Monge government also created two new antiterrorist Civil Guard units for duty outside the capital. One was a 100-man force for the Atlantic Coast region, where local banana unions were striking. These guardsmen were to be trained to "intervene in labor conflicts" and conduct searches for arms caches and "clandestine groups." Another Civil Guard antiterrorist unit, the 260-man Chorotega Company, was assigned to the San Juan River area and based out of Los Chiles. Under Security Minister Solano, its ostensible mission was to rout out anti-Sandinista encampments.[17] In practice these border guards developed a closely protective relationship with the contras, and most rebel camps were "found" only after the guerrillas had vanished. After Benjamín Piza became Security Minister in mid-1984, the main task of the border patrols was redefined as stopping Sandinista incursions.[18]

In addition to providing "security" assistance, the United States also increased its direct military visibility in Costa Rica. Between 1983 and 1989, there were nine U.S. military "civic action" projects and five "humanitarian assistance" programs in Costa Rica that were also billed as training exercises for American servicemen. These included Air Force high-altitude training, emergency medical-reaction-team exercises, disaster-relief seminars, medical readiness exercises, maritime search and rescue activities, flood and hurricane disaster relief, and an unspecified number of ship visits.[19] Olive-green C-130 military transport planes regularly landed at San José's international airport. Off the Atlantic and Pacific coasts, U.S. warships were allowed to cruise in territorial waters and to make occasional "goodwill" visits to Costa Rican ports. Crew members, dressed in military garb, undertook "civic" projects such as repairing schools, giving medical and dental care, and promoting sports events. Such frequent U.S. shows of force were apparently designed both to intimidate the Sandinistas and to convince Costa Ricans that a U.S. military presence in the region was commonplace as well as helpful.

Over the years, Monge, a political juggler without much vision, tried to walk a tightrope between Costa Rica's antimilitary traditions and the country's pressing need for substantial U.S. economic support.[20] During his June 1982 visit to Washington, Monge warned of a "massive offensive on the part of totalitarian Marxist-Leninists" in Central America, charging that Costa Rica was threatened by a "Marxist-Leninist encirclement directed from Nicaragua." But despite such high-pitched rhetoric, Monge did, over the years, manage to resist some of the U.S. pressure and reject a number of proposals. Over time, however, pressured by threatened cutoffs of U.S. economic aid—and enticed, the evidence indicates, by personal bribes[21]—President Monge did agree to accept the most important of the U.S. military and CIA proposals. These included the Murciélago training base; road, bridge, and airport construction by U.S. military engineers; the Santa Elena airstrip; and a secret communications system.

Monge's Declaration of Independence

In the first half of his administration, Luis Alberto Monge attempted to gain some political distance from the United States and protect Costa Rica's nonaligned image through his Neutrality Proclamation, announced September 15, 1983. At a solemn public ceremony, Monge used Central American Independence Day to declare Costa Rica's "determination to be neutral in all military conflicts." He called it a policy of "perpetual, active and unarmed neutrality" with respect to the political crisis in the region. Monge explained that while Costa Rica would continue to participate in the United Nations and the Organization of American States, it would ask to be relieved of its military obligations under the Río Treaty and would send doctors and nurses, not troops, to any international conflicts. Under the Proclamation, Costa Rica pledged not to permit its territory to be used by either the United States or the contras to invade Nicaragua. Monge was careful, however, to assure Washington that ideologically and politically, Costa Rica was still an ally. As the Costa Rican President put it, "Costa Rica reaffirms its faith in the political and social conception that it has shared and still shares with the Western democracies."

The Neutrality Proclamation was welcomed by the vast majority of Costa Ricans. In a poll taken at the time, 76 percent expressed support, while only 6 percent were opposed. The same poll showed that 83 percent of Costa Ricans were opposed to rebuilding a national army. The Proclamation was also hailed internationally.[22]

The negative reaction was, however, swift and strong. Costa Rica's right wing, its major news media, and the Reagan administration immediately launched a campaign against the Proclamation. In addition, Monge's foreign minister Fernando Volio spoke out against it, caustically calling it a proclamation for "perpetual defenselessness." Washington retaliated by suspending disbursement of previously agreed-upon AID loans. The reason, U.S.

officials said, was because Costa Rica had failed to comply fully with the technicalities of an IMF loan. The message was not lost on the Costa Rican government: Washington was not willing to extend economic aid if Costa Rica was not on board militarily as well as politically in the war against Nicaragua.

A Bad Day for Washington

Besides economic reprisals, the Reagan administration countered with various forms of political and military pressure. The first was a proposal to send between 400 and 1,000 U.S. Army Corps of Engineers troops to build and upgrade roads, bridges, and airports in northern Costa Rica. On September 25, 1983, just ten days after Monge's Neutrality Proclamation, the head of the U.S. Southern Command, General Paul Gorman, visited Costa Rica and made the offer. U.S. officials subsequently claimed that the idea originated after Monge complained that implementation of AID's recently approved Northern Zone Development Project, designed to put substantial infrastructure in the border region, would take too long. In fact, the idea of using military engineers was first proposed by the U.S. Embassy in 1982, just six months after Monge took office.[23]

Shortly after Gorman's visit, Monge indicated his conditional agreement. In November 1983, during a visit by Under Secretary of Defense Fred Ikle, Ambassador Winsor announced that Costa Rica had approved the plan and the military engineers would arrive in February. He said the construction project would be financed by the Defense Department and would last from two to four years. Winsor called the scheme a $9 to $12 million "freebie" financed by the Defense Department.

Despite such persuasive salesmanship, it was at this point that the real controversy started. Ikle returned to Washington and announced that "the dispatch of combat engineers would be the first such joint exercises in Costa Rica." Ikle's comment caused an uproar in Costa Rica, where there was already concern that this project was modeled on U.S. military road-building projects along the Honduran border, the scene of heavy contra activity. The scheme also violated both the just-announced Neutrality Proclamation and the constitution. Many feared this was intended to allow the U.S. military to do a detailed survey of Costa Rica's strategic northern zone as well as to install a Southern Front infrastructure for the contras.

Asked at a press conference about Ikle's statement, Monge was visibly angry. He demanded confirmation of the understanding "that Costa Rica will not participate in any military maneuvers," adding, "Any such force would require approval of the Legislative Assembly, regardless of its purpose here."[24] Off the record, top Costa Rican government officials explained that when Gorman had proposed the plan, Monge had set specific preconditions to accepting it. These included guarantees that all the projects would be of a purely civilian nature; projects would be located mainly in southern Costa Rica (not in the north, as the United States wanted), the engineers would be unarmed and protected only by Costa Rican guardsmen; and that engineers from Panama, Venezuela, and Colombia would also take part in the construction. According to one official, "Anyone who knows President Monge would realize immediately that these criteria were tantamount to saying 'No.' " The Americans, however, ignored the conditions laid down by Monge, pushing instead for the "expansion of several airstrips in the northern zone to receive military cargo planes" and insisting that the engineers be accompanied by a contingent of armed military police, the officials interviewed explained.[25]

In San José, U.S. diplomats tried to downplay the military rationale for the scheme, calling the 1,200 National Guardsmen whom they proposed sending "citizen soldiers." Contrary to what President Monge said, U.S. diplomats contended that if the National Guard came without arms, no Legislative Assembly approval was necessary. They also pointed out that there were already thirteen U.S. Army engineers in the north assembling prefabricated barracks at border points. Further, the year before Costa Rica had permitted twenty-two U.S. Navy Seabees (from the Navy corps of construction engineers) to carry out a three-month well-drilling project in the drought-stricken Guanacaste area. The Seabees had carried out a similar project in Honduras's border region, digging wells for military camps and local communities.

Only years later did interviews reveal evidence that the Seabees in Guanacaste had also been involved in clandestine training of contras on private farms and had secretly brought in equipment that was left for use by the contras.[26]

Ultimately, the public outcry and opposition from within Monge's Liberation party doomed Washington's plan to send military engineers to northern Costa Rica. On January 23, 1984, Liberation party legislators circulated a manifesto opposing "the presence in our territory of any advisers or military engineers of whatever nation or foreign power." Shortly afterward, Monge called an emergency Cabinet meeting. Each minister was asked to express his opinion and, according to the *Tico Times,* members then voted unanimously to reject the U.S. proposal. Monge then announced that the engineers would "definitely not" work near the Nicaraguan border, although he left open the possibility that they might participate in construction projects in the southern part of the country.[27]

While the Embassy did not give up on Costa Rica, it was not until January 1986 that the Cabinet finally signed onto an agreement allowing U.S. military engineers to build roads and bridges—but only in southern Costa Rica. The Costa Rican government also insisted that the soldiers be unarmed and be protected by a contingent of Costa Rican guardsmen. The Cabinet avoided further public debate by not asking for Legislative Assembly approval, as should have been constitutionally required.

For the rest of the decade, uniformed U.S. soldiers from Panama's Southern Command and National Guardsmen from several states arrived periodically for "training exercises." These included building roads, bridges, classrooms, and dispensaries in the southern region as part of the so-called "Roads for Peace" and "Bridges for Peace" projects. Between 1986 and 1990, there were five such projects, as well as three more well-drilling projects—two carried out by Navy Seabees and one by the Army Corps of Engineers.[28] Each year the numbers increased and their stay lengthened: in 1986, 182 engineers came for one and a half months; in 1988, 430 came for about three months; and in 1989, 740 came for about four months. Throughout, controversy continued to simmer about the true intention, cost, and political impact of these projects.

Hidden from public view was the issue of the real cost of these construction projects. While Ambassador Winsor argued repeatedly that they were a "freebie" for Costa Rica, Arias government officials say this turned out not to be the case. Under the agreements, the U.S. Army supplied the equipment and donated the soldiers' time, while the Costa Rican government, using the PL-480 account overseen by the Minister of Planning, was obligated to pay for all materials, fuel, and other local expenses. This arrangement and the total cost to Costa Rica were not publicly known. The press did report that the cost of a March 1986 project to build and repair five bridges along the southern Pacific coast highway was $400,000 for the Costa Rican government and approximately $375,000 for the U.S. Army. In 1987, *Aportes* reported that Costa Rica had paid about $3 million (250 million colones), while the United States' share was equivalent to about $2.5 million (200 million colones), presumably for all the projects to that date.[29]

Preventing a "Backsliding into Neutrality"

Back in the fall of 1983, Costa Rica's neutrality stand was tested by the first of a series of CIA- and contra-precipitated border incidents. Just before dawn on September 28, less than two weeks after Monge's declaration, shooting broke out at the Peñas Blancas border crossing on the Pan American Highway and continued sporadically throughout the day. Damage was heaviest on the Nicaraguan side, where at least three border officials were killed and a number of buildings were destroyed. On the Costa Rican side there were no casualties and only minor damage to the border post. By nightfall Sandinista troops were several hundred yards inside Costa Rica. The situation was defused only after Costa Rica's pro-neutrality Security Minister, Angel Edmundo Solano, called his Nicaraguan counterpart, Interior Minister Tomás Borge, and demanded that the Sandinistas leave Costa Rican territory. Borge agreed.

The next morning's headline in *La Nación* read, "Civil Guard Attacked by Nicaraguan Army." Its editorial the following day declared, "Our country, which is practically disarmed, cannot tolerate aggression from a nation in which the nine *comandantes* are naturally dogmatic and expansionist . . . Wednesday's events should make President Monge reconsider the appropriateness of proclaiming a Statute of Neutrality. . . . Now more than ever Costa Rica needs support from its traditional allies." Costa Rica's Cabinet met in emergency session and ordered the recall of Costa Rica's ambassador in Managua. It also requested an extraordinary meeting of the Organization of American States. Solano was able to fend off the hawks who wanted to ask Washington to send troops by assuring them that no Sandinista soldiers remained on Costa Rican soil. Years later Solano recalled that this incident "was the closest Costa Rica had ever come to being at war."

Years later, too, it became apparent that the incident had been orchestrated by the CIA and contras to scuttle the new Neutrality Proclamation and escalate the war against Nicaragua. According to both Solano and Pastora aide Carol Prado, ARDE forces began the attack from the Costa Rican side of the border. The Sandinistas only counter-attacked after several Nicaraguan border guards had been killed. The attack was organized by two CIA operatives, Harold Martínez ("Ramón"), a top ARDE commander, and "Iván," one of the CIA's Latin assets who was handling logistics for the Southern Front contras.[30] While it did not lead to the entry of U.S. troops, the incident did serve to undermine support for Monge's Neutrality Proclamation.

Just eight months later, in another incident at Peñas Blancas, Washington again attempted to exploit a border skirmish to sabotage Monge's neutrality stand and enlist Costa Rica as a military ally. This incident followed several months of an escalating ARDE offensive, including the battle for San Juan del Norte from April 11 to 14 and the April 29, 1984, attack on the Sandinista garrison of El Castillo and resultant Nicaraguan strafing of two Costa Rican border towns. Then, on May 3, 1985, the Costa Rican Civil Guard border post was attacked with mortars and machine guns. The Nicaraguan government immediately sent a diplomatic note charging that it was an ARDE "hoax"—that the attack had been carried out by contras posing as Sandinistas. Costa Rican Foreign Minister Carlos Gutiérrez called the Sandinista version "ludicrous," and Ambassador Winsor said the incident "proved once and for all that the Sandinistas are a threat to Costa Rican democracy."

In Washington, State Department spokesman Alan Romberg termed the situation "extremely grave," saying there was "the possibility of a Nicaraguan invasion of Costa Rica." The Reagan administration immediately offered to deploy U.S. combat troops to Costa Rica. A U.S. military strategist in Tegucigalpa announced that at least 1,500 U.S. troops in Honduras and Panama were prepared to move to the Nicaraguan–Costa Rican border within eighteen hours. He went so far as to say the operation was code-named "Absalom."[31] Defense Secretary Caspar Weinberger told a Senate committee that Costa Rica had agreed to joint military exercises. This was not true.

The United States also responded by announcing it was speeding up, to within seventy-two hours, deliveries to Costa Rica of vehicles, boats, uniforms, and other military supplies from an aid package already in the pipeline. On May 7 General Gorman made an unannounced visit to Costa Rica where he met, not with Security Minister Solano, but privately with the hard-line, right-wing Vice President Armando Aráuz, who was coordinator of the Security Council. When asked about Gorman's visit, Aráuz said it was "unofficial or personal," and so he had not felt it necessary to inform the rest of the Security Council. On May 10, 1984, some-one leaked to the *Washington Post* a draft of a secret fourteen-page State Department document entitled "U.S. Response to Costa Rica's Urgent Request for Security Assistance." The memo, dated May 5, said that in the wake of the El Castillo and Peñas Blancas attacks, the Costa Rican government had made a "formal written request" for $7 million in additional military aid—more than three times greater than the $2.15 million already appropriated for fiscal year 1984. The memo called the request "potentially an important milestone in our relations" with Costa Rica and urged quick approval as "the only way to stiffen their resolve and prevent a backsliding into neutrality."

It continued, "[New aid] could lead to a significant shift from [Costa Rica's] neutralist tightrope act and push it more explicitly and publicly into the anti-Sandinista camp." The memo noted further that "a visible shift in Costa Rica's position will strengthen our position in Central America. This is the principal argument for responding positively, quickly and in full to the GOCR [Government of Costa Rica] request." The State Department document proposed that President Reagan use his emergency authority to provide the funds, thereby bypassing an unwanted congressional debate.

The State Department document went on candidly to discuss the need to neutralize "the ARDE factor" in the Costa Rican–Nicaraguan conflict. The clear pattern in border incidents, they noted, was that ARDE attacked first, the Sandinistas counter-attacked, Costa Rica made a public outcry—and thus, it might have added, the United States stepped forward to offer supplies and soldiers. The report argued that the United States should, somehow, "try to demonstrate the pattern of Sandinista incursions, shelling and intimidation predated ARDE's establishment of an effective military response." It proposed, "The story should be Nicaragua vs. Costa Rica, not GRN [Nicaragua] vs. armed opposition."[32]

Costa Rican officials interviewed about these events and the memo had a different story—one that revealed considerable U.S. pressure and diplomatic hype. Government officials at the time said that the bulk of the Costa Rican aid request—$7.6 million for light arms, patrol boats, jeeps, and two helicopters—had been made three months earlier as part of normal procedures and had nothing to do with the border troubles. But off the record, Costa Rican officials complained that they had been strong-armed into asking for more U.S. military aid. The *Washington Post* quoted a prominent Costa Rican as saying that Monge was trying to handle the situation diplomatically, but was "being pushed to create a scandal" by the Reagan administration. The *New York Times* also quoted Costa Rican officials as saying the Reagan administration was putting pressure on the Monge government to abandon its neutrality policy. A Monge adviser said the pressure on the Costa Rican president had "increased ten-fold over the last two months. . . . What Reagan needs from Costa Rica is the moral support for an invasion of Nicaragua." Diplomats in San José said the pressure was working: the Monge government was showing a "greater receptivity" to military cooperation.[33]

The Reagan administration tried to minimize the memo's damage by claiming it had been written by unnamed "junior people" and had since been "superseded by more balanced and relaxed thinking." Nevertheless, the document was a candid representation of U.S. intentions. It was, in fact, a prelude to arguably the most intense and overt period of U.S. pressure, when Costa Rica was being pushed toward open war with Nicaragua and strong-armed into passing the controversial bank denationalization bill, the Ley de la Moneda.

On May 15, schools and public offices closed to allow some twenty to thirty thousand Costa Ricans to take to the streets for a march "against war and for peace and neutrality." The march, the largest to that date in the country's history, was endorsed by Monge and other Liberation party leaders, as well as Archbishop Román Arrieta as a way of reviving the Neutrality Proclamation. It was supported by a broad coalition of trade unions, youth and university groups, former presidents Figueres and Daniel Odúber, University of Costa Rica Rector Fernando Durán, a number of government officials, and a contingent of U.S. residents. An editorial in La Nación denounced the event as "communist inspired," and a headline in La Prensa Libre declared, "Communists Take Over the March." The U.S. Embassy sent around a flyer warning U.S. citizens to stay away, because communists were known to be among the organizers.

Just after the demonstration, Monge and a large entourage left for a twelve-nation European visit intended to secure foreign aid and boost Costa Rica's tarnished image as an unarmed, neutral country. At the request of a majority of his cabinet, Monge left Vice President Alberto Fait as acting President, instead of Armando Aráuz, whom many distrusted because of his close allegiance to the U.S. Embassy. Rumors were widespread that the United States was planning an imminent invasion of Nicaragua, and, as one cabinet member put it, "We feared Aráuz would welcome the gringo troops with open arms." Rather than an invasion, it was the May 30 La Penca bombing which threw Costa Rica into an even higher state of confusion and fear. Monge's return only heightened the dissension within his government, the pressure from the Embassy, and calls from the right, spearheaded by the Chambers of Commerce and Industry, to abandon the neutrality policy and support the U.S. war against Nicaragua. The crisis came to a head in August with the passage of the banking-reform law and a cabinet reshuffle which replaced Security Minister Solano with Benjamín Piza.

The Green Berets at Murciélago

"We don't want a group of jack-booted young men here, goose-stepping, saluting, and clicking their heels. I see this as another U.S. mistake in Latin America in the making."

—José Figueres, May 1985, referring to the
opening of the Murciélago Military Base

Under arch-conservative Piza, U.S. influence over the police and security apparatus greatly increased. The most controversial of Washington's military programs was the creation of the U.S.-run civil guard military base located just ten miles from the Nicaraguan border. It was constructed on an ocean-side hacienda that had once been a summer vacation home for Nicaragua's rulers, the Somozas.[34] The base was to be run by Green Beret instructors and used to train a new Costa Rican battalion to patrol the border with Nicaragua.

Before the plan could be put in operation, Washington once again had to get around the 1974 congressional ban on U.S. training of Latin American police forces. This time it was done through a March 1985 amendment to the Foreign Assistance Act of 1961, which stated that the ban on police training "shall not apply with respect to a country which has a long-standing democratic tradition, does not have standing armed forces, and does not engage in a consistent pattern of gross violations of internationally recognized human rights."[35] Costa Rica was the only country in Latin America that met these criteria, and congressional sources confirmed that this amendment was intended to permit the United States to carry out police training there.

Construction at Murciélago began in April 1985, when three U.S. military engineers were sent from Panama to supervise the conversion of the *hacienda* into a military training camp. A group of Israeli engineers also came to build the landing docks at

Murciélago, which sits on a natural deep-water port. The access road and landing strip were improved, so that the camp was accessible by road, sea, and air and ideally situated for an invasion of Nicaragua. In May 1985, military instructors—two dozen U.S. Army Special Forces (Green Berets) sent from Panama—arrived to train a new 800-man Civil Guard "Lightning Battalion" (*Batallones Relámpagos*) to patrol at four different points along the northern frontier. This battalion was to supplement the recently formed border patrol, the Chorotega Company, which had been trained at the School of the Americas.

The Murciélago base seriously challenged in a number of ways Costa Rica's policies of nonmilitarism and neutrality. From Washington, a Pentagon official frankly but undiplomatically explained that the Murciélago training program was intended to create the "first military unit in Costa Rica since it dismantled its army in 1949." The base had not been approved beforehand by either the Legislative Assembly or President Monge. Rather, Security Minister Piza secretly arranged the training program with the U.S. Embassy, even though the base appeared to violate Costa Rica's constitution, the president's Neutrality Proclamation, and the Contadora peace plan.

When Monge first learned of the agreement, he was furious, saying he would have preferred Panamanian trainers. "We will pay a political price for this," he accurately predicted. But because he was heavily dependent on U.S. economic aid and had already turned down several other U.S. military offers, he felt he could not veto the Murciélago base. As news of the Green Beret trainers spread, there was an outcry from trade unionists, student and university groups, pro-neutrality activists, and the left wing of the Liberation party. Several former government ministers demanded that Monge abide by his own Neutrality Proclamation. The Legislative Assembly tried unsuccessfully to pass a motion censoring Piza for not obtaining their prior permission before permitting foreign troops to enter the country.[36]

The debate over the new base and the U.S. military advisers ended abruptly on May 31, 1985, when two Costa Rican guardsmen were killed and ten others were injured in an attack at the Costa Rican hamlet of Las Crucitas, near the Nicaraguan border. Costa

Rican and U.S. officials immediately blamed the Sandinistas. In a solemn television address to the nation, President Monge accused the Sandinista army of launching a "premeditated attack" against Costa Rica and announced he was downgrading the nation's diplomatic relations with Nicaragua. He called upon the Organization of American States to send an investigating commission.

U.S. officials could hardly contain their delight. While Costa Ricans buried the guardsmen at a military-style funeral, a U.S. Embassy spokesman told journalists that the incident was what the United States and Costa Rica "have been hoping for." Piza immediately ordered 400 Civil Guard reinforcements to the border and accepted a U.S. offer for quick delivery of military supplies, including M-16 rifles, grenade launchers, mortars, ammunition, reconnaissance planes, and a helicopter. Within a week the first planeload had arrived. The Reagan administration also offered to send U.S. troops to the border. Piza and several other right-wing ministers urged Monge to accept, but the Costa Rican leader refused, favoring instead a multinational OAS force if border troubles continued. Monge also resisted U.S. pressure to break diplomatic relations with Managua completely.

Overnight, anti-Sandinista tirades reached a fevered pitch and took on nationalist overtones, as protesters demanded that all Nicaraguans, not just Sandinista sympathizers, get out of Costa Rica. A group of taxi drivers burned the Sandinista flag. Then, on June 10, thousands of citizens poured into the streets at 1:00 P.M. for a civic act called "five minutes for Costa Rica," during which they sang the national anthem and silently mourned for the two dead guardsmen. Following this peaceful show of patriotism, about three hundred right-wing demonstrators, led by young men wearing Free Costa Rica Movement (MCRL) arm bands, stormed the Nicaraguan embassy.

Simultaneously, a handful of even more far-right militants, break-aways from the MCRL, were preparing to carry out their own commando-style action in Guanacaste. At 1:50 A.M. a powerful homemade bomb brought down the electricity tower near El Salto de Bagaces, outside Liberia, knocking out power in northern Costa Rica as well as parts of Nicaragua and Honduras.

Early the next morning, in the picturesque mountain town of

Naranjo, police stopped to check the occupants of a pay telephone booth. They found two brothers—Juan José (Comandante Javier) and Ricardo Alberto Saborio—busy notifying the media of the sabotage act. In the brothers' car, officials found a Rural Guard uniform, grenades, knives, a revolver (registered to right-wing Costa Rican rancher Victor Wolf), and a press communiqué signed by Patria y Verdad (Fatherland and Truth) that claimed responsibility for the bombing. The communiqué listed six demands, including that Costa Rica stop selling electricity to Nicaragua and collect a $200 million debt owed by the Managua government. It also warned that all groups and individuals perceived as sympathetic to the Sandinistas or the "communist mafia" should cease their activities "or we will be obligated to subject them to similar actions."

After arresting the Saborio brothers, OIJ investigators announced that the bomb had contained C-4 chemical explosive and was similar to the La Penca bomb. Subsequent interviews suggested that the C-4 may have come from John Hull and the CIA. Mercenary Peter Glibbery recalled that in April 1985, Hull complained that he had given Juan José Saborio some C-4 that the CIA had sent for contra use against strategic targets inside Nicaragua. Hull said that Saborio, who was a military trainer for right-wing para-military groups, had apparently "lost" or "sold" the powerful explosive. The electrical tower case was never prosecuted and the Saborio brothers were quietly released from jail.

The government's failure to prosecute the MCRL rock throwers or the Saborio brothers was a sign of the country's rapid drift to the right. Another was a public opinion poll done just after the May 1985 Las Crucitas incident that showed, for the first and only time, that a majority of Costa Ricans favored passage of U.S. aid to the contras (although the issue being debated in the U.S. Congress was "humanitarian," not military aid). For months afterward, U.S. officials cited this poll, which found that 69 percent of Costa Ricans supported (nonlethal or so-called "humanitarian") U.S. aid to the contras. A subsequent survey, taken that November by the same polling company, showed that a majority of Costa Ricans (61%) opposed contra aid, both military and nonmilitary. However, U.S. officials chose not to distribute these results.

Gradually a few politicians and guardsmen began to raise

doubts about the government's version of the Las Crucitas border incident. Figueres, a frail but respected voice of sanity, said, "I don't think it's been sufficiently proved that the attackers were the Sandinistas. I think it's part of a ploy concocted internationally." Three leftist legislators who interviewed the wounded guardsmen held a press conference to enumerate a long list of discrepancies in the official story.

In July, the Special OAS Commission investigated the border incident and concluded that some artillery fire had come from the Nicaraguan side of the river, where the Sandinista forces had taken up positions. The Commission said there also had been unidentified armed men (presumably contras) in the area, and it was impossible to say definitely that Sandinista fire had been responsible for the deaths or whether the firing came from more than one direction. No definitive conclusion was ever reached on the identities of the attackers. It appears most probable that the Costa Rican guardsmen were caught in cross fire between rebel and Nicaraguan army troops.

War rhetoric, fueled by the press, government hard-liners, and the U.S. Embassy, remained high for months, and this was the mood that prevailed at Murciélago's first graduation ceremony in late June. As top brass from the U.S. Southern Command, newly arrived Ambassador Lewis Tambs, Piza, Vice President Aráuz, and other high-level government officials stood at attention, the sun-baked hills resounded with the Costa Rican and U.S. national anthems, patriotic speeches denouncing the Nicaraguan threat, and the pounding of military boots hitting the hard Guanacaste earth. During their ten-week course, the Costa Ricans had been trained in antiterrorism, jungle survival, night fighting, and guerrilla warfare. They were taught the use of automatic rifles, 50-caliber machine guns, 90-millimeter recoilless rifles, grenade launchers, and mortars. They received ideological training as well; one of their chants was "*Comunista bueno, comunista muerto*" ("A good communist is a dead communist").

In August 1985, ostensibly to control the transfer of weapons, the Legislature approved a new "Law of Arms," which legitimized the security forces' use of sophisticated arms. It stated that the Civil and Rural Guards, OIJ, and other state entities could possess machine guns, bazookas, grenade launchers, mobile equipment including tanks and armored vehicles, high explosives, and so forth. Many of these weapons were already in use at Murciélago.

Piza said in interviews at the time that he hoped the entire Civil Guard could receive U.S. training at Murciélago and that the number of Green Beret instructors could be increased to thirty or more. Instead, the U.S. trainers stayed for only five months, graduating two groups of Costa Ricans, each numbering 400. Starting in January 1986, the base was formally turned over to Costa Rican trainers and gradually expanded into Costa Rica's main training base.

Officially, Murciélago was only a training base for the Civil Guard. But former security officials say that, especially during Monge's administration, a variety of people came to Murciélago for military instruction. These included OIJ, DIS, and Ministry of Government agents, MCRL militants, Cuban Americans working with the contras, and possibly soldiers and intelligence agents from Guatemala, Panama, and El Salvador.[37] If true, this indicates that Murciélago had become a sort of mini-School of the Americas.

At the second graduation ceremony in October 1985, U.S. and Costa Rican military brass and politicians pronounced the training program "highly successful." But even as the Green Berets packed their bags to depart, the local press was reporting that a number of Costa Rica's new crack troops—more than one hundred of Murciélago's graduates—had already resigned. The soldiers complained of low pay and poor working conditions in the isolated mud and jungle border region. Most had found jobs in the private sector, working as security guards at factories, offices, and hotels, many owned by Americans.

In terms of its stated mission—training troops to protect against a Sandinista invasion—Murciélago fell short. Instead, the facility ended up mainly training military men to be used, as some observers had foreseen, against Costa Ricans. These Murciélago graduates that remained within the Civil Guard, as well as those from other Costa Rican security units, did not see their main action along the northern frontier. With increasing frequency in the 1980s, the forces that were "modernized" and "professionalized" by the United States were called into action to put down local dissent, including demonstrations by campesino organizations, trade unionists, student groups, peace activists, local communities, and the homeless and landless. As a local publication *Crisis* put it in 1985, "The relation of the police to the people changes as they become armed with U.S. anti-communism, with U.S. weaponry." The publication continues,

> The manner in which the militarization is directed against our own people is perhaps more insidious and runs deeper. . . . Now a people's protest of poor water services is met with anti-riot squads and tear gas. A peaceful building takeover to protest governmental corruption results in several hospitalized demonstrators, while police are without a scratch. Popular leaders are "disappeared" for 24 hours and abused while in custody. In last year's banana strike the police shot and killed two unarmed strikers, wounded several others, and got away without a major scandal.[38]

During the 1980s, it was not just the Civil Guard and others trained at Murciélago who were undergoing these disturbing changes. The United States was facilitating a broader transformation by providing training and equipment to a variety of other police and security units.

Special Forces, Special Courses—and Rights Abuses

During the 1980s, the core units of Costa Rica's security forces, the Civil and Rural Guards, were overhauled, upgraded, modernized, and professionalized, but because of low pay and often-difficult working conditions, their overall numbers remained fairly constant. The fourfold expansion in the size of the nation's security forces was due instead to the growth, on the one hand, of quasi-governmental police organizations, and on the other to the rapid expansion of a bevy of new, often shadowy, specialized intelligence, antiterrorist, and antinarcotics bodies.

One of the oldest and largest was the Organization for National Emergencies, known as OPEN, a rough equivalent to the

U.S. National Guard. In November 1982, just six months after taking office, Monge issued an executive decree creating a volunteer 10,000-member "para-police" to be made up of persons of "proven democratic faith." (Members of the officially recognized communist party, the Partido Vanguardia Popular, were barred from joining.) The impetus came from private business, particularly the Costa Rican Association of Managers, and behind the scenes it was pushed by the U.S. Embassy. OPEN's purpose was to assist the Civil Guard in preserving order and handling national emergencies such as foreign (i.e., Sandinista) aggression and internal terrorism, subversion, and protest. It was under the control of the Security Minister and could be made active on orders of the President and Minister. Although up to ten thousand people are estimated to have taken OPEN's training course, they were activated only a few times.

The tone of the new organization was set by its first director, Colonel Rodrigo Paniagua Salazar, himself an ultra-right-winger and one of the contras' closest collaborators in Costa Rica. Paniagua used his position to carry on a wide range of contra and CIA activities, including providing OPEN training to paramilitary groups such as the MCRL and Patriotic Union, as well as to Cuban Americans and other foreigners fighting with the contras.

OPEN set up thirty-five training centers scattered throughout the country, where recruits practiced with M-16 rifles and other weapons supplied by the Security Ministry. During the courses, which ran from seven to fourteen weeks, male and female volunteers received basic infantry training and instruction in dealing with natural disasters, as well as internal and external threats. On one weekend encampment at a farm outside San José, which the press was barred from covering, they staged a mock attack on "a group of communist guerrillas" who had infiltrated "across the northern border." By the end of the 1980s, the Security Ministry reported that OPEN (or the Reserve of the Public Force, as it was officially renamed in 1985) had an estimated five thousand members.

In late 1982 OPEN made its debut by attacking demonstrators protesting President Reagan's visit. In mid-1983 OPEN broke up a hospital strike in Ciudad Quesada, and 1,500 OPEN members also helped with crowd control during the Pope's visit to

San José. In August 1987, as Arias promulgated his peace plan and cracked down on contra and CIA activities in Costa Rica, its activities were suspended indefinitely. Security Minister Hernán Garrón said he took the decision because the country was now "tranquil" and because "very serious internal differences" had developed within OPEN. He did not elaborate.[39] By the end of the decade, OPEN's training courses had been stopped, but those already trained could still be called up for duty in the event of a national emergency.

Also under the Security Ministry is the Auxiliary Police, which provides guards and security for private businesses, government offices and institutions, embassies, and wealthier neighborhoods. During the 1980s, the number of private guard companies grew rapidly, with few regulations and little oversight of their operations. The private guards include former Civil or Rural Guards or ex-members of other government security units, OPEN-trained volunteers, people drawn from the various paramilitary groups, ex-contras, and recruits with no military or police training. The Security Ministry provides some training courses for the Auxiliary Police, but it is only for the officers; many private guards licensed to carry guns have had no proper training. In August 1990, 17,000 private guards were officially registered, but press reports estimated the real figure was about 36,000, or nearly double all the other police and security units combined, including OPEN.[40] By the end of the decade, concern had grown about the size and lack of controls over the Auxiliary Police, which one legislative assistant termed "a large standing private armed force within Costa Rica—the security arm of the parallel state."

In addition to OPEN and the Auxiliary Police, there were numerous other new security, police, intelligence, antiterrorist, and antinarcotics units created during the 1980s, invariably with U.S. funds, equipment, and training. These units fall under four different ministries: Government, Public Security, the Presidency, and the Judicial Power of the Public Ministry (that is, the court system). Between 1982 and 1984, the number of official security units increased from six to thirteen, and 40.6 percent of new government posts were security or police-related. By 1990, there were nineteen different police units. During the decade, the size of the public security forces grew 400 percent, from around 7,000 in 1980 to 28,159 in 1989. While social services such as health and education were being compelled to trim their budgets, the Ministries of Security and Government continued to receive large annual increases. Between 1981 and 1986, for instance, spending for the public security forces increased 250 percent, thanks to U.S. military assistance.

As Max Peltz concludes in his important study on Costa Rican militarization, "Perhaps the most notable consequence" of the Reagan administration policies in Costa Rica "was the transformation of [the] Public Security Force . . . [which] is now the strongest, largest and most specialized, modernized, and professionalized force since the proscription of the army."[41] Likewise, abuse of power and human rights violations by the security forces have never been higher. According to the Costa Rican human rights organization CODEHU, the principal violations of civil and political rights are carried out by the Security Ministry, the Government Ministry, and the Judicial Power. They include arbitrary arrest and detention, physical and psychological torture, and ideological discrimination.[42]

Both the Monge and Arias administrations instituted reorganizations that were intended to gain some executive control over the proliferating security forces. In 1983 Monge set up the National Security Council, composed of all top government officials and chaired by Vice President Armando Aráuz, to improve coordination among the various security and police units. However, this was hardly a watch-dog committee, given Aráuz's hawkish, pro-U.S. political leanings. In July 1987, Arias announced several more substantial and controversial reforms, including the abolition of military ranks and terminology, and the creation of a national training school for the Rural and Civil Guard to instill the concept of the police as a peacekeeping force. He explained, "We will look to best take advantage of what resources we already have and will insist that the training programs faithfully obey a non-militarized concept of Costa Rican police."

While many of the reforms Arias proposed were never carried out, his presidency did set a new tone that allowed more public scrutiny of the police and security forces.

"The Babies" and Papi's Other Unsavory Progeny

One of the first to fall under the spotlight of public exposure was the Directorate of Intelligence and Security (DIS), formed in 1982. As conceived by Security Minister Angel Solano, DIS was to be composed of well-trained intelligence agents who would work to preserve the policy of neutrality and rout out contra camps and facilities, particularly in the border region. Wary of becoming too dependent on the United States, Solano appealed to Israel to train the new DIS agents as well as members of another antiterrorist unit.

The U.S. Embassy, wanting a strong foothold within Costa Rica's security and intelligence services and not wanting to be muscled out by the Israelis, came forward with its own proposal. In October 1982, according to one top Costa Rican security official, CIA station chief Phil Holts offered to train a special team of DIS intelligence agents "to give them a high level of professionalism."[43] The Costa Rican government accepted, and fifteen trainees were selected. Most were young men, former law students or university graduates, who came to think of themselves as an elite group, above the other DIS agents. "Real smart-asses," was how one agent described them. The leader of the group was Douglas Coblentz ("Lonny Chávez"), a tall, muscular Costa Rican of German parentage who had lived for many years in the United States and had received training from both the CIA and FBI. The U.S. trainer of this new unit was the older Greek American CIA agent Dimitrius Papas, who was known as "Papi"; his young trainees became known simply as "The Babies."

While Security Ministry official Francisco Tacsan described The Babies as a "pure intelligence-gathering unit," those close to it say the team's real mission was "dirty tricks"—a sort of Costa Rican equivalent to the Watergate Plumbers. Papi and other CIA agents taught The Babies a variety of covert skills, including how to break into houses and offices; follow, interrogate, and blackmail suspected leftists; manufacture phony documents; circulate false rumors; bug homes and offices; and tap telephones. According to one of his superiors, Coblentz once offered to manufacture fake documents to be used to accuse a North American journalist of unprofessional ties to the Sandinistas. The Babies also produced and circulated phony documents purporting to show that the FMLN guerrillas and "leftists" in the Costa Rican government were responsible for the La Penca bombing and that Arias and several of his ministers, including Guido Fernández, were involved in drug trafficking.

While the Embassy's offer was to upgrade the professionalism within DIS, the CIA in fact set out to create a parallel institution. The Babies should have answered directly to DIS Director Carlos Monge. However, within a month Papas had moved his operation outside DIS headquarters, partly because the CIA did not trust Carlos Monge and partly because the other DIS agents became jealous of this CIA-pampered unit. Carlos Monge says he then lost touch with the agents, even though they remained on the DIS payroll. Papas rented and furnished an office and several safe houses and purchased vehicles for the exclusive use of The Babies. The special agents also received a monthly "topping up" of 5,000 colones or more, based on the level of their modest DIS salaries. Coblentz received a more generous monthly bonus. For a brief period, The Babies reported to Vice Minister Johnny Campos and Colonel Francisco Tacsan, the Security Ministry's number three man. In reality, The Babies worked for and reported to the CIA. As one former DIS agent put it, "The Babies, they weren't the territory of anyone in the Costa Rican government."

One of The Babies' first "projects" was to help orchestrate a campaign against both DIS Director Monge and Security Minister Angel Solano. Solano says that although he had had a very cordial relationship with Ambassador McNeil, Winsor disliked him and stopped all contact. Instead, the Embassy began to deal on security matters with Solano's subordinate, Tacsan, or with Vice President Aráuz. Within a short time, rumors were circulating that both Carlos Monge and Solano were Sandinista agents, and the Chambers of Commerce and Industry and the Free Costa Rica Movement were demanding their resignations. Solano says that once, at a U.S. Embassy reception, Winsor casually told Foreign Minister Carlos Gutiérrez that Solano "had become a lawyer at the Patrice Lumumba University of Moscow." He said "it is not possible" for the United States to give aid to "a product of a Soviet university." Gutiérrez, himself a former law professor, informed Winsor that his "information" was incorrect: Solano was a graduate of the University of Costa Rica, where he had been Gutiérrez's student for six years.

In the case of DIS director Monge, The Babies created and circulated phony documents charging that he was corrupt, involved in immoral practices, unprofessional, also a graduate of the Patrice Lumumba University, married to a leftist Chilean woman, and involved in secret meetings with Sandinista diplomats. Monge was not amused: "My wife is Costa Rican and her father is a wealthy coffee grower and an extreme right-winger. I've never been in Moscow; I've only been in the U.S.," he said in an interview.

Why the United States targeted Carlos Monge is not altogether clear. ARDE officials say he was one of their most important government supporters, although Monge apparently angered the United States because he would not fully cooperate with certain U.S.-backed schemes. As Monge put it, "I'm a friend of the U.S., but I'm first of all a Costa Rican. There were many things the CIA asked me to do which I could not do."

The Babies carried out surveillance of other top officials whom the Embassy deemed to be in the neutrality camp. These included Minister of the Presidency Fernando Berrocal, Vice Minister Manuel Carballo, and President Monge himself. According to several of these officials, their offices were bugged, their telephones were tapped, and they were followed. Solano relates that the day he was fired as Security Minister, he packed up his most sensitive personal papers and locked them in his office, with the intention of collecting them the next morning. He believed that he possessed the only key to his office, but when he entered the following day, the box had mysteriously vanished. He blames The Babies.

Once Solano had been replaced by Piza, Carlos Monge was even more isolated. Piza offered him another post in the ministry if he would agree to leave DIS. He declined and in late 1984 resigned and set up his own private security company. His replacement, Sergio Fernández, was a long-time confidant of the CIA. The upshot of this change of leadership at the Security Ministry and within its DIS division was that U.S. influence and assistance expanded, including new cars, radios, and other equipment. Between 1982 and 1989, DIS's budget increased 1400 percent, from 4.2 million to nearly 60 million colones.[44]

After Carlos Monge's departure in late 1984, The Babies themselves were brought back within the Security Ministry structure, and they gradually ceased to function as a separate entity. As one ex-DIS agent said in an interview in 1985, "Now all DIS agents are Babies." Papas himself set up an office within the DIS building.

When the Calderón government took office in 1990, Security Minister Víctor Emilio Herrera—who, like Piza, was a wealthy businessman and a founding member of the Free Costa Rica Movement—was said to have quietly implemented a policy requiring that all new Ministry employees be members of this ultra-rightist, paramilitary organization.[45] According to a well-placed former intelligence agent, The Babies continued to exist, although their operations had become "more clandestine." By the end of the decade the Security Ministry had, therefore, been transformed from an institution that, as envisioned by Solano, was to safeguard Costa Rica's neutrality and sovereignty into an organ primarily to protect the interests of both Costa Rica's powerful right wing and the United States.

Back in 1982, as Dimitrius Papas was creating The Babies, he was working simultaneously to penetrate another key Costa Rican police institution, the Organization of Judicial Investigation (OIJ), to assure its loyalty to the CIA. Again the way in the door was to offer CIA assistance in giving courses, this time a training program in antiterrorism, and in creating a new unit, the Office of Special Affairs, to handle crimes involving state security. This early linkage between OIJ and DIS was facilitated by Rodolfo Jiménez, the number two official at DIS, who had previously worked at OIJ. Jiménez, who was known as "Flaco" ("Slim"), was a close confidant of the CIA and, during the Arias government, headed the Security Ministry's Narcotics Division, which worked closely with both the DEA and the Agency.

Office of Special Affairs agents were trained by Papas and other CIA agents side by side with The Babies, and eventually the combined "Babies" units within DIS and OIJ totaled about twenty-five agents. CIA equipment and money were funneled to the new OIJ unit through Papas's DIS operation. Government prosecutors later found that the unit had illegally developed "a true economic dependency" on the CIA: "that the office was furnished not only telephone tapping equipment, recorders and photographic equipment, but also money in cash that was used for the purchase of supplies, payment of vehicle rentals, rentals of apartments for surveillance and per diem." As with the DIS Babies, the CIA was giving these OIJ agents "a monthly or fortnightly bonus in cash," a practice that government prosecutors concluded was "totally irregular . . . and in contradiction to the payment system of the State that is controlled by the Finance Ministry." These bonuses grew from a total of 30–40,000 colones initially to 1.6 million colones per month. To conceal the origin of the funds, they were passed through a previously unknown local organization, the Costa Rican Civic Assistance Association, which claimed to receive the money from several sources, including another unknown "private organization" in New York known as the Cardenal Association.

Papas maintained "a relation of great camaraderie" with OIJ personnel and had particularly close personal ties with Alberto Llorente, who worked in the Office of Special Affairs, where (as in DIS) Papas maintained a desk. Llorente, who coordinated relations between the U.S. Embassy and the OIJ, even chose Papas to be the *padrino* or godfather of one of his sons.[46] The CIA was able to cash in on these ties by using Llorente and his assistant, Alan Solano, to stall politically embarrassing investigations into contra and drug-related crimes and to derail the inquiry into the La Penca bombing. (see chapter 11). By the end of the decade, the Office of Special Affairs had only brought three cases to trial, all involving leftists.

Under Papas's guidance, the Office of Special Affairs, together with The Babies, was also involved in covert and illegal operations for the CIA. According to a former OIJ agent, the Office ran an internal spy operation which kept special files on OIJ and court employees, including psychological profiles and notes on any "leftist tendencies." These files could, the official said, be used to blackmail or fire "people the CIA did not like."

Another operation involved illegal telephone taps. Under Costa Rican law, telephones could only be tapped if a police agency got written permission from a judge giving the telephone company permission to put a recording device on the line. According to former Security Minister Johnny Echevarría, the CIA had long "been tapping phones on its own, behind our backs." In the

1980s, a former OIJ official says, at least some of this illegal tapping was handled by the Office of Special Affairs and The Babies, who used CIA funds to pay telephone company employees about 50,000 colones to put an unauthorized tap on a line. These numbers never showed up on the official government list of tapped phones.[47]

This relationship between the CIA and the OIJ "Babies" within the Office of Special Investigations continued into 1988, when judicial prosecutors reopened the La Penca case and began uncovering these gross improprieties and illegalities. At the end of the Arias administration, judicial prosecutors brought charges of "illicit enrichment" and "negligence of duty" against Llorente and Alan Solano for their collaboration with the CIA in the La Penca cover-up. About this time, Dimitrius Papas packed up his Costa Rican operations and moved to Panama, where he was reportedly working out of the U.S. Embassy. Despite Papas's departure, an indication of continuing CIA influence within Costa Rica's security services is that, in May 1990, the Calderón government appointed Alberto Llorente as head of the Security Ministry's Narcotics Division. This was done despite the pending legal action against him and over the objections of judges on Costa Rica's Supreme Court.

During this period, the OIJ also gained notoriety "as responsible for carrying out arbitrary detentions and practicing physical and psychological torture."[48] In March 1989, members of the Legislative Assembly, accompanied by other government officials, discovered a secret underground cell, a 6-by-3-foot windowless room that was apparently used as a torture chamber, hidden below the basement of the OIJ building. Three other possible torture cells were discovered in the building, and there were reports of other such chambers, including on the prison island of San Lucas in Puntarenas, long viewed as a model minimum-security facility. Since the early 1980s there had been court testimony and rumors of torture by OIJ officials.

The human-rights organization CODEHU gave legislators a list of fourteen persons who claimed they were tortured while in government custody. Legislator José María Borbón said the evidence of torture indicates "the problem is structural." He told the press that

OIJ "has created a repressive administrative structure" and went on to denounce the type of instruction OIJ has received from the United States, Argentina, Chile, Israel, South Korea, and Taiwan.

The Supreme Court immediately ordered an internal investigation, and Borbón demanded an independent inquiry by the legislature. However, no congressional commission was ever set up, apparently because of a secret deal struck between top legislators and the Supreme Court. According to press accounts, after the legislature's drug commission issued a November 1987 report recommending the removal of three Supreme Court judges for collaboration with drug traffickers, members of the legislature met with the Supreme Court and agreed, in the future, to let the judicial branch handle its own house cleaning. In August 1989, the judicial investigators announced they had reviewed the allegations concerning the OIJ torture chamber and found them groundless.[49]

In addition to the rapid expansion of the numbers, size, and types of police, security, and intelligence units, U.S. training courses for Costa Ricans also accelerated, especially after 1985 when Congress exempted Costa Rica from its prohibition on police training. According to one former OIJ agent, "There were so many courses. People went all the time to the U.S. and a steady stream of gringos—from the CIA, FBI, military, police, Customs, DEA, State Department, Justice Department—came here to give us courses." Costa Rica was one of the "beneficiaries" of the United States' antiterrorist training programs, which expanded greatly during the 1980s in order to circumvent the 1974 congressional prohibition on police training as well as other legal, political, and logistical difficulties. According to an investigative report in the *Los Angeles Times,* this was "one of the most closely held U.S. intelligence and military programs" which "covertly trained counterterrorism squads in dozens of countries in the Middle East, Africa, Asia and Latin America." The article quotes a senior counterterrorism official as saying, "Virtually everyone is now in on the action—all branches of the military, the State Department [through its Anti-Terrorism Assistance Program], the CIA, the FBI, even the FAA [Federal Aviation Administration]."[50]

As has long been standard practice in other Latin countries, the U.S. Embassy in Costa Rica used scholarships to these courses as a way to reward loyalists or get rid of potential political problems—people who knew too much, had been involved in human rights abuses and were liable to be publicly exposed, or were themselves too vigorously investigating U.S.-linked dirty deeds. One ex-OIJ officer complained in an interview that two agents who collaborated closely with the CIA were rewarded again and again with courses in the United States. Another case was that of Major Harry Barrantes, a Rural Guard intelligence officer who in April 1985 began working under special orders of the Vice Minister of the Presidency, Manuel Carballo, to help us in our La Penca investigation. Suddenly, in mid-August 1985, the U.S. Embassy military attaché offered Barrantes a scholarship to attend a three-month counter-terrorism course at the School of the Americas, which had been relocated to Fort Benning, Georgia. Normal procedures had been bypassed, all the paperwork had been completed in less than twenty-four hours, and Barrantes was whisked out of the country, without informing either his superior within the Rural Guard, Colonel Pedro Arias, or his boss in the La Penca investigation, Vice Minister Carballo. The government's special La Penca investigation closed down. In relating the details later, Barrantes said the scholarship was "too good an offer to pass up." In fact Barrantes was the lucky recipient of twelve such overseas training courses during his fourteen years with security.[51]

These U.S. scholarships and courses for members of the security forces received little publicity, although there were periodic perfunctory notices in the paper. However, considerable detail could be gathered about one course held at New York City's Roosevelt Hotel in November 1985 for a group of Ecuadorian police and twenty-four Costa Rican OIJ agents. The two-week course was run by the Nassau County Police Department, which obtained a contract from the State Department's Anti-Terrorism Assistance (ATA) Program. The course involved anti-terrorism training, psychological operations, surveillance, and hostage negotiations. According to the commanding officer in charge of the course, it also included use of firearms and surveillance equipment, responses to bomb threats, eavesdropping technology, infiltration techniques, evasive driving maneuvers, intelligence gathering, and protection of leaders. One of those involved said the Costa Ricans and Ecuadorians were "taught" about U.S.-based "terrorist" organizations, all of them left wing, including CISPES (Committee in Solidarity with the People of El Salvador),[52] the academic research organization North American Congress on Latin America (NACLA), the National Lawyers Guild, and the Puerto Rican pro-independence group the FALN (Armed Forces for National Liberation). At one point, the lecturer held up a copy of the left-leaning weekly *Nation* as an illustration of a "communist" publication. One of those involved described the instruction as "very violent," and said several of the OIJ participants were "disgusted" by a course that seemed to provide little that was applicable to the real situation in Costa Rica.[53]

Even the most senior security and police officials took part in these courses in the States. In 1985, for instance, Piza, Minister of Government Enrique Obregón, Civil Guard Colonel José Montero, along with members of OIJ, the Supreme Court, and the electricity company ICE (sections of which collaborated closely with the Security Ministry and the contras) participated in a week-long seminar held at the Civil Defense Training Center in Maryland and conducted by the Federal Emergency Management Agency (FEMA). Established in 1977, FEMA has responsibility for developing a national preparedness program for "continuity of government" in the wake of a national emergency such as a natural disaster or nuclear war. Between 1981 and 1984, President Reagan signed a series of National Security Decision Directives which gave FEMA greatly expanded powers to undertake nationwide readiness exercises, counterintelligence, and law-and-order maintainence in the event of terrorist incidents or civil disturbances. The readiness exercises included a scheme to round up and put in detention camps thousands of undocumented Central Americans and possibly American political activists who were considered security threats, as the United States had done with Japanese Americans during World War II. FEMA's exercises also included a secret plan calling for the suspension of the Constitution, appointment of military commanders to run state and local governments, and a declaration of martial law.

Details of FEMA's activities were among the Reagan administration's most guarded secrets, and they were never explored during the Iran contra hearings. Oliver North served as the NSC liaison to FEMA from 1982 to 1984 and was instrumental in drawing up the plans, but when Iran-contra panel members broached the subject during North's testimony, Chairman Daniel Inouye ruled that this highly classified operation could only be discussed in executive session.[54] It apparently never was.

Costa Rica's connection with FEMA is intriguing. FEMA is ostensibly purely a domestic program, and this is the first indication that it had become involved in training foreign governments. Piza said the course, given exclusively to the group from Costa Rica, concerned organizing emergency systems to deal with both "natural and man-made disasters" and involved both government functionaries and private business people. Piza said he met with FEMA director Colonel Louis Giuffrida, who expressed "an interest in organizing [a civil defense plan including] medical services, firemen, the Red Cross and the authorities of the country with the aim of handling in the best way whatever type of emergency is present in the country." Giuffrida, a right-wing Republican, had played a key role when Reagan was governor of California in the 1970s in developing the state's antiterrorist plans to deal with peace and African American activists. A U.S. Embassy spokesman said that Giuffrida's offer to Piza for FEMA to come to Costa Rica to assist with civil defense planning was never implemented.[55]

As the decade neared an end, the *Tico Times* covered another scandal that dramatized the inappropriateness of at least some of the U.S. military training in Costa Rica. In late August 1989, as the Arias administration was priding itself on the near-successful implementation of the Central American Peace Plan and on closing down the Southern Front, two California tourists and their Costa Rican guide stumbled upon a Green Beret and Civil Guard training camp in the Braulio Carrillo National Park, just off the highway to Limón. As the trio drove into the park for a day of hiking and bird watching, they heard gunfire and then saw soldiers dressed in camouflage uniforms with painted faces and vegetation attached to their helmets crouching behind sandbags with machine guns mounted on tripods. "There was a lot of action, and they were shooting all around," related tour guide Sergio

Volio. As the trio of visitors was assessing the unusual scene, a van carrying a group of North American soldiers pulled up. "They seemed to be the bosses," Volio recalled. One soldier told the startled tourists, "You're lucky you didn't get shot. You better get out of here."

After a heated exchange, the trio left, followed out of the park by the U.S. soldiers' van. "We didn't understand why Americans in camouflage uniforms were throwing us out of a national park in Costa Rica. We thought it was outrageous," lawyer Donna Williamson told the *Tico Times* later in a telephone interview from San Francisco. Volio, who has been a conservationist for fifteen years, added, "I was very upset at finding a military camp in the park. Parks are very sacred places in Costa Rica."

Nonsense, was the official response from Costa Rica's Security Minister Hernán Garrón and U.S. Ambassador Deane Hinton. "Why is it illegal? What law were they breaking?" demanded Minister Garrón. He dismissed the incident, which was not covered by any of Costa Rica's major news media, as "not a big deal. . . . You are looking for a hair in the soup." Ambassador Hinton retorted in a similar vein that the incident "was not of transcendental importance," adding that a national park is a good place for such training.

Under questioning, Costa Rican and U.S. authorities admitted that the ten Green Berets were members of a Special Forces Group from Fort Bragg, North Carolina, who were spending four weeks in Costa Rica doing "joint field exercises" with sixty-three Civil Guardsmen and eight Costa Rican trainers. They had been in the park for three days doing military-style antinarcotics training. The U.S. Embassy said this was just one of a number of antinarcotics exercises taking place in Costa Rica. A similar one had been held at the beginning of 1989, and three more such programs were scheduled for the coming year.[56]

This issue became increasingly important in Costa Rica and elsewhere in the region as Bush's "war on drugs" together with the "war on terrorism" supplanted both the Cold War and the war against Nicaragua. Increasingly the U.S. military was getting a boot in the door of Latin American countries under the guise of fighting "narco-terrorism." Between 1984 and 1990, the U.S. military carried out nine "counter-narcotics" operations and training exercises in Costa Rica. These were in addition to DEA and State Department drug interdiction programs in Costa Rica that included training, equipment, and a new radar station. Depite all these programs, by the end of the decade, drug trafficking and money laundering had become increasingly serious problems. According to DEA figures for 1990, at least a ton of cocaine was passing through Costa Rica every month, and Costa Rica had become third among Latin American countries in money laundering. The U.S. continued, however, to prescribe the same medicine. In September 1991, the Calderón government announced the Murciélago base would be reopened and U.S. military instructors would return to give antidrug training.[57]

These issues—the appropriateness of U.S. military training and its new antidrug slant—came tragically to a head just over a week after the Calderón administration took office in May 1990. Early on the morning of May 19, 1990, thirty-four heavily armed members of the Security Ministry's Narcotics Division, hooded and in camouflage dress, and the Immediate Action Unit (UAI), dressed in black uniforms and their faces smeared with camouflage paint, stormed into Jardines de Cascajal, a working-class barrio of Desamparados, south of San José. In the commando-style assault, they targeted three houses of suspected marijuana traffickers. Finding the door to one small wooden row home locked, twenty-one-year-old UAI agent Erick Valverde aimed his 12-gauge shotgun and blasted the door. This failed to open the door, so Valverde took the butt of his rifle and smashed a window, reached inside, and undid the lock so the agents could enter. Inside they found Wagner Alfonso Segura, a twelve-year-old boy, shot four times in the heart and back. As the boy lay bleeding to death, the agents forcibly prevented his parents from calling an ambulance and handcuffed his father, Roy Segura. No drugs or arms were found in any of the houses, and no one was detained.[58]

The killing of the Segura youngster was not the first by government forces. The human rights organization CODEHU documented thirteen cases in which people had died as a consequence of police actions between January 1988 and May 1990.[59] However, the Segura case caused an outcry of public shock and horror. Oto Castro, the attorney for the dead boy's family, declared, "This isn't the Colombian drug wars, this isn't a Rambo movie. This is Costa Rica." Protesters marched on the Legislative Assembly, demanding a special investigating commission and more details about the Immediate Action Unit, one of the growing number of shadowy "special" police divisions.

Most members of the UAI received U.S. military training, either at the School of the Americas at Fort Benning, in Costa Rica from the Fort Bragg Green Berets (such as those training in the national park), or by U.S.-trained Costa Rican officers at Murciélago. Two UAI agents were trained in Guatemala (one of these was Erick Valverde), and fifteen received training in El Salvador. The Embassy tried to downplay the role of the U.S. military, arguing that the training it provided was only in rural antidrug campaigns, not in urban operations. Coincidentally, two days before the fatal shooting, ten to fifteen more Fort Bragg Green Berets arrived to train another group of sixty Costa Ricans.

In August 1990, the special bipartisan legislative commission looking into Wagner Segura's death released a fifty-one-page report that concluded that the raiding party had used unnecessary force and had not first warned the Segura family that they were police and had a warrant to enter. The commission recommended that in the future Costa Rican security forces should receive only police training in order "to avoid situations that could evolve into behavior of a military nature."[60] For many this was the heart of the issue: what type of training had the Costa Rican security forces been receiving, and what was its impact?

It was, in a sense, chickens coming home to roost. At the beginning of the decade, the Reagan administration had sold Costa Rica on the need for U.S. military training and equipment to "professionalize" and "modernize" its security forces so as to protect against Nicaraguan aggression. These newly upgraded and expanded forces were largely ineffectual in stopping the violence in the border region. Costa Rican guardsmen frequently turned a blind eye or actively helped the contras, and many of the border clashes were deliberate CIA-contra provocations. Instead, by the end of the decade, Costa Rica's militarized police and security forces were being largely used internally, against Costa Ricans.

It Couldn't Happen Here

One of the darker questions raised by the increased militarization of the 1980s is whether Costa Rica has moved toward developing death squads tied to or tolerated by its security forces. According to investigative journalist Jean Hopfensperger, at least six paramilitary military groups, ranging in size from a few dozen to about 1,000 members, became active during the 1980s. She describes their existence as "a well-kept secret guarded by national-security officials and the influential members of the press." They carried out military training exercises on private farms, and four of the groups became integrated into the National Reserve (originally called OPEN) where they received military instruction with U.S. weapons donated to Costa Rica's Civil Guard.

With the exception of the Free Costa Rica Movement which was founded after the Cuban Revolution, the others—Patriotic Union, North Huétar Democratic Association, National Reserve, North Chorotega Democratic Association, and Fatherland and Truth—formed in the wake of the Sandinista victory. All worked closely with the contras, were backed by large landowners and big businessmen, and were protected by the Ministry of Security. In addition, Hopfensperger writes, "Most of these groups include members with ties to the United States, through military training, collaboration with the CIA, friendship with U.S. Embassy personnel, or work as security officers with U.S. multinational corporations." Their mission—to fight communism—involved assisting and sometimes fighting with the contras, evicting squatters from large ranches, busting up peasant and peace demonstrations, infiltrating student organizations, spying on Nicaraguan diplomats and Sandinista sympathizers, and compiling dossiers on suspected leftists.

Hopfensperger says these rightist forces had not yet resorted to death squad activity, but she warns that "they are planting the seeds of internal repression that could ripen in the future."[61] With hindsight its possible to see that, during the 1980s, death squads began to take root in Costa Rica. Several former DIS and OIJ agents say they believe this is the case. According to a DIS agent, The Babies' activities involved possibly even killing people." An OIJ agent who took a CIA training course given by Dimitrius Papas recalls, "The course was preparing people for the future, but it began very lightly. Papi did not teach killing or bombing directly, but the ground was being prepared. Papi did say we had to eliminate all communists. That was our mission. In this atmosphere they could be trained to do anything. If ordered to kill a person, I'm sure they would."

Elements of the far-right paramilitary groups and the contras had similar objectives. Beginning in 1983, John Hull and some of his associates were clearly preparing the terrain for political killings. Hull's sidekick and self-confessed CIA operative Bruce Jones matter-of-factly told journalists Jon Lee and Scott Anderson how he and other large landowners had formed "a kind of La Mano Blanca," modeled after the Guatemalan death squad. Jones said that the North Huétar Democratic Association was a paramilitary group trained to protect their cattle farms from both Sandinista invaders and Costa Rican squatters and to carry out surveillance of suspected leftists in the San Carlos area. The group included members of MCRL's *Boinas Azules* (Blue Berets), and its members used Hull's and other ranches for private paramilitary training. One of their military instructors, Adolfo Louzao, a Costa Rican who had fought in Vietnam, said he had enlisted retired American military specialists to help with the training. Louzao, who worked as a security guard at both the U.S. Embassy and the VOA station, described the North Huétar group as the sort of "special forces" of OPEN. From the outset a number of thoughtful Costa Ricans voiced concern that OPEN, with its anti-Communist ideology, loose organization, and sophisticated training, could evolve into a Guatemalan- or Salvadoran-type death squad.

Another of the North Huétar military instructors was Juan José Saborio, alias Comandante Javier or "Carlos Sánchez," who was responsible for killing a Nicaraguan racehorse imported to Costa Rica and blowing up the Guanacaste electricity tower. In the 1970s Saborio had fought in Nicaragua with Somoza's National Guard; then he moved to Guatemala, where he worked as an "ideological trainer" with Mano Blanca's "rural vigilance" program. Originally from Guanacaste, Saborio trained militants on Victor Wolf's farm near Cañas and served as an ideological trainer for the Free Costa Rica Movement. He broke with the organization, considering it too moderate, and formed a string of smaller anti-Communist terrorist groups—the Black Berets, Costa Rican People's Army, and Fatherland and Truth (Patria y Verdad). His recruits included the sons and daughters of the wealthy, former contras from the FDN and FARN, and ex-Rural Guardsmen. He approached high-level Rural Guard officers about dropping out of government service and forming a Mano Blanca–type organization. He told Colonel Carlos Camacho, deputy director of the Rural Guard, that the group's goal was "the elimination of Marxist-Leninists in the country, including those in the government." At the same time, he became deeply involved in meetings with Hull.

Bruce Jones and John Hull developed a close relationship with the Civil and Rural guardsmen in the area. Jones had been honored with a membership card in the security forces, and those familiar with Hull's operations say guardsmen were frequently at his farmhouse pouring over maps, discussing the logistics of the contra-supply network, and laying plans for military forays into Nicaragua. One contra based on Hull's ranch referred to the group of "Hull's colonels" who were, in practice, based there and took their orders from Hull and the CIA.

Jones showed Jon Lee and Scott Anderson written intelligence reports on supposed Sandinista sympathizers that he collected several times each month from Rural Guard officials posted along the border. "This man is a known communist and is believed to travel often to Nicaragua," read one entry. Jones said he prepared copies of these intelligence reports for his contacts in the Costa Rican government and in the U.S. Embassy. Anyone showing up on the Embassy's list, Jones claimed, "is denied a visa to the U.S., if they ever apply."

Jones's group also kept the list "of all the communists in northern Costa Rica." The reason, he frankly admitted to the Andersons, was "in case we ever have to do an Operation Phoenix here."[62] Jones was referring to the CIA's notorious counter-insurgency program during the Vietnam war that was responsible for assassinating between twenty and fifty thousand Vietnamese, mainly civilians.

Beginning in August 1983, a mini-Operation Phoenix appeared to be underway in the border town of Upala.[63] About a dozen people had been murdered, and there were widespread rumors of a "hit list." The tranquil hamlet had been converted "into a little hell," according to an editorial in *La Nación*.[64] Residents and local officials interviewed at the time said their tranquility had ended when, several months earlier, Pastora's ARDE guerrillas began operating from camps near the town. Since then the town had experienced, in addition to the murders, a series of other "mysterious incidents," including the fire bombing of eleven businesses and houses, burning of a private plane, and bomb threats against the town's only bridge, electricity company, social security office, and secondary school. In July, a teacher was murdered after he said publicly he knew the whereabouts of some contra camps. Another teacher interviewed said he had been "warned that I am on the hit list." One headmaster, Tito José Somarriba, told government investigators where contra camps were located and asked that they be closed down. In an interview afterward, he said, "I know that I am writing my death sentence, and that from this moment they will be looking for me to assassinate me as they have done with other persons." A number of teachers, fearing for their lives, had requested transfers, four schools had closed, and many parents had withdrawn their children. In late August 1983, the government announced that it was placing guards in all the remaining schools.

This once sleepy backwater was seriously divided by the Nicaraguan war, with residents lining up for and against the contras. Town official Carlos Fonseca accused "the communists" of moving a network of spies into Upala, while other residents said that Pastora could enter Upala "whenever he wants, and the worst part is that the police seem not to even see him."[65] From interviews conducted at the time, it was apparent that most government and police officials in Upala were sympathetic to the contras. According to Civil Guard Captain Víctor Julio Quirós, who was stationed there, "What I found in Upala was that the civil guards, on orders from their superiors, functioned as logistical or rearguard support for the contras. That was their purpose for being there. We were just one more element of the counterrevolution."[66]

The Upala murders shocked Costa Ricans. Given the intertwined changes underway—the U.S.-supported expansion and militarization of the police and security forces, the growth of paramilitary organizations, and the build-up of contra operations—political assassinations and at least the beginnings of death-squad activities were probably inevitable. As former legislator and Communist party leader Arnoldo Ferreto told Hopfensperger, "We're playing with fire. People talk about the Central Americanization of Costa Rica. How do they think the death squads began in El Salvador? Do they want that to happen here?" By the end of the decade, Costa Rica had not become as violent as its neighbors, but it was also no longer immune to human-rights abuses and political terrorism. It had been drawn into both the war against Nicaragua and international drug trafficking. And, like the other "democracies" in Central America, Costa Rica had been taking the same medicine—U.S. economic and military aid—and while the country's traditions of nonmilitarism, respect for human rights, and the rule of law provided some protection, it also suffered serious side effects.

ELEVEN

Unconventional Warfare: La Penca, Drugs, and Other Dirty Tricks

These people are involved in drug and arms trafficking and they are making money off the blood of my Nicaraguan brothers.

—David, contra defector

For the Costa Rican public and press, as well as Tony and me personally, the La Penca bombing, May 30, 1984, became the watershed event in the U.S-contra/Sandinista war along the Southern Front. It represents the centerpiece around which all other events in the war seem to fall. As we began unraveling the mysteries surrounding La Penca, we gradually uncovered evidence of plots by three different covert networks, each of which wanted, for different reasons, to remove the troublesome contra commander, Edén Pastora. The first network we stumbled upon was the one being run out of the U.S. Embassy and off John Hull's ranches, the Costa Rican end of Oliver North's operation. It included Americans, Cuban Americans, foreign mercenaries, FDN contras, and right-wing Costa Rican officials who viewed Pastora as too independent, a closet communist who was blocking the unity of the Northern and Southern Front contra groups. The mission of this network was to remove Pastora, dismantle his army, and create border clashes and terrorist attacks that could be blamed on the Sandinistas and would help build U.S. public and congressional support for the war. The second were the drug and arms trafficking operations closely intertwined with the CIA/North/Hull network. Pastora opposed involving ARDE in drug trafficking, and so some of his pilots, Hull, the Cuban Americans, and others involved in the trade began to plot his removal. Only much later did our La Penca investigations lead geographically and ideologically in the opposite direction, to a spy and assassination cell—the Fifth Directorate—housed deep within the Sandinista's Interior Ministry in Managua. This included a group of leftist Argentine guerrillas, a Cuban intelligence officer and spy master, a network of spies and collaborators in Costa Rica, and top Sandinista security officials. This unit carried out attacks in several countries, including against key Southern Front leaders.

In the year preceding the bombing, all three of these networks—the CIA/North/Hull, the drug trafficking, and the Sandinista's Fifth Directorate—were plotting against Edén Pastora. In ways that remain partly shrouded, all three appear to converge at La Penca. The journalist-cum-bomber, Vital Roberto Gaguine, was working for the Sandinistas' Fifth Directorate. The coverup was orchestrated by the CIA. By the end of the decade the Sandinistas were out of office and the CIA/North operation discredited and dismantled, and only the drug trafficking through Costa Rica continued to flourish.

For the CIA and North network, La Penca signals the point at which Costa Rica is converted from a base for conventional warfare against Nicaragua into an arena for "unconventional" warfare[1] Before La Penca, the United States had been attempting to build up the Southern Front as the mirror image of the Northern Front in Honduras with a large, unified, conventional contra army. Afterward the Sandinistas launched a major offensive against ARDE, sending hundreds of guerrillas fleeing into Costa Rica. Political in-fighting, the bombing, and the Sandinista assault left ARDE badly crippled. However, rather than regrouping and rebuilding the Southern Front forces, U.S. strategists moved, over the coming months, to swiftly dismantle those that remained and to replace them with a small "dirty tricks" network whose main task was not to fight against the Sandinista army but to stage terrorist actions designed to be blamed on the Sandinistas.

In the process Costa Rica, the region's only real democracy, was to become the base for what is known in the covert trade as "simulated terrorism," actions designed to be blamed on one's enemy and to cause a public outcry. Simulated terrorism is a well-established CIA tactic. Miami Cubans involved with the Southern Front adopted it in their war against Fidel Castro, John Hull employed it as a CIA operative in Brazil,[2] and the contras used it in border incidents.[3] After La Penca, the CIA/North/Hull network laid plans an ambitious program of terrorism: a 1985 assassination attempt on Pastora, a phony "Sandinista" attack on the border town of Los Chiles, a series of bombings against the U.S. embassies in Costa Rica and Honduras, and the murders of U.S., Costa Rican, and contra officials in both these countries.

Parallel to these plots, this same group became increasingly involved in drug trafficking for both personal profit and to help finance the contra war after Congress cut off funding. Contra operations provided a perfect womb for securely moving cocaine from Colombia through Costa Rica to the United States: personnel, airplanes, landing strips, loose financial records, and, most important, protection under the aegis of a clandestine CIA operation. In Costa Rica, guardsmen and contras protected private landing strips and farms in Guanacaste and San Carlos that were used for arms deliveries and military training. On some of these same farms, planes were reloaded with sacks of cocaine for their return run to the States. When planes landed at commercial or military airports in the United States, DEA and customs agents were routinely kept away, told not to inspect because this was a covert Agency mission. In some cases, CIA operatives within the anti-Sandinista network made deals to give drug cartel officials immunity from prosecution. In return, drug dollars flowed into the contras' war chest and into the private bank accounts of certain rebel leaders and CIA officials. As Miami-based former federal attorney John Mattes put it, "There was a marriage of convenience between the contras and the coke smugglers. The smugglers had access to intelligence, airstrips, and, most importantly, unimpeded access into the U.S. And that to a drug smuggler is worth all the tea in China."

These activities—terrorism and drug trafficking—were among the most closely guarded secrets of the Iran-contra scandal. The La Penca bombing represented the union of U.S.-sponsored murder and narcotics smuggling under the banner of fighting communism, but La Penca itself was just one event in a much broader and more complex panorama. Even after years of our own investigations, coupled with those of the Christic Institute and other journalists and researchers, as well as judicial and congressional inquiries in both the United States and Costa Rica, many mysteries remain. But enough had been revealed about the underworld surrounding Washington's war against Nicaragua to show that, as the young frightened contra "David" whispered to Carlos Rojas, "These people are involved in drug and arms trafficking and they are making money off the blood of my brothers."

The CIA's Campaign for ARDE/FDN Unity

Edén Pastora's relationship with the CIA was a marriage of convenience. This meant that, from the start, some in the Agency were involved in schemes to untie the knot. Argentine CIA operative Héctor Francés related that as early as 1982, officials in Washington were discussing plans to assassinate Pastora.[4] Almost from the moment Pastora declared the formation of his political movement in April 1982, the CIA began pressuring him to unite with the FDN. "They didn't like popular struggles. They wanted an army they could manage like chess pieces," Pastora explained. But some of the CIA higher-ups apparently had another, more fundamental, concern about the type of government Pastora and ARDE would establish if they toppled the Sandinistas. Pastora relates that the Colombian CIA operative Armando "told us that, within the high leaders of the CIA there was worry about the possibility of a triumph of our centrist position."[5] These CIA operatives wanted the FDN to seize power since, as the reincarnation of the Somocistas, they had a proven track record of loyalty and obedience to Washington.

By the spring of 1983, several of the key Southern Front field commanders and officials had also concluded that they could not work with Pastora. Alfonso Robelo and the conservative businessmen within his Nicaraguan Democratic Movement (MDN) wing of

ARDE found Pastora unprofessional and dictatorial. Robelo worried that because as a businessman and politician he controlled only a handful of fighters, he would be marginalized should the contras come to power, just as had occurred within the Sandinista junta. Many in the MDN became convinced that the Southern Front could only flourish in alliance with the CIA and FDN, and that ultimately victory would have to come through a U.S. invasion. Luis Rivas, a darling of the CIA and later the North network, complained that Pastora was erratic and too left-leaning. John Hull and Bruce Jones openly accused Pastora of being "the tenth comandante" to the nine members of the Sandinista Directorate in Managua. Some of the ARDE pilots and Guanacaste cattle ranchers were annoyed that Pastora was opposed to using the contra network for drug trafficking. Costa Rican right-wingers such as Víctor Wolf and Juan José Saborio, as well as Miami Cuban extremists, were particularly angered with Pastora's statement that, if the United States invaded Nicaragua, he and his ARDE forces would fight with the Sandinistas to expel the foreign aggressors. That, they said, proved he was a communist.[6]

In plotting against Pastora, the CIA and Oliver North's network assembled a coalition of its most trusted ultra-right-wing loyalists, including John Hull, Robert Owen, Cuban American operatives, contras from the FDN and inside ARDE, General Noriega, and collaborators within the Costa Rican security forces and government. Their objectives were multiple: to replace the politically unpredictable and too left-leaning Pastora with a more compliant commander such as Fernando ("El Negro") Chamorro, who would align with the FDN; to clear the way for expanding drug trafficking through Costa Rica; and to blame this and other incidents on the Sandinistas in order to turn public opinion and trigger an escalation in the war against Nicaragua.

Distrust of Pastora came from other quarters as well. Much of the FDN leadership based in Honduras, including Colonel Enrique Bermúdez and Adolfo Calero, also considered the ARDE commander to be too independent and left-wing. They were not keen to have a strong Southern Front rivaling their Northern Front. From the start they were reluctant to share supplies, training, and manpower with ARDE. At the end of 1983 or in early

1984, Hull met with Calero and told him he was disappointed with Pastora and asked FDN help in organizing a new Southern Front. The FDN sent a Nicaraguan, "Comandante Jesús" (Santiago Moncada Guardia), who was placed in charge of the Cuban contingent and, later, of the group of five foreign mercenaries. According to the Public Prosecutor's report, " 'Jesús' kept his center of operations in John Hull's office in San Carlos."[7]

The tale told by a low-level Atlantic coast contra leader, Rudi Sinclair, helps shed light on the linkages between the anti-Pastora plotting and the dirtiest elements of the contras—persons tied to Somoza's old National Guard, the Argentine military dictatorship, and the CIA, as well as to drug trafficking and death squads. In interviews and in sworn testimony Sinclair related that in February 1984 he met outside Tegucigalpa, Honduras, with FDN military chief Enrique Bermúdez,[8] FDN political leader Aristides Sánchez (who was also involved in drug trafficking), and an infamous FDN hitman, Ricardo "El Chino" Lau,[9] who asked him to return to Costa Rica and take part in plans to murder both Pastora and Brooklyn Rivera. They told Sinclair that he and three other Atlantic coast contras should infiltrate as bodyguards for Pastora and that they would be well paid for this operation. Sinclair said that "Alex," a CIA agent in Honduras, set up the meeting and told him that "the CIA was not willing to fund the Southern Front as long as Pastora and Brooklyn were in charge." When he returned to San José in mid-February, Sinclair met with the FDN intelligence officer, Colonel Isidro Sandino,[10] and a mustached Argentine CIA operative, "Ramiro," who continued to try to enlist him in the murder plot. Both Sandino and Ramiro had been part of Héctor Francés's original team, and Sinclair says that by 1984, the Argentine Ramiro was "working under the direction of Hull" and closely with Felipe Vidal.

Sinclair contends that he turned down the offer, even though the FDN promised to fund his Atlantic coast movement, known as NICOPA, in return. "I got nervous," he recalls. "I said I don't agree with this policy. Pastora is our brother. I said this is really a network—CIA and everything, and I don't want to get involved in it." Even after Sinclair turned them down, Vidal and others kept pressuring and threatening him to take part. Sinclair says he came to realize he "was a vein in their project; one beam of their building" and that the CIA/FDN had a multifaceted plan to eliminate Pastora.[11] Another "vein" in the anti-Pastora "project" may have involved Roger Lee Wong (alias Roger Lee Pallais or Roger Lino Hernández), a Nicaraguan of Chinese descent who ended up in La Reforma prison outside San José. In a series of interviews, Wong said he had been part of a five member FDN hit team, including a woman, which was sent from Honduras to Costa Rica some time in early 1984 on a mission to kill Pastora. Wong said the plan went awry when he got into a fight with the woman, she contacted the OIJ, and he shot a policeman in an effort to avoid arrest.[12]

In February 1984, a Pastora supporter in Miami secretly recorded a conversation of MDN and FDN officials discussing plans to get rid of Pastora in order to achieve unity among the various contra groups. The recording was then sent to Pastora and Carol Prado. Throughout the lengthy conversation "gringos" refers to the CIA and "the military people" to the FDN. The most important part goes as follows:

Voice: "How is ARDE going to turn out? And Edén?"

Voice: "Edén? (laughter) We'll see what's going to happen."

Voice: "Forget about Edén." . . .

Voice: "Yes, they, the gringos, are going to eliminate Pastora now. They are going to put in just the military people."[13]

Carol Prado says they received another warning that the FDN was involved in a plot against Pastora. Just one day before the La Penca press conference, a Nicaraguan woman called him from Houston, Texas saying she had learned from an FDN person working with Nicaraguan refugees that there was an FDN plot to kill Pastora.

Rumors of a plot to eliminate Pastora had been circulating in Miami's Cuban community for several months. According to a Costa Rican arms dealer with good connections in Cuban terrorist groups such as Alpha 66 and Omega 7, "Two months beforehand, these people had begun to refer to Pastora as only a 'bench warmer,' saying it was time to replace him," He said the talk was that Pastora would be replaced as Southern Front commander by El Negro Chamorro, which is precisely what happened.

Accoring to Jesús García, a Miami Cuban who says he was privy to discussions before the bombing, those involved weighed the pros and cons of targeting the press. While a few raised some objections, the majority finally decided that journalists, particularly Americans, should be killed and the murders blamed on the Sandinistas as a way of escalating the U.S. war against Nicaragua. García recalls that the plotters drew an analogy to the June 1979 murder by Somoza's national guardsmen of ABC correspondent Bill Stewart. Stewart was shot in the head at point blank range on a Managua street, and his cameraman secretly managed to film the gruesome event. When the footage was shown on U.S. television, it almost overnight turned public and congressional opinion against the dictatorship. The Carter administration then decided to usher Somoza out of power. García says the Cubans involved hoped that their "simulated" terrorist act would lead to a similar outcry against the Sandinistas and thereby turn the tide of the contra war.[14]

The specific origins of the CIA/FDN campaign against Pastora can be traced from two events in mid-1983. On June 5, 1983, just six weeks after Pastora had declared the official start of Southern Front military operations, Vidal and sixteen other "private volunteers," dubbed the International Brigade, arrived on a commercial flight from Miami. While some of these mercenaries helped to form the first splinter group from ARDE, M-3, Vidal set his sights on getting close to Pastora. Pastora was wary, sensing that Vidal's group was working for the CIA or the FDN and was trying to penetrate his operation. By the fall, Vidal had managed, through the intervention of Hull, Bruce Jones, and Colonel Paniagua, to get himself and a half dozen others accepted into an ARDE camp near the Nicaraguan riverside town of El Castillo. From there Vidal was ideally positioned to watch Pastora.

ARDE officials who knew Vidal during the period leading up to the bombing say that he began to agitate against Pastora and to talk about the need to "liquidate" the ARDE commander. Pastora aide Carol Prado recalls that Vidal "spoke like a terrorist, about attacks, about bombs." One ARDE militant said he had become convinced that Vidal "originally came to Costa Rica with the intention of killing Edén. What he wanted to do was to be in the camp and wait for him. One of the Cubans with him fled because he became afraid he would be implicated, and he came and told me about this, months before La Penca." An ARDE intelligence officer said that Vidal was "the only person I know of who mentioned the possibility of eliminating Pastora with a bomb."

On a political level, the move to oust Pastora dates from a July 1983 trip John Hull, pilot-businessman Bill Crone, and contra leader Luis Rivas made to Washington. Crone says the trio went with the intention of convincing Reagan administration officials, members of Congress, and private contra supporters that Pastora was militarily ineffectual and politically suspect. They wanted CIA support for him stopped. The delegation stayed at the Virginia home of Colonel Joseph Yurko, a friend of Hull's who owned land in Costa Rica and had been based at the U.S. Army's Southern Command in Panama. In contrast to Hull, Yurko supported Pastora. He said later he found the trio's mission curious since, at this point, Pastora's operation was beginning to have success in the field, and Pastora was by far the most popular and credible of the contra leaders.[15] In most Washington offices, Hull's group found a cool reception. Pastora had recently been there and had managed to win considerable support, particularly on Capitol Hill.

But in the office of Indiana Senator Dan Quayle they got a sympathetic hearing. After meeting briefly with Quayle, Hull, Crone, and Rivas detailed their concerns to his aide, Robert Owen, who then took them over to the National Security Council and introduced them to Lieutenant Colonel Oliver North. Anticipating that Congress was about to cut off funds, North was being readied to take covert and illegal control of contra operations, including identifying and surveying Southern Front airstrips, something Hull, Rivas, and Crone were all deeply involved in (see chapter 12). Shortly after this visit, Owen left Quayle's office and began working more directly with North on contra affairs. His salary was paid first by the public relations firm Gray and Company and then by the State Department's Nicaraguan Humanitarian Assistance Office (NHAO). His specialty became the Southern Front, and in September he came to Costa Rica—at the invitation, he says, of Hull. Just how much these July 1983 meetings with Owen and North were happenstance, which is the impression Crone conveys, and how much was prearranged remains unclear. What is clear is that from this time on, Hull, Rivas, Owen, and North developed a close working relationship that included lobbying against Pastora.

Hull also pursued his anti-Pastora campaign among Costa Rican ultra-rightists. Shortly after returning from Washington, Hull and Crone met in San José with anticommunist farmer/pilot Víctor Wolf and others to discuss the problem of Pastora and other Sandinista "infiltrators" within the Southern Front ranks. Wolf agreed that Pastora was a communist. Such meetings continued over the coming months and included Patria y Verdad terrorist Juan José Saborio. They also met at the San José law office of attorney Carlos Manuel Coto Albán; the Minister of Government, Dr. Alfonso Carro, attended on occasion. The topic was always the same: that Pastora "had to be eliminated or taken out of the Southern Front."[16]

In late 1983 and early 1984, as Pastora repeatedly resisted unity, the CIA escalated its campaign against him. Pastora says the CIA "sabotage" including offering him "mansions in Miami and bank accounts" if he would quit the struggle. It also included, he says, "corrupting my compañeros with money" in order to convince them to align with the FDN. Pastora requested more weapons and ammunition, saying he had several thousand recruits who could not fight because they lacked supplies. CIA airdrops, however, were few and included worthless supplies. "They sent us suppositories, sanitary napkins, extra large underwear," Pastora bitterly recalled. "And a very typical Nicaraguan food, *gallo pinto*, which is rice and beans—only it arrived spoiled, mixed with salt and insects in plastic bags." The CIA airdrops also included size 12 army boots, World War I Mauser rifles, and little ammunition. Since the parachutes frequently would not open, the supplies were often damaged on impact. Carol Prado described these air drops as "cruel jokes from the CIA. It was a way of jesting at us—vulgar, rude, worse than Columbus giving mirrors to the Indians."

Pastora protested with his usual flair. One time, when a supply plane was requesting a signal from ARDE ground troops to make a drop, Pastora got on the radio and demanded to know what the plane was carrying. "Clothing" came the reply from the cockpit. "Permission denied," Pastora shot back. "We need weapons. Go back to Ilopango." And then he ordered his men to shoot down any more such supply planes. Another time, during a heated discussion with Ambassador Winsor and several CIA officials at the ambassador's residence, Pastora suddenly dropped his trousers. He was wearing enormous, U.S. Army-issue boxer shorts which came nearly to his knees. "See the shit you are sending! How can my men fight a war with this?" he screamed at the startled agents.

The CIA also tried to use ARDE chief political spokesman Alfonso Robelo to put the screws on Pastora. Robelo, leader of the Nicaraguan Democratic Movement (MDN) faction of ARDE, came to support unity with the FDN as the only pragmatic solution to the Southern Front's problems. Robelo controlled the distribution of CIA funds within ARDE, and by the fall of 1983, Pastora was accusing him of not slicing the pie fairly. Robelo was also a cousin of FDN political chief Alfonso Callejas; under the CIA's unity plan, the two would share political power within the new organization. Toward the end of 1983, Robelo quietly sent some MDN cadres to Honduras to undergo military training with the FDN. Pastora found out and was incensed. He accused Robelo of trying to form his own army and of being a "traitor."[17]

Robelo recalls his frustration during these months: "Pastora announcing, 'I'm quitting,' and then, 'No, I won't quit,' hours of meetings, days spent on the river working out responsibilities within the ARDE alliance, and then Pastora throwing the agreements to the wind." "It was Pastora's egocentrism," Robelo concluded. "It became impossible to deal with."

In October 1983, Hull organized a powwow at his ranch house for the ARDE directorate: Robelo, Pastora, Brooklyn Rivera, and José Dávila of the Christian Democrats. Hull acted as "referee." Rivera and Dávila sided with Pastora in opposing unity with the FDN, but neither had much clout within the directorate or with the CIA. It was an all-night meeting, loud and stormy, and little was resolved. In early November, Hull wrote a sarcastic note to Owen about "the hero's" reluctance to join with the FDN.

Then in December General Noriega sent his personal representative, José Blandón, to assess the Southern Front situation.

Noriega, at this point the CIA's most important asset in Central America, had played a key role in supplying arms for the Southern Front. He was also involved in the increasing drug trade through the contra network. Blandón met with Hull at the home of former Costa Rican President Daniel Odúber, a friend and political ally of Noriega's. (Odúber had long been rumored to be involved in drug trafficking and, in 1988, the Legislative Assembly's special drug commission, which accumulated a substantial case against him, recommended that he renounce all political positions.) At this meeting, Hull bluntly said he was convinced Pastora was a communist and had to be replaced.[18]

Not long after this, the head of the CIA's Latin American division, Dewey Clarridge ("Moroni"), called Pastora, El Negro Chamorro, Robelo, and Brooklyn Rivera to a meeting with Noriega in Panama. According to Pastora, Noriega proposed that the ARDE directorate agree to unify its forces with the FDN. Pastora turned down the plan.[19]

Clarridge then turned to another CIA ally, the Honduran military, to put the screws on Pastora. In late 1983, Clarridge ordered the ARDE directorate to Tegucigalpa. Pastora agreed, but asked to meet only with the Honduran army chief, General Gustavo Alvarez, with whom he had had an earlier confrontation. To the ARDE commander's annoyance, also present were the head of Honduran intelligence, General Walter López Reyes, the Costa Rican station chief "John Hull," and an Argentine Army intelligence officer, Colonel Osvaldo Riveiro, who was the CIA's head of political operations with the contras.

Pastora came with a proposal of his own: that the FDN let ARDE open a political and military front out of Honduras—a quid pro quo for the FDN's operations out of Costa Rica. The plan was not well received. Station chief "Hull" and Colonel Riveiro pushed for joining the FDN and ARDE under one directorate. Pastora says Alvarez was "very rude," and Robelo recalls, "Alvarez only talked to me, totally ignoring Pastora. And being very critical, complaining about Pastora." Again, no meeting of the minds.

Just after this meeting, Pastora ordered another cease-fire; he said he did not have enough supplies to carry on fighting. Although he didn't publicly accuse the CIA of intentionally withholding support, the message was clear. Clarridge again tried to negotiate with him. Pastora refused, saying he wanted to talk directly "to the people who make decisions . . . to the head of the National Security Council." There were phone calls, and within a day a meeting had been arranged.

In January, Pastora and Robelo went to Washington. They met in the White House with NSC adviser Robert McFarlane and with Clarridge and North. Pastora later recalled, "I think that there is where my death sentence was signed. McFarlane . . . had an imperial attitude. I felt that I was speaking with the representative of an Empire. . . . I remember we were looking eyeball to eyeball. I thought, 'If I take my eyes off him he'll defeat me.' "

Robelo recalls, "When we went out Pastora said, 'This was a dog fight, between a gringo bulldog—bow, wow—and a *chapiollo* [a little Latin street dog]—gaw, naw, naw.' It was a hell of a meeting."

While no agreement on unity was reached, the upshot was that, for a time, the CIA did send enough supplies. The airdrops increased and so did the war. But Pastora was being given only a temporary respite. While in the United States he went to see Sarkis Soghanalian, one of his favorite arms dealers. Just before meeting with the comandante, the Miami-based Iranian businessman received a telephone call from McFarlane. "When you greet Pastora, hug him, but don't kiss him," was McFarlane's cryptic message. The arms merchant took this as a signal that those running the contra war were distancing themselves from Pastora.[20]

This is precisely what happened. In April, the CIA suddenly resuspended its monthly financial allowance to Pastora. After that the ARDE commander received no further CIA funds. Again, according to Pastora, the CIA also gave the green light for Costa Rican authorities to raid ARDE's clandestine installations inside Costa Rica, including its command headquarters, "San Pedro," located in a suburb just outside San José. Hull joined in by ordering Pastora to stop using any of his properties.

In late April 1984, top ARDE officials—Alfonso Robelo, El Negro, Popo Chamorro, Harold Martínez (Comandante Ramón), and Carlos Coronel—again went secretly to Honduras, where they met with the CIA station chief, his boss, Dewey Clarridge, the top

leadership of the FDN (minus Enrique Bermúdez), and General
Walter López, who had just successfully replaced General Alvarez
in a surprise March 31 coup. The FDN and ARDE officials present
signed a unity agreement by which a new general staff would be
made up equally of representatives from the FDN, ARDE, and the
Atlantic coast groups. Carol Prado relates, "When Robelo came
and talked with Pastora and said it was the moment for unity,
Pastora was totally against it. This was the true break between
Robelo and Pastora."

Pastora retaliated by gathering up five of his commanders and
traveling, in full military gear, to Tegucigalpa. There they had a
long meeting with Honduran military chief General López and
other top officers, while a group of CIA agents awaited the
outcome in an adjoining room. Pastora did not fare any better with
the new Honduran strongman than he had with Alvarez. "It was a
meeting of oil and water," Prado recounted. López urged an
alliance, pledging "they would give us everything." Pastora countered that the FDN did not want an equal partnership; it wanted to
"absorb the South." "We did not arrive at anything," recalled
Prado. Just after this, Pastora told others in ARDE that on May 1 he
had received a thirty-day ultimatum from the CIA: unity by the
end of the month or Pastora's story would be stopped. Pastora said
the message was passed to him via Robelo, who said he had
received it from Dewey Clarridge in Honduras. Robelo denies he
was the messenger.[21] A few weeks after this, Carlos Valverde, a
Costa Rican intelligence agent with the CIA's dirty tricks unit The
Babies began frantically trying to contact Pastora. Through a
friend who worked at the Channel 7 television station, Valverde
left a series of urgent messages for Orión Pastora, but the ARDE
press chief never called back. In interviews, Valverde's father and
brother both said that in mid-May Valverde came to them extremely agitated, saying that there was going to be a murder
attempt against Pastora before the end of the month, that it would
take place at a meeting, and that "innocent people would be
killed." They and the Channel 7 friend said that after La Penca
Valverde was extremely upset and tended to blame himself for not
successfully warning Pastora.

ARDE officials took the CIA's ultimatum to mean that, as of

May 30, the Agency would completely cut off all support. The contra organization was thrown into turmoil. As the crisis deepened, ARDE political leaders, commanders, and rank-and-file fighters chose sides between Robelo's and Pastora's factions. Every group within the alliance became seriously divided over the unity question.

Pastora, fearing for his life and looking for allies, left his river camp and went to Panama to seek guarantees of continued assistance from General Noriega. What Pastora did not realize was that Noriega, who was working simultaneously for the CIA, the Sandinistas, Cuba and the drug cartel, was also involved in plotting against him. Press reports at the time claimed Pastora was en route to Cuba to sign an accord with the Sandinistas. This false story further undermined Pastora's credibility with his fellow contras.

Notations in Oliver North's diaries show that he was tracking Pastora's movements in Panama and elsewhere. North was also complaining to associates about the ARDE comandante. Arturo Cruz, Jr., who during this period was dating North's secretary, Fawn Hall, told Pastora that North had said "he was sick and tired of us." Pastora answered, "We knew what imperialists do with people who bother them."[22] While Pastora was in Panama, North called Nestor Pino, a Cuban American in the Pentagon, to ask when Pastora would return to Costa Rica. The entry indicates that Pastora was due back Monday, May 27.[23]

This is correct. Pastora returned, clandestinely, to take part in that day's heated unity debate with ARDE's twenty-seven-member Democratic Assembly, the organization's top decision-making body. After hours of discussion, a majority of the Assembly voted for unity with the FDN. That day, and again on May 29, Pastora and his followers walked out. After the second walkout, Pastora's people decided not to return.

It was only in these days just before the bombing, when CIA pressure was at its peak, that Pastora and his lieutenants said publicly for the first time that ARDE had been receiving CIA support and that Pastora's faction had now locked horns in battle with their U.S. sponsors. At first the references were oblique. On May 22, for instance, Pastora, José Dávila of ARDE's Christian Democratic wing, and Donald Castillo, head of ARDE's workers' organizations, placed a half-page ad in La Nación stating that "dark forces" were using "pressure, manipulation and false expectation," to force ARDE to join with the FDN.

The next day, in an interview with Costa Rica's *Radio Monumental,* Pastora was explicit. He said, "There are strong pressures by the CIA. And they have blocked all help to us. For the last two months, we have not received a bullet or a pair of boots, we have not received anything." In an interview with Costa Rica's Channel 6 television, the ARDE commander said that the CIA was putting great pressure on his organization to join with the FDN. "But," he added, "the CIA will have to kill me first."[24]

On Monday, May 27, North himself made a brief, clandestine visit to Costa Rica. According to one of those present, North met at the airport restaurant in the late afternoon with contra leader Luis Rivas and Colonel John Taylor, the Embassy's military attaché, who was one of the links to the contras. There is no record of North's entering or leaving Costa Rica, and it seems probable that, as he did on other covert missions, he traveled under another name. Most curiously, the pages of his diary for May 27 and 28 have never been released. Either these pages contained no entries, or they were removed before his famed spiral notebooks were turned over to investigators.

During the evening of May 27, after North had departed, Luis Rivas, Hull, Robelo, and others gathered for a party in honor of Robert Owen, North's envoy, who had arrived the day before, together with a Vaughn Forrest, a congressional aide for a conservative congressman. Owen later admitted in his testimony to the Iran-contra congressional hearing that he was in Costa Rica "on a survey for Colonel North."[25]

On May 29, the press conference was hastily arranged at the insistence of several right-wing Costa Rican officials. Late that day, Pastora was urgently contacted, first by Colonel Rodrigo Paniagua and then by Security Vice Minister Johnny Campos, both of whom told the ARDE chief that the Security Council, chaired by Vice President Armando Aráuz, wanted him to depart immediately and hold a press conference at one of his camps. They said that Pastora's presence in the country had become known publicly and was potentially embarrassing to President Monge, who was on his European tour trying to promote Costa Rican neutrality. Pastora resisted but finally consented to get out of Costa Rica. He had his own reasons for wanting to hold a press conference: he had decided to publicly denounce the CIA, whose deadline for unity with the FDN ran out May 30, and to announce he would carry on his fight without American support. Late that night the ARDE commander set out driving to the border. His cousin Orión Pastora, who handled the press for ARDE, started calling journalists and notifying them of the press conference.

The night of the bombing, May 30, Owen and Forrest were in a CIA safe house in the Pavas section of the capital, along with Hull, CIA station chief Phil Holts, two of Pastora's chief pilots, and others. Owen testified that he was "somewhat saddened" when, about 3:30 A.M., some contras arrived and told him that "reporters and Americans" had been killed in the bombing. Owen and Forrest flew to Honduras early that morning, May 31.[26]

Other eyewitnesses related that news of the bombing sent the CIA network into a frenzy. At Hull's safe house in San Jose and at his farm and office in San Carlos there was a great deal of confusion and activity. Hull's secretary Sheila Ugalde recalls a steady stream of people—Bruce Jones, Dr. Max Pacheco, and a Rural Guard collaborator—arriving at the office (which she lived above) and asking for Hull. The group of dissident ARDE pilots, including Mariano Montealegre and Marcos Aguado who had been at the San José safe house, also showed up at Hull's farm. Hull called his former business partner Bill Crone early in the morning and told him that if he were asked, he should refuse to fly up to La Penca to help evacuate the wounded. "It could be a trap," Hull said without elaborating.

According to contra defector David who claims Hull's CIA network was involved in the bombing, the original plan had been for "Hansen" to fly out from San José's main international airport the morning after the bombing, probably aboard a small private plane. Key members of the CIA network were around the airport: Owen was there boarding a plane to Honduras, former M-3 director Eduardo Sánchez Renazco also flew out, René Corvo and Armando López-Estrada arrived on two different flights from Miami, and Colonel Rodrigo Paniagua, Colonel Antonio Pereira, and other Costa Rican officials who collaborated with the CIA and the contras were stationed at the airport. But security was also being tightened, so that at the last moment, David says, the plans were shifted. "Hansen" went instead to a rice farm in Guanacaste and from there he was flown to Panama aboard a private plane. A Panamanian intelligence officer recalls that just after the bombing he saw "Hansen" with Noriega at one of the general's private residences. This officer says he was told that "Hansen" was being outfitted with an American passport and new identity. From Panama, "Hansen" went to Miami where, according to several sources, he lived for a time under cover in the Cuban community.[27]

The Medellín Cartel, General Noriega, and the Southern Front

Parallel to these political and military pressures on Pastora to put the Southern Front under the control of the FDN and the CIA, another drama was being played out. It involved efforts to open the Southern Front to drug trafficking, a move that was opposed, although not always vigorously, by Pastora. While in the 1970s there had been some drug trafficking through Costa Rica and other Central American countries, the trade grew enormously during the 1980s with the formation of the Medellín cartel in Colombia and the opening of the contra war in Central America. Costa Rica, along with other countries in the isthmus, became an important "bridge" for moving cocaine from Colombia to the United States.[28]

During the 1980s, the burgeoning cocaine trade through Costa Rica was not all contra-related, and there are indications of competing rings and turf wars among traffickers. However, the contra-linked drug trade appears to have been the biggest, best organized, and most protected. The Southern Front drug trafficking involved John Hull and other farmers in San Carlos and Guanacaste; Felipe Vidal and other Cuban Americans; some of the contra leadership; pilots supplied by General Noriega and the contras; companies such as Frigoríficos de Puntarenas; and Costa Rican politicians and officials, particularly a group of colonels who provided protection for drug shipments. Some of the contras involved—Edmundo Chamorro, Octaviano César, Norman Meneses-Canterero, among others—had been involved in drug trafficking in Nicaragua before they became based as contras in Costa Rica. According to Scott and Marshall's excellent analysis of the contra-cocaine connection, "[E]ach major contra faction in Costa Rica was strengthened with a drug connection, and each contra drug connection in Costa Rica arose (and in at least some cases fell) with a political change in the overall direction of the contras."[29]

This Southern Front–linked cocaine trade had at least four different tentacles: the Noriega–Floyd Carlton network, the Hull–George Morales network, the Miami Cuban network, and the network within El Negro Chamorro's UDN-FARN. There was considerable intertwining of these Costa Rican networks: they involved some of the same Colombian drug barons, pilots, contra leaders, landing strips, and Costa Rican guardsmen and politicians. Some of the major players, such as John Hull, were linked into several of the networks. One additional common thread is that these different operations all appear to have involved, in various ways, CIA operatives, some of whom personally benefited from the profits.

Like the contras, the Medellín cartel was organized in the early 1980s, but initially the two operations were unconnected. The cartel was formed in late 1981, after the leftist Colombian guerrilla movement M-19 kidnapped and held for ransom the youngest sister of drug lord Jorge Ochoa. The traffickers assembled at Ochoa's restaurant on the outskirts of Medellín and took up a $7-million-plus collection, which they used to form a two-thousand-man, heavily equipped force to liberate the young woman and to wipe out the guerrillas. Over the next two months, scores of M-19 members were kidnapped or killed. In early 1982, M-19 appealed to General Noriega, who was facilitating their weapons shipments through Panama, to help end the bloodbath by mediating the dispute. The negotiations, held in Panama City, were successful: Ochoa's sister and other captives were freed, the M-19 backed away from assaults on members of the drug oligarchy, and, according to a 1988 Senate Foreign Relations Sub-Committee on Terrorism, Narcotics, and International Operations report on drug trafficking, sectors of M-19 forged an alliance with the cartel, providing protection in return for money and arms.

The summit mediator, General Noriega, took advantage of the occasion to work out a new business relationship with the Colombian traffickers. Noriega had long been involved in drug trafficking and money laundering, a fact well known but ignored by U.S. officials, because the Panamanian general was providing Washington important intelligence information and political support.[30] In 1982, the Medellín cartel connection offered an opportunity for a considerable expansion of his drug activities. For cover in this new venture, Noriega turned to his "civilian group" of loyal and well-pampered Panamanian pilots: Floyd Carlton, César Rodríguez, Teofilo Watson, and a few others. These were Noriega's personal pilots as well as his middlemen, who, since the late 1970s, had been trafficking arms from Panama to the region's various guerrilla groups: M-19 and the National Liberation Front in Colombia; the FMLN in El Salvador; first the Sandinistas and then the contras in Nicaragua. (Carlton testified, for instance, that beginning in 1980, he made seventeen weapons runs for the FMLN.) Noriega also oversaw a thriving trade with Cuba, circumventing the U.S. trade embargo by selling the Castro government advanced American technology in exchange for Cuban shrimp and seafood. The Panamanian general was the boss of each of these operations, but his name was never mentioned. The same ground rules applied when his pilots began flying drugs for the cartel.

In 1982, Noriega authorized Floyd Carlton and César Rodríguez to negotiate with cartel kingpins Pablo Escobar and Gustavo Gaviria to work out the details of a business relationship. (According to various accounts, including that of Ramón Milián Rodríguez, the cartel's Miami accountant, Noriega had already struck a personal deal in 1979 to launder money on behalf of some of the major Colombian traffickers.) Under the new agreement, Noriega provided government-controlled runways, refueling, storage facilities, and security for cocaine flights through Panama, as well as confidential banking services for the profits. In the first four flights, each carrying more than three hundred kilos of cocaine, Noriega was paid, via Carlton, $100,000, $150,000, $200,000, and $250,000 respectively.

Carlton and the other pilots also flew the drug dollars, packed in cardboard boxes, from Miami to Panama, where Panama Defense

Forces armored cars met the planes and transported the money to the Banco Nacional de Panamá, the notorious Bank of Credit and Commerce International (BCCI), and other local banks. Those involved say the cartel laundered billions of dollars in Panama, and Noriega received millions of dollars in commissions.[31]

By 1983 the Medellín cartel's U.S. operation was a sophisticated, multifaceted international network involving coca leaf production zones in the jungles of Bolivia, Peru, Brazil, and Ecuador; processing plants in Colombia; temporary storage and refueling facilities in Mexico, Guatemala, Honduras, Panama, Costa Rica, Nicaragua, Cuba, the Bahamas, Jamaica, and the Cayman Islands; and distribution centers throughout the United States. Profits were laundered through scores of front companies and banks in Miami, the Cayman Islands, Panama, and, increasingly, Costa Rica. In each country the cartel assured its ease of operation with bribes and campaign contributions to police and military officials and politicians.

The Noriega-Carlton cocaine-trafficking operation had a Costa Rican connection as well. Carlton and the other pilots occasionally used contra airstrips for refueling their planes or temporarily storing cocaine en route to the United States. They purchased fuel for their flights from José Angel Guerra, owner and manager of three private aviation companies, who was also selling fuel to ARDE. Guerra, whom Pastora and others say collaborated with the CIA, was eventually indicted in Costa Rica, along with contra pilot Gerardo Durán (also a Costa Rican), on drug trafficking charges.

Guerra was a partner with Carlton in a Miami aircraft dealership and parts supply company, DIACSA, which in 1986 received some of the U.S. "humanitarian" aid funds for the contras. Company president Alfredo Caballero, a Miami Cuban, was, according to the Costa Rica Public Prosecutor's La Penca indictment, "in charge of money laundering from the narcotics trafficking and of plane purchases for Floyd Carlton." In addition, Caballero "gave his help to Edén Pastora between 1983 and 1984," by "acting as a middleman in the purchase of planes for ARDE." DEA agent Daniel Moritz, who infiltrated the company as an undercover agent, reported that Carlton used the offices for planning drug

smuggling operations and handling distribution of his multimillion-dollar profits. One of those connected with DIACSA was
Cecilio Saenz-Barría, a Panamanian described by a Moritz confidential informant as "in charge of supervising the landing and
refueling at airstrips on the Panama/Costa Rica border" and "ar-
rang[ing] for bribe payments for certain Costa Rican officials to
ensure the protection of these aircraft as they head north loaded
with cocaine."[32]

In addition to the drug trafficking through Panama and Costa
Rica, by 1984 Noriega was providing the cartel with other services
as well. In March, police in Colombia raided Tranquilandia in the
Amazon, the largest cocaine laboratory in the world, seizing
fourteen *tons* of cocaine and closing down the plant. On April 30,
the cartel retaliated by murdering Colombia's distinguished justice minister, Rodrigo Lara Bonilla. The national outrage after
Lara's murder forced Pablo Escobar and other cartel leaders to
seek temporary refuge in Panama. Noriega housed the drug lords
in luxurious and well-protected comfort and later boasted to
friends that he pocketed between $4 and $7 million for his
services.[33]

However, on May 21, 1984, just nine days before the La Penca
bombing, the cartel suffered another loss. While Noriega was off in
Israel and the drug kingpins were still in Panama, the Panamanian
Defense Forces staged a surprise raid on a new cocaine processing
plant in the Panamanian province of El Darién, near the Colombian border. Following the Tranquilandia raid, the cartel had paid
$5 million to Noriega underling Lieutenant Colonel Julián Melo
for permission to construct a new lab in the Panamanian jungle.
Twenty-three cartel personnel, a helicopter, the plant, and equipment were seized. The cartel was furious. The Israelis warned
Noriega that his life was in danger, and the general prolonged his
overseas tour.

What happened in the wake of the raid is subject to controversy. The official version, based largely on testimony of former
Noriega confidant José Blandón, is that Noriega initially permitted
construction of the lab, but then, feeling heat from the DEA, had
decided to authorize the raid to take U.S. eyes off his other drug
operations. According to this account, Noriega (and Blandón,

among others) went to Cuba, where Fidel Castro, acting as mediator, worked out a deal: Noriega apologized to the cartel, gave back
their $5 million, returned the helicopter, fired Melo, released the
twenty-three captives and the equipment, and dropped the case; in
return, the cartel lifted the death threat against the Panamanian
strongman. After that, Noriega and the cartel are said to have
resumed business as usual. This is the version which became part
of the U.S. government's legal case against Noriega as well as part
of the rationale for the Reagan administration's December 1989
invasion of Panama.

However, investigative journalist John Dinges persuasively
musters evidence which indicates that, after the Darién raid,
Noriega got out of the drug-trafficking business and threw his
energies into Panamanian politics and less risky forms of profiteering. Based on the testimony of drug pilots Floyd Carlton and
Steven Kalish and a careful rereading of the record, Dinges concludes that Melo, without Noriega's knowledge, authorized construction of the cocaine lab and pocketed the cartel's $5 million.
Noriega learned of the plant and ordered the raid to signal that he
was getting out of the drug business. As Dinges writes, "After the
Darién raid Noriega seemed to be closing up shop, paying off
outstanding obligations and creating a new image for himself—
that of the statesman-soldier standing behind a democratically
elected president."[34] This tale is relevant to the Southern Front
because, even after Noriega apparently dropped out of the drug
trade, Carlton, moving cocaine for Colombia's Cali cartel, stepped
up his transshipments through Costa Rica.

Beginning in October 1984, Carlton's drug operations through
Guanacaste were expanded with the assistance of local businessman Eduardo Zaporoli and the area's guard commanders, Colonel
José Montero, head of the Civil Guard in Guanacaste, and Colonel
Edwin Viales, head of the province's Rural Guard. This network
provided landing strips, police protection, safe houses, and gasoline. The traffickers were also bringing in arms and transporting
cocaine for El Negro Chamorro's forces and for the Costa Rica–
based FDN.

Carlton no longer flew the planes. As general manager of the
operation, he cleared a handsome million dollars per load, and

hired an international mix of pilots, many of whom also flew for the contras. Most trusted was Carlton's long-time friend and business partner, Teofilo Watson. In mid-May 1985, Watson took off alone from Tamarindo, on Costa Rica's Pacific coast, and flew to Colombia, where he collected 538 kilos of cocaine. The next day he was due back at Tamarindo for refueling before making the final leg of his journey to the States. He never arrived.

Carlton said later that he had learned that Eduardo Zaporoli, who was in charge of ground operations, had guided Watson's plane into one of Hull's ranches, where they murdered Watson and stole the $3 million cocaine shipment. The Cali cartel was furious and retaliated by summoning Carlton to Colombia and sending hit men, who briefly kidnapped Hull's son and stole some jewelry—an incident which Hull, predictably, blamed on "the communists." This marked the beginning of the end for Carlton, who quickly fled from Panama.

One of the few people who located Carlton in his Miami hideout was his old friend, the Panamanian doctor-cum-contra leader Hugo Spadafora, who was carefully compiling evidence of Noriega's drug trafficking activities. Spadafora had been working closely with Hull and Felipe Vidal and had stumbled upon the interconnections among the contras, Noriega and the Colombian cocaine cartels. Spadafora decided to use this information as part of his campaign to bring down his long-standing personal and political foe, Noriega. He gently appealed to Carlton to help by confirming the dates of various drug flights. Reluctantly, Carlton gave the information and Spadafora took it to Robert Nieves, the new DEA chief in Costa Rica. On Friday, September 13, a few days after his second meeting with Nieves, Spadafora's headless body was discovered on the Costa Rican/Panamanian border.

Nieves said later he'd done nothing with Spadafora's information. But numerous contra and Panamanian sources say they believe the CIA and DEA were involved in Spadafora's murder. One of the most vocal was Panamanian lawyer Rodrigo Miranda, who was appointed the government's special prosecutor to investigate the case. He said publicly Spadafora "was the victim of an international conspiracy" involving the DEA, CIA and Noriega. Panama President Guillermo Endara fired Miranda in 1990, a move which the ex-special prosecutor said was engineered by CIA agent Felipe Vidal. Miranda said Vidal was sent to Panama following the U.S. invasion to "wipe out the tracks" of Spadafora's killers. In August 1993, as eight men went on trial for Spadafora's murder, Miranda predicted that "the connection with the CIA or the Iran-contra affair will never come out in the trial because there is no interest in bringing it to light." All were acquitted.

Back in September 1985, Floyd Carlton was hiding out from both the cartel and drug enforcement agents and watching his luck go from bad to worse. His old buddy Spadafora was murdered, his wife and seven other relatives were seized and tortured by cartel-hired hit teams, a $2 million load of his cocaine was seized by Miami agents, another close friend, César Rodríguez, was executed by the cartel in Colombia, and Carlton and his Miami partner Caballero were indicted. In July 1986, Carlton flew to Costa Rica to meet Caballero, who was out on bail. It was a trap arranged by Caballero, who had cut a deal with the DEA. As Carlton and Caballero were meeting in Carlton's room at the luxurious Cariari Hotel, DEA and Costa Rican narcotics agents burst in and arrested Carlton.[35]

While John Hull apparently attempted to siphon off some of Carlton's cocaine, the American rancher was also directly involved in running his own drug-trafficking operation, some of it in partnership with Miami-based Colombian George Morales. On June 25, 1983, just prior to the trip to Washington that signaled the start of the political campaign to get rid of Pastora, Hull flew to Miami in a private plane with ARDE members José María Robelo,[36] Marcos Aguado, Emigdio Prado, Roberto Espinoza, and Costa Rican pilot Gerardo Durán, all of whom were working with ARDE. The purpose of this trip was to set up an arms-for-drugs operation independent of Pastora's weapons supply system.

In Miami, Hull's delegation checked into the Quality Inn at the airport. A Colombian friend, Gustavo Vélez, then took Hull, Aguado, and Durán to the office of George Morales, who ran one of the cartel's most important transportation operations. Morales had a "stable" of about thirty pilots (which included Durán) and an aviation company at Hangar No. 1 at Opa-Locka airport, the private-plane airport on the outskirts of Miami. A multimillionaire naturalized American and world-class speedboat racer, Morales was one of the top drug distributors in southern Florida. "On his payroll," writes Leslie Cockburn, "were presidents and generals throughout the Caribbean and Central America. His was a one-man Caribbean Basin Initiative,"[37] and Hull wanted to tap this resource.

The cautious Morales was leery of meeting with Hull directly because of his CIA connections. However, through an intermediary, Morales agreed to Hull's request for help in illegally transporting forty M-79 grenade launchers destined for the contras from Miami to the Southern Front warehouse at Ilopango Air Force base. The launchers were moved from a downtown warehouse to one of Morales's planes. Two of Morales's pilots, Gary Betzner and Richard Healey, made the clandestine flight, stopping en route at the U.S. naval air station at Boca Chica in southern Florida to pick up antivessel mines (which may well have been those used to mine the Nicaraguan ports), and finally landing at Ilopango. From there the pilots flew to Colombia, picked up a load of marijuana, and returned to Miami.

By March 1984, the DEA had caught up with Morales, and he was indicted for conspiracy to import and distribute cocaine. Shortly afterward, another delegation from Costa Rica—once again pilot Marcos Aguado and two contra officials, Popo Chamorro and Octaviano César—arrived at Morales's Opa-Locka airport office. Accounts vary about whether they were summoned by Morales or whether they initiated the meeting. César and Aguado identified themselves as CIA agents, a fact Morales said he already knew. This time the Colombian trafficker was ready for direct negotiations. They discussed a package deal: that Morales fly weapons to Central America for the contras and, on the return flights, bring cocaine into the United States under CIA protection. The Nicaraguans offered to supply Morales with "clean" contra pilots, since his own has been implicated with the indictments, and they stipulated that Morales give the contras a cut of the profits. But most importantly, Morales related, in exchange for his financial and material support "they offered to take care of my legal problems with the Washington people." A deal was struck.

For the next eighteen months Morales's planes and about ten Southern Front pilots flew weapons, explosives, and ammunition out of Opa-Locka and Fort Lauderdale to landing strips in Costa Rica, Honduras, and El Salvador, and on the return runs they brought back cocaine. Morales says that during this period he donated a number of planes to the contras and paid César, Aguado, and Chamorro $3–3.5 million in cash, most of it packed in "cardboard boxes" and shipped to Central America along with the weapons. For a time, Morales says, his drug charges "died away," which convinced him that the CIA and high officials in Washington had successfully run interference to squelch the DEA's case against him. (In 1986, about the time the Iran-contra scandal broke, Morales was brought to trial and sentenced to sixteen years in jail. "They dropped me like a hot potato. I became dispensable," he says.)

Chamorro, César, and Aguado claimed that the donated funds were for ARDE, but Morales says that he later became convinced that the trio siphoned off much of it. In early 1986 Morales met Pastora at the Marriott Hotel in Panama City, and, Morales said, "I told him my concern and he was very surprised to hear that I had sent so much money." Asked if Pastora condoned dealing with drug traffickers, Morales said, "Pastora did not know that. I never had no discussions with Pastora about the drug business." Pastora acknowledges receiving at least one suitcase of cash from Morales (containing about $50,000), but says when he learned the Colombian's line of business, he ordered Popo Chamorro to cut the ties and return a plane Morales had sent to ARDE.

When the contra trio—Chamorro, César, and Aguado—met with Morales they were, in reality, in the process of breaking with Pastora and working with Hull to organize the FDN-connected Southern Front. By claiming to represent Pastora, they were helping to set up the troublesome comandante on drug charges. In the future, Pastora became the fall guy, repeatedly accused by U.S. officials of drug trafficking. As Alan Fiers boldly but incorrectly asserted in his 1987 congressional testimony, "There was a lot of cocaine trafficking around Edén Pastora. . . . None around FDN, none around UNO."[38] (Four years later, Fiers pled guilty to lying to Congress about the resupply operations.)

While Pastora may not have been fully aware of the deal his lieutenants had stuck, Morales said "the CIA knew" and its man in northern Costa Rica, John Hull, was a main beneficiary. By August 1984, Morales was doing a brisk business through Costa Rica, much of it centered on Hull's farms. Hull was paid, Morales recalls, $300,000 per flight. Pilot Betzner says that twice in 1984 he flew into Hull's properties, and he remembers chatting with the farmer while ranch hands unloaded the weapons and put sacks of cocaine aboard. In 1990, another of Morales's pilots, Fabio Ernesto ("Tito") Carrasco, testified that he flew arms and cocaine through Hull's ranch.[39]

George Morales said that as early as 1981, years before he began doing business with Hull, he had heard of the CIA operative from his Colombian drug trafficking buddies. Pilots and others "many times" mentioned using Hull's properties for refueling their planes and storing arms and drugs. The Senate subcommittee took testimony from four other witnesses, in addition to Morales, who said Hull was involved in cocaine trafficking.[40] Convicted Colombian drug lord Carlos Lehder said in a television interview, "I do know the situation for a fact that John Hull in Costa Rica . . . he was taking about 30 tons of cocaine into the United States a year. Now this is a kingpin."[41]

A third tentacle of the contra-drug network involved the arrival in June 1983 of Vidal's International Brigade. Despite their bravado about fighting communism, their real mission was two-fold: to eliminate Pastora and to expand drug trafficking under the protection of the Southern Front. They worked under the direction of Hull and, besides making approaches to ARDE, they also quickly began working with other Cuban Americans based in Costa Rica and already involved in drug trafficking. These included Adolfo Jiménez, Armando López-Estrada, Frank Castro, and Dagoberto Núñez, who had long ties with Costa Rica. According to Miami Cuban Jesús García, who was close to this group, "The CIA gave the cover for drug trafficking through Central America" because it hired back onto the payrolls a number of Cubans and sent them to Central America to work with the contras. He said, "Every known freedom fighter's organization is involved in drugs. In Central America, they do drugs and the CIA looks the other way." Vidal, for instance, was a self-described "enforcer" (or debt collector) for Miami drug barons. When Vidal first came to Costa Rica in 1983, he had broken parole on an outstanding narcotics conviction in Dade County.[42]

By late 1982, pilot Bill Crone, along with Hull, Luis Rivas, and José ("Chepón") Robelo had been tapped by CIA officials to locate landing strips for use by the contras. Almost simultaneously, Crone says he was approached by Frank Castro, Armando López-Estrada, and Adolfo Jiménez, who asked him to find private airstrips for their use (see chapter 12). These three were all Bay of Pigs veterans with a long history of Agency and drug trafficking connections. In January 1983, Crone says he and Hull met the Cuban trio at Jiménez's Guanacaste farm, where they discussed integrating some Miami Cubans (Vidal's group) into El Negro Chamorro's operation. At the same time that Hull was seeking his first meeting with George Morales, Crone flew to Miami to visit a contra and Cuban training camp being run by Corvo and Vidal. It seems probable these contacts really involved expanding drug operations through the Southern Front contra network: Hull, Adolfo Jiménez and the other principal Cubans, as well as some top officials in El Negro's UDN-FARN, were already involved in cocaine trafficking, and several were subsequently arrested.

There is no indication that Crone was involved in drug trafficking, and he evidently was nervous about the company he was keeping. He says he asked his CIA contact at the Embassy, "Tomás," if it was all right for him to deal with Frank Castro. At first "Tomás" told him, "Frank is okay" and he should go ahead and meet with him. After several months, however, the CIA warned him to stay clear of Castro, because "he was being investigated for arms trafficking from the Dominican Republic and some other island."[43] But the Embassy did not warn Crone that Frank Castro was involved in drug trafficking, or that Vidal had been arrested at least seven times in Miami on narcotics and weapons charges. Nor did the CIA tell Crone about the drug activities of López-Estrada, who during this period was serving as a CIA-hired contra military trainer on Jiménez's farm. The evidence indicates the opposite: that the CIA facilitated the creation of these contra–drug trafficking connections using Southern Front landing strips and pilots. An ARDE official working in Guanacaste, for instance, tells of seeing what he believes were small bundles of cocaine being loaded onto contra planes at several locations, including Jiménez's farm. He says these apparent drug shipments were overseen by Costa Rican and CIA officials.

In addition, this same network of Miami and Costa Rican–based Cuban Americans also used the boats and business cover of the Costa Rican seafood exporting company Frigoríficos de Puntarenas, which, like DIACSA, became a recipient of congressionally allotted contra "humanitarian" aid funds. Frigoríficos, a preexisting Costa Rican company, was bought by Miami Cubans in 1982, and became one of the hundreds of front companies managed by cartel accountant Ramón Milián Rodríguez. In a prison interview, Milián Rodríguez explained that Frigoríficos and its sister company, Ocean Hunter in Miami, were mainly used for money laundering. Drug money, passed from other cartel companies, was deposited into Frigoríficos accounts; then the so-called business transactions between it and Ocean Hunter were used to hide these profits. Eventually the funds moved to cartel companies on Caribbean island tax shelters. Some of this money was also passed to the contras, as well as to Costa Rican politicians. As stated in the Costa Rican Public Prosecutor's La Penca indictment, "Through Ocean Hunter, Inc. and Frigoríficos de Puntarenas, monies coming from the narcotrafficking were delivered to the Nicaraguan 'contras.' "[44]

Milián Rodríguez said that Frigoríficos also used its fleet of boats to export shrimp (a lucrative business) as well as cocaine to Miami. Three Miami Cubans who came briefly to Costa Rica to join the International Brigade—Orlando Ponce, José Sosa, and Marcelino Rodríguez—say they were taken to a farm near the Nicaraguan border for training. However, they quickly became disillusioned and left because they discovered the Cubans were involved in smuggling drugs, believed to be cocaine, to the United States in shrimp containers belonging to Frigoríficos.

The stateside owners of Frigoríficos included Luis Rodríguez, along with Carlos Soto and Ubaldo Fernández, both convicted drug traffickers. According to Massachusetts law enforcement officials, Luis Rodríguez directed the largest marijuana smuggling ring in the state's history. Francisco Chánes, another Miami drug trafficker, was also a partner in Ocean Hunter and one of the main financial backers of Vidal's International Brigade. Frank Castro was also said to be a partner in Ocean Hunter.[45]

In Costa Rica, the Frigoríficos manager was Dagoberto Núñez, a close associate of Vidal and Hull. Interpol's drug registry lists Núñez as "a narcotrafficker who passes himself off as an intelligence agent to cover his activity." A Miami Cuban, he had lived in Costa Rica since the late 1970s and had cultivated relationships with politically powerful people. He became the Liberation party's chief fund raiser in Puntarenas as well as a close friend of Colonel Luis Barrantes, director of the Security Ministry's narcotics police until 1987. Barrantes gave Núñez an ID card making him a Costa Rican narcotics agent, and Núñez collaborated in carrying out drug raids with Barrantes, other Costa Rican police divisions, and the DEA.

In 1987, a Legislative Assembly drug commission, headed by legislator Alex Solís, found substantial evidence that Barrantes was involved in accepting bribes from drug traffickers, including Mexican marijuana kingpin Rafael Caro Quintero. It recommended that Barrantes be fired, which he was, and be barred from ever again holding public office.

In 1989, Núñez, together with DEA agent Juan Pérez, helped Hull flee to Miami to avoid prosecution on drug and murder charges. Shortly afterward, Núñez himself left Costa Rica and resettled in Miami. In 1992, Núñez and several DEA officials in Miami were arrested for stealing money confiscated in drug busts—a scam reminiscent of his Costa Rican activities.[46]

The fourth tentacle of Costa Rica's contra-drug labyrinth involved some of the leadership of El Negro Chamorro's tiny guerrilla group, UDN-FARN. The Cuban Americans originally hoped to join forces with El Negro, and this may well have been because of these drug activities rather than FARN's pitiful military record. In the spring of 1983, El Negro met with these Miami Cuban "volunteers," including Vidal and Ernesto Cruche, a CIA agent with long ties to Costa Rica and a close relationship with Colonel Rodrigo

Paniagua.[47] By the time Vidal's group arrived in June, El Negro had, for political reasons, moved his tiny operation to Honduras.

Prior to this, UDN-FARN had been involved in one of the earliest contra- and CIA-linked drug busts, known as the Frogman case.[48] In January 1983, San Francisco police broke up what they called "a major Bay Area cocaine ring [helping] to finance the contra rebels in Nicaragua."[49] Two Nicaraguans, Julio Zavala and Carlos Cabezas, were arrested after divers seized nearly two hundred kilos of cocaine wrapped in plastic and taped to the bottom of a Colombian fishing boat. Police also seized $36,000 in cash and some weapons from Zavala's home.

In their trial three years later, the pair argued in defense that they were smuggling cocaine to help finance UDN-FARN contra activities in Costa Rica. Zavala's lawyer said the U.S. government had "either sanctioned use of cocaine trafficking to raise funds for the contras or had led Zavala to believe it was sanctioned." The court's behavior added credence to these claims. Court records connected with the case were sealed under the "Classified Information Procedures Act," and prosecutors returned the cash after Zavala presented letters from UDN-FARN and the Nicaraguan Conservative Party stating the money belonged to them. Both letters were signed by Francisco Aviles, FARN's international secretary and cousin of ARDE official César Aviles. Zavala claimed to have delivered $500,000 to Francisco Aviles, mostly from cocaine profits, but Aviles put the amount at $35,000.

Zavala and Cabezas were linked with a Costa Rican–based contra drug trafficker, Horacio Pereira. Wiretap transcripts introduced in Pereira's 1985 trial included conversations with M-3 leader Sebastián González ("Wachán"), who had fled Costa Rica for Panama in November 1984 after being accused of drug trafficking. In 1985, Pereira was sentenced to twelve years in prison in Costa Rica. Also named in the case was El Negro's brother Edmundo, himself a top FARN official and, according to other contras, a well-known drug trafficker.

Even more damaging for Washington was an FBI teletype, obtained and declassified five years later by Senator John Kerry's Subcommittee on Terrorism, Narcotics, and International Operations, which revealed that the cocaine came both from Colombia and from "Nicaraguans living in Costa Rica associated with the Contras"—Horacio Pereira, Troilo Sánchez, and Fernando Sánchez. Troilo and Fernando are brothers of FDN Directorate official Aristides Sánchez, who, along with Bermúdez, tried to recruit contra Rudi Sinclair into a pre–La Penca plot to kill Pastora. In 1986, Troilo was arrested in Costa Rica "with pillows full of cocaine," according to a former contra.[50] About this time, Robert Owen warned in a memo to North that Aristides and his brother were alleged to have overseas bank accounts in the Netherlands Antilles. If true, Owen wrote, the U.S. government "is being had."[51] Despite this, Washington stuck with Aristides to the end: he became a director of the final contra umbrella group, the Nicaraguan Resistance.

These burgeoning Southern Front drug activities in the year leading up to La Penca became an increasing concern to Pastora and some of his lieutenants. Pastora claims he has never had any connection with drug traffickers, but by 1985 the CIA and State Department were putting out information that Pastora was involved in trafficking.[52] The reality appears to be that Pastora turned a blind eye to some monies and equipment, particularly planes, coming from suspected drug traffickers. However, he did try to prevent drugs from moving through ARDE landing strips or his pilots from transporting drugs. As early as 1983, he shifted around the ARDE commanders in Guanacaste when he learned that they were allowing cocaine to pass through the contra-controlled airstrips.

Pastora's chief of security, Miguel Urroz Blanco ("Bigote"), told the OIJ that Pastora "considers that to accept help originating from narcotrafficking means the political death of ARDE and his own" and for this reason "he was opposed to this type of financing." In the months leading up to the La Penca bombing, a group of ARDE pilots met with John Hull and Costa Rican terrorist Juan José Saborio to discuss the need for a coup against the contra commander, so that drug trafficking via the Southern Front could be expanded. The pilots, including Mariano Montealegre, the head of ARDE's air force whose family was closely tied to Somoza's national guard, Marcos Aguado, and Yamil Frech ("Turco") informally discussed their desire to continue drug trafficking as a way of funding the contra war. Montealegre outlined for the group the specific changes he wanted to make on the ARDE helicopter which he piloted so that it would be better suited for moving cocaine. All expressed their frustration with Pastora because he opposed their drug trafficking. The night of La Penca, Montealegre and another pilot met with North's envoy, Rob Owen, and told him Pastora was "finished." They said they were "willing to fly for anyone." Those involved in the trafficking—Hull, Vidal, the Costa Rican guards-men, and some contra commanders and pilots—therefore came to view Pastora as an obstacle who had to be eliminated. As the Costa Rican Public Prosecutor's indictment on La Penca puts it, "Be-tween mid-1983 and 1984, John Hull became Pastora's principal opponent, backed by Oliver North, the FDN, Adolfo Calero, the Cubans and the narcotraffickers."[53]

Sandinista Dirty Tricks on the Southern Front: Targeting Pastora

Pastora had his strong opponents among the Sandinistas as well. In Managua the campaign to neutralize him was spearheaded by Interior Minister Tomás Borge, master poet turned master con-spirator, and by Renan Montero, an illusive Cuban intelligence officer. The two men harbored a deep and bitter hatred for the turncoat contra commander. Together with security chief Lenin Cerna, Borge and Montero ran the Fifth Directorate, a clandestine unit that was ideologically the flip side but tactically remarkably similar to the CIA/North/Hull operation in Costa Rica. Over the years the Fifth Directorate had botched several attacks against Pastora and other Southern Front commanders. In March 1984 the steps that culminated in the La Penca bombing were set in motion.

Sometime during that month, Swedish television producer Peter Torbiornsson and his young Bolivian assistant Luis Fer-nando Prado were invited to a private party attended by some top Sandinista intelligence officials. Torbiornsson says he was intro-duced to another invited guest, a tall, handsome Danish photogra-pher with drooping eyes and an angular nose. They nodded greetings but did not converse. Sitting with this journalist and acting as his host was an older man whom Torbiornsson says he learned later was "a high ranking but obscure Sandinista official," Colonel Renan Montero. Montero is in reality a legendary colonel with Cuba's Interior Ministry's elite Special Forces and international revolutionary who ran the ultra-secret counterintelligence unit, the Fifth Directorate, under Borge's Interior Ministry.

In early May, Torbiornsson again met the "Danish" journalist, this time at the reception desk of the Gran Via hotel in downtown San José. Torbiornsson says the "Dane" introduced himself as Per Anker Hansen, a free lance photographer on assignment for a Paris-based agency, "Europe 7." Torbiornsson agreed that "Hansen" could tag along with him and Fernando Prado in seeking an interview with Pastora. They made only an oblique, coded reference to "Hansen" 's real mission. Torbiornsson asked, "Didn't I see you at a party in Managua?" and the "Dane" acknowledged that this was correct. "I knew right away that he was a Sandinista agent," Torbiornsson admitted eight years later. The Swede says he did not ask any further questions, not even the man's real name or nationality. He realized he was meant to discretely assist the "Dane" in his job, which, he says he assumed, was "collecting information." Torbiornsson swears he believed "Hansen" was sent to simply spy on, not to murder, Pastora.

This was an educated guess based on Torbiornsson's own experience. Like much of the European left, Torbiornsson, who had covered Latin America for a decade, was a strong supporter of the Sandinista and Cuban revolutions. Like a handful of other journalists, he had developed a symbiotic relationship with officials in Managua and Havana. Torbiornsson says that he regularly gave copies of his contra footage to Nicaragua's Interior Ministry and in return was rewarded with access to officials and stories frequently denied to other journalists. During 1983, for instance, Torbiornsson was in Cuba and, he says, "Fidel gave me a gift." He was permitted an exclusive interview with Enrique Gorriarán Merlo, a famous Argentine guerrilla leader. Gorriarán, at the behest of the Sandinistas, had commanded an Argentine hit squad that pulled off the spectacular September 1980 assassination of ousted Nicaraguan dictator Anastasio Somoza on the streets of Asunsión, Paraguay. It was a dramatic story: in broad daylight Gorriarán had personally pumped dozens of bullets into Somoza while his comrades fired a rocket propelled grenade that destroyed the deposed dictator's armor-plated limousine. Swedish television was thrilled with Torbiornsson's scoop. Torbiornsson says it was not until years after the La Penca bombing that he realized Gorriarán, Renan Montero, and "Per Anker Hansen" were part of the same espionage and assassination cell—a cell that he, too, was drawn into.[54]

As Torbiornsson documented in his television program, Enrique Gorriarán Merlo had been involved in armed struggle since the early 1970s and was the sole surviving member of the People's Revolutionary Army's (*Ejécito Revolutionario del Pueblo* or ERP) original directorate. The ERP, the armed wing of the Trotskyist Revolutionary Workers Party, was together with the *Montoneros,* the most important guerrilla movement fighting against the Argentine military in the 1970s. While the Somoza hit made Gorriarán an international revolutionary folk hero, his combat record at home had brought him little praise from the left. In 1974, he led a failed attack on an army base in Azul and shortly after he was demoted for brutally torturing a ERP member he wrongly accused of being an army infiltrator. Gorriarán regained leadership of the ERP in 1976, but by then the guerrilla group had been heavily infiltrated by military spies and agent provocateurs and had been largely destroyed. Gorriarán therefore "remained a rather marginal figure on the outer fringe of Argentina's revolutionary left."

Over time, many of this former comrades and other Argentine progressives accused him of having an amoral love of violence and of being out of touch with political realities. Others suspected that Gorriarán himself was a double agent, in part because he was never arrested and in part because many of his actions were tactically and politically ill-conceived.[55] In the late 1970s, Gorriarán and a cadre of ERP militants went into exile in Spain and France, joining the thousands fleeing Argentina's "Dirty War." In Europe, Gorriarán formed an ultra-leftist splinter group within the ERP, which preached " 'a putschist notion of politics . . . that 40 people could provoke a popular insurrection.' "[56]

One ex-member of this faction, Jorge Masetti, recalls that some time in 1978 or 1979 Gorriarán convened a clandestine meeting in Paris of his ERP followers. There he met for the first time the man he later identified as the La Penca bomber. The new recruit was brought into Gorriarán's inner circle by his brother-in-law, a seasoned ERP guerrilla.[57] He became known as "Martin El Inglés" and sometimes more derogatorily, "El Lord," because he spoke English with an affected accent, smoked a pipe, was lazy, and preferred reading books to doing any heavy lifting. Over the next three years, Masetti says he crossed paths with "Martin" several more times, in Nicaragua, Cuba, and Mexico. He never knew this man's real name—Vital Roberto Gaguine, or the false identity he soon was given—"Per Anker Hansen."

During this period Gaguine/"Martin" was living in England with his wife, America Garcia Robles ("Maura"), and, according to immigration records, he was enrolled in the Shakespeare School of English. He hung around in the exile leftist Argentine community but apparently at this point had had no military training or guerrilla experience. Gaguine was born in Buenos Aires in 1953, the oldest of two sons of Samir, a Sefardic Jew who had immigrated to Argentina from Turkey, and Loretta, a strikingly beautiful Jewish woman, also from Europe. The family were in the fur and mica business and stayed out of politics. But, according to an aunt, the Gaguines, like other Jewish families in Argentina were antimilitary, in part because so many soldiers came from German or Italian fascist families. In the 1970s, many of Argentina's Sefardic Jews fled into exile to Spain, Israel, Venezuela or Mexico.

Vital Gaguine went abroad also, first during high school on a cultural exchange to the U.S. He returned to Buenos Aires in 1972 and became a medical student. In 1978, a few years after his parents divorced, he moved to England with his young wife and several years later, America gave birth to a daughter. In 1979, he applied for political asylum and was turned down. About this same time, he attended for the first time a gathering of ERP combatants.[58]

In early June 1979, Gorriarán, Gaguine's brother-in-law, Masetti, and four other ERP comrades—but not Gaguine/"Martin"—flew to Panama, passed through Costa Rica, crossed into Nicaragua, and joined Edén Pastora's Sandinista forces fighting against Somoza troops in southern Nicaragua. Forty-four days later, Somoza fled, his National Guard collapsed, and the Sandinistas triumphantly seized power. Gorriarán and his ERP militants were among the potpourri of international revolutionaries—Chileans, Venezuelans, Costa Ricans, Salvadorans, Basque separatists from ETA, Guatemalans, German Bader-Meinhoffs, Italian Red Brigades, Palestinians, and others—who were given safe haven, new passports and identities, and, sometimes, military, espionage, and sabotage training in Managua. According to Pastora, Cuban instructors ran a training school for foreign revolutionaries which was located on Lake Managua.

The new Nicaraguan government was short on counterintelligence and espionage expertise and so Renan Montero, (a colonel with the Cuban Interior Ministry's elite Special Forces), was tapped to organize its foreign operations. Montero's ultrasecret unit, the Fifth Directorate, came under the General Directorate of State Security (*Dirección General de Seguridad del Estado* or DGSE), run by the Sandinista's security chief, Lenin Cerna. Cerna, in turn, reported to Interior Minister Tomás Borge. Montero's boss in Cuba was Manuel Piniero, the head of the Cuban Community Party's Latin American Department.

Montero ran espionage and covert operations throughout Latin America. He had a network of leftists in Costa Rica who worked with him but who also, those interviewed say, maintained some independence. Most of these Costa Ricans were members of either the pro-Soviet/Cuban communist party, *Partido Vanguardia Popular,* headed by Manuel Mora or the *Movimiento Nueva Republica* (MNR), a splinter of which supported armed struggle. Typically, these Costa Ricans had fought on the Sandinistas' Southern Front, received military training from the Sandinistas and, in the early 1980s returned to Costa Rica to work as spies, arms couriers, and, on occasion, kidnappers for Montero. There is no evidence that any of these Costa Rican leftists participated in La Penca or any other assassination plot. The Fifth Directorate's assassination squads employed operatives who were sent in from Managua.

The Cuban Montero knew both Costa Rica and Edén Pastora well. Pastora says that when he first organized his Sandinista

Revolutionary Front in 1961, Montero "joined the FRS with me."[59] Afterwards he worked with Che Guevara in Bolivia and only escaped the CIA hit team because he was traveling in Argentina and Peru. During the 1970s, Montero was appointed consular officer in the Cuban Embassy in San José, a position he used to liaise with Sandinistas running military operations along the Southern Front. One Costa Rican leftist who was part of Montero's network, recalled, "We knew him as 'El Vaquero' (The Cowboy).[60] He was practical, not dogmatic, but with a strong personality. He was not a public person, but he had great weight within the [Sandinista] Front. He had a nexus with many groups through the Sandinistas, but he also had his own agents."

Whether Montero took his orders from Sandinista or Cuban intelligence agencies is murky. "It was hard to tell if Renan [Montero] was working for the Front or had a role as a Cuban agent within the Front," said one of his Costa Rican agents. Top Sandinista officials indicated Montero had considerable discretionary powers in running his operations. Daniel Ortega described Montero as "a very closed person, a man with hundreds of secrets." Tomás Borge gave a similar description: "introverted, a mystery, a man of a thousand secrets."

Within months of the Sandinista's July 1979 victory, Montero had recruited Gorriarán and about 15 other Argentines. They called themselves the "Nucleus of Steel" and they became Montero's strike force. Within a year they carried out two successful assassinations: the October 1979 murder in Honduras of Somocista Major Pablo Emilio Salazar ("Comandante Bravo") who was lured into a death trap by "Barbara," his lover turned Sandinista agent.[61] Next came the assassination of Somoza, in September 1980. In December, Argentine military trainers based in Guatemala retaliated by sending a newly formed commando team of ex-Somoza National Guardsmen to attack the Costa Rican-based *Radio Noticias del Continente,* a leftist station run by Argentine guerrilla exiles. The contra war was underway, and guerrillas and military foes from Argentine's "Dirty War" were playing key roles in this Central American conflict.

In the early 1980s, Gorriarán and his ERP followers set up another base of operation, in Sao Paulo, Brazil. This sprawling cosmopolitan city of ten million afforded the guerrillas the sort of anonymity that they could not be guaranteed in Managua. Gorri-arán and his cadre also wanted to be closer to Argentina as the military dictatorship began losing power in the wake of the Falkland/Malvinas Islands war. According to some accounts, Gor-riarán's faction began to use their military expertise to hire them-selves out as free lance terrorists, working for the left, the right, and the drug cartels. Their specialties included kidnapping ultra-rich Latin Americans for ransom, a trade Gorriarán already knew. (In Argentina in the mid-1970s, he had masterminded the kidnap-ping of an American oil executive which had netted the ERP $12 million in ransom.) Throughout the decade, until the 1989 La Tablada attack, these ERP militants continued to move in and out of Nicaragua and to work with the Fifth Directorate.

During the early 1980s, Montero's "Nucleus of Steel" struck at several ARDE and CIA targets inside Costa Rica, and their success rate was mixed. In February 1982, a lone assassin working for Montero tossed a fragmentation bomb into El Negro Chamorro's San José apartment, injuring the contra commander's son and a visiting Canadian woman.[62] In October 1982, Montero's strike force kidnapped Argentine military intelligence agent "Héctor Francés" off the street in a San José suburb. Some Costa Rican leftists helped in the operation. Gorriarán personally inter-rogated "Héctor Francés" before the Argentine soldier made his declarations to the press (see pp. 00–00).[63]

Then, in June 1983, just as two Nicaraguan men were getting into their blue FIAT in a downtown San José parking lot, a bomb hidden in their briefcase accidently exploded.[64] The man carrying the case—Rodrigo Cuadra Clachar—was blown to pieces, and his companion, Mario Gutiérrez, was badly injured and rushed to a local hospital. Cuadra, a former deputy health minister, was a Sandinista agent working for a special counterintelligence cell within Nicaragua's telephone company. Several days earlier, Cuadra had contacted ARDE officials saying he wanted to defect. At the time of the explosion he was en route to meet Alfonso Robelo at ARDE's political headquarters in La Sabana Sur, on the outskirts of the city.

The local press and Costa Rican and U.S. Embassy officials quickly denounced this as a Sandinista terrorist plot intended to kill Pastora. Several days beforehand, Ambassador McNeil and the CIA had warned Robelo that Cuadra was a Sandinista assassin, not a defector, a fact ARDE officials say they had independently confirmed. Pastora was not in San José and, for security reasons, Robelo arranged to meet Cuadra at ARDE's public relations office rather than their military command center.

Right after the explosion, Security Minister Angel Edmundo Solano called Tomás Borge, his counterpart in Managua, and berated him for attempting such a stupid, provocative attack in the heart of San José. Solano says Borge promised that the Sandinistas would never again try to kill contra leaders inside Costa Rica. In return, Solano agreed to quietly drop the case rather than expose the presence of contras in the country and increase tensions between Costa Rica and Nicaragua. The injured Gutiérrez and Cuadra's body were returned to Managua, and Costa Rica never issued a report on the incident. Borge, who gave the eulogy at Cuadra's funeral, said in an interview years later, "Montero coordinated that operation."[65]

Just two months after the Cuadra bomb, Costa Rican officials claimed to have foiled an assassination plot targeting Pastora. In September 1983, authorities arrested Gregorio Jiménez (alias "Pistola"), a Basque terrorist with ETA who was wanted in Spain for armed assault and bombing electrical stations. Also arrested was Jorge Chaverri, a Costa Rican agricultural machinery salesman and auto mechanic.[66] The pair was accused of being part of an international hit team sent by Managua to bomb Pastora's car near Naranjo, on the mountain road the contra leader regularly traveled to the border. Through Chaverri, Jiménez' team had rented cars and several apartments near Pastora's military command post in Escazú.

After their arrest, both men were tortured and Jiménez signed a confession saying his group was preparing to kill Pastora and other contra leaders. Police confiscated maps and notes, but no weapons or explosives, and Jiménez's companions—about a dozen Europeans and Latin Americans—managed to slip out of Costa Rica. After three years in jail, Jiménez was deported to Spain where he was again imprisoned. Chaverri, who was released after several months, frankly admitted in an interview that he was a Sandinista supporter who traveled frequently to Managua and had knowingly assisted what he said was Jiménez's spy network. He explained that the group was tracking the movements of various contra leaders, not just Pastora.

Years later, a Costa Rican who collaborated with Renan Montero said he understood Jiménez's "operation" could have involved "laying the groundwork" to kill Pastora. He said Jiménez's group "included three people directly involved in planning the operation and others who collaborated. They worked in solidarity with the Front but had much independence. It's possible Jiménez had a connection with Borge or Renan or someone else in the MINT (the Interior Ministry)."[67] He added that ETA guerrillas in Central America did not normally engage in violent actions. Instead they "helped get passports, transit people in trouble, give mutual help to other leftists, all in solidarity with the Sandinistas."[68]

In 1979, when Enrique Gorriarán Merlo's cell left to join the Sandinistas, Vital Roberto Gaguine, alias "Martin El Inglés," stayed in England and Paris. He arrived in Managua in late 1979 and, according to another ERP militant, first showed up among "a large group" of internationalists receiving military training at a school outside Managua. Afterwards, this guerrilla saw Gaguine/"Martin" in Havana where he was getting training in intelligence and special operations. There is no evidence Gaguine took part in any of the Fifth Directorate's early operations in Costa Rica or in the Somoza assassination.

In April 1982, Gaguine surfaced in Panama with the Danish passport and posing as a photo-journalist named, "Per Anker Hansen." He was there about three months and his arrival coincided with a rumored Sandinista team sent in to tail Pastora. In April 1982, Pastora declared the start of his armed conflict against the Sandinistas and he traveled frequently to Panama seeking Noriega's financial support and assistance in setting up ARDE front companies. Augusto Montealegre, Nicaragua's then-ambassador to Panama who later defected said he heard that the Sandinistas had sent a three or four-person cell to Panama to keep an eye on Pastora. He said this spy team operated autonomously, without diplomatic cover, in order to conceal Managua's hand. It is conceivable Gaguine was part of this team.

What is concretely known of his activities in Panama points, however, towards involvement with Noriega, the CIA, and/or Israelis. He stayed in the Las Vagas Hotel, a luxury, high-rise apartment-hotel frequented by diplomats, businessmen, and Noriega's intelligence agents. "Hansen" 's 6th floor room overlooked a house used by Gen. Noriega's secret police. A receptionist recalled that "Hansen" always paid his rent promptly and in cash, had no friends or fixed routine, and though amiable was a man of "very few words." (The receptionist, also, had few words to say after an initial conversation. She said security officials had come around and warned her and the rest of the staff not to talk with the press about "Hansen.") In Panama, "Hansen" bought a pick-up truck from an American G.I. attached to an intelligence unit, then sold it to an Israeli company which had business ties to Michael Harari, the notorious Israeli intelligence agent who was working with both Noriega and the contras. Several sources claim to have seen "Hansen" in the presence of Noriega and Harari, before and after the bombing.[69]

In the end, although some details are known of Gaguine/ "Hansen" 's time in Panama and a crucial photo was retrieved from Panamanian immigration files, no conclusions can be drawn about who was giving the bomber his orders. Panama was a witches brew of political intrigue. As one of our sources put it, "Panama is the point of confusion, the crossroads of interests. Mossad, the Sandinistas, drug traffickers, CIA, Cubans, all had close relations with Noriega and all exist together even though they are supposedly enemies."

During at least part of his stay in Panama, "Hansen" shared his room with a woman who was traveling on a stolen French passport in the name of Patricia Anne Boone Mariscot. Immigration records show that over the coming year, the couple traveled together to Ecuador, Peru, Venezuela, Amsterdam, back to Panama, Mexico, Honduras and, several times, to Costa Rica. Torbiornsson says "Hansen" told him that he had recently been in New York and Miami, as well.

The couple's longest stay after Panama appears to have been in Honduras. According to immigration records, "Hansen" and "Boone" entered on March 3 and left for Costa Rica on March 26. They were seen together at one hotel, and between March 9 and

26, "Hansen" rented cars in Tegucigalpa from Molinari Car Rental Agency. The owner recalled that "Hansen" showed credit cards for security purposes but paid the bill in cash, using local currency, and oddly, asked to change cars three times as if "he had something to hide." According to the original OIJ report, the couple traveled extensively and stayed at hotels in other Honduran cities as well. Torbiornsson and Prado recall "Hansen" saying he had been to an American military base and some of the FDN camps in Honduras. Since Torbiornsson recalls being introduced to "Hansen" in Managua sometime in March, it appears likely he traveled there clandestinely (since there is no immigration record of the trip) or under another name.

On March 26, immigration records show "Hansen" and "Boone" entered Costa Rica from Honduras. This is the final entry for the couple. They were seen together at one San José hotel, but "Hansen" checked in alone to the Gran Via hotel. There is no official exit for either "Hansen" or "Boone" after the bombing, one of the indications that they were flown out illegally or left with other passports. "Boone" has never been conclusively identified and there are indications that Gaguine/"Hansen" had several female accomplices.

Over the next few weeks, Torbiornsson, Fernando Prado, and "Hansen" traveled together, seeking an interview with Pastora. They received permission to visit ARDE's contra camps and so, on May 14, the trio and a Mexican cameraman flew to the northern Costa Rican fishing hamlet of Barra del Colorado where they hired two boats. For ten days, they traversed the San Juan River, stopping at a half dozen rebel camps including La Penca, interviewing contra commanders. Throughout this journey, "Hansen" carried his oversized metal camera case which he carefully covered with plastic garbage bags to keep out moisture. Several times Torbiornsson and Prado told him a canvas sack would be much more convenient for carrying his gear. But "Hansen" insisted he needed this case which he said, he'd recently purchased in Mexico after his other gear had been stolen. What became tragically clear after the bombing was that the case was equipped with a false bottom that was used to hide the powerful C-4 bomb.

On May 23, "Hansen" and the others stopped at a contra camp and Torbiornsson called via two-way radio to Pastora, requesting an interview. Pastora said it would be impossible, that he was too involved in fighting and also had to travel outside the country. He would not be available for an interview for another two months. Disappointed and frustrated, "Hansen" and the Swedish crew returned to San José the next day.

Back in San José was another of Montero's agents, but her exact role, if any, in the La Penca plot remains unclear. Maria Lourdes Pallais, a Nicaraguan journalist, arrived May 22, saw Pastora and other ARDE officials over the next few days, and then disappeared. In conversation several years later, she said that Pastora had invited her "the day before" to attend the La Penca press conference but she turned him down because she had to leave for Honduras. Pastora denies this, pointing out the decision to hold the press conference was not made until very late the night before. Immigration records show no legal exit for Lourdes and the commercial flight she later said she took to the U.S. (not Honduras) did not exist.

Pastora and Prado suspected she might be one of several women described as seen with "Hansen." She is fluent in Spanish, French and English, has a Peruvian mother, and is tall and good looking, all traits said to fit one of the suspected female accomplices. She is also the niece of Somoza, the sister of a Sandinista war hero, adept at moving in various political circles, and long rumored to be working for the CIA, the Sandinistas, or both. Pastora says that Lourdes acted as a CIA-hired translator during a trip he made to the U.S. in late 1983, leading him to conclude she must be a CIA agent.

In May 1988, Borge made a highly unusual public announcement that Lourdes was "a [Sandinista] counter-intelligence agent who had worked within the enemy's ranks," i.e., inside the CIA and she deserved the nation's respect. In an interview, Borge would not elaborate on what Lourdes had done as a spy, could not remember if she was working for the Interior Ministry at the time of La Penca, and said this "relationship" with Lourdes had been "terminated." Borge admitted that Pallais "at one time committed the indiscretion of saying she was [with the] CIA" but that she "was working for the Front all the time." He added that he had agreed to publicly claim her as Sandinista spy "as a personal favor [because] she came and asked me to." He said that right afterwards he realized he "shouldn't have done it." Again, he did not elaborate.

No longer in San José at the time of La Penca was another Sandinista spy, "Nanci" (Marisol Serrano) who for many months had been Pastora's lover and confidante at his military command head-quarters in Escazú. Other ARDE officials had warned Pastora that "Nanci" was a spy. Pastora, supremely confident of his prowess with women, said he knew "Nanci" had been sent by Borge, but that he'd "turned her" and Nanci was now deeply in love with him. There are conflicting accounts of her departure. Some say she was withdrawn for her own protection just three days before the bombing. Pastora disputes this. He says he sent Nanci back to Managua several weeks earlier, after he discovered she was having an affair with his lieuten-ant Carlos Coronel. He asked her mother to come to collect her. Borge basically supported this version, explaining Nanci was pulled out because she engaged in "unauthorized activities" and he "was afraid that Pastora was turning her." If true, Nanci's departure was unrelated to the La Penca preparations.[70]

May 29, the day before La Penca, the Swedish crew and "Hansen" met again with ARDE information chief Orión Pastora who reassured them that they would soon get an interview with Comandante Cero. Late that evening, "Hansen" received a call in his hotel room from Orión Pastora informing him that Edén Pastora would be holding a press conference the following day, at his main camp, La Penca, along the San Juan river. Early the next morning, the Swedish film crew and other journalists gathered at the Hotel Irazú, ready to depart for La Penca. So, too, did Gaguine/ "Hansen," carrying his large metal camera case.

Crosscurrents and Cover-Up

> *"Six different stories as to the identity of the killer have crossed my desk, all depending on the ideology of the person making the report."*
>
> —Security Minister Angel Solano

Pastora was, as he himself often says, a man with many enemies. The evidence of multiple plots by the CIA/North/Hull network, drug traffickers, and Sandinista's Fifth Directorate is overwhelming. Now that it has been finally determined that the bomber was Vital

Roberto Gaguine, a leftist Argentine who had worked for a counter-intelligence cell inside Borge's Interior Ministry, the most straight forward explanation is that the Sandinistas were responsible for La Penca. This was the conclusion of several news reports.[71]

Not surprisingly, the man who would know, Tomás Borge, denies this. In several interviews with Doug Vaughan and Carl Deal, Borge refuted Torbiornsson's story of meeting "Hansen" and Renan Montero at a private party in Managua. "Renan never would have associated with the bomber if he was going to use him in his operation. Furthermore," Borge says, "Renan never went to parties." He said that Montero had personally investigated and prepared a report on La Penca but, "unfortunately all the MINT [Interior Ministry] files were burned after the [Sandinista's 1990] electoral defeat." Montero, he suggested, "would have more information," but, again, "unfortunately, he is sick with an incurable disease and had gone to either Cuba or England for medical treatment." Borge tried, he said, but could not locate him.

More compelling than these excuses, are the indications that the Sandinista directorate had taken a decision several months before La Penca that Pastora was useful alive, causing divisions within the contra ranks and headaches for the CIA. Among those who heard this was a Costa Rican leftist who spied for Montero. He says that some time in late 1983, after the Cuadra bomb and Jiménez arrest, the Sandinistas abandoned plans to kill Pastora and decided instead to neutralize his operation with infiltrators. He says that if Gaguine were working for Borge and Montero, it was probably as a spy, not a terrorist. But even he, like nearly every one else interviewed, did not rule the possibility that for the sake of old vendettas, Borge and Montero might have defied the Sandinista dictorate and continued their plots against Pastora.

Clearly, then, the Sandinistas had a hand in the operation that culminated at La Penca. But within the complexities of the case are strong indications that the CIA and contra linked-drug traffickers also played a role in the bombing and its cover-up. There are, for instance, eyewitness accounts by contras and their collaborators who identify the bomber as a CIA-hired mercenary and who give descriptions which seem to fit Gaguine. The contra defector David who passed information to us via Carlos Rojas (see chapter 2) said he personally saw the bomber with John Hull, Felipe Vidal, René Corvo, right wing Costa Rican security officials, and others. He said he was told the bomber had lived for a long time in South America, that he was a Libyan, and that went by an Arabic name, "Amac Galil." Within Miami's Cuban community the bomber was also known as "Amac Galil" or simply "the Arab." Others close to the contra network said they believed he was really Israeli. In fact the bomber Gaguine was all of the above: an Argentine Jew of Turkish parents and Middle Eastern—either Arab or Jewish—physical features.

There is as well a story which appears to place Felipe Vidal with the bomber and to implicate rightwing Costa Rican officials in the plot. In early December 1983, San José undercover cops with Costa Rica's Unit on Crime Prevention (UPD) arrested two men—"Hansen" and/or Vidal—who were overheard discussing a bomb they had supposedly hidden in a television set in their hotel room. One of the men had a gun, press identification in the name of "Peter Jensen," and a passport identifying him as Cuban American. The arresting officers thought they had made an important catch, but to their shock, shortly after they arrived at headquarters a phone call came from Dr. Luis Fernando Lamicq, a medical doctor who worked for the UPD and collaborated closely with the contras. (Lamicq had, for instance, signed a permit allowing Vidal to carry a gun.) Lamicq ordered that the pair be released. They were. No search was made of their hotel room, no report of the arrest was written, and the case was dropped.

After La Penca, an anonymous memo about this arrest was sent to the local media saying that Costa Rican authorities had been ordered to release the bomber. When interviewed, one of the arresting officers said he was certain from the news photos that "Per Anker Hansen" was one of the two men he had arrested. Curiously, "Hansen" was erroneously identified as "Peter Jensen" in an early press report by Benigno Quesada, one of the journalists involved in the La Penca cover-up. In 1985, when I asked Felipe Vidal about this incident, he admitted he was arrested but denied that the other man was the bomber. Lamicq refused to be interviewed. Whatever the truth, this incident indicated that the anti-Pastora plotter's operatives had government contacts ready to protect them.[72]

Then there is an apparent convergence of information about where the bomber fled after La Penca. Informant David said the bomber went first to Panama and then to Miami where he was living in the Cuban community. From there, David said, he traveled to both Honduras and Nicaragua, including Managua. A Panamanian intelligence officer also said that the bomber was briefly in Panama, Noriega supplied him with a new passport and identity, and from there he traveled to Miami. In a series of interviews, this Panamanian military official said the La Penca bomber was linked to the CIA and Israeli intelligence. Jesús García said "the Arab" was in Miami, living with a woman and hanging out with René Corvo. This information, which comes from those who say La Penca was carried out by the CIA, appears correct. Gaguine's father has lived in Miami since 1980 and both he and the younger son admit that Vital Roberto visited them there in the mid 1980s.

There is as well the issue of infiltration. The ERP cell within the Fifth Directorate—the "Nucleus of Steel"—was infiltrated by military informants and agent provocateurs. Their final action— the 1989 attack on La Tablada in which Gaguine was reportedly killed—was politically and personally suicidal, leading many to conclude that military intelligence had infiltrated the sect and that Gorriarán Merlo may be a police agent.[73] Documents released by the Paraguay government show that the Nucleus of Steel's first action, the Somoza assassination, was also wired. The documents reveal that one member of the hit team was working simultaneously for Sandinista, Cuban, Chilean and Paraguayan intelligence.[74] The right could have stopped the Somoza hit, but chose not to in order, it seems, to protect its agent. Are there parallels here to La Penca? We don't yet know.

It is known that the CIA and U.S. Embassy warned Pastora and Robelo about several other Sandinista assassination plots. But no warning was passed beforehand about the La Penca bomb plot. The bombing coincided with a fierce CIA campaign against Pastora and it fell on the very day the Agency's 30-day ultimatum was up. Does this mean that the CIA knew about the bomb plot and decided to let it happen? Again, we don't yet know.

More puzzling and incriminating than these tidbits of information is Washington's behavior in the wake of La Penca. Beginning within hours of the bombing, the Reagan administration and its contra and Costa Rican government allies began leaking a stream of false leads, which pointed towards Managua, but which named, over and over, the wrong leftwing terrorist group. During the first two years the bomber was falsely identified as an ETA terrorist, a Tupermaro guerrilla from Uruguay, a leftist Swede working in Nicaragua, a Libyan, a Dane, a Palestinian, among others. (Curiously, only Pastora mentioned that the bomber might be a member of the Borge/Montero hit team which had killed Somoza. Shortly after La Penca, Pastora said he thought "Per Anker Hansen" looked similar to a Colombian "Calvo," who was one of the Somoza assassins. However, he subsequently retracted this, saying that once he had studied the photos of "Hansen", he realized "Calvo" was "too old" and physically quite different from the La Penca terrorist.) Coupled with these false identities, U.S. officials worked to close down and derail all serious investigations by the Costa Rican government and journalists and to stop any official inquiries in the U.S. This remains one of the most perplexing aspects of the La Penca story.

The cover-up was two-pronged: it involved blocking serious police and press investigations and putting out false stories to implicate the Sandinistas. In the hours after the bombing, as Dr. Pacheco was supposed to be attending to the wounded, he was plotting how to get to La Penca. Outside the emergency room in Ciudad Quesada I overheard him talking with several men whom I took to be Costa Rican security officials. They were discussing getting quickly up to La Penca to see what remained. Bruce Jones, who worked with Hull in business and contra affairs, says that shortly after the bombing he was asked by CIA agent Phil Holts to "get up to La Penca . . . and get any sort of residues that were available" for analysis in Washington. Jones recalls Holts saying that every lot of C-4 plastic explosive has a slightly different chemical texture so that it can be traced back to its source. Jones says he asked Pastora's people for permission to go to La Penca, but it was denied.[75]

The following day ARDE combatants did go to La Penca, where they collected several bags of debris, which they turned over to the OIJ. The remains of the bomb, including the detonator, were spread out on a table in the Office of Special Affairs. This office was run by Alberto Llorente and Alan Solano and overseen by CIA agent Dimitrius Papas, and it became a sort of command post for the judicial and police cover-up.[76] The Public Prosecutor's report on La Penca confirms that "Dimitrius Papas was allowed access to the information on the case." OIJ immediately turned to the CIA for help, despite the fact that a preliminary intelligence report on the case, apparently prepared by Carlos Monge's DIS agents, concluded that either the Sandinistas or the CIA carried out the bombing.[77] OIJ forensic expert Gustavo Castillo says that the U.S. Embassy supplied an expert, apparently from the Southern Command in Panama, to help with the lab work. Instead, this man took the detonator away, saying he was going to have it analyzed. This vital piece of evidence was never returned. Ambassador Curtin Winsor confirmed in a PBS "Frontline" program that the detonator was sent "to Langley."[78]

Over the next year, Llorente and Solano, under the tutelage of Papas, collected a voluminous file on the case, but most of it consisted of worthless leads or false information purposely inserted to confuse the investigation. For instance, the photocopy of "Boone"'s passport which appeared in the OIJ files contained several pages showing she visited Nicaragua in 1983 and obtained a multiple entry visa. In the weeks after the bombing, this was used by the Costa Rican government and press to finger the Sandinistas. However, a careful examination of these photocopied passport pages reveals that the Nicaraguan pages are larger and in a different type face—clearly not part of the original passport. Dimitrius Papas's agents should have noticed this, unless, of course, they were the ones who doctored "Boone"'s passport.

The only significant fact they determined was that the man responsible for the bombing was the false Danish photographer, "Per Anker Hansen." As OIJ Director Minor Calvo admitted a year after the bombing, they had no concrete leads. In December 1989, the Public Prosecutor's report concluded that Solano and Llorente could have been charged with "the crime of unfulfillment of their duties" but for the fact that the four-year statute of limitations had already expired. The report also found that Papas personally tried to "disorient the investigation"[79] by pushing several of the false stories: that the bomber was José Miguel Lujúa Gorostiola from the Basque separatist group ETA; that he was the Uruguayan Héctor Amodio Pérez, who had been with the leftist Tupamaro guerrilla group; and that he was a Swedish leftist, Per *Arvid* Hansen, who was working in Nicaragua. The story of the Swedish Hansen was also circulated by Francisco Tacsan and Security Minister Piza more than a year after the bombing, long after Llorente and Solano had dropped it.

In the weeks after the bombing, others in the anti-Pastora network linked to the CIA also circulated false information. Hull told associates, perhaps as soon as a few hours after the bombing, that the terrorist was a Libyan hit man sent by Colonel Qadhafi. According to this false story, Qadhafi accused Pastora of stealing a Libyan donation to the Guatemalan guerrilla movement and using it to set up the Southern Front. Bruce Jones, Víctor Wolf, Robert Owen, and G-2 intelligence agents in Panama all circulated this same story. Alfonso Robelo had his own variant, which combined two of these false stories. He told several journalists that the bomber was the Uruguayan Héctor Armodio Pérez, who had been hired by Qadhafi, and that he was killed by Libyan hit men in Brussels shortly after the bombing. The *Tico Times* and Associated Press (AP) checked with Belgian police, who said they had no information about such a murder. Years later, Robelo admitted in an interview that he had been given this story by a CIA agent.

Papas's dirty-tricks unit, The Babies, which functioned parallel to the DIS, also concocted an elaborate phony story, complete with fabricated documents on DIS letterhead. According to this version, left-wing guerrillas from the FMLN in El Salvador, the Sandinistas, and leftists within the Costa Rican government, including DIS director Carlos Monge, were behind the bombing. This story and the stack of phony documents were circulated by both Carlos Bravo, a former Somoza national guardsman who was with the FDN, and by Carlos Valverde, an ex-Babies agent who was working for Francisco Tacsan. While the tale was false, what became certain was that Valverde himself had known of an assassination plot targeting Pastora several weeks beforehand.

One of the clearest indications that the cover-up reached into Washington was the phony ETA story. Not only did CIA agent Papas push this story within OIJ, but just hours after the bombing, literally before some of the wounded journalists had reached the hospital, the Washington press corps began receiving calls from government officials who asked to remain anonymous, telling them that the Basque terrorists from ETA were responsible for the bombing. Several U.S. journalists later said they suspected the story was not true and chose not to use it.

However, the story was widely run, including by ABC "World News Tonight," Cable News Network (CNN), the "MacNeil/Lehrer News Hour" (PBS), the *Washington Times,* and the Interpress News Service (IPS). John McWethy, then ABC's Pentagon correspondent, says he was given the story by his contacts in the State Department's Office of Public Diplomacy (OPD) and the Pentagon. McWethy's two ABC reports, on June 1 and 6, went so far as to identify the bomber as José Miguel Lujúa Gorostiola, a Basque hit man who bore some resemblance to the La Penca bomber. McWethy said Lujúa was hired by the Sandinistas and fled after the bombing to Nicaragua and then Cuba. However, as the *Tico Times* and AP quickly established, Lujúa was at the time under house arrest in southern France and had been since January. There was no way he could have planted the bomb at La Penca.[80]

What eventually became clear was that the Office of Public Diplomacy, the CIA, and the FDN, in alliance with certain Costa Rican officials, had carefully laid the foundation for accusing ETA. Former FDN chief of communications Edgar Chamorro recalls that in mid-1983 a CIA agent in Honduras ordered him to distribute a stack of posters showing a hand holding a gun superimposed on a map of Central America. The text said that ETA was planning terrorist activities in the region. Chamorro says he threw the posters away because he didn't believe that ETA posed a threat in Central America. Shortly after this, Costa Rican authorities arrested a Basque, Gregorio Jiménez, and accused him of plotting to kill Pastora. This was never proved because Jiménez was deported instead of being brought to trial.

ETA next made headlines in March 1984, when José Miguel Lujúa's name and photo suddenly, and very curiously, appeared in the Costa Rican press. On March 14, 1984, both *La Nación* and *La República* carried stories, based on information from DIS, Interpol, the FBI, and Spanish police, warning that a group of ETA members were possibly en route to Costa Rica. The lists in both papers were virtually identical, except that *La República*'s included Lujúa, while *La Nación* listed someone else.[81] None of these people ever turned up in Costa Rica, and the story was dropped.

The evidence indicates that this story, along with Lujúa's photo, was intentionally planted to prepare the ground for subsequently blaming ETA for the bombing. A senior DIS official said that Colonel Francisco Tacsan, an overseer of The Babies and the Security Ministry's liaison to the CIA, used to prepare articles which *La República* would publish without any by-line. The March 14 Lujúa story had no by-line.

The next day, March 15, the Office of Public Diplomacy at the State Department contracted a private consultant, Luis Miguel Torres, to write a report on ETA terrorism in Central America. OPD head Otto Reich told Torres the report was urgently needed by March 26, less than two weeks later. He followed up with three memos demanding the report be finished by that date. Despite the pressure, Torres did not hand over his report until May 5, and it contained only one piece of evidence. This was an interview with Alejandro Montenegro, a Salvadoran guerrilla defector and friend of Torres', who claimed to know about two failed ETA assassination attempts in Central America, one against Pastora and another against a Salvadoran defense minister. Allegations from this interview were leaked to the press right after La Penca and used by ABC's McWethy, among others. However, David MacMichael, a former CIA analyst who handled El Salvador at the time, said the CIA was unaware of the alleged ETA actions.

There is a footnote to this story. In response to a subpoena served in connection with the Christic Institute's La Penca lawsuit, the State Department refused to turn over the OPD's ETA report. It did, however, release the cover page of a twenty-page report on the Christic Institute's lawsuit which contained a curious handwritten note in the upper corner. The note read: "Delib. [Deliberate] CIA effort to throw people off track of real perpetrators" and was signed by Peter Olson, a State Department official.[82]

This was the assessment Costa Rican investigators privately held of the ETA story. A top OIJ official said in an interview during this period, "The ETA story, the U.S. invented it." A DIS agent said simply, "ETA was launched in the street to cover the truth." As such, it was successful. Breaking only hours after the bombing, the ETA story had a decided impact on the course of the press investigation. All the major local press named the ETA terrorist Lujúa as the bomber stories, mainly citing the ABC reports as the source. This helped halt any serious investigation within Costa Rica or internationally.

In the end, the phony stories circulated by The Babies, OIJ's Special Affairs unit, and the Vidal-Tacsan network succeeded in muddying the waters so much that even dedicated police investigators and journalists had difficulty getting any clarity. Immediately after La Penca, Oliver North personally interceded with congressional allies to spike a bill that would have given the FBI jurisdiction to investigate terrorist acts in which U.S. citizens were injured aboard. In dozens of other ways the U.S. Embassy, CIA, State Department, and NSC orchestrated a cover-up, put out false leads, "disappeared" crucial evidence, derailed any serious investigation, and inteferred with or prevented journalistic, legal, police, and congressional inquiries. This is not logical. The Reagan administration repeatedly argued that Nicaragua under the Sandinistas was a terrorist state. The Reagan White House, obsessed with winning public and congressional support for its campaign to topple the Sandinistas, should have wanted to quickly turn up evidence proving that the leftist Gaguine and his Sandinista patrons were responsible for the La Penca bombing. The fact that they did not raises the question of why Washington had an interest in blocking the true story behind the La Penca bombing.

More Terrorist Plots

> "I'm a right-winger from way back, but the U.S. is backing the most corrupt bunch of sons of bitches. . . . Drugs, gun running, assassination, you name it."
>
> —Ex-mercenary Jack Terrell, December 1985

Side by side with this cover-up, the CIA-North network plotted new terrorist actions, including a 1985 scheme to kill Pastora. It began with a meeting at the Shamrock Hilton Hotel in Houston attended by Hull, Owen, and Jack Terrell and Lanny Duyck, two members of the Alabama-based Civilian Military Assistance (CMA), which was sending men and military supplies to the FDN.[83] Adolfo Calero participated in the meeting by phone from Miami. Terrell recalls the conversation "would have curled your hair." It involved two plans, one to eliminate Pastora and another ambitious plot to systematically assassinate the Sandinista leadership and prominent civilian Sandinista supporters inside Nicaragua in the event that the FDN managed to reach Managua. Code-named "Pegasus," it was first proposed by the CMA and was modeled on the Operation Phoenix assassination program in Vietnam. Pegasus called for air-dropping about thirty Americans and two hundred contras into Managua to take out strategic economic targets—electric utilities, dams, bridges—and to kill Tomás Borge, Daniel Ortega, Miguel D'Escoto, Nora Astorga, some unnamed politicians, priests, and a nun.[84]

Three days later, Hull, Owen, Duyck, and Terrell flew to Miami, where they and others—including Enrique Bermúdez, Aristides Sánchez, Felipe Vidal, Tom Posey, Bruce Jones, and Joe Adams ("Shooter," Calero's bodyguard)—gathered at Calero's house for another meeting. Terrell says that during the meeting he noticed two men "sitting on Adolfo's patio," looking in at the gathering through sliding glass doors. One, whose hair had a strange orange tint as if it had been dyed badly, was, Terrell says, "someone I didn't know. Later someone told me it was the Pastora bomber." (Terrell later repeated this startling information under oath to the OIJ, in our 1986 libel trial, and in his book.)[85] Terrell, one of those who insists that La Penca was a right-wing plot, says this meeting consisted of "the same group that did the original Pastora bombing. This was a rerun of the same thing. The purpose of the meeting was to obtain approval of the FDN Directorate to carry out the Costa Rican plan."

Afterward, Terrell summarized the meeting in a handwritten diary entry which began, "the 'termination' of Zero." In interviews during this period, Terrell explained that the plan was to lure Pastora to a meeting in Costa Rica with Adolfo Calero and then kidnap him. The kidnappers, dressed in Sandinista uniforms, would then "take him to El Castillo [in Nicaragua] and publicly hang him." This scheme apparently didn't get very far off the drawing board, perhaps because the larger plan (Pegasus) ran into trouble. Joe Adams says that in January the hit list was drawn up and a date—March 1, 1985—set for beginning the assassinations. But the project was nixed after a press report revealed that CMA mercenaries were operating out of Honduras, and the embarrassed Honduran government ordered them expelled.[86]

There was, however, another scheme waiting in the wings. This one involved bombing the U.S. embassies in Costa Rica and Honduras, as well as the Costa Rican presidential offices, killing Brooklyn Rivera and several contra leaders aligned with Pastora, and assassinating the newly appointed ambassador to Costa Rica, Lewis Tambs.[87] Tambs, who had been U.S. ambassador to Colombia, was said to have angered the cartel by his efforts to extradite narcotics traffickers to the United States. The cartel had put out a million-dollar reward for Tambs.

According to Terrell this multifaceted project "started as a bull session" in Memphis in January 1985, when a group of CMA types and Mario Calero, the FDN's supply officer and brother of Adolfo, were sitting around discussing the million-dollar bounty for Tambs.[87] Tambs had been withdrawn as ambassador to Colombia and, at the urging of Oliver North, had been named ambassador to Costa Rica. The cartel's bounty tempted this crowd.

"Here's where the drug money comes in," Terrell said in an interview. "These guys cooked up the scheme to bomb the Embassy in San José and kill Tambs, blame it on the Sandinistas, and collect the million dollar reward. Everyone got something out of the deal." Terrell said the plan "was something that developed like ice in a tray. It kept getting harder and harder. And more and more people began to think it was a good action."

But not everyone was enthusiastic. Jesús García, an anti-communist Cuban American corrections officer in Miami, says he first heard about the plan in February 1985, at a meeting in a Howard Johnson motel and restaurant near Miami's international airport, one that offered a special "freedom fighters discount." Gathered there were a number of Americans and Cuban Americans who were heading for Costa Rica—Hull, Jones, mercenaries

Steven Carr, Robert Thompson, Claude Chaffard, Posey, Corvo, and Vidal. García recalls joining some of this group, who were sitting around a table in the bar. One had a blueprint of the U.S. Embassy in San José and another counted heads and divided the million dollars, calculating what each participant would make.

Later, after his arrest, García detailed the plan in a memorandum to the Federal Public Defender, Theodore Sakowitz in Miami. "We were all to fly to San José, where we were to meet and be provided back-up by Mr. John Hull and Mr. Bruce Jones. This operation was being coordinated by Mr. Tom Posey of Decatur, Alabama, who is providing support here in the United States." García said he was told this plan "was sanctioned from up there in Washington. Somebody big was covering them." He said he assumed "it was a CIA operation. Nobody moves in this town without the blessing of the CIA."[88]

García says when he heard about the plot, he got up and walked away from the table. "I don't want to kill Americans. I'm not here to kill my own kind. I picked up too many American bodies in Vietnam," García says he told the others. Shortly afterward Tom Posey approached him directly. "He dropped that particular incident in front of my wife while we were all drinking coffee together in a hotel restaurant," he recalled. García again said he did not want to discuss it. García's court-appointed lawyer, John Mattes, became convinced that his client was later set up for arrest because he said no to the Embassy plot.

While at the Howard Johnson, García stopped in Bruce Jones's room, where he found crates of supplies awaiting shipment to Central America. One of the boxes contained C-4 plastic explosive, and García says he was told "it was going to be used to dynamite the American embassy." García says that over the course of several days, Steven Carr, Robert Thompson, René Corvo, and he drove around Miami in a pick-up truck, collecting donations of civilian clothing, boots, fatigues, and half a field hospital, plus an impressive assortment of military hardware: G-3 automatic rifles, M-16 rifles, two AR-15 rifles, a .50-caliber machine gun, a 308 sniper rifle, a Remington shotgun, a 9 mm Browning pistol, a 60 mm mortar launcher, mortar rounds, ammunition, claymore mines, and a fourteen-foot-long 22 mm cannon. All of it was destined for the Southern Front.

One of the stops was the house of Francisco Chánes (of the money-laundering company Ocean Hunter), where Carr said he inadvertently opened a desk drawer and found about three kilos of cocaine inside. García recalls, "I told Carr to close the drawer. He was getting close to some dirty business." Corvo later claimed to the FBI that all the military supplies came from "unidentified contributors [in the Miami area who] were all private citizens with no ties to the United States government."[89] Jesús García disagrees. He said the supplies were partly private or organizational donations and partly from the CIA. In interviews later, García, Carr, and British mercenary Peter Glibbery all indicated that the C-4 plastic and claymore mines were probably intended for the U.S. Embassy bomb plot[90] and that the cannon was for a border incident. Hull subsequently talked to Carr and Glibbery of using "a 14-foot cannon" to attack the Costa Rican border town of Los Chiles, which would be blamed the Sandinistas. Clearly this was a shipment of CIA supplies destined for the "unconventional" war of terrorism being run out of Costa Rica.

On March 6, 1985, the four men loaded the several tons of military hardware onto an Air Florida charter at the Fort Lauderdale airport. Corvo paid the Cuban pilot $8,000 in cash. Then Carr, Thompson, and Corvo boarded the plane and flew to Ilopango Air Base in El Salvador, where they were met by seven U.S. Air Force flight instructors, who acted as if such charter flights were a common occurrence. As Carr explained, "They didn't speak but they witnessed that we were Americans and we definitely had arms. We unloaded the aircraft and stored our weapons in their warehouse. From their behavior, I knew that there had to be connections through our government." The trio waited in El Salvador for about a week, and then loaded the military hardware into a small twin-engine plane belonging to the FDN, which flew to a northern Costa Rican landing strip controlled by Hull. Hull and Owen, who was in the country, went to meet the small plane from Ilopango and oversee the unloading of the supplies. Carr and Thompson then took a commercial flight from San Salvador to San José.

At this same time, three other foreign adventurers—Brits Peter Glibbery and John Davies, and Frenchman Claude Chaffard—arrived in Costa Rica to work as part of Hull's FDN group. Their commander was "Jesús" (Santiago Moncada Guardia), a Nicaraguan sent from Honduras at Hull's request. Carr said their mission was to "wreak havoc" along the border. He said Hull discussed plans to stage an attack on the Costa Rican border town of Los Chiles and blame it on the Sandinistas. Hull told Carr that they would bring the fourteen-foot cannon from Ilopango in order to shell the town and would scatter around a few dead contras dressed in Sandinista army uniforms. According to Terrell, these mercenaries were part of the CIA-FDN plan outlined at the Houston and Miami meetings to assassinate Pastora and others, create border incidents, bomb the U.S. Embassy and other targets, and blame them all on the Sandinistas. The aim, Terrell said, was "to provoke a possible [U.S.] invasion of Nicaragua from Costa Rica and justify this form of U.S. intervention in defense of this country, Costa Rica."[91]

But the mercenaries' mission was short lived. In mid-April Corvo led Carr and a group of contras in an attack on the small Nicaraguan town of La Esperanza. Hull and his CIA bosses were furious, blaming the raid for the narrow defeat of a contra aid bill. A few days later, Costa Rican guardsmen raided "Jesus's" camp and arrested the five foreign mercenaries and nine Nicaraguans. It is possible that the CIA authorized this raid, having concluded the mercenaries were too uncontrollable and that it was better to remove them from the war front. The problem was that, once behind bars, Carr and Glibbery began to talk, vowing that they would not take the rap for what they said were CIA-approved activities.

Just before the mercenaries were arrested, another member of this CIA-FDN cell, the young contra "David," decided to talk. He said he had been part of the La Penca plot, but, like Jesús García, David decided to draw his personal line at the bombing of the U.S. Embassy. He wanted out, he told us, but first he wanted to expose the entire network. In passing information to us, he managed to foil the plot to bomb the embassy. Unfortunately, his cell realized they had an informer in their midst; they captured David, took him to Hull's farm, and killed him.

Although some of its activities had been exposed and partially foiled, the North-CIA network was far from broken. In fact, at this point, August 1985, two other major covert projects were getting off the ground. One was the secret Santa Elena airstrip; the other was the final "Project Pastora" (discussed in chapters 12 and 13). Parallel and at times intertwined with their past and future plots was another ongoing CIA-FDN mission: the elimination of Brooklyn Rivera, leader of the Atlantic coast contra movement, Misurasata. While Pastora was, as Calero's bodyguard Joe Adams put it, "the biggest 'bad guy,' "[92] Rivera had long been a target as well. "Agents of the CIA have been trying to neutralize Misurasata because we are the only effective resistance fighting [on the Atlantic coast] and we are an independent organization," Rivera said in an April 1987 interview.

Beginning in late 1983, Rivera was involved in autonomy and peace talks with the Sandinistas, to the displeasure of the CIA handlers, his Atlantic coast rivals, and the FDN. In early 1984, Enrique Bermúdez and Aristides Sánchez tried to recruit Rudi Sinclair to kill both Pastora and Rivera; in mid-1985, David's CIA-FDN cell was plotting to murder Rivera as well as bomb the U.S. Embassy. Then in mid-1986, Rivera said, Felipe Vidal using a new alias, "Max Morgan" (previously he had used "Morgan" and "Max Varges", tried to hire an Atlantic coast commander for 60,000 colones (about $1,000) to kill the Misurasata leader. ("It seems that I'm not worth very much," Rivera commented wryly.) Rivera said other CIA agents—"Tom Castillo" (Joe Fernández), "Risa" (Victoriano Morales), a Major Lee, Charles Harrington (a U.S. Embassy political officer in San José), and Tim Brown and Richard Chidester (both stationed in Honduras)—were among those working to sabotage the peace talks, buy off his commanders, create rival movements, cut off his supplies, and split his organization. "The CIA definitely is undermining in every way efforts for peace," commented one Rivera loyalist.

Rivera's most serious peace and regional autonomy initiative began in 1987, when he became leader of a new Atlantic coast coalition, Yatama, which refused to join the U.S.-backed, pro-FDN coalition, the Nicaraguan Resistance. Rivera instead embarked on talks with a Sandinista delegation headed by Tomás Borge and mediated by the Moravian church. Again the CIA moved in with an array of covert tactics aimed at disrupting the negotiations. One of the dirtiest involved a plot in November 1987, organized by Vidal, to kidnap the three-year-old daughter of John Paul Lederach, one of the two main Moravian church mediators shuttling between Sandinista and Yatama officials. Lederach was tipped off about the plot, and his child and pregnant wife quickly moved out of Costa Rica. A month later, Lederach was detained by Costa Rican narcotics agents[93] as he entered Costa Rica from Nicaragua. They photocopied all his documents pertaining to the peace negotiations, took his mug shot, and accused him of being involved in drug trafficking. About the same time, several contras warned him of a second plot—this one targeting him and two other church mediators for murder. The assassin was to be paid $50,000 for the three murders. With each instance of harassment, Lederach, an effective and courageous mediator, sought to protect himself and the peace process by protesting to the Arias government, the U.S. Embassy, and to members of Congress, as well as by notifying the press.[94]

Behind the Reagan administration's anti-Sandinista rhetoric vowing to protect Costa Rica's democracy and "return" democracy to Nicaragua, a much more complex and sinister drama was being played out. Beginning in 1984, the North network and CIA operatives overseeing the contra war shifted from trying to build a large standing contra army along the Southern Front to using Costa Rica as a base for unconventional warfare. Their proclaimed intention was to blame assorted border incidents and other attacks and killings on the Sandinistas and thereby provoke an expanded war between the United States and Nicaragua at a time when Congress was moving to cut off funding. But the North-Hull network of contras, Costa Ricans, Cuban Americans, and "civilian" collaborators was made up of ultraright and criminal extremists who in practice proved more intent on profiteering through drug and arms deals than on toppling the Sandinistas. As the following chapters elaborate, they set about both dismantling Pastora's and Brooklyn's fighting forces and undermining President Oscar Arias's peace plan. In the end they waged neither an effective war against the Sandinistas nor worked for a lasting peace.

TWELVE

The Santa Elena Airstrip and the Opening of the Southern Front

Back in the summer of 1985, as the first guardsmen were graduating from Murciélago, just over the ridge a major CIA–North network covert project, the Santa Elena airstrip, was getting off the drawing board. Murciélago and Santa Elena were originally part of one grand design to build a joint Costa Rican/contra/U.S. military complex on the Santa Elena peninsula just south of the Nicaraguan border. The project was first conceived in 1982 (not 1985, as U.S. officials testified to the Tower Commission and Iran-contra congressional hearings), and it was begun by a top-secret U.S. Army unit known as Yellow Fruit. It was completed by Oliver North's Project Democracy using front companies, individuals with phony identities, and secret bank accounts in Switzerland, Panama, and Liberia. Ultimately it became part of a larger scheme to reorganize (what Ambassador Tambs termed "to open") the Southern Front.

When the project was first discovered by the press in September 1986, phony documents released by Costa Rican security officials claimed the two-kilometer-long landing strip was a tourist project sponsored by a group of U.S. investors. In official inquiries—the Tower Commission, Iran-contra hearings, various court cases, Costa Rican judicial and legislative cases—U.S. officials "conceded" the airstrip was built in early 1986 for two military purposes. One was to provide a base near the Nicaraguan border where an "international force"—what Tambs cynically described as "a platoon of Panamanians, half a company of Venezuelans, and the 82nd Airborne"[1]—could land in the face of Sandinista aggression against unarmed Costa Rica. The other purpose was to provide facilities to resupply the contras inside Nicaragua and get them away from the border area. As spun out by officials in Washington and San José, both of these rationales were intended to allow the United States to protect and uphold Costa Rica's neutrality and sovereignty.

According to North, Tambs, and CIA station chief Joe Fernández, the 1984 Boland amendment, by which Congress forbade U.S. aid to the contras, was not violated, because the landing strip was financed and built by private citizens (what Tambs termed "private benefactors" or PBs), who were voluntarily aiding the contras. The Tower and Iran-contra investigations did manage to peel away part of this cover story and reveal that the facility was financed by North's network through the Saudi contributors and profits from Iranian arms sales. Scandalous as these revelations were at the time, much of the true history and purpose of the Santa Elena airstrip, including its use for drug trafficking, was successfully covered over.

U.S. operatives selected the Santa Elena peninsula in late 1982 after General Noriega, then head of G-2, Panama's powerful military intelligence service, nixed plans to construct a large Southern Front training facility on Panama's Pacific Ocean island of Coiba. At the time, Santa Elena was one of a number of private landing strips surveyed jointly by the U.S. Army, CIA, contras, and drug traffickers. Bill Crone, a North American pilot and businessman, says that about mid-1982 he met at John Hull's ranch contra official Luis Rivas, who was working on contract for the CIA. Rivas had fought in the late 1970s on the Southern Front against Somoza and then had left Nicaragua in the early 1980s to rejoin Pastora in the new war against the Sandinistas. Blond, German-looking, Rivas was described by many as intelligent and capable, and he was someone Pastora quickly perceived as a rival to his own authority. Crone recalls that Rivas asked him to make "reconnaissance" flights, surveying landing strips to be used for air drops of contra supplies. Crone and Hull, partly because they were both pilots, were the main civilian Americans in Costa Rica helping the anti-Sandinistas during this early period.

From the latter part of 1982 until the beginning of 1983, Crone made a series of flights over northern Costa Rica with Rivas, Costa Rican–North American farmer and pilot Robert Bradford Brenes, contra logistics official José "Chepón" Robelo, and other rebel officials. Crone coordinated these flights with CIA agents at the U.S. Embassy, and frequently either station chief Phil Holts or an agent known as "Duke" would go along. They flew over the arid, brush-covered Santa Elena peninsula to take photos of two sites: Murciélago and the runway on the Hacienda Santa Elena, located at Potrero Grande on the Pacific Coast. The CIA's intention was to connect the two properties by road and construct a large airstrip, a multipurpose military training camp, and an infantry, naval, and air base to be run by Green Berets and utilized jointly by the contras and Costa Ricans. Beginning in at least 1983, contras connected with M-3 and El Negro's FARN had been operating on the peninsula. Located just ten miles south of the Nicaraguan border on a strip of land between the sea and the Pan American highway, this new base was to be the equivalent of the U.S.-financed Aguacate Air Base in Honduras and would truly have earned Costa Rica the name "Honduras South."[2]

However, because of problems at both the Washington and Costa Rican ends, including the 1986 election of the pro-peace candidate Oscar Arias, this plan was never developed. Instead, the Murciélago area became a Civil Guard training camp run initially by Green Berets, and the long, unpaved Santa Elena runway[3] became a clandestine landing and refueling base for the contra resupply and drug flights.[4]

Phase I: From Yellow Fruit to Project Democracy

Some of these early reconnaissance flights were part of Yellow Fruit, an ultra-secret U.S. Army project begun in July 1982 by an elite group of intelligence officers with close ties to the CIA. Following accusations of massive corruption, the project was closed down in December 1983 and became the subject of a three-year (1983–86) Army and Justice Department investigation and a series of secret military courts martial the first such in twenty years.

Initially housed within the Pentagon, Yellow Fruit eventually moved under a cover company, Business Security International (BSI), a "private" consulting firm in Annandale, Virginia. With a staff of just nine, it had access to virtually unlimited funds. According to one Army official involved, Yellow Fruit was "an organization that was a hidden circle within a circle within a circle" so it would be very difficult to discover "it was really an Army unit."[5]

By mid-1983 Yellow Fruit was involved in implementing a secret plan intended to provide continued support to the contras in the event that Congress passed the Boland amendment and cut off aid. Yellow Fruit financial manager William "Tom" Golden, who had twenty years' experience in covert operations, recalls reading an unsigned thirty- to forty-page document proposing three contra-related projects: setting up offshore bank accounts; funneling weapons to the contras through Latin American allies such as Honduras, Guatemala, and Argentina; and constructing a large airstrip in Costa Rica. Golden says that there was a draft Presidential Finding authorizing the covert activities either attached to or discussed within the plan.[6] Golden believes the draft document was drawn up jointly by Army intelligence and the CIA. "This was blueprint for circumventing Boland. It included proposals for padding military aid to certain countries and syphoning off money," Golden recalled in an interview. When the first Boland amendment was passed in December 1982, "We went into high gear," he said. Before the end of 1983, Yellow Fruit was embroiled in financial scandal and was being closed down, and a new covert operation, Oliver North's Project Democracy, was being readied to fill the void. Golden says, "There's no doubt in my mind" that Yellow Fruit was one of the precursors, a sort of prototype for North's covert operation.

Golden, the Yellow Fruit whistle blower, told the Iran-contra Select Committee hearings that the plan he read included a proposal for the CIA, Army, Department of Defense, and possibly other agencies jointly to construct a large airfield in Costa Rica to support the "supply system." This fits with statements from Costa

Rican and contra sources who say that by late 1983 some construction was underway, even though President Monge had not yet agreed to the plan. Golden explained that John Hull was Yellow Fruit's chief contact in Costa Rica, heading the aerial surveys, and that retired Air Force officer Richard Gadd was contracted in the United States to build the airstrip. Initially Yellow Fruit considered using Hull's property, but according to both Golden and pilot Bill Crone, Hull was considered "a little unstable" and a security risk, and this contributed to the decision to select a more discrete venue.

The Yellow Fruit team eventually selected the 15,000-acre Hacienda Santa Elena, which belonged to a group of five U.S. investors who had bought it from the Somoza family for about $1.8 million in the early 1970s. These investors never developed the property, which they registered under a Costa Rican corporation known as "Desarrollo Hacienda Santa Elena" or "Compañía del Desarrollo de Santa Elena." This, in turn, became a wholly owned subsidiary of a parent company, Santa Elena Development Corporation, registered in Monrovia, Liberia, a location frequently used by international financiers and offshore investors seeking anonymity. Liberia was also the name of the Costa Rican town nearest the Santa Elena airstrip. As shown below, the North network moved to capitalize on the fortuitous coincidence.

In August 1982, Joseph Hamilton, a wealthy North Carolina textile manufacturer who was one of the original investors, was named president of the company. In mid-1984 he moved permanently to Costa Rica, where he also owns three "máquila" factories assembling shirts, pants, and shorts for the U.S. market. He has taken advantage of the AID-CINDE export-promotion strategy and been caught cheating on his claims for CATs benefits. Model planes hang from the ceiling of his office, which overlooks the shop floor where hundreds of women sit bent over sewing machines, stitching pre-cut pieces of garments for export to the United States.

Hamilton bears many similarities to John Hull, but the two gringos claim not to know each other. Like Hull, he's an elderly, balding American with a southern drawl and a love for flying his small plane around Costa Rica. A former Air Force pilot, he is a right-wing Republican and avid anticommunist. But while Hull relished the limelight and often captured headlines in the local press, Hamilton was elusive and secretive about his political connections and involvements. A business associate described Hamilton as very "patriotic" and "close to the Embassy." He says Hamilton was approached "by the boys," who appealed to his patriotism and asked him to be "a front" for the project.

During this early phase it is not known what financial arrangement, if any, the CIA and the contras made to use the Santa Elena property. It is possible they paid the owners or managers a certain fee each time it was used, as was done with other landing strips and farms in the Guanacaste area. No effort was made, at this point, to set up a dummy company and buy the land. As contra operations and plans for the Santa Elena airstrip got underway, one person put on the CIA payroll was Colonel José Ramón Montero, the Civil Guard commander for Guanacaste. Contra officials say Montero became one of the CIA's highest paid Costa Rican collaborators. He was officially named administrator of the Hacienda Santa Elena property in January 1986, but prior to that he had actively facilitated U.S. military projects in Guanacaste, including the Green Beret training camp at Murciélago. He built a large, conspicuous house just outside the town of Liberia which area residents termed "a palace," and it was commonly said the house was partially paid for with drug trafficking profits.[8]

There are indications that, from the outset, the Santa Elena airstrip, like other Guanacaste landing strips surveyed by the CIA and contras, was used for transshipments of drugs as well as arms. Members of the Legislative Assembly's special commission on drug trafficking said that they found such evidence, and a California pilot, Tosh Plumlee, provided maps and details of what he claims were his repeated arms and drug runs through Santa Elena between 1982 and 1984. From at least 1983 onward, M-3 and El Negro's FARN, both contra groups involved in drug trafficking, had camps in the Santa Elena peninsula. In 1984, El Negro's troops were reported to be at Potrero Grande, site of the airstrip. Colonel Montero testified in a court case that in mid-May 1985, well before the major expansion of the airstrip had started and before Montero was officially put in charge of the property, the Guanacaste Rural Guard commander Edwin Viales offered him $7,000 per flight if he would leave the Santa Elena airstrip unguarded two days a week. Montero, of course, denied he accepted the offer.[9]

Although in the aerial survey Santa Elena's seclusion and proximity to the sea made it appear ideal for covert operations, once the groundwork began, the North network encountered serious logistical problems. For six months of the year, the Santa Elena area is buffeted by high sea winds and the ocean is generally too rough for boat landings. In the dry season it is difficult to get equipment into the area over the rough dirt track, and in the rainy season it becomes virtually impassable. The soil was soft on the runway itself, and when it rained planes got stuck in the mud. Former ambassador Frank McNeil dubbed it "Air Swampy."[10]

There were also delays due to political problems in San José and Washington. Officials from the CIA and Pentagon were having trouble convincing President Monge to permit the project. Costa Rican sources say that some improvement on the landing strip began in 1983, but by August 1984 Monge had still not signed on to this and several other contra projects. Monge's resistance to U.S. pressure almost led to a coup intended to install Vice President Armando Aráuz. Instead, the coup was defused and Monge quietly agreed to a series of U.S. demands, including the airstrip project and the appointment of Benjamín Piza as Security Minister. Piza quickly became Santa Elena's principal sponsor.

The Santa Elena airstrip scheme ran into delays in Washington as well, as the corruption-ridden Yellow Fruit was being closed down in late 1983 and its Costa Rican operations moved over to North's Project Democracy. William Golden, who handled finances for Yellow Fruit's covert operations, says that before its demise, the project had established a bank account for the Costa Rican airfield. While Golden was working at BSI, Yellow Fruit's front company, he was asked by his boss, Colonel Dale Duncan, and by Joel Patterson, who Golden describes as "a money launderer for the Defense Department," to sign a number of bank signature cards to open accounts for the different clandestine projects. Golden says he "didn't pay much attention at the time," and he assumed that these accounts were closed down when Yellow Fruit was terminated.

It was not until April 1987 that Golden found out, through a journalist with CBS News, that one card had been used in 1983 to open a secret account at Credit Suisse, Switzerland's third largest bank, and that the account was never closed. Golden was told by the journalist and later he confirmed it directly with Credit Suisse officials in Geneva, that North, Secord and, Albert Hakim (Secord's Iranian-born business partner) were also signatories to this same account. Golden discovered that not only had this account continued to function, but that it had also "evolved into other accounts." Press and congressional investigators discovered that this original Credit Suisse account and its offspring were used to channel money, illegally and secretly, to the contras, contra-related projects, and a variety of other covert schemes never investigated by Congress. These accounts had been established by North, Secord, Hakim, and Thomas Clines using the "discreet financial services" of Willard I. Zucker, a former IRS lawyer in Switzerland who ran the Geneva-based Compagnie de Services Fiduciaries (CSF). Secord, Clines, and Hakim had worked together in the past on other covert financial projects, and Zucker had provided banking-related services to Hakim since 1971.[11]

It is these Swiss and other offshore bank accounts and shell companies that constituted what Secord termed the Enterprise, which was the covert business structure for North's Project Democracy. Among the dummy companies created with the Credit Suisse accounts were three—Lake Resources,[13] Dolmy Inc.,[14] and Udall Research Corporation—established between April and September 1985 by the prestigious Panamanian law firm of Quijano and Associates, which had handled the incorporation of a number of such companies.[15]

Of the three, Udall Research Corporation[16] was the most important for the Southern Front operations; North termed it a "Project Democracy proprietary." It bought and operated contra supply planes, mortgaged the Santa Elena property, and eventually modernized the airstrip and a road, and built military barracks. At the time it was set up—April 29, 1985—Udall listed its capital as only $10,000, although a ledger of Enterprise financial transactions shows various transfers to the company including $100,000, $60,000, $25,000, and $35,000. Udall bought at least three planes and sent wire transfers to ACE, another Enterprise company in Panama.

First contacted just after the airstrip came to public light in September 1986, Quijano firm officials were predictably circumspect. They described Udall as "a shelf company" which they had incorporated on behalf of some "clients abroad." (It later became known that Quijano had used the services of Zucker and his associates in Switzerland to set up the Udall and other accounts.) They said they had nothing in their records about the airstrip in Costa Rica, had never met or heard from North, Secord, Hakim, Owen, Clines, et al., and had no bank statements or other communications from Udall, even though theirs was the only known address of the company, and three officers listed on Udall's incorporation documents were from the Quijano firm. Indeed, Udall's director was the head of the firm, Julio Antonio Quijano, a prominent and wealthy Panamanian in his mid-fifties and a close friend of Eric Delvalle, Noriega's handpicked President, who was installed in September 1985. Another Quijano partner was Juan Castillero, who, according to the counsel for the Iran-contra congressional committee, handled some of Noriega's legal business.[17]

By late spring 1985, most of the preparations had been completed for the Santa Elena project: the airstrip had been surveyed by CIA-hired pilots, it had been used intermittently for contra-linked arms and drug runs, and, the evidence indicates, it had been somewhat improved and extended. Control of the project had been transferred from the Army's Yellow Fruit unit over to North's Project Democracy. The North-Secord financial structure, the Enterprise, included Udall as a dummy company to handle the finances and provide the cover story of a tourist scheme. But the more grandiose plans for a joint U.S./contra/Costa Rican military base on the Santa Elena peninsula had been slowed by complications in Washington and Costa Rica. Then, during the last half of 1985, as the North-Secord network moved to extend its hegemony over all aspects of the contra operations and geared up to take over the air resupply network, including air drops inside Nicaragua, they worked on completing the Santa Elena airstrip project with a new sense of urgency.

Phase II: Restructuring the Southern Front

During the summer of 1985, the Embassy and envoys from Washington increased the pressure on President Monge to approve the airstrip expansion and another, even more sensitive covert project: an intelligence-gathering center tuned to Nicaragua. Monge admits to meeting two or three times with map-carrying men from Washington. Their arguments that these facilities were essential to protect Costa Rica from Sandinista military incursions were bolstered by the May 31 attack at Las Crucitas, the most serious of the border incidents orchestrated by the contras. Sandinista troops were blamed for the killing of two and wounding of ten Costa Rican Civil Guardsmen. Overnight anti-Sandinista hysteria in Costa Rica reached a boiling point.

In June, the U.S. Congress passed a $27 million "humanitarian" aid package for the contras which, coupled with the North-Secord covert "private sector" military funds, provided the finances for these two Southern Front projects. At this point, North moved in to consolidate financial control of contra operations in the hands of Secord's group. In early July, North met at a hotel at Miami International Airport to lay out plans for reorganization of the contra air supply system and the Southern Front. Present at the meeting were FDN leaders Adolfo Calero and Enrique Bermúdez, Secord, Clines, and their long-time Cuban American underling in CIA and nefarious business affairs, Rafael "Chi Chi" Quintero. According to Secord, "The meeting commenced on a pretty hard note, with Colonel North being worried about and critical of the contras, because he had been receiving reports that the limited funds they had might be getting wasted, squandered or even worse, some people might be lining their pockets."

Until this point, funds from Saudi Arabia had been deposited in Calero's bank account and contra officials, including most importantly his brother Mario, had purchased arms, airplanes, and other supplies from a number of different brokers. Now North decreed that these contra leaders would be cut out of the money pipeline and that Secord and his associates—basically, the Enterprise—would handle all funds, arms purchases, and logistics for the covert war effort.[18]

North argued that these changes would control corruption and improve efficiency. In fact what ensued was a more massive and sophisticated level of profiteering. Congressional investigators found that between 1984 and 1986, almost $48 million flowed into Enterprise accounts from arms and missile sales to Iran, donations from third countries, sale of arms to the CIA and contras, and "private" donations solicited by North and his associates. Of the $16.1 million surplus generated from the Iranian arms sales, a mere $3.8 million went to the contras. The Enterprise was carefully and covertly structured so as to make large profits for its directors. Secord, Hakim, and Clines took $4.4 million in self-determined commissions, averaging a whopping 38 percent on weapons purchases. Secord and Hakim siphoned off another $2.2 million for personal use and private business ventures, and they put the Enterprise's assets in their names. The financial records also showed what congressional investigators termed "unexplained cash expenditures," which included cash transfers to unspecified places. At the time the scandal broke and the Enterprise was closed down in November 1986, $5.6 million remained in Enterprise accounts, funds which Secord and Hakim arrogantly told Congress were rightfully theirs.

Under the scheme North outlined at the Miami meeting, Secord was put in overall control. Clines was made the procurement officer in charge of obtaining weapons. Quintero, along with, first, retired Air Force lieutenant colonel Richard Gadd and then, beginning in 1986, retired Air Force colonel Robert Dutton was put in charge of running from Miami the contras' air resupply operation out of Ilopango Air Force base in San Salvador, Cuban American Felix Rodriguez oversaw the on-site operations at Illopango, and Hakim was charged with setting up the secret Swiss and other overseas bank accounts and front companies. Most immediately, Hakim was told to establish Lake Resources, a Swiss company which from this point on replaced Calero's accounts as the main recipient of the North network's funds for the contras.[19]

Beginning at this point plans were laid to upgrade Santa Elena into a runway and base for refueling larger planes resupplying contras operating inside Nicaragua. This was part of a larger scheme to reorganize the Southern Front, a scheme overseen by the new U.S. ambassador, Lewis Tambs, who arrived in late July to fill the post which had been vacant since Curtin Winsor's departure in February 1985.

A cigar-chomping cold warrior, Tambs was a professor of Latin American history from Arizona State University and another political appointee. He had been one of the authors of the 1980 Santa Fe document, the key Reagan-era strategy paper which viewed Soviet domination as the main threat in Central America. During 1982 and 1983, Tambs had worked as a consultant at the NSC, where he developed a close relationship with Oliver North. From 1983 to early 1985, he served as ambassador to Colombia, his first diplomatic posting. One of his primary missions there was to crack down on drug trafficking to the United States. He had been given these instructions not by the State Department, his official employer, but by NSC adviser William Clark, to whom he reported through back channels. Tambs later testified that because of his efforts, what he labeled the "narco-terrorists"—which he identified as the Medellín cartel in alliance with leftist Colombian guerrillas, Cuba, and Nicaragua—retaliated by putting a bounty on his head, threatening his family, and bombing the Embassy and ambassador's residence. North, then Clark's underling at the NSC, came to Tambs's rescue, sending members of Delta Force, the army's elite counter-terrorist unit, to Colombia to provide protection for the ambassador and his family. In November 1984, Tambs, as well as other U.S. diplomats and dependents in Colombia, was recalled to Washington because of the threats, but a lasting friendship had been struck between Tambs and North.

Almost immediately, North requested that Tambs be reassigned to Costa Rica, a curious move for a diplomat whose life was threatened by drug lords. Costa Rica, like other parts of Central America, was becoming increasingly important as a "bridge" or transit point for moving cocaine from Colombia to the United States. Costa Rica's growing importance was due to the drug traffickers' alignment not with leftists, as Tambs and North contended, but with the contras, a connection which grew during the period Tambs served in Costa Rica. The week Tambs arrived, he was scheduled to be the target of a CIA-contra terrorist attack which, was to be blamed on the Sandinistas. The attack, which was aborted at the last minute, was supposedly being bankrolled by Colombian drug traffickers, who had agreed to pay participants a million-dollar reward for killing Tambs.

Most Costa Ricans anticipated that Tambs's academic training, previous ambassadorship in Colombia, and fluency in Spanish would make him a more professional, reflective, and perhaps sympathetic U.S. envoy; but although less flamboyant, he turned out to be little different than his predecessor Winsor. During the Iran-contra hearings, Congressman Dante Fascell described Tambs as "a rock-em, sock-em, no nonsense type of person, cut the red tape, damn the torpedoes, and all that kind of stuff." Without a hint of shame, the silver-haired, grim-faced Tambs admitted that he had never read the Boland amendment, attended the Foreign Service Institute, or received any instructions from the State Department regarding his assignment in Costa Rica. He justified this by indicating that he believed he was following President Reagan's orders, as passed to him through North. As he cryptically put it, "One who takes the king's shillings does the king's bidding."[20] As had been true in Colombia, Tambs's marching orders came not from Secretary of State George Shultz but from the NSC, and in this instance from staffer North.

In the Embassy, most closely involved in promoting the Santa Elena airstrip project were Tambs, CIA station chief Joe Fernández/"Tomás Castillo," chargé d'affaires James Tull (brought by Tambs from Bogotá), and defense attaché John Lent, who had served in the U.S. Embassy in Managua and knew all the contra players. The day following Tambs's arrival, the four assembled at the ambassador's walled, heavily protected suburban mansion to discuss his mission—to "open up the Southern Front."[21]

The mission involved several covert projects which had, as always, the ultimate goal of welding the northern and southern contras into a unified army firmly under U.S. and FDN control, commanded out of Honduras, and fighting inside Nicaragua rather than in the border regions. Key to this goal was the reorganization of Ilopango Air Force Base[22] in El Salvador and the construction of the Santa Elena airstrip. Tambs and Fernández recognized that their own roles in these operations would need to be carefully concealed.

Their progress was carefully monitored in Washington by Oliver North, whose trusted courier, Robert Owen, frequently visited Costa Rica to facilitate negotiations with the Costa Rican government and to help negotiate use of the Santa Elena property jointly owned by Joe Hamilton and four other Americans. Owen wrote to North, following an inspection tour of the property in August 1985, saying that the land could be rented for a reasonable price and, by way of providing the airstrip with a cover, it could publicly be described as an extension of the nearby Murciélago training base.[23]

Also participating in negotiations over Santa Elena was William Haskell, an H&R Block tax agent who had lost an eye in Vietnam combat and who North supplied with a passport and identity in the name of Robert Olmsted (sometimes spelled "Olmstead"), president of the dummy company Udall Research. One of the "private volunteers" who helped hide the Reagan administration's illegal support for the contras, Haskell's qualifications for international covert operations appeared to be solely his right-wing political bent and unquestioning loyalty to his old Marine buddy North. In September 1985, he was assigned by North and Secord to negotiate the agreement to use the land and airstrip. He recalls that they described Udall as "simply a shell corporation, an untraceable corporation, that I could use in acquiring the land." In late September and early October, he met in New York with Joe Hamilton and another of the Santa Elena owners and reported that the partners had tentatively agreed to lease the property.[24]

Between October 1985 and June 1986, Olmsted/Haskell made half a dozen trips to Costa Rica to participate in various legal negotiations. At one point, at Oliver North's request, Ambassador Tambs contacted Hamilton to vouch for "Olmsted" (whom Tambs referred to as "One-Eyed Jack") and the Udall Research Corporation, and personally to lend a hand in the negotiations. At first, Olmsted anticipated no problems. Both the U.S. and Costa Rican governments (through Security Minister Benjamín Piza and Colonel José Ramón Montero, the Civil Guard commander in Guanacaste) backed the project, owner Hamilton was politically supportive of the contra war, and Owen had estimated that the property, which was not in active use, could be obtained for $20,000 or less a year.

Then the airstrip project hit a snag. In January 1986, Hamilton switched law firms, and the new attorneys—Vargas, Jiménez and Peralta, who worked regularly for the U.S. Embassy, AID, and CINDE—decided to play hardball.[25] After some delay, "Olmsted" signed a legal document stating that Udall would buy rather than lease the Santa Elena property for the incredible sum of $5 million. Hamilton says he was delighted by this offer, since the property had been rendered virtually "useless" by the "Sandinista problem." "I thought they were the biggest suckers in the world, but it seemed they could afford to pay anything," Hamilton said in an interview. The money was to be paid in three, highly uneven, installments: $125,000 in February 1986, $50,000 in January 1987, and $4,825,000 in January 1988. However, records indicate only $125,000 was ever paid, in a transfer from CSF Investments in Geneva to Hamilton's account in Charlotte, North Carolina.[26]

Ownership of the airstrip property was also transferred—first to "Olmsted" and Udall Research, and subsequently to "Olmsted" and two silent partners, North and Secord, who became owners of the parent company, Santa Elena Development Corporation, registered in Monrovia, Liberia.[27] They later tried unsuccessfully to sell the property to the CIA at its overvalued price of $5 million.[28] Although North said in September 1986 that the company had been closed, by the early 1990s it still existed.[29] Whether North and Secord continued, in essence, to be the real owners of the Santa Elena property and to maintain a secret bank account in Monrovia remains one of the unsolved mysteries of the Iran-contra scandal.

On the surface the Monrovia, Liberia, connection appears truly bizarre; coincidentally, the nearest Costa Rican town to the airstrip is also known as Liberia. But there are pieces of evidence indicating that the North-Secord network intentionally to use this West Africa registration in order to hide their own profiteering. In international finance and business circles, Liberia is considered the Panama of Africa, a country known for its flexibility and anonymity in registering companies. Both countries permit, for instance, bearer shares, that is, titles which contain no name and can be transferred anonymously. The *Iran-Contra Affair* report states that a Swiss fiduciary such as CSF normally uses Panamanian- or Liberian-registered companies, along with Swiss bank accounts and offshore trust accounts, to give "a triple layer of secrecy, a formidable barrier against identification of the location of money."[30]

The odd coincidence of Liberia, in West Africa, and Liberia, Costa Rica, appears to have been used to advantage by the North network to facilitate siphoning off money officially allocated for the airstrip construction. Although the North-Secord network was frequently portrayed as the gang that couldn't shoot straight, its financial dealings appear well calculated to bring them maximum profit and to permit "plausible deniability" when caught. According to Rafael Quintero's testimony at the North trial, money for the airstrip expansion was sent via wire transfers to Colonel Montero's bank account; at one point "instead of going to Liberia, Costa Rica, the check went to Liberia, Africa" and was thereby "lost for several months."[31]

Quintero describes this as a sort of comical and harmless bureaucratic screw-up, similar to the so-called clerical error which occurred in August 1986, when North's secretary, Fawn Hall, deposited a $10 million contribution from the Sultan of Brunei into the wrong Swiss bank account, because two numbers of the account were inadvertently transposed. The money should have gone into a secret bank account for the contras; instead, the Iran-contra hearings disclosed, it went into the account of an unnamed businessman. This man immediately transferred the money to another of his accounts, claiming later that, coincidentally, he had been expecting a $10 million wire transfer from the sale of a ship. Congressional investigators let the matter drop after they "were assured by the Swiss Magistrate . . . that the individual is neither a principal in the investigation, nor related to any of the principals."[32]

As it turned out, this was not quite so. In 1989, Swiss authorities told the State Department that the lucky recipient was Bruce Rappaport, a Swiss-Israeli oil man, financier, and shipping magnate deeply involved in Middle East business deals, arms-for-hostage negotiations, and influence peddling. Rappaport had hired Attorney

General Edwin Meese's close friend E. Robert Wallach to get Reagan administration support for a proposed billion-dollar Iraqi pipeline. (Wallach had already used his influence with Meese to win favors for the Wedtech Corporation, a crime for which he was subsequently tried.) In June 1985, Wallach arranged for Rappaport to meet with Robert McFarlane and other NSC staffers at the White House. Just after this the NSC took the unusual step of urging the Overseas Private Investment Corporation (OPIC) to indemnify the Iraqi pipeline project. A year later, the Sultan's $10 million was deposited into Rappaport's account. Conservative columnist William Safire, outraged at this "diversion" of funds *from* the contras concluded that "the lesson in this apparent new connectedness of insidership is never to let an assumption of stupidity overwhelm your suspicion of venality." Rappaport and Credit Suisse officials denied the story but refused to reveal where, if not into this account, the $10 million actually went. The Iran-Contra congressional panel was assured, however, that the $10 million was eventually returned to the Sultan of Brunei.[33]

There were other such seemingly odd screw-ups in the Enterprise's accounting system. For instance, Hakim set up a company, Defex SA, to receive commissions and profit distributions. The *Iran-Contra Affair* report states, "The choice of name was not random. Defex (Portugal) was a major arms dealer from whom the Enterprise bought weapons. Defex SA was owned by the Enterprise and, according to Hakim and Secord, had no connection with Defex (Portugal). Hakim testified that when he transferred funds to Defex SA 'people' would think that the funds were being used to purchase arms from Defex (Portugal). Secord testified that Defex SA was a 'cover mechanism' set up by Hakim to disguise the source of money paid to arms dealers."

The report continues, "The ledgers indicated that one of the main uses of Defex SA was the Enterprise's distributing profits. Often, commissions were moved into the Defex SA account, creating wire records and ledger entries that looked like payments to Defex [the arms company]. Then the profits were wired out of Defex SA to members of the Enterprise."[34]

The Monrovia, Liberia, account could have been used to provide a similar clever cover: if caught, they could simply plead clerical error, noting that, as Quintero testified, they had managed to successfully "discover" and retrieve one such error. This is yet another indication that North, as well as the profiteering business partners Secord, Clines, and Hakim, used the Enterprise for illegal personal enrichment.

While these legal and financial maneuvers were underway, the expansion of the airstrip and construction of barracks were being simultaneously handled by two other members of the Enterprise, former Air Force officer Richard Gadd and Cuban American CIA operative Rafael Quintero. Gadd, a covert-operations specialist, had met Secord in connection with the failed Desert One hostage rescue mission in 1980. He had retired from the military in 1982, formed several companies, and continued to work on classified government operations, including Yellow Fruit. Between 1983 and 1985, Gadd's companies provided office space and staff assistance to Secord's businesses. Secord, in turn, funneled lucrative contra-related work to Gadd, including contracting him to arrange air charters for the weapons deliveries, purchase resupply planes and spare parts, hire crews, and draw up a supply drop plan from the flights out of Ilopango. Through the good offices of North and Owen, Gadd also secured a contract to move U.S. "humanitarian" aid supplies to the contras through one of his companies AIRMACH.

In the fall of 1985, North and Secord put Gadd in charge of supervising the expansion of the Santa Elena airstrip. Through his subsidiary, EAST, Inc., he hired three people who came to Costa Rica in early 1986 to undertake the airstrip expansion. Gadd's testimony is somewhat unclear, but it appears he made a profit of over $100,000 from the airstrip project.[35] According to Costa Rican immigration records, Gadd himself never came to Costa Rica.

Rather, it was long-time CIA operative Rafael (Ralph or "Chi Chi") Quintero who supervised the construction. A Miami Cuban and Bay of Pigs veteran, Quintero is an assassinations and sabotage specialist trained in the 1960s by his CIA case officer in Miami, Tom Clines. Beginning in the mid-1970s, Quintero worked with Secord, Clines, Ted Shackley, and Ed Wilson in military intelligence activities in Southeast Asia and the Middle East. In 1976, he signed a $1 million contract with Wilson to assassinate a Qadhafi dissident in Egypt. But he backed out when he became worried that the operation might not be CIA-sanctioned. Quintero and his partners were also tied to the Sydney-based Nugan Hand Bank, which, Australian government investigators found, was used to launder money from weapons and drug sales.

In late 1984 or early 1985, Quintero says he was contacted by Secord and brought into the Enterprise's expanding resupply activities. Quintero had no illusion that he was involved in a "private" operation. He testified at the North trial that when he was recruited, he was assured "that this operation was approved from the highest in the White House" and he subsequently found himself "working with the people who were working out of the U.S. Embassies," including Fernández and Tambs.

Quintero described his specific function as coordinating air and sea transportation, locating drop points and airfields in Central America, and unloading the supplies. He was paid $4,000 a month in salary, plus bonuses for each weapons shipment by air or sea.[36] Known as "The Traveler," Quintero shuttled between El Salvador, Honduras, Costa Rica, and Miami.

By mid-April 1986, North's resupply operation out of Ilopango was making almost daily supply drops to the FDN in the north. But the resupply operation to the Southern Front troops got off to a slower start, in part because of logistical difficulties and in part because the FDN was reluctant to share its hardware with the Southern Front, which was still dominated by Pastora loyalists. On March 28, Owen outlined in a memo to North that he and the operatives at Ilopango had reached agreement on how to resupply the south. He wrote that Southern Front lethal and nonlethal supplies stockpiled at Ilopango would be loaded into transport planes and airdropped to the Southern Front contras; then the planes would land at the Santa Elena airstrip for refueling before returning to Ilopango. In early April there was more than $1 million in arms stockpiled at Ilopango for the Southern Front, and the first delivery of supplies was made to these contras. According to Fernández, between April and September 1986, when the airstrip was discovered by the press and finally closed by the Arias administration, there were nine successful supply drops to the Southern Front, two with nonlethal supplies and seven with weapons.[37] There were, in addition, other supply flights made out of the Aguacate base in Honduras.

Parallel to these military supply flights, contra-linked drug flights through Santa Elena continued and, North's diary entries indicate, they were officially protected and even facilitated. In January 1986, North spent four days in Costa Rica. Following a January 20 meeting with Security Minister Piza about the airstrip, North made a series of curious notations in his diary. One reads, "Look to bringing in fuel by shrimp boat"; another states, "D.E.A. will be briefed to leave hands off [of Santa Elena]." That same day North also had, he notes, "Meeting with Buck, et al" (apparently the CIA team), and an entry underneath reads, "NEED TO HAVE: Felipe Vidal." An earlier note, on January 10, states, "Joe [Fernández] wants to use Felipe Vidal." What this shows is that North and Fernández (with the consent, it appears, of Piza) were enlisting Vidal, a Miami drug trafficker, to help with Santa Elena and other Southern Front projects. They knew who they were dealing with. In secret testimony to the Iran-contra committee, Fernández admitted that both Vidal and his partner René Corvo were "our people" (that is, with the CIA) and had a "problem with drugs" but the Agency had to protect them. Costa Rica's special legislative commission on drug trafficking found that Vidal had received large payments from Frigoríficos de Puntarenas, a company involved in smuggling cocaine to Miami in frozen shrimp containers. As researcher Carl Deal writes, "Wild speculation is not necessary to appreciate the significance" of North's twin entries about using shrimp boats and keeping the DEA away.[38]

By March, with the legal papers and construction work mostly completed and the Santa Elena airstrip ready for use,[39] Fernández and North had succeeded in arranging a reward (a free trip to Washington) for their most important Costa Rican collaborator, Security Minister Piza. Evidence introduced in the 1989 North trial revealed Piza was a CIA asset, that is, a person who systematically assisted covert U.S. operations and was on the Agency's payroll.[40] While Piza readily admits he worked closely with the CIA, the only reward he says he received was this trip to Washington for himself and his wife, which included a "photo opportunity" with President Reagan. In a mid-March memo to

Poindexter, North noted that "Piza had been instrumental in helping the U.S. organize the Southern Front [and] had intervened with another senior Costa Rican official [presumably President Monge] on numerous occasions and had personally assisted in the development of a logistics support base for Resistance forces deployed north from Costa Rica."[41]

Piza described the March 19 White House visit as "purely social" and said he and his wife were "escorted" by their "good friends" Joe Fernández and his wife. They met first with Oliver North, who then ushered the Pizas and Fernándezes into the White House Oval Office for a three-minute photo session, during which Piza presented Reagan with a picture book of Costa Rica.[42] Chief of Staff Donald Regan and others were also present. Piza and Fernández contend nothing of substance was discussed. Despite its supposed "social" nature, Piza's visit to the Oval Office was not listed on President Reagan's calendar, and the Costa Rican Embassy was not informed he was in Washington.

Fernández, however, said that the trip was CIA-approved. He testified that CIA "headquarters was fully aware of this invitation, the trip, the arrangements hour by hour." In addition, as North wrote to his boss, Admiral John Poindexter, President Reagan knew at the time that meetings such as this were intended to thank those who had collaborated with the covert contra supply network.[43]

While at the White House, Piza, Fernández, and North also met for about twenty minutes with Poindexter. Piza recalls, "I told him what I thought of the Nicaragua thing and all that. That," he added emphatically, "I call [a] social [visit]." Clearly not social was a meeting later that day at the Four Seasons Hotel in Washington, where Piza, Secord, Quintero, and Fernández discussed the landing strip.[44] Piza took the opportunity to tidy up some of the airstrip's paperwork. The late March visit took place only six weeks before Piza's and President Monge's departure from government and the May 8 inauguration of the pro-peace candidate Oscar Arias. Piza evidently wanted to be sure that the paper trail he left behind matched the airstrip's phony cover story. So, according to Joe Fernández and Quintero, they huddled together to draw up a letter to Piza from "Robert Olmsted" and typed it on Udall's rather crude stationery.[45] The letter, which was largely dictated by Piza and back-dated to December 19, 1985, stated that "Per your verbal request, the UDALL RESEARCH CORPORATION is pleased to make available to the Government of Costa Rica the use by the Government of the airfield at Potrero Grande area. It is our understanding that this area is needed for Civil Guard training and as an emergency alternate airfield for Murciélago." The letter concluded, "The period of this authorization will extend as long as UDALL RESEARCH CORPORATION is the owner in control of Hacienda Santa Elena."[46]

Southern Front Communications Center

As North's mid-March 1986 memo to Poindexter states, top Reagan administration officials were grateful to Piza for his help with other Southern Front projects as well. An even more closely guarded secret than the Santa Elena airstrip was a covert communications center to facilitate Washington's war but which, like the airstrip, was "sold" to President Monge and Piza as something vital to Costa Rica's security.

The "Quid Pro Quo" document released during the North trial states that "in August 1985, Costa Rican President Monge indicated to U.S. officials that he would be willing to provide assistance to the Resistance if the United States government would help fund a certain operation in Costa Rica. The U.S. officials concluded that the operation could be funded if President Monge would take certain specified actions to assist the Resistance." (After this document became public, an embarrassed Monge denied discussing the Santa Elena airstrip or U.S. help with another "project.")[47]

It seems likely that the "certain operation" referred to in the North document is the top-secret intelligence gathering facility for monitoring Nicaraguan communications and troop movements and coordinating aerial supply drops to the contras. Like the Santa Elena airstrip and Murciélago complex, this sophisticated listening post was proposed and financed by Washington and was used by Costa Rican security, the CIA, and the contras.

Former President Arias and others in his government say that officials from the Embassy and Washington—including Joe Fernández, Central American Task Force Director Alan Fiers, and NSC adviser Frank Carlucci—repeatedly pushed the project. According to one Arias government minister, "The argument was that since the Sandinistas can intercept all our communications why not allow the U.S. to do the same for the government of Costa Rica so we can know what is going on on the other side. They claimed that this is exactly a replica of what the Sandinistas were doing with East German assistance vis-a-vis Costa Rica. They presented it as if it was a favor. They said they wanted to help us a little."[48] In late November 1985, Congress agreed that the CIA would be granted $3 million to provide communications equipment and training to the contras,[49] and it appears that these funds were used to finance construction of the covert communications center.

In November 1986, Arias's Security Minister, Hernán Garrón, who had replaced Piza, admitted that the Directorate of Intelligence and Security (DIS) was running a communications tracking center on a hill near the northern Costa Rican town of Zarcero. Garrón made this admission after residents in the area complained of interference on their televisions and radios and reported spotting unidentified aircraft flying late in the day and at night in the area. Garrón said the installation was supplying information to the "executive power," the Civil and Rural Guard, and "other entities" he refused to identify. He announced that because of the complaints from local residents and for "other strategic reasons" the base would "soon" be relocated to a new location in San Carlos de Alajuela, closer to the northern border. The Security Minister declared that any further details about the center were "a state secret,"[50] and journalists who attempted to enter the remote, well guarded compound were refused permission.

Further details of this covert eavesdropping operation were revealed in the Iran-contra hearings testimony of Joe Fernández. According to the former CIA station chief, what he called "the Southern Front communications center" was constructed in late 1985 and was used in 1986 to coordinate supply drops to the Southern Front contras in both Nicaragua and Costa Rica. Fernández coordinated these drops from his office in the Embassy, using information received from the contra field commands and passed through the communications center. Fernández made the dubious argument that, despite the Boland amendment, this project and his participation in it were legal since the new "humanitarian" aid package signed by Reagan in August 1985 permitted the CIA to exchange information with the contras.

Fernández explained that he also obtained information from CIA headquarters in Washington, including "flight path information," weather reports, and the location of Sandinista troops (the "hostile risk situation"). He then communicated this package of information from the CIA and the contra field commanders to the "private benefactors" (the North-Secord pilots based at Ilopango Air Force Base) "who flew the airplanes to make the deliveries." He kept both North and Tambs informed about the outcome of each supply drop.

"Secure" communications between the contras and the North network were facilitated in January 1986, when North, with the approval of CIA Director William Casey and National Security Adviser Admiral John Poindexter, obtained fifteen KL-43 encryption devices from the National Security Agency. He distributed these computer-like machines to the main players involved in covert operations in the United States and Central America.

But as the months passed, Fernández and his bosses at the CIA became increasingly nervous about the legality of the Costa Rican station chief's role in the resupply operation. His nervousness increased when, on April 8, 1986, the Intelligence Oversight Board, which was appointed by the President to monitor the propriety and legality of covert operations, ruled that under the "communications" and "advice" provisions approved by Congress, the CIA and other U.S. agencies could "provide basic military training" to the contras, but they were barred from "participation in the planning or execution" of military actions. Fernández therefore moved to take himself out of the loop: he cooked up a plan for the CIA to train a Nicaraguan contra to "communicate directly with the clandestine communications center . . . and relay messages from the commanders . . . [and] the private benefactors. . . ." This plan involved setting up the newly trained contra communicator at a location outside the Embassy. According to Fernández, a contra was selected and trained in using the radio and coding/decoding equipment and given travel documents and visas for El Salvador and elsewhere in Central America. Contra sources confirm that ARDE's former chief radio operator, Ricardo Espinoza, was trained, and he worked out of a new location in the Central Valley under the direction of Felipe Vidal and another CIA operative, former Pastora commander Gustavo Peterson.

Fernández told the congressional panel that training a contra to handle communications for the supply drops seemed like an ideal solution, because the CIA "would be essentially cut out of the operation" but "we would still, of course, have received the information because we monitored the activities of the communication center since we were the communications advisors. So we still would have derived the benefit of the information transmission without having been involved in the actual passing of that information."[51] Thus by the time the Monge administration was preparing to leave office in May 1986, the North network had managed to finish constructing its two main contra infrastructure projects in Costa Rica: the Santa Elena airstrip and the clandestine communications center, successfully concealing their role in these operations.

THIRTEEN

The Success of Washington's "Project Pastora" and the Dismantling of the Southern Front

As the North-Secord network was beginning to cheer the relatively successful completion of the Santa Elena airstrip and construction of the clandestine communication center, it chalked up another triumph. On May 16, 1986, Edén Pastora and seventy-nine loyalists left the last bit of Nicaraguan territory they occupied, the small Morgan Islands in the middle of the San Juan River, and waded to the Costa Rican shore, where they deposited an arsenal of ancient, rusty weapons at the feet of Costa Rican Vice Minister of Security Rogelio Castro Pinto and a contingent of Civil Guardsmen.[1] Pastora, dressed in camouflage fatigues and carrying his field radio and a picture of Nicaraguan revolutionary hero Augusto Sandino, signed a neatly typewritten paper asking Costa Rica to give political asylum to him and his men. In return, he pledged he would permanently give up the armed struggle. The graying, bearded, forty-nine-year-old commander then positioned himself under the shade of a tree and told the group of about fifty journalists gathered in a sunbaked field that although on other occasions he had "suspended" his fighting for lack of supplies, "this is the first time we have decided to pull out of the armed struggle. We retire from the war because we think there is no possibility of military victory. We have been shut down by the CIA." He added, "We don't want to be soldiers of the United States, we want to be soldiers of Nicaragua. Ours is a nationalist war, a civil war, not a North Americans' war."

The night before, in an interview with the author and two other especially invited journalists, Pastora sat under the stars and detailed the events leading to his decision to quit his four-year contra war. Pointing up the darkened river, he explained Sandinista troops were encamped only a few kilometers away, but that he had had to spend more time recently in battles with Washington than with Managua: "I can no longer fight both the Sandinistas and the CIA at the same time." The CIA, he said, had cut off all his funds and supplies for the last two years, and in recent months several CIA agents had visited his camps to urge desertions. A week before, all but one of his field officers had switched alliance to Washington's newest creation, the FDN-controlled United Nicaraguan Opposition (UNO).

Deep in the bowels of the U.S. Embassy in downtown San José, at NSC and CIA headquarters up in Washington, and at John Hull's breezy ranch house in San Carlos, this was a moment for great celebration. It marked the successful conclusion of "Project Pastora," as Carlos Coronel termed Washington's three-year-long effort to remove Pastora from the contra war.

Pastora says he believes the plan originated with the three-member Restricted Interagency Group or the mini-RIG (or Riglet), which was also known as the Committee 208, after the room where they met. Pastora testified that "Arturo Cruz Jr. one time in a moment of sincerity, told me that Oliver North, Alan Fiers, and Elliott Abrams were part of an organization to try to eliminate . . . and to 'dry up' Pastora . . . to destroy me politically, morally and militarily.[2]

In Costa Rica, the campaign to "dry up" Pastora was led by Felipe Vidal and overseen by Joe Fernández, who, in his Iran-contra committee testimony, complained that the Agency had had "many . . . difficulties" with Pastora, and he went on to describe several. One was ARDE's September 1983 air attack on Managua when, at the last minute and without (Fernández claimed) CIA authorization, ARDE pilots changed targets and bombed Managua's international airport (see pp. 00–00).

Fernández cited another example of what he called Pastora's

"unthinking . . . unseemly behavior that made it impossible for us to deal [with him]":[3] the August 1985 capture by Southern Front contras of twenty-nine U.S. pacifists and a dozen international journalists who were on a two-day peace voyage down the San Juan River. Pastora was angered by the Witness for Peace mission because he believed the pacifists were pro-Sandinistas ("politicians disguised as shepherds of peace"), and he ordered his men along the river to shoot at the flotilla.

This is precisely what happened. Early on the morning of August 7, 1985, a band of contras fired shots across the bow of the forty-foot, flat-bottomed barge and forced the pacifists and members of the press to disembark onto the Costa Rican bank. After being held, unharmed, for a tense thirty hours, the delegation was permitted to continue their journey. The incident, however, caused considerable consternation, both within the Costa Rican government and the U.S. Embassy in San José, as well as in Washington, where Oliver North's diaries confirm that he was following the situation. A Costa Rican helicopter, two Civil Guard patrols, and three U.S. Embassy officials were dispatched to the border area to look for the pacifists. Joe Fernández telephoned Pastora, berating him, "Are you out of your mind? Do you realize that you are going to be labeled an international terrorist bandit?" Pastora relates that Fernández was most concerned about the safety of what he said were "several" of his own agents, who had infiltrated the Witness for Peace entourage and were among those kidnapped.[4]

Pastora says that the campaign to "terminate" him politically and economically involved "a thousand" different tactics. Beginning in May 1984, the CIA and North network refused to fund Pastora's ARDE faction,[5] and after La Penca they stole his helicopters, light planes, and vehicles and gave them to Hull, the FDN in Honduras, and Robelo's faction. Rumors were leaked to the press and Congress that Pastora (as well as Carol Prado) was involved in drug trafficking and the Spadafora murder. In addition, the Agency blocked aid from most other sources—from Cubans in Miami, private donors, Portugal, South Africa, and General John Singlaub, and other arms dealers. Most importantly, the CIA mounted a campaign to buy his field commanders out from under him.

The North network and CIA sought to win support by promising other Southern Front commanders, including Leonel Póveda, El Negro Chamorro, and Popo Chamorro, that they had been chosen by Washington to replace Pastora as military leader. One of the first offered Pastora's job was Popo Chamorro, who had been ARDE's liaison to the CIA in Costa Rica. In 1984, he had clashed with Pastora after becoming involved in CIA-authorized arms-and-cash-for-drugs deals with Colombian George Morales. He was expelled from Costa Rica in early 1985 after he described himself at a press conference as a top Southern Front military commander, an open affront to Costa Rica's neutrality policy.[6] In July 1985, Oliver North met with Popo and Leonel Teller, Pastora's chief representative in Washington, and offered ammunition, military supplies, uniforms, and $50,000 if Popo would muscle aside Pastora as the top military commander and convince Pastora to play a purely political role. Popo ultimately declined North's offer, probably because the near-starving troops were angry at the entire San José leadership, Popo included. Instead he settled in Miami where, after the UNO government took office in Nicaragua in 1990, he was appointed the new Nicaraguan consul.

North's July 1985 proposition to Popo was part of the broader plan to try to win over Pastora's commanders in the field by offering them economic and military support to switch en masse over to UNO/FDN. This operation was overseen by Fernández and Armando in San José, and carried out in the field by several of the Cuban assets, including Felipe Vidal, René Corvo, and Dagoberto Núñez, who were assisted by Popo Chamorro, Tito Chamorro, and Octaviano César. The CIA's plan was simply to weld Pastora's estimated 2,500–3,000 troops and the defecting commanders into the FDN and run military operations regionally out of Honduras.

In November 1985, several of Pastora's commanders met inside Nicaragua with some FDN commanders and, according to Fernández, "they wrote an agreement in the field that they would cooperate with each other, that they would share information and whatever supplies they could." Then, in December, Pastora's eight regional commanders met secretly in San José and wrote an impassioned appeal for a more democratic and collective administration of ARDE, better communications, and more equitable distribution of the organization's limited supplies. The commanders charged that 80 percent of the resources remained with the rear-based troops along the San Juan River, a claim denied by the commander of that zone. Alluding to Pastora's egocentric and high-handed leadership style, the commanders charged that a "lack of humility in the superior structure" along with "external forces" had led to "our organization's frank regression." They did not break with Pastora, but they demanded that he confine himself strictly to the political field and let his commanders run the war. Verbally, the commanders proposed a three-month waiting period before formally aligning with FARN and the FDN. They wanted to see if the CIA would really deliver supplies to them.

Fernández ordered the supply tap turned on. First, a column of seventy contras from the San Juan River was sent to make contact with Southern Front forces inside Nicaragua. Eight days after this column arrived in the zone, a DC-6 from Aguacate in Honduras airdropped knapsacks, boots, ponchos, and uniforms for a thousand men. Fifteen days later, the plane returned and dropped rifles, 200,000 rounds of ammunition, RPG rockets, and grenade launchers into one of the FARN camps. Over the next few weeks, several more drops were made. The supplies were then distributed "as bait" to those of Pastora's commanders and men who agreed to align with UNO. The CIA did not inform Pastora about these clandestine airdrops. During this same period Felipe Vidal and the Panamanian "Risa" (Victoriano Morales) made a trip by boat up Nicaragua's Atlantic coast, bringing money, 80,000 rounds of ammunition, and other supplies to another field commander in a bid to convince him to abandon Pastora.[7]

Singlaub Tries to Cut a Deal

By late March 1986, the Fernández-Vidal efforts seemed on the verge of successfully driving a wedge between Pastora and his field commanders. Then they hit a small but irritating snag in the form of retired Army Major General John Singlaub, who suddenly showed up in San José with a proposal to deliver supplies directly to Pastora. Singlaub, a covert-operations specialist and chairman of the U.S. branch of the World Anti-Communist League

(WACL),[8] wanted Pastora in return to align his forces with the UNO-FDN. By this point, however, North and his allies did not want Pastora to convert; they wanted him out of commission.

Singlaub seems to have been driven by both his ideological fervor to help the contra cause and his own business interests. Together with his partner, arms dealer Barbara Studley,[9] Singlaub had handled weapons sales for Calero and the FDN, and, with North's blessing, Singlaub had solicited contra funds from third countries and raised donations through the World Anti-Communist League. Following the July 1985 Miami meeting at which North and Secord maneuvered to take full control of the resupply system, Singlaub and other arms dealers were frozen out of any further sales to the Honduran-based contras. North piously testified that he took this action in an effort to cut down on corruption, even though Singlaub had been delivering weapons at about half the price charged by Secord. Cut out of Honduras, Singlaub turned his sights to Costa Rica, hoping to work a deal with Pastora.

Before heading for San José in late March, Singlaub met secretly in Miami with a recently organized group of contra dissidents and reformers, known as CONDOR (Nicaraguan Coalition of Opposition to the Regime). They gave him an English translation of their manifesto in which they complained that massive corruption by the contra leadership was preventing field commanders from effectively fighting the Sandinistas. CONDOR hoped to circumvent the contra hierarchy and CIA by going directly to Singlaub whom they viewed as leader of the private aid network. They wanted Singlaub to help secure arms and clean up contra operations.

In San José, Singlaub did not mention his conversations with CONDOR. Instead he said that he had met with Assistant Secretary of State Elliott Abrams and his staff and secured approval to attempt to convince Pastora to join the UNO alliance and remove himself as military commander, in return for sufficient U.S. military support for his troops.[10] Singlaub admitted he had not consulted with either North or CIA Director Casey and claimed he was unaware that the Agency had embarked on "a denigration campaign against Pastora." However, he added that he assumed that

Abrams would brief North and Casey and that "if this was not a good idea, someone would let me know."

On March 26, Pastora and Singlaub wrote the agreement, which Barbara Studley typed up in English. It stated that the "United States will provide Pastora with" eight items already being supplied to the FDN, including boots and uniforms, medicines, food, ammunition, "encrypted communications systems" (the KL-43), training advisers, and "all military needs for additional men joining his forces." The supplies were to come from UNO-FDN stockpiles. In return, Pastora agreed that his troops would depart "from the borders of Costa Rica," move into Nicaragua, and "willingly act in a co-operative and good-faith manner with the other elements of the Nicaraguan Resistance." Pastora himself agreed to become a roving contra ambassador, thereby removing himself as the Southern Front military commander.[11]

Upon learning of the agreement, Tambs, an old friend of Singlaub's, instructed it be sent to the mini-RIG (Abrams, Fiers, and North) via a highly restricted CIA "back channel," together with a cable from him which made no disclaimer of U.S. government involvement in the deal. This agreement accomplished the essence of what the CIA and North network proclaimed was their objective: to forge unity and remove Pastora as military commander. But when Tambs reported it, he was roundly reprimanded, in part because the cable left a dangerous paper trail of the Administration's illegal contra activities. But the real reasons were that North and his associates wanted Pastora out of the way altogether, and they did not want Singlaub or any other competitors negotiating arms deliveries to the contras. The response was swift and harsh.

Station chief Joe Fernández, who had been out of town when Singlaub arrived, became "extremely upset" when he learned of the cable. "[T]his whole Singlaub affair raised—was contradictory to strategy, policy and legality . . . to say nothing of the fact that we didn't want to give Pastora any encouragement whatsoever," Fernández told congressional investigators. In Washington, Abrams, giving no hint that he had ever endorsed Singlaub's mission, sent a strongly worded cable demanding that Tambs tell Pastora the agreement was canceled. He demanded that Tambs "inform Pastora that Singlaub is not authorized to negotiate on behalf of the United States [and] that the United States Government does not consider it is bound by Singlaub's agreement."

Tambs never informed Pastora, but Singlaub later told the ARDE commander that the CIA had stopped in Mexico the plane bringing the promised military supplies.[12] In the end, Carol Prado says, the only thing Pastora got from Singlaub was "the cheap pen" used for signing their agreement.

This episode marked the start of an ongoing conflict between Abrams and Tambs. Fernández testified, "I thought Tambs would not survive a month . . . and from then on their relationship went down hill." Shortly afterward, in July 1986, Tambs wrote the president of Arizona State University that he was planning to return and take up his teaching post in the spring of 1987. However, he hedged his bets and did not publicly announce his resignation until December,[13] just after three even bigger scandals broke: the public disclosure of the Santa Elena airstrip, the downing of the Hasenfus plane, and the admission by Attorney General Edwin Meese of the diversion of Iranian arms-sales profits to the contras.

The South African Connection

In the post–La Penca period, Pastora's most serious and substantial offer of help came from South Africa.[14] In November 1984, a high-level South African military delegation made a secret visit to meet with contra and Costa Rican officials. The five-member South African delegation was composed of Brigadier Alexander Potgieter, the defense and armed forces attaché at the South African Embassy in Washington, and four top intelligence and military officials from Pretoria. The visit was conducted under tight security, it received no press coverage, and the Legislative Assembly was not notified. The Costa Rican organizers say that Washington had approved the visit, although no U.S. Embassy officials participated in the San José talks.

The host for the delegation was Antonio Capella, a Costa Rican businessman who since 1969 had served as South Africa's consul general (the diplomatic equivalent of ambassador) in San José. Capella was also president of the Chamber of Basic Grain Producers, a large rice farmer, and, despite the international trade boycott against South Africa, an active promoter of economic links with Pretoria.[15] Also involved was Daniel Pacheco, vice president of the Basic Grains Chamber, a large rice grower and cattleman, and an arms supplier for the contras. Both men were said to be close to the U.S. Embassy; Pacheco told Pastora he worked for the CIA. He was subsequently arrested in a cocaine bust.

In a letter arranging the trip, Potgieter wrote to Antonio Capella that the purpose was to discuss "a threat originating from the same source, i.e. communist expansionism." The letter requested that the South Africans visit Costa Rican police and security forces' "security installations" and offered his country's expertise "on measures to counter propaganda and the accompanying psychological onslaught." The letter made no mention of meetings with the contras, which, Capella later explained, was the "real purpose" of the trip: "They said they wanted to know the situation and compare it to the guerrilla wars they were involved in."[16] Both Pastora and Robelo admit they held talks with South Africans to solicit aid.

For reasons of comfort and security, the delegation stayed at Capella's countryside villa, whose view is reminiscent of a gently rolling African savannah. After spending the morning with Pastora, the South Africans met with El Negro Chamorro and Alfonso Robelo at a barbecue luncheon beside Capella's swimming pool. That night Capella put on a party attended by contra collaborators such as Victor Wolf and Security Minister Piza. Capella recalls that President Monge informed him upon his arrival that "since he didn't speak English he was just going to get drunk—which he did."

One of the Costa Ricans involved described the South African delegation as "very professional [and] different from the CIA agents here who just gossip rather than analyze." Their discussions centered on two projects: financial and military support for the contras and the formation of a united front of right-wing guerrilla movements in Nicaragua, Angola, Mozambique, Ethiopia, Afghanistan, Laos, Cambodia, and Vietnam. The South Africans went on to Honduras to meet with FDN officials, and then they reported back their impressions and made their proposals.

Capella says that El Negro told the Pretoria delegation that he was "very interested" in getting some South African–made "mini tanks"—small armored vehicles with wide wheels especially designed for guerrilla warfare. In early 1985, the South Africans sent seven via Panama to Chamorro's main camp on the Santa Elena peninsula.

One participant in the talks, who asked to remain anonymous, says the Pretoria delegation was most impressed with Pastora, whom they equated with the South African–backed Angolan rebel leader Jonas Savimbi. "They were talking about supplying [Pastora's] Southern Front with whatever it needed—arms, money, etc. No amount was discussed, but it was clear it would be whatever was necessary," this person related. In early 1985, help for Pastora appeared to be en route. On January 5, North wrote in his diary that Clarridge had called, telling him that "200 T [tons] arms en route to C.R. from South Africa" and that the ship would be "offloading 70 t[tons]/night." But following a meeting of CIA officials in Central America, North wrote an entry on January 17 or 18 that the shipment should be transferred to the FDN: "Move S/A delivery from ARDE to FDN."[17] Pastora and his aides say no South African supplies ever reached them.

In March 1985, a Costa Rican businessman who supported Pastora went to South Africa to try to cut another deal. He was taken by helicopter to visit Savimbi in Angola and to Mozambique, where he met with an unnamed top leader of RENAMO, the notoriously brutal South African–backed counter-revolutionary movement. However, nothing concrete materialized out of this trip either. "Washington stopped the project. They [the Americans] did not like Edén," said the Costa Rican who traveled to South Africa.

In mid-1985, an international anticommunist front was officially forged without Pastora when FDN leader Adolfo Calero, along with Laotian Pa Kao Her and Afghani Colonel Ghulam Wardak, visited South Africa, also meeting with UNITA leader Savimbi in southern Angola. The trip was officially sponsored by conservative U.S. millionaire Lewis Lehrman, a Rite Aid drugstore heir and one-time New York gubernatorial candidate who in 1983 had founded the pro-contra lobbying group Citizens for America. Lehrman carried with him a letter of endorsement from President Reagan. The four right-wing rebel leaders announced the formation of the Democratic International to fight, they said, against "the Soviet Empire."[18]

Although there was no overt U.S. role in these South African negotiations with Southern Front contra leaders, the Reagan administration had embarked on an effort to enlist Pretoria in the war against Nicaragua. The earliest-known South African aid began in August 1983, when Safair Freighters, a South African air-freight carrier with ties to the Pretoria government, incorporated in New Jersey and began leasing two Lockheed Hercules L-100 aircraft and a C-130 transport plane to the CIA front company Southern Air Transport for supply runs to the contras.

In January 1984, the month Congress began debate to cut off aid to the contras, Casey and Dewey Clarridge met in Washington with a prominent South African official to discuss assistance. In April, Clarridge visited South Africa, but the timing was bad: he later testified that upon arriving he received word from CIA headquarters to "hold off" because of the "big hullabaloo" over the mining of Nicaragua's harbors. During this same period, Casey also urged Saudi Arabia to provide financial assistance to the UNITA rebels and the contras (they did, far more than any other country, to the tune of $32 million), as well as to facilitate oil deliveries to the South African government.

South Africa consistently denied providing any support to the contras. In fact, covert cooperation remained alive and South African assistance began to flow to the contras. It is likely that the South African military delegation's October 1984 visit to Costa Rica and Honduras, while ostensibly arranged by Costa Rican businessmen, was really part of these ongoing discussions between Pretoria and Washington.

In March 1986, Casey himself visited South Africa to discuss channeling U.S. weapons and intelligence data to UNITA and to confirm President Reagan's continued opposition to U.S. economic sanctions against South Africa. The CIA chief concluded a deal whereby South Africans and other "third country nationals" would be contracted to fly contra resupply missions out of Ilo-pango Air Force Base. A 1987 House Foreign Affairs Subcommittee on Africa staff paper on these dealings stated, "if true, they would indicate that the U.S. government directly and systematically violated the Clark Amendment [which, when in effect from 1976 until July 1985, barred covert aid to Angola] over a period of several years, and that a far more intimate—and insidious—relationship existed between the U.S. and South Africa than the American public was led to believe."[19]

In addition to the planes and pilots, Miami arms dealer David Duncan says that South Africa financed through a Liechtenstein holding company a $72 million military complex (including industries, port facilities, and a hospital) in Honduras, sold arms to the contras, and provided fifteen to twenty military trainers, pilots, and cargo handlers at Aguacate and Swan Island military bases in Honduras. Others were stationed at Ilopango.

According to published reports, Pretoria's aid to the contras involved several illegal quid pro quos, including Washington's resumption of covert support to the Angolan rebels and arms sales to South Africa.[20] It also involved a triangular arrangement with King Fahd of Saudi Arabia by which, beginning as early as 1981, the Reagan administration sold the Arab state AWAC reconnaissance aircraft in return for a Saudi agreement to provide oil to South Africa and to assist several of Washington's pet rightist movements, including eventually the contras.

From Fighter to Fisherman, Again

After Pastora's offers from South Africa, Portugal, Singlaub, and others had all fallen through, the beleaguered rebel leader received one other proposition, and his response was an indication of how desperate he had become. In early April 1986, David Sullivan, a legislative assistant for Idaho's conservative Republican Senator James McClure, flew into the reconstructed La Penca camp to meet with Pastora. An exceptionally tall man known as "Mad Dog" Sullivan, the congressional aide wanted Pastora to write a statement he could use to make a last-ditch effort to plead the comandante's cause in Washington. The statement contained Pastora's rebuttals to a number of the charges circulating around him: that he was involved in drug trafficking, that his top leadership was heavily infiltrated by the Sandinistas, and that he was anti-U.S. Pastora wrote, "We recognize the United States as our great ally and in the same way we hope that the U.S. Government will extend to us the same consideration."[21] But even this remarkably conciliatory April statement proved too little, too late. Washington operatives running the contra war were determined to get rid of Pastora once and for all, and they sensed success was near at hand.

Only with hindsight did it become evident that a curious incident in late April 1986 might be tied to the CIA's final move against Pastora. Sketchy press reports said that a private plane originating in Miami and carrying Popo Chamorro was seized by Costa Rican officials when it mistakenly landed on the Guanacaste farm of a Liberation party member of the Legislative Assembly. (According to press reports, its flight plan called for it to land in Limón.) Legislator Víctor Julio Román called the authorities because contra military leader Popo Chamorro had been officially expelled from the country in 1985. Chamorro claimed he was trying to enter the country so he could talk personally with President Monge about returning to Costa Rica and working in the political field for Alfredo and Octaviano César's organization, the Southern Opposition Bloc (BOS). Instead he was held for several days and then deported. The plane's other passenger, a Cuban American, was never arrested or identified in the press.

The mystery passenger was Nino Díaz, owner of the plane and a Bay of Pigs veteran with long CIA ties.[22] Carol Prado says he was tipped beforehand that Chamorro and Díaz were coming from Miami with a mission to sign (along with Joe Fernández, Vidal, and the César brothers) the new pact with Pastora's commanders and "make a coup against Edén." The plan was to name Popo Chamorro as the new military commander and Alfredo César as the new political chief. With Popo Chamorro expelled, the CIA operatives tapped their old standby, El Negro, for Pastora's job.

The clandestine ceremony was finally held on May 9, 1986. It was attended by six of Pastora's eight field commanders (Leonel, Oscar, Ganso, Navegante, Omar, and Pedro Rafa), who claimed to represent 4,500 combatants but really had about 1,500 fighters under their control. They signed a statement saying they were switching their alliance to FARN, under the banner of UNO-Southern Front. Also present were Alfonso Robelo, El Negro Chamorro, and other contra leaders, plus three "witnesses," all prominent conservatives who had closely collaborated with the contras. They were Joaquín Vargas Gene, a senior editor of *La República* (whose brother Carlos had been among the journalists most seriously wounded at La Penca), Oscar Saborio, owner of a grocery-store chain, and Enrique Villalobos, a loan sharker and black marketeer. The ceremony followed a week or more of long, heated meetings at a safe house in Escazú, during which several CIA men—the Colombian Armando, Felipe Vidal, Dagoberto Núñez, Octaviano César, and possibly Joe Fernández—bribed, cajoled, and strong-armed Pastora's commanders into aligning with UNO. They offered the Southern Front a slice of the $27 million "humanitarian" aid package; they promised them a chunk of the $100 million in military aid which appeared on the verge of being approved by Congress. (It passed in June.) They gave each one, once they had signed, $5,000 in cash for their personal use.

The signing ceremony illustrated the brazenness with which the contras violated Costa Rica's neutrality policy. El Negro and the other contra military leaders were officially barred from entering the country. President Arias had been sworn in just one day before, on May 8, on a pledge to stop contra operations inside Costa Rica and negotiate an end to the Nicaraguan war. The contra signing ceremony took place at a CIA safe house just a few blocks from Arias's home. This new alliance symbolized Washington's determination to keep the war going despite Costa Rica's new pro-peace president.

El Negro was named as the figurehead commander. It was, however, two of the Costa Rican–based UNO directors, Robelo and Arturo Cruz, Sr., who viewed themselves as the main beneficiaries. They hoped to be able to claim, for the first time, that they controlled the Southern Front forces and therefore have more clout vis-à-vis Adolfo Calero and the FDN forces. In addition, Alfredo César hoped his organization, BOS, would benefit.

Just a week after the signing ceremony, Pastora abandoned war. It was May 16, almost two years after the La Penca bombing.

He did not blame his troops or even his field commanders. Pastora was hurt, however, by the fact that many of his oldest colleagues and even some of his family turned against him. Pastora's older brother Félix became an aide to Arturo Cruz, Sr., and, using UNO funds, spread the story among Cubans in Miami that Edén was a communist. Pastora was particularly upset that longtime political and military allies such as Alfredo César, Popo Chamorro, Tito Chamorro, and José Dávila yielded, he said, to the CIA's maneuvers and money.

Pastora had expected to be granted immediate political asylum in Costa Rica. Instead, he had found himself in a new and unanticipated political predicament. The Costa Rican officials waiting on the riverbank arrested him and his seventy-nine fighters, loaded them into three tour buses, and carted them off. Pastora was taken to the aging Civil Guard barracks in the old capital city of Cartago; his loyalists were transported to several other detention centers. In the following days, at Rural Guard posts along the border, more poorly clad and ill-equipped ARDE guerrillas arrived, straggled across the river, surrendered their weapons, asked for asylum—and were arrested. In all, 158 fighters were detained. By the end of the month, the government had released these guerrillas on their own recognizance while their requests for political asylum were being studied.

Faced with his first political crisis, President Arias announced he would consider granting Pastora asylum if he promised to "stop being what he is today, one more comandante in the anti-Sandinista fight." The U.S. Embassy, however, applied pressure to have Pastora expelled to another country where he would have no chance of making a military or political comeback. As Costa Rican officials studied and debated the issue, Pastora was officially charged with two crimes: "hostile acts against the security of the country" and negligence in child support for one of his score of children born out of wedlock.

From his Cartago cell he met with a steady stream of journalists, former guerrillas, political associates, one-time financial supporters, prominent Costa Ricans, and a few Washington envoys. As the weeks passed, his patience grew increasingly thin. On May 30, the anniversary of the La Penca bombing, Pastora declared a hunger strike. Two days later, he received a telephone call from the Costa Rican Foreign Ministry saying the Arias government had agreed to grant him political asylum. Visibly relieved, Pastora called off the hunger strike, packed his few belongings, and walked out of prison into "retirement."

For the next several months, the war-weary and now relatively wealthy field commanders stayed in San José, enjoying the fruits of the deal with the CIA. ("It is a great drama. They fight with each other to pay the bills at the bars now," Pastora said bitterly.)[23] Pastora's departure marked the final death knell to any serious Southern Front contra activities. What forces remained either gradually came into Costa Rica as refugees or bandits, or grafted themselves onto the FDN's operations out of Honduras.

Meanwhile, Costa Rican authorities and the U.S. Embassy continued to keep a nervous eye on Pastora to assure that he did not try to return to the battlefield. But Pastora upheld his pledge to retire; he spent much of his time over the next several years running a fishing business at San Juanillo, a tranquil beach on a horseshoe-shaped bay along Costa Rica's Nicoya peninsula. The enterprise was a sort of retirement project for several dozen former contras, and it had many of the trappings of Pastora's contra operation. The contras-as-fishermen wore remnants of their military uniforms—cut-off khaki green pants, camouflage T-shirts, jungle caps. A number of their boats and their two-way, olive-green radios had been CIA issue to the guerrilla war. The setting itself looked like a contra camp, with several thatched huts, a communal kitchen, and the usual fare of rice, beans, fried plantains, and heavily sweetened black coffee. Pastora called himself "Cero," and the workers still addressed him as Comandante. Like his contra operation, Pastora's fishing business was poorly organized and ill-fated: for weeks on end the boat engines were broken, the sea was too rough, the fishermen were too hung-over, and the fish weren't running. Through it all, the graying guerrilla commander continued to scheme and dream of returning to his homeland, this time as leader of a new "third way" political movement. But after the Sandinistas were voted out and the opposition coalition, the "second UNO" (United National Opposition), was in office, Pastora remained in Costa Rica, saying he was tired of Nicaragua's turbulent political waters and preferred to cast his nets into the Pacific Ocean.

Creation of UNO and the Demise of FARN

With the covert signing ceremony in May 1986, the CIA and North network pledged to throw their support and some of their funds behind the UDN-FARN, the Costa Rican–based groups aligned with the FDN. (To a lesser extent they also supported Kisan-South, the Atlantic coast movement set up by the North network to exclude Brooklyn Rivera.) The publicly stated policy was to align FARN under the newest contra political-military umbrella group, the first UNO (United Nicaraguan Opposition or Unidad Nicaraguense Opositora), thereby unifying the Northern and Southern Fronts as Pastora had steadfastly refused to do. But the covert game plan was different. For months, CIA operatives had been carrying out policies which led to the dismantling not only of Pastora's and Brooklyn Rivera's military units, but also of those of El Negro's FARN.

The Southern Front commanders were integrated under the UNO umbrella, but this CIA-inspired contra coalition had more to do with winning votes in Congress than winning military battles inside Nicaragua. Efforts to build UNO had been underway for several years. Just after the November 1984 Nicaraguan election— in which the CIA had ordered Arturo Cruz, Sr., to run and then withdraw from the presidential race, leaving the field to the Sandinistas—North had proposed "longer-range planning for a Calero-Cruz coalition" that would eventually become a "liberation government" either in Costa Rica or, preferably, inside Nicaragua.[24] Although most international observers and journalists in Nicaragua for the elections accepted that, although held while the country was at war, they were free and democratic, President Reagan immediately branded them a "Soviet-style sham."[25]

During the early months of 1985, contra leaders, North, and his associates shuttled between Washington, Miami, and San José for intense negotiations about the new alliance and common political platform. As President Reagan was telling the American people that the contras were "the moral equal of our Founding Fathers,"[26] North, FDN leader Adolfo Calero, and other contras gathered in a

Miami hotel room to lay plans for an "elaborate legislative strategy" aimed at convincing Congress to resume contra aid. It included an anti-Sandinista and pro-contra propaganda blitz, a contra "peace" initiative, and the creation of the new umbrella organization, UNO. Rebel officials interviewed at the time complained this strategy was "dictated" by Reagan administration officials.[27]

The first step was the San José Declaration, signed March 2, 1985 by Honduran- and Costa Rican–based contra leaders to demonstrate their unity around a common political platform and to give, the document said, "a last option for the Sandinistas" to negotiate. Eighteen exiled political and military leaders endorsed the document, including Cruz, Calero, Robelo, Pedro Joaquín Chamorro, Jr., Steadman Fagoth, El Negro Chamorro, and Carlos Coronel. (One exiled official described the signers as "a coalition of the right and the ultra-right" who wanted "to return Nicaragua to the days of the dictator.")

The five-page declaration gave the Nicaraguan government just until March 20 to implement a series of sweeping (and at the time totally unacceptable) reforms, including a ceasefire, suspension of the state of emergency, restoration of civil liberties, and a general amnesty for political prisoners. It proposed a one-month period, beginning March 20, for a ceasefire, negotiations between the Sandinistas and contras around ten points, and the organizing of new elections. If the Sandinistas did not make substantial concessions by April 20, the rebels vowed to end any dialogue and intensify the guerrilla war.

This was no serious negotiating proposal. It was pure p.r., a ploy aimed at winning more congressional aid to expand the war. In an interview just days before the ceremony, Robelo termed the new unity document "a final take-it-or-leave-it" ultimatum to the Sandinistas. Cruz was even more blunt, terming the document "simply something on behalf of motherhood and apple pie." The Nicaraguan government refused to allow Cruz to enter Managua to deliver the document, and President Daniel Ortega quickly dismissed the proposal, saying that his government would only negotiate with "the puppet master" (the Reagan administration) and not with the "puppets" (the contras).

Not among the signatories were Edén Pastora and Brooklyn

Rivera. Rivera was in the process of trying to negotiate with the Sandinistas his own peace settlement for the Atlantic coast, an effort CIA and North operatives were actively trying to disrupt. By late May Washington's covert operatives had, they believed, succeeded. A secret May 31 memo from North to McFarlane reported that "after nearly two months of careful coordination with Rivera, he agreed on Saturday to break-off his discussions with the Sandinistas."[28]

Pastora had announced his interest, under certain conditions, in supporting the agreement. But because Pastora was officially barred from entering Costa Rica, he could not attend the signing ceremony. Pastora suspected that the location was chosen purposely to block him from joining the new pact. Several days later Pastora and Alfredo César, who also did not sign the San José Declaration, announced the formation of the Southern Opposition Bloc (BOS), a supposedly independent movement supported by the Socialist International. In reality, though, most of its funds came from the CIA.[29]

Curiously, Calero was present at the San José Declaration signing ceremony, despite the fact that he, like Pastora, was classified as a military leader and could not legally enter Costa Rica. However, the CIA's man of the hour, Security Minister Piza, defied directives from Monge and two fellow ministers and ordered security officials to permit the signing ceremony and Calero's participation in it. The next day the local press carried photos of the smiling Alfonso Robelo, Arturo Cruz, and Adolfo Calero at the ceremony.[30]

In the wake of the San José Declaration and as Congress debated a new aid package, North decided it prudent to refrain from any contra military actions, because it might appear that the rebels were breaking their own ceasefire proposal. But contrary to North's instructions, on April 16, René Corvo, along with mercenary Steven Carr and a handful of contras, carried out a cross-border raid against the Nicaraguan hamlet of La Esperanza, and on April 23 and 24 the House narrowly voted down both the Administration's proposal and a congressional compromise plan. North's operatives blamed the defeat on wild-card Corvo and the undisciplined mercenaries. Overnight Corvo fell from grace and was marginalized, and, on April 25, Carr and the other foreign mercenaries were arrested, perhaps on CIA orders so as to prevent any future free-lance ventures.

Despite this glitch in North's strategy, in June 1985 Congress finally approved $27 million in "humanitarian" aid, the first official U.S. aid to the contras since funds had run out in late 1984. Passage was helped both by the announcement that Cruz, Robelo, and Calero would jointly head the new UNO umbrella movement and by Nicaraguan President Ortega's unfortunately timed "Moscow trip," which was vigorously condemned by Washington. (In reality, this was a long-scheduled twelve-nation European visit to solicit foreign aid and oil.) Reagan signed the contra aid bill into law in August and by executive order created a new State Department unit, the Nicaraguan Humanitarian Assistance Office (NHAO), to handle the purse and delivery of the nonlethal supplies to UNO. Robert Duemling, described in the *Iran-Contra Affair* report as "a seasoned diplomat, but with no prior experience in administering an aid program," was named NHAO director. Elliott Abrams was responsible for day-to-day policy guidance.[31]

Although NHAO was created specifically to avoid the CIA's being involved in the aid deliveries, North immediately began utilizing this new "humanitarian" system for channeling weapons to the contras and lucrative contracts to Owen, Gadd, and their other business associates. As congressional and press investigations subsequently revealed, the contras on the ground devised a myriad of scams for ripping off funds, including exchanging the money on the local black markets and illegally selling the food and medical supplies. Some of the funds went into offshore bank accounts of contra leaders in the Bahamas, Cayman Islands, and elsewhere and to pay bribes to top Honduran military officials. From top to bottom the "humanitarian" aid program served as a financial windfall for the North network and certain contra leaders.

In addition, UNO directors Calero, Cruz, and Robelo—who became known as the "Triple A" because their first names all started with A—were all on a secret payroll managed by North and passed through one of Calero's bank accounts. Calero received $12,500, Robelo $10,000, and Cruz $7,000 per month, an indication of the skewed power balance within the organization. About forty other UNO staff members, consultants, and collaborators (such as Hull, who received $10,000 per month) were also on covert salaries arranged by North. Within UNO, Pedro Joaquín Chamorro, Jr., the former editor of Nicaragua's opposition newspaper *La Prensa*, served as information director. In November 1984, apparently on orders from the CIA, Pedro Joaquín moved to San José to edit the pro-FDN syndicated newspaper supplement *Nicaragua Hoy* ("Nicaragua Today"). Another key UNO operative was Arturo Cruz, Jr., a close CIA and North confidant who arranged meetings for Southern Front contras in Washington. He also helped to establish an UNO office and residence for his father in San José.

Robelo, Cruz, Sr., and Chamorro all maintained homes in San José, and UNO's headquarters were officially in the Costa Rican capital, but real power within the alliance remained with Calero and the Honduran-based FDN. Calero exercised control over the FDN's estimated 12,000 to 15,000 contras, while Robelo and Cruz, both of whom had separated from Pastora, had no combatants. Robelo and Cruz therefore argued that political decisions should determine military strategy and not the other way around.

But this never happened. Within months of UNO's formation Cruz was threatening to quit, bitterly complaining that he was being used as simply "a fig leaf" for Calero and the FDN. Robelo had similar complaints. In an August 1985 memo to North, Owen reported that Robelo told him, "I'm tired of the lack of equivalency in the Triple A. Cruz and I were integrated into the FDN to clean their face."

Yet as Owen laid out in a frank memo to his boss, UNO was intended to be an unequal alliance, dominated by the FDN and directed by the U.S. government. In a March 1986 memo entitled "Overall Perspective," with a section on the "FDN/UNO Political Situation," Owen wrote, "I put it as FDN/UNO because the FDN is now driving UNO, not the other way around. UNO is a creation of the USG [U.S. government] to garner support from Congress. When it was founded a year ago, the hope was it would become a viable organization. In fact, almost anything it has accomplished is because the hand of the USG has been there directing and manipulating."

Owen continued, "No doubt the hope was Cruz and Robelo would turn into strong leaders to somewhat counter-balance the strength of Calero and the FDN. Both Cruz and Robelo have been disappointments. Calero, on the other hand, has used his strength and will and the FDN to further consolidate his hold on the resistence [sic] and to gain control of UNO. Perhaps UNO is the correct acronym, for there is only one leader in the Democratic Resistence [sic], Adolfo Calero." He added, "As long as the USG understands this to be true, then it can go forward with planning."[32]

Calero, for his part, extended his control into Costa Rica even though he was officially persona non grata. Not only was the Hull-Cuban network already aligned with the FDN, but Calero also handpicked which Southern Front contras were to receive financial support. As Owen wrote North as early as April 1985, "Sparkplug [Calero] has decided to go with El Negro Chamorro as the military commander of the South." Based on this the North network stated its intent to channel funds to FARN, but only after FARN underwent considerable reorganization.

FARN leaders were told the plan was to increase by early 1986 the number of their combatants from several hundred to several thousand by absorbing Pastora's defecting troops, to move these guerrillas inside Nicaragua, and to displace Pastora's remaining fighters. The problem was that the operatives handling the war did not fully trust FARN—either its unstable leader, El Negro Chamorro, military commander José "Chepón" Robelo, or political adviser Carlos Coronel. Owen accused José Robelo of black-marketeering and of ordering the torture and execution of a FARN prisoner; he described Coronel as "the manipulator behind the scenes [who] is pulling everyones [sic] strings."[33] The real "crime" of both Chepón and Coronel, however, was their past ties to Pastora and unwillingness to fully accept CIA control. FARN officials say that Chepón had successfully built up El Negro's forces to close to 500 by October 1985. But he clashed with Station Chief Joe Fernández, accusing the CIA of interfering with military operations and failing to furnish adequate military hardware.

While FARN suffered from a myriad of problems—El Negro's heavy drinking, lack of leadership and military incompetence; widespread corruption; connection with Corvo and other Miami

Cubans involved in drug trafficking—these were largely ignored as CIA handlers zeroed in on the "problem" of Coronel, Chepón Robelo, and other suspected Pastora loyalists. The proposed solution was to require all top FARN military, political, and administrative officials to take lie-detector tests to gauge their loyalty to UNO (that is, the FDN) and to weed out "Pastoristas." The official story, however, was that the CIA was looking for Sandinista infiltrators. FARN was told the tests were a prerequisite to reorganizing its leadership, creating a new military command structure, receiving U.S. "humanitarian" aid funds, and expanding the Southern Front. Between September 1985 and March 1986, about forty FARN officials were ordered to take the tests, which were given at several CIA-contra safe houses.[34]

A half dozen FARN officers interviewed about the test said its real purpose was a crude attempt to intimidate FARN and other anti-Sandinista leaders and force them to accept more stringent CIA control. Said Miguel Chibel, FARN's chief of logistics, who quit soon after being forced to take the test, "I believe the objective was to weed out people who are less than obedient. The CIA is scared of the Southern Front because it has had a more dignified and independent position [than the FDN in the north]. We accept U.S. advisers and aid, but not people who come to give orders." Added FARN's second-in-command Juan Zavala, who repeatedly refused to take the test, "What right has the CIA to say who can and who cannot be a contra?" Those interviewed described the procedures as degrading (CIA agents strapped a belt around the subject's chest and attached sensors to his fingertips), and they dubbed the polygraph machine *la chimichu,* the name of an electric-shock torture instrument used in dictator Somoza's prisons.

The CIA's compulsory polygraph program had disastrous repercussions on FARN's already weak organization, but this may well have been the Agency's and North network's real intent. FARN's ex-accountant Roger Monge says he became convinced that "the CIA's objective was to destroy FARN." He and others said that the CIA failed, as well, to provide air cover or supplies for the FARN forces that it forced to move inside Nicaragua and that the CIA set up raids by Costa Rican gaurdsmen against FARN military personnel and installation inside Costa Rica. One FARN official related that in late 1985 or early 1986, "Costa Rican security who captured our radio repeater and the captain in charge of the raid told us the gringos had given the location. The communications network was our lifeline in terms of military commands and control." Another former FARN official concluded, "The [the CIA] decided they did not want to struggle in the South"

U.S. officials, of course, painted a different picture, blaming FARN's demise on contra incompetence. Joe Fernández testified to the Iran-contra panel that he had hoped to build FARN up to about 2,500 guerrillas by early 1986.[35] Instead, virtually all the top leadership quit or was removed, and El Negro simply named himself and FARN official Ulises Fonseca to fill the vacancies. After Chépon was removed, most of FARN's troops deserted. By March 1986, FARN's forces numbered less than twenty, and the organization never recovered.

Ironically, however, during this period when the CIA's polygraph program and other manuevers were dismantling FARN, El Negro's organization was receiving increased amounts of U.S. funds. Nearly $2 million was earmarked for nonlethal supplies for the South, although much of it never left Miami and some of that which came to Costa Rica was used, illegally, for arms purchases and to buy off Pastora's commanders with gifts and military hardware.

According to the General Accounting Office report, there were business irregularities at all levels, and when auditors finally scrutinized the accounts, millions were missing. Among the "humanitarian" aid purchases, for instance, were color televisions, volleyball uniforms, and living-room sets. There was also an intertwining of the nonlethal supplies with the covert, illegal contra military supply network. NHAO chief Duemling admitted that, on orders from Under Secretary of State Elliott Abrams, he twice authorized his planes to carry to the contras "mixed loads" of lethal and nonlethal supplies.[36]

In addition, NHAO awarded contracts to a number of companies and individuals involved in North's network, several of whom were also simultaneously being investigated for drug trafficking. NHAO hired, for instance, at least three air cargo companies—

the Honduran-based Setco Aviation and two Miami-based firms, DIACSA and Vortex Inc.—which were at the time under federal investigation for drug trafficking. (DIACSA was partly owned by José Angel Guerra, a Costa Rican businessman involved in arms supplies for the contras.) When reporter Brian Barger asked why these firms were being used, State Department officials responded that "they had been told to hire these companies by the 'boys across the river,' meaning the CIA."[37]

Robert Owen was among those who personally benefited from the "humanitarian" aid, even though he was deeply involved in procurement of weapons and military equipment for the contras. NHAO awarded Robert Owen $50,675 in consulting fees between September 1985 and May 1986; a State Department official told CBS television that Owen's job with NHAO "was a payoff" for his work as North's courier. During this time, Owen arranged for NHAO planes to carry military supplies to the contras. The Iran-contra panel concluded that North "exploited" Owen's position "by using his trips, funded by humanitarian aid dollars, to transfer and receive information about the contra war and the fledgling resupply operation."

In addition, Richard Gadd's company, AIRMACH, received at least $487,000 in classified NHAO contracts to transport nonlethal supplies to the contras. The contracts were requested by Abrams, North, and Owen. North personally accompanied Gadd to meet Duemling and urge that he be awarded an NHAO contract. Air Mach in turn hired Southern Air Transport to fly "humanitarian" aid down to Ilopango, where the planes were reloaded with military supplies to be airdropped to the contras inside Nicaragua.[38]

The bulk of NHAO funds intended for Central America was deposited in Miami bank accounts controlled by contra leaders and businessmen, who were expected to use it to reimburse Costa Rican and Honduran suppliers. NHAO officials in Washington, however, were able to verify to GAO investigators only $8.4 million out of the total $17 million reported as spent on goods and services in the region.[39] Further, GAO investigators discovered that many of the covering receipts were phony, indicating that an even greater, undetermined amount was unaccounted for. Following GAO and press revelations of apparent corruption, the House

Foreign Affairs Committee subpoenaed records from fourteen of the U.S. bank accounts. According to GAO testimony examination of these records " 'for the most part only raised more questions,' " including evidence indicating that " 'humanitarian assistance may not be reaching the intended beneficiaries.' " A senate report concluded, "The relationship between contra suppliers and U.S. funds supporting the contras has been fraught with the appearance of deceptive business practices and false invoicing as standard operating procedure."[40]

This clearly was the case in Costa Rica. FARN purchases made in Costa Rica were handled by Ulises Fonseca, who became the chief administrator for the U.S. "humanitarian" aid funds. He submitted receipts to the NHAO office, and funds were then deposited in the Miami bank account of Iván Fonseca, Ulises's brother, who acted as FARN's broker. U.S. officials cited by the *Miami Herald* said FARN received $1.87 million, based on its claim that it was purchasing supplies for three thousand guerrillas. At the time it made the claim, however, FARN had no more than sixty-five combatants.[40]

Ulises Fonseca was in charge of the bookkeeping: collecting receipts for various purchases in Costa Rica, paying bills, and filing financial claims with NHAO. NHAO itself had no representative based in Central America to provide oversight to the aid disbursement. According to FARN's chief accountant, Roger Monge, El Negro and Fonseca conspired to falsify the accounts they submitted to NHAO. In an interview in 1986, Monge said, "All the receipts were collected in October [1985] in blank form" in anticipation that FARN was about to receive a portion of the "humanitarian" aid. Another rebel source concurred, saying that as soon as the $27 million was approved, "we began to get blank receipts from all over the place."

In San José, Ulises and Iván Fonseca's family business, Farmacía San Luis, was listed as one of the largest recipients of contra business. According to NHAO records, FARN spent $47,853 at the pharmacy during a three-month period in late 1985 and early 1986. Ulises Fonseca told the *Miami Herald* that such large purchases were necessary because the rebels were stocking a clinic and supply warehouse.[42] Not only does this constitute a clear conflict of interest for the Fonseca brothers, but sizable purchases of medicines should not have been necessary, since NHAO had awarded its largest contract, $3.75 million, to Project Hope to buy medicines in the United States and ship them to the contras.

One of the most popular places for collecting receipts was the muddy border hamlet of Upala, where most of FARN's dwindling forces were based. NHAO records contain one receipt, for example, showing that FARN had purchased $26,766 worth of food-stuffs at Upala's Abastecedor El Puente. The large, one-room shop sells only clothing, not food, and its owner, Coralía Valverde, said in a June 1986 interview that she had sold the contras only about $360 worth of clothing. "At no time did I receive that kind of money from them," she said.

Similarly, according to NHAO records, a tiny Upala pharmacy sold FARN foodstuffs and medicines valued at $16,764, all on November 6, 1985. Like El Puente, however, it sells no foodstuffs, and its proprietor, Judith Sánchez Alfaro, said, "I never made out receipts that big. As you can imagine, such a sale would have taken almost all our merchandise."

The only Upala store where employees admitted to doing a massive business with FARN was the Almacén Upala, which stocks both food and clothing. According to NHAO records, the store sold $50,211 worth of goods to the contras in late 1985. Records kept by FARN accountant Monge, however, show the store only sold FARN about $10,000 worth of supplies in that period. Ex-FARN members said that Almacén Upala maintained "an open line of credit" for over-invoicing and covering personal expenses for certain FARN leaders.

Then there was the case of Frigoríficos de Puntarenas, the Costa Rican–based frozen-seafood exporting company, which, on the recommendations of Oliver North and Robert Owen, received a $261,937 contract from NHAO.[43] Not only is a seafood company an odd choice to handle contra supplies but its Miami-based sister company, Ocean Hunter, was being investigated at the time by federal law enforcement agencies for involvement in cocaine traf-ficking. Two owners of these companies, Francisco Chánes and Luis Rodríguez, were subsequently convicted of cocaine trafficking. Senate investigators determined that $206,399 in NHAO funds were transferred from Miami to the Frigoríficos account in San José. A portion of these funds was used for illegal weapons shipments to contras connected with Kisan-South, the North network's Atlantic coast creation.[44]

In yet another case, GAO and Justice Department officials discovered that $25,870 supposedly spent on a thousand sets of T-shirts, jeans, and rubber boots was actually diverted in January 1986 by a "CIA employee"—Felipe Vidal, according to contra sources—to purchase military supplies for Kisan. Reporter Tim Golden interviewed two managers of Creaciones Fancy, a "closet-sized discount clothing store" where the clothing purchases were allegedly made. The managers related that three men had come to the store to inquire about prices and collect blank receipts, but ultimately purchased nothing. One of the three was later identified as Robert Owen.[45]

In early 1986, a group of contra reformers, known as CON-DOR, drafted a document denouncing this and other forms of corruption. A Senate investigator who interviewed several signatories of the document wrote, "The fundamental complaints of the reformers are [that] after five years and nearly $200 million they [the contras] hold not one square inch of Nicaragua. They compare their situation unfavorably to the Salvadoran guerrillas, a much smaller force with much less money, which controls up to a quarter of El Salvador."[46] Contras who provided press, congressional, and GAO investigators with details of the "humanitarian" aid scandal charged that virtually the entire contra leadership—the "Miami mafia"—was corrupt. Javier Gómez Ortega, a contra commander who resigned in March 1986, told the *New York Times* that the rebel leaders "don't want to win—it's too profitable. They don't want to see it end. They're doing too well."[47] Ron Rosenblith, an aide to Senator John Kerry who was involved in investigations of contra and North network illegalities, echoed these sentiments. "The contras don't want to win," he said. "They have a big business in supplies and drugs and guns, and they're not interested in risking the business [by doing serious fighting]," Rosenblith told United Press International.[48]

Beginning in mid-1984, the CIA and North network abandoned plans to build "Honduras South," that is, a large contra guerrilla force operating out of Costa Rica which paralleled the FDN in Honduras. Ambassador Tambs' mission was not, as he testified, to build the Southern Front; it was rather to dismantle the existing contra armies led by Pastora, Brooklyn Rivera, and even El Negro Chamorro, all of whom were never fully trusted by the Americans. The contras, under the umbrella of FDN/UNO, were to be based in Honduras and to penetrate into Nicaragua from the north. Left in tact inside Costa Rica were the operations of John Hull, Felipe Vidal, their cronies, and a handful of FDN contras. Their main mission was to provoke Sandinista aggressions and attacks against unarmed, neutral Costa Rica and thereby provide the pretext for the U.S. to escalate the war. The Hull/Vidal network, in turn, used their CIA protection to profiteer through financial rip-offs, black marketeering, and arms and drug trafficking. Costa Rica continued to play a distinct role in Washington's regional infrastructure for the war against Nicaragua. It became the most important political, propaganda and communications base in Central America. It housed the VOA sation, Radio Impacto, *Nicaragua Hoy,* the clandestine communications center, and the dozens of contra political and civic organizations. The Santa Elena airstrip was built as part of the region-wide contra resupply operation and Costa Rica's humanitarian traditions and good public health system were put to the service of wounded contras and Nicaraguan refugees. But, beginning in May 1986, the multifaceted U.S. game plan for Costa Rica suddenly faced a formidable challenge: Oscar Arias and the Central American Peace Plan.

FOURTEEN

Arias: Making Peace

Arias, more than any other Latin leader, single handedly undid U.S. policy in Nicaragua.
—High-level State Department official, 1988

I propose to show the world that, small and poor as my Costa Rica may be, we can have our own ideas, independent judgment, autonomy and dignity.
—Oscar Arias, August 1988[1]

By May 1986, the month the Arias administration took office, U.S. policy was on something of a roll in Costa Rica: Pastora was out of the way; human assets and physical infrastructure were in place and functioning; and Congress was on the verge of renewing military aid to the contras. But just as things looked promising for those running the U.S. war against Nicaragua, the Reagan administration's clandestine operation began to come unraveled.

Blow No. 1: The Arias Victory

On February 2, 1986, Oscar Arias, Costa Rica's first "peace candidate," won the presidential election. It was a victory the Reagan administration had neither wanted nor predicted. On the eve of the election, as Costa Rica's leading pollsters were terming the race "a real squeaker" and "too close to call," Embassy officials were quietly but confidently predicting that their preferred candidate, Rafael Angel Calderón, would be the victor.

Calderón, a center-right lawyer from the conservative Social Christian Unity party, also had the backing of the major Costa Rican media, big business, and the country's sizable Nicaraguan exile and contra community. (He had grown up in Nicaragua and his *padrino* was the deposed Anastasio Somoza.) He capitalized on the political legacy of his father, a populist president in the early 1940s credited with beginning many of Costa Rica's social welfare programs. He adopted a stridently anti-Sandinista posture, pledging opposition to Monge's Neutrality Proclamation and vowing to send Costa Rican guardsmen to fight alongside the Honduran army in the event of a Sandinista attack on that country.

In a variety of ways, Washington had quietly assisted Calderón's candidacy. The Republican party had helped finance his campaign, the CIA sent an operative, a Puerto Rican named José Luis Fernández (the second Joe Fernández) to lend his services, and Reagan invited Calderón to Washington for a photo opportunity while turning down Arias's request for a similar visit. Calderón had similar photo ops with conservative British Prime Minister Margaret Thatcher and Pope John Paul II.

But Arias won anyway. At forty-five, he became Costa Rica's youngest president; one of his vice presidents was, for the first time, a woman; and Arias played on the generational theme, building his support around the "young Turks" within the Liberation party. His victory was due in part to Monge's perceived success in pulling Costa Rica out of the depths of economic crisis.[2] Arias's victory upset the almost unbroken precedent of the incumbent party's being voted out of office every four years. On only one other occasion in the post–World War II period, the Liberation party victories in 1970 and 1974, had the candidate from the party in power won a presidential election.

However, it was the peace issue that ultimately set the Arias candidacy apart and brought his administration to loggerheads with the Reagan administration. Initially, peace appeared to be simply an Arias campaign tactic; the Embassy seemed convinced, should Arias win, they could bring him into line. Only gradually did the full implications of Arias's peace position become apparent. His peace platform declaring that contra activities would not be tolerated inside Costa Rica and pledging his support for negotiations to end the region's conflicts was not adopted until the latter stages of his year-long campaign for the presidency.

He was encouraged to put peace in his platform by Joe Napolitan, a seasoned New York–based political consultant who met with the Arias campaign team in September 1985. Until this point, Arias had been trailing in the polls and there was little to distinguish him from Calderón. Both candidates had stressed their dislike for the Sandinistas. Napolitan looked at Costa Rica's public-opinion surveys and gave his advice: play down domestic economic issues and play up peace.

Arias walked a political tightrope, careful not to appear pro-Sandinista or anti-U.S. He began to talk about the need to learn to live with one's neighbors and not give armed contras "hospitality" inside Costa Rica. This message immediately found popular appeal. In October the Liberation party put out a pro-peace series of newspaper ads and shortly afterward Arias moved ahead in the polls. It was a lead he held through the election.

As election day neared, Calderón sought to soften some of his most hawkish stands. It was all to no avail. Arias won 54 percent of the vote to Calderón's 45 percent. The Liberation party also gained a majority, with twenty-nine seats, in the Legislative Assembly, the Unity party won twenty-five, and the two leftist parties got one seat each.

In his victory speech and earliest postelection interviews, Arias clearly signaled that peace, neutrality, and negotiations would become central themes of his presidency. He pledged that Costa Rica would be "inflexible with the contras," adding that "the solution to problems in the area is dialogue." While expressing ideological opposition to the Nicaraguan government, Arias continued, "One does not choose one's neighbors. They are there and we have to learn to live with them." He added that Costa Rica should become "an agent of peace and catalyst of solutions" rather than "part of the problem in Central America."

Arias was the embodiment of Costa Rica's strongest values and traditions. He was a staunch constitutional democrat and civil libertarian, but also an anticommunist and sharp critic of the leftist Sandinista government. He believed that problems could be solved through rational discourse and dialogue, and he had a somewhat smug self-assurance that Costa Rica was the model that other Latin American nations should emulate. Indeed, his peace plan was aimed both at preventing the region's troubles from further undermining Costa Rica's way of life and at exporting Costa Rica's political and social system to the other countries of the isthmus.

The Arias victory came at an inopportune time for the Reagan administration, which was vigorously pushing for congressional approval of a $100 million contra aid package. This was to be the first military aid package since passage of the 1984 Boland amendment, and the last thing the administration wanted was for Central American leaders to speak out against aid to the rebels or the war against Nicaragua.

Less than two weeks later, however, in his first in-depth interview for U.S. television the president-elect came out against the $100 million contra-aid package: "If I were Mr. Reagan, I would give the money to Guatemala, El Salvador, Honduras and Costa Rica for economic aid, and not military aid to the contras," he told John McLaughlin, host of the syndicated program "One on One." He added, "I don't think that with the aid [Reagan] is going to obtain what he wants. On the contrary, the result of the aid to the contras has been a more dictatorial, more totalitarian government in Nicaragua."

Just after the "One on One" interview aired, AID failed to deposit a scheduled $15 million payment into the Costa Rican government's account at the New York branch of Manufacturers Hanover Trust. Several high-level Costa Rican government officials termed the delay "a direct punishment" for Arias's open opposition to contra aid. There were other repercussions as well. In early March, the Embassy and State Department and *La Nación* began circulating a public-opinion poll to "prove" that Costa Ricans and other Central Americans favored U.S. military aid to the contras, and that president-elect Arias was out of step with popular sentiment. The multicountry poll, carried out over a number of months in mid-1985, showed that 69 percent of those Costa Ricans surveyed and between 52 percent and 55 percent of respondents in Honduras, Guatemala, and El Salvador favored U.S. aid to the contras.

At least the Costa Rican portion, was, however, both outdated and misleading.[3] It was based on a public-opinion sampling of eight hundred people carried out in Costa Rica just after the May 31, 1985, Las Crucitas border incident. According to Arias pollster Víctor Ramírez, "This was a hyper-tense time and completely different from other periods." Further, this poll by CID (Interdisciplinary Consultants on Development), a Gallup affiliate, asked only about "humanitarian" and not military aid to the contras. Most importantly, subsequent polls not circulated by the State Department indicated a far lower level of support for such aid. Polls done by the Liberation party found that only 9.5 percent of Costa Ricans supported contra aid, while nearly 80 percent were opposed. Even a CID poll, done in November 1985 only in Costa Rica, showed that just 39 percent of those surveyed supported contra aid. This poll was not distributed by the U.S. Embassy or State Department.[4] Thus even before Arias was sworn in, he was involved in political warfare with Washington.

Oscar Arias was born in 1941, just as Costa Rica's social welfare system was beginning to be constructed. His mother came from one of the wealthiest coffee-growing families in the town of Heredia, the seat of the country's oldest university. His father, in contrast, was from a much poorer family, but through hard work and good marriage rose, so the story goes, from rags to riches.

He grew up in a tradition of public service. His grandfather had been a government minister, and his father directed the Central Bank. His father also instilled in him a lifelong love of books. "I am a man of books," Arias explained in an interview; according to his wife, he sleeps only four or five hours a night in order to find time to read.

After a year and a half at Harvard Medical School, Arias dropped out because he could not stomach dissections. He returned to the University of Costa Rica to study law and economics. In 1967, he won a British government scholarship to the London School of Economics and Essex University, where he obtained a master's degree and, in 1974, a Ph.D. in political science. His doctoral thesis was entitled, "Who governs in Costa Rica?" Arias never doubted that one day his name would be included. The quote underneath his first-year photo in the 1967 University of Costa Rica Law School yearbook reads, "I'm studying to be president."

Upon his return to Costa Rica, Arias began a methodical climb toward this political pinnacle. In addition to teaching political science at the university and writing a series of academic books, he became vice president of the Central Bank, Minister of Planning twice, and then a legislator. In 1979 and again in 1983, he was elected Secretary General of the National Liberation party. He resigned in 1984 to begin his political campaign.

Just as Arias saw his studies as preparation for the presidency, so he saw his academic training as influencing his style of government. During the campaign he said in an interview, "My life has been academics, the university and politics. I would like to take with me into the political arena the rigor and honesty of the intellectual." This he did, in sharp contrast to Monge, the portly political wheeler and dealer who rose through union and party ranks. Arias took office with a stubborn and straightforward determination to enforce Costa Rica's policy of neutrality and to win international recognition as a statesman and peacemaker.

Yet Arias proved that he, too, was a master politician, although he held his political discourse and made his political deals on a higher plane than his predecessor. In pursuing his peace plan, he repeatedly confounded both foes and allies with his almost naive conviction that dialogue could bring peace, his astute assessment of Washington's no-win war policies, and his ability to get consensus among the region's leaders through a blend of personal persuasion and carefully balanced political programs.

He, too, cut a deal with Washington, and with the powerful local right-wing. Throughout the campaign and in his initial speeches as well, Arias appeared as a fervent advocate of Costa Rica's welfare state. This, as well as his peace stand, pitted him against not only the United States, but also the IMF and World Bank. In a speech on the eve of the elections Arias said, "The IMF will have to understand that we cannot destroy our welfare state. They have to concede to Costa Rica that we were right when we preferred a welfare state to a garrison state. And that Costa Rica is what it is: a stable country with peace due to the welfare state we started forty years ago." But once in office, Arias came to realize he could not fight Washington on both the economic and political-military fronts at once. As detailed in earlier chapters, Arias chose to take on the Reagan and Bush administrations on the issue of peace, but to buy into Washington's economic programs for Costa Rica, particularly the "agriculture of change" and privatization.

Arias repeatedly stressed he is not anti-American and reiterated Costa Rica's longstanding friendship and shared political philosophy with the United States. He was, however, fond of saying that such "a well-founded friendship between two brotherly peoples allows us to agree at times but also to differ; that when the small one always does what the big one wants, that is not friendship, but slavery." His British education helped to make him more European in outlook than many Costa Ricans who view Miami as their cultural, material, and social mecca. Arias much preferred, for instance, negotiating with U.S. envoy Philip Habib, a smooth, seasoned, urbane diplomat, than with Elliott Abrams, the State Department's brash, aggressive, and politically rigid top Latin American official.

Arias did not look the part of either a great statesman or an astute political negotiator. Stoop-shouldered, low-key, somber, introspective, and at times socially awkward, Arias often shows little personal charisma, warmth, or sense of humor. He has had to overcome a painful shyness in order to sell himself to the public. His close friend and confidant John Biehl says, "He was born in a golden cradle, with everything you could ask for. He could have enjoyed an easy life, but it was obvious he has taken the most difficult road, one he had no talent for. He didn't know how to communicate. I think that is why he chose politics, simply because it was hardest for him. The bigger the challenge, the more he grew."

As his international prestige rose, those close to him complained that his vanity also increased. He developed a fetish for highly polished shoes, liked being photographed in his bathing suit, and became an aggressive womanizer. But he had a gift for articulating the pulse of public concern for peace and neutrality, and his personal popularity rose steadily in the polls. By the time he left office, the public opinion polls showed that 87 percent of Costa Ricans surveyed had a favorable opinion of him, up from just 50 percent at the time of his election.

As Costa Rica's youngest president, Arias described himself as "representative of a new generation" in the populist style of John Kennedy, whom he admired and frequently quoted. While Monge's government had a small and increasingly isolated proneutrality faction within his cabinet, Arias's original government included highly educated, articulate, and forthright critics of Reagan's policies: Guido Fernández (Minister of Government, ambassador to Washington, and Minister of Information), Fernando Zumbado (Minister of Housing), Ottón Solís (Minister of Planning), Alberto Esquivel (Minister of Agriculture), Alvaro Umaña (Minister of Natural Resources), and as well as more quiet liberals such as Muni Figueres (Minister of Exports), Danilo Jiménez (Minister of Development, ambassador to Washington), Dr. Edgar Mohs (Minister of Health), and Luis Paulino Mora (Minister of Justice). Arias relied heavily on an informal "kitchen cabinet," a politically well-balanced trio made up of his outspokenly liberal friend John Biehl, his centrist wife Margarita Peñón, and his conservative brother Rodrigo Arias, who was also Minister of the Presidency.

The Reagan administration also had its allies within the Arias government. The most important were Rodrigo Madrigal (Foreign Minister), Hernán Garrón (Minister of Security), Jorge Dengo (Vice President), Eduardo Lizano (Central Bank president), and Fernando Naranjo (Minister of Finance). Three other officials with close ties to the CIA were Sergio Fernández (DIS director), Rogelio Castro Pinto (Vice Minister of Security), and Alvaro Ramos (Vice Minister of Government).

As Arias was assembling his team in the months between the February election and May inauguration, he was also meeting with Monge and U.S. Embassy officials to be briefed on CIA and contra operations inside Costa Rica. Arias says he first learned of the Santa Elena airstrip during a breakfast meeting with Tambs and Monge at Monge's Spanish-style suburban home. Arias recalls, "We met to converse over many issues and the Ambassador informed me that this airport existed to supply the forces fighting in southern Nicaragua. He told me that it didn't put into danger the security of Costa Rica because the planes would never fly across the border between Costa Rica and Nicaragua, that they would come by sea from the Caribbean. I took a decision that I would not permit this."[5]

Oliver North's notebooks refer to this meeting. An entry on February 28 reads: "Call from San José . . . Lew [Tambs] met w/ Arias & Monge. Brief on Spec. Air Force; explained roles of . . . Arias was stunned."

John Biehl also recollects this and other such conversations. "As the elected president, Oscar was officially, but reluctantly, informed of certain things that had already happened within Costa Rica. The head of the CIA [Joe Fernández] used to arrive on orders of the Ambassador [Tambs]. They thought they had to tell him something—the number of people being trained in Panama and elsewhere, plans for a huge radar installation, the Santa Elena airstrip. And they were taking for granted that nothing was going to change and more things were to come. I remember how very, very angry and terrified Oscar was many nights before the swearing in as president. He never thought things had gone so far."[6]

Blow No. 2: Closing the Santa Elena Airstrip

The day of Arias's inauguration, May 8, 1986, was an occasion for both public pageantry and high-level, behind-the-scenes diplomacy. Ten Latin American heads of state, along with Vice President George Bush, attended the ceremony in the National Stadium. Afterward Arias met with his Latin colleagues, all of whom had been active participants in the Contadora peace process which since 1983 had been seeking a negotiated end to the Nicaraguan war. By mid-1986, the eight Contadora countries—Panama, Colombia, Venezuela, Mexico, Brazil, Argentina, Uruguay, and Peru—appeared near agreement. Conspicuously absent from the ceremony was Nicaraguan President Daniel Ortega, whom Arias had specifically asked not to attend. The new Costa Rican President feared Ortega's presence would provoke public demonstrations by Nicaraguan contras and Costa Rican right-wingers, thereby stealing the limelight and complicating his own nascent peace initiative.

Arias had a private breakfast meeting at his home with Vice President Bush, who came with an agenda of his own. In a confidential State Department briefing memo, Bush was advised to order Arias to "tone down" his rhetoric and not be so "loose in denouncing" U.S. policy and aid to the contras. Bush was to insist that the

United States and Costa Rica work "quietly and privately [to] resolve questions and divisions, not openly like Arias wants." The memo further said that Bush was to inform the Costa Rican President that he must accept a two-track policy toward the Sandinistas: endorsing the Contadora peace plan aimed at finding a diplomatic solution to the war in Nicaragua and supporting aid to the contras. Bush was told to "take the message that military pressure on Nicaragua is a necessary part of the two track approach."[7]

Arias placated Washington a bit, first by not inviting Ortega and second, in his inaugural address, by not reiterating his opposition to contra aid. He used the occasion to pledge publicly that Costa Rica would sign the Contadora agreement. However, privately he had already concluded that neither the Contadora peace process nor Washington's war could succeed in bringing peace or western-style democracy to Nicaragua. Indeed, Arias was in the process of evolving a two-track policy of his own. It involved, on the one hand, working to halt contra military operations, including those inside Costa Rica, and, on the other, initiating a new peace process involving Central America's leaders and excluding Washington.

Arias hinted at this new diplomatic approach in his inaugural address. He said that negotiations such as Contadora "should not be prolonged" and vowed he would "demand the fixing of a timetable for the complete fulfillment of agreed-upon commitments" in any peace accord. A timetable became one of the cornerstones of Arias's own peace proposal. He first presented it publicly in February 1987, at another San José summit to which Nicaraguan President Daniel Ortega was, once again, not invited.

The day of his inauguration Arias also quietly began the second track: he ordered Tambs to shut the Santa Elena airstrip.[8] Arias also fired Colonel José Montero, the local administrator of the airstrip, and ordered his Security Minister, Hernán Garrón, to station a Civil Guard patrol at the airstrip to prevent it from being used. Arias and a handful of his most trusted officials debated whether to make the existence of the airstrip public. Minister of Government Guido Fernández argued a press announcement should be made since, as a former journalist, he was sure the press would eventually discover it. Arias, not wanting to upset the

United States further or embarrass his and Monge's Liberation party, ruled out any public announcement.

Then, on June 4, Arias's orders to shut the airstrip were quietly countermanded. The official story is that a legislator from Guanacaste, José Joaquín Muñoz of the Unity party, complained to Security Minister Garrón that guardsmen should not be permanently stationed at a private airstrip when more guardsmen were needed to protect against crime in the town of Liberia. Garrón and his Vice Minister, Rogelio Castro, took the decision to remove the five guards and ordered that patrols be sent in periodically to check on conditions. Over the coming months, patrols checked out the airstrip "on eight opportunities," Garrón said later.[9] Arias was not told of these developments.

The North-Secord network immediately accelerated their plans to expand Santa Elena's use and facilities, and there are indications that it was never really closed down. Cuban CIA operative Rafael Quintero, who was overseeing the supply flights, was registered at a hotel in Liberia from May 13 to June 28 and was in and out of the country after that date. A North network document prepared during this period says the Santa Elena facilities were to be completed by late May, and it does not mention that the landing strip had been officially closed. The two-dozen-odd supply flights to the Southern Front between May and late September were all coordinated by CIA chief Fernández in the Embassy and Quintero at Santa Elena. Other planes were using the airstrip as well to deliver fuel, bring in people, and transit drugs. Tambs testified that three or four times planes got stuck in the mud at Santa Elena.[10]

The most infamous incident occurred on June 9, when a camouflage-painted C-123 loaded with ten thousand pounds of munitions, uniforms, and medicines sunk in the rain-soaked runway. The plane had tried, unsuccessfully, to drop its supplies to FDN troops fighting in southern Nicaragua. It could not find the ground forces, began to have engine trouble, ran low on fuel, and made an emergency landing at Santa Elena.

Immediately alarms went off up and down the network. Quintero, who was in a San José hotel at the time, received an urgent call from Richard Secord to get to the site and get the plane out.

Fernández arrived at the hotel just after this to find Quintero "upset" by the "bad news." U.S. officials had always assured Costa Rican officials that the airstrip would only be used for refueling planes that had already dropped their loads and, just a month earlier, they had assured Arias "the airstrip would not be used" at all. Now, Fernández realized, they faced the unpleasant prospect of telling the Costa Rican President "not only that it was being used, but that we had a plane in neutral Costa Rica loaded with lethal supplies." Tambs, Fernández, and Quintero quickly arranged to borrow some trucks from around Liberia, but before they could reach the airstrip, the plane managed to take off on its own.[11]

More problems were on the way. On its next arms run, the same C-123 hit a treetop, managed to limp back to Ilopango, and was out of action for months. Only a C-7 aircraft remained for the Southern Front drops, and it needed to refuel before returning to El Salvador. The Santa Elena airstrip was closed because of rain and mud, so Tambs and Fernández made arrangements through their Costa Rican collaborators for the supply plane to refuel at San José's international airport. Twice, on June 21 and July 12, the C-7 landed in the early morning hours at the international airport, quickly refueled, and took off for Salvador. Arias was never notified; he read about it later in the Tower Board report.[12]

By early July, the airstrip had become common knowledge to area residents. They feared a retaliatory air attack by the Sandinistas and suspected drug traffickers were using the airstrip. The La Cruz municipal council became so concerned that, on July 2, it passed a unanimous resolution asking the Rural Guard to investigate the airstrip,[13] but no investigation was made.

Minister of Natural Resources Alvaro Umaña says Arias had told him about the airstrip (which was adjacent to a national park), and he had heard the rumors it was still in use. Umaña saw it for the first time July 4, 1986. "It's an easy date to remember," said the U.S.-educated Minister. "A group of park officials and I overflew the entire park and we also overflew the airstrip. To me it was surprising that it was so long and very well built." Umaña explained that although "nothing had been said publicly I had talked to the President and I was pretty clear on what his position was. He stated that this was against the basic policy of Costa Rica keeping away from any military activities. And he said Garrón was guaranteeing that this would not be used."

By August Garrón was also hearing rumors that not only were large airplanes landing at the airstrip, but that about four hundred contras were based there. Minister of Government Guido Fernández was hearing the same stories.

On Friday, September 5, Arias met with ministers Garrón and Fernández and ordered guards sent to reoccupy the Santa Elena airstrip. Arias also instructed Garrón to hold a press conference and announce what he had done. That same day Arias met with U.S. Embassy officials to inform them of the impending raid. Tambs was in the United States, and his underlings were quite abrasive with the Costa Rican President. According to Biehl, one of them replied something to the effect, "We don't have control over the contras. So if they need this [airstrip] for their security reasons or whatever, they will go ahead [and use it]." Arias, in turn, replied, "Well, I have no army to send there and clean this up, but I can send the journalists." Biehl says that conversation was "hysterically reported to Washington." North's notebooks reveal that it was CIA chief Joe Fernández who called with the news: "Call from Joe—Security Minister plans to make public . . . Base West [Santa Elena] and allege violation of CR [Costa Rican] law by . . . North, Secord, et al."[14]

Late that Friday night, Arias, Guido Fernández, and others were gathered at John Biehl's home, celebrating the Chilean's birthday. About 2:00 A.M. an urgent call came from North Carolina. It was Lewis Tambs looking for the President. Arias recalls, "I told him I had already decided to send a group of Civil Guards to inspect the airport and corroborate this information that there were contras there. Garrón and I decided that we must do this. What he asked me then was that I not announce it. He swore to me that this was absolutely false, that there were not contras there."

The next day Oliver North sent his boss, Admiral Poindexter, a cable outlining the previous day's events and falsely bragging that he personally had threatened Arias that if the press conference were held, Arias "w[ould] never see a nickel of the $80m [AID package]." North wrote that Arias responded that there would be no press conference and no team of reporters sent to the airfield. North added, "I recognize that I was well beyond my charter in dealing w/ a head of state this way and in making threats/offers that may be impossible to deliver, but under the circumstances it seemed like the only thing we could do. Best of all, it seems to have worked." Poindexter responded, "Thanks, Ollie. You did the right things, but let's try to keep it quiet." Arias, however, never talked with North. Only Tambs called him.

Guido Fernández recalls that afterward Arias told the others about the conversation. He explained that Tambs was "very much concerned because he realized that I was going to go on the record saying that the Santa Elena strip should be closed. And there were several threats implied. [Tambs insinuated,] 'I don't want to put in jeopardy your trip to the U.S.' At that time there was talk that he [Arias] was going to be invited, but they had not said exactly what were the dates. And the second is 'this is going to be detrimental to your getting more [U.S.] aid for Costa Rica.' It wasn't a threat to cut aid. He said, 'I'm doing my best to get more help for Costa Rica, but what can I do if you do this?' It's not very subtle."

Tambs raised a third issue as well. He argued that public disclosure of the airstrip would not be prudent in light of the Nicaraguan government's case against Costa Rica in the International Court of Justice at The Hague.[15] This was a theme that the Reagan administration and Costa Rica's right-wing played again and again to deter closure of contra operations, and it did strike a genuine chord of concern with some in the Arias government. In July 1986, the Nicaraguan government had brought separate World Court suits against both Costa Rica and Honduras (as it had successfully done earlier against the United States), accusing them of complicity with the contra war. The Costa Rican government, unlike the U.S. or Honduran governments, agreed to accept the jurisdiction of the World Court. Washington tried to use the court case to its advantage, warning the Arias government that public disclosure of the airstrip or a crackdown on contra activities would constitute an admission of Costa Rican involvement in the war against Nicaragua.

After being leaned on by Tambs and, earlier, the other Embassy officials, Arias agreed to call off the press conference, but not the government's raid. Three days later, early in the morning of September 8, sixty Costa Rican guardsmen arrived by land and sea and reoccupied the Santa Elena base. They impounded seventy-seven drums of aviation fuel, rolling some of them onto the runway to prevent its use, and left twenty-five guardsmen behind as a permanent security force. Two days after the raid, a furious Rafael Quintero cabled Richard Secord: "Alert Ollie Pres. Arias will attend Reagan's dinner in New York Sept. 22nd. Boy [Arias] needs to be straightened out by heavy weights."[16]

Although Arias sought to soften the blow by, once again, refraining from any public announcement, journalists were about to discover the airstrip on their own. In early September, the *Tico Times* received a call from a North American farmer in La Cruz, just above Santa Elena, telling them that the airstrip was "a big open secret in the north" and he was "surprised it hadn't hit the papers." Based on this tip, a group of journalists from the *Tico Times,* NBC, *Time,* and the *Miami Herald* went to the Guanacaste park, where several scientists pointed out the airstrip's location on a relief map. The reporters returned to Liberia and hired a plane, telling the pilot they were doing a documentary on tourism. Just as they landed on the airstrip, they were detained by Costa Rican guardsmen, but they managed to see the L-shaped barracks, a radio antenna, and a weather monitoring station. The layout and construction seemed similar to that in U.S.-built contra camps in Honduras.

The journalists returned to San José and began seeking the government's explanation. Arias was away at the United Nations (discussing Costa Rica's neutrality policy), so Security Minister Garrón was left in the uncomfortable position of explaining a clear violation of official policy. John McPhaul of the *Miami Herald* cornered Garrón just as he was leaving a meeting at the presidential offices. He said he and others had been to the airstrip, showed him the photos, and asked for an explanation. "He was a little taken aback but he didn't deny anything. We all assumed it was for the contras. He confirmed that the Civil Guard had taken over the airstrip and that Montero had been fired the day Arias took office."

The next day, September 24, at the Security Ministry's regular weekly press conference, Garrón was ready for the unusually large turnout. He brought with him the phony December 19, 1985, letter from "Olmsted" to Piza giving Udall Corporation's permission for the Civil Guard to train at Santa Elena. Garrón's rendition was part fact, part fiction. He said that the Panamanian company Udall had begun a tourist project on the property, but had abandoned it in late 1985 and turned the facilities over to the Monge administration for use by the Civil Guard, who used it until the change of government. Garrón said his men occupied and closed the airstrip in early September, because they suspected it was being used by either drug traffickers or contras. The only name mentioned was the one on the Udall letter, "Robert Olmsted." The press didn't buy this sanitized version: no tourist project would include a two-kilometer-long runway and military-style wooden barracks. The reporters went away to look for Udall, Olmsted, and Piza and get more answers.

The damage control began immediately. In San José, Vice Minister of Security Rogelio Castro, a close U.S. Embassy collaborator, led the charge, claiming the press reports were "all just a part of a disinformation campaign perpetrated by the Sandinista regime."[17] In Washington, North wrote in a September 25 memo to Poindexter, "Damage assessment: Udall Resources, Inc., S.A. is a proprietary of Project Democracy. It will cease to exist by noon today. There are no USG fingerprints on any of the operations and Olmstead [sic] . . . does not exist. We have moved all Udall resources [$42,000] to another account in Panama, where Udall maintained an answering service and cover office. The office is now gone as are all files and paperwork."[18] Among themselves, Poindexter, North, and Abrams blamed Tambs for not heading off the public disclosure, noting caustically in memos that he was still on vacation in the United States.

The trio also blamed Arias, and North told Poindexter that steps must be taken to "punish" the Costa Rican government. North claimed that because Arias "had disclosed the existence of the Santa Elena airstrip [and thereby] had breached his understanding with the U.S. government," both Elliott Abrams and Secretary of State George Shultz "wanted to cancel Arias' scheduled visit with President Reagan and replace his appointment by scheduling a meeting with President [Vinicio] Cerezo of Guatemala. Admiral Poindexter agreed."[19] Arias did not meet with Reagan until December 1986.

Philip Habib, Reagan's special envoy to Central America, and CIA director Casey both came to Costa Rica to pressure Arias. The Costa Rican leader met with Habib, a diplomat whom he respected. However, when Casey arrived unannounced in November and demanded a secret meeting, Arias refused. He said he had nothing to discuss with Casey, and that in Costa Rica "it is very hard to hold a secret meeting." The President offered to receive Casey publicly at his home or office. Casey refused and instead, Minister of the Presidency Rodrigo Arias and the conservative Foreign Minister Rodrigo Madrigal went to the airport to meet with the crusty CIA chief. Minister Arias later reported that "nothing out of the ordinary" was discussed.[20]

Arias confidants suspected that once again AID disbursements were deliberately held up. Costa Rican officials told the *New York Times* that "a long delay in releasing $40 million of American economic aid" in 1986 "may have been an attempt to pressure Costa Rica." In addition, U.S. aid in 1987 dropped by 21 percent, which some Costa Rican officials took as a further sign of Reagan administration displeasure with Arias.[21]

In a memo to Poindexter, North admitted that "the damage done by this revelation is considerable."[22] Indeed it was. It marked the beginning of the end of North's covert contra operation. The press was finally onto the story and looking hard for another smoking gun. It came on October 5, when a young Sandinista soldier in southern Nicaragua shouldered his surface-to-air missile launcher and shot down an arms-laden C-123 cargo plane out of Ilopango. Two American pilots and a young Nicaraguan radio operator died, but "kicker"[23] Eugene Hasenfus survived, was captured, and began talking. He told reporters that he believed he was working for the CIA and that his contra supply plane had on earlier flights stopped for refueling at "a secret airstrip in Costa Rica."

The airstrip fit the description of Santa Elena. Documents found in the wreckage linked the plane to Southern Air Transport and Ilopango Air Force Base. Soon reporters in El Salvador had located the safe houses used by Hasenfus and other crew members and obtained their telephone records. They showed calls to Joe Fernández's home and his unlisted Embassy number, to Rafael Quintero's hotel in San José, to Southern Air Transport in Florida, Secord's office in Virginia, and to North and other officials in Washington. Asked if there was any U.S. government connection, President Reagan replied, "Absolutely none"; but behind the scenes the North-Secord "private" resupply operation was closed down.

Ironically, this sudden and unceremonious suspension of Project Democracy came just as the North network's resupply operation was due to be phased out. On October 1, the $100 million in authorized contra aid began flowing, and the CIA was legally back on the books. The Santa Elena and Hasenfus revelations had given the contra supporters in Washington a couple of black eyes, but they were far from being down for the count. The near-dormant Condeca, the U.S.-backed Central American Defense Council intended to isolate Nicaragua, had been reactivated, and Garrón announced that Costa Rica was joining.[24] The Contadora peace process, a continual headache to Washington's war strategists, was once again mired by divisions, while contra activities were picking up. Within a few weeks, light arms and other military supplies were arriving at FDN camps in Honduras, and more Americans had shown up in Tegucigalpa to run the contra war. The first group of contras had been sent to an undisclosed military base in the United States to undergo training. The war was gearing up to coincide with the onset of the dry season in December.

On November 24 and 25, the contra umbrella organization UNO attempted a bold political move. It called a two-day General Assembly at San José's country club–style Cariari Hotel to polish its international image and produce documents to be used by the provisional government they planned to set up in exile or in contra-controlled territory inside Nicaragua. In attendance were several hundred top and middle-level contra officials, plus representatives from several Latin American political parties and the State Department.

The first day, the tone was optimistic, as contra representatives, meeting under tight security, worked out details of a constitution and bill of rights. The draft constitution failed to mention land reform, but, predictably, was detailed on the protection of private property and private enterprise. Arturo Cruz, Sr., with self-effacing frankness, explained in an interview that in the future corruption within the contra organization would be controlled because "all the money flow will be handled by Americans. There will be very, very little participation in that connection by Nicaraguans."

The second day promised more of the same. But midway through the morning session, word spread that President Reagan had called a White House press conference to announce he had fired Oliver North and accepted the resignation of Admiral John Poindexter. Minutes later, Attorney General Edwin Meese was on the screen, revealing that between $10 million and $30 million in profits from illegal U.S. arms sales to Iran had been diverted to the contras as a way to circumvent the Boland amendment. The Iran-contra affair was out in the open. The contra leadership in San José reacted like rats jumping off a sinking ship. Within minutes every important rebel official had vanished from the conference room. Many hastily packed their bags and caught the next plane to Miami, Washington, or Honduras. Their bewildered underlings were left to deal with the press. One observer on the scene commented, "This could mean curtains for the contras."

While the contras still had a few more acts to play out, the Santa Elena, Hasenfus, and diversion-of-funds scandals did bring down the curtain for the Embassy overseers of the Southern Front, Tambs and Fernández. By December Tambs, already embroiled in a bitter dispute with his boss, Elliott Abrams, decided it was time to bail out. He informed Arias he was resigning as they flew together to Washington for the Costa Rican President's first meeting with Reagan. When he returned to Costa Rica, Tambs publicly announced he was resigning "for personal reasons" and returning to his university teaching post.

At a final press conference, Tambs exuded arrogance. Chomping on a cigar, he snapped, "That was a September story" when asked to comment on the Santa Elena airstrip. Asked if he had investigated who in the Embassy had received the calls from the safe houses in San Salvador, he replied, "No, I had no reason to do so." He did, however, expound at length on his favorite theme, "narco-terrorism." At his airport departure, no Costa Rican government officials came to say good-bye. Surrounded by a cordon of armed Embassy security guards, Tambs refused to comment on press reports that he and other U.S. diplomats had been deeply involved in illegally assisting the contras.

In contrast with Tambs, CIA station chief Joe Fernández literally slipped out of town. Costa Rican Foreign Ministry officials said that "the CIA man" left in late 1986, following press reports that he had provided military and logistical advice to the contras. He was recalled and suspended by the CIA for violating the 1984–86 congressional ban on helping the contras. It was only at this point that a number of the contras and Costa Ricans who had worked with the CIA station chief realized that "Tom Castillo" and Joe Fernández were one and the same person.

That spring Tambs and Fernández were called to give testimony, first to the Tower Commission (the president's Special Review Board, a three-member Iran-contra investigating commission composed of Senators John Tower and Edmund Muskie and Former National Security Adviser Brent Scowcraft) and then the Iran-contra congressional committees. Both denied charges that they were renegade officers. Tambs said his orders came from the RIG, composed of North, Abrams, and Alan Fiers, head of the CIA's Central American Task Force. "There was no doubt in our minds that this was a triumvirate," Tambs told the *New York Times*.[25] No criminal charges were brought against Tambs. He resumed his academic post at Arizona State University, but remained so fearful that "narco-terrorists" were out to get him that he taught with a bodyguard in the classroom.

In his testimony, Fernández told government and congressional investigators that he acted on orders of his CIA superiors, including Fiers. He complained bitterly that, after the scandal broke, the Agency hung him out to dry. Fernández was charged by the Iran-contra Special Prosecutor Lawrence Walsh with four counts of obstruction of justice and lying to his CIA superiors. The ex-CIA station chief planned to defend himself by presenting five thousand classified documents to prove that the CIA had authorized his involvement in Santa Elena and other contra projects. In November 1989, Attorney General Richard Thornburgh ruled these documents constituted "government secrets" and could not be released. This scuttled the case: Walsh was reluctantly forced to drop the charges on the grounds that, without these documents, Fernández could not properly defend himself.

The Attorney General reaffirmed his controversial decision in October 1990, after a federal appeals court upheld the dismissal of all charges against Fernández. Thornburgh said he made his decision after being told by officials from several U.S. intelligence agencies that a Fernández trial threatened to reveal classified information about CIA operations in Costa Rica. The intelligence officials told Thornburgh this could cause "potentially serious damage to the national security."

Special Prosecutor Walsh complained to Congress that there was "an appearance of conflict of interest" in Thornburgh's actions, because "the agency refusing disclosure [the CIA] is itself a subject of the investigation." Walsh argued that the Attorney General's decision showed "a lack of concern for applying the rule of law to officials in the intelligence community." He contended, "There is no question that the overprotective attitude toward classified information forced the dismissal of this important case." He contended that the documents contained only "fictional secrets" since much of it had already appeared in the press.[26]

In Costa Rica, there was similar jockeying for jurisdiction among the judicial, legislative, and executive branches, with the Embassy and its local collaborators trying to keep a lid on the scandal. Following publication of the Tower Board report in late February, the Legislative Assembly attempted to set up a special commission to investigate the Santa Elena airstrip, including U.S. pressure on the Costa Rican officials first to build it and then keep it open. Members of both political parties called for former President Monge to appear before the legislature and explain how and why the clandestine airstrip was built. Arias initially endorsed the special commission, but in a surprise last-minute move, he reversed his position and instructed Liberation party legislators to vote against it. Sources close to the debate said they suspected that the U.S. Embassy had brought pressure to block this potentially wide-ranging investigation. In addition, Arias apparently feared that such an investigation would further embarrass his party and hurt Costa Rica's defense in the World Court case brought by Nicaragua.

Instead, Arias instructed Foreign Minister Madrigal to write a strongly worded letter to Secretary of State George Shultz demanding "clarifications" to several allegations in the Tower Board report. This marked the first time ever that a Costa Rican government had sent an official protest to Washington. Arias told the press that if contra planes had used the Santa Elena airstrip after his inauguration, this would constitute "a flagrant violation of national sovereignty and the repeated promise of the United States Government to respect Costa Rican neutrality." Shultz replied, untruthfully, that the airstrip had not been used, and that it was "simply not true" that Tambs's mission in Costa Rica had been to build the Southern Front, as the ex-ambassador had testified. Arias did not answer the letter and quietly let the matter drop.[27]

In November 1987, the Costa Rican judiciary opened a case against ex-Security Minister Piza and Colonel José Montero,—but not former President Monge, for their roles in the Santa Elena airstrip. Piza was charged with dereliction of duty because he failed to notify either the cabinet or the civil aviation authority about the construction of the airstrip. Montero was charged with fraud and conflict of interest for lending fifty Civil Guardsmen and government vehicles to the project and accepting funds and a $15,000 car donated from "U.S. sources." Although judicial investigators compiled a thick file of incriminating testimony, the case went nowhere. After three years, the court suspended it for "lack of evidence."

In July 1987, the Costa Rican government tackled the issue of what to do with the ecologically valuable Santa Elena property. At an outdoor ceremony attended by conservationists and school children, Arias announced the expansion of the Santa Rosa National Park to include the Santa Elena airstrip and several smaller properties, thereby creating the largest protected dry tropical forest anywhere in Central America or Mexico. In his speech Arias made oblique reference to the secret airstrip. He declared, "As a result of the tragic conflict that continues to affect the people of Nicaragua, people have tried to involve this region, its inhabitants and our government in someone else's conflict." The Costa Rican president then asked, "What do we do with this region of conflict? We make it into an area to study nature. We don't send soldiers with instruments of death. We send students, scientists and naturalists with the instruments they need for their intellectual work."[28]

The swords-into-plowshares symbolism was apt, but the paperwork turned into a legal nightmare. It centered around the questions of who really owned the Santa Elena property and what was a fair purchase price. The day after the scandal broke, North told Poindexter that the front company, Udall Research Corporation in Panama, had been dissolved and all U.S. government "fingerprints" removed. The Costa Rican government, therefore, assumed that ownership of the property had reverted to the original investors, Joseph Hamilton and his partners. However, in September 1987, just after Arias announced that Santa Elena was being incorporated into the park, Hamilton's high-powered team of lawyers, Vargas, Jiménez and Peralta, were suddenly named as the new board of directors for the Costa Rican–registered company, "Compañía del Desarrollo de Santa Elena." Once again, this law firm, which also represented the U.S. Embassy, dug in their heels and refused to negotiate a selling price.

Neither the lawyers nor the U.S. Embassy, citing rules of confidentiality, would say who the real owner was behind the corporate façade. Adding to the confusion was the discovery that the Panama-based Udall Corporation, which had bought the land in 1985, had never been closed. Further, Hamilton told the *Tico Times* that he was "no longer the [company's] representative" and that he could not discuss the matter because "it's gotten very complicated." However, the lawyers ominously warned Costa Rican National Parks Foundation officials who were handling the negotiations that the owners were "very prominent and politically powerful Americans," and they were asking $5 million for the property.

Matters were further complicated in 1991, when the State Department, largely at the instigation of Senator Jesse Helms, withheld $10 million in AID funds, claiming that no progress had been made on paying indemnization on Santa Elena and six other Costa Rican properties owned by U.S. citizens. Costa Rica had, in fact, collected over $1 million for the Santa Elena property, but the lawyers kept raising the ante, which in negotiations ranged from about $5 million to as high as $40 million. In the waning months of the Bush administration, the stakes were hiked. Bush not only issued a 1992 Christmas eve pardon of top officials who had been convicted or faced trial for Iran-contra crimes, but his administration also moved to block Inter-American Development Bank loans to Costa Rica totaling several hundred million dollars. Infuriated, Independent Counsel Lawrence Walsh who had labored six years to bring these convictions, said the presidential pardons of Caspar Weinberger, Elliot Abrams, Robert MacFarlane, Duane Clarridge, Alan Fiers and Clair George (another top CIA official) demonstrated that "powerful people with powerful allies can commit serious crimes in high office—deliberately abusing the public trust—without consequence." Likewise infuriated, Costa Rican negotiators demanded proof that the owners of Santa Elena were really American citizens. If they were not, the United States had no grounds for blocking Costa Rica's loans. U.S. officials gave verbal assurances that Hamilton was, once again, the principal partner, but said that for reasons of privacy, the names of the other owners could not be revealed.

By early 1993, the situation remained murky, but scrutiny of various corporate records and numerous interviews revealed the possibility that North and Secord continued to own, as "Olmsted"/ Haskell testified, the Santa Elena Development Corporation, the parent company tucked away in Monrovia, Liberia. Lawyers for Quijano and Associates, the Panamanian firm which incorporated Udall, said that, contrary to North's statement, Udall Research Corporation was never dissolved and as far as is known, remained connected to the Santa Elena Development Corporation. It therefore remained possible that the "powerful politicians" blocking a final settlement on the Santa Elena airstrip debacle were not simply disinterested "private benefactors" but were, in fact, North and Secord.[29]

Despite all that has been revealed, certain mysteries still surround the Santa Elena airstrip: its origins apparently within the womb of the Army's top-secret Yellow Fruit project, its corporate cover in far-off West Africa, and those "powerful politicians" who even now are attempting to profit from it. In the end, no one was convicted for building the secret landing strip. However, those behind it—North, Secord, Fernández, Tambs, Monge, colonel José Montero, and Piza—all had their reputations tarnished and their careers disrupted. Only President Arias emerged with his image intact. A careful reading of the record shows that he pursued, as a matter of principle, the closure of the Santa Elena airstrip and other contra and CIA facilities. He often acted less vigorously and publicly than his liberal critics wanted. Yet he was walking a political tightrope. His orders were often circumvented, sabotaged, and countermanded by U.S. officials and their Costa Rican collaborators. Despite this, by the end of his administration, Arias had succeeded in implementing one track of his Nicaraguan policy: he had dismantled the Southern Front contra operations inside Costa Rica. Parallel with this domestic strategy, Arias pursued his other track: formulation and implementation of the Central American Peace Plan.

Blow No. 3: The Central American Peace Plan

Oscar Arias is a paradox. September 24, 1986, the day before Security Minister Garrón announced that Costa Rica had closed the covert contra airstrip, Arias addressed the United Nations General Assembly and denounced, not the Reagan administration for violating Costa Rica's neutrality, but the Nicaraguan government for what he termed its "new dogmatic totalitarianism." Arias told the world body, "As Costa Ricans, we are concerned about the consolidation of a totalitarian regime of Marxist ideology on our border." His remarks could have been written by a White House speech writer.

Ideologically, Arias was in fact not far from the Reagan administration. However, his solution for the "Nicaraguan problem" was profoundly different. He prescribed political negotiation and dialogue by the region's leaders, including those of Nicaragua, rather than a contra war financed by the United States. He encapsulated his concepts in a shrewdly balanced peace plan which, over the course of three years, he maneuvered through a mine field of political obstacles. In the eyes of Washington right-wingers, Arias's peace plan put the Costa Rican president in the enemy camp. In the end, this plan succeeded, as the contra war had not, in paving the way for the Sandinistas' defeat. The defeat came at the ballot box, not the battlefield.

Arias's main concern, however, was protecting Costa Rica's way of life, which was threatened by contra war. "The economic development I want for my country is incompatible with war in Nicaragua. That is why I don't agree with armed struggle. That is why I favor a peaceful negotiated solution."[30] Arias said further that unless the contra rebels were expelled, Costa Rica would be forced to abandon its nonmilitarism and build an army, not to protect itself against the Sandinistas, but to project itself against the armed anti-Sandinistas inside its territory.

The concept of a Central American peace plan was born during the Arias election campaign, but it was not fully articulated until February 1987. Several developments toward the end of 1986 helped provide an opening for the new peace initiative. In mid-1986, the Contadora peace process appeared close to agreement. By November, however, it was hopelessly stalled. In January 1987, the foreign ministers of eight Latin American countries, along with UN and OAS officials, made a final tour through Central America. After visiting all five countries in the isthmus, they announced that they had not found "the necessary political will to reach a negotiated peace in Central America."[31]

On top of this, the Iran-contra scandal, including the removal of North, Poindexter, Tambs, and Fernández, helped weaken and discredit the backers of the war against Nicaragua. The Tower Board report documented U.S. pressure on the Arias government, as well as violations of both Costa Rica's neutrality and the Boland amendment. In November, Democrats gained control in the Senate and increased their margin in the House. In January, Jim Wright, a Texas Democrat deeply interested in Central America, took over from Tip O'Neill as Speaker of the House. Wright, along with Senators Christopher Dodd, John Kerry, and Terry Sanford, became key backers of the Arias peace plan, helping to provide a counterweight to the Reagan administration and conservatives in Congress.

In December 1986, Arias at last received an invitation to meet with President Reagan at the White House. The Costa Rican leader took with him a large delegation of foreign-policy and economic advisers and a sketchy outline of a new peace plan. In the meeting, Arias stressed two points: the need for democratization in Nicaragua, and for a new peace initiative to replace Contadora. Afterward, the Arias delegation concluded the meeting had accomplished nothing of substance, but they were relieved there had also been no hostility, no threats.

It was elsewhere, apparently, that Arias was supposed to be leaned on. His schedule included a one-on-one meeting with CIA Director William Casey at the Langley, Virginia, headquarters. Arias protested that he had nothing to discuss with the CIA, especially in private. Finally it was agreed that Casey would come to Arias's hotel suite for "semi-private" talks. Arias extended invitations to his entire delegation and the Costa Rican Embassy staff. "Mr. Casey was very surprised when he entered the room. So many people, and he came only with Alan Fiers and Elliott Abrams," recalls Guido Fernández, who was by then Costa Rica's ambassador to Washington.

"Arias was sitting on the couch, with Casey, next to him. And in front twenty people," recounted Fernández. "Casey could only hear in his left ear. Arias talked very low into his right ear and it was impossible for Casey. All of us were leaning from side to side trying to hear. We assumed they were talking about something very secret. But it was only niceties, about the weather, the trip, nothing of substance. My perception was that Casey wanted to discuss the airstrip, treating wounded contras in our hospitals, and the intelligence and interception communications system, but nothing could be mentioned because the meeting was not secret." Just a few days after this meeting, on December 15, Casey was disabled by a stroke and forced to retire.

As the Costa Rican delegation met with Administration and congressional leaders, they became increasingly convinced that no one in Washington—neither the White House nor Congress, the Republicans, nor the Democrats—had a clear, coherent position on Nicaragua. Arias and his aides returned from Washington convinced the time was right for their peace initiative.

However, they left in their wake some nervous Reagan administration officials. In early January, Foreign Minister Madrigal, viewed by Washington as a man of confidence, was summoned to Miami to discuss terms for a new peace plan. Madrigal and three staff members met at the airport Sheraton Hotel with Philip Habib, Elliott Abrams, and two other State Department officials, William Walker and Richard Melton, and drew up the broad outlines of a four-point peace plan. It was based around a "democratic alliance" of the region's pro-U.S. states (Costa Rica, Honduras, El Salvador, and Guatemala) who, together with Washington and Western Europe, would create a "quarantine" around Nicaragua. Madrigal then took this proposal, which several Arias aides dubbed the "Abrams plan," to Europe, where he discussed it with officials from Spain, Belgium, Britain, Germany, Italy, France, and the Vatican. It had not been approved by Arias.

Indeed, during this same period, presidential staff members in San José began to draft what became known as the ten-point "Arias peace plan," which included Nicaragua at the negotiating table. Arias argued that a two-stage process was necessary to get all the Central American presidents on board, because José Napoleón Duarte of El Salvador and José Azcona of Honduras would not come if Ortega was present. The first summit was thus intended to get these two committed to the plan; then Ortega would be brought in. Contrary to the Abrams-Madrigal proposals, therefore, "the Sandinistas were in and the contra were out" of the negotiating process, one Arias official explained. A summit meeting of the four pro-U.S. states was set for February 14.

Three days before the San José summit, Arias's two most trusted advisers, his brother Rodrigo and John Biehl, left San José in a small propeller plane to hand-deliver the Arias plan to the presidents of Guatemala, El Salvador, and Honduras. Guatemalan President Vinicio Cerezo enthusiastically endorsed the plan, Honduran President Azcona was noncommittal, and Salvadoran President Duarte was openly hostile. Biehl recalls, "Duarte said the American Ambassador had just been there for four hours. He had brought a copy of the plan. Duarte said 'sorry, the plan was all wrong.'" But the Costa Ricans accomplished their mission: all three presidents agreed to attend the summit.[32]

Nicaraguan President Daniel Ortega was also briefed the day

before the presidential meeting. In the weeks leading up to the summit, he had became deeply suspicious at once again being excluded from negotiations. He denounced the plan as merely "the most recent demonstration of U.S. interventionist policy." The Nicaraguan government was further annoyed that Arias met personally with contra leaders Arturo Cruz and Alfonso Robelo to brief them on the plan. (Both said they endorsed it, in principle.) But when Ortega learned what was in the plan, his attitude began to soften. According to a member of Arias's staff, "The Nicaraguans were very quick to react. They accepted it the next day."

At the end of the one-day summit the four presidents signed the preamble to the Arias plan and gave their verbal endorsement to the entire seven-page document. They termed it "a viable, opportune and constructive instrument for finding peace by means of a negotiated political settlement." Arias had urged them to sign the full plan, but, a Costa Rican close to the talks said, Salvadoran President Duarte and Honduran President Azcona wanted to "check it back home" first (that is, with Washington), and Cerezo argued it should not be signed until Ortega was present. The presidents announced another summit would be held June 25, 1987, in Guatemala. Guatemalan President Cerezo then went to Managua to brief Ortega on the summit results and invite him to the next gathering. Ortega gave his endorsement to the plan.

The Reagan administration, on the other hand, found much to be concerned about. Their plan, which Foreign Minister Madrigal had circulated to the other Central American foreign ministers, was now dead in the water. In its place was the Arias plan, which called for a compromise between the positions of Washington and Managua. As a Center for International Policy analysis put it, "Essentially, Washington would call off the contras; Nicaragua would allow complete political pluralism. Each would gain something essential from the deal: Nicaragua would get peace, and Washington would bar what it perceives to be the consolidation of a one-party Sandinista regime."[33] But Washington wanted more than that: they wanted the Sandinistas out of power and the contras in, and the Arias peace plan contained no such guarantee.

Further, the Arias peace plan was equally binding on all five

Central American countries, and it sought to end the guerrilla wars in El Salvador and Guatemala, as well as in Nicaragua. Although Arias's main intent was to end the war in Nicaragua, his plan avoided singling out and thereby isolating the Sandinistas. It laid out a precise timetable for implementation; accepted the legitimacy of all the region's existing governments, including the Sandinistas; and called for a cease-fire in the region's three wars, suspension of external aid to the contras, and democratic elections according to schedules set in the separate countries' constitutions. It did not, therefore, demand that the Sandinistas immediately hold new elections. While proposing "democratization" within sixty days, it only specifically mentioned two types: freedom of the press (through a lifting of Nicaragua's national state of emergency, imposed because of the war) and political pluralism.

While the Arias peace plan was widely and correctly hailed as an astute and carefully chiseled work of international diplomacy, it was also, in a way, a highly parochial and nationalistic proposal. Arias was deeply convinced that Costa Rica's unarmed democracy was the model that should be adopted throughout the isthmus. He believed that all of Central America's problems could be solved, on the one hand, by the region's governments adhering to a Costa Rican–style nonmilitarism, respect for human rights, and democratic electoral systems, and, on the other, by the armed opposition's simply laying down their weapons and rejoining the internal political process. What his peace plan failed to recognize was that the popular struggles in El Salvador and Guatemala had different origins and objectives than the contra war in Nicaragua. The latter could largely be ended by suspending U.S. funding and support. The civil wars in El Salvador and Guatemala, in contrast, were home grown, not wholly dependent on outside support, and based on struggles to end grave human rights violations and to make major land and economic policy reforms. Conventional political processes had, so far, proved incapable of making such fundamental changes.

While giving a general verbal endorsement to Arias's peace initiative, the Reagan administration had a long list of specific objections. It did not like at least four of its ten provisions. One called for amnesty and dialogue with the unarmed internal opposition; Washington wanted the Nicaraguan government to talk directly with the armed external opposition, the contras. Another called for an immediate cease-fire upon signing of the peace plan. The Reagan administration wanted a cease-fire only after Managua-contra talks. Third, the United States doubted that Nicaragua would comply with the sixty-day calendar for democratization, and fourth, Washington did not like the international verification procedures. On top of this, Costa Rican negotiators say, the administration objected to two of the proposal's most innovative concepts, "simultaneity"—that is, that steps toward democracy and peace would proceed at the same time—and "symmetry," which made it equally binding on all Central American countries. Fundamentally, Costa Rican foreign ministry official Guillermo Solís said, Reagan and then Bush officials "did not like the plan because it recognized the legitimacy of the Sandinista regime."

Despite U.S. coolness to the plan, some top contra leaders expressed their general support, perhaps in order to keep up their democratic appearances and chances of continued U.S. congressional funding. With money again legally flowing to the contras, administration officials were making promises of yet another new alliance, the Nicaraguan Resistance (which in April 1986 officially replaced UNO led by Colero, Cruz, and Robelo), and predictions of a major fall offensive. However, contra unity still remained paper thin. In April, Southern Front commander El Negro Chamorro quit, complaining, as Pastora had before him, of CIA meddling and cutoffs of funds and supplies. In a much more serious blow, administration favorite and UNO leader Arturo Cruz, Sr., announced his resignation that same month.

In the months after the San José summit, Costa Rica's Foreign Ministry began what one official termed "frantic activity, trying to get from the other Central American countries reactions to the peace plan." Some on Arias's staff accused Foreign Ministry officials of doing Washington's bidding: gathering criticism and drafting new versions of the plan which brought it more into line with the discarded Abrams-Madrigal plan. Arias is said to have become extremely annoyed when he found that revised versions of his plan were being circulated; he ordered the Foreign Ministry to stop drawing up new plans. However, throughout the peace process, Arias continued to face such problems with his Foreign Minister.

Right after the January summit, State Department officials sent word through the Foreign Ministry that they were very angry at not being consulted beforehand. In Washington, Abrams called a meeting of all the Central American ambassadors to complain about Costa Rica's behavior. Philip Habib made two tours of the region, to raise objections to the plan and try to forestall the next summit, which was to include Nicaragua. El Salvador, the closest U.S. ally in the region, led the attack on the plan. Arias say that Duarte "presented a book of reservations."

Arias himself toured Central and South America as well as Europe to drum up support for the plan. Costa Rican–Nicaraguan relations gradually improved, and Arias agreed to send an ambassador to Managua. The Contadora Group endorsed the peace plan and, in April, the U.S. Senate voted 97–1 to support it. In late July 1987, the House followed suit, voting unanimously to "strongly support" the Arias initiative.

Despite growing international support for the plan, in early June, just after meeting with Philip Habib, Salvadoran President Duarte demanded that the next summit be postponed. Publicly, he argued that the foreign ministers and technicians needed more time to iron out the differences. However, Biehl says Duarte called Arias and was "very open. He said 'Habib told me that they [the Americans] can't accept it. They are my friends. I couldn't carry on this war for 15 minutes if I antagonize them.' " Arias reluctantly agreed to put off the summit until August.

Just after this disappointment, Arias traveled to Indianapolis to give a speech. There he received an urgent call that President Reagan wanted to meet with him. Arias thought it would be a private meeting or photo opportunity and was surprised on arriving at the White House to find the top administration officials—Vice President Bush, Chief of Staff Howard Baker, NSC Chief Frank Carlucci, NSC Director of Latin American Affairs José Sorzano, Under Secretary of State John Whitehead, Habib, and Abrams—gathered there. Arias was accompanied only by Biehl and Guido Fernández. Both sides were extremely tense. Biehl recalls, "This was the famous meeting where President Reagan gave his standard warning about the dangers of communism and need to support the contras. He said the peace plan was full of loopholes and that the U.S. would continue to aid the contras, whether or not the peace plan is signed by the Central American presidents."

Biehl says, "When Reagan stopped, Oscar moved to the edge of his seat and took the opportunity to allow them to listen. He spoke for about ten minutes, and he was very tough. 'I'm sorry, Mr. President, but I have a different view of Central America. You listen to me. Without peace, the Central American countries will get poorer and poorer every day. If you have as much interest as I do in the consolidation of the Central American democracies, you have to improve their standard of living. But that is incompatible with war.' Then Oscar told Reagan, 'You are completely isolated with regard to your contra policy. No one, not Contadora, the Latin American Support Group, Western Europe, not even [British Prime Minister] Margaret Thatcher supports the contras.' At the end Reagan looked at all his aides, as if to say, 'How the hell did you let this midget in here?' "[34]

Arias returned to San José deeply depressed. He told an airport press conference, "I have tried by all means to persuade the Reagan administration that this is the way out [of the Nicaraguan conflict], but I have not succeeded." He reiterated two points: that "my peace proposal is incompatible with continued U.S. aid to the contras," and that "there can be no peace in Central America" if Nicaragua is excluded from the negotiating table. He pledged, however, to "do everything necessary" over the next few weeks to salvage the plan and the summit.

As the delegates gathered for the August 7 summit in Guatemala City, the atmosphere was not optimistic. The Central American foreign ministers, coming from their own pre-summit meeting in Tegucigalpa,[35] told the presidents that there was virtually no chance of success. And the situation was only to get worse. On the day before the summit's opening, President Reagan suddenly announced a new bipartisan peace plan on Nicaragua which, he said, had been agreed upon by House Speaker and Democrat Jim Wright.[36] The so-called Reagan-Wright plan, which was distributed soon after by the U.S. Embassy in Guatemala City, differed from the Arias plan in several crucial ways. It only dealt with Nicaragua, not the entire region, and it called for a continuation of U.S. aid to the contras until after the Sandinistas had implemented democratic reforms. It also proposed direct talks between the contras and Managua and direct U.S. participation in future talks with the five Central American states. Reagan announced that he was sending the plan immediately to Guatemala City to be placed on the summit table for discussion by the five presidents.

To many of the participants and press, Reagan's astonishing announcement appeared to be a desperate, last-minute attempt to derail the talks and upstage the Central American presidents. It seemed the U.S. leadership had suddenly realized that the Central American leaders were about to make peace by themselves and largely on their own terms. Washington's plan was obviously hastily written, and Reagan's attempt to place it on the negotiating table alongside, or perhaps instead of, the Arias plan was an affront to Central American pride.

The Reagan-Wright plan was never considered; Arias had made it clear, and the other presidents had agreed beforehand, that the only document to be discussed was the Arias plan. Arias reflected in an interview later, "I believe that it [the Reagan-Wright plan] favorably served our cause. It touched the pride of all five Central American presidents. It was so inopportune that for us to accept that plan was really to declare that we had no sovereignty or independence, no honor. That we were puppets."

The five presidents met alone, without their foreign ministers or advisers. This was the pattern at all subsequent summits, and it set up a dynamic which allowed for frankness, flexibility, and sense of unity. According to Biehl, "Ninety-nine percent of the pressure put on these countries is put toward the ministers and the group of technicians. It's difficult for presidents to arrange meetings without their foreign ministers. But it was necessary to break the protocol. They're a pain in the neck and they want to be included. And I think all the presidents felt they gained political space by being able to meet on their own."

Arias recalls that, despite the aura of pessimism surrounding the summit, he personally felt confident an agreement could be reached. As the summit began, Arias told his colleagues, "We have created a lot of expectations and I don't want to leave this room without arriving at an agreement because it would be a failure that wouldn't be pardoned by history or by our people."

Arias wanted to keep all the presidents isolated in the conference room until agreement was reached. At dinnertime he asked
Cerezo if the meal could be served to them in that room. The
Guatemalans, however, had asked the hotel to prepare a banquet
in a large dining hall, with a separate table for each delegation. He
said it was impossible to change the arrangements. Arias was
worried, particularly about Duarte and Ortega. "I knew if Duarte
had time to consult his military there could be problems and if
Daniel Ortega had to consult the rest of the Sandinista *comandantes,* there might be. Nevertheless, we suspended the meeting and
went down to eat."

Ortega ate little, soon leaving the room with his aides, apparently for consultation with Managua. "I indicated to the people at my
table that this worried me," Arias recounted. It was a long dinner,
with music, and after the main course, an impatient Arias went over
to the host Cerezo and said, "Let's go. We shouldn't spend any more
time here. If we don't reach an agreement now, it's going to be very
difficult tomorrow." Arias returned to his dessert and soon the
Nicaraguan delegation came back to the room. Ortega went over to
Cerezo and echoed Arias's feelings, saying something like, "It's better
if we continue this today because tomorrow will be very difficult."
Arias was heartened. The presidents returned to the conference
table, where they finally reached agreement at four in the morning.

The plan was largely the same as the January document,
except for changes in the timetable. It called for the creation, by
August 29 (fifteen days later), of national reconciliation commissions in each country to hold talks with the internal opposition. By
November 7, three months after signing, they were to have implemented cease-fires, democratization, cutoff of aid to the contras
and other insurgents, and the removal of contra bases from
Honduras and Costa Rica. On December 7, four months after
signing, an international verification commission was to report on
implementation. On January 7, 1988, 5 months later, the presidents were to meet at another summit and certify that the plan had
been fully implemented. Finally, multiparty and internationally
supervised elections would be held in each country, according to
their constitutions.

Several hours later the Hondurans changed their mind, telling the others that they were going to issue their own document. The other four agreed that they would sign the Arias plan. Before the Hondurans backed out, Guido Fernández, with the permission of Arias, had called Jim Wright to tell him agreement had been reached. Several journalists had also been tipped. Early in the morning, Wright announced in Washington that the Central American presidents had signed the peace plan. Wright's announcement proved fortunate. He did not know Honduras had quietly backed out and so announced there was unanimous agreement to sign the peace plan. This was reported around the world. When the presidents reassembled at mid-morning, Azcona was too embarrassed to break publicly with the others. He did not want to be the odd man out, so he agreed to sign what from that moment on became known as the Central American Peace Plan.

Arias arrived home to a hero's welcome. All along the fifteen-mile highway leading to the capital people gathered, waving flags and banners, tossing white roses, shouting support. Church bells rang and car horns honked throughout the city. Overnight he became not only an immensely popular president but an international figure.

As euphoria swept Central America, gloom and confusion settled over the White House. Reagan administration officials had not really believed the five presidents would sign the Central American Peace Plan, and a deep split formed within the White House over how to deal with it. Philip Habib saw the peace plan as an honorable way for the United States to extract itself from the Nicaraguan quagmire. Elliott Abrams saw it as a sellout of the contras. Habib, backed by Shultz, wanted to make an immediate tour of the region to show U.S. willingness to help with implementation of the plan. Abrams, backed by National Security Adviser Frank Carlucci, Defense Secretary Caspar Weinberger, and NSC official José Sorzano, opposed Habib's mission. Reagan was asked to make the call, and he sided with the hardliners. Reagan denounced the Central American Peace Plan as "fatally flawed." Habib quit his post, and was replaced by Morris Busby.[37]

By late August, the Nicaraguan government announced it was dropping without condition its World Court suit against Costa Rica, an act of good will not required by the peace plan. Soon after, the Nicaraguan government took a major step toward complying with the new peace plan by agreeing to lift press restrictions.[38] In a further compliance with the peace plan, Nicaragua named Catholic Cardinal Miguel Obando y Bravo, an outspoken Sandinista critic, to head the National Reconciliation Commission and to act as a mediator in ceasefire talks between the contras and the government. Over the next three years, the Nicaraguan government, more than any other in the region, implemented most vigorously and thoroughly the provisions in the peace plan.

At the same time, Speaker Wright announced his wish to bring Arias to explain the peace plan to a joint session of Congress on September 22. The White House, however, nixed the plan. Formal joint sessions of Congress are only held for persons on state visits; Carlucci informed Wright that the President would not invite Arias. The excuse was that Arias had already been to the White House, twice. The real reason was that Congress was again debating contra aid, and the Reagan administration did not want Arias speaking out against it.

Wright and other congressional Democrats arranged instead for Arias to address an informal congressional gathering. An overflow crowd showed up to hear the Costa Rican leader, and he received a standing ovation when he asked Congress to give the peace plan a chance to work. Despite Arias's appeal, just twenty-four hours later, the House approved another $3.5 million in "humanitarian" contra aid.[39]

Costa Rican ambassador Guido Fernández, a persuasive proponent of the peace plan, soon found that he, too, was being muzzled by administration officials. In February 1988, after Fernández briefed several congressmen on Arias's position regarding contra aid, Elliott Abrams attacked the ambassador for inappropriately lobbying on Capitol Hill. In fact, Fernández was simply performing the routine diplomatic function of clarifying his government's position. However, the administration's criticism became so shrill that, on April 1, Arias removed Fernández. He returned to San José, where he was named Minister of Information.

By the time the peace plan was ratified at the Guatemala summit in August 1987, Arias officials could tick off a list of hostile actions by Washington that dated from the start of the

Arias peace process. These included: the suspension of all U.S. economic assistance; maneuvers to block international bank loans to Costa Rica and cut the country's exports to the United States; a campaign to force the resignation of presidential adviser John Biehl; and the delay in appointing a new U.S. ambassador. While U.S. officials had explanations for each of these actions, Costa Rican officials and political observers began to see a pattern in Washington's behavior. Former ambassador Frank McNeil, for instance, told a House Foreign Affairs Subcommittee in July, 1987, "It is impossible to avoid the suspicion that Costa Rica's 'less favored nation treatment' is a form of revenge for having the temerity to disagree with us about the contras."[40]

Between February and August 1987, no AID funds were disbursed in Costa Rica. An Embassy official put the amount withheld at $85 million, while Costa Rican and U.S. congressional officials said it totaled $140 million. "Costa Rica has not received a penny since almost the beginning of the peace plan effort. That, of course, is purely coincidental," one Arias insider remarked sarcastically at the time. After congressional Democrats, particularly Senator John Kerry, threatened AID with a scandal, the tap was quietly reopened.

In addition, the Reagan administration slapped unusually strict bans and restrictions on flowers, clothing, and some other Costa Rican exports to the United States, thus hurting foreign exchange earnings. Further, in August 1987 the U.S. government refused for the first time to intervene with American commercial banks on Costa Rica's behalf. The banks rejected an Arias proposal for rescheduling the country's staggering $4.5 billion foreign debt, one of the highest per capita in the world. The failure to reach agreement with the banks made Costa Rica ineligible for further bank loans and held up agreements with the IMF, World Bank, and European donor countries.

Arias officials also charged that the local media and Embassy, together with U.S. officials and leading Republicans such as Senator Robert Kasten, UN Development Program director William Draper, and Vice President Bush, launched a campaign against John Biehl. Biehl was one of the most important architects of the peace plan. However, as a foreigner who held no official Costa

Rican government post, he was vulnerable. During the summer of 1987, Biehl was accused of using his position as a United Nations employee to promote Arias's policies and was forced to resign. A year later, he was again attacked after he revealed AID's "Parallel State." In August 1988, he left Costa Rica and returned to Chile.

The second wave of the campaign against Biehl was in part orchestrated by the new U.S. ambassador, Deane Hinton. Hinton finally arrived in November 1987, almost a year after Tambs's unceremonious departure. Some Arias officials saw the long delay as politically convenient. They complained that during the crucial months leading up to and through the signing of the peace plan, the U.S. Embassy was in disarray and unable to deal with policy matters or even provide a reliable channel to Washington.

Hinton was the first career diplomat named ambassador to Costa Rica in nearly five years. He had previously been ambassador in Pakistan, El Salvador, and Zaire. The Reagan administration picked Hinton because it decided "a big gun" was needed in Costa Rica. In an interview, Hinton said his mission was "to have good relations with a democracy, support their economy, and get them to think straight about the menace in Managua." He added that in the wake of the Iran-contra scandal and the departure of Tambs, Fernández, and AID director Chaij (who left, at Arias's request, in June 1987), "there wasn't much sense of morale [within the Embassy]."[41] In essence, Hinton's mission was two-fold: to straighten out the Embassy and to straighten out Arias.

Once again, Costa Rican officials hoped for an American envoy who would be both professional and sympathetic, but they found Hinton, like his predecessors Tambs and Winsor, was a cigar-smoking, boisterous, and blunt conservative with little understanding of Costa Rica. One Arias aide described Hinton as "a blind right-wing guy with no subtlety whatsoever."

Relations between the Arias administration and the Embassy continued to worsen. In June 1988, in an effort to ease the tensions, Hinton asked Arias, Biehl, and Guido Fernández to dinner at the suburban home of a mutual friend, a wealthy Salvadoran businessman. Their wives were there and it was supposed to be a relaxed social occasion. But things went badly. Hinton lectured the others. He accused Fernández of "lobbying"

Congress before a close contra-aid vote in February. The diminutive, soft-spoken Fernández, who had just resigned as ambassador to Washington, politely defended himself.

Hinton then launched into a defense of Reagan administration policy in Central America. Biehl, looking like a paunchy, rumpled college professor, cut him off: "The analysis you make shows total ignorance of the problems of Latin America." Hinton shot back, "Don't get aggressive with me." Then, looking directly at Arias, the ambassador declared, "The problem with you Costa Ricans is you are all very naive."

A silence fell over the dinner party. Arias winced. His drooped shoulders, which always seemed to be bearing the full weight of Central America's problems, sank even lower. Slowly Arias's wife, Margarita Peñón, rose to her feet. In a dignified, silky, and yet icy, tone she said to Hinton, "You are known as a distinguished diplomat and we felt honored when the United States named you to our country. But you don't know us well, Mr. Ambassador. I invite you to come, talk to the people and get to know the far corners of this country. We are intelligent, bright, mature. You [Americans] are the ones who are naive."[42]

Two months later, Biehl left Costa Rica to return to Chile.

This dinner exposed, rather than closed, the deep gulf which had grown during the decade between top policy makers in Washington and San José. In the face of these wide-ranging maneuvers and attacks by Washington, the Arias government had, as one Costa Rican official put it, "very few cards to play." However, two months after the signing of the peace plan, Arias did manage to come up with one major trump card: the Nobel peace prize. It took both him and the Reagan administration by surprise.

Arias and his family were off at a remote Guanacaste beach house with no telephone when the news reached San José early on the morning of Tuesday, October 13, 1987. Arias aides in San José tried without success to contact the President by radio. Arias says that his daughter Silvia shook him in the morning and said they were announcing on the radio that he had won the Nobel peace prize. "I told her, 'I'm tired, let me sleep.'" Later another family member appeared with the same news, and again Arias dismissed it, saying that perhaps the news was that he had been proposed for the following year; certainly not that he had won. Finally he heard the news himself and, now convinced, flew quickly back to San José in a small plane.

At the airport a group of friends, relatives, government officials, and reporters had been waiting for several hours. In his brief tarmac press conference, and in interviews and statements throughout the day, Arias said that although he was the recipient of the prize, it was really meant for all Costa Ricans and for all the Central American presidents who had signed the peace plan. He said, "I have done nothing more than interpret the conscience and values of the Costa Rican people. This prize is a recognition of Costa Rica, of the way we are and the way we think, and of what Costa Rica is worth to the whole world. It has been given to a magnificent country and to the values we share: freedom, peace and democracy." He added the second reason: "They are giving us this prize so that we will redouble our work for peace. Peace has not yet happened. It is about to happen." His first congratulatory phone call came from Daniel Ortega.

Although Arias did not know the full story at that time, he spoke correctly when he said that the Nobel Prize had been given to him partly because he was the architect of the Central American Peace Plan and partly because he was the President of Costa Rica. Unbeknownst to him, he had been nominated the previous January by a Swedish member of parliament, Bjorn Molin.[43] Molin had done so at the request of Swedish medical doctor Lars Hanson, who had worked in Costa Rica in the early 1980s and been very impressed by the country. Beginning in 1983, Hanson nominated Costa Rica, as a country, for the Nobel peace prize every year. His efforts were supported by a small group of Costa Ricans including Dr. Edgar Mohs, who was director of the children's hospital and then Arias's Minister of Health. During his presidency, Monge had hoped his Neutrality Proclamation would bring Costa Rica the prize, but his government's collaboration in the U.S. war against Nicaragua became too obvious. Then, in January 1987, after witnessing Costa Rica's election campaign, meeting Arias, and learning of his peace initiative, Lars Hanson decided to propose Arias himself. The timing was perfect.[44]

The nomination of Arias was unusual because it recognized a recent achievement, the August signing of the peace plan, whose outcome was very much in doubt. However, the Nobel committee clearly saw the prize as a way to strengthen the peace plan and provide a counterweight to Washington's opposition. As Egil Aarvik, president of the committee said in Oslo, "We in the committee do not operate in a vacuum. We saw that the Central American problem has been in focus over the last months and the past year. I think it is important that the Peace Prize can be given to a person who is currently active, that the prize can have an influence."

Under the peace plan, November 7, 1987, or three months after the signing, was set for implementing a ceasefire, democratization, cutoff of contra aid, and elimination of contra bases. However, within a few weeks after the Guatemala summit, it was clear this timetable was too ambitious. November 7, therefore, was quietly redefined as the beginning of a process of compliance.

By the time the presidents gathered in San José for their second peace-plan summit on January 15 and 16, 1988, a number of the points had been at least partially implemented: creation of National Reconciliation Commissions, internal political dialogue with the unarmed opposition parties, amnesty decrees in all five countries; and expanded press freedoms in Nicaragua, El Salvador, and Guatemala. There had been other less tangible results as well. While in the past the Central American leaders generally communicated with one another via Washington or through the press, now they were in regular, direct contact. Arias, especially, was spending long hours on the phone with his colleagues discussing implementation.

The Sandinista leadership, for its part, was by now firmly committed to the plan, seeing it as the best hope for ending the crippling U.S.-orchestrated war and economic boycott against Nicaragua. But the viability of the peace plan depended on the simultaneous progress of many steps toward demilitarization and democratization. A major stumbling block was the refusal of Honduras to comply with the treaty by closing down contra camps in its territory. In addition, the Reagan administration, although not a signatory, continued to violate the peace plan by its support for the contras and call for a new contra aid vote in Congress on January 3, 1988.

The second Central American Peace Plan summit, held at a technical institute outside San José, appeared to be going nowhere. The meeting was supposed to verify that every point in the plan with the exception of elections had been implemented. Many had not, and the talks quickly became deadlocked over whether to extend the timetable for implementation, which was due to expire with this meeting. Arias played the mediator, talking with the other presidents one-on-one during breaks and meals. Along with Cerezo, he argued that the peace plan should be extended for another thirty to sixty days. This would keep it alive until after the U.S. congressional vote on new contra aid.

The two strongest U.S. allies, Honduran President Azcona and Salvadoran President Duarte, had unexpectedly arrived in Costa Rica a day early, intent on enlisting Arias's support for a hard anti-Sandinista line. Both vigorously attacked the Nicaraguan government for not complying with the peace plan and argued that its timetable should not be extended "for even one minute more." Summit insiders say Duarte was "the most verbose and intransigent" in his attacks on Nicaragua. Azcona fought to disband (in the end successfully) the international verification commission, which had found that Nicaragua had taken "positive steps" toward democratization and was now proposing unannounced "snap" inspections of the Honduran border region where the contras had their camps. A Costa Rican adviser complained that, behind the scenes, there was "very, very heavy pressure from the U.S. administration for the peace plan to end." He described Washington as the "invisible and uninvited guest at the conference table."

Then, suddenly, the Nicaraguan leaders showed that they still had the ability to pull off a well-timed political move. The Sandinistas' political offensive began Saturday afternoon, January 16, just before final deadlines for the U.S. networks and Sunday newspapers. While the five Central American presidents were cloistered in their conference room, Donald Casey, from a New York public-relations firm representing the Nicaraguan government, circulated through an awaiting crowd of several hundred journalists. "This is it. Go with it," he said as he distributed the one-page communiqué written in English. The journalists, many of whom had already filed stories about the failure of the summit, sprinted for the bank of phones in the press room.

The communiqué, signed by Daniel Ortega, announced that the Sandinistas would immediately lift the six-year-old state of emergency which had restricted press and political freedoms, open direct cease-fire talks with the contras, free 3,200 remaining political prisoners, and hold scheduled municipal elections. On the eve of the summit, Ortega had also said, in a *New York Times* op-ed piece, that Nicaragua was willing to negotiate limits on the size of its armed forces, removal of foreign military advisers, and a ban on foreign military bases. With these two documents, the Sandinistas agreed to implement virtually all the major reforms being demanded of them.

The final communiqué signed by the five presidents was a balancing act. Despite the Sandinistas' concessions and Arias's mediation efforts, Azcona and Duarte succeeded in blocking two points Ortega and Arias wanted: a joint condemnation of contra aid and a new timetable for implementation of the peace plan. However, the presidents did agree verbally to meet again in about thirty days, thus extending the peace process past the contra aid vote.

Probably largely because the Central American Peace Plan remained alive, Congress voted no on contra aid by a narrow margin of just 219–211. Arias, who had been privately warned by U.S. officials to keep quiet in the days leading up to the vote, now called for all outside powers—the United States, as well as Cuba and the Soviet Union—to halt their military support for insurgent groups in Central America. "I think that now the path toward a ceasefire is much easier. We have removed a very important obstacle, and I do hope that very soon we can reach a ceasefire both in Nicaragua as well as in El Salvador and Guatemala."

The Guatemala and San José summits were followed by two meetings between the contras and the Sandinistas, mediated by Nicaragua's Catholic leaders. They produced no results, in part because Cardinal Obando y Bravo suddenly suspended the second round of talks being held in Guatemala City before they even began. Sandinista negotiators suspected he was working in alliance with the contras and Washington to avert a ceasefire.

The Sandinistas then made a new concession, one that went beyond what was required under the Central American Peace Plan. On March 2, 1988, Ortega announced that the Nicaraguan government was willing to hold direct, high-level talks with the contras inside Nicaragua, in the hamlet of Sapoa, just over the border from Costa Rica. The meeting was to have an open agenda and no mediation. However, in the days leading up to the March 21–23, 1988, Sapoa talks, there was an ominous development. The Sandinista army launched a major military offensive against contra strongholds along the Honduran border, as it had done in previous years. This time, the United States responded by airlifting over three thousand troops into Honduras in what Reagan called an "emergency exercise." Distressed by this military escalation, Arias publicly condemned the ill-timed Sandinista drive.

Despite the Sandinista and U.S. military actions, the talks went forward. The Sandinista delegation was headed by the President's brother, Defense Minister Humberto Ortega, an astute and flexible negotiator. The contra delegation, composed of Adolfo Calero, Alfredo César, Aristides Sánchez, and two military commanders, stayed in a hotel in Liberia, on the Costa Rican side of the border. Arias granted special permission for Calero and others involved in waging the war to enter Costa Rica. Two months earlier, in January 1988, Arias had ordered all contra leaders living in Costa Rica to renounce the armed struggle or leave the country. Two officials, Alfredo César and Pedro Joaquín Chamorro, Jr., moved permanently to Miami. Alfonso Robelo, who had family and business ties in Costa Rica, including with Arias's brother Rodrigo, chose to stay. He resigned his position as one of the directors of the Nicaraguan Resistance and did not participate in the Sapoa talks.

For three days, the two delegations were holed up in the immigration building at Sapoa, while several hundred journalists camped on the barren, windswept field outside. By late Wednesday night, March 23, it was clear something important was about to happen. A Nicaraguan flag and one microphone were placed on a crude outdoor platform. Security was reinforced and the press was moved back from the podium. Word spread that President Daniel Ortega had arrived from Managua. Then five busloads of contras crossed the border from Costa Rica. As midnight approached, the two sides emerged and mounted the platform. President Ortega greeted the three contra officials—César, Calero, and Sánchez. They stood at attention while a static-filled tape played Nicaragua's national anthem. Then the chief observer to the talks, OAS Secretary General Joîo Baena Soares, read a nine-point ceasefire agreement. Three delegates from each side signed the accord.

The Sapoa agreement largely implemented, and at points went beyond, the Central American Peace Plan. Prior to this, Nicaragua had taken a number of steps toward democratization, and Congress had, in both February and March, voted down contra aid. Now a mechanism was laid out for the contras peacefully to reenter their homeland with guarantees for their safety and protection of human rights. The accord called for a sixty-day temporary ceasefire, beginning April 1, during which a permanent halt to hostilities would be negotiated. Over the first fifteen days, the contras would regroup into protected zones within Nicaragua. There they were to be allowed to keep their arms and receive U.S. humanitarian aid channeled through neutral organizations such as the International Red Cross. The Sandinistas agreed to grant amnesty to half of its remaining political prisoners after the contras arrived in their zones and to the rest once a permanent ceasefire was signed. Once in zones, the contras could send up to eight delegates to the National Dialogue (talks between the government and the internal opposition) already underway, where the compulsory military draft was to be among the topics discussed. The government also guaranteed unlimited freedom of expression, repatriation without prosecution of all exiles and contras, and guarantees that returnees could run for political office.

Starting June 1, stage two was scheduled to begin as a permanent ceasefire would take effect. At this point, the contras would begin to lay down their arms and be fully reintegrated into civilian life. The entire process was to be monitored by a Verification Commission composed of OAS Secretary Baena Soares and Cardinal Obando y Bravo.

After the midnight signing ceremony, the contra leadership drove in a high-speed caravan back to their Liberia hotel in Costa Rica, where the press also gathered. Sources within the talks said that Alfredo César played a key role in getting the contra delegation to reach agreement. César, a banker and one-time Sandinista who was considered part of the contras' liberal wing, said in an interview that the final agreement "incorporates 90 percent of our demands," including a pledge that the Nicaraguan government would implement more democratic reforms before the contras disarmed.

Only later did the extent and complexity of César's role become known. Two months before the Sapoa agreement, César quietly opened a "back channel" to the Nicaraguan government via Washington lawyer Paul Reichler, who was a member of the Sandinista negotiating team. Through a chance meeting with Alfonso Robelo in the Miami airport, Reichler says he learned that César had become convinced that "the military option was a lost cause for the contras," and he wanted to make contact with someone on the Sandinista negotiating team. Beginning February 25, 1988, and continuing through the end of May, Reichler and César held eight secret meetings in Washington, Miami, and Managua and hammered out most of the points incorporated into the Sapoa agreement.

Neither Reagan hardliners nor the ultra-rightists among the contras anticipated an agreement. FDN military chief Enrique Bermúdez had boycotted the talks and was vowing in broadcasts on the CIA-financed Radio Impacto to continue the war. In the early morning hours following the signing ceremony, as the press was packing up their gear, Charles Harrington, a tall, lanky CIA agent from the Embassy in San José, came racing through the front door of the hotel. He was all business. "Where's Alfredo?" he demanded to the first contra he saw. "I need to speak with him, now—in private."

Arias, however, was elated with the agreement. He proclaimed in the flowery language which reflected his vision, "What Sapoa shows us is that you can expect miracles from dialogue. Rationality has prevailed again." The next steps were often rocky, painfully slow, and sometimes backward. They did eventually lead to a disarming of the contras and, in February 1990, presidential elections in Nicaragua. Yet after Sapoa, the negotiations largely moved beyond Costa Rica's borders and out of Arias's close scrutiny.

Over the next year and a half leading up to the Nicaraguan

elections, there were several more Central American summit meetings, but none was as significant as the initial ones. Arias continued to play a key role, to be consulted by all sides, to give his views, and, on occasion, to speak out against U.S. attempts to derail the peace process.

However, with the Sapoa agreement, his major role was finished. The Central American Peace Plan was a reality. Arias eventually achieved his twin goals by negotiating a peace accord and Western-style democratic elections, if not to the entire region, at least to Costa Rica's neighbor to the north. He was delighted with Violeta Chamorro's and the opposition's victory in Nicaragua, but he was not responsible for it, and unlike Washington he could have lived as well with a peaceful Sandinista government.

During his presidency, Arias showed himself to be complex and sometimes contradictory, but he was no one's puppet. He is, as he says, an idealist and a dreamer and, as such, he managed to stand what passes for conventional wisdom on its head. He showed that strength and security can come through dialogue and disarmament, not through building armies and waging war. He showed that the leader of a tiny country located deep within what the United States calls its "backyard" can craft an independent diplomatic strategy without Washington's approval. In pursuing his regional peace plan, Arias took the best of Costa Rica's traditions—its commitments to peace, social and economic justice, and rational discourse—and elevated them to a level of international diplomacy.

APPENDIX 1

Acronyms and Abbreviations

ADC: *Asociación Democrática Costarricense* (Costa Rican Democratic Association)

Agricultura de Cambio: Agriculture of Change

AID: U.S. Agency for International Development

ARDE: *Alianza Revolucionaria Democrática* (Democratic Revolutionary Alliance)

BOS: *Bloque Opositor del Sur* (Southern Opposition Bloc)

CACM: Central American Common Market

Caja or CCSS: *Caja Costarricense de Seguro Social* (Costa Rican Society Security System)

CATs: *Certificados de Abono Tributario* (Tax Credit Certificates)

CBI: Caribbean Basin Initiative

CDDN: Committee in Defense of Democracy in Nicaragua

CENPRO: *Centro de Promoción de las Exportaciones* (Center for the Promotion of Investment and Exports)

CIA: U.S. Central Intelligence Agency

CINDE: *Coalición de Iniciativas de Desarrollo* (Coalition for Development Initiatives)

CMA: Civilian Military Assistance

CNP: *Consejo Nacional de Producción* (National Production Council)

CODESA: *Corporación Costarricense de Desarrollo Sociedad Anónima* (Costa Rican Development Corporation)

CONDECA: *Consejo de Defensa Centroamericana* (Central American Defense Council)

DINADECO: *Dirección Nacional de Desarrollo de la Comunidad* (National Directorate of Community Development)

DIS: *Dirección de Inteligencia y Securidad* (Directorate of Intelligence and Security)

EARTH: *Escuela de Agricultura de la Región Tropical Húmeda* (School of Agriculture for the Humid Tropical Region)

ESF: AID's Economic Support Funds

ETA: *Euzkadi Ta Askatasuna* (Homeland and Liberty)

FDN: *Fuerza Democrática Nicaraguense* (Nicaraguan Democratic Force)

FMLN: *Frente Farbundo Marti Liberación Nacional* (Farabundo Martí National Liberation Front)

FRS: *Frente Revolucionario de Sandino* (Sandino Revolutionary Front)

FSDC: *Frente Solidaridad Democrática Cristiana* (Christian Democratic Solidarity Front)

FSLN: *Frente Sandinista Liberación Nacional* (Sandinista National Liberation Front)

GAO: U.S. Government Accounting Office

IMF: International Monetary Fund

KISAN: *Kus Indian Sut Asla Nicaragua Ra* (Coast Indians All Unite in Nicaragua)

Ley de la Moneda: Money Law

M-3: *Movimiento Tercera Via* (Third Way Movement)

MCRL: *Movimiento Costa Rica Libre* (Free Costa Rica Movement)

MDN: *Movimiento Democrático Nicaraguense* (Nicaraguan Democratic Movement)

MISURA: Unity of Miskito, Sumu and Rama

MISURASATA: Unity of Miskito, Sumu, Rama and Sandinistas

NHAO: Nicaraguan Humanitarian Assistance Office

NSC: National Security Council

NTAE: Nontraditional Agricultural Exports

OIJ: *Organismo de Investigación Judicial* (Organization of Judicial Investigation)

OPEN: *Organización para Emergencias Nacionales* (Organization for National Emergencies)

OPIC: Overseas Private Investment Corporation

PATRIA Y VERDAD: Fatherland and Truth (also translated as Country and Liberty)

PIC: *Corporación de Inversiones Privadas* (Private Investment Corporation)

PL-480: AID's Public Law 480 or Food for Peace Program

PLN: *Partido Liberación Nacional* (National Liberation Party)

PUSC: *Partido Unidad Social Cristiana* (Social Christian Unity Party)

PVP: *Partido Vanguardia Popular* (Popular Vanguard Party)

Terceristas: Followers of the Third Way

UCR: *Universidad de Costa Rica* (University of Costa Rica)

UDN-FARN: *Unión Democrática Nicaraguense-Fuerzas Armardas Revolucionarias Nicaraguenses* (Nicaraguan Democratic Union-Nicaraguan Revolutionary Armed Forces)

UNO: *Unidad Nicaraguense Opositora* (United Nicaraguan Opposition—1985 contra umbrella group)

UNO: *Unidad Nacional Opositora* (United Nicaraguan Opposition-Violeta Chamorro's 1990 election campaign coalition)

VOA: Voice of America

WACL: World Anti-Communist League

YATAMA: *Yapti Tasba Masraka Nani Aslatakanka* (Children of the Motherland)

Principal Figures

Aráuz, Armando: Vice President under Monge. Strong supporter of U.S. policies. Involved in massive embezzlement scandal.

Arias Sánchez, Oscar: President, 1986–1990. Architect of Central American Peace Plan and winner of 1987 Nobel Peace Prize.

Barrantes, Harry: Israeli and U.S.-trained Major (later Colonel) and intelligence officer in Rural and Civil Guards who collaborated with U.S. Embassy, John Hull, and contras.

Biehl, John: Chilean friend and adviser to Arias who played major role in Central American Peace Plan and in exposing the Parallel State.

"Boone Mariscot, Patricia Anne": Name used by La Penca bomber's female accomplice whose true identity was never determined.

Borge, Tomás: Sandinista's Interior Minister.

Calderón, Rafael Angel: President, 1990–1994, who led conservative, generally pro-U.S. government.

Calero, Adolfo: Political leader of FDN and one of three leaders of contra umbrella group, UNO.

Carazo, Rodrigo: President, 1978–1982, who fought with international financial institutions.

Carlton, Floyd: Panamanian drug pilot working for Noriega. Arrested by DEA in Costa Rica and extradited to U.S. where he became a key witness against Noriega.

Carr, Steven: Jailed American mercenary who revealed details of CIA and North network operations in Costa Rica. Found dead under mysterious circumstances in Dec. 1986, just after release from prison.

Castillo, Carlos Manuel: Key government economist promoting AID's development strategy. Unsuccessful Liberation Party candidate for president in 1990.

Castro, Frank: Miami Cuban terrorist and drug trafficker involved with Southern Front.

Castro, Oto: Lawyer who successfully defended Honey and Avirgan from Hull's libel suit in 1986.

César, Alfredo: U.S.-educated banker, Washington favorite and leader of Southern Front BOS (Southern Opposition Bloc) faction and of Nicaraguan Resistance. After 1990, President of Nicaragua's Congress and opponent of Violeta Chamorro government.

César, Octaviano: Southern Front contra leader, brother of Alfredo, CIA operative, and involved in drug trafficking.

Chaij, Daniel: Powerful chief of AID mission in Costa Rica, Feb. 1982–June 1987, and principal architect of the Parallel State.

Chamorro, Pedro Juaquín Jr: Son of Violeta Chamorro. Southern Front contra leader and editor, *Nicaragua Hoy*.

Chamorro, Edgar: Former CIA operative and information director for FDN who became outspoken critic of the contras.

Chamorro, Adolfo ("Popo"): ARDE's logistics chief, CIA collaborator, and involved with drug traffickers. Left after La Penca to join FDN. In 1990, named Violeta Chamorro's consul in Miami.

Chamorro, Fernando ("El Negro"): Head of small, Costa Rican-based UDN-FARN contra faction. Picked by CIA to succeed Pastora.

Chavarria Guzman, Jorge: Costa Rican prosecutor who courageously investigated John Hull, the La Penca bombing, and contra-linked drug trafficking in Costa Rica.

Clarridge, Duane ("Dewey Moroni"): Chief of CIA's Latin American Division, Core Group member, and key implementer of covert policies in Central America.

Coblentz, Douglas: CIA trained as leader of "The Babies."

Coronel, Carlos: Adviser to Pastora. Suspected of maintaining ties with CIA, Sandinistas, and Cubans.

Corvo (Corbo), René: Cuban American extremist, drug trafficker, and CIA operative, and leader of Cuban contingent along Southern Front.

Crone, William: Costa Rica resident, business associate of John Hull, and contra collaborator.

Cruz, Jr., Arturo: ARDE adviser and close with North who played role in La Penca cover-up.

Cruz, Sr., Arturo: Ex-Sandinista ambassador, and elder statesman who joined contras and worked as ARDE liaison to Washington. Director of several contra unity movements until he quit in protest.

Cruz, Fernando: Chief Costa Rican prosecutor who tried to honestly investigate La Penca and other crimes.

Cruz, Roberto: Journalist badly injured at La Penca who worked tirelessly to investigate the crime.

"David": Member of CIA's terrorist group working under John Hull. Involved in La Penca and plot to bomb U.S. Embassy in San José. Disappeared and believed to have been murdered after he began to pass information about the bombing.

Dávila, José: German educated leader of Christian Democratic wing of ARDE. Received covert funds from Konrad Adenauer Foundation.

Dyer, Dery and Richard: Crusading editor and publisher of *Tico Times*.

Fernández, Guido: Arias's ambassador to Washington and Information Minister. Strong supporter of Central American Peace Plan.

Fernández, Joe ("Tom Castillo"): July 1984–Jan. 1987, CIA station chief in Costa Rica. In charge of Santa Elena airstrip and other illegal projects. Declared *persona non grata* by Legislative Assembly.

Fiers, Alan ("Albert Fenton"): CIA Central American Task Force Director and member of the RIG.

Figueres, José ("Don Pepe"): Three-time Costa Rican president who abolished army, nationalized banks, and founded Liberation Party. Defender of neutrality and opponent of contras.

"Francés, Héctor" (Estánislao Valdez): Argentine Army Lieutenant who helped set up early CIA/FDN infrastructure in Costa Rica and later revealed details to Sandinistas.

Frazier, Linda: *Tico Times* reporter killed in La Penca bombing.

Gadd, Richard: Covert operations specialist and part of North network who organized expansion of Santa Elena airstrip.

"Galil, Amac": One of several names used by La Penca bomber.

García, Jesús: Cuban-American prison guard and contra supporter in Miami who provided details about 1985 CIA-backed plot to bomb U.S. Embassy in Costa Rica.

Gaguine, Vital Roberto: Real identity of La Penca bomber. An Argentine leftist who worked for Nicaragua's counterintelligence unit, the Fifth Directorate, his pseudonyms included "Per Anker Hansen," "Amac Galil," and "Martin El Inglés."

Garrón, Hernán: Arias' conservative Security Minister who collaborated with U.S. embassy.

Glibbery, Peter: British mercenary who after arrest in April 1985 disclosed details of Hull's contra network.

Golden, William "Tom": Intelligence agent who became the whistle blower on the U.S. Army's top secret Yellow Fruit project.

González, Sebastián ("Wachán"): Early Southern Front contra leader accused of drug trafficking and with ties to CIA, Israelis, and Noriega.

Gorriarán Merlo, Enrique: Leader of the ERP, an Argentine leftist guerrilla group. Fought with Sandinistas and worked for Nicaragua's Fifth Directorate carrying out assassinations and intelligence operations, including killing of exiled dictator Somoza.

Halvorsen, Tor: Norwegian-born Venezuelan business and conduit for CIA funds to FDN and Southern Front.

Hamilton, Joseph: Wealthy conservative North Carolina businessman with factories and land in Costa Rica. CIA collaborator and owner of Santa Elena airstrip property.

"Hansen, Per Anker": Phony identity used by La Penca bomber.

Harrington, Charles: CIA agent under cover as political official in U.S. Embassy in Costa Rica. Oversaw contra operations after Joe Fernández departed.

Haskell, William ("Robert Olmsted"): Member of North's private network who negotiated purchase of land for Santa Elena airstrip.

Hinton, Deane: U.S. Ambassador to Costa Rica, 1987–1991.

Holts, Phil ("Felipe"): U.S. Embassy economic officer and CIA agent in Costa Rica from early 1980s until just after the La Penca bombing.

Hull, John: Wealthy U.S. landholder and important CIA operative who ran contra operatives in northern Costa Rica. Fled the country after Costa Rica charged him with drug trafficking, murder, and "hostile acts."

"Hull, John": CIA station chief in Costa Rica when ARDE was first organized who worked under U.S. Embassy cover.

Jiménez, Adolfo: Cuban-American Bay of Pigs veteran and CIA operative whose Guanacaste ranch was used for training contras and trafficking drugs.

Jiménez, Gregorio: ETA guerrilla arrested in Costa Rica in September 1983 and accused of being part of Sandinista hit team sent to kill Pastora. Was tortured, never tried, and finally deported to Spain.

Jiménez, Rodolfo ("Flaco"): CIA collaborator who worked in top posts in Costa Rica's security and narcotics departments in the 1980s.

Jones, Bruce: Contra-CIA collaborator, citrus farmer, and partner of Hull who was expelled from Costa Rica in early 1985 after *Life* published photos of Jones leading armed contras.

Lizano, Eduardo: President of Central Bank and key AID ally.

Llorente, Alberto: CIA collaborator and head of OIJ's Office of Special Affairs which handled official cover-up of La Penca bombing.

López-Estrada, Armando: Cuban-American involved with terrorist groups and drug trafficking. Trained contras in Costa Rica.

McFarlane, Robert: Reagan's National Security Adviser, Oct. 1983–Dec. 1985, McFarlane became first administration official sentenced for Iran-contra scandal misdeeds.

McNeil, Frank (Francis): Career diplomat and U.S. Ambassador to Costa Rica, June 1980–June 1983. Rumored removed because of disagreements with Reagan hardliners over contra policies. Later quit State Dept. after clashing with Under Secretary Elliott Abrams.

Monge, Luis Alberto: Costa Rican president, 1982–1986 who collaborated with Reagan administration and Southern Front contras.

Montero, Col. José Ramón: Civil Guard commander in Guanacaste who oversaw construction of Santa Elena airstrip.

Montero, Renan: Cuban intelligence agent and revolutionary who became head of the Sandinista's counterintelligence unit, the

Fifth Directorate, which carried out assassinations and spy missions.

Naranjo, Fernando: Key government economist in supporting AID's strategy.

Noriega, Manuel: Ex-Panamanian military leader who collaborated simultaneously with CIA, contras, Sandinistas, and Cubans.

North, Col. Oliver: Oversaw illegal contra support and supply operation out of Costa Rica which became intertwined with drug trafficking.

Núñez Ruíz, Moisés Dagoberto: Cuban-American CIA operative and head of Frigoríficos de Puntarenas. Heavily involved in contras and drug trafficking operations in Costa Rica.

Odúber, Daniel: Costa Rican president, 1974–1978. Part of Liberation Party's pro-neutrality faction. Accused by Legislative Assembly of involvement with drug traffickers.

Ortega, Daniel: Sandinista revolutionary leader and president of Nicaragua, 1979–1990.

Owen, Robert: Oliver North's go-between to contras who traveled often to Costa Rica, including at time of La Penca bombing.

Paniagua, Col. Rodrigo: Security Ministry official and key CIA operative working with the contras.

Papas, Dimitrius ("Papi"): CIA agent who set up and ran intelligence agents known as "The Babies."

Pastora, Edén ("Comandante Cero"): Ex-Sandinista hero, leader of FRS faction of ARDE, and main military commander of Southern Front. Target of La Penca bombing.

Piza, Benjamín: CIA and contra collaborator who held key post as Security Minister in Monge administration, mid-1984–mid-1986.

Poindexter, John: National Security Adviser, Dec. 1985–Nov. 1986.

Póveda, Leonel ("Comanche"): Early Pastora lieutenant and CIA collaborator who broke and joined with FDN.

Prado, Carol: A non-aligned Nicaraguan nationalist who was Pastora's closest aide and became highly critical of CIA ineptitude and domination over the contras.

Quintero, Rafael ("Chi Chi"/"The Traveler"): Cuban-American

terrorist and CIA agent who supervised on-the-ground construction of Santa Elena airstrip.

Quirós, Jorge: Young Costa Rican cameraman killed in La Penca bombing.

Rivas Leal, Luis ("Wichard" or "Comandante Roger Aleman"): One of CIA's and North network's favorite Southern Front commanders. Involved with M-3 and La Penca bombing.

Rivera, Brooklyn: Leader of Misurasata faction of ARDE and first contra leader to open talks with Sandinistas. Had stormy relationship with CIA.

Robelo, Alfonso: Wealthy Nicaraguan businessman, leader of MDN faction of ARDE, and CIA's "money man." Aligned with FDN at time of La Penca bombing. In 1991 became Nicaraguan ambassador to Costa Rica.

Robinette, Glenn: Elderly CIA agent sent to Costa Rica in 1986 by North and Secord to collect compromising evidence on author and Avirgan. Also installed security fence at North's house.

Rodríguez, Félix ("Max Gomez"): Cuban American CIA operative in charge of contra resupply operations out of Ilopango Air Force Base in El Salvador.

Rohrmoser, Ernesto: Costa Rican businessman who became part of Chaij's inner circle. Benefited greatly from AID policies and funds.

Rojas, Carlos: Go-between to "David." Received death threats and was forced into exile with his family.

Saborio, Juan José ("Carlos Sánchez" or "Comandante Javier"): Right-wing terrorist who worked closely with John Hull. Head of tiny, extremist "Patria y Verdad."

Secord, Richard: Ex-Air Force General and chief businessman for North's operations. Declared *persona non grata* by Legislative Assembly.

Sequeira, Evelio: Costa Rican television station employee who died as result of injuries from La Penca bombing.

Singlaub, John: Retired Army Major General and leader of World Anti-Communist League. Supplied arms and funds to contras.

Solano, Alan: CIA collaborator with OIJ's Office of Special Affairs who helped orchestrate La Penca cover-up.

Solano, Angel Edmundo: Monge's first Security Minister, who tried to uphold Costa Rica's neutrality policy. Removed in August 1984.

Solís, Ottón: Arias's first Minister of Planning and critic of AID's policies, including denationalization of the banking system.

Spadafora, Dr. Hugo: Panamanian doctor who fought with Pastora in wars against Somoza and the Sandinistas. Leading opponent of Noriega. His grisly September 1985 murder remains unsolved.

Tacsan, Col. Francisco: Monge government Security Ministry liaison to CIA who was involved in La Penca plot.

Tambs, Lewis: U.S. Ambassador to Costa Rica, July 1985–Jan. 1987, who worked closely with North to construct Santa Elena airstrip. Left in wake of Iran-contra scandal and later declared *persona non grata* by Legislative Assembly.

Taylor, Col. John: Head of security at U.S. embassy and AID throughout much of 1980s. Heavily involved in covert activities and met secretly with North just before La Penca bombing.

Terrell, Jack: Worked with contra private aid network, became disillusioned, and played important role in uncovering covert activities.

Torbiornsson, Peter: Swedish journalist with whom La Penca bomber traveled in weeks before attack.

Vidal, Felipe: Cuban-American terrorist, CIA operative, and drug dealer who headed the International Brigade and worked with John Hull. Fugitive from Costa Rican murder charges stemming from La Penca bombing.

Winsor, Curtin: U.S. Ambassador to Costa Rica, June 1983–early 1985. Outspoken opponent of Sandinistas and Costa Rican neutrality.

Wolf, Victor: Costa Rican CIA collaborator who allowed his Guanacaste ranch "Las Loras" to be used by contras and drug traffickers.

Chronology of Events

1948–1949 • Costa Rican Civil War followed by abolition of army, enfranchisement of women, outlawing of Popular Vanguard Party (PVP), and nationalization of banks.

1951 • National Liberation Party (PLN) formed by José Figueres.

1961 • Free Costa Rica Movement (MCRL) founded.

1975 • PVP again legalized.

1978 • Rodrigo Carazo becomes president. • Costa Rica's severe economic crisis begins. • Costa Rica quietly supports Sandinistas' military operations along border with Nicaragua.

Aug. 22, 1978 • Sandinista guerrillas, led by Edén Pastora, seize Gen. Anastasio Somoza's National Palace in Managua.

July 19, 1979 • Sandinistas topple Somoza dictatorship in Nicaragua.

Oct. 10, 1979 • Sandinista hit team kills Somocista leader *Comandante Bravo* (Major Pablo Emilio Salazar) in Honduras.

June 1980 • U.S. Ambassador Frank McNeil arrives.

Sept. 17, 1980 • Argentine led hit team working for the Sandinistas assassinates deposed Nicaraguan dictator Anastasio Somoza in Paraguay.

Dec. 13, 1980 • Contra war launched with attack by September 15th Legion against *Radio Noticias del Continente*, a leftist radio station in Costa Rica.

Jan. 20, 1981 • Ronald Reagan sworn in as U.S. President.

1981 • U.S. resumes military assistance after 14-year hiatus.

March 9, 1981 • Reagan signs his first Presidential Finding authorizing $19.5 million for CIA operations in Nicaragua.

July 8, 1981 • Pastora resigns as Nicaragua's Vice Minister of Defense and goes into exile.

Aug. 1981 • Brooklyn Rivera goes into exile. • Costa Rica becomes first Latin American country to cease debt payments.

Aug. 11, 1981 • In Guatemala City, FDN (Nicaraguan Democratic Force) formed.

Nov. 1981 • Misura launches "Red Christmas" offensive along
Coco River, marking start of contra war on Nicaragua's
Atlantic Coast.

Feb. 1982 • Pastora meets with CIA official Duane Clarridge and
agrees to open Southern Front. • Daniel Chaij, Director of
AID (U.S. Agency for International Development) in Costa
Rica arrives. • A Sandinista commando unsuccessfully tries
to kill Negro Chamorro in his San José apartment.

April 1982 • Alfonso Robelo leaves Nicaragua for exile in Costa
Rica.

April 15, 1982 • Pastora publicly breaks with Sandinistas at San
José press conference.

May 8, 1982 • Luis Alberto Monge sworn in as Costa Rican
president and quickly negotiates agreements with IMF (International Monetary Fund) and AID.

Sept. 1982 • Pastora, Robelo, Fernando ("El Negro") Chamorro,
and Rivera form ARDE (Democratic Revolutionary Alliance).

Oct. 7, 1982 • Héctor Francés "kidnapped" in San José and later
reveals details of CIA/FDN operations in Costa Rica.

Late 1982 • CIA begins locating airstrips and training camps for
contras in Costa Rica.

Dec. 21, 1982 • Congress passes first Boland Amendment prohibiting use of CIA and other U.S. funds for toppling the
Nicaraguan government.

Jan. 8–9, 1983 • Foreign Ministers of Panama, Venezuela, Colombia, Mexico form the Contadora Group to seek negotiated
end to Nicaraguan war.

April 15, 1983 • ARDE issues call for armed struggle.

May 1, 1983 • ARDE's first military action, against El Castillo
Viejo on San Juan River.

May 1983 • Felipe Vidal's Cuban contingent, later known as the
International Brigade, arrives to join Southern Front. • The
CIA and the Defense Department arrange for Israel to transfer
captured PLO weapons to contras. Known as "Operation
Tipped Kettle," the deal is overseen by Richard Secord, who
had just retired from the military under a cloud of scandal.

June 5, 1983 • Felipe Vidal and sixteen other "private volunteers" from Miami arrive in Costa Rica to join the contras. Some members of this "International Brigade" work for the CIA, are involved in drug trafficking, and plot to replace Pastora and Brooklyn Rivera with commanders aligned with the FDN.

June 29, 1983 • Bomb carried by two Nicaraguans explodes prematurely in San José parking lot, killing one. The pair were Sandinista agents sent to kill ARDE political leader Alfonso Robelo.

June 1983 • Ambassador Curtin Winsor arrives, replacing McNeil.

July 21–23, 1983 • John Hull, Luis Rivas, and Bill Crone visit Washington to lobby against Pastora. They meet with Oliver North, Sen. Dan Quayle, and Robert Owen.

Sept. 8–9, 1983 • ARDE air attack against Managua airport and oil tanks at Corinto port.

Sept. 9, 1983 • ETA guerrilla Gregoria Jiménez is arrested and jailed in Costa Rica and accused of being part of a Sandinista hit team sent to kill Pastora. Jiménez claims he was to spy on, not kill, Pastora and other contra leaders.

Sept. 15, 1983 • Monge's Neutrality Proclamation.

Sept. 15–17, 1983 • ARDE attack Sandinista garrison at El Castillo on San Juan River.

Sept. 25, 1983 • U.S. proposes sending military engineers to Costa Rica's northern zone.

Sept. 28, 1983 • ARDE attack at Peñas Blancas, first in series of CIA-orchestrated border incidents.

Oct. 1, 1983 • Immigration records show La Penca terrorists, "Per Anker Hansen" and "Patricia Anne Boone Mariscot" first arrive in Costa Rica.

Oct. 24, 1983 • CIA-orchestrated M-3 ("Third Way") faction splits from ARDE.

Dec. 8, 1983 • Congress passes $24 million aid package to contras, stipulating that when funds run out, CIA must withdraw. This prompts Reagan administration to approach third countries for support and to set up covert North network to run war.

Jan. 1984 • Pastora visits Washington and has hostile meeting at

National Security Council (NSC) with Robert McFarlane, North, and Clarridge.

March 24, 1984 • Contra supply plane crashes in northern Costa Rica.

April 11–14, 1984 • ARDE attacks and occupies San Juan del Norte, marking its biggest military victory.

May 1, 1984 • Pastora receives CIA's 30-day ultimatum demanding he align ARDE with FDN.

May 10, 1984 • Leaked draft of secret State Dept. memo says U.S. military aid can prevent Costa Rica from "backsliding into neutrality."

May 15, 1984 • Largest peace march in Costa Rica's history held in San José.

May 26, 1984 • North's envoy Robert Owen arrives in San José.

May 27, 1984 • North arrives in San José for clandestine meeting with U.S. embassy and contra officials.

May 29, 1984 • Monge leaves for 6-week European tour.

May 30, 1984 • Bomb explodes at La Penca during Pastora's press conference.

July 1984 • Joe Fernández becomes CIA station chief in Costa Rica.

Aug. 16, 1984 • Monge reshuffles cabinet, replacing pro-neutrality Security Minister Angel Solano with CIA collaborator Benjamín Piza.

Aug. 19, 1984 • Legislature passes *Ley de la Moneda*, the first major bank privatization bill.

Oct. 1984 • Rivera and Sandinistas begin peace talks.

Oct. 10, 1984 • Congress passes second Boland amendment prohibiting "direct and indirect" U.S. aid to the contras.

Nov. 1984 • South African military delegation makes secret visit to Costa Rica to meet Southern Front contras. • Pedro Joaquín Chamorro takes asylum in San José and begins publishing *Nicaragua Hoy*. • Nicaraguan throws grenade into car, injuring Alfonso Robelo and his girlfriend. The attacker escapes and is suspected of working for the Sandinistas.

Jan. 30, 1985 • $3.2 million VOA (Voice of America) station, "Radio Costa Rica," beamed at Nicaragua opens in northern Costa Rica.

March 1985 • U.S. amends Foreign Assistance Act to permit police aid to Costa Rica.

March 2, 1985 • Contra leaders sign San José Declaration giving Sandinistas list of demands and ultimatum.

April 16, 1985 • René Corvo leads attack on Nicaraguan border town of Esperanza which North network blames for defeat of congressional contra aid package.

April 25, 1985 • Five foreign mercenaries and nine Nicaraguans arrested in contra camp on Hull's property.

May 1985 • U.S. Green Berets arrive to train Civil Guard at battalion at Murciélago. • Carlos Rojas comes forward with "David's" story about La Penca.

May 31, 1985 • Two Civil Guardsmen killed in Las Crucitas incident. U.S. and Costa Rica blame Sandinistas.

June 10, 1985 • MCRL demonstrators stone Nicaraguan embassy. • *Patria y Verdad* terrorists bomb electrical station in Naranjo.

June 11, 1985 • CIA creates contra umbrella organization, UNO (United Nicaraguan Opposition), announced in San José with "Triple A" (Alfonso Robelo, Arturo Cruz, and Adolfo Calero) as directors.

June 12, 1985 • Congress passes $27 million "humanitarian aid" package for contras and in Aug. Reagan signs order creating State Department's Nicaraguan Humanitarian Assistance Office (NHAO) to oversee program.

July 1, 1985 • North gives exclusive right to purchase contra military supplies to Richard Secord's group, the Enterprise, cutting out other businessmen and Calero brothers.

July 19, 1985 • Ambassador Lewis Tambs arrives with orders from North to "open" the Southern Front.

Late July 1985 • Ultra rightist plot to bomb U.S. embassy and other targets exposed. "David" disappears and presumed murdered.

Aug. 1985 • North network begins expansion of Santa Elena airstrip for contra resupply operations.

Aug. 7–8, 1985 • Twenty-nine Witness for Peace pacifists captured by ARDE on San Juan River.

Sept. 13, 1985 • Beheaded body of Hugo Spadafora found near
Costa Rican–Panama border.

Sept. 25, 1985 • Honey and Avirgan release La Penca report
implicating CIA and FDN in bombing.

Feb. 2, 1986 • Oscar Arias, running as peace candidate, elected
president.

Feb.–March 1986 • After years of controversy, 173 U.S. military
engineers arrive, but only permitted to work in southern
Costa Rica.

March 19, 1986 • Security Minister Piza goes to Washington
with Joe Fernández to meet Reagan, NSC Adviser John Poindexter, North, and Secord and to draft cover story letter for
airstrip.

Late March 1986 • Singlaub makes unsuccessful last ditch effort
to negotiate an arms-for-FDN-alliance deal with Pastora.

April 1986 • Nicaraguan Resistance, a new contra umbrella
group with expanded leadership, formed to replace UNO.

May 8, 1986 • Arias inaugurated and informs Ambassador Tambs
to close down Santa Elena airstrip.

May 9, 1986 • At CIA-organized ceremony, six top Pastora commanders sign document shifting allegiance to FARN and FDN.

May 16, 1986 • Pastora gives up armed struggle and asks for
political asylum in Costa Rica.

May 22–23, 1986 • Honey and Avirgan win libel case brought by
Hull.

May 24–25, 1986 • At Esquipulas, Guatemala summit, five Central American presidents reiterate intention to sign Contadora peace plan.

June 4, 1986 • North network contravenes Arias's orders and
secretly reopens Santa Elena airstrip.

June 9, 1986 • A C-123 cargo plane loaded with contra military
supplies gets stuck in mud at Santa Elena airstrip.

July 1986 • Top Noriega drug pilot Floyd Carlton arrested in San
José in DEA sting operation. Eventually extradited to U.S. and
becomes key witness against Noriega.

Aug. 13, 1986 • Senate approves $100 million in aid for contras.
House had approved similar package in June. This marks
resumption of official CIA role in war.

Sept. 5, 1986 • In late night telephone call, Tambs warns Arias not to publicly reveal Santa Elena airstrip.

Sept. 24, 1986 • Journalists who had discovered Santa Elena publicly confront Security Minister Hernán Garrón. He describes the mile-long airstrip as a "tourist" project owned by private investors from Udall Research.

Sept. 25, 1986 • In memo to his boss Poindexter, North falsely writes he has closed down Udall and removed all "USG fingerprints" from the airstrip project.

Oct. 5, 1986 • Sandinistas shoot down supply plane carrying Eugene Hasenfus who reveals covert resupply network.

Nov. 3, 1986 • Lebanese magazine reports U.S. secretly sold arms to Iran.

Nov. 1986 • Casey makes unannounced visit to Costa Rica and Arias refuses to meet with him.

Nov. 25, 1986 • Nicaraguan Resistance's General Assembly in San José abruptly terminated when Reagan and Attorney General Edwin Meese announce on TV the arms sales to Iran and diversion to contras. Poindexter resigns and North is removed. Iran-contra scandal officially becomes public.

Dec. 1986 • Arias visits Washington and meets Reagan and Casey.

Dec. 4, 1986 • Arias visits Washington and meets Reagan and Casey, who try to win his cooperation in the war against Nicaragua.

Dec. 13, 1986 • Steven Carr, American mercenary who had revealed important details of CIA operations in Costa Rica dies in Van Nuys, Calif., reportedly of cocaine overdose.

Dec. 19, 1986 • Reagan appoints Independent Counsel Lawrence Walsh to investigate Iran-contra affair. Over next four years, Walsh convicts eleven. Two cases overturned on appeal and one dismissed before Bush issues presidential pardons.

Jan. 11, 1987 • Tambs, who resigned in wake of Santa Elena airstrip scandal, leaves Costa Rica. CIA Station Chief Fernández is recalled and departs secretly shortly afterward.

Jan. 17, 1987 • San José Summit convened by Arias to launch peace plan. Attended by presidents of Honduras, Guatemala, and El Salvador, but not Nicaragua.

Jan. 1987 • Contadora Group finally announces it has been unsuccessful in negotiating Nicaraguan peace agreement.

Feb. 26, 1987 • Tower Commission Report on Iran-contra scandal released.

Feb.–Aug. 1987 • AID withholds funds to Costa Rica as sign of
displeasure with Arias peace plan.

April 1, 1987 • Arias, under pressure from Washington, removes
Guido Fernández as ambassador.

May 6, 1987 • Casey dies of a brain tumor.

May 7, 1987 • Congressional Iran-contra hearings open.

June 1987 • AID Director Chaij recalled at request of Arias.

June 17, 1987 • Arias summoned to White House and has hostile
exchange with Reagan and top administration officials over
peace plan.

July 25, 1987 • Arias incorporates Santa Elena property into
national park, touching off years of complex legal battles with
U.S. owners.

Aug. 7–8, 1987 • Central American presidents sign "Arias Peace
Plan" at summit in Guatemala.

Oct. 13, 1987 • Arias wins Nobel Peace Prize.

Nov. 1987 • Costa Rican judiciary opens case against Piza and
Col. José Montero for involvement in Santa Elena airstrip
project. • Ambassador Deane Hinton arrives.

Nov. 5, 1987 • Peace accords begin to go into effect.

Nov. 17, 1987 • The *Iran-Contra Affair* of the U.S. Congress
report released.

Jan. 12, 1988 • Arias expels contra leaders who refuse to renounce armed conflict and adhere to peace accords.

Jan. 15–16, 1988 • Sandinistas make important concessions at
second San José Summit on the Central American peace plan.

Jan. 21, 1988 • State Dept. Inspector General's memo and audit
regarding AID malpractice in Costa Rica made public.

Feb. 3, 1988 • Congress votes down administration's contra military aid package.

March 21–23, 1988 • Ceasefire agreement between Nicaraguan
government and contras signed at Sapoa, Nicaragua, marking
official end of war.

April 1, 1988 • Sandinistas and contras begin truce in fighting. • Arias recalls Ambassador Guido Fernández whom Washington accused of "lobbying" against contra aid. Fernández becomes Information Minister.

May 23–29, 1988 • Biehl publicly denounces AID's Parallel State in small Chilean magazine, *APSI*.

Aug. 1988 • Biehl leaves Costa Rica.

Oct. 24, 1988 • Legislature passes second bank denationalization law.

Nov. 23, 1988 • Legislative Assembly's first Special Drug Commission report links leading politicians and officials to drug traffickers.

Dec. 1988 • U.S. Senate report, *Drugs, Law Enforcement and Foreign Policy,* documents links between contras, the CIA, Noriega and the drug cartel. • Enormous new AID complex, a symbol of the parallel state, opens in San José suburb. Nearby, U.S. Embassy headquarters had opened two months earlier.

Dec. 26, 1988 • Costa Rica judiciary report blames La Penca bombing on contras, CIA and drug traffickers, accuses CIA and OIJ officials of conspiring to derail the investigation, and charges Hull and Vidal with first degree murder for their involvement in the bombing.

Jan. 12, 1989 • Costa Rica's public prosecutor charges Hull, Octaviano César, and pilot Gerardo Durán with drug and arms trafficking and "hostile acts" for his contra activities. Hull arrested and subsequently released on bail.

Jan. 20, 1989 • George Bush sworn in as U.S. President.

Jan. 23, 1989 • The La Penca bomber Gaguine is reported to be among 28 leftist guerrillas killed in an attack on La Tablada, Argentina's main military base.

Jan. 26, 1989 • Seventeen Congressmen write letter threatening aid cutoff if Costa Rica continues to pursue Hull. Arias sends strong reply.

Feb. 14, 1989 • Five Central American presidents agree contras should be demobilized and Nicaraguan president Daniel Ortega agrees to free elections in 1990.

March 3, 1989 • McFarlane sentenced in Washington court to two years' probation, a $20,000 fine, and 200 hours of community service for withholding information from Congress.

April 13, 1989 • Congress agrees to allocate the contras $4.5 million in non-lethal aid each month until Nicaragua holds elections.

May 4, 1989 • North convicted on several minor counts for role in Iran-contra scandal. Fined and sentenced to community service in July.

July 18, 1989 • Hull jumps bail and DEA illegally flies him out of Costa Rica to avoid prosecution.

July 20, 1989 • Legislative Assembly's second Special Drug Commission report links U.S. officials, Noriega, and drug traffickers to Costa Rican contra operations. It recommends Joe Fernández, North, Poindexter, Tambs, and Richard Secord be declared *persona non grata* and that Hull be tried and sentenced, and then stripped of his Costa Rican citizenship and expelled.

Aug. 6–7, 1989 • At Tela, Honduras summit, Central American presidents reject U.S. pressure and unanimously call for demobilizing contras by Dec. 8. They ask United Nations and Organization of American States for help.

Aug. 23, 1989 • Tourists discover Green Berets and Civil Guard carrying out military and anti-drug operations in national park.

Aug. 1989 • Anti-Noriega "contras" reported operating out of southern Costa Rica.

Oct. 26–28, 1989 • Arias hosts hemispheric summit attended by Bush and fifteen other presidents to celebrate one hundred years of Costa Rican democracy. Leaders discuss the "Six D's": development, drugs, democracy, debt, disarmament and deforestation.

Nov. 24, 1989 • Washington judge dismisses case against Joe Fernández after Attorney General Dick Thornburgh blocked disclosure of relevant CIA documents.

Dec. 1989 • Enormous new AID complex • symbol of the Parallel State • opens in San José suburb. Nearby embassy headquarters had opened two months earlier.

Dec. 20, 1989 • U.S. invasion of Panama.

Jan. 24, 1990 • In Washington court, Secord sentenced to two years probation for role in Iran-contra scandal.

Feb. 1, 1990 • Albert Hakim sentenced to two years probation for illegally supplementing North's salary.

Feb. 4, 1990 • Conservative Unity Party candidate Rafael Angel Calderón elected Costa Rican president.

Feb. 25, 1990 • Sandinistas defeated in elections by opposition coalition UNO, led by Violeta Chamorro.

Feb. 1990 • Costa Rica starts extradition proceedings against Hull, asking that U.S. government return him so he can be tried on murder and other charges.

March 1990 • EARTH university finally opens.

March 13, 1990 • Bush lifts 5-year-old trade embargo and asks Congress for $300 million in aid for Nicaragua, including $45 million for demobilization of contras.

March 23, 1990 • Contras and Sandinistas reach agreement for disarming and moving rebels into UN-monitored zones.

April 2–3, 1990 • In Montelimar, Nicaragua, Central American presidents hold final summit on impementation of peace plan and agree to immediate demobilization of the contras and destruction of their weapons.

April 25, 1990 • Violeta Chamorro inaugurated as president of Nicaragua.

May 8, 1990 • Arias leaves office and Calderón inaugurated.

May 19, 1990 • U.S.-trained narcotics agents kill twelve-year-old boy in anti-drug raid.

June 8, 1990 • José Figueres, the "father" of modern Costa Rica, who abolished the army, nationalized the banks, and founded the Liberation Party, dies.

Aug. 1990 • Calderón government reacts cautiously to Bush's Initiative for the Americas, which is intended to eliminate trade barriers and increase investment.

Late Nov. 1990 • Legislature appoints special 4-member commission to investigate La Penca bombing.

Sept. 16, 1991 • North's convictions are thrown out on appeal.

Oct. 28, 1991 • Costa Rica closes last of the Nicaraguan refugee camps.

Nov. 15, 1991 • In Washington, former Under Secretary of State Elliott Abrams sentenced to two years probation and 100 hours' community service for lying to Congress about his role in Iran/contra scandal. • Washington judge reverses conviction of Poindexter on five felony counts for role in Iran-contra scandal.

Jan. 31, 1992 • CIA official Alan Fiers sentenced to one year's probation and 100 hours' community service for withholding information from Congress about illegal financing of contras.

May 25, 1992 • Ex-CIA official Tom Clines begins serving sixteen month prison term for tax felonies related to Iran-contra financial deals.

Dec. 9, 1992 • In Washington trial, CIA official Clair George found guilty of two felony charges.

Dec. 11, 1992 • Bush agrees to turn over to Independent Prosecutor Walsh his personal diary notes on the Iran-contra affair kept after November 1986.

Dec. 24, 1992 • Bush gives presidential pardons to former Defense Secretary Caspar Weinberger, Clarridge, George, Abrams, Fiers, and McFarlane, effectively ending Walsh's prosecution of government officials involved in the Iran-contra scandal.

Aug. 1, 1993 • The La Penca bomber is identified as Vital Roberto Gaguine, a leftist Argentine guerrilla who worked for the Sandinista's Fifth Directorate counter-intelligence unit.

Notes

Chapter 1: Coming to Costa Rica

1. Mitchell Seligson, "Implementing Land Reform: The Case of Costa Rica."

2. U.S. General Accounting Office, "Costa Rica: Country Summary," draft, p. 3. No date but released Feb. 1989. Obtained through a congressional aide.

3. Charles Ameringer, *Don Pepe: A Political Biography of José Figueres,* pp. 179–89, 218–226.

4. Edgar Chamorro, the FDN's public relations officer in Honduras who was working for the CIA, wrote that at the time Torgerson and Cross were killed, "It was being said in some *contra* camps that the death of a journalist . . . could cause an uproar if it were blamed on the Sandinistas, and could be very destructive for them." Chamorro, who had arranged permissions for the two American reporters to visit the border region, related that although they were killed on the Honduras side of the border by the type of mine used by the contras, the initial reports said they were killed by a grenade and machine-gun fire from Nicaraguan territory. "The manner in which the Hondurans and Americans, in support of the *contras,* were to make rash statements about the deaths and fail to make a very full investigation of the kinds of mines that were involved, was very strange," wrote Chamorro who later quit the FDN. Edgar Chamorro, *Packaging the Contras: A Case of CIA Disinformation,* monograph series, no. 2 (New York: Institute for Media Analysis, 1987), 31–33.

Chapter 2: The Road from La Peuna

1. We assumed that "Amac Galil" was probably a pseudonym and that the Libyan identity might be a confusion with Lebanese or simply signify an Arab or someone from the Middle East.

2. Charles Mohr, "U.S. in Warning to Nicaraguans on Terror Plans," *New York Times,* July 19, 1985.

3. These included Martha Honey, "Right Plot to Hit US Envoys," *Sunday Times* (London), July 28, 1985.

4. In one of the more bizarre twists of the case, Hull several months later produced a young Nicaraguan contra whom he claimed was "our

David." At a "special" closed-door press conference given by Hull and DIS, Costa Rica's security and intelligence agency, this "David" said simply that he did not know Carlos Rojas, Tony, or me. We, along with the *Tico Times*, were labeled as "leftists" and barred from attending. However, we obtained a videotape of the press conference, and Carlos easily confirmed this was not the David he knew. Crude as this maneuver was, Hull continued to trot out this man over the years in a vain effort to discredit our investigation. The original articles include "La Penca: interrogan a supuesto informante," *La Prensa Libre*, Nov. 9, 1985; "Rancher Seeks to Discredit Report," *Tico Times*, Nov. 15, 1985.

5. "Nuevas pistas sobre 'La Penca,'" *La República*, Aug. 31, 1985.

6. In the weeks leading up to the press conference, we had solicited a private meeting with Tambs to tell him what we had learned about La Penca, the Embassy plot, and the plans to assassinate him. He refused to see us.

7. There were several journalistic investigations into Carr's death including Dennis Bernstein and Vince Bielski, "Conspiracy of Hopelessness," *In These Times*, Apr. 15–21, 1987; Michael Fessier, "An American Contra," *Los Angeles Times Magazine*, May 31, 1987; Leslie Cockburn, *Out of Control*, New York: Atlantic Monthly Press, 1987; Peter Dale Scott and Jonathan Marshall, *Cocaine Poltics: Drugs, Armies, and the CIA in Central America*, pp. 154–56.

8. Tony Avirgan and Martha Honey, *La Penca: On Trial in Costa Rica—The CIA vs. the Press*. Also published in Spanish.

9. The defendants in our lawsuit were: John Hull, Richard Secord, Albert Hakim, John Singlaub, Rafael "Chi Chi" Quintero, Robert Owen, Ronald Joseph Martin, Theodore Shackley, Thomas Clines, James McCoy, Mario Delamico, Adolfo Calero, René Corvo, Thomas Posey, Francisco Chanes, Moisés Dagoberto Núñez, Héctor Cornillot, Bruce Jones, Ricardo Gris, William Gris, Jorge González, Frederico Saenz, Felipe Vidal, Ramón Cecilio Palacio, Amac Galil, Alvaro Cruz, Pablo Escobar, and Jorge Ochoa.

10. Peter Dale Scott and Jonathan Marshall, *Obstruction of Justice: The Reagan-Bush Coverup of the Contra Drug Connection*, and *Cocaine Politics: Drugs, Armies and the CIA in Central America*. See also Jack Terrell with Ron Martz, *Disposable Patriot: Revelations of a Soldier in America's Secret Wars*.

11. Costa Rican Legislative Assembly, *Special Commission Appointed to Investigate the Acts Reported on Drug Trafficking*, San José, July 10, 1989.

12. Jorge Chavarria, Public Prosecutors, Costa Rican Judiciary,

Investigation on the La Penca Case, San José, Dec. 26, 1989; Christic Institute English translation.

Chapter 3: AID's Privatization Solution

1. Author's interviews; Lisa Jones, "U.S. Embassy Building Opens to Mixed Reviews," *Tico Times,* Oct. 14, 1988.

2. Douglas Eldred, special assistant to the media operations coordinator, Bureau of External Affairs, AID, Washington, D.C., letter to author, Nov. 3, 1989.

3. Tom Barry and Deb Preusch, *The Soft War,* p. 33.

4. Colin Danby, "Stabilization and Transformation: Bilateral U.S. Economic Aid in Central America," p. 24.

5. Quoted in Barry and Preusch, *Soft War,* p. 47.

6. Theodor Galdi, *Development Assistance Policy,* pp. 20–21.

7. Quoted in Barry and Preusch, *Soft War,* p. 36.

8. The document was written by a team of Cold Warriors headed by Arizona State University professor and future ambassador to Costa Rica Lewis Tambs. Committee of Santa Fe, "A New Inter-American Policy for the Eighties," pp. 3–5.

9. The author of this plank, an aide to Senator Jesse Helms, said this meant overthrowing the Sandinistas. Roy Gutman, *Banana Diplomacy: The Making of American Policy in Nicaragua 1981–1987,* pp. 18–22.

10. Gutman, *Banana Diplomacy,* pp. 85–86.

11. Senate Development Policy Committee, "Foreign Aid to Central America, FY 1981–1987," pp. 1, 5–6.

12. Senate Policy Committee, "Foreign Aid," pp. 5–6.

13. Danby, "Stabilization," p. 35; Senate Policy Committee, "Foreign Aid," p. 10.

14. Danby, "Stabilization," p. 34.

15. USAID, "The Effectiveness and Economic Development Impact of Policy-Based Cash Transfer Programs: The Case of Costa Rica," *Evaluation Highlights,* No. 1, Washington, Oct. 1988, p. 7.

16. Senate Policy Committee, "Foreign Aid," p. 7.

17. Senate Policy Committee, "Foreign Aid," pp. 2, 8.

18. Robert E. Sánchez, *The Central American States and Panama: Country Background Reports,"* Congressional Research Service Report, Sept. 18, 1987, p. 37.

19. In the 1950s, Monge was secretary general of the Inter-American Regional Organization of Labor (ORIT), which received CIA funding, and also a member of the board of directors of another CIA-financed

organization, the Institute for International Labor Research (IILR). Together with José Figueres, Monge set up the Inter-American Institute of
Political Education (IIEP), a Liberation Party leadership training school
and ideological center. The IIEP (later known as CEDAL) received funds
from the IILR, and IIEP's first secretary/treasurer was Sacha Volman, a
Rumanian refugee who had been recruited into the CIA in Europe. In the
1970s, Volman worked closely with anti-Castro Cubans involved in
terrorist activities. His son Dennis was a diplomat in the U.S. Embassy in
Managua and then a *Christian Science Monitor* reporter; according to a
top contra, he also worked for the CIA. Author's interviews; Ameringer,
Democracy in Costa Rica, pp. 122–25, and *Don Pepe,* various sections.

20. As U.S. Ambassador to Costa Rica Curtin Winsor, a Reagan
administration appointee, said of Monge, "He was a labor leader and a lot
of people were very afraid of him, but he turned out to be a staunch
democrat and anticommunist. He recognized the spot Costa Rica was in
. . . so he was willing to trade off some out of control programs of the
state." Interview with Ambassador Curtin Winsor, conducted by Charles
Stuart Kennedy, Association for Diplomatic Studies, Foreign Affairs Oral
History Program, Lauinger Library, Georgetown University, Washington, Feb. 29, 1988, p. 33.

21. Black, "Costa Rica: Into the Eye of the Storm," *NACLA: Report
on the Americas* (July/August 1982): p. 38.

22. Whereas AID funds were mainly grants, the IMF, World Bank,
and IDB gave only loans. IMF loans were, like most AID funds, for
balance-of-payment support and debt servicing. In contrast, World Bank
and IDB loans were for large infrastructure projects.

23. Marc Edelman, "Back from the Brink," *NACLA: Report on the
Americas* (Nov./Dec. 1985): pp. 42, 45.

24. USAID, "AID in Costa Rica: 1982–1992"; USAID, "USAID
Assistance to Costa Rica: 1946–1989."

25. Seligson and Gómez, "Political Economy of Voting in Costa
Rica," in Booth and Seligson, *Elections and Democracy in Central America,*
p. 164.

26. Court document, "U.S. Government Stipulation on Quid Pro
Quos with Other Governments as Part of Contra Operations," Apr. 6,
1989, introduced in case of United States of America v. Oliver L. North,
Defendant, pp. 3–4. Reprinted in full of Peter Kornbluh and Malcolm
Byrne, ed., *The Iran-Contra Scandal: The Declassified History,* pp. 85–97.

27. Court document, "Stipulation," pp. 3–4.

28. Senate Policy Committee, "Foreign Aid," p. 52.

29. Herbert Beckington, confidential Manager-to-Manager memo to AID administrator Alan Woods, Oct. 1987, p. 10.

30. Winsor interview by Kennedy, p. 25; John Newton, et al., *The Effectiveness and Economic Development Impact of Policy-Based Cash Transfer Programs: The Case of Costa Rica,* Nov. 1988, pp. 24–25.

31. USAID, "Effectiveness," *Evaluation Highlights,* pp. 4–5.

32. USAID, "Assistance Agreement between the United States of America and the Central Bank of Costa Rica for Economic Stabilization and Recovery II," AID Loan No. 515-1K-040, Dec. 13, 1982.

33. GAO, "Foreign Assistance: U.S. Use of Conditions to Achieve Economic Reforms," p. 27.

34. Newton et al., *Effectiveness,* p. A–3.

35. Neil Billig, AID officer in Costa Rica, Jan. 5, 1989, quoted in Danby, "Stabilization," p. 106.

36. USAID, "Effectiveness," *Evaluation Highlights,* p. 5.

37. Newton et al., *Effectiveness,* p. 39.

38. USAID, Washington worldwide cable #327494/02, Sec. 2.80. Copy in author's permission.

39. Alexander Tomlinson and Ismael Benavides, *Evaluation of the Divestiture Program of Corporación Costarricense de Desarrollo, S.A. ("CODESA"),* p. 41.

40. The commission was made up of the Minister of the Presidency, Rodrigo Arias; President of the Central Bank Eduardo Lizano; Minister of Finance Fernando Naranjo; and the Minister of Planning, Jorge Monge, who replaced Ottón Solís in late 1988.

41. John Bennett, "Wealthy Costa Ricans Enriched by U.S. Aid Program, Audit Shows," Scripps Howard News Service, Jan. 21, 1988; Beckington, Manager-to-Manager memo.

42. Associated Press, "Probers: Costa Rica Aid Abused," *Miami Herald,* Feb. 13, 1988.

43. Curiously this memo does not mention the two practices most troubling to the Arias administration: charging interest and keeping the Special Account in AID's name.

44. Lezak Shallat, "Oscar [Arias] ha sido tremendo," *APSI,* May 23–29, 1988; Shallat, "U.S. Aid to C.R.—The Story behind the Uproar," *Tico Times,* July 15, 1988.

45. John Biehl del Río, "No me sentí extranjero en Costa Rica," *La Nación,* June 17, 1988.

46. CEPAS, "La privatización de lo público," *Costa Rica: Balance de la Situación,* No. 27, San José, Aug.–Oct. 1988, p. 10.

Chapter 4: Privatization of the Banks

1. Ameringer, *Don Pepe,* p. 70.

2. Costa Rica's national banking system consists of four state banks: *Banco Anglo de Costa Rica,* registered in 1863; *Banco de Costa Rica,* registered in 1877; *Banco Nacional de Costa Rica,* registered in 1914; and *Banco Crédito Agrícola de Cartago,* registered in 1918.

3. Ameringer, *Democracy in Costa Rica,* p. 42.

4. Julio Jurado, Liberation party official and legislator during the Monge years, quoted in "Unidad no vota Ley de Moneda si se incluye en presupuesto," *La Prensa Libre,* June 18, 1984.

5. Interview by Bruce Wilson, for Ph.D. dissertation, Washington University, July 1990.

6. Lidiette Brenes, *La nacionalización bancaria en Costa Rica,* p. 74.

7. Edward Cody, "Costa Rican Leaders Irked by 'Lip Mistakes' of U.S. Ambassador," *Washington Post,* Feb. 4, 1984; Jacqueline Sharkey interview with Curtin Winsor, *Mesoamérica,* San José, Aug. 1984.

8. USAID, "Three-Year Strategy," p. 1.

9. USAID, "AID: 1982–1992," p. 6.

10. Newton et al., *Effectiveness,* p. B-1.

11. Newton et al., *Effectiveness,* p. 25.

12. The agreement specified interest rates to be applied to the final user which would give the private banks a "spread" of 9.0 percent. Of this, 4.0 percent would be redeposited in the Central Bank as insurance for the private banks. The result was that the private banks were receiving a comfortable 5 percent profit for acting as intermediaries channeling Central Bank funds to the private sector, while the Central Bank was responsible for insuring these funds. Central Bank of Costa Rica, "Reglamento para la utilización de los recursos de los convenios de asistencia AID-515–0185, 0186, 0192 y 0194 (Préstamos AID-515-K-037, 040 y 043)," approved by the board of directors of the Central Bank in session No. 4173, Art. 5, Oct. 29, 1986.

13. USAID, "Emphasis on Private Sector: Summary," San José, Jan. 1987, p. 4.

14. USAID, "Project Loan Agreement between the United States of America and the Central Bank of Costa Rica for Economic Stabilization and Recovery," AID Loan No. 515-K-037, July 14, 1982, Sec. 6.1.C.

15. USAID, "Assistance Agreement," AID Loan No. 515-K-040, Dec. 13, 1982, Sec. 3.3.

16. USAID, "Strategy Update," San José, Mar. 1988, p. 21.

17. For an excellent analysis of the intertwining of U.S.-pushed

political and economic changes see Manuel Gutiérrez S. and Jorge Vargas C., *Costa Rica es el Nombre del Juego.*

18. Winsor interview by Kennedy, p. 23; "Embajador de Estados Unidos Visitó la Asamblea Legislativa," *La República,* May 18, 1984.

19. Sam Dillon, "Debt, Rebels Undercut U.S. Relations with Costa Rica," *Miami Herald,* June 17, 1984.

20. Brenes, *La nacionalización bancaria,* note 66, p. 87.

21. "La Dogma de la Nacionalización Bancaria," *La Nación,* Aug. 14, 1984.

22. "FMI Flexibiliza Posición," *La Prensa Libre,* Aug. 10, 1984.

23. Edelman, "Back from the Brink," p. 43. This cutoff also related to U.S. pressure to force Costa Rica to accept its military engineers.

24. Gutiérrez and Vargas, *Costa Rica,* pp. 29, 43. Winsor later boasted, "I ended up withholding aid—something no ambassador had done in Costa Rica—for a month. To the point where, literally, the country was on the brink of problems." Winsor interview by Kennedy, p. 28.

25. "AID reitera que no ayudará sin reforma a Ley de Moneda," *La Nación,* May 4, 1984.

26. Edelman, "Back from the Brink," p. 43.

27. Sharkey, *Mesoamérica,* Aug. 1984; "$23 millones Dió E.U. Ayer a Gobierno," *La República,* Aug. 21, 1984.

28. "¡El país está al borde del colapso!" *La Nación,* Aug. 6, 1984.

29. Gutiérrez and Vargas, *Costa Rica,* p. 55.

30. Author's reporting; interviews with Solano and other government officials; "Monge" Coup rumors are No Big Deal," *Tico Times,* Aug. 10, 1984.

31. Winsor acknowledged he pressured President Monge to get rid of Solano, whom he characterized as "about as extreme left as you can get without being communist." Solano's firing effectively halted several investigations, including those into the La Penca bombing and John Hull's ties to the contras and drug traffickers. Author's interviews; Brian Donovan, "US Reportedly Pressured Costa Rica," *Newsday,* July 27, 1987; UPI, "Costa Rican's Cabinet resigns; shake-up linked to coup rumors," *Miami Herald,* Aug. 13, 1984; Edward Cody, "Coup rumor, shake-up, and democracy rolls along," *Philadelphia Inquirer,* Aug. 27, 1984.

32. "Ha caído el telón: La historia tiene la palabra," *La Semanario Universidad,* Aug. 24, 1984.

33. USAID, "Three-Year Strategy," p. 32.

34. "Record de cocaína confiscada," *La República,* Nov. 20, 1987;

"Capturado con 3 toneladas de cocaína en EE.UU.," *La Prensa Libre,* Nov. 20, 1987.

35. Rafael A. Ugalde and Marco Sibaja, "El Castigo de los Dioses," *La Semanario Universidad,* Feb. 12, 1988.

36. José Miguel Fonseca, "Estado reconoce responsibilidad por quiebra de financieras," *La Prensa Libre,* June 20, 1989.

37. Luis Paulino Vargas Solís, "Todo sea por la banca privada," *Aportes,* Sept. 1988.

38. USAID, "Three-Year Strategy," pp. 32–33.

39. Costa Rica Central Bank, Auditor General for Financial Entities, "Información financiera y contable por tipo de entidad financiera al 31 de Mayo de 1990," published in *La Nación,* June 24, 1990. The number of finance companies had dropped from a peak of sixty-eight in 1987, on the eve of the crash.

40. Author's interviews; USAID, "Three-Year Strategy," p. 2.

41. USAID, "Emphasis on Private Sector," p. 6.

42. Newton et al., *Effectiveness,* p. 3.

43. USAID, "AID: 1982–1992," p. 5.

44. USAID, "Three-Year Strategy," p. 30.

45. Ameringer, *Don Pepe,* p. 234.

46. Brenes, *La nacionalización bancaria,* pp. 165–66.

47. USAID, "Strategy Update," pp. 20–21.

48. Leonel Villalobos, "La Banca Nacionalizada," speech to Legislative Assembly, October 1987.

49. Brenes, "Banca privada," *La Nación,* Apr. 16, 1990.

50. Solís, "Cierre de bancos," *La Nación,* Mar. 9, 1990.

51. "Bank Shuts 7 Branches," *Tico Times,* Oct. 12, 1990; Yanancy Noguera C., "Cierran 7 oficinas del banco Nacional," *La Nación,* Oct. 1, 1990.

52. USAID, "Strategy Update," p. 21.

53. AID, "Strategy Update," pp. 10, 20–23.

54. Brenes, *La Nacionalización Bancaria,* pp. 147, 140.

55. USAID, "Three-Year Strategy," pp. 2–3.

56. Central Bank statistics for 1989, for instance, showed that 64 percent of private bank credit went to industry, 12 percent to agriculture and cattle, and only 1 percent to housing. In contrast, 27 percent of state bank credit went to industry, 37 percent to agriculture and cattle, and 8 percent to housing. While state bank credit was roughly divided between investment and operational activities, well over 90 percent of private bank credit went into operational activities.

57. Private finance companies were also having a hard time. Of the fifty-eight finance companies listed in the May 1990 Auditor General's report, twenty-three had been prohibited from new transactions because of insufficient funds and eleven were on the verge of closing. Interview with Ottón Solís; "Información financiera," *La Nación,* June 24, 1990.

58. Walter Coto, "Fortalecimiento de la banca privada: ¿Avance financiero o retroceso político?" in "Comentarios sobre asuntos económicos" No. 66 (San José: Central Bank, 1987), p. 12.

Chapter 5: The Parallel State

1. Lezak Shallat, "Biehl's 'Parallel State': Duplication of Efforts," *Tico Times,* July 22, 1988.

2. Brian Donovan, "U.S. AID a Boon to Pro-Contra Rancher," *Newsday,* May 17, 1987; Tom Barry, *Costa Rica,* p. 65.

3. Interviews with CINDE officials by Mary Clark for Ph D dissertation, University of Wisconsin-Madison, Tom Barry, *Costa Rica,* p. 65.

4. USAID, "US Emphasis on Private Sector: Summary," Jan. 1987; USAID "Project Summaries," Costa Rica, n.d.

5. Abelardo Morales Gamboa, "Ricos y famosos se benefician con AID," *Áportes,* Mar. 1988.

6. Beckington, Manager-to-Manager memo, p. 1.

7. Larry Jordan, "Goodwill and Friendship . . . Denied," *Tico Times,* May 31, 1991.

8. Shallat, "Biehl's 'Parallel State' "; Peter Brennan, "Party Protests Kerry Document," *Tico Times,* July 7, 1989; USAID, "Private Sector: Summary," pp. 9, 15; author's interviews.

9. Fax to Deputy Alberto Fait, Costa Rican Legislative Assembly, from Sen. John Kerry, Washington, D.C., June 26, 1989.

10. Vicki Kemper, "Exporting Politics: How Federal Funds Boosted Costa Rica's Opposition Party," *Common Cause,* Jan./Feb. 1990.

11. USAID, "Program Assistance Approval Document (PATE)" #515–0240, Costa Rica, Annex B, Mar. 1989, p. 3.

12. Tomlinson and Benavides, *CODESA,* p. 1.

13. Beckington, Manager-to-Manager memo; Editorial, *Tico Times,* June 16, 1989.

14. Richard Dyer, "Doom Soon for White Elephant," *Tico Times,* May 24, 1991.

15. USAID, "Approval Document," p. 2.

16. Tomlinson and Benavides, *CODESA,* p. 20.

17. Brenes, *La nacionalización bancaria,* pp. 130–31; Tomlinson and Benavides, *CODESA,* p. 20.

18. Tomlinson and Benavides, *CODESA,* pp. 4, 20.

19. Tomlinson and Benavides, *CODESA,* p. 5.

20. The money FINTRA received from sales was then applied against CODESA's deficit with the Central Bank. In effect, this was a book transfer: the colones were withdrawn from the AID Special Account and applied against CODESA's deficit.

21. Tomlinson and Benavides, *CODESA,* pp. 5, 40.

22. Beckington, Manager-to-Manager memo, pp. 36, 20.

23. Beckington, Manager-to-Manager memo, pp. 20–21; Tomlinson and Benavides, *CODESA,* p. 32.

24. Journalist Carol Weir's interview (for author) with Irvin Geiger of the AID Private Sector Department, San José, Sept. 1992.

25. Caitlin Randall, "Politicos Still Haggling over Fate of CODESA," *Tico Times,* June 7, 1985.

26. Yanancy Noguera C., "CODESA: Reconversión industrial pasará a sector privado," *La Nación,* June 28, 1990.

27. USAID, "Approval Document," Annex B, p. 3.

28. USAID, "Project Summaries," Costa Rica, n.d.

29. Tomlinson and Benavides, *CODESA,* p. 10.

30. Weir interview with Geiger. By 1990, 42.5 percent of CODESA's assets had been liquidated, 21.5 percent transferred to other government agencies, 22.5 percent sold to coops or private buyers, and 13 percent had not been handled. AID, "Approval Document."

31. Tomlinson and Benavides, *CODESA,* p. 5.

32. USAID, "Private Sector," p. 13.

33. Beckington, Manager-to-Manager memo, p. 6; author's interviews.

34. Beth Hawkins, " 'EARTH' Approval Sparks University Protests," *Tico Times,* Aug. 29, 1986. A copy of this study could not be located in the libraries at the University of North Carolina or in those at EARTH, AID, or the University of Costa Rica.

35. USAID, computer printout of ESF and PL-480 project funding in Costa Rica.

36. Ronald Bailey, "EARTH Hopes to Conquer Initial Controversy," *Tico Times,* Jan. 18, 1991.

37. Frank Heileman, Project Manager, AID, Costa Rica, letter to author, Jan. 12, 1989.

38. Newton et al., *Effectiveness,* p. 60.

39. USAID, "Approval Document," Annex F, p. 4.

40. Jim McNeill, "A parallel state: U.S. AID drains Costa Rican democracy," and "CINDE: A 'well-oiled job-stealing machine' paid for by U.S. taxpayers," *In These Times,* Sept. 19–25, 1990.

41. CBS's "60 Minutes" on Sept. 27, 1992, did a critical exposé of AID's business promotion agency in El Salvador, Fusades.

42. The figures claimed by CINDE are for jobs projected by investors. At this time, only about half had been filled.

43. Letter to CBS from Carlos Eduardo Robert, general manager, CINDE, and Rodrigo Ortiz, general manager, Costa Rican Investment Promotion Program, Oct. 24, 1989.

44. Bell et al., *Evaluation of CINDE,* p. 4.

45. Beckington, Manager-to-Manager memo.

46. Beckington, Manager-to-Manager memo, pp. 6–7.

47. Bell et al., *Evaluation of CINDE,* Executive Summary.

48. Beckington, Manager-to-Manager memo, pp. 6–11.

49. In interviews, both Guido Fernández and former Ambassador McNeil defended this procedure, which they argued violated no Costa Rican laws.

50. Bennett, "Wealthy Costa Ricans," Scripps Howard News Service, January 21, 1988. For a fairer version of the scandal see Jelinek, "Probers: Costa Rica aid abused," *Miami Herald,* Feb. 13, 1988.

51. Neil Roland, "Billions in U.S. Foreign Aid Untraceable, Auditors Say," UPI, Jan. 1, 1989.

52. USAID, "Private Sector," pp. 3, 4; Beckington, Manager-to-Manager memo; Costa Rican Legislative Assembly, Special Commission on CINDE and AID, 1988, partial transcript in possession of author; Mary Clark, "The Politics of Economic Adjustment in a Democracy: International Relations, Domestic Coalitions, and Nontraditional Export Promotion in Costa Rica," University of Wisconsin-Madison, draft of Ph.D. dissertation in progress, 1993), chapter 4, pp. 31–33; Alicia Korten, "Structural Adjustment, the Environment and the Poor: Case Study of Costa Rica," Brown University senior honors thesis, May 1992, pp. 27–31.

53. CINDE, "Costa Rica: The Right Business Climate," San José, 1989.

54. Between 1980 and 1986, OPIC insured more projects in Costa Rica than in any other Latin American country. Kal Waggenheim, "Costa Rica," special advertising section, *Wall Street Journal,* Oct. 20, 1988.

55. U.S. Congress, *Drugs, Law Enforcement and Foreign Policy,* p. 57.

56. Martin Tolchin, "A Contra Supplier in Costa Rica Got $375,000, U.S. Agency Says," *New York Times,* Oct. 31, 1987.

57. William Crone deposition to Christic Institute, Jan. 5–7, 1988, Vol. I, p. 160.

58. Brian Donovan, "Probing Hull's Bad Debt," *Newsday,* Oct. 5, 1987; Jonathan Kwitny, "Figure in Contra," *Wall Street Journal,* Oct. 30, 1987.

59. CINDE, "CBI: Costa Rica, The Right Business Climate," San José, n.d.

60. CINDE, "Costa Rica."

61. Bell et al., *Evaluation of CINDE,* p. 31. Once again AID and CINDE were backed up by an AID-funded Arthur D. Little study which concluded that textiles represented the highest potential profits in the short term. Brenes, *La Nacionalización Bancaria,* p. 128.

62. Bell et al., *Evaluation of CINDE,* p. 27.

63. Waggenheim, "Costa Rica"; USAID, "Approval Document," Annex F, p. 4.

64. CINDE, "Costa Rica."

65. An excellent *Tico Times* series by Emma Daly and Cyrus Reed investigated the poor working conditions in these new, foreign-owned factories which resulted in workers filing hundreds of complaints about a broad spectrum of abuses, including wages under the minimum; compulsory, unpaid overtime; sexual harassment; union blacklisting; and unjustified dismissals. Labor Ministry official Alvaro Sojo described the textile industry, which employed mainly young single mothers, as having the "most unstable worker-employee relations" of any industrial sector. The *Tico Times* series ran on May 4, 11, 25 and June 8, 1990.

66. McNeill, "CINDE."

67. Carol Weir interview with Luis Guillermo, director, Administrative Office of Quotas (for the textile industry), Aug. 31, 1992.

68. Cyrus Reed, "Changes in Textile Industry—Hopes, Fears," *Tico Times,* June 8, 1990.

69. USAID, "Approval Document," Annex F, p. 6.

70. USAID, "Approval Document," Annex F, p. 6; author's interview with Torres.

71. USAID, "Approval Document," Annex F, p. 10; Carol Weir interview with AID officer Arturo Villalobos in Sept. 1992.

Chapter 6: Health Care in the 1980s

1. World Bank, *World Development Report,* and "Costa Rica: Country Economic Memo," p. 38.

2. In 1981, the IMF recommended that rural clinics and schools be closed. The government objected and this became one of the reasons prompting President Carazo to break off negotiations and expel the IMF representatives. Author's interviews.

3. Quoted in Abigail Adams, "Sterilization in Costa Rica," *Links* (National Central America Health Rights Network, Inc. [NCAHRN]) 4, no. 4 (Winter 1987).

4. Leonard Bird, *Costa Rica,* p. 134; Phillip W. Rourk, "Equitable Growth: The Case of Costa Rica" (AID/Washington Development Studies Program, 1979), p. 43.

5. Edgar Mohs, "Evolution of Paradigms of Child Health in Developing Countries," *Pediatric Infectious Disease* 4, no. 5 (1985):532.

6. Rourk, "Equitable Growth," p. 43.

7. Mohs, "Evolution of Paradigms," p. 532.

8. Luis Rosero-Bixby, "Infant Mortality in Costa Rica: Explaining the Recent Decline," *Studies in Family Planning* 17, no. 2 (1986):58.

9. By the end of the 1980s, there were twenty-nine government and four government-regulated private hospitals.

10. Rosero-Bixby, "Costa Rica Saves Infants' Lives," *World Health Forum* 9(1988): pp. 439–43.

11. Catherine Overholt, Peter Cross, and Catherine Linderberg, "Costa Rica: Health Sector Overview" (AID, Technologies for Primary Health Care [PRITECH] Project, Dec. 1985), p. 13; Lynn Morgan, "Health Effects of the Costa Rican Economic Crisis," in *The Costa Rica Reader,* ed. Marc Edelman and Joanne Kenen, pp. 215–16.

12. AID regional funds not included. AID, "Report on the Health, Population and Nutrition Activities," San José 1972, 1973, and 1974.

13. Morgan, "Health Effects," p. 216.

14. Mohs, "Evolution of Paradigms," p. 535; María Isabel Solís, "El laberinto de cáncer gástrico," *La Nación,* Sept. 3, 1990.

15. Morgan, "Health Effects," p. 214.

16. Rosero-Bixby, "Infants' Lives," pp. 439–43; Richard M. Garfield and Pedro F. Rodríguez, "Health and Health Services in Central America," *Journal of the American Medical Association* 254, no. 7 (Aug. 16, 1985): p. 939.

17. Interviews with Caja officials; Morgan, "Health Effects," p. 215; Rosero-Bixby, "Infant Mortality," p. 57.

18. "Costa Rica: Doctors' Strike Reflects Crisis," *Mesoamérica,* June 1982.

19. Morgan, "Health Effects," p. 215.

20. Overholt, "Overview," p. 13; World Bank, "Economic Memo," p. 35; Rosero-Bixby, "Infants' Lives," p. 442.

21. Author's interviews; Dr. Guido Miranda Gutiérrez, "Aporte económico-financiero de la C.C.S.S. a la gestión del gobierno" (Caja confidential document, Sept. 1987).

22. Mohs, "Infectious Diseases and Health in Costa Rica," *Pediatric Infectious Disease* 1, no. 3 (1982):215.

23. Morgan, "Health Effects," p. 216.

24. Garfield and Rodríguez, "Health," p. 942.

25. Garfield and Rodríguez, "Health," p. 942; USAID, "AID in Costa Rica: 1982–1992," Annex III.

26. USAID, "Project Summaries," n.d.; USAID, "Private Sector," p. 13; USAID, "Action Plan FY 1990–FY 1991," pp. 36, 55.

27. While decentralization frequently means empowering local communities, in this context it was being used by the medical elite to build up urban hospitals at the expense of rural and poorer areas.

28. Nicolás Aguilar, María Isabel Solís, and Ronald Moya, "Grave Situación en hospitales del país," *La Nación,* Feb. 17, 1990.

29. Morgan, "Health Effects," p. 217.

30. By 1990, the Caja paid medical specialists about 100,000 colones or just over $1,000 per month, while in the late 1970s salaries were about $1,700.

31. USAID, "Three-Year Strategy," p. 37.

32. UNICEF/WHO Joint Committee on Health Policy, "National Decision-Making for Primary Health Care," 1981, pp. 54–55.

33. Milton Roemer and Ruth Roemer, "Global Health, National Development, and the Role of Government," *American Journal of Public Health* 80, no. 10 (Oct. 1990): pp. 1188–92.

34. Rosero-Bixby, "Infant Mortality," p. 59, and "Costa Rica Saves," p. 443.

35. Interpress News Service (IPS), "Development: UNDP Cites Costa Rica as Outstanding Example," May 22, 1991.

36. World Bank, "Costa Rica," p. 39; USAID, "Action Plan, FY 1990–FY 1991," p. 36.

37. Solís, "El laberinto"; Garth Fraga, "Health Care: Fact and Fiction Behind Costa Rica's Health Care System," *Mesoamérica,* Sept. 1990; Lynn Morgan, "Health, Economic Austerity, and Structural Adjustment

in Costa Rica" (paper presented at Latin American Studies Association, Miami, Dec. 1989), p. 2.

38. "Private Medical Services Eyed as Boost for System," *Tico Times,* June 22, 1990.

39. The Calderón government cut $7.8 million from the health budget in 1991 and another $2 million in 1992. According to Ministry of Health statistics, the percentage of the national budget spent on health care dropped from 7.4 in 1989 to 6.9 in 1991. Throughout the 1980s, the percentage steadily declined from a peak of 11.4 in 1979.

40. Morgan, "Health, Economic Austerity," pp. 6, 14.

41. Quoted in Barry, *Low Intensity Conflict,* p. 51.

42. Author's interviews; Tony Avirgan, "Medicine for the Contras," *Links* (NCAHRN) 4, no. 4 (Winter 1987).

43. Cable from U.S. Ambassador Deane Hinton, Costa Rica, to U.S. Secretary of State Howard Baker (Subject: Expansion of Medical Supply and Service Program), July 1988. Obtained through Freedom of Information Act. Copy in possession of author.

44. "The Humanitarian Assistance Medical Supply and Service Program in Costa Rica," U.S. Embassy document released Sept. 14, 1988; USAID, "Task Force on Humanitarian Assistance for Central America."

45. Jake Dyer, "Rebel Clinic a Problem for Arias," *Tico Times,* Sept. 23, 1988.

46. Editorial, "If It Was a Blunder, It Shouldn't Have Happened," *Tico Times,* Sept. 23, 1988.

47. Costa Rican Ministry of Public Security, "Comunicado del gobierno de la república," Sept. 19, 1988.

48. Author's interviews; Security Ministry, "Comunicado"; Dyer, "Rebel Clinic."

49. Ken Ward and Rosalind Wiseman's interviews with AID and clinic officials; cable, Hinton to Baker, July 1988.

50. Barry and Preusch, *The New Right Humanitarians,* p. 56.

51. Carlos Briceno, "Medical Supplies Worth $2 Million Shipped to Refugees," *Miami Herald,* Feb. 15, 1985.

52. For more on these organizations see Barry and Preusch, *The New Right Humanitarians,* pp. 49–50, 63; Sklar, *Washington's War,* pp. 236–39.

53. Author's interviews; documents collected by Costa Rican legislator Javier Solís; Avirgan, "Medicine for the Contras"; numerous Costa Rican press articles, including Jake Dyer, "US Rancher Probed for Dona-

tion, Default," *Tico Times*, Aug. 7, 1987, and "Social Security Officials Defend Gift Involving Hull," *Tico Times*, Aug. 14, 1987.

54. Memo to North from Owen, Nov. 5, 1984.

55. Wiseman interview with Pat Irish, U.S. Task Force on Humanitarian Assistance, San José, 1990; USAID Task Force on Humanitarian Assistance documents.

56. Author's and Ken Ward's interviews with relief agency officials.

57. Friends of the Americas border projects included centers to aid contra families in the La Mosquitia area, where AID also had a $7.5 million medical and road- and bridge-building program.

58. Trans World Mission, a Los Angeles–based evangelical Christian organization, had eleven missions in Costa Rica. The Washington, D.C.–based Concerned Women of America, a fundamentalist Christian group headed by Beverly LaHaye, opposes the Equal Rights Amendment, abortion, homosexuality, and premarital sex, and it supported the contras. In the late 1980s, it claimed to be the fastest growing women's organization in the United States.

59. Author's interviews; Kathy Holub, "Ex-salesman's Pitch for Nicaraguan Refugees," *San José Mercury News*, San José, California, Oct. 30, 1986.

60. Author's interviews; USAID Task Force memo from N. R. Billig (Subject: Issuance of Clothing to Newly Arriving TFHA Center Patients), Mar. 15, 1989.

61. See Mario Ramírez, *Refugee Policy Challenges*, and Gilda Pacheco Oreamundo, *Nicaraguan Refugees in Costa Rica*.

62. Statistics from the Costa Rican government's Department for Refugee Protection and Assistance (DIGEPARE).

63. Author's interviews; Kathy McHugh, "ICM Brought First Refugees Here in 1957," *Tico Times*, Oct. 14, 1983; Sam Dillon, "US-Aided Refugee Camp Sits Idle and Empty in Honduras," *Miami Herald*, Dec. 10, 1984.

64. Author's interviews, including with an inmate of the Tilerán camp in 1983 who said he had lived in Costa Rica for eighteen years and had crossed the San Juan River into Nicaragua to visit his ailing mother. When he returned, he was seized by police and sent to the refugee camp, even though he had a wife, children, and property in Costa Rica. He and five other bogus refugees subsequently staged a hunger strike, demanding to be released.

65. Author's interviews; Ramírez found that 93 percent of the refugees were males in the Tilerán camp and 71 percent male in the Limón camp. Mario Ramírez, *Refugee Policy Challenges*, p. 52. One camp

administrator admitted that he was frequently given lists of contras to admit as refugees. In 1984, just after ARDE had received new supplies from the CIA, fifty of a group of ninety-seven ex-fighters who had earlier entered Costa Rica as refugees "escaped" from the Tilerán camp. It was widely presumed they returned to the war front. "Escapan pastoristas de centro de refugio," *La Nación,* Mar. 9, 1984.

66. Statistics from DIGEPARE; Ken Ward's interviews.

67. Mohs, "La salud en la década de los 80," speech reprinted in *La Prensa Libre,* Jan. 31, 1990.

Chapter 7: Nontraditional Agricultural Exports

1. USAID, "Three-Year Strategy," p. 7.

2. Cam Duncan, "Costa Rica: Conditionality and the Adjustment Policies of USAID in the Eighties" (paper presented at the Latin American Studies Association, Dec. 1989).

3. Stephen Lack and C. Kenneth Laurent, "Agricultural Crop Diversification/Export Promotion: Cross-Cutting Evaluation," Draft Executive Summary and Part C: Costa Rica USAID, Wash., 1988. This report gives no total for AID funding of Costa Rica's NTAE programs, but it lists some $110 million in loans and grants between 1982 and 1988. In addition, AID funneled multimillion-dollar loans and grants for NTAE programs through regional banks and institutions.

4. In Costa Rica "small farmer" means food producers or growers of cash crops such as coffee who rely only on family labor. Some Costa Rican experts say the term describes farmers with five or fewer hectares. However, AID and the World Bank consider small farmers to be those with up to ten hectares, which allows them to claim that their programs are "targeting" campesinos.

5. Miguel Martí, "La estrategía agroindustrial de exportaciones," *Aportes* 21 (Sept.–Oct. 1984), pp. 16–18.

6. The Monge government did so under the banner, "Return to the Land," while the Arias government adopted the slogan, "No farmer without land, no land without a farmer."

7. Statistics from CENPRO and SEPSA (Executive Secretary of Planning for Agricultural Development), Ministry of Agriculture.

8. USAID, "Congressional Presentation Fiscal Year 1989: Main Volume," Washington, D.C., p. 422.

9. Alicia Korten, "Structural Adjustment, the Environment and the Poor: Case Study of Costa Rica" (Brown University, Latin American Studies Dept., senior honors thesis, May 1992), pp. 62–63.

10. Cyrus Reed, " 'Agriculture of Change' Squeezes Farmers," *Tico Times,* June 1, 1990.

11. Armando González, "El fenómeno de la popularidad," *La Nación,* Mar. 11, 1990. Under Costa Rica's constitution, presidents cannot run for a second term.

12. Marc Edelman, "Extensive Land Use and the Logic of the Latifundio: A Case Study in Guanacaste Province, Costa Rica," *Human Ecology* 13, no. 2 (1985), and "Rethinking the Hamburger Debate: Deforestation and the Crisis of Central America's Beef Exports" (unpub. manuscript, Yale University, Dept. of Anthropology, 1990).

13. Robert Williams, *Export Agriculture and the Crisis in Central America,* p. 206, table A-10 (1960–80); 1980s figures from CENPRO.

14. Louis Andrews, "C.R. Leads in Deforestation," *Tico Times,* July 13, 1990. Satellite photos of Costa Rica taken in the late 1980s revealed that only 5 percent of the land outside nationally protected areas was still densely wooded.

15. By 1973, large farms (over 200 hectares) represented less than 6 percent of the total number of cattle ranches, but they controlled over half of all grazing land. Irene Aguilar and Manuel Solís, *La Elite Ganadera en Costa Rica;* Williams, *Export Agriculture,* pp. 102–12, 226.

16. USAID, "Regional Strategic Plan for Latin America and the Caribbean," p. 11.

17. USGAO, "Foreign Assistance: U.S. Use of Conditions to Achieve Economic Reforms," GAO/USAID-86-157, Aug. 1986, p. 8.

18. "Latins Warned on Sale of Assets," *Miami Herald,* May 4, 1990.

19. USAID, "Three Year Strategy," p. 7.

20. Michael Conroy, "The Diversification of Central American Exports: *Chimera* or Reality?" (paper presented at the "Coloquio sobre las crisis económicas del siglo XX," Madrid, Apr. 17–19, 1990), p. 19.

21. USGAO, "Foreign Assistance," p. 44.

22. William Bolton and Henry Mannion, *Evaluation of USAID/ Costa Rica Nontraditional Agricultural Export Strategy,* AID Contract no. 515-0000-C-00-9035-00, July 1989, p. 73.

23. Bea Bezmalinovic, et al., "*Agricultura de Cambio:* Mad about Macadamia?" (unpub. paper, San José: Associated Colleges of the Midwest program, Nov. 11, 1987), pp. 16–20.

24. Bolton and Mannion, *Export Strategy,* p. 41.

25. Lise Kirsten Nelson, "The Burden of Development: The Effects of *Agricultura de Cambio* on the Small Farmer in Costa Rica" (unpub. paper, San José: Association of Colleges of the Midwest program, May 1988), p. 24.

26. Eduardo Ramírez, "Las flores de la ruina," *Aportes* 44 (May 1988); Thomas Thacher, "Foreign Investment," p. 10.

27. Bolton and Mannion, *Export Strategy*, pp. 67–68.

28. Mary Clark, "Politics of Economic Adjustment," chapter 4, p. 7. Based on interview with AID director Daneil Chaij.

29. Clarence Zuvekas, "Central America's Foreign Trade and Balance of Payments: The Outlook for 1988–2000," Table 3, revised version, USAID, Washington, June 17, 1988; CENPRO, "Tabulados de la Dirección General de Estadísticas y Censos Período 1984–1989."

30. USGAO, "Central America: Impact of U.S. Assistance in the 1980s," GAO/NSIAD-89-170, July 1989, p. 51.

31. Lack and Laurent, "Crop Diversification," Summary, pp. 4, 7, 8; Section 3, p. 2.

32. Reed, "Squeezes Farmers."

33. USGAO, "Food Safety and Quality: Five Countries' Efforts to Meet U.S. Requirement on Imported Produce," Appendix 1, GAO/RCED-90-55, Mar. 1990; and "Five Latin American Countries' Controls over the Registration and Use of Pesticides," GAO/T-RCED-90–57, Mar. 28, 1990, incl. pp. 32, 49; Karen Cheney, "8 of 12 Worst Pesticides are used in Costa Rica," *Tico Times,* July 6, 1990.

34. Nelson Murillo, "País perdió $362 millones por rechazo de alimientos," *La Nación,* Feb. 22, 1989.

35. Bolton and Mannion, *Export Strategy*, p. 42.

36. Cheney, "It all started in the '50s," *Tico Times,* July 6, 1990; in a landmark legal case brought in Texas in the late 1980s, eighty-two Costa Rican banana workers and their spouses sued Dow Chemical, Shell Oil, and Standard Fruit, charging that they are among more than a thousand workers sterilized by DBCP, a hazardous pesticide used in the late 1970s to kill a worm which eats the roots of banana plants. David Weir and Constance Matthiessen, "Will the Circle Be Unbroken," *Mother Jones,* June 1989.

37. Thacher, "Foreign Investment," p. 50.

38. Information supplied by Costa Rican Central Bank's Department of Statistics and Census. In mid-1990, exonerations given to nontraditional exporters and others had become so great that for each colón collected on imports, the government was losing 1.36 colones on imported goods that were allowed to enter duty free. Carlos Roverssi, "Falta de Control en Exoneraciones Provoca Evasión Fiscal," *La República,* Oct. 16, 1990.

39. CENPRO chart "Movimiento anual de CAT otorgados en el

período 1973–1989"; internal document provided to author by CENPRO economist.

40. Central Bank statistics; Wilmer Murillo, "Cancelarán Incentivos a más de 500 empresas," *La República,* May 26, 1990.

41. María Elena Carvajal, "Court Case Hits Export Subsidies," *Tico Times,* Feb. 8, 1991.

42. "70% de exportadores no reciben los CAT," *La República,* July 10, 1990.

43. Lana Bennett, agricultural attaché, U.S. Embassy, San José, Costa Rica, "Costa Rica Agricultural Situation Annual 1988," pp. 16–18; Cyrus Reed, " 'Agriculture of Change' Costly, Complicated," *Tico Times,* June 22, 1990.

44. Dixie Mendoza, "Gobierno urge fallo sobre los CAT," *La Nación,* Feb. 7, 1991.

45. Wilmer Murillo, "Cancelarán incentivos", *La Republica,* May 26, 1990.

46. Of the top eight recipients of CATs in 1989, owners of one, the jewelry exporter Aurind, were Peruvian fugitives wanted for defrauding that country of $8 million; another, Corporación Aires de Paz, which exported handicrafts, was investigated for financial fraud, drug trafficking, and money laundering; and a third, the seafood company A. M. Inversiones, whose owners included Honduran military officers, mysteriously closed up just after receiving $1.2 million in CATs. Interviews by author and Ken Ward; Ministry of External Trade, "Monto de CAT otorgados, marzo 88–septiembre 89," confidential report, Dec. 1989; numerous local press reports.

47. Carol Weir's interviews, Nov. 1992; Murillo, "Cancelarán incentivos"; Korten, "Structural Adjustment," p. 29.

48. Author's interview; Bolton and Mannion, *Evaluation,* p. 68.

49. USAID, "Strategy Update," p. 12.

50. Ken Ward's interviews, Oct. 1990.

51. Ministry of Planning, "El deterioro socioeconómico del año 1989."

52. Foreign control in the nontraditional industrial sector is even greater than in the new agricultural export sector. Cited in Thacher, "Foreign Investment," pp. 63–64; Reed, "Squeezes Farmers."

53. Wilmer Murillo, "Transnacionales aumentan su poder económico en C.R.," *La República,* Oct. 28, 1988.

54. Bolton and Mannion, *Export Strategy,* pp. 67–68.

55. Thacher, "Foreign Investment," pp. 16–18.

56. Lack and Laurent, "Crop Diversification," Costa Rica, p.IV.C-30.

57. Costa Rica is the number one exporter of ornamental plants in the world. By 1990, there were just two national cooperatives, accounting for only about 7 percent of this sector's total exports. Thacher, "Foreign Investment," pp. 9–10, 13.

58. USAID, "Action Plan FY 1990–1991" (Costa Rica, n.d.), p. 26; Bolton and Mannion, *Export Strategy*, p. 30.

59. Bezmalinovic et al., "Mad about Macadamia?" pp. 16–17.

60. Economy and Commerce Ministry, "Enquesta de Hogares, 1989."

61. Thacher, "Foreign Investment," pp. 7–8, 11–12.

62. Lack and Laurent, "Crop Diversification," Part C: Costa Rica, p. IV.C-24–28.

63. Thacher, "Foreign Investment," p. 43.

64. Thacher, "Foreign Investment," p. 18.

65. CENPRO, "Requisitos para solicitar los beneficios del contrato turístico" and "Incentivos a las actividades turísticas" (undated; received July 1990). The Calderón government reduced some of these privileges.

66. "Mejores playas en manos de extranjeros," *La República*, July 11, 1990.

67. U.S. Congress, *Drugs*, pp. 45–47.

68. "Seminario sobre narcotráfico en las exportaciones" and "Costa Rica: Es utilizada como puente de drogas de América del Sur hacia Norteamérica," *Exportación* (Costa Rican Chamber of Exporters) 25, 1990; Peter Brennen, "2 Drug Busts, New Charges Shake Country," *Tico Times*, Apr. 21, 1989; Virginia Medina, "Analizan el narcotráfico en la exportación" and "Dos toneladas de cocaína pasan mensualmente por Costa Rica," *La República*, Apr. 17 and 18, 1990.

69. Korten, "Structural Adjustment," p. 51.

70. Alvaro Alvarez Desanti, Agriculture Ministry, "Un diálogo permanente," Oct. 1987.

71. Ken Ward's interviews; Bolton and Mannion, *Export Strategy*, p. 20; Thacher, "Foreign Investment," pp. 38, 40.

72. Nelson, "The Burden of Development," p. 53.

73. Interview with Peter Rosset, Centro Agronómico Tropical de Investigación y Enseñanza (CATIE).

74. Cyrus Reed, "New Government," *Tico Times*, June 29, 1990.

75. Contrary to AID's assertions, two traditional exports, bananas and coffee, have a history of high labor efficiency and productivity in terms of yields and, bank officials and economists say, small farmers have a good track record in paying back loans. It is the big producers,

cattlemen, manufacturers, and exporters, often politically well connected, who most often default.

76. USAID, "Regional Strategic Plan," Dec. 1983.

77. Bennett, Agricultural attaché, San José, "Costa Rica Grain and Feed Annual," Sept. 30, 1987, pp. 5, 11; René Vermeer, "La política agraria de la administración Arias en el marco del ajuste estructural," in Rubén Soto, ed., *Los campesinos frente a la nueva década,* p. 75.

78. U.S. Embassy, "Economic Trends Report, Costa Rica," Costa Rica, July 8, 1988, p. 5. In 1988, Costa Rica was forced to import 25 percent of its rice needs. David Dye, "Fate of 'Central American Switzerland' may be Bleak," *In These Times,* Nov. 23, 1988.

79. Reed, "New Government."

80. "Dice Lizano 'No sé por qué avergüenza importar maíz y fríjoles,' " *La República,* Jan. 14, 1989.

81. Statistics from *Oficina de la Agregada Agrícola,* U.S. Embassy, San José. Somewhat different statistics are given in Reed, "Squeezes Farmers."

82. USAID, "Loan Agreement between the United States of America and the Central Bank of Costa Rica for Economic Stabilization and Recovery III," AID loan no. 515-K-043, May 7, 1984.

83. Vermeer, "La política agraria," p. 59.

84. PL-480 agreement between the United States and Costa Rica, Sec. 5.B.1.b, in *La Gaceta,* Dec. 26, 1985.

85. Bank Information Center, ed., *Funding Ecological and Social Destruction* (Washington, D.C., Sept. 1990), p. 20.

86. Vermeer, "La Política Agraria," p. 59.

87. Weir interview with Alberto Fernández Mono, head of the CNP's Import and Export Section, Dec. 1992; Bennett, Agricultural attaché, "Grain and Feed," 1987, pp. 6–9.

88. In 1989, Costa Rica again exported rice but, according to Antonio Capella, this was the surplus remaining from an over-importation in 1988, rather than a surplus of local production.

89. Author's interview. According to a U.S. Embassy report, "The sowing of the 1989 crop has been financed to a large extent (60 percent) by mills as banks . . . reduced the amount of new lending to 20 percent of the total area planted (compared to 35 percent the year before). . . . Mills charge 2 percent above bank rates." Bennett, Agricultural attaché, San José, "Grain and Feed Annual Report," Oct. 1, 1989, n.p.

90. Author's interview; Dye, "Central American Switzerland."

91. Weir interview with Fernández, CNP.

92. Rose Mary Monge, Marvin Barquero, and Nelson Murillo, "Perdidas por $1.890 millones en vías," *La Nación,* Nov. 11, 1988.

93. Heather Williams et al., "*Agricultura de cambio,* n.p.

94. Abelardo Morales, "Labriegos sencillos frente a la guerra del hambre," *Aportes,* Aug./Sept. 1986.

95. Reed Karaim, "Food Aid: A Noble Cause Is Tainted," *Miami Herald,* Oct. 2, 1989.

96. Danby, "Stabilization," chart, p. 27, and other sections.

97. USAID, "Regional Strategic Plan," p. 25; Karaim, "Food Aid."

98. "Informe Semestral," Planning Ministry, Dec. 1989; Bolton and Mannion, *Export Strategy* p. 123; Reed, "Costly, Complicated."

99. Barry and Preusch, *Soft War,* p. 68.

100. Bennett, Agricultural attaché, San José "Grain and Feed," pp. 2, 7.

101. "Fueran eliminados," *La República,* Dec. 30, 1988.

102. "Politics of Costa Rican Agriculture," *Mesoamérica,* Jan. 1989.

103. Author's interviews with Esquivel, Lizano, and others; Betsy Lordan, "Cabinet Shakeup Defies Party's Old Guard," *Tico Times,* May 1, 1987; "Agriculture," *Mesoamérica,* Jan. 1989.

104. Cyrus Reed, "Food Aid OK'd Despite Protests," *Tico Times,* July 27, 1990. See also Tom Barry and Rachel Garst, *Feeding the Crisis: U.S. Food Aid and Farm Policy in Central America,* pp. 81–83.

105. The Sala Cuarta is modeled after the U.S. Supreme Court, and, like that body, it interprets the nation's constitution. It is a division of Costa Rica's Supreme Court, a body that hears important cases, receives appeals from the lower courts, and oversees prosecutors and the OIJ (roughly equivalent to the FBI).

106. Interviews with AID, State Dept., and Costa Rican government officials; Nelson Murillo, "PL-480 aprobado en primer debate," and "Reservas sobre capítulo de garantías económicas," *La Nación,* Aug. 9 and Sept. 13, 1990; Murillo and Armando Mayorga, "Fallo de la sala IV: Inconstitutional PL-480," *La Nación,* Aug. 30, 1990; "En tercer debate: Aprobado PL-480," *La República,* Sept. 14, 1990; Ronna Montgomery and Martha Brant, "Costa Rica: AID Assistance to Costa Rica," *Mesoamérica,* Oct. 1990.

107. Conroy, "*Chimera* or Reality?" p. 19.

108. Williams, *Export Agriculture,* pp. 184–85.

109. Quoted in Bank Information Center, *Funding,* p. 20.

110. Korten, "Structural Adjustment," pp. 40–43.

111. Reed, "Squeezes Farmers" and "Costly, Complicated."

Chapter 8: The Southern Front: "Honduras South"

1. A Finding is a classified document signed by the President authorizing a covert operation and taking responsibility for its consequences.

2. Peter Kornbluh, *Nicaragua: The Price of Intervention*, pp. 22–23.

3. Holly Sklar, *Washington's War on Nicaragua*, p. 144; Kornbluh, *Nicaragua*, p. 57.

4. Kornbluh, *Nicaragua*, pp. 20–22.

5. U.S. Congress, *Iran-Contra Affair*, p. 34.

6. The CIA is barred by law from conducting propaganda or other operations inside the United States. To get around this, CIA director William Casey transferred his leading propaganda specialist, Walter Raymond, Jr., to the National Security Council to oversee the Office of Public Diplomacy and other propaganda operations. Ross Gelbspan, *Break-ins, Death Threats and the FBI* (Boston: South End Press, 1991), pp. 122–25, 176–78; also U.S. Congress, *Iran-Contra Affair*, p. 34; Robert Parry and Peter Kornbluh, "Iran-Contra's Untold Story," *Foreign Affairs* (Fall 1988): 11.

7. U.S. Congress, *Iran-Contra Affair*, pp. 34–36.

8. U.S. Congress, *Iran-Contra Affair*, p. 42.

9. Kornbluh, *Nicaragua*, pp. 54–61, 270.

10. The Enterprise and Project Democracy became the centerfold of what was later termed the Iran-contra scandal. For an overview see: Kornbluh and Byrne, ed., *The Iran-Contra Scandal*; Kornbluh, *Nicaragua*; Robert Parry and Brian Barger, "Reagan's Shadow CIA," *New Republic*, Nov. 24, 1986; Leslie Cockburn, *Cover Up*, (New York: Atlantic Monthly Press, 1987); Holly Sklar, *Washington's War*; U.S. Congress, *Iran-Contra Affair*; and President's Special Review Board, *Report of the Special Review Board* (hereafter referred to as the *Tower Commission Report*), Feb. 26, 1987.

11. Hakim unabashedly told the Iran-contra hearings, "I never pretended to undertake the tasks I was asked to perform for philanthropic purposes and I made that clear to all of those with whom I [w]as involved—including General Secord, Lieutenant Colonel North, the CIA, and the Iranians." U.S. Congress, *Iran-Contra Affair*, pp. 331, 343; Sklar, *Washington's War*, pp. 251–52.

12. Lewis Tambs to U.S. Congress, Iran-contra hearings, May 27, 1987. Tambs was not asked why he reported to North, a middle-level bureaucrat, rather than to the Secretary of State, or why he permitted U.S. Embassy funds and personnel to be used to assist in violating not only the

Boland amendment and other U.S. laws, but also Costa Rica's neutrality policy.

13. For the connections between the Free Costa Rica Movement (MCRL) and the Taiwan-headquartered WACL, see Anderson and Anderson, *Inside the League,* pp. 242–51, 268, 272. Joel Millman documented MCRL's close relationship with the Taiwan embassy in San José. Millman, "The Pacific Rim, Part II: Taiwan's School of the Americas" (Institute of Current World Affairs, New York, May 26, 1988).

14. Quoted in Lloyd Jansen, "Coming Soon: Gulf of Tonkin in Costa Rica?" *Nicaraguan Perspectives* 86 (Winter 1983).

15. Edén Pastora deposition to Christic Institute, San José, July 1987, pp. 2–3; Christopher Dickey, *With the Contras,* pp. 32–33.

16. The Proletarian group, another faction led by Jaime Wheelock and influenced by leftist politics in Chile, argued that urban workers were the legitimate vanguard of a revolutionary movement. The Prolonged Popular War group, led by Tomás Borge, was influenced by the Cuban revolution, which called for a protracted struggle in the countryside and building *focos* (liberated areas) among the peasantry. By 1979 the three factions had reached a unity agreement which permitted them to co-exist within the Front.

17. Dickey, *With the Contras,* pp. 33–40; Shirley Christian, *Nicaragua: Revolution in the Family* (New York: Random House, 1985), pp. 61–65.

18. John Dinges, *Our Man in Panama,* pp. 100–102.

19. This may have marked Pastora's first contact with the CIA. Seven years later, Pastora again met Singer, who became part of the Oliver North's network and who told him that, back in 1979, the CIA had decided not to help his troops reach Managua quickly because they "believed it would be easier for Somoza to regain power if the [Marxists within the] Sandinista Front won." Interviews with Pastora, Prado, and former Costa Rican government officials; Héctor Francés testimony in Chamorro, *Packaging the Contras, pp. 52, 66.*

20. Pastora speech, Friends Peace Center, San José, May 1988.

21. Interviews; Roy Gutman, *Banana Diplomacy,* p. 108.

22. Years later, Pastora's chief aide Carol Prado commented, "We gradually came to realize that the U.S. administration would not tolerate even this mild type of socialism in Central America. I don't think it was ever possible for the 'third way' to succeed in partnership with the U.S. government."

23. Christian, *Nicaragua,* pp. 270–71.

24. Interview with Pastora; Dinges, *Panama,* pp. 121–22.

25. Interviews; Robert Pastor, *Condemned to Repetition,* p. 239; Dickey, *With the Contras,* pp. 148–49.

26. Years later, the CIA and Pastora's right-wing enemies spread the false story that Pastora had received the money and, over Qadhafi's objections, used it to start the contras' Southern Front. Qadhafi's revenge, it was wrongly rumored, was the reason for the La Penca bombing.

27. The mastermind of the Wackenhut-Cabazon scheme was tribal administrator John Philip Nichols, a globe-trotting evangelical social worker with a jail record and friends in high places. It included plans to develop biological weapons, manufacture night-vision goggles and combustible cartridge cases, and provide security for Saudi Crown Prince Fahd's palace, all the while taking advantage of the sovereignty of the Indian reservation to circumvent government taxes and the CIA's prohibition against working within the United States. For more details see the three-part series by Jonathan Littman, *San Francisco Chronicle,* September 4–6, 1991; Mike Kataoka, "Dead Writer has Cabazon Connection," *Press-Enterprise,* Riverside, Calif., August 24, 1991; John Connolly and Eric Reguly, "Badlands," *Spy* (April 1992); Connolly, "Inside the Shadow CIA," *Spy* (Sept. 1992).

28. Interviews; information obtained from free-lance investigative journalist Doug Vaughan.

29. Pastora depositions, p. 5, and interviews with the author. John Hull is the real name of the Indiana farmer. The true identity of "John Hull," the CIA station chief who worked out of the U.S. Embassy, is not known.

30. Based on author's interviews.

31. Ideologically, Prado and Pastora were both democratic socialists who shared a distrust of Soviet, Cuban, and U.S. intervention in Nicaragua and a commitment to land reform, a mixed economy, and human rights. But in their personal habits they were like oil and vinegar. Prado is hardworking, meticulous, practical, and a responsible family man. While Pastora was the pied piper of the Southern Front, Prado was its scribe: he kept the books, preserved the files, and analyzed its complex history. Recognizing Prado's organizational skills and anti-imperialist politics, the CIA and Oliver North's network later tried to discredit him by falsely accusing him of being a drug trafficker and Sandinista agent.

32. U.S. Congress, *Iran-Contra Affair,* pp. 31–33 and Appendix A, vol. 2, pp. 1019–22; Sklar, *Washington's War,* p. 120.

33. Pastora deposition, pp. 11–12; "Comandante Cero Dissolves his Organization," *Mesoamérica,* Sept. 1982.

34. Cruz never formally joined ARDE, but he became an unofficial adviser and a mediator between the Southern Front and Washington.

35. In 1991 Wolf, a cousin of President Calderón and friend of John Hull's, claimed that he still had about five thousand militants (certainly an exaggeration) undergoing training at Las Loras. Myers interview; Martha Honey and David Myers, "US Probing Drug Agent's Activities in Costa Rica," *San Francisco Chronicle,* Aug. 14, 1991.

36. This cover was blown even before ARDE declared war: on April 4, 1983, an ARDE helicopter made an emergency landing in the border town of Los Chiles. A string of such military faux pas gradually helped reveal ARDE's extensive operations inside Costa Rica.

37. The first time was in October 1983, when North, then an unknown, middle-level bureaucrat at the NSC, visited San José as part of the Kissinger Commission. Robelo attended the reception at the posh Cariari Hotel, where, he recalled in an interview, "I was going around talking to Dr. Kissinger and [UN ambassador Jeane] Kirkpatrick and here is this guy I don't know. I shake hands with him, and there is a little paper between both our hands, and I don't know what to do with it because there is another guy waiting to shake my hand. So I quickly put it in my pocket. Later I read it and it says, 'Next time you're in Washington, contact me. Oliver North.' " Robelo did so, often.

38. "Robelo is my friend," Arias repeatedly said, even when they stood on opposite sides of the Central American Peace Plan. Robelo is a director and part owner, along with members of Arias's family, of Taboga, Costa Rica's largest sugar plantation, mill, and cane alcohol plant. This plant indirectly received a $3 million loan from AID, passed through the AID-created investment bank, the Private Investment Corporation (PIC). Sandra Peddie and Brian Donovan, "Business Before Neutrality," *Newsday,* June 21, 1987.

39. Author's interviews.

40. "Sandinista Foe Backs Exile Accord," *Miami Herald,* May 4, 1983.

41. Dickey, *With the Contras,* p. 117.

42. Author's interviews.

43. Carlos Vargas, "A Visit to the Southern Front," *Tico Times,* Apr. 22, 1983; José Luis Fuentes, "Ticos combaten en el frente norte," *La República,* July 15, 1983.

44. Memo, Owen to North, "Southern Trip," Aug. 2, 1985.

45. Memo, "The Hammer" (North) from T.C. (Owen), Apr. 1, 1985; Memo, B.G. (North) from T.C., July 31, 1985.

46. Interviews; Sklar, *Washington's War,* p. 101–5; Bernard Niet-

schmann, *The Unknown War: The Miskito Nation, Nicaragua and the United States,* Focus on Issues, no. 8 (Washington, D.C.: Freedom House, 1989), pp. 24–37.

47. Indian leaders and refugee officials say Fagoth rapidly showed himself to be ruthless and corrupt. At one point he shocked two U.S. Senators by showing them a "death list" of twelve Indian leaders who opposed him, boasting that five had already been killed. In an interview, Fagoth snapped, "Despite the rumors that I am a psychopath, a killer, and a kidnapper, I'm the leader the people follow." Frederick Kempe and Clifford Krauss, "US Policy on Indians in Nicaragua Damages Anti-Sandinista Effort," *Wall Street Journal,* Mar. 2, 1987.

48. Interviews; Guy Gugliotta, "Nicaragua Indians Divided," *Miami Herald,* Oct. 1, 1984.

49. Misurasata leaders accused the "Spaniards" leading ARDE of being arrogant and racist and of not understanding the nature of their struggle for autonomy. As one put it, "The contras are treating us the same way we were treated by Somoza and by the Sandinistas."

50. In March 1984, for instance, Reagan accused the Sandinistas of attempting "to wipe out an entire culture, the Miskito Indians, thousands of whom have been slaughtered or herded into detention camps where they have been starved or abused." Human rights and religious groups, while often critical of Sandinista policy on the Atlantic coast, found little to support Reagan's and Nietschmann's lurid descriptions of the situation. According to a 1985 Americas Watch report, "There has never been evidence of racially-motivated or widespread killing of Miskitos." Nietschmann, *The Unknown War;* transcript of Reagan's speech, *New York Times,* May 19, 1984; Americas Watch Report, "Human Rights in Nicaragua: Reagan, Rhetoric and Reality," July 1985, pp. 49–56.

51. Sklar, *Washington's War,* pp. 262–63. Other academics served as Office of Public Diplomacy consultants. Gelbspan, *Break-ins,* pp. 122–25.

52. Kempe and Krauss, "Indians in Nicaragua."

53. This is different from the earlier contra UNO of Robelo, Cruz, and Calero, which was purely an exile/guerrilla organization.

Chapter 9: The Southern Front: CIA Network

1. The Contadora Group, named after the Panamanian resort island on which it was formed, consisted of Venezuela, Panama, Colombia, and Mexico and was later supplemented by the "Support Group," which included Argentina, Peru, Uruguay, and Brazil. It functioned between

January 1983 and late 1986, trying unsuccessfully to work out a negotiated end to the Nicaraguan war. In early 1987 it was superseded by the Arias peace plan, which became, in August 1987, the Central American Peace Plan, endorsed by the five Central American presidents.

2. Marshall, Scott, and Hunter, *Iran-Contra Connection,* pp. 110, 266.

3. Interviews; Manuel Jirón, *Exilio, S.A.;* Chamorro, *Packaging the Contras,* p. 18.

4. Francés testimony in Chamorro, *Packaging the Contras,* p. 65. Oduber was also said to have lent his farm in Guanacaste for early training of the contras and possibly for drug trafficking.

5. This included a vigorous attack against the author and Tony Avirgan, including a court case in 1987 demanding that the two journalists be expelled as Sandinista spies. The case was eventually dismissed for lack of evidence.

6. Between 1980 and 1982, the Foundation was used to funnel CIA money to the political party of Vinicio Cerezo, who in 1985 was elected Guatemala's first civilian president in more than two decades. Guatemala's return to democracy was, however, fragile; in 1993 the military ousted the elected president. In El Salvador, the Foundation channeled money to José Napoleón Duarte's presidential campaign. Robert McCartney, "US is Seen Assisting Duarte in Sunday's Salvadoran Vote," *Washington Post,* May 4, 1984.

7. Marshall, Scott, and Hunter, *Iran Contra Connection,* various sections.

8. Congress, *Iran-Contra Affair.* The earlier *Tower Commission Report* did contain numerous references to Israel which could have been expanded upon by the congressional hearings. As journalist Seymour Hersh put it, the cover-up was facilitated by Israel's "unchallenged refusal . . . to provide witnesses and other evidence" and by Congress's fear "of exposing the extent to which Israel had been doing the United States' dirty work around the world." Hersh, "The Iran-Contra Committees: Did They Protect Reagan?" *New York Times Magazine,* April 29, 1990.

9. Court document, "Stipulation."

10. Author's interviews, Jane Hunter, "Israel: The Contras' Secret Benefactor," *NACLA Report on the Americas,* Mar.-Apr. 1987; Marshall, Scott, and Hunter, *Iran Contra Connection,* pp. 83–124, 167–186; James Dunkerley, *Power in the Isthmus,* pp. 491–92; Sklar, *Washington's War;* Jíron, *Exilio, S.A.*

11. Interviews; Marshall, Scott, and Hunter, *Iran Contra Connection,* pp. 14, 89–90, 99; Hunter, "Israel," *NACLA,* pp. 122–23.

12. Interviews; Emerson, *Secret Warriors*, pp. 122–23; Marshall, Scott, and Hunter, *Iran Contra Connection*, pp. 96–98; "Nicaragua, Honduras and Israel," *Mesoamérica*, Jan. 1983; court document, "Stipulation," p. 1; Marshall, "Israel, the Contras and the North Trial," *Middle East Report*, Sept./Oct. 1989.

13. The CIA viewed Panama, a member of the supposedly neutral Contadora Group, as especially important to compromise. By involving the Contadora countries, the CIA undermined their credibility with other Latin American countries and, more importantly, with the Sandinistas.

14. Bob Woodward, *Veil*, pp. 229–33; interview with Wachán in Panama, who said Leahy and Clarridge also clashed over the CIA/Israeli/ Panama supply operation.

15. Dickey, *With the Contras*, p. 89; Sklar, *Nicaragua*, pp. 84–85; Chamorro interview with Martin Edwin Andersen, quoted in Anderson, *Dossier Secreto: Argentina's Desaparecidos and the Myth of the "Dirty War"*, p. 298.

16. In early 1980, Lt. Col. Vernon Walters, the former CIA deputy director who became Reagan's UN ambassador, traveled to Buenos Aires for negotiations, together with his close friend Francisco Aguirre, a Nicaraguan newspaper editor and former National Guard colonel with close ties to the Argentine army. Several months later the Argentines were again approached by Aguirre and two anticommunist activists: Nat Hamrick, a North Carolina arms merchant and Somoza family business partner, and John Carbaugh, an aide to Senator Jesse Helms. Carbaugh followed up the discussions in September while attending the World Anti-Communist League's meeting in Buenos Aires. Interviews; Dickey, *With the Contras*, pp. 89–90; Héctor Francés testimony in Chamorro, *Packaging the Contras*, pp. 67–68; Sklar, *Washington's War*, p. 86; Gutman, *Banana Republic*, pp. 50–55.

17. Chamorro, *Packaging the Contras*, pp. 5–7, and Héctor Francés testimony in Chamorro, *Packaging the Contras*.

18. Andersen, *Dossier Secreto*, pp. 292–93; Dickey, *With the Contras*, pp. 89–90; Salinas and Villalonga, *Gorriaran*, pp. 45–61.

19. Sources on the *Radio Noticias* attack include: Dickey, *With the Contras*, pp. 90–92, 245–47; Interview with Hugo Villagra, done by senior analyst, Peter Kornbluh, National Security Archive June 4, 1986; Chamorro, *Packaging the Contras*, pp. 91, 113, 245; Edelman and Kenen, *Costa Rica Reader*, pp. 269–70, 276, 308; "Radio Station Attack Provokes Fear, Protests" and "Suspects in *Radio Noticias* Attack Caught," *Tico Times*, Dec. 16 and 23, 1980.

Costa Rican authorities produced a captured rebel document implicating U.S officials as well as the MCRL. The document, according to a July 1981 U.S. Embassy cable from Ambassador McNeil, "cites this Embassy as offering five thousand dollars a month to support MCRL activities and mentions a plan to destroy far left shortwave radio station (now closed) *Radio Noticias del Continente.*" Cable from McNeil, San José, to Secretary of State, Washington, Subject: Terrorist document charges collusion between right-wing group with Panamanian dissident and with Embassy, July 1981, obtained by investigative journalist Carl Deal through the Freedom of Information Act. See also Frank McNeil, *War and Peace,* p. 147.

20. Costa Rican immigration records show Valdez, using the name Francés, traveled in and out of Costa Rica frequently between December 1981 and October 1982.

21. Early FDN and UDN leader José Francisco "El Chicano" Cardenal, quoted in Dickey, *With the Contras,* p. 154.

22. Francés testified that he reported to two Argentine officers in Honduras: José Hoyas (or "Villegas"), head of logistics, and Col. Osvaldo Riveiro, an intelligence officer and political head of operations. Francés and other Argentine trainers received between $2,500 and $3,000 from the CIA. In welding the various contra groups into the FDN, this Argentine network worked closely with General Gustavo Alvarez and others in the Honduran military.

23. Christopher Dickey, "Argentine Defector Tells of Multinational Plot for Sandinistas' Ouster," *Washington Post,* Dec. 2, 1992; McNeil, *War and Peace,* p. 148.

24. Diplomats and journalists in Central America widely believed that Francés had been jailed or killed by either the Nicaraguan or Cuban government. However, in 1993, several Argentine journalists said they had information that Francés had been living clandestinely under Sandinista protection during the 1980s, that his wife had been permitted to join him, and that toward the end of the decade the couple returned to Argentina. For more details on Francés see Salinas and Villalonga, *Gorriarán.*

25. Much of Francés's testimony is translated and reprinted in Chamorro, *Packaging the Contras,* pp. 61–69. Author possesses another, slightly different translation, based on Francés's testimony, which was reprinted in Managua's Sandinista-controlled newspaper, *Barricada.*

26. Francés did not give the names of other Argentine trainers in Costa Rica, but contra sources say there were several, including one known as "Ramiro," who worked closely with Brooklyn Rivera and later with John Hull and a group of Cuban Americans.

27. Translation of Héctor Francés testimony in author's possession.

28. Francés testimony; Chamorro, *Packaging the Contras,* pp. 67–68.

29. It is possible that this "John Hull" was the same person whom Francés said he knew as Leckson or "Delicado" and who "was in charge of the area for the CIA, [and had] been permanently in Costa Rica in the last few months." Francés testimony; Chamorro, *Packaging the Contras,* pp. 67–68.

30. Interviews; North's diary page for July 26, 1984, contains notes of a phone conversation with Owen relating that Hull is "concerned about Phil leaving." After Brazil, Holts was posted in Turkey and then back in Washington.

31. Following the December 1989 U.S. invasion of Panama, Papas and CIA agent Felipe Vidal were seen in Panama where they were involved in training a new security force for the Guillermo Endara government.

32. Fernández claimed to have been born in Spain. A number of press reports described him as Cuban American.

33. Embassy chargé d'affaires James Tull, Iran-contra congressional hearings, U.S. Congress May 6, 1987, Appendix B, vol. 27, p. 181, 213; Sklar, *Washington's War,* pp. 177–86.

34. CIA collaborator and pilot Bill Crone says one of his Embassy contacts was "Buck." Robert Owen mentions Buck, indicating that he was working as an intelligence agent. Memo from TC [Owen] to BG [North], Subject: Overall Perspective, Eyes Only, Mar. 17, 1986. North also mentions meeting with "Buck" in San José (North diary entry, Sept. 20, 1985).

35. Kempe and Krauss, "Indians in Nicaragua." In 1982, for instance, the CIA station in Honduras roughly doubled, to about twenty-five agents. Peter Kornbluh, *Nicaragua,* p. 23.

36. Interviews. This agent did not say how many agents were based in Costa Rica. However, according to a book on the CIA by two German journalists, there were forty-three CIA agents in Costa Rica between 1980 and 1983. Gunter Neuberger and Michael Opperskalski, *CIA in Mittelamerika* (Bonn-Merten, FRG: Lamuv Verlag, 1983), pp. 180–83, 188–200.

37. Carter administration Latin American expert Robert Pastor writes, "Intelligence was weak because State and CIA gave the region low priority." Pastor, *Condemned to Repetition,* p. 128.

38. Owen comments, "Seems a waste to miss this opportunity." Memo, Owen to Oliver North, Nov. 5, 1984.

39. Former Iran-contra prosecutor Jeffrey Toobin writes that the

investigation into North network bribes to Costa Rican and other officials collapsed because "our friends at the agency did not remember anything. . . . With a few courageous exceptions most of our CIA witnesses suffered stunning memory lapses." Jeffrey Toobin, *Opening Arguments* (New York: Penguin, 1991), pp. 96–115; David Johnston, "Book Accuses the CIA in a Contra Aid Scheme," *New York Times,* Feb. 5, 1991; AP, "CIA Book," Feb. 2, 1991.

40. Interviews; Tim Golden, "Long Odyssey," *Miami Herald,* June 29, 1986; testimony of José Sosa, investigative report of the bombing of the Continental National Bank in Miami, May 27, 1983, supplied by investigator Diosdado Díaz, Special Investigations Unit, Miami Police Department, to Special Agent George Kiszynski, September 26, 1984.

41. Title of a song by Costa Rican artists Rubén Pagura and Juan Carlos Urena which describes the power of Costa Rica's press. It is part of their marvelous musical history, "The Central American Cantata."

42. Frederick says the Reagan and Bush administrations used a "familiar modus operandi" of combining "modern statecraft"—the VOA—with clandestine, CIA-run radio stations. Howard Frederick, "Electronic Penetration," in Thomas Walker, ed., *Reagan versus the Sandinistas.*

43. There are a number of excellent studies of the Costa Rican press, including Jean Hopfensperger, "US and Contras Find Ally in Costa Rica's Three Major Dailies," *Christian Science Monitor,* Aug. 18, 1986; Andrew Reding: "Unhidden Agenda," *Channels,* Apr. 1986; "The Costa Rican Press," *Mesoamérica,* Jan. 1985; Mario Zeledón Cambronero, *La Desinformación de la Prensa en Costa Rica: Un grave peligro para la paz* (San José: ICES, 1987); Miguel Sobrado, Gabriel Coronado, Leda Trejos, *¿Quién quiere la guerra en Costa Rica?* (San José: ICES, 1988); Howard Friel and Michelle Joffroy, "The Continuing War: Media Manipulation in Costa Rica," *Covert Action* 26 (Summer 1986); and Frederick, "Electronic Penetration."

44. "Press," *Mesoamérica,* Jan. 1985; Patricia León and Isabel Ovares, "La prensa llama a la guerra," in Zeledón, *La Desinformación,* pp. 169–224.

45. "Un disturbio finalizó ayer marcha hacia embajada nica," *La Nación,* June 11, 1985; "La mancha en la camisa," and "Conclusión de la Vergüenza," *El Semanario Universidad,* University of Costa Rica, June 21, 1985; Hopfensperger, "US and Contras Find Ally"; Friel and Joffroy, "Continuing War."

46. All Costa Rican journalists pledge in their contracts to exercise "ethical conduct," and *La Nación* and most other media have specific rules prohibiting outside income which may conflict with journalistic

activity. The CIA, for its part, is not legally prohibited from paying foreign journalists. After a 1977 Senate Select Committee on Intelligence report disclosed the CIA was paying fifty American journalists for information, the Agency announced new rules barring it from entering into "any paid or contractual relationship" with U.S. journalists, including free-lancers and stringers. Although difficult to prove, there are indications that this ban was violated with certain American reporters covering Central America.

47. Author's interviews.

48. Quoted in Martha Honey, "Contra Coverage-Paid For by the CIA," *Columbia Journalism Review*, Mar./Apr. 1987.

49. When, prior to the invasion, we went to Puerto Viejo to videotape these facilities, security guards aggressively tried to stop us, contending they were secret. They refused to say if the towers belonged to Radio Impacto, but we knew we were at the right location when we noticed that a small grocery store across the road was named "Impacto." According to several of those close to Radio Impacto, the facilities beamed toward Panama were financed from $10 to $12.25 million in CIA funds channeled to anti-Noriega forces. Some of this money was also used for training anti-Noreiga rebels ("contras" for Panama), which included ex-contras from Nicaragua's Atlantic coast who could pass as Panamanians.

50. I am grateful to Gordon Durnin for doing much of the investigation and interviews on Radio Impacto, especially its anti-Noriega phase. Information is also based on author's interviews with Manuel Jirón, "Comandante Marcos," and others, as well as Jirón, *Exilio*, and Chamorro, *Packaging the Contras*, p. 26.

51. Author's coverage of Winsor's inaugural speech. In what Costa Ricans dubbed "the Battle of the Airwaves," right-wing government officials, along with large landowners and businessmen in the northern zone, complained that Costa Rica's landless laborers, who made up about three-quarters of the rural population, were being encouraged to stage land takeovers by the Sandinista propaganda beamed across the border. However, Costa Rica was the electronic "superpower," having six television stations and one hundred commercial and religious radio stations which were received in Nicaragua. Frederick, "Electronic Penetration."

52. ACIC officials included Channel 7 Director of Programming Rodrigo Fournier, Guido Fernández, former Foreign Minister Gonzalo Facio, and representatives from Radio Colombia, CINDE, the Chambers of Industries, and *La Prensa Libre*.

53. Lezak Shallat, "Uneasy Ticos Meet Transmitter," *Tico Times*, Mar. 1, 1985.

54. Tony Avirgan, "Beam Them Up, Costa Rica: Church-Funded Transmitters Once Used for U.S. Propaganda," *National Catholic Reporter,* Mar. 13, 1992.

55. For a period, *La República* carried its own pro-contra supplement.

56. Interviews; Sharkey, "Back in Control," *Channels,* Sept./Oct. 1986.

57. Interviews; Andrew Reding, "Costa Rica: Democratic Model in Jeopardy," *World Policy Journal* 3, no. 2 (1986).

58. The raids were overseen by a CIA agent, but no Americans went on the flights. The Salvadoran military also served as a conduit for airplanes and fuel to the contras and provided special infantry training to a hundred-odd ARDE guerrillas.

59. The CIA gave the contras three Pentagon-surplus Cessna airplanes. U.S. Congress, *Iran-Contra Affair,* p. 35.

60. In late June 1983, Investair, a shady McLean, Virginia, brokerage firm whose two directors had worked for other CIA airplane companies, "sold" a Cessna 404 to ARDE's Panamanian front company, Servicios de Mar, Aire y Tierra run by Wachán. Through his Defense Forces contacts, Wachán got Panamanian tail numbers and an air-worthiness certificate. Just two months later, the plane crashed during an ARDE attack on Managua's international airport. Another ARDE front company, Piña Loca ("Crazy Pineapple"), based at the Pavas airport in San José, obtained a Beechcraft Baron via Dudley, Inc., a farm implements and trucking company in Sioux City which had been sold to unnamed Americans. Interviews with Gerardo Durán, Carol Prado, José Robelo, and other contra officials; Juan Tamayo, "The Contra Air Force: Clues Point to CIA," *Miami Herald,* Oct. 8, 1983.

61. Memo, Owen to North, "Costa Rica," June 11, 1984.

62. Interviews with George Morales, Pastora, Alfredo César, Prado; Cockburn, *Out of Control,* pp. 168–88; 1986 CBS-TV "West 57th Street" series on the Southern Front contras, drug trafficking, and John Hull; Sklar, *Washington's War,* p. 295.

63. This served the dual purpose of promoting Pastora among liberals in the United States, Latin America, and Western Europe and of ultimately allowing the Reagan administration to dismiss Pastora as a Sandinista agent.

64. Memo, TC ("Trusted Courier" Owen) to BG ("Blood and Guts" North), May 20, 1985.

65. Peddie and Donovan, "Hull's Partner had Ties to Klan," *Newsday,* May 17, 1987.

66. Kwitny, "Rancher in Costa Rica was Big Help to U.S. against the Sandinistas," *Wall Street Journal,* May 21, 1987.

67. Syd Rubinow and Stephen Schmidt, "Showdown in Bitter Land War," *Tico Times,* Oct. 3, 1976.

68. "Resume of John Hull," OPIC document included in Christic Institute's deposition of William Crone.

69. Syd Rubinow and Stephen Schmidt, "Showdown in Bitter Land War," *Tico Times,* Oct. 3, 1975. Williams, *Export Agriculture,* pp. 183–89.

70. Interviews; "The Misadventures of El Patron," *Time,* Nov. 16, 1987; U.S. Senate, *Drugs,* Dec. 1988, pp. 53–58.

71. Kwitny, "Rancher."

72. "El Patron," *Time.*

73. Clint Duke, "Iran-Contra Inquiry Reaches Lakeland Man," *The Ledger,* Lakeland, Florida, Jan. 12, 1988; Dennis Bernstein and Jessica Jiji, "John Hull Accused in Planning CIA Terrorism in Brazil," *Guardian,* Feb. 17, 1988; affidavit to congressional and journalistic investigators, signed by Robert M. Hayes in front of Notary Public Elizabeth B. Jones, Jan. 7, 1988.

74. Hull's ex-business partner Bill Crone says that in the mid-1970s, Hull and Klansman Shoff were involved in an alfalfa pellets plant for animal feed in Brazil. Interviews; information gathered by Christic Institute investigators.

75. Duke, "Iran-Contra Inquiry"; Bernstein and Jiji, "John Hull Accused."

76. Bruce Jones deposition to Christic Institute, Dec. 3, 1987, p. 22.

77. Kwitney, "Rancher"; Sklar, *Washington's War,* p. 234; Cockburn, *Out of Control,* p. 257.

78. Among the articles on these U.S. farmers/investors/contra supporters see: Clark Spencer, "Farming on the Edge of a War," *Top Producer Extra* (published by *Farm Journal,* Philadelphia), Nov. 1984; "Costa Rica: Taming a New Frontier," *State Journal-Register* (Springfield, Ill.), Feb. 22, 1988; Jacqueline Sharkey, "Disturbing the Peace," *Common Cause,* Sept./ Oct. 1985; James Ridgeway, "American Farmers: The Contras' New Friends," *Village Voice,* July 30, 1985; John Piowaty, "Contra Air," *Soldier of Fortune,* Oct. 1987; Chuck Clark, "On War's Edge," *Evansville Courier* (Indiana), June 11, 1986.

79. Jon Lee Anderson, "CIA Agent in Costa Rica," *Life,* Feb. 1985.

80. Senate, *Drugs,* pp. 53–59.

81. Articles on James Denby include: George Skelton, "Scheme to Spring Denby: A Tale of Intrigue, Luck," *Los Angeles Times,* Feb. 2, 1988; Milton McGriff, "Nicaragua Releases U.S. Pilot," *Herald Examiner* (Los

Angeles), Jan. 31, 1988; Daniel Browning, "Farmer Lives 2nd Life on Costa Rican Ranch," *St. Louis Post-Dispatch,* June 21, 1987; June Erlick, "Controversy Clouds Downing of U.S. Pilot in Nicaragua Airspace," *Miami Herald,* Dec. 10, 1987; David Gollob and Martha Honey, "Managua's Capture of U.S. Pilot Reopens Contra Arms Issue," *Times* (London), Dec. 7, 1987.

82. In May 1989, just seven months before the U.S. invasion of Panama, Hylton's company acquired over 6,000 hectares along Costa Rica's southern border with Panama. The CIA also set up a clandestine radio transmitter near the border and there were unconfirmed reports of anti-Noriega guerrillas operating in the area. Marc Edelman, *The Logic of the Latifundio: The Large Estates of Northwestern Costa Rica Since the Late Nineteenth Century* (Stanford: Stanford University Press, 1992), pp. 240–46, 408–10; author's interviews.

83. In mid-1993 eight men accused of the Spadafora killing went on trial in David, Panama. They were, as one local lawyer put it, "the small fry." Who ultimately ordered the grisly beheading of Spadafora remained undetermined. The U.S. government said that it was ordered by Noriega, but a number of Panamanian and contra sources said the CIA (for whom Noriega was working at the time) had a hand in it. Just before his murder Spadafora met with the DEA in Costa Rica and was also threatening to go public with evidence of contra and CIA involvement in drug trafficking (through Hull, Felipe Vidal, Noriega, and others).

There are intriguing parallels between the Spadafora murder and the La Penca bombing. The CIA's phony story (as told by Hoffman) that Spadafora was murdered by Salvadoran leftists is virtually identical to one circulated by the CIA's "dirty tricks" unit The Babies following the La Penca bombing. Colonel Roberto Díaz, who was fired by Noriega from the Panamanian Defense Forces in 1988, said at the trial that the real reason for Spadafora's murder could be linked to the CIA. He pointed as evidence to the fact that "CIA operatives based in Costa Rica" had "commissioned" Hoffman to put out a fake cover-story. Interviews with Spadafora, Hoffman, Floyd Carlton, and others; documents from Costa Rican government judicial investigation of the Spadafora murder; information from investigative journalist Hugh Graham; John Dinges, *Our Man in Panama,* p. 220; Silvio Hernández, "Panama: Was Beheaded Guerrilla Killed in an International Plot?" IPS, Aug. 13, 1993.

84. He also appears to have pocketed much of the $375,000 OPIC loan and at least $10,000 of the $50,000 sent him by James Keyes, a Boston businessmen working with North, to bail out the five jailed mercenaries.

85. During Easter week of 1984, I went to the ranch as part of an

ABC television team to find that Hull and his family were away at the beach. But Edén Pastora's red and white Cessna was in the front yard and its pilot, a Costa Rican named Mario Alvarado, was surprisingly talkative and explained on camera the workings of Hull's contra operations inside Costa Rica. While we were there, another light plane landed and a group of five men, apparently Nicaraguans, got off and quickly disappeared when they saw the cameras. Just after this report aired, Hull stationed security guards on his farm to keep out, he said, "the communists"—a euphemism, in this instance, for inquisitive journalists.

86. "El Patron," *Time.*

87. He built a legal shield around himself. He never divorced his American wife, but his Costa Rican family (Margarita Acosta and their son) afforded Hull some legal protection against deportation. In June 1984, at the request of the CIA, Hull took out Costa Rican citizenship. He retained his U.S. passport, even though both countries rarely recognize dual citizenship.

88. Author's interviews and inspection of Costa Rican land registry records; CIA Office of the Inspector General, Cole Black and George Jameson, CIA interview with Joseph Fernández, Jan. 24, 1987, reprinted in Kornbluh and Byrne, *Iran-Contra Scandal,* p. 157.

89. CIA interview with Fernández in *Iran-Contra Scandal,* p. 154.

90. Letter to Oscar Arias Sánchez, President of Costa Rica, from U.S. Congressmen David Dreier and Lee Hamilton and seventeen others, Jan. 26, 1989. Arias, infuriated, wrote back on Mar. 3, 1989: "I deeply regret your letter. . . . Mr. John Hull is accused of serious crimes, among them that of participating in the illegal traffic of drugs to the United States. It pains me that you insinuate that the exemplary relation between your country and mine could deteriorate because our legal system is fighting against drug trafficking, no matter how powerful the people who participate in it."

91. According to another DEA agent based in Central America at this time, Pérez "was in charge of the contra war out of Costa Rica." An internal DEA investigation into Pérez for illegal CIA and drug trafficking activities was finally dropped in the summer of 1993. Author's interview with former DEA agent Celig Castillo; Martha Honey and David Myers, "U.S. Probing Drug Agent's Activities," *San Francisco Chronicle,* Aug. 14, 1991; Brian Donovan, "CIA Operative Cites U.S. Help in Getaway" and "Who Killed Linda Frazier?" *Newsday,* Oct. 19 and Dec. 16, 1992.

92. Interviews with Gil, Paz, Pérez, Vidal, Héctor Cornillot, José Coutin, Jesús García, and others linked to International Brigade; statement of José Coutin in report on Continental Bank bombing which

Diosdado Díaz, investigator, Special Investigations Unit, Miami Police Department furnished to Special Agent George R. Kiszynsk, Sept. 26, 1984, released in *U.S.* v. *Calero* and *U.S.* v. *Corvo*, both Southern District of Florida; Joseph Treaster, "A Cuban-American 'Adviser' Tells of Combat with Nicaraguan Rebels," *New York Times*, Dec. 22, 1986.

93. There was another Max Vargas, a Nicaraguan dissident in Miami working with UDN-FARN and the CIA.

94. Interviews with Vidal and others; Carl Deal, "Chronologies of Felipe Vidal Santiago and René Corbo," prepared for Christic Institute La Penca case; U.S. Senate, "Report on Contra/Drug Connection" (unpub., prepared by staff of Sen. John Kerry, 1986).

95. Warren Hinckle and William Turner, *The Fish is Red: The Story of the Secret War Against Castro* (New York: Harper and Row, 1981), pp. 321–23.

96. Interviews; Sandra Dibble, "Cuban Exile Boosts Contras," *Miami Herald*, June 29, 1986.

97. In August 1988, Corvo and "Papito" Hernández were two of six Cuban Americans indicted for U.S. Neutrality Act violations by the Southern District of Florida federal court in Fort Lauderdale for their involvement in the paramilitary training camp near Naples and two arms shipments, in March and June 1985, to the Costa Rican–based contras, via El Salvador. Sources: Frank Cerabino and Linda Robertson, "Six Indicted on Charges of Helping Arm Contras," *Miami Herald*, Aug. 24, 1988; Don Finefronc, UPI, "Six Men Face Charges of Recruiting, Training Contras," Aug. 23, 1988; AP, "Six Accused of Contra Arms Ring," Aug. 22, 1988.

98. Memo, TC (Owen) to BG (North), Subject: Southern Trip, July 31, 1985 and Aug. 2, 1985 (memo has two dates).

99. López-Estrada participated in the founding meeting of CORU, held in the Dominican Republic in 1976. Also present was CIA agent Sacha Volman, who had lived in Costa Rica and worked closely with presidents Monge and Figueres. Donald Freed and Fred Landis, *Death in Washington: The Murder of Orlando Letelier* (Westport, Conn.: Lawrence Hill and Company, 1980), p. 149; Hinckle and Turner, *Fish is Red*, pp. 322, 341–42. For more on Volman see chapter 3, note 19.

100. Costa Rican immigration records and López-Estrada's statement obtained by the author.

101. Author's reporting; "Dejaron salir a López-Estrada sin resolver denuncia planteada por Vargas Carbonell," *Libertad*, Aug. 22, 1986.

102. Felipe Vidal, letter to Candido de la Torre, May 12, 1986.

103. This amount comes from the U.S. Senate report. Some accounts say Frigoríficos received either $231,587 or $261,932 in U.S.

humanitarian aid funds. Núñez and other Frigoríficos directors deposited some of this money in Israeli and South Korean bank accounts. Both countries were supplying arms to the contras. U.S. Senate, *Drugs*, pp. 45–47; U.S. General Accounting Office, *Central America: Problems in Controlling Funds for the Nicaraguan Democratic Resistance*, Dec. 1986; Cockburn, *Out of Control*, pp. 152–67; Sklar, *Washington's War*, p. 294; Alan Levin, "On Trial: Seafood Company with a Contra Connection," *Boston Herald*, Dec. 11, 1988.

104. Author's interviews; Ameringer, *Democracy in Costa Rica*, pp. 122–25 and *Don Pepe*, various sections.

105. Interviews; "Anuncia Costa Rica la Captura de 7 Antisandinistas," *Diario de las Américas*, Dec. 20, 1983; "Falta de Mérito para un M-3," *La República*, Jan. 6, 1984; John McClure, *Soldier Without Fortune*, pp. 108–11. McClure was a trained psychologist and right-wing adventurer who spent time with the Southern Front contras with his wife.

106. This section is based on the author's investigation and reporting of the Managua airport bombing, plus subsequent interviews with Pastora, Prado, José Robelo, Modesto Watson, Gerardo Durán, and others; Woodward, *Veil*, pp. 271–76; "Thirty Seconds over Managua," *Time*, Sept. 13, 1983; Tamayo, "Contra Air Force."

107. Sandinista and ARDE communiqués both wrongly claimed the Cessna had been shot down by anti-aircraft fire. The Sandinista statement also incorrectly reported that the planes had left from Costa Rican territory.

108. Author's conversation with Nugent. John McClure in interview with Christic Institute investigator Richard McGough identified Nugent as a CIA agent and said that in Feb. 1984 he met Joe Fernández in Nugent's office.

109. Woodward, *Veil*, pp. 271–76.

110. Interviews; "Tomás Castillo" testimony to Iran-contra congressional hearings, May 29, 1987, morning and afternoon sessions. Cohen, an Iran-contra panel member, disputed Fernández's account, saying that he and Hart had been told by a CIA official that Pastora's bombing target had been approved beforehand.

111. In addition to Golden, the sources who said there were Americans on board included Security Minister Solano; Felipe Vidal; a socialist member of the Legislative Assembly, Sergio Erik Ardón; Benigno Quesada, a Ciudad Quesada journalist with close ties to the contras, Hull, and the CIA; and area residents. Pastora said he does not know who was on board, and Carol Prado said he was assured by Costa Rican investigators that there were no Americans on the plane.

112. Loria's articles ran on Apr. 7, 9, and 10, 1984.

113. CIA contract agents are hired for specific projects. They are not full-time, salaried employees.

114. Investigation and reporting by author; "Avión accidentado en zona norte procedía de Honduras," *La Nación,* May 17, 1984; "Misterio rodea avión siniestrado," *La República,* April 11, 1984. The government's inquiry was overseen by Vice President Armando Arauz and the Minister and Vice Minister of the Government, Alfonso Carro and Enrique Chacón, all strong contra supporters close to the U.S. Embassy. Through a mixture of truth, lies, and misleading information, they were able to block a more thorough investigation.

115. Dave Todd, Southern News Service of Canada, Ottawa, Canada, May 24, 1984; Sandra Peddie and Brian Donovan, "Ex-Contras Allege Cover-up, Say CIA Behind Orders," *Newsday,* May 24, 1987.

116. Brian Donovan, "Army Has Secret Files on Crash," *Newsday,* Dec. 24, 1987.

Chapter 10: Militarizing Costa Rica

1. U.S. State Department, "US Response to Costa Rica's Urgent Request for Security Assistance," secret, first draft, May 5, 1984, reprinted in Edelman and Kenen, eds., *Costa Rica Reader,* pp. 279–90. Although the United States repeatedly accused the Sandinistas of posing a military threat to Costa Rica, this memo documents that virtually all the border incidents were precipitated by ARDE.

2. Costa Rica's army could be abolished by decree largely because it was a weak institution whose main role had been to quell labor and peasant unrest. Figueres also banned the Communist party and, through a variety of legal means, circumscribed labor organizations and activites, including strikes, thereby severely crippling the trade unions. Gradually paternalistic and largely benevolent state institutions expanded to fulfill many of the functions performed in other countries the military, labor, and popular organizations.

3. For a good overview of these early U.S. military and police programs in Costa Rica see John Saxe-Fernández, "The Militarization of Costa Rica," *Monthly Review,* May 1972.

4. *CRISIS* (Costa Rican Information Services in Solidarity) 1 (1985), p. 3. This was an excellent, short-lived, mimeographed bulletin, published anonymously in English by Costa Rican students and faculty and distributed informally. Only a few issues were published during the height of the contra war.

5. Marc Edelman and Jane Hutchcroft, "Costa Rica: Modernizing the Non-Army," *NACLA Report on the Americas,* Mar./Apr. 1984, p. 9; Saxe-Fernández, "Militarization."

6. José Romero and David Romero, *El Caso Chemise* (San José: Editorial D. Mora, 1991), pp. 78, 83, 90–91, 156–67.

7. By 1974, DEACON I had not contributed to any drug busts and "had apparently sanctioned drug smuggling by its own agents," including Hernández Rumbaut. Scott and Marshall, *Cocaine Politics,* p. 28.

8. George Crile, "The Informant Who Jumped Bail" and "The Colonel's Secret Drug War," *Washington Post Magazine,* June 13, 1976; Romero and Romero, *Chemise,* p. 159.

9. Interviews; Escuela de Las Américas, *US ARSA Fact Book 1983,* Fort Gulick, Panama; Mary Day Kent and Eva Gold, "The U.S. Army School of the Americas," NARMIC, American Friends Service Committee, May 1984; U.S. Embassy handout, "History of U.S. Aid Program to Costa Rican Public Forces" (1986), p. 4.

10. Edelman and Hutchcroft, "Non-Army."

11. Tord Haivik and Solveig Aas, "Demilitarization in Costa Rica: A Farewell to Arms?" *Journal of Peace Research* 18, no. 4 (1981), pp. 347–49.

12. U.S. Embassy handout, "History of the Current U.S. Aid Program to the Costa Rican Public Security Forces" (no date, about 1988).

13. Interviews; Joanne Kenen, "Practically Neutral," *Atlantic Monthly,* Mar. 1984.

14. "Costa Rica: From Democracy to . . .?" *Mesoamérica,* Jan. 1986.

15. By 1988, an estimated 200 to 300 Costa Ricans—Civil and Rural guardsmen, immigration officials, police detectives, intelligence specialists, and presidential bodyguards—had attended the two-month course "Political Warfare," which included counter-insurgency strategy and anti-communist propaganda. Millman, "Pacific Rim."

16. CODEHU, *Informe sobre la situación de los derechos humanos en Costa Rica* (Nov. 1987), pp. 8–9.

17. APIA (a pro-Sandinista news agency based in Managua), "Costa Rica Joins Central American Arms Race," Nov. 2, 1982; Edelman and Hutchcroft, "Non-Army."

18. According to Civil Guard Captain Víctor Julio Quirós, who was stationed on the border for about two years, beginning in May 1985, "[M]y orders were to prevent the entry of foreign forces, that is, to enforce neutrality. But . . . the truth is that we have never been neutral. . . . They [top Civil Guard officers] coordinated their border operations with the contras instead of with the Costa Rican government. Orders were

given verbally to avoid generating compromising documents." Manuel Bermúdez, " 'The Government Can Be Neutral, but not the Police.' An Interview with Civil Guard Captain Víctor Julio Quirós," reprinted in Edelman and Kenen, eds., *Costa Rica Reader,* pp. 338–39.

19. Information from U.S. Embassy.

20. Costa Rican officials complained, generally off the record for fear of reprisals, of U.S. pressure for military cooperation. As one official explained, "There is a definite feeling in the government that acceptance of economic aid is conditioned on acceptance of military aid." Joel Brinkley, "Costa Ricans at Odds over U.S. Army Advisers," *New York Times,* May 19, 1985; Tina Rosenberg, "Costa Rica's Dilemma: Neutral but Needy," *Miami Herald,* Apr. 27, 1986.

21. Jeffrey Toobin, a lawyer who worked for Iran-contra Independent Prosecutor Lawrence Walsh wrote that Monge was apparently offered a considerable sum of money in exchange for his cooperation in building the clandestine contra resupply airstrip at Santa Elena. Toobin, *Opening Arguments,* pp. 96–115; David Johnston, "Book Accuses the C.I.A.," *New York Times,* Feb. 5, 1991.

22. Maxwell Peltz, "Costa Rica and the Reagan Administration," pp. 50–51; Frank Kendrick, "The Nonmilitary Neutrality of Costa Rica," in Ralph Lee Woodward, Jr., ed., *Central America: Historical Perspectives;* Edelman and Hutchcroft, *"Non-Army."*

23. "Los Ingenieros Militares en el Gobierno de Monge," *El Semanario Universidad,* Feb. 21, 1986.

24. "Monge Hints He May Ban Troops," *Tico Times,* Nov. 18, 1983.

25. Author's interviews; Linda Ferris and Dery Dyer, "Official Cites U.S. 'Pressure,' " *Tico Times,* Feb. 24, 1984.

26. Interviews by McGough; Seabee funds were channeled through a newly formed Emergency Commission headed by Vice President Armando Arauz and set up to handle the drought. Subsequent legislative and judicial investigations found that Arauz, Monge, and their cronies syphoned off large amounts from this fund for their personal use.

27. "U.S. Guard Offer Turned Down," *Tico Times,* Jan. 20, 1984.

28. U.S. Embassy statistics.

29. William Vargas y Eduardo Ramírez, "Ingenieros militares: entrenamiento que trae progreso," *Aportes,* Apr. 1989; Julia Meeks, "U.S. Army Engineers Arrive Amid Protests," *Tico Times,* Mar. 7, 1986.

30. Tony Avirgan and Martha Honey, "The CIA's War in Costa Rica," *The Nation,* January 31, 1987.

31. "Estados Unidos intercede para disminuir tensiones," *La Nación,* May 5, 1984; "C.R. Asks for Arms," *Tico Times,* May 11, 1984.

32. Joanne Omang, "Secret Report Says Costa Rica Asks More," *Washington Post,* May 10, 1984; U.S. State Department, "US Response to Costa Rica's Urgent Request for Security Assistance," May 5, 1984 in Edelman and Kenen, eds., *Costa Rican Reader,* pp. 278–90. The report contains a "Chronology of Events Concerning Costa Rica–Nicaragua Border Incidents" which makes clear that U.S. officials were privy to private communiqués between the Nicaraguan and Costa Rican governments.

33. Author's interviews and reporting; Omang, "Secret Report"; Richard Meislin, "US Said to Seek Costa Rica Shift," *New York Times,* May 11, 1984; Hedrick Smith, "2 Senators Call on Pentagon to Make Its Plans in Costa Rica Public," *New York Times,* May 13, 1984; Linda Frazier, "C.R. Asks for Arms," and "Monge, Envoy Deny 'Pressure' on Arms Aid," *Tico Times,* May 11 and 18, 1984; Peltz, "Costa Rica and the Reagan Administration," p. 56.

34. After Somoza's overthrow the Carazo administration had expropriated the hacienda for 12 million colones. Edelman, "The Somozas' Properties in Northern Costa Rica," in Edelman and Kenen, eds., *Costa Rica Reader,* pp. 242–49.

35. Quoted in *CRISIS,* p. 7.

36. Article 121.5 of the Costa Rican constitution states that the legislature must approve the "arrival of foreign troops into national territory." Peltz, "Costa Rica and the Reagan Administration," pp. 59–60; "The Militarization of Costa Rica," *Mesoamerica,* June 1985.

37. Based on author's interviews and reporting of these events; interviews by McGough and Steinberg; "2 Held in Bombing of Electrical Tower," *Tico Times,* June 14, 1985; Peltz, "Costa Rica and the Reagan Administration," p. 60; transcript, William Vargas, CODEHU, interview with Col. Harry Barrantes, ex-director of the Immediate Action Unit (UAI), Aug. 31, 1990.

38. *CRISIS,* p. 3.

39. Interviews and visit to OPEN training session; Peltz, "Costa Rica and the Reagan Administration," p. 48; Edelman and Hutchcroft, "Non-Army"; "Costa Rica: Paramilitary OPEN Formed," *Mesoamerica,* Dec. 1982; "Suspenden la reserva de la fuerza pública," *La Nación,* Aug. 27, 1987

40. Francisco Gamboa and José Alberto Briceno, "Cinco veces más policía privada que estatal" and "Seguridad privada indica inseguridad pública," *La Prensa Libre,* Aug. 30 and 31, 1990; Eduardo Ramírez and Gaetano Randolfo, "La vigilancia se privatiza ante incapacidad estatal," *El Semanario Universidad,* Jan. 24, 1986.

41. Peltz, "Costa Rica and the Reagan Administration," p. 85.

42. CODEHU, *Informe sobre la situación de los derechos humanos en Costa Rica*, 1988–1st Trimester 1989.

43. Jorge Chavarria, Costa Rica Public Prosecutors, Public Ministry, "Investigation on 'La Penca' Case," San José, Dec. 26, 1989, from Christic Institute English translation, p. 25.

44. Author's interviews; CODEHU, *Situación*, 1988, p. 27.

45. Barrantes interview by Vargas.

46. Public Prosecutors, "La Penca," pp. 26–29.

47. Author's interviews. In late 1990, Costa Rica's "legal" wiretap system was declared an unconstitutional invasion of privacy by the *Sala Cuarta*, a newly created constitutional court. Police and security officials protested, arguing that particularly in drug cases, phone taps were vital in gathering evidence. A new drug law authorized taps for drug-related investigations.

48. CODEHU, *Informe* (1988–89):23.

49. Peter Brennan, "Congressmen Denounce Policy 'Torture Chamber,' " and "Deputies Debate Probe of Alleged Torture by OIJ," *Tico Times*, Mar. 31 and Apr. 7, 1989; Nicolás Aguilar, "Clausurado foso en San Lucas," *La Nación*, July 25, 1989; Carlos Arguedas, "Corte niega uso de foso para torturas," *La Nación*, Aug. 12, 1989; Boris Andrés Ramírez, "Denuncias sobre foso resultaron ser falsas," *La República*, Aug. 12, 1989; CODEHU, *Informe* (1988–89):43.

50. Robin Wright and John Broder, "US Secretly Aids Anti-Terror Units," *Los Angeles Times*, July 2, 1989.

51. Barrantes interviews by Vargas and author.

52. During the 1980s, CISPES was the object of intense FBI infiltration and surveillance. See Ross Gelbspan, *Break-Ins, Death Threats, and the FBI* (Boston: South End Press, 1991).

53. "The program is a reflection that terrorism has become a worldwide problem. It's the most comprehensive program we know of which involves countries from all corners of the earth," said State Department spokesman Michael Kraft. He added that during 1985, police officials from more than thirty countries were expected to participate in the program. "Police in Nassau Teach Foreigners," *New York Times*, Nov. 22, 1985; interviews with course participants, ex-OIJ official, and academic who investigated the course.

54. Alfonso Chardy, "Reagan Advisers Ran 'Secret' Government," *Miami Herald*, July 6, 1987; Oliver North, Iran-contra hearings, U.S. Congress, including questioning by Rep. Jack Brooks, summer 1987.

55. Interview with Piza; "Capacitarán contra terrorismo a Cuerpos

policiales del país," *La Nación,* February 19, 1985; Diana Reynolds, "FEMA and the NSC: The Rise of the National Security State," *Covert Action* 33 (Winter 1990); Sklar, *Washington's War,* pp. 158–59; Gelbspan, *Break-ins,* pp. 184–85; Chardy, "Reagan Aides and the 'Secret Government' " and "North Denies Role in Plan to Suspend Constitution," *Miami Herald,* July 5 and 16, 1987.

56. Brennan, "US Troops Oust Park Tourists" and "Hinton: Troops in National Park No Big Deal," *Tico Times,* Sept. 15 and 22, 1989.

57. Alex Todorovic, "Costa Rica: Of Drugs and Thugs, "*Mesoamerica,* Aug. 1990; Edward Orlebar, "Murcielago Base Will Reopen," *Tico Times,* Sept. 20, 1991.

58. Interviews. Most important articles include: Cyrus Reed, "Boy's Death Sparks Call for Probe" and "Four Foreign Nations Cited in Anti-Terrorist Training," *Tico Times,* May 25, 1990; Louis Andrews, "Report Blames 'Aggressive' Cops for Boy's Death," *Tico Times,* August 17, 1990; William Vargas, "¿Se militariza Costa Rica?" CODEHU, *Informe,* Segundo Trimestre de 1990; Karen Brown, "Rambo-style Drug Raid Leaves Boy Dead, No Drugs," *Mesoamérica,* June 1990; Patricia Muse, "Costa Rica: Searching for Justice in Needless Shooting of Young Boy," *Mesoamérica,* Sept. 1990; "Métodos policíacos ajenos al país generan indignación," *El Semanario Universidad,* May 25, 1990; "La U.A.I. es 'casi' un cuerpo paramilitar," *Esta Semana,* May 25, 1990; "Los cuerpos especiales de policía," *Esta Semana,* June 7, 1990.

59. CODEHU, "¿Se Militariza?" pp. 11–14.

60. Muse, "Searching for Justice."

61. Jean Hopfensperger, "Costa Rica's Right-Wing Paramilitary Groups," in Edelman and Kenen, eds., *Costa Rica Reader,* pp. 313–20.

62. Another American, John McClure, told Christic Institute investigators he, too, had seen a hit list. He says that in the spring of 1987, René Corvo set up a meeting with DIS officials who complained that they were frustrated in their attempts to thwart "Sandinista terrorism" and they "proposed the idea of forming a death squad in Costa Rica." McClure says they gave him "a computer print-out of the names of the people they wanted eliminated." Hopfensperger says the Patriotic Union maintains computer files on suspected leftists and subversives. Author's copies of interviews and reports by Christic Institute investigators, including Richard McGough and Susan Steinberg; Anderson and Anderson, *Inside the League,* pp. 249–50; Hopfensperger, "Costa Rica's Right-Wing;" "Electrical Tower," *Tico Times.*

63. Author's interviews and reporting on Upala, numerous local articles, and two books: Zeledón Cambronero, ed., *La desinformación de*

la Prensa en Costa Rica, and Sobrado, Coronado, Trejos, *¿Quién quiere la guerra en Costa Rica?*

64. "Editoriales: Las vicisitudes de upala," *La Nación,* Aug. 6, 1983.

65. Giselle Cubillo, "Adoptan severas medidas de seguridad en Upala," and "Solicitan en Upala diálogo con Pastora," *La Nación,* Aug. 5 and 6, 1983. See chapter 13 for more on Fonseca's complicity with the contras.

66. Quirós interview by Bermúdez, " 'The Government can be Neutral, but not the Police,' " in Edelman and Kenen, eds., *Costa Rica Reader,* pp. 339–40.

Chapter 11: Unconventional Warfare

1. The Nicaraguan war as a whole has generally been viewed as being an "unconventional" or "low intensity" conflict because it involved covert operations by U.S. financed, trained and equipped rebels, psychological warfare techniques, and attacks on civilian targets. The terms "conventional" and "unconventional" warfare are used here to signify two distinct U.S. military strategies toward the FDN and ARDE contras and toward Honduras and Costa Rica. In building the FDN forces, the U.S. set out to regroup and reconstruct Somoza's National Guard as a conventional army. Since its inception in the 1920s, the National Guard had been modeled after the U.S. army, its top officers were U.S. trained, and it used mainly American equipment. The CIA intended to build the FDN into a conventional standing army with a hierarchical chain of command, privileged officers corps, large base camps, and training in standard military warfare techniques. In Honduras as well, the U.S. openly trained and equipped the Honduras military, conducted joint military maneuvers, and built large military bases used by both the Honduran and U.S. armed forces. The situation was very different in Costa Rica. It had no army and was prescribed by law from both building one or allowing foreign troops to be be based in its national territory. In addition, the ARDE's top leaders were mainly disaffected Sandinistas (rather than former National Guardsmen), who resisted aligning with and taking orders from either the CIA or the FDN. Gradually the U.S. advisers running the covert war against Nicaragua abandoned their attempts to build ARDE and Costa Rica along the lines of the FDN and Honduras.

2. See discussion of Hull and Cubans in chapter 9.

3. Several such contra/CIA-provoked attacks, particularly against the border post of Peñas Blancas, are described elsewhere. In addition,

former Security Minister Angel Edmundo Solano said in an interview that he learned that during a 1983 attack at the border hamlet of Cerro de la Mercedes, a handful of contras dressed as Sandinista soldiers staged an "invasion" into Costa Rica. Solano recalls that Costa Rica's all-news station *Radio Monumental* "went overboard and broadcast that Costa Rica was being invaded by a thousand EPS [Sandinista army] soldiers."

4. Francés in *Packaging the Contras,* pp. 66–67.

5. Pastora deposition, pp. 17, 30.

6. McGough and Steinberg, unpublished chronology based on their investigation of the La Penca bombing, Christic Institute, June 1988, p. 11.

7. Public Prosecutors, "La Penca," p. 20.

8. In February 1991, Bermúdez, one of the most disliked rebel leaders, was gunned down by an unknown assassin as he left Managua's Intercontinental Hotel.

9. Lau had been Somoza's chief of intelligence operations, and according to Sinclair he was "heading a death squad group in Honduras, for the FDN."

10. Sinclair says ex-National Guard colonel Isidro Sandino told him that "Brooklyn and Pastora were the biggest obstacles and the only way around this thing was to give them bullets."

11. Sinclair said he was told that "a special guy would arrive from Honduras" to carry out the assassination projects and that later he suspected this had referred to the La Penca bomber. He realized that one of the men he saw during his meeting with Bermúdez "resembled this guy at La Penca." When the La Penca bombing occurred, Sinclair said he assumed it was part of the same project he had discussed with the FDN and CIA officials. Interviews; Sinclair, sworn statement to McGough and Oto Castro, San José, Sept. 9, 1988.

12. Wong's declarations to author and attorney Ricardo Lankaster. Wong first mentioned that he was involved in an FDN plot to kill Pastora to fellow inmate Peter Glibbery. While many details Wong told us did not check out, he did seem to know personally the key figures involved with the contras, including a number whose names had not appeared in the press and to have knowledge of contra bases in both Honduras and Costa Rica.

13. Taped copy of conversation and English transcript in possession of author. The voices on the tape are Rafael Espinoza (the Pastora sympathizer who made the recording), José Wenceslao Mayorga, Carlos Lacayo of the MDN, Ludendorf Huack ("Captain Hook"), and Rommel Castaneda.

14. Edgar Chamorro also says that in the contra camps there was discussion that the death of a journalist "like the death of Bill Stewart, could cause an uproar if it were blamed on the Sandinistas." Chamorro, *Packaging the Contras,* p. 31.

15. McGough and Steinberg interviews with Yurko and Crone.

16. Public Prosecutors, "La Penca," pp. 21–22; McGough and Steinberg chronology, pp. 12, 15.

17. Pastora deposition, pp. 25–26, 28–29, 46; Prado deposition, p. 48.

18. McGough and Steinberg chronology, p. 10.

19. Public Prosecutors, "La Penca," p. 17.

20. Soghanalian conversation with journalist Joe Trento. Despite the CIA's warning, the arms dealer continued to deal with Pastora. According to a May 1986 cable exchange between CIA headquarters and station chief Joe Fernández in Costa Rica, Soghanalian was shipping Pastora "a 707 aircraft loaded with 250 complete sets of military gear (rucksacks, uniforms, boots, etc.) along with five hundred thousand rounds of small arms ammunition." Fernández, who was on the verge of successfully buying off most of Pastora's field commanders and forcing the troublesome ARDE leader to quit the war permanently was furious. "Station strongly urges that above resupply mission be thwarted at all cost," he cabled headquarters. It was. According to Pastora and Carol Prado, the CIA stopped the shipment in Mexico. CIA cable to Joe Fernández, "Possible Shipment of Lethal Materials from Miami," May 10, 1986; CIA Cable from Joe Fernández, [Pastora] Machination, May 10, 1986. Obtained through a FOIA suit filed by the National Security Studies (a project of the National Security Archive), Washington, D.C. See Chapter 13 for Fernández' other maneuvers to remove Pastora.

21. Interviews; Pastora deposition, p. 69; McGough and Steinberg chronology, pp. 10–11; Arturo Cruz, Jr., *Memoirs,* pp. 169–70.

22. Pastora deposition, p. 32.

23. North's diary entry for May 26, 1984, reads, "Call from Nestor Pino. Pastora arriving Monday P.M."

24. Press reports cited in Honey and Avirgan, *La Penca,* p. 3.

25. Interviews, including with an anonymous eyewitness; North's diary; Owen testimony to Iran-contra congressional hearings, May 19, 1987; Costa Rican immigration records for Robert Owen and Vaughn Forrest. Forrest was on the staff of Bill McCollum (R-Fl).

26. Owen's written report to North about his Costa Rica trip makes only passing mention that a "bomb went off" and includes no speculation about who did it. This silence and his hasty departure from Costa Rica

appears odd since Owen was supposed to be North's "eyes and ears" to the contras and determining who had attempted to kill the main Southern Front leader would seem to be an important task. Memo, Report of eleven-day trip to Costa Rica and Honduras, Owen to North, June 11, 1984; Owen testimony, Iran-contra hearings, U.S. Congress, May 12, 1987, vol. 2, p. 402; Costa Rican immigration records for Robert Owen and Vaughn Forrest.

27. Author's interviews with Sheila Ugalde, Bill Crone, Panamanian officer, and others; information from "David."

28. As the Chemise case reveals (see pp. 00–000), since the early 1970s some Costa Rican narcotics agents and politicians, together with some CIA and DEA agents, had been involved in drug (initially marijuana) trafficking. According to Legislative Assembly investigators interviewed by the author, this activity grew in the 1970s after fugitive U.S. financier Robert Vesco was given political asylum in Costa Rica. Vesco set himself up as a high-level middleman between influential Costa Ricans and Mexican marijuana and Colombian cocaine barons.

29. Scott and Marshall, *Cocaine Politics,* p. 104. The authors delineate four somewhat different contra–drug trafficking rings, but I believe they do not sufficiently recognize the contradictions between Pastora and El Negro Chamorro or that Pastora was viewed as an obstacle to rather than a promoter of drug trafficking.

30. U.S. Congress, *Drugs,* pp. 27–29, 80; Public Prosecutors, "La Penca," For an excellent overview of U.S.-Panamanian relations see Dinges, *Panama;* Frederick Kempe, *Divorcing the Dictator;* and Philip Wheaton, *Panama Invaded* (Trenton, N.J.: Red Sea Press, 1992).

31. Public Prosecutors, "La Penca," p. 4; Dinges, *Panama,* pp. 132–36.

32. In the 1970s, Caballero was a business partner with Alfonso Robelo in a Nicaraguan cotton fumigation company. Public Prosecutors, "La Penca," p. 6; U.S. Congress, *Drugs,* pp. 47–48.

33. U.S. Congress, *Drugs,* p. 86.

34. Dinges, *Panama,* pp. 185–86.

35. After his arrest, Carlton was eventually extradited to the United States, where he, in turn, cut a deal to help the U.S. government prosecute an even bigger fish, Manuel Noriega. Interviews with Carlton (while he was jailed in Costa Rica), Hull, Glibbery, Carr, Vidal, and Terrell; Costa Rican court documents from 1987 case against Edwin Viales, Carlos Eduardo Zaporoli, and Fernando Loaiciga; Hernández, "Panama: Was Beheaded Guerrilla Killed in an International Plot?" IPS,

Aug. 13, 1993; and various sections in Dinges, *Panama;* Scott and Marshall, *Cocaine Politics;* Kempe, *Divorcing,* and U.S. Congress, *Drugs.*

36. Not the same person as José "Chepón" Robelo.

37. Cockburn, *Out of Control,* pp. 168–69. In early 1992, Morales was killed in a car crash in Colombia, shortly after he was released from prison in the United States.

38. Interviews including with Morales; U.S. Congress, *Drugs,* p. 55; Public Prosecutors, "La Penca," pp. 6–8; Scott and Marshall, *Cocaine Politics,* pp. 112, 229; Cockburn, *Out of Control,* pp. 170–71; Paul Eddy, with Hugo Sabogal and Sara Walden, *The Cocaine Wars* (New York: W.W. Norton, 1988), p. 335.

39. Testimony of Fabio Ernesto Carrasco, trial of United States vs. José Rafael Abello Silva, Tulsa, Oklahoma, Apr. 6, 1990.

40. They were Floyd Carlton, José Blandón, Werner Lotz, and Gary Betzner. U.S. Congress, *Drugs,* p. 54.

41. Associated Press, "Lehder Says Colombia Drug Lords Funded Contras," New York, May 4, 1990.

42. Author's interviews; information collected by Christic Institute researcher Carl Deal.

43. William Crone deposition to Christic Institute, Washington, January 6–7, 1988, vol. 1. At the end of the decade Frank Castro was in jail in the Dominican Republic, convicted of·cocaine trafficking.

44. Public Prosecutors, "La Penca," p. 11.

45. Documents obtained from Vidal; interviews with Joseph Coutin; Public Prosecutors, "La Penca," p. 12.

46. In an interview Oscar Arias said he had no idea Núñez was a drug trafficker when he accepted a campaign contribution from him in 1985. Public Prosecutors, "La Penca," pp. 13–14; Information from Richard Cole, AP, Miami.

47. Public Prosecutors, "La Penca," p. 15.

48. Information for this section comes from U.S. Congress, *Drugs,* pp. 58–59; Scott and Marshall, *Cocaine Politics,* pp. 106–9; Seth Rosenfeld, "Big Bay Area Cocaine Ring Tied to Contras," *San Francisco Examiner,* Mar. 16, 1986; Jacqueline Sharkey, "The Contra-Drug Tradeoff," *Common Cause,* Sept./Oct., 1988; and numerous newspaper articles and interviews.

49. Rosenfeld, "Cocaine Ring."

50. U.S. Congress, *Drugs,* p. 58; Scott and Marshall, *Cocaine Politics,* p. 107.

51. "Overall Perspective," To "BG" [North], From "TC" [Ownen]," Mar. 17, 1986, p. 2.

52. In March 1985, Pastora told a press conference in Miami that State Department and CIA officials were spreading false stories that he was involved in drug trafficking. During this same period, Ambassador Tambs told a Costa Rican newspaper editor that Pastora and his people were trafficking. The editor asked for proof, but Tambs never provided any. Interviews; Andres Viglucci, "Pastora Charges U.S. Officials are Linking Him to Drug Trade," *Miami Herald*, March 27, 1985; Cockburn, *Out of Control*, p. 171.

53. Public Prosecutors, "La Penca," p. 21; McGough and Steinberg chronology, pp. 17–18; memo, Owen to North, June 11, 1984.

53. Based mainly on extensive investigation by Doug Vaughan.

54. Author's interviews with Torbiornsson and others; I am also grateful to fellow journalists Doug Vaughan, Julio Villalonga, Tony Avirgan, David Adams, Susie Morgan, and Juan Tamayo for investigations and interviews on the Sandinista and Argentine guerrilla links to the La Penca. Articles relevant to this section include Martha Honey, "Contra War Mystery Bomber Identified," *San Francisco Chronicle*, Aug. 2, 1993; Tony Avirgan, "Unmasking the La Penca Bomber," *Nation*, Sept. 6–13, 1993; Martha Honey, "Nine-Year Manhunt Ended Quietly, Family Confirmed Identity," *Tico Times*, Aug. 6, 1993; Martha Honey, "The La Penca Bombing: Case Reopened," *National Review*, Dec. 13, 1993.

55. From the mid-1970s on, Argentina's guerrilla movements were heavily infiltrated and many of their actions were known beforehand to the authorities. The leader of the *Montoneros*, Mario Firmenich, was a double agent working for the Argentine military. Argentine human rights activist Emilio Mignone says of Gorriarán, " 'All his life he appears, disappears, no one ever finds him. In his long trajectory as a terrorist, he has never been arrested. That's why many believe him to be a double agent." Joe Schneider, "Argentina: The Enigma of La Tablada," *NACLA Report on the Americas*, September 1989; Martin Edwin Andersen, "Dirty Secret of the 'Dirty War,' " *Nation*, Mar. 13, 1989; Andersen, *Dossier Secreto: Argentina's Desaparecidos and the Myth of the 'Dirty War'*, various sections on the ERP and Gorriarán; Juan Salinas and Julio Villalonga, *Gorriaran, la Tablada y las 'querras de inteligencia' en American Latina*, various sections.

56. Ex-ERP militant Carlos Ponce de León, quoted in Schneider, "Argentina," *NACLA Report*, Sept. 1988.

57. Notes from interviews by Juan Tamayo and Susie Morgan; investigative notes compiled by Doug Vaughan; Tamayo, "Nicaragua Assassin Finally Unmasked," *Miami Herald*, Aug. 1, 1993; Martin Arostegui, "The Case of the Danish Assassin," *National Review*, May 24, 1993.

58. Author's interviews with Gaguine family members; Vaughan and Avirgan interviews with Samir and Eduardo Gaguine.

59. Author's interviews. Pastora says that during the time that Fidel Castro was fighting the Batista dictatorship, Montero was a student in New York. His brother, however, was one of only twelve guerrilla leaders to survive the Sierra Maestra campaign. After Castro's victory, "Renan took the first plane back to Cuba. He saw his brother with a huge beard on the runway. His brother was furious and told him to go back to his imperialist friends. Renan vowed to overcome this bad image. He made a pledge to join the next revolutionary struggle in Latin America, and it was ours in Nicaragua." Some who worked with him believe that Montero was originally from South America, probably Chile. After the Sandinista victory, Montero took out Nicaraguan citizenship and married a Nicaraguan woman.

60. Pastora called Montero "Moleón," while his nom de guerre with Che Guevara was "Ivan."

61. During the final phases of the war against Somoza, Comandante Bravo had held the Southern Front guerrillas to a standoff and successfully deprived Pastora the glory of marching into Managua with the other Sandinista commanders. Pastora welcomed Bravo's murder. Author's interviews; Dickey, *With the Contras,* pp. 63–67.

62. Interview with Pastora and a Montero operative in Costa Rica.

63. Although many details Francés revealed proved true it is possible the Sandinistas forced him to insert some of the information. Salinas and Villalonga, *Gorriarán,* pp. 211–21.

64. In 1990, Juan Tamayo reported in the *Miami Herald* that evidence indicated the La Penca and Cuadra bombs were so similar that "it would be easy to believe that La Penca was also the work of Sandinistas." But a close examination of the evidence and numerous interviews by investigator Ken Ward shows there are major differences between the two bombs. The Cuadra bomb was mainly TNT and composed of steel ball bearings of 4 different sizes. In contrast, the La Penca bomb was mainly C-4 plastic, was much more powerful, and contained various types of shrapnel, screws, rivets, and ball-bearings. Sources: Interviews; Ward interviews and report; John McPhaul, "Bomb Rocks Downtown Area; 1 Dead," *Tico Times,* July 1, 1983; "El OIJ confirmo similitud entre el atentado de La Penca y el parqueo," *La República,* June 26, 1984; Juan Tamayo, "Costa Rica reopening mystery of 1984 bombing," *Miami Herald,* Dec. 30, 1990.

65. Author's reporting and extensive Costa Rican press coverage at time of Cuadra bombing; interviews with Pastora, Prado, Solano, Sandinista infiltrator into ARDE; Vaughan/Deal interview with Borge.

66. The arrest of an ETA terrorist connected to the Sandinistas came at an awkward moment for Managua since Borge was in Spain seeking support President Felipe González' government and from the Socialist International of which González was a leading member. Borge denied Nicaragua had given ETA guerrillas military training in Nicaragua, although he admitted individual ETA members had been in his country. But the damage was done and afterwards González became an important supporter of Pastora's faction of ARDE. Honey and Avirgan, "La Penca," pp. 4–5.

67. Author's interviews and reportirg; extensive Costa Rican press coverage of the event.

68. A handful of the ETA militants became trainers for the FMLN guerrillas in El Salvador, Noriega permitted others to live temporarily in Panama, some went to Cuba, and others to Nicaragua. It is possible Jímenez' network was linked to a huge warehouse of armaments, passorts, dossiers, and other documents discovered years later—in May 1993—when some weapons accidently exploded at an auto repair shop in the Santa Rosa neighborhood in Managua. An archives of evidence exposed by the blast revealed that this was a base of operations for an international ring whose activities included supplying arms to the Salvadoran guerrillas and hemisphere-wide kidnappings for ransom. The auto repair shop was run by a Basque who had come to Nicaragua in 1982. At least three people were killing in the explosion, and another three Basques, described as top-ranking ETA members living in Nicaragua under assumed names, were arrested and quickly deported to Spain. Author's interviews; Tracy Wilkinson, "Stalking the Rich for Ransom," *Los Angeles Times,* July 28, 1993; Tim Johnson, "Blast Blows Kidnapping Ring's Cover," *Miami Herald,* June 21, 1993; Douglas Farah, "Managua Blasts Rip Lid Off Secrets," *Washington Post,* July 14, 1993.

69. Based largely on Doug Vaughan's investigations, plus author's interviews in Panama.

70. Author's interviews including with Borge, Maria Lourdes Pallais, Pastora, Carol Prado.

71. Tamayo, "Nicaragua Assassin," *Miami Herald,* Aug. 1, 1993; Martin Arostegui, "The Case of the Danish Assassin," *National Review,* May 24, 1993; Glenn Garvin, "Who Bombed in La Penca?" *Washington City Paper,* Aug. 6, 1993.

72. Anonymous memo regarding arrest presumably written by a Costa Rican detective and circulated in June 1984. Copy in possession of author; "Hechos" ["Matters"—concerning the La Penca case], from Jorge Chavarría, Fiscal, Pubic Ministry to Fourth Court of Instruction, San

José, April 16, 1990. David Myers thoroughly investigated this incident but found a number of key witnesses, most importantly Dr. Lamicq, unwilling to cooperate. No definitive conclusion was reached about who had been detained.

73. In the January 23, 1989 leftist attack on the La Tablada military base outside Buenos Aires, was politically counter-productive. The first guerrilla action in Argentina in a decade, it came as the country was returning to civilian democracy and it unleashed an anti-left witch hunt. The attackers said they acted to pre-empt an ultra-rightist military coup, but there is no evidence one was about to occur. There was evidence the military expected the guerrilla attack. Gorriarán's guerrillas which included several Nicaraguans and ERP militants who had worked for the Sandinistas, were decimated: 28 guerrillas died, 79 were wounded, and about 20 arrested. Six bodies, among them (police initially said) Gaguine's, were so badly burned they could not be positively identified. In late 1993, Costa Rican and Argentinian police said Gaguine might still be alive, and they issued a warrant for his arrest. Gorriarán, the leader, escaped unharmed and may not even have been on the scene. John McPhail, "Last Photo of Bomber is Revealed," *Tico Times,* Nov. 19, 1983. For a discussion of possible military infiltration of Gorriarán cell see: Salinas and Villalonga, *Gorrarian*; Schneider, "Argentina," *NACLA,* Sept. 1989; Andersen, "Dirty Secrets," *Nation,* Mar. 13, 1989.

74. Salinas and Villalonga, *Gorriaran,* pp. 50–61.

75. Bruce Jones deposition to Christic Institute. McGough and Steinberg chronology, p. 32.

76. In an interview, an ex-OIJ agent recalled that on the day of the bombing, "people [in Special Affairs] were all locked up together in that office as if waiting for something. I recall thinking this was very unusual because they were usually all working separately and were never all together."

77. Public Prosecutors, "La Penca," p. 40. This is apparently the DIS report which both Security Minister Solano and DIS director Carlos Monge mentioned in interviews.

78. "Murder on the Río San José," produced by Charles Stewart for PBS's "Frontline" TV program (Boston: WGBH, Apr. 19, 1988).

79. Public Prosecutors, "La Penca," pp. 51, 64.

80. Author's interviews; Joan Carlisle, "Anatomy of a Disinformation Campaign," *Propaganda Review,* Winter 1988.

81. "Alerta por Posible llegada de terroristas de la ETA," *La Nación,* Mar, 14, 1984; "Buscan comando Etarra aquí," *La República,* Mar. 14, 1984.

82. Olson was posted in Africa and could not be deposed about the cryptic note. Author's interview; Carlisle, "Anatomy."

83. Interviews. For more details about CMA see Terrell, *Disposable Patriot.*

84. Several months after this meeting, in March 1984, Hull told mercenary Peter Glibbery that the CIA had sent him C-4 plastic for economic sabotage actions inside Nicaragua. This C-4 was apparently used instead to blow up an electrical tower inside Costa Rica.

85. Interviews; Terrell's declarations to OIJ, May 23, 1986; Avirgan and Honey, *La Penca,* p. 87; Terrell, *Disposable Patriot,* pp. 225–30.

86. Allan Nairn, "The Contras' Little List," *Progressive,* Mar. 1987.

87. Although Tambs did not arrive in Costa Rica until July 1987, it was announced in the press in early January that he had been appointed. According to several of those involved, the actions were postponed several times because Tambs' arrival was delayed. John Riley and Fred Strasser, "In Search of Justice: The Story That Wouldn't Go Away," *National Law Journal,* Mar. 16, 1987.

88. Author's interviews with García, Carr and Terrell; "Statement of Jesus Garcia," given to Theodore Sakowitz, Federal Public Defender, Southern District of Florida, U.S. Courthouse, Miami, n.d. Copy in author's possession.

89. Corvo interview with FBI agents Kevin Currier and George Kiszynski, Miami, June 13, 1986.

90. Glibbery recalled that at one point he found the claymore mines hidden in a sawmill. When he proposed taking them to his contra camp, Hull told him sternly, "Put them back. We may need them for an embassy job." Glibbery said, "I didn't ask any questions. That wasn't the kind of thing I wanted to know."

91. These weapons, which were key pieces of evidence in U.S. and Costa Rican legislative and judicial investigations, were, according to Carr and others, ferreted out of the country by unnamed Miami judicial officials. The politically explosive judicial investigation and grand jury probe in Miami was later aborted on instructions from the Justice Department in Washington. The whereabouts of the weapons is unknown. In a 1986 interview at La Reforma prison, Carr said he had been told that Senate Republicans had determined that the flight that took him and others from Florida to El Salvador contained only three back packs, no weapons. "A charter flight for back packs? That's ridiculous," retorted Carr. In May 1986, the Justice Department announced there was "no foundation" for charges that contra and their American supporters were involved in gunrunning. "We ran everything down and didn't find

anything. It comes to nothing," a senior department official told the *New York Times*. Author's interviews with Carr and others; "Contras Clear on Gunrunning," *New York Times*, May 7, 1986; Riley and Strasser, "In Search of Justice," *National Law Journal*, Mar. 16, 1987.

92. Terrell testimony to OIJ, May 23, 1986.

93. Nairn, "Little List."

94. Lederach says he was interrogated by Rodolfo ("Flaco") Jiménez, who had been with DIS at the time of the La Penca bombing and was in 1987 head of its Narcotics Division.

95. Interviews; Honey and Avirgan, "The CIA's War," *The Nation*, Feb. 6, 1988, and "Reagan Disrupts Nicaraguan Peace Talks," *San Francisco Bay Guardian*, Jan. 13, 1988.

Chapter 12: The Santa Elena Airstrip and the Opening of the Southern Front

1. Tambs, Iran-contra hearings, U.S. Congress, May 27, 1987, p. 149.

2. Crone deposition, Christic Institute, Jan. 6–7, 1988, plus author's numerous interviews with Crone, an ARDE pilot, and others.

3. The landing strip, which was first built in 1948, was officially closed in 1976 because it did not meet Costa Rican safety standards. However, like other airstrips scattered around the country, light aircraft continued to use it illegally. Interviews; Lyle Prescott and John McPhaul, "Costa Rica Puzzled by Mystery Airstrip," *Miami Herald*, Sept. 27, 1986.

4. According to a March 1986 entry in Oliver North's notebooks, a second covert landing strip was being built, with Monge's approval, on a U.S.-owned and -managed ginger farm at Siquerres, on Costa Rica's Atlantic coast. This was partially confirmed by the farm's manager, George Hogan, who is mentioned in North's entry. Interviews; North notebooks, Mar. 10, 1986.

5. Steven Emerson, *Secret Warriors: Inside the Covert Military Operations of the Reagan Era*, pp. 8–9, 96. Emerson traces Yellow Fruit's origins back to the 1980 failed rescue mission of U.S. hostages in Iran, which involved a number of the Iran-contra players: Richard Secord, Albert Hakim, Richard Gadd, and Robert Dutton (pp. 8–9, 96).

6. William Golden, to Iran-contra hearings, U.S. Congress May 6, 1987, vol. 12, Appendix B, pp. 409–10, 433; Emerson, *Secret Warriors*, pp. 151–52.

7. Golden said that Yellow Fruit "was planning other things in Costa Rica but the only mission carried out was the airstrip." Author's interview with Golden; Emerson, *Secret Warriors*, p. 9.

8. Between February and July 1986, for instance, Montero received $193,233 into his bank account, ostensibly for construction of the airfield. Costa Rica's Legislative Assembly drug commission questioned "the origin of Mr. Montero Quesada's income," which "bears no relation to his salary." Former Ambassador McNeil writes that Montero "apparently made a pile" and that local residents believed the airstrip was used "by more than Contra planes, probably for drug flights." Legislative Assembly, *Special Commission Appointed to Investigate the Acts Reported on Drug Trafficking*, pp. 52–53; McNeil, *War and Peace*, pp. 236–37; U.S. Congress, *Iran-Contra Affair*, p. 338; and bank records in same, vol. 2, Appendix A, p. 330.

9. Interviews; Cockburn, *Out of Control*, pp. 178, 268; Neal Matthews, "I Ran Drugs for Uncle Sam," *San Diego's Weekly Reader*, April 5, 1990; "Presencia de tropas Somocistas en Costa Rica," paid ad by legislator Ricardo Rodríguez, *La Nación*, Sept. 9, 1984; "Witness: Guard Sought Airstrip for Drugs," *Tico Times*, May 19, 1989.

10. McNeil, *War and Peace*, p. 237; Tambs, Iran-contra hearings, U.S. Congress various references. Although remote and largely inaccessible by road, the landing strip was easily visible by air, a fact that ultimately led to its discovery by the press.

11. The *Iran-Contra Affair* report describes Zucker as "a covert operator's model banker, accountant, lawyer, and money manager." U.S. Congress, *Iran-Contra Affair*, p. 332. Author's interviews; Golden Iran-contra hearings, U.S. Congress, May 6, 1987, pp. 425–26; "Report: Army Had Secret Contra Fund," *Miami Herald*, Apr. 22, 1987; Charles Babcock, "Army Denied Report on Swiss Bank," *Philadelphia Inquirer*, July 3, 1987.

12. Hakim unabashedly told the Iran-contra hearings, "I never pretended to undertake the tasks I was asked to perform for philanthropic purposes and I made that clear to all of those with whom I [w]as involved—including General Secord, Lieutenant Colonel North, the CIA, and the Iranians." Congress, *Iran-Contra Affair*, p. 331, 343; Sklar, *Washington's War*, pp. 251–52.

13. Lake's account at Credit Suisse received Iranian arms sale money and was controlled exclusively by North. "Complex Money Network Revealed," *Miami Herald*, Dec. 21, 1986; Sklar, *Washington's War*, pp. 230–59; John Tagliabue, "Concerns in Switzerland Were Apparently Fronts," *New York Times*, Dec. 15, 1986; William Safire, "Man in the Middle," *New York Times*, July 27, 1989.

14. Dolmy featured in another North-Secord financial scandal: the purchase of a small Danish steamer, *Erria*. No reasonable explanation was given as to why Project Democracy needed its own ship. In 1986, North tried unsuccessfully to sell this ship and other Project Democracy assets to

the CIA, apparently, it seems, with the intention that he and Secord would keep the proceeds. William Golden, Iran-contra hearings, U.S. Congress, vol. 12, Appendix B, pp. 402–25; U.S. Congress, *Iran-Contra Affair,* pp. 341, 356 (note 75), 367–68; Sklar, *Washington's War,* p. 253.

15. Another company incorporated by Quijano, Stanford Technology Corporation, was owned by Hakim and Secord and connected to a string of other similarly named companies in Europe and the United States, dating back to the mid-1970s. Beginning in 1974, Hakim, a CIA asset, along with former CIA agents Edwin Wilson and Frank Terpil used Stanford Technology Corporation, located in the heart of California's Silicon Valley, and its subsidiary Intercontinental Technology, to sell a vast array of explosives, electronics, and surveillance equipment, weapons, and other military and covert operations hardware to, among others, the Shah of Iran, Qadhafi in Libya, and Idi Amin in Uganda. During this period they teamed up with Secord, chief of the Air Force Military Assistance Group in Teheran, and CIA officers Ted Shackley and Tom Clines.

In 1979, while covering the overthrow of Idi Amin in Uganda, I came across evidence of these transactions in the State Research Bureau, Amin's notorious torture chambers and security headquarters in Kampala. Among the files, I found a three-page contract signed by Amin and "F. Terpil" of Intercontinental Technology for the $3.2 million sale of spy equipment. Terpil and Wilson were, at the time, being prosecuted by the U.S. government. Just after this, Terpil skipped bail and dropped from site. Wilson was convicted and went to jail, while others in their gang—Secord, Hakim, Clines, and Rafael Quintero—soon turned up in the thick of the Iran-contra scandal. Avirgan and Honey, *War in Uganda,* pp. 21–25, 123; Honey and David Ottaway, "Foreigners Aided Amin," *Washington Post,* May 28, 1979; Peter Maas, *Manhunt,* entire; Sklar, *Washington's War,* pp. 254–55.

16. In his memoirs, Secord writes that the company was "named, appropriately, after Morris Udall, the noted conservationist." Richard Secord with Jay Wurts, *Honored and Betrayed: Irangate, Covert Affairs, and the Secret War in Laos,* (Philadelphia: John Wiley & Sons), 1992, p. 214.

17. Former ambassador Frank McNeil makes the interesting speculation that the CIA asset Noreiga may have arranged for the Enterprise to use Quijano and Associates for incorporating its dummy companies. McNeil, *War and Peace,* p. 237. Record of incorporation obtained in Panama; National Security Archive, *The Chronology,* pp. 282, 321; Joseph Treaster, "Leading Panamanian Lawyer Set Up Companies Tied to Contra Supplies," *New York Times,* Dec. 16, 1986; John Tagliabue, "Concerns in Switzerland were Apparently Fronts," *New York Times,* Dec. 15, 1986; U.S. Congress, *Iran-Contra Affair,* vol. 2, Appendix A, pp. 225–350.

18. As the Tower Commission stated, this new arrangement in-cluded doing what Congress had refused to fund—the air resupply of lethal materials for the contra forces inside Nicaragua. *Tower Commission Report,* p. 452.

19. U.S. Congress, *Iran-Contra Affair,* pp. 61–63, 343.

20. Tambs's behavior did not sit well with Arias officials. When he packed his bags and left Costa Rica seventeen months later, no Costa Rican officials came to see him off, a considerable diplomatic snub. Tambs, along with North, Poindexter, Secord, Owen, and Joe Fernández, was subsequently declared persona non grata by the Costa Rican legisla-ture's special commission on drug trafficking. Legislative Assembly, *Drug Trafficking;* Tambs, Iran-contra hearings, U.S. Congress, May 27, 1987; speech by Tambs to Ravenscroft School, Raleigh, North Carolina, June 1, 1985; Ben Bradley, Jr., *Guts and Glory: The Rise and Fall of Oliver North* (New York: Donald Fine, 1988), pp. 253–54; interviews, investigation, and reporting by author.

21. Tambs, Iran-contra hearings, U.S. Congress, May 27, 1987, pp. 131, 240; James Tull, Iran-contra hearings, U.S. Congress, vol. 27, Appendix B, May 6, 1987, p. 177.

22. Members of the North network claimed that Ilopango was used for contra operations only from 1985 onwards, when in fact, as shown earlier, it had been used since 1982.

23. Memo, "August 1989. Trip," To BC [North]: For Your Eyes Only, From: TC [Owen], Aug. 25, 1985.

24. William Haskell testimony, Oliver North trial, Washington: U.S. District Court, Apr. 4, 1989; North notebooks, Sept. 17 and Oct. 3, 1985; U.S. Congress, *Iran-Contra Affair,* p. 62.

25. Hamilton, who had apparently been willing to make a cheap deal, recalls that his new lawyers bluntly ordered him "to get out" of the way and let them handle the negotiations. The reason why this U.S. Embassy–connected law firm decided to raise the price is not clear, although Hamilton says most of the money paid to him went for legal fees. Interviews with Hamilton and others; Haskell testimony, North trial.

26. Udall Research Corporation order for wire transfer of $125,000 to account of Joseph Hamilton, unclassified, document 22–67 in U.S. Congress, *Iran-Contra Affair,* Appendix A, vol. 2, p. 832.

27. Haskell testified that North and Secord were both listed in the corporate records by their frequently used aliases: William C. Goode for North and Richard S. Copp for Secord. Haskell testimony, North trial, pp. 6589–92; Santa Elena legal documents obtained by the author from Costa Rica's registry of corporations and Costa Rican government officials.

28. Beginning in May 1986, North and Secord set up a new front company known as B.C. Washington for the Santa Elena airstrip and other Project Democracy assets. They claimed it belonged to unnamed private individuals. (They did not, however, dissolve either Udall or Santa Elena Development Corporation.) But, as Col. Robert Dutton, the operational chief for the resupply flights, told the Iran-contra panel, "B.C. Washington was a facade that North and Secord developed in order to cloak their role."

In the summer of 1986, Congress passed a $100 million contra aid package, thereby allowing the CIA to take over from North's network the running of the war against Nicaragua. In July North wrote his boss Poindexter, "We are rapidly approaching the point where the Project Democracy assets in CentAm need to be turned over to CIA." He proposed the CIA buy them for between $4.5 and $5 million, estimating it would cost the Agency $8 to $10 million to replace the facilities. North went on to deny, falsely, any U.S. ties to Project Democracy: "All of the assets—and the personnel—are owned/paid by overseas companies with no U.S. connection." Both Casey and Deputy Director of Operations Clair George turned North down. This appears to indicate that North himself was trying to use his covert activities for personal profit.

Interviews and investigations by author; Robert Dutton, Iran-contra hearings, U.S. Congress, May 4, 1987, Appendix B, vol. 9; U.S. Congress, *Iran-Contra Affair,* pp. 68–78.

29. Interviews with Quijano and Associates and Costa Rican government officials.

30. U.S. Congress, *Iran-Contra Affair,* p. 332.

31. Quintero, testimony, North trial, Mar. 2, 1989, p. 2919.

32. U.S. Congress, *Iran-Contra Affair,* p. 353.

33. Safire, "Man in the Middle," *New York Times,* July 27, 1989; Safire, "No August Doldrums," *New York Times* Aug. 3, 1989; "Note from William Safire: A Follow-Up on Mr. Rappaport," *New York Times,* Aug. 16, 1989; "More on Those Mission Millions," *Newsweek,* Aug. 7, 1989.

34. U.S. Congress, *Iran-Contra Affair,* p. 348.

35. Richard Gadd, Iran-contra hearings U.S. Congress, May 1, 1987, Appendix B, vol. 11, p. 211–16; U.S. Congress, *Iran-Contra Affair,* p. 62.

36. Jonathan Kwitny, *The Crimes of Patriots,* p. 379; Maas, *Manhunt,* pp. 65–81; Quintero, North trial, pp. 2885, 2906, 2959, 3018.

37. A chart in the Iran-contra congressional report lists thirteen successful drops to Southern Front forces and a number of aborted flights. TC (Owen) to BG (North), Subject: Trip Report, March 28, 1986;

"Thomas Castillo," Iran-contra hearings, U.S. Congress, vol. 3, Appendix B, May 29, 1987, morning and afternoon sessions; "Table 3–1. Resupply Flights Made by the North/Secord Resupply Operation During 1986," U.S. Congress, *Iran-Contra Affair*, pp. 79–81.

38. North notebooks, various entries in early 1986; Cockburn, *Out of Control*, p. 89; Legislative Assembly, *Drug Trafficking*, p. 53; Carl Deal, "Administration Blocks CIA Trial: Defendant Threatened to Expose Deals Between CIA, Drug Traffickers," *Convergence*, Winter 1991.

39. It took another six weeks to finish the project. "By May, the Santa Elena airstrip, along with emergency fuel storage space and temporary housing, was finished." U.S. Congress, *Iran-Contra Affair*, p. 67.

40. Alfonso Chardy, "CIA Agents Named in North Papers," *Miami Herald*, Jan. 13, 1989; AP, "Documents Kept from Iran-Contra Probe Name CIA Contacts," Jan. 12, 1989.

41. Court document, "Stipulation," p. 35.

42. These photos were later hand-carried to San José by Quintero, who was stopped and searched by customs agents. They found maps and papers relating to the airstrip, but Quintero successfully hid the photos, which Piza afterward hung in his house. However, when asked if they might be available for use in this book, Piza said that unfortunately they had been misplaced by his wife. Quintero, testimony, North trial, p. 2999; author's interviews with Piza.

43. North wrote Poindexter that "the President obviously knows why he has been meeting with several select people to thank them for their 'support for Democracy' in CentAm." U.S. Congress, *Iran-Contra Affair*, p. 70; Sklar, *Washington's War*, p. 277; "Tomás Castillo," Iran-contra hearings, U.S Congress.

44. Fernández said Piza and Poindexter discussed "Costa Rican problems . . . views of the new President . . . all political military stuff." Piza said that he did not recall Secord being present even though Fernández testified that Piza and Secord did most of the talking and he and Quintero "were only observers." Apparently Piza, like his friend Fernández, did not want to be linked to Secord. Fernández told CIA investigators, "My impression of Secord was . . . negative. I nicknamed him 'dickhead.' Ollie would get very upset when I called him that. He'd say, 'Don't say that.' " Author's interviews with Piza; interview with Joe Fernández, Cole Black, and George Jameson, 1987; CIA Office of the Inspector General Investigative Reports, January 24, 1986 [sic:1987], released through FOIA to Center for National Security Studies. Document appears in Peter Kornbluh and Malcolm Byrn, eds., *The*

Iran-Contra Scandal: The Declassified History; "Tomás Castillo," Iran-contra hearings, U.S. Congress, May 29, 1987, morning session.

45. Fernández testified that the letterhead "looks like it was done with a typewriter rather than a printed letterhead." "Tomás Castillo," Iran-contra hearings, U.S. Congress; Quintero testimony, North trial.

46. Copy of letter obtained from Arias government.

47. Court document, "Stipulation," p. 27; Dan Morgan and John Goshko, "Costa Rican Disputes North Trial Document," *Washington Post*, Apr. 15, 1989.

48. Interview. It could not be ascertained whether the Sandinistas did have such an East German–supplied eavesdropping system.

49. U.S. Congress, *Iran-Contra Affair*, p. 64.

50. "Centro de Comunicaciones es 'Secreto de Estado,' " *La República*, Nov. 5, 1986.

51. U.S. Congress, *Iran-Contra Affair*, p. 61, 65; "Tomás Castillo," Iran-contra hearings, U.S. Congress, April 20 and May 29, 1987, vol. 3, Appendix B, various references; Woodward, *Veil*, p. 465.

Chapter 13: The Success of Washington's "Project Pastora" and the Dismantling of the Southern Front

1. "75 percent de Armas que Entregó Pastora Están Inservibles," *La República*, May 18, 1986.

2. Pastora deposition to Christic Institute, 1987, San José, p. 54. The RIG campaign against Pastora is also the subject of an undated, five-page memo submitted by GeoMilitech president Barbara Studley, an arms dealer, to the congressional Iran-contra committee. Most of the text is blacked out by the committee, but one line reads, "North's policy to terminate Eden Pastora and the southern front in Nicaragua." Sent by her attorney Frank Koszorus, Jr., to Kenneth Ballen, Assistant Counsel, House Select Committee to Investigate Covert Arms Transactions with Iran, *Iran-Contra Hearings*, vol. 12, pp. 1040–44.

3. "Tomás Castillo," Iran-contra hearings, U.S. Congress, May 29, 1987, morning and afternoon sessions. Ambassador Curtin Winsor had an equally low opinion of Pastora, whom he described as "singularly ineffective." Winsor told an interviewer, "As a guerrilla he lived up to his name, Comandante Zero. I found that singularly appropriate for him. He did nothing effective as a guerrilla whatsoever." Winsor interview by Kennedy, p. 40.

4. Witness for Peace officials later identified a New York–based

free-lance photographer who they suspect may have been one of Fernández's agents. Interview and correspondence with Witness for Peace; "Witness for Peace Newsletter," Sept./Oct. 1985; Richard Dyer, "Peace Group Found After Being Freed," and "Pacifists' Abductor Identified as ARDE Member," *Tico Times,* Aug. 9 and 16, 1985; "Nicaragua Rebels Said to Abduct 29 U.S. Activists and 18 Others," *New York Times,* Aug. 8, 1985; Stephen Kinzer, "29 American Peace Activists Reported Freed in Nicaragua," *New York Times,* Aug. 8, 1985; AP, "Freed U.S. Activists in Nicaragua Town," *New York Times,* Aug. 10, 1985.

5. Pastora says that of the $27 million "humanitarian" aid package voted by Congress in June 1985, he received a mere $384.81 (reimbursement for a plane ticket), and this he angrily sent off as a donation to an American Vietnam War veterans' organization. Interviews; Julia Preston, "Contras' Bad Boy Reflects on Defeat," *Washington Post,* July 3, 1986.

6. Kathy McHugh, "Rebel SOS Plea Begs for Funds," *Tico Times,* Feb. 10, 1985. The expulsion order was never officially rescinded but Popo managed to go in and out secretly.

7. Interviews; copies of letters; "Castillo" testimony, pp. 372–75, 500–503, 535.

8. Singlaub, who was removed by President Jimmy Carter as U.S. commander in South Korea, retired from the military in 1980 but carried on his far-right ideological warfare through the World Anti-Communist League (WACL) and its U.S. branch, the Council for World Freedom. With chapters in over ninety countries, WACL was founded in 1966 by the South Korean and Taiwanese military dictatorships and former East European Nazis and fascists. For an excellent history of WACL see Anderson and Anderson, *Inside the League.*

9. Studley, a former Miami radio talk show host, was president of the Washington-based arms brokerage firm GeoMilitech, for which Singlaub was a consultant.

10. In mid-March, just before Singlaub's trip to Costa Rica and perhaps as part of the same plan, Abrams and other State Department officials suddenly announced that Pastora would receive $400,000 of the humanitarian aid package and a portion of the $100 million being debated by Congress. They said Pastora had agreed to unity with UNO, and in San José a Pastora aide told the press that "progress towards unity has been achieved." There had been months of quiet diplomacy and this announcement appeared to signal that, desperate for aid, Pastora had softened his position on aligning with the FDN. The announcement appeased Pastora's supporters in Congress and helped the White House secure passage of the

$100 million. But Pastora never got the funds. Pastora deposition, p. 55; Prado deposition, p. 40; Doyle McManus, "U.S. Quietly Resumes Funding Contra Leader Edén Pastora," *Miami Herald,* Mar. 13, 1986; Beth Hawkins, "Rebels Try Again for unity," *Tico Times,* Mar. 14, 1986; Jonathan Winer, Staff report for U.S. Senator John Kerry, "Contra Corruption: An Overview," Summer 1986, unpublished, pp. 8–9.

11. "Castillo" testimony, pp. 403–8, 538–41; agreement between Maj. Gen. John K. Singlaub and Edén Pastora, March 26, 1986, copy in possession of author.

12. Singlaub testimony, Iran-contra congressional hearings, April 29, 1987, p. 1051–59; Tambs testimony, Iran-contra congressional hearings, May 27, 1987, pp. 176–93; "Castillo" testimony, pp. 401–7; Prado deposition, Christic Institute, 1987, San José, p. 70; Alfonso Chardy, "General Says Abrams Told of Contra Aid," *Miami Herald,* Feb. 26, 1987. See also p. 577, note 20, for Fernandez's success in stopping an arms shipment in May 1986 from Sarkis Soghanalian to Pastora.

13. "Castillo" testimony, pp. 406–8; Tambs testimony, pp. 176–93, 199–204.

14. This section is based largely on interviews and reporting done by the author. Journalist Peter Shinkle supplied an extensive and valuable chronology as well as documents and analysis about the CIA-contra–South African connection. Other sources, in addition to those cited below, include: Gutman, *Banana Diplomacy;* Emerson, *Secret Warriors;* Karen Burnes's report on ABC's "World News Tonight," Feb. 25, 1987; Stephen Engelberg, "US Planned in '84 for South Africa to Help Contras" and "Shultz Tie to Pretoria Aid is Denied," *New York Times,* Aug. 20 and 21, 1987; James Ridgeway, "Iran-Contra-Apartheid," *Village Voice,* Sept. 8, 1987; Dan Morgan, "Pretoria Offered to Aid Contras," *Washington Post,* Aug. 20, 1987; David Corn, "South Africa Link," *The Nation,* Sept. 12, 1987.

15. Despite Costa Rica's espoused support for human rights, it had diplomatic relations with South Africa until July 1986, two months after the Arias government took office. Two decades earlier, in 1967, the Legislative Assembly had voted to cut commercial links, but trade as well as sports ties continued, despite a international boycott of the racist government.

16. Interviews; letter from Brigadier Alex Potgieter, defense and armed forces attaché, South African Embassy, Washington, to A. S. Capella, consul general for South Africa, Oct. 12, 1984. Copy of letter in possession of author.

17. North notebook entries Jan. 5 and 17 or 18 (date of entry

unclear), 1985; Sklar, *Washington' War*, p. 225; Emerson, *Secret Warriors*, p. 222.

18. Interviews; "Disclosures: Declaration of Dependence," *Briarpatch* (Canadian) Dec. 1985/Jan. 1986, p. 31.

19. House Foreign Affairs Sub-Committee on Africa, "Recent Reports on Southern Africa/Contra Ties," undated 1987 report supplied to author by New York *Guardian* journalist John Bennett.

20. In December 1986, for instance, the British *Independent* reported that sixty tons of U.S. arms, including machine guns and rocket launchers, had been shipped to South Africa in three separate airlifts. The arms were apparently intended for UNITA. Ken Fireman, "US May Have Sent Arms to S. Africa in Deal to Aid Contras," *Miami Herald*, March 5, 1987; interviews; Sklar, *Washington's War*, p. 225.

21. Pastora also included in the letter the following: "With reference to the attempt on my life at La Penca on May 30, 1984, I assure you categorically that I have never accused any U.S. government entity. [The evidence] leaves little doubt that my assassination was an integral part of a military plan of the EPS [Sandinista army] under Cuban direction." On all other occasions, both before and after this letter, Pastora had either blamed the bombing on his "enemies on the left or the right" or the CIA–Oliver North network. Pastora says that he wrote this at the insistance of Sullivan. Unsigned, typed statement from Pastora to Elliott Abrams and David Sullivan, Apr. 10, 1986, reprinted in U.S. Senate, *Drugs*, pp. 275–76; interviews with Pastora and Carol Prado.

22. Interviews; "Chamorro pretende regresar al país," *La Nación*, Apr. 26, 1986. For background on Nino Díaz see Hinckle and Turner, *Fish is Red*, pp. 80–88.

23. Glenn Garvin, "U.S. Urged Pastora Not to Quit, He Says," *Washington Times*, June 4, 1986; Roland Evans and Robert Novak, "Commander Zero, Deserted," *Washington Post*, May 23, 1986; "Pastora Still Held in Jail," *Tico Times*, May 30, 1986; Tim Golden, "Pastora Crosses River, Retired from Anti-Sandinista Fight," *Miami Herald*, May 17, 1986.

24. Memo from North to McFarlane, Nov. 7, 1984, *Iran-Contra Hearings* Appendix vol. 2, pp. 463–65.

25. Sklar, *Washington's War*, pp. 192–209.

26. Gerald Boyd, "Reagan Terms Nicaraguan Rebels 'Moral Equal of Founding Fathers,'" *New York Times*, Mar. 2, 1985.

27. Interviews; Congress, *Iran-Contra Affair*, p. 48; Sklar, *Washington's War*, pp. 261–65.

28. Memo, North to McFarlane, May 31, 1985, *Iran-Contra Hearings*, Appendix vol. 2, pp. 530–32.

29. Interview with a high contra official in June 1985 who said BOS was receiving financial support in cash from the CIA in Washington.

30. "Nicaragua Rebels Request 'Dialogue,'" *Tico Times*, Mar. 8, 1985.

31. U.S. Congress, *Iran-Contra Affair*, p. 61; Sklar, *Washington's War*, p. 269.

32. TC [Owen], Memo to BG [North], "Overall Perspective," Mar. 17, 1986.

33. Owen, various memos to North, April 1, May 20, August 25, 1985, and March 17, 1986; author's interviews.

34. This section is based on author's interviews and reporting, including Honey, "Contra Polygraphs," *The Nation*, Mar. 29, 1986.

35. "Castillo" testimony, afternoon session.

36. U.S. General Accounting Office, *Central America: Problems in Controlling Funds for the Nicaraguan Democratic Resistance*, Dec. 1986; Sklar, *Washington's War*, pp. 269–70.

37. Interview with Barger.

38. John Kerry, "'Private Assistance' and the Contras: A Staff Report," U.S. Senate, Oct. 14, 1986, p. 9; letter from Calero, Cruz, and Robelo to Ambassador Duemling, Oct. 3, 1985 and Owen contract in U.S. Congress, *Iran-Contra Affair*, Appendix, vol. 2, pp. 829, 835, plus pp. 63–65; Sklar, *Washington's War*, p. 269.

39. U.S. General Accounting Office, *Controlling Funds*, p. 10.

40. Winer, U.S. Senate, "Contra Corruption," pp. 10, 13.

41. Interviews. Tim Golden, "Contras Bilked U.S.," *Miami Herald*, June 1, 1986. NHAO and CIA officials apparently turned a blind eye to such corruption, either through negligence or because those involved, including the Fonseca brothers, were deemed to be important U.S. collaborators.

42. Golden, "Contras Bilked U.S."

43. Levin, "On Trial: Seafood Company with a Contra Connection," *Boston Herald*, Dec. 11, 1988.

44. Interviews; U.S. Senate, *Drugs*, pp. 45–47; Schoot and Marshall, *Cocaine Politics*, various ref.; Kerry, "'Private Assistance,'" pp. 9–10.

45. Interviews; Golden, "Contras Bilked U.S."

46. Winer, U.S. Senate, "Contra Corruption," p. 9; Chardy, "Contra Aid Wasn't Misused, U.S. Says," and "Panel Seeks Bank Records of Suppliers of Contra Aid," *Miami Herald*, June 26 and Sept. 5, 1986.

47. David Shipler, "Ex-Officers Accuse Contra Chiefs of Siphoning Off U.S. Aid Money," *New York Times*, June 21, 1986.

48. Neil Roland, UPI, "Ex-Contras Tell Senate Investigators of Corruption," June 21, 1986.

Chapter 14: Arias: Making Peace

1. Quotes from Stephen Kinzer, "Officials Assert U.S. is Trying to Weaken Costa Rican Chief," *New York Times*, Aug. 7, 1988.

2. Mitchell Seligson and Miguel Gómez, "Ordinary Elections in Extraordinary Times: The Political Economy of Voting in Costa Rica," in Booth and Seligson, *Elections and Democracy in Central America*. Because Seligson and Gómez focus on the impact of Costa Rica's economic crisis and do not examine how the issues of peace and neutrality affected voters, they fail to explain adequately the phenomenon of the Arias victory. They do not correctly interpret the extent to which Costa Ricans *believed* that the economy had improved under Monge, even though they and I both agree that the economic improvements were superficial and long-term structural problems remained unaddressed.

3. Investigation and reports by Honey and Avirgan, including Avirgan report on National Public Radio, Apr. 16, 1986; UPI, "Poll: 60 percent Oppose Aid Bid Despite Reagan Campaign," *Miami Herald*, Mar. 9, 1986; UPI, "Poll: Most Americans Oppose Contra Aid," *Miami Herald*, Apr. 16, 1986.

4. Press spokesman Mark Krishik said he had no explanation for why the Embassy was promoting the eight-month-old figures instead of current data. CID President Charles Denton was more frank, saying that the older poll was being circulated "because it's a hot issue now."

5. Interviews with Arias; Richard Boudreax, "The Bashful Peacemaker," *Los Angeles Times*, Nov. 2, 1987.

6. Arias explained, "I didn't know that we were doing all that we were doing. And for me it was a blow that Ambassador Tambs said, 'We want to open up a Southern Front and we need the help of Costa Rica.' Of course, I had to say no."

7. Author was shown copy of this secret State Department memo prepared for Bush as talking points to be covered with Arias.

8. After the inauguration ceremony Tambs informed Abrams that Arias had "misgivings about the airstrip." Abrams responded, "We'll have to squeeze his balls and get tough with him." CIA Office of the Inspector General, partial chronology of Fernández's activities in Costa Rica, late summer 1985 to Feb. 2, 1987, one of investigative reports released through FOIA to the Center for National Security Studies, p. 18; Tambs testimony, p. 172; James LeMoyne, "US Envoy Linked to Rebel Airstrip Inside Costa Rica," *New York Times*, December 26, 1986.

9. Hernán Garrón Salazar, Ministro de Seguridad Pública, "Comunicado de prensa," Mar. 6, 1987.

10. Undated document, compiled between May and July 1986,

outlining reorganization of Project Democracy, [Richard] Dutton exhibit 14 from Iran-contra congressional hearings, copy in possession of author; Rafael Quintero testimony, North trial, March 2, 1989, pp. 2821–2924; Tambs testimony, Iran-contra hearings, pp. 166–68; hotel and immigration records; Quirós declarations in Edelman and Kenen, *Costa Rica Reader,* pp. 337–44.

11. U.S. Congress, *Iran-Contra Affair,* p. 68; Tambs testimony, pp. 166–68; "Castillo" testimony, no page numbers on author's copy.

12. U.S. Congress, *Iran-Contra Affair,* pp. 69, 80; Tambs, testimony, pp. 194–96; "Castillo" testimony, afternoon session, n.p.

13. The council's resolution was apparently never sent to the government in San José. Jake Dyer, "Network: U.S. Used Airstrip," *Tico Times,* Oct. 10, 1986.

14. North notebooks, Sept, 5, 1986.

15. Author's interviews with Guido Fernández, Arias, Biehl; U.S. Congress, *Iran-Contra Affair,* pp. 142–144 and Poindexter note, Appendix A, vol. 2, pp. 922–23; North notebook, Sept. 6, 1986; Tambs testimony, pp. 172–75; *Tower Board Report,* pp. 470–74.

16. "A Memo From Rafael 'Chi Chi' Quintero to General Richard Secord," in Edelman and Kenen, *Costa Rica Reader,* pp. 354–55.

17. Jake Dyer, "Minister: Strip Not Used," *Tico Times,* Oct. 31, 1986; James LeMoyne, "Airstrip Near Nicaragua is Linked to Americans," *New York Times,* Sept. 29, 1986.

18. Copy of memo in possession of author.

19. Congress, *Iran-Contra Affair,* p. 76; Court document, "Stipulation," pp. 40–41.

20. Interviews; Arias press conference, Mar. 13, 1987; "Costa Rica: Explanations Demanded from US," *Mesoamérica,* Apr. 1987; AP, "Costa Rican President Says He Snubbed Casey," *Washington Post,* Mar. 13, 1987.

21. LeMoyne, "Costa Rica Weighs Protest to U.S. on Use of Airstrip to Aid Contras," *New York Times,* Mar. 9, 1987; Jake Dyer, "CR Asks U.S. for 'Information,' " *Tico Times,* Mar. 20, 1987.

22. Memo, Poindexter from North, "Press Guidance re Costa Rican Airstrip," National Security Council, Sept. 30, 1986. North proposed publicly denying any U.S. government funds were used for the airstrip's construction or that the United States had violated Costa Rican neutrality.

23. Hasenfus's was a low-tech job—literally kicking the supplies out the cargo door— but he happened to be the only crew member supplied wearing a parachute.

24. "Costa Rica," *Mesoamérica,* Dec. 1986.

25. Joel Brinkley, "An Ex-Ambassador says U.S. Ordered Aid for Contras," *New York Times,* May 3, 1987.

26. Deal, "Administration Blocks CIA trial," *Convergence,* Winter 1991; James Vicini, "Thornburgh After New Review, Withholds Iran-Contra Secrets," Reuters, Oct. 12, 1990.

27. Interviews and reports by author; Jake Dyer, "CR Asks U.S. for 'Information' " and "Shultz Claims U.S. Didn't Know of Airstrip's Use, *Tico Times,* Mar. 20 and Apr. 10, 1987; LeMoyne, "Costa Rica Weighs Protest."

28. Author's interviews and reporting.

29. Author's interviews; Peter Kornbluh and Martha Honey, "Iran/Contra in Costa Rica: The Case of Ollie's Airstrip," *Nation,* Feb. 22, 1993.

30. Joanne Omang, "Reagan Rallied for Aid Till the Hill Surrendered," *Washington Post,* January 2, 1987.

31. "Costa Rica: Contadora Group Tours Region," *Mesoamérica,* Feb. 1987.

32. Interviews with Fernández, Biehl, Guillermo Solís, and Arias. Fernández, *El Desafío,* pp. 27–35, 50–55. Arias's staff does not know how the United States got an advance text of the plan.

33. Center for International Policy, "Arias Primer," "International Policy Report," Washington, D.C., June 1987.

34. Fernández also records his recollection of this visit in *El Desafío,* pp. 119–29.

35. At this foreign ministers' meeting, which was supposed to iron out last-minute differences in the Arias plan, Honduras suddenly produced its own, totally different plan, written in English. Guillermo Solís, who was present, recalls, "Everyone was highly suspicious. The reaction was so negative that the plan back-fired."

36. This section is based on the author's reporting from the Guatemala summit and subsequent interviews with Costa Rican government officials, as well as accounts in Gutman's *Banana Diplomacy* and Fernández's *El Desafío.*

37. Interviews; Gutman, *Banana Diplomacy,* pp. 349–57.

38. The opposition paper, *La Prensa,* edited by Violeta Chamorro, had been banned since June 1986 and before that subject to strict censorship under Nicaragua's wartime emergency decree.

39. "Costa Rica: Arias Asks for Dialogue," *Mesoamérica,* Oct. 1987.

40. Honey and Avirgan, "Leaning on Arias," *The Nation,* Sept. 12, 1987.

41. Interview; "Hinton Selected as U.S. Envoy to Costa Rica," *Miami Herald,* Apr. 23, 1987; Jake Dyer, "US Envoy Presents Credentials to Arias," *Tico Times,* Nov. 20, 1987.

42. Interviews with Arias, Biehl, Fernández, Hinton.

43. Serge Schmemann, "Costa Rica Leader Wins Nobel Prize for Peace Plan," *New York Times*, Oct. 14, 1987.

44. Interviews; Lars Hanson, "Child Health and the 1987 Nobel Peace Prize," *Pediatrics* 81, no. 5 (May 1988).

Selected Bibliography

Among the sources not listed here are author's interviews, the testimony of scores of witnesses taken during various trials, and related court documents. The National Security Archive in Washington, D.C., holds the most complete collection of Iran-contra documents, including the author's La Penca investigation and case files; Oliver North's notebooks; Robert Owen's memos; the Iran-contra hearings; documents, depositions, and testimonies from various trials and from the independent prosecutor's investigation; and declassified documents obtained through the Freedom of Information Act.

Books

Aguilar, Irene, and Manuel Solís. *La Elite Ganadera en Costa Rica*. San José: Editorial de la Universidad de Costa Rica, 1988.

Ameringer, Charles D. *Democracy in Costa Rica*. New York: Praeger, 1982.

———. *Don Pepe: A Political Biography of José Figueres*. Albuquerque: University of New Mexico Press, 1978.

Anderson, Scott, and John Lee Anderson. *Inside the League*. New York: Dodd Mead and Company, 1986.

Avirgan, Tony, and Martha Honey. *La Penca: On Trial in Costa Rica—The CIA vs. the Press*. San José: Editorial Porvenir, 1987.

———. *War in Uganda: The Legacy of Idi Amin*. Westport, Connecticut: Lawrence Hill and Company, 1982.

Barry, Tom. *Costa Rica: A Country Guide*. Albuquerque: The Resource Center, 1989.

———. *Low Intensity Conflict: The New Battlefield in Central America*. Albuquerque: The Resource Center, 1986.

Barry, Tom, and Rachel Garst. *Feeding the Crisis: U.S. Food Aid and Farm Policy in Central America,* Lincoln: University of Nebraska Press, 1990.

Barry, Tom, and Deb Preusch. *The New Right Humanitarians*. Albuquerque: The Research Center, 1986.

———. *The Soft War: The Uses and Abuses of U.S. Economic Aid in Central America*. New York: Grove Press, 1989.

Bell, John Patrick. *Crisis in Costa Rica: The 1948 Revolution*. Austin: University of Texas Press, 1971.

Bird, Leonard. *Costa Rica: The Unarmed Democracy*. London: Sheppard Press, 1984.

Booth, John A., and Mitchell A. Seligson, eds. *Elections and Democracy in Central America*. Chapel Hill: University of North Carolina Press, 1989.

Brenes, Lidiette. *La Nacionalización Bancaria en Costa Rica*. San José: FLACSO, 1990.

Bulmer-Thomas, Victor. *The Political Economy of Central America since 1970*. Cambridge: Cambridge University Press, 1987.

Chomsky, Noam. *The Culture of Terrorism*. Boston: South End Press, 1988.

Cockburn, Leslie. *Out of Control*. New York: Atlantic Monthly Press, 1987.

Cockcroft, James D. *Neighbors in Turmoil: Latin America*. New York: Harper and Row, 1989.

Cruz, Arturo, Jr. *Memoirs of a Counter-Revolutionary*. New York: Doubleday, 1989.

Dickey, Christopher. *With the Contras: A Reporter in the Wilds of Nicaragua*. New York: Simon and Schuster, 1985.

Dinges, John. *Our Man in Panama*. New York: Random House, 1990.

Dunkerley, James. *Power in the Isthmus: A Political History of Modern Central America*. London: Verso, 1988.

Edelman, Marc. *The Logic of the Latifundio: The Large Estates of Northwestern Costa Rica since the Late Nineteenth Century*. Stanford: Stanford University Press, 1992.

————, and Joanne Kenen, eds. *The Costa Rica Reader*. New York: Grove Weidenfeld, 1989.

Emerson, Steven. *Secret Warriors: Inside the Covert Military Operations of the Reagan Era*. New York: Putnam, 1988.

Fernández, Guido. *El Desafío de la Paz en Centroamérica*. San José: Editorial Costa Rica, 1989.

Gelbspan, Ross. *Breaking In, Death Threats, and the FBI*. Boston: South End Press, 1991.

Gutiérrez S., Manuel, and Jorge Vargas C. *Costa Rica es el nombre del Juego: Análisis de la crisis de 1984*. San José: ICES, n.d.

Gutman, Roy. *Banana Diplomacy: The Making of American Policy in Nicaragua 1981–1987*. New York: Simon and Schuster, 1988.

Hall, Carolyn. *Costa Rica: A Geographical Interpretation in Historical Perspective*. Boulder: Westview Press, 1985.

Hamilton, Nora, et al., eds. *Crisis in Central America: Regional Dynamics and U.S. Policy in the 1980's*. Boulder: Westview Press, 1988.

Holleman, Edith, and Andrew Love (principal authors). *Inside the*

Shadow Government: Declaration of Plaintiff's Counsel, Filed by the Christic Institute, U.S. District Court, Miami, Florida, March 31, 1988. Washington, D.C.: Christic Institute, 1988.

Honey, Martha, and Tony Avirgan, eds. *La Penca: Reporte de una Investigación.* San José: Editorial Porvenir, 1989.

Jirón, Manuel. *Exilio, S.A.* San José: Ediciones Radio Amor, 1983.

Kempe, Frederick. *Divorcing the Dictator: America's Bungled Affair with Noriega.* New York: G. P. Putnam's Sons, 1990.

Kinzer, Stephen. *Blood of Brothers: Life and War in Nicaragua.* New York: G. P. Putnam's Sons, 1991.

Kornbluh, Peter. *Nicaragua: The Price of Intervention.* Washington, D.C.: Institute for Policy Studies, 1987.

————, and Malcolm Byrne, eds. *The Iran-Contra Scandal: The Declassified History.* New York: New Press, 1993.

Kwitny, Jonathan. *The Crimes of Patriots: A True Tale of Dope, Dirty Money, and the CIA.* New York: Simon and Schuster, 1987.

Maas, Peter. *Manhunt: The Incredible Pursuit of a CIA Agent.* New York: Random House, 1986.

Marshall, Jonathan. *Drug Wars: Corruption, Counterinsurgency and Covert Operations in the Third World.* Forestville, California: Cohan and Cohan Publishers, 1991.

————, Peter Dale Scott, and Jane Hunter. *The Iran-Contra Connection: Secret Teams and Covert Operations in the Reagan Era.* Boston: South End Press, 1987.

Mayer, Jane, and Doyle McManus. *Landslide: The Unmaking of the President, 1984–1988.* Boston: Houghton Mifflin, 1988.

McClure, John L. *Soldier Without Fortune.* New York: Dell, 1987.

McNeil, Frank. *War and Peace in Central America.* New York: Macmillan, 1988.

Morgan, Susie. *In Search of the Asssassin.* London: Bloomsbury, 1991.

National Security Archive. *Documented Day-by-Day Account of the Secret Military Assistance to Iran and the Contras.* New York: Warner, 1987.

Pastor, Robert A. *Condemned to Repetition.* Princeton: Princeton University Press, 1987.

Peeler, John A. *Latin American Democracies: Colombia, Costa Rica, Venezuela.* Chapel Hill: University of North Carolina Press, 1985.

Roddick, Jackie. *The Dance of the Millions: Latin America and the Debt Crisis.* London: Latin American Bureau, 1988.

Rodríguez, Félix I., and John Weisman. *Shadow Warrior.* New York: Simon and Schuster, 1989.

Rovira Mas, Jorge. *Costa Rica en Los Años '80*. San José: Editorial Porvenir, 1987.

Rubén Soto, William, ed. *Los Campesinos Frente a la Nueva Década*. San José: Editorial Porvenir, 1989.

Salinas, Juan, and Julio Villalonga. *Gorriaran: La Tablada y las "guerras de inteligencia" en America Latina*. Buenos Aires: Mangin, 1993.

Scott, Peter Dale, and Jonathan Marshall. *Cocaine Politics: Drugs, Armies and the CIA in Central America*. Berkeley: University of California Press, 1991.

————. *Obstruction of Justice: The Reagan-Bush Coverup of the Contra Drug Connection*. Washington, D.C.: Christic Institute, 1990.

Seligson, Mitchell A. *Peasants of Costa Rica and the Development of Agrarian Capitalism*. Madison: University of Wisconsin Press, 1980.

Sklar, Holly. *Washington's War on Nicaragua*. Boston: South End Press, 1988.

Sobrado, Miguel, Gabriel Coronodo, and Leda Trejos. *¿Quién Quiere la Guerra en Costa Rica?* San José: ICES-CRIES, 1988.

Terrell, Jack, with Ron Martz. *Disposable Patriot: Revelations of a Soldier in America's Secret Wars*. Washington, D.C.: National Press Books, 1992.

Toobin, Jeffrey. *Opening Arguments: A Young Lawyer's First Case; The United States vs. Oliver North*. New York: Viking, 1991.

Tower, John, Edmund Muskie, and Brent Scowcroft. *The Tower Commission Report*. New York: Bantam Books, 1987.

Walker, Thomas, ed. *Reagan versus the Sandinistas: The Undeclared War on Nicaragua*. Boulder: Westview Press, 1987.

Williams, Robert G. *Export Agriculture and the Crisis in Central America*. Chapel Hill: University of North Carolina Press, 1986.

Woodward, Bob. *Veil: the Secret Wars of the CIA 1981–1987*. New York: Simon and Schuster, 1987.

Woodward Jr., Ralph Lee, ed. *Central America: Historical Perspectives on the Contemporary Crisis*. Westport, Conn.: Greenwood Press, 1988.

Zeledón Cambronero, Mario, ed. *La Desinformación de la Prensa en Costa Rica: Un Grave Peligro para la Paz*. Costa Rica: ICES, 1987.

Articles, Pamphlets, and Reports: Published and Unpublished

Anderson, John Lee. "CIA Agent in Costa Rica." *Life* (Feb. 1985).

Annis, Sheldon, et al. *Costa Rica's Dual Debt: A Story about A Little*

Country That Did Things Right. Washington, D.C.: World Resource Institute, June 1987.

Avirgan, Tony. "Unmasking the La Penca Bomber." *Nation,* Sept. 6–13, 1993.

Blachman, Morris J., and Ronald G. Hellman. "Costa Rica." In *Confronting Revolution: Security through Diplomacy in Central America,* edited by Morris J. Blachman, William M. LeoGrande, and Kenneth E. Sharpe. New York: Pantheon Books, 1986.

Booth, John A. "Representative Constitutional Democracy in Costa Rica: Adaptation to Crisis in the Turbulent 1980s." In *Central America: Crisis and Adaption,* edited by Steve C. Ropp and James A. Morris, 387–422. Albuquerque: University of New Mexico Press, 1984.

Carlisle, John. "Anatomy of a Disinformation Campaign." *Propaganda Review* (Winter 1988).

Chamorro, Edgar. *Packaging the Contras: A Case of CIA Disinformation.* New York: Institute for Media Analysis, 1987.

Christic Institute. *The Contra-Drug Connection.* Washington, D.C.: Christic Institute, 1987.

Clark, Mary. "The Politics of Economic Adjustment in a Democracy: International Relations, Domestic Coalitions, and Nontraditional Export Promotion in Costa Rica." Ph.D. diss. in progress, University of Wisconsin–Madison, 1993.

Comisión Costarricense de los Derechos Humanos (CODEHU). *Informe sobre la Situación de los Derechos Humanos en Costa Rica.* San José: CODEHU, 1987, 1988, 1989, 1990.

Committee of Santa Fe. "A New Inter-American Policy for the Eighties." May 1980.

Danby, Colin. "Stabilization and Transformation: Bilateral U.S. Economic Aid in Central Ameria." Policy Alternatives for the Caribbean and Central America (PACCA). Unpublished, March 1989.

Feinberg, Richard E. "Costa Rica: The End of the Fiesta." In *From Gunboats to Diplomacy: New U.S. Policies for Latin America,* edited by Richard Newfarmer. Baltimore: Johns Hopkins University Press, 1984.

Friel, Howard, and Michell Joffroy. "The Continuing War: Media Manipulation in Costa Rica." *Covert Action Information Bulletin* (Summer 1986).

Furlong, William. "Costa Rica: Caught between Two Worlds." *Journal of Inter-American Studies and World Affairs* 29, no. 2. (Summer 1987).

González-Vega, Claudio. "Fear of Adjusting: The Social Costs of Economic Policies in Costa Rica in the 1970s." In *Revolution and*

Counterrevolution in Central America and the Caribbean, edited by Donald E. Schulz and Douglas H. Graham. Boulder: Westview Press, 1984.

Haivik, Tord, and Solveig Aas. "Demilitarization in Costa Rica: A Farewell to Arms?" *Journal of Peace Research* XVIII, no. 4 (1981): 333–51.

Honey, Martha. "Contra Coverage—Paid for by the CIA." *Columbia Journalism Review* (March-April 1987).

———. "Contra War Mystery Bomber Identified." *San Francisco Chronicle,* Aug. 2, 1993.

———. "Nine-Year Manhunt Ended Quietly: Family Confirmed Identity. Personal Report." *Tico Times,* Aug. 6, 1993.

———, and David Myers. "U.S. Probing Drug Agent's Activities in Costa Rica." *San Francisco Chronicle,* Aug. 14, 1991.

Kirsten Nelson, Lise. "The Burden of Development: The Effects of *Agricultura de Cambio* on the Small Farmer in Costa Rica." Unpublished field research paper for the Association of Colleges of the Midwest (ACM), May 1988.

Korten, Alicia. "Structural Adjustment, the Environment and the Poor: The Case Study of Costa Rica." Senior honors thesis, Brown University, Latin American Studies Department, May 1992.

Marshall, Jonathan. "Israel, the Contras and the North Trial." *Middle East Report* (Sept./Oct., 1989).

Mohs, Edgar. "Evolution of Paradigms of Child Health in Developing Countries." *Pediatric Infectious Disease* 4, no. 5 (1985).

———. "Infectious Diseases and Health in Costa Rica: The Development of a New Paradigm." *Pediatric Infectious Disease* 1, no. 3 (1982).

Pacheco Oreamundo, Gilda. *Nicaraguan Refugees in Costa Rica: Adjustment to Camp Life.* Washington, D.C.: Georgetown University Center for Immigration Policy and Refugee Assistance, 1989.

Peltz, Maxwell. "Costa Rica and the Reagan Administration: Sparring with a Giant." Honors thesis, International Relations Program, Stanford University, May 1989.

Ramírez, Mario. *Refugee Policy Challenges: The Case of Nicaraguans in Costa Rica.* Washington, D.C.: Georgetown University Center for Immigration Policy and Refugee Assistance, 1989.

Reding, Andrew. "Costa Rica: Democratic Model in Jeopardy" and "Voices from Costa Rica." *World Policy Journal* 3, no. 2 (1986): 301–45.

Rosero-Bixby, Luis. "Costa Rica Saves Infants' Lives." *World Health Forum* 9, 1988.

————. "Infant Mortality in Costa Rica: Explaining the Recent Decline." *Studies in Family Planning* 17, no. 2 (March/April 1986).

Rubinow, Syd, and Stephen Schmidt. "Showdown in a Bitter Land War." *Tico Times,* Oct. 3, 1975.

Saxe-Fernández, John. "The Militarization of Costa Rica." *Monthly Review* (May 1972).

Seligson, Mitchell A. "Implementing Land Reform: The Case of Costa Rica." *Managing International Development* (March/April 1984).

Tamayo, Juan. "Nicaraguan Assassin Finally Unmasked." *Miami Herald,* Aug. 1, 1993.

Thacher, Thomas. "Non-Traditional Agricultural Export Expansion in Costa Rica: The Role of Foreign Investment: An Obstacle to National Participation in the Export Sectors of Ornamental Plants, Flowers and Foliage." B.A. honors thesis, Carleton College, Northfield, Minn., April 1990.

Vaughan, Douglas "The Jackal of La Penca is Named." *The Times* (London), Aug. 13, 1993.

Williams, Heather, et al. *"Agricultura de Cambio:* The Solution to Costa Rica's Development Problems?" Unpublished thesis, Institute for Central American Development and Economic Studies (ICADES), San José, November 1987.

Government and Legal Documents

Avirgan, et al., versus Hull, et al. Documents and depositions related to La Penca lawsuit, U.S. District Court for the Southern District of Florida, Case No. 86–1146, 1986–91.

Bell, Charles, Checchi and Company Consulting and Louis Berger International. *Evaluation of CINDE's Progress towards the Attainment of Its Objectives and Long-Term Goals.* Prepared for AID Latin America and Caribbean Bureau. IQC no. PDC-0085-I-6097-00. Washington, D.C., May 1988.

Bolton, William, Checchi and Company Consulting, and Harry Mannion, ATMA International. *Evaluation of USAID/Costa Rica Nontraditional Agricultural Export Strategy.* AID Contract No. 515-0000-C-00-9035-00. Washington, D.C., July 1989.

Chavarria Guzman, Jorge. "Public Prosecutors Investigation on 'La Penca' Case." San José, Dec. 26, 1988. English translation for Christic Institute by John Anderson, certified court interpreter, Dade County, Florida.

Costa Rican Legislative Assembly. *Special Commission Appointed to Investigate the Acts Reported on Drug Trafficking.* Document 10.684, Final Report, San José, July 10, 1989. Translation by Congressional Research Service, Washington, D.C.

Court document. "U.S. Government Stipulation on Quid Pro Quos with Other Governments as Part of Contra Operations." *United States v. Oliver North.* Docket No. 88-0080-02-GAG. Washington, D.C., April 6, 1989. Reprinted in full in Kornbluh and Byrne, ed., *The Iran-Contra Scandal: The Declassified History,* pp. 85–97.

Galdi, Theodor. *Development Assistance Policy: A Historical Overview.* Congressional Research Service Report for Congress. Washington, D.C., April 6, 1988.

Lack, Stephen, and C. Kenneth Laurent. "Agricultural Crop Diversification/Export Promotion: Cross-Cutting Evaluation." Draft executive summary. Washington, D.C.: USAID, 1988.

Ministry of Planning (MIDEPLAN). "El Deterioro Socioeconómico del Año 1989: Principal Reto de la Economía Costarricense en el Año 1990." San José, July 1990.

Newtonarry, John, et al. *The Effectiveness and Economic Development Impact of Policy-Based Cash Transfer Programs: The Case of Costa Rica.* AID Evaluation Special Study No. 57. Washington, D.C.: U.S. Government Printing Office, November 1988.

North, Oliver. Personal daily diaries. Obtained through Freedom of Information Act by National Security Archive.

Owen, Robert. Various memos to Oliver North: 1984–87. Uncensored version obtained by Christic Institute and available at National Security Archive.

Tomlinson, Alexander C., and Ismael Benavides. *Evaluation of the Divestiture Program of Corporación Costarricense de Desarrollo, S.A. ("CODESA"): Costa Rica 1984–1988.* Center for Privatization Project No. 71. Washington D.C., May 1988.

Tower, Sen. John, Sen. Edmund Muskie and former National Security Adviser Brent Scrowcroft. Executive Office of the President. President's Special Review Board 1987. *Report of the President's Special Review Board [Tower Commission Report].* Washington, D.C.: Government Printing Office, Feb. 26, 1987.

United States Agency for International Development (USAID). "AID in Costa Rica: 1982–1992." San José: USAID, October 1988.

——— (USAID). "The Effectiveness and Economic Development Impact of Policy-Based Cash Transfer Program: The Case of Costa Rica." *Evaluation Highlights.* No. 1. Washington, D.C., Oct. 1988.

————. "Emphasis on Private Sector: Summary." San José: USAID, January 1987.

————. "Non-Traditional Agribusiness Export Strategy 1986–1990." San José: USAID, January 1987.

———— (USAID). "Regional Strategic Plan for Latin America and the Caribbean." Washington, D.C., Dec. 1983.

———— (USAID). "Strategy Update." San José, Costa Rica: AID Mission. March 1988.

————. "Task Force on Humanitarian Assistance for Central America." Washington, D.C.: USAID, April 1988.

————. "USAID Assistance to Costa Rica: 1946–1989." San José: USAID, n.d.

————, Costa Rica Private Sector Office. "Three-Year Strategy." San José: USAID, December 1987.

United States Congress. Senate Sub-committee on Narcotics, Terrorism and International Operations of the Committee on Foreign Relations (John Kerry, chmn.). *Drugs, Law Enforcement and Foreign Policy.* Senate Report 100–165. Washington, D.C.: U.S. Government Printing Office, 1989.

United States Congress. Senate Development Policy Committee. "Foreign AID to Central America, FY 1981–1987." February 18, 1987.

United States Congress. Senate Select Committee on Secret Military Assistance to Iran and the Nicaraguan Opposition; and House Select Committee to Investigate Covert Arms Transactions with Iran. *Report of the Congressional Committees Investigating the Iran-Contra Affair, With Supplemental, Minority and Additional Views.* Nov. 1987. Plus: Appendix A: Source documents, 2 vols.; Appendix B: Depositions, vols. 1–27 (televised); Appendix C: Chronology of Events; Hearings 100-1 to 100-11, incl. parts I and II of 100-7, 12 vols. (non-televised testimony).

United States General Accounting Office (GAO). "Central America: Impact of U.S. Assistance in the 1980s." GAO/NSIAD-89-170. Washington, D.C.: U.S. Government Printing Office, July 1989.

————. "Central America: Problems in Controlling Funds for the Nicaraguan Democratic Resistance." GAO/NSIAD-87-35. Washington, D.C.: U.S. Government Printing Office, December 1986.

————. "Costa Rica: Country Summary." Washington, D.C.: U.S. Government Printing Office, February 1989.

————. "Food Safety and Quality: Five Countries' Efforts to Meet U.S. Requirements on Imported Produce." Appendix I. GAO/RCED-90-55. Washington, D.C.: U.S. Government Printing Office, March 1990.

————. "Foreign Assistance: U.S. Use of Conditions to Achieve Economic Reforms." GAO/USAID-86-157. Washington, D.C.: U.S. Government Printing Office, August 1986.

United States v. Oliver North. Docket No. CR 88-0080-02-GAG. Trial before Gerhard Gesell, U.S. District Judge and Jury. Washington, D.C., 1989. Including depositions by William Haskell and Rafael Quintero.

World Bank. "Costa Rica: Country Economic Memo." Washington, D.C.: USAID, December 1988.

————. *World Development Report 1988*. New York: Oxford University Press, 1988.

Yu, Alan K. *Central America and U.S. Foreign Assistance: Issues for Congress*. Congressional Research Service Issue Brief, The Library of Congress, IB84075. Washington, D.C.: Congressional Research Service, May 1989.

Newspapers, Magazines, and Journals

Aportes (Costa Rica)
Esta Semana (Costa Rica)
La Nación (Costa Rica)
La Prensa Libre (Costa Rica)
La República (Costa Rica)
Mesoamérica (Costa Rica)
Miami Herald
New York Times
Semanario Universidad (Costa Rica)
Tico Times (Costa Rica)

Index

The following individuals and organizations granted permission to reproduce photographs in this book:

Oscar Arias: 34, 36, 37, 38
Chris Covatta: 25

La Nación: 2, 3, 5, 6, 17, 23
La República: 7
Tico Times: 4, 9, 11, 12, 13, 15, 16, 18, 19, 20, 27, 28, 29, 30, 31, 33, 35
Doug Vaughan: 8
Julio Villalonga: 22